Musselman
Library

Purchased with
John D. Unruh, Jr
Memorial Funds

Bluffton
College

THE PAPERS OF ULYSSES S. GRANT

THE PAPERS OF

ULYSSES S. GRANT

Volume 20:
November 1, 1869–October 31, 1870

Edited by John Y. Simon

ASSISTANT EDITORS
William M. Ferraro
Brian J. Kenny
J. Thomas Murphy

TEXTUAL EDITOR
Sue E. Dotson

———

SOUTHERN ILLINOIS UNIVERSITY PRESS

CARBONDALE AND EDWARDSVILLE

Library of Congress Cataloging in Publication Data (Revised)

Grant, Ulysses Simpson, Pres. U.S., 1822–1885.
    The papers of Ulysses S. Grant.

    Prepared under the auspices of the Ulysses S. Grant Association.
    Bibliographical footnotes.
    CONTENTS: v. 1. 1837–1861—v. 2. April–September 1861.
—v. 3. October 1, 1861–January 7, 1862.—v. 4. January 8–March 31,
1862.—v. 5. April 1–August 31, 1862.—v. 6. September 1–December 8, 1862.—v. 7. December 9, 1862–March 31, 1863.—v. 8.
April 1–July 6, 1863.—v. 9. July 7–December 31, 1863.—v. 10.
January 1–May 31, 1864.—v. 11. June 1–August 15, 1864.—v. 12.
August 16–November 15, 1864.—v. 13. November 16, 1864–Feb-
ruary 20, 1865.—v. 14. February 21–April 30, 1865.—v. 15. May 1–
December 31, 1865.—v. 16. 1866.—v. 17. January 1–September 30,
1867.—v. 18. October 1, 1867–June 30, 1868.—v. 19. July 1, 1868–
October 31, 1869.—v. 20. November 1, 1869–October 31, 1870.
    1. Grant, Ulysses Simpson, Pres. U.S., 1822–1885. 2. United
States—History—Civil War, 1861–1865—Campaigns and battles
—Sources. 3. United States—Politics and government—1869–1877
—Sources. 4. Presidents—United States—Biography. 5. Generals—
United States—Biography. I. Simon, John Y., ed. II. Ulysses S. Grant
Association.
E660.G756   1967   973.8′2′0924   67–10725
ISBN 0–8093–1965–9 (v. 20)

Contents

Introduction   xi

Editorial Procedure   xiv

Chronology   xix

The Papers of Ulysses S. Grant,
     November 1, 1869–October 31, 1870   3

Calendar   331

Index   477

Introduction

AFTER ULYSSES S. GRANT'S first months in office, he continued to encourage economic expansion, to promote peaceful Reconstruction in the southern states, to advocate passage of the Fifteenth Amendment, and to urge humane treatment of Indians. In his annual message, Grant clearly stated that he wanted a nation where all citizens were productive, showed mutual respect, and lived in peace. Realities of political intrigue, racial tension, Ku Klux Klan violence, and clashes between Indians and western settlers and business interests made turmoil the order of the day. Passage of the Fifteenth Amendment, prohibiting denial of suffrage based on race, pleased Grant so much that he sent a special message to Congress calling this achievement "of grander importance than any other one act of the kind" since the founding of the government.

Faced with largely intractable domestic problems, Grant turned to foreign policy. His major initiative involved the annexation of Santo Domingo. He believed that the troubled island nation contained valuable natural resources of great economic potential. It could also provide the United States with a strategic port in the Caribbean and a possible answer to racial conflict, since he thought the territory "capable of supporting the entire colored population of the United States, should it choose to emigrate." Grant based his glowing opinion of Santo Domingo primarily upon the report he received from private secretary Orville E. Babcock. Babcock's discussions with Buenaventura Báez, Santo Domingo's nominal president, formed the basis of an annexation treaty. The Senate's rejection of this treaty, and particularly the vociferous opposition of U.S. Senator Charles Sumner of Massachusetts after he had hinted his support for the measure, infuriated Grant and set the stage for future battles with Sumner. While Grant was beguiled by Santo Domingo, he also directed considerable attention to Cuban insurgency, the Franco-Prussian War, and negotiations with England over the Alabama Claims, a thorny and politically sensitive issue unresolved since the Civil War. These issues intertwined, since each involved questions of international law regarding neutral conduct during armed hostilities.

Grant's experiences as president ineluctably drew him into the political fray. He actively intervened through exhortations and executive patronage to influence state and local politics. He lashed back at Sumner by removing his friend John Lothrop Motley as minister to England. His motivation at times may have been personal, but Grant thought that the actions of congressional Republicans had "put the party in a very bad light" and likely believed his intervention important to Republican electoral success in coming elections.

Willingness to engage in politics overreached Grant's skill in obtaining political results. He supported the interests of Horace Greeley only to have the *New York Tribune* editor become his presidential opponent in 1872. He unseated Motley but spent months finding a replacement. He suffered an embarrassing rebuff when the Senate rejected his nomination of Ebenezer R. Hoar for the U.S. Supreme Court. Grant then decided to nominate the desperately ill Edwin M. Stanton, who died before he could be seated. Disruption afflicted Grant's cabinet, with Attorney General Hoar and Secretary of the Interior Jacob D. Cox departing under duress in favor of Amos T. Akerman and Columbus Delano. Rumors regarding the resignation of Secretary of State Hamilton Fish abounded.

Grant escaped the trials of politics and presidential duties as often as possible. He enjoyed his seaside "cottage" at Long Branch, took a fishing trip to Pennsylvania, visited St. Louis to inspect his property, and traveled to New York and New England to see his son Frederick at West Point and to take his son Ulysses, Jr., to Harvard. These excursions combined relief, recreation, and fulfillment of family obligations and yet allowed citizens to come in contact with their president. His schedule was demanding and, as Grant noted frequently, left little time for extensive correspondence.

By the middle of his first term as president, Grant had begun much but finished little. His experience had acquainted him with the many challenges of his office, but he had not developed the political finesse necessary to meet or to overcome these challenges effectively. His popularity, however, remained high, and he puffed contentedly on his cigar.

We are indebted to Timothy Connelly for assistance in searching the National Archives; to Harriet F. Simon for proofreading; and to Rebecca A. Phillips and Aaron M. Lisec, graduate students at Southern Illinois University, for research assistance.

Financial support for the period during which this volume was prepared came from Southern Illinois University, the National Endowment for the Humanities, and the National Historical Publications and Records Commission.

JOHN Y. SIMON

September 30, 1993

Editorial Procedure

1. Editorial Insertions

A.   Words or letters in roman type within brackets represent editorial reconstruction of parts of manuscripts torn, mutilated, or illegible.

B.   [. . .] or [— — —] within brackets represent lost material which cannot be reconstructed. The number of dots represents the approximate number of lost letters; dashes represent lost words.

C.   Words in *italic* type within brackets represent material such as dates which were not part of the original manuscript.

D.   Other material crossed out is indicated by ~~cancelled type~~.

E.   Material raised in manuscript, as "4th," has been brought in line, as "4th."

2. Symbols Used to Describe Manuscripts

AD	Autograph Document
ADS	Autograph Document Signed
ADf	Autograph Draft
ADfS	Autograph Draft Signed
AES	Autograph Endorsement Signed
AL	Autograph Letter
ALS	Autograph Letter Signed
ANS	Autograph Note Signed

D	Document
DS	Document Signed
Df	Draft
DfS	Draft Signed
ES	Endorsement Signed
LS	Letter Signed

3. *Military Terms and Abbreviations*

Act.	Acting
Adjt.	Adjutant
AG	Adjutant General
AGO	Adjutant General's Office
Art.	Artillery
Asst.	Assistant
Bvt.	Brevet
Brig.	Brigadier
Capt.	Captain
Cav.	Cavalry
Col.	Colonel
Co.	Company
C.S.A.	Confederate States of America
Dept.	Department
Div.	Division
Gen.	General
Hd. Qrs.	Headquarters
Inf.	Infantry
Lt.	Lieutenant
Maj.	Major
Q. M.	Quartermaster
Regt.	Regiment or regimental
Sgt.	Sergeant
USMA	United States Military Academy, West Point, N.Y.
Vols.	Volunteers

4. *Short Titles and Abbreviations*

ABPC	*American Book-Prices Current* (New York, 1895–)

CG	*Congressional Globe* Numbers following represent the Congress, session, and page.
J. G. Cramer	Jesse Grant Cramer, ed., *Letters of Ulysses S. Grant to his Father and his Youngest Sister, 1857–78* (New York and London, 1912)
DAB	*Dictionary of American Biography* (New York, 1928–36)
Garland	Hamlin Garland, *Ulysses S. Grant: His Life and Character* (New York, 1898)
HED	*House Executive Documents*
HMD	*House Miscellaneous Documents*
HRC	*House Reports of Committees* Numbers following *HED, HMD,* or *HRC* represent the number of the Congress, the session, and the document.
Ill. AG Report	J. N. Reece, ed., *Report of the Adjutant General of the State of Illinois* (Springfield, 1900)
Johnson, Papers	LeRoy P. Graf and Ralph W. Haskins, eds., *The Papers of Andrew Johnson* (Knoxville, 1967–)
Lewis	Lloyd Lewis, *Captain Sam Grant* (Boston, 1950)
Lincoln, Works	Roy P. Basler, Marion Dolores Pratt, and Lloyd A. Dunlap, eds., *The Collected Works of Abraham Lincoln* (New Brunswick, 1953–55)
Memoirs	*Personal Memoirs of U. S. Grant* (New York, 1885–86)
O.R.	*The War of the Rebellion: A Compilation of the Official Records of the Union and Confederate Armies* (Washington, 1880–1901)
O.R. (Navy)	*Official Records of the Union and Confederate Navies in the War of the Rebellion* (Washington, 1894–1927) Roman numerals following *O.R.* or *O.R.* (Navy) represent the series and the volume.
PUSG	John Y. Simon, ed., *The Papers of Ulysses S. Grant* (Carbondale and Edwardsville, 1967–)
Richardson	Albert D. Richardson, *A Personal History of Ulysses S. Grant* (Hartford, Conn., 1868)
SED	*Senate Executive Documents*
SMD	*Senate Miscellaneous Documents*
SRC	*Senate Reports of Committees* Numbers following

SED, *SMD*, or *SRC* represent the number of the Congress, the session, and the document.

USGA Newsletter   *Ulysses S. Grant Association Newsletter*

Young   John Russell Young, *Around the World with General Grant* (New York, 1879)

5. *Location Symbols*

CLU	University of California at Los Angeles, Los Angeles, Calif.
CoHi	Colorado State Historical Society, Denver, Colo.
CSmH	Henry E. Huntington Library, San Marino, Calif.
CSt	Stanford University, Stanford, Calif.
CtY	Yale University, New Haven, Conn.
CU-B	Bancroft Library, University of California, Berkeley, Calif.
DLC	Library of Congress, Washington, D.C. Numbers following DLC-USG represent the series and volume of military records in the USG papers.
DNA	National Archives, Washington, D.C. Additional numbers identify record groups.
IaHA	Iowa State Department of History and Archives, Des Moines, Iowa.
I-ar	Illinois State Archives, Springfield, Ill.
IC	Chicago Public Library, Chicago, Ill.
ICarbS	Southern Illinois University, Carbondale, Ill.
ICHi	Chicago Historical Society, Chicago, Ill.
ICN	Newberry Library, Chicago, Ill.
ICU	University of Chicago, Chicago, Ill.
IHi	Illinois State Historical Library, Springfield, Ill.
In	Indiana State Library, Indianapolis, Ind.
InFtwL	Lincoln National Life Foundation, Fort Wayne, Ind.
InHi	Indiana Historical Society, Indianapolis, Ind.
InNd	University of Notre Dame, Notre Dame, Ind.
InU	Indiana University, Bloomington, Ind.
KHi	Kansas State Historical Society, Topeka, Kan.
MdAN	United States Naval Academy Museum, Annapolis, Md.

MeB	Bowdoin College, Brunswick, Me.
MH	Harvard University, Cambridge, Mass.
MHi	Massachusetts Historical Society, Boston, Mass.
MiD	Detroit Public Library, Detroit, Mich.
MiU-C	William L. Clements Library, University of Michigan, Ann Arbor, Mich.
MoSHi	Missouri Historical Society, St. Louis, Mo.
NHi	New-York Historical Society, New York, N.Y.
NIC	Cornell University, Ithaca, N.Y.
NjP	Princeton University, Princeton, N.J.
NjR	Rutgers University, New Brunswick, N.J.
NN	New York Public Library, New York, N.Y.
NNP	Pierpont Morgan Library, New York, N.Y.
NRU	University of Rochester, Rochester, N.Y.
OClWHi	Western Reserve Historical Society, Cleveland, Ohio.
OFH	Rutherford B. Hayes Library, Fremont, Ohio.
OHi	Ohio Historical Society, Columbus, Ohio.
OrHi	Oregon Historical Society, Portland, Ore.
PCarlA	U.S. Army Military History Institute, Carlisle Barracks, Pa.
PHi	Historical Society of Pennsylvania, Philadelphia, Pa.
PPRF	Rosenbach Foundation, Philadelphia, Pa.
RPB	Brown University, Providence, R.I.
TxHR	Rice University, Houston, Tex.
USG 3	Maj. Gen. Ulysses S. Grant 3rd, Clinton, N.Y.
USMA	United States Military Academy Library, West Point, N.Y.
ViHi	Virginia Historical Society, Richmond, Va.
ViU	University of Virginia, Charlottesville, Va.
WHi	State Historical Society of Wisconsin, Madison, Wis.
Wy-Ar	Wyoming State Archives and Historical Department, Cheyenne, Wyo.
WyU	University of Wyoming, Laramie, Wyo.

Chronology

November 1, 1869–October 31, 1870

Nov. 18. USG held a Thanksgiving dinner for his staff and their families.

Dec. 6. USG submitted his annual message to Congress.

Dec. 11. USG addressed a delegation from the predominately black National Labor Convention.

Dec. 14. USG nominated Ebenezer R. Hoar as associate justice, U.S. Supreme Court. On Dec. 22, the Senate tabled this nomination.

Dec. 15. USG accepted the resignation of Robert C. Grier, associate justice, U.S. Supreme Court, to take effect Feb. 1, 1870.

Dec. 20. USG nominated Edwin M. Stanton as associate justice, U.S. Supreme Court. Orville E. Babcock returned from Santo Domingo.

Dec. 22. Congress revoked the statehood of Ga. and required ratification of the Fifteenth Amendment for readmission, a standard subsequently applied to all unreconstructed states.

Dec. 24. Stanton died.

Jan. 10. USG submitted to the Senate the Santo Domingo annexation treaty.

Jan. 20. USG met a delegation from the Cherokees and Creeks.

Jan. 24. USG received Prince Arthur of England at the White House and, on Jan. 26, held a dinner and ball in his honor.

Jan. 26. Congress readmitted Va.

Feb. 3. The Senate rejected Hoar's nomination.

FEB. 7.   USG nominated Joseph P. Bradley and William Strong as associate justices, U.S. Supreme Court.

FEB. 9.   USG nominated Jesse Root Grant to continue as postmaster, Covington, Ky.

FEB. 25.   Hiram R. Revels of Miss. was seated as the first black U.S. senator two days after Congress readmitted Miss.

MAR. 9.   USG discussed events in Cuba with U.S. senators and Gen. Manuel Quesada.

MAR. 14.   USG urged Senate action to ratify the Santo Domingo annexation treaty before its expiration on March 29.

MAR. 23.   USG issued a special message on the decline of the U.S. merchant marine.

MAR. 24.   Meeting with U.S. Representative James H. Platt, Jr., of Va. and Republican members of the Va. legislature, USG sustained the actions of Bvt. Maj. Gen. Edward R. S. Canby to prevent riots in the state.

MAR. 29.   In a subsequently published interview, USG expounded on the advantages of annexing Santo Domingo.

MAR. 30.   USG marked the passage of the Fifteenth Amendment with a special message to Congress. Congress readmitted Tex.

MAR. 31.   USG submitted to the Senate a treaty with Colombia for construction of an "Interoceanic canal across the Isthmus of Panama and Darien."

APRIL 8.   USG attended the funeral of Maj. Gen. George H. Thomas at Troy, N.Y.

APRIL 9.   USG, Gen. William T. Sherman, Lt. Gen. Philip H. Sheridan, and Maj. Gen. George G. Meade attended a reunion of the Army of the Potomac in Philadelphia.

APRIL 21.   USG nominated Adam Badeau as consul gen., London.

APRIL 28.   USG and Julia Dent Grant left Washington, D.C., for West Point.

MAY 1.   USG and Julia Grant were guests of Abel R. and Virginia Grant Corbin in Elizabeth, N.J.

MAY 16.   Wishing to discuss foreign policy, USG convened a special cabinet meeting.

MAY 17.   USG advised Attorney Gen. Ebenezer R. Hoar to prevent the Union Pacific Railroad from falling into receivership at the dictum of a territorial judge.

MAY 24.   USG issued a proclamation, directed at Fenians, prohibiting armed expeditions against Canada originating in the U.S.

MAY 31.   USG submitted to the Senate an agreement stipulating an extension for ratifying the Santo Domingo annexation treaty.

MAY 31.   Congress passed a bill known as the Ku Klux Klan, or Enforcement, Act to protect the new constitutional rights of blacks.

JUNE 6.   USG gave an evening reception for the delegations of Spotted Tail and Red Cloud and the diplomatic corps. He met representatives of Brulé and Oglala Sioux on June 2 and 9.

JUNE 9.   USG, Julia Grant, and a party of friends left Washington, D.C., for a fishing trip in Pa., returning on June 13.

JUNE 15.   USG accepted the resignation of Attorney Gen. Ebenezer R. Hoar. The following day, USG nominated Amos T. Akerman as attorney gen.

JUNE 22.   Congress established the Dept. of Justice.

JUNE 30.   A vote of 28 to 28 in the Senate defeated the Santo Domingo Republic annexation treaty.

JULY 1.   USG advocated the removal of John L. Motley as minister to England and suggested Frederick T. Frelinghuysen for the post. On July 27, Frelinghuysen declined this nomination.

JULY 7.   USG returned to Washington, D.C., after visiting Conn. since July 2 and speaking at Stamford, New Haven, and Plainfield.

JULY 20.   USG ordered a pay increase of $1.50 per month for enlisted naval personnel and appointed Charles F. Hall to command an expedition toward the North Pole.

JULY 21.   USG and family went to Long Branch.

JULY 22.   Upon the request of Governor William W. Holden of N.C., USG ordered troops to the state to suppress Ku Klux Klan violence.

JULY 25.   USG authorized Lt. Gen. Philip H. Sheridan to visit Europe.

AUG. 2.   To interdict filibustering expeditions, USG put troops in San Francisco at the disposal of the U.S. marshal.

AUG. 4.   USG went to Washington, D.C., for two days.

AUG. 10.   USG traveled to St. Louis. USG stayed at the home of William H. Benton.

AUG. 12.   After looking into property matters and considering the purchase of a cemetery plot, USG left St. Louis for Chicago.

AUG. 17.   USG arrived in Long Branch after leaving Chicago on Aug. 14.

AUG. 18.   USG wrote to Sherman trying to reconcile differences between him and Secretary of War William W. Belknap over proper command of the army.

AUG. 22.   USG proclaimed U.S. neutrality in the Franco-Prussian War.

AUG. 23.   USG and Julia Grant went to Newport, R.I.

AUG. 28.   USG and Julia Grant visited West Point.

SEPT. 8.   Back in Washington, D.C., on account of events in Europe, USG declined an invitation to visit U.S. Senator Roscoe Conkling of N.Y. at his home in Utica.

SEPT. 9.   USG received Santiago Perez, Colombian minister, and acknowledged the importance of negotiations related to construction of an interoceanic canal.

SEPT. 10.   From New York City, USG telegraphed Secretary of State Hamilton Fish that U.S. Senator Oliver P. Morton had accepted appointment as minister to England. At Morton's request, USG withheld public announcement.

SEPT. 14.   In response to a formal welcome, USG spoke briefly at the Monmouth County Agricultural Fair, Freehold, N.J.

SEPT. 26.   USG and Julia Grant left Long Branch to take Ulysses S. Grant, Jr., to Harvard and Ellen Grant to Miss Porter's School, Farmington, Conn.

SEPT. 30.   USG attended the New York City funeral of Admiral David G. Farragut and dined that evening at the Union League Club.

OCT. 2.   USG returned to Washington, D.C.

OCT. 4.   USG asked Governor Marshall Jewell of Conn. to keep Ellen Grant at his home following her withdrawal from school.

OCT. 5.   USG accepted the resignation of Secretary of the Interior Jacob D. Cox effective upon completion of his annual report.

OCT. 8.   USG issued a proclamation prohibiting French and German vessels from using U.S. ports for any military purpose.

OCT. 12.   After several weeks consideration, USG simultaneously pardoned Fenians then in U.S. custody and issued a proclamation warning against violations of U.S. sovereignty.

OCT. 20.   USG privately acknowledged Morton's decision to decline appointment as minister to England.

OCT. 21. Troubled by problems related to the surveying of Chickasaw lands, USG called Cox and Ely S. Parker, commissioner
of Indian Affairs, to the White House.

OCT. 29. USG commissioned Columbus Delano as secretary of the
interior, effective Nov. 1.

The Papers of Ulysses S. Grant
November 1, 1869–October 31, 1870

To Hamilton Fish

Washington. D. C. Nov. 6th *1869.*

DEAR GOVERNOR:

If the appointment of Wing has not been made out for the place declined by Mr. Nunn of Tenn. it may be offered to Judge James H. Embry,[1] of Tenn. but now living in Washington, who I know will decline it. He is a man that I would like to offer a place to and who would appreciate the offer   It can afterwards be given as agreed yesterday.

> Respectfully
> your obt. svt.
> U. S. GRANT

TO HON. H. FISH,
SEC. OF STATE.

ALS, DLC-Hamilton Fish. On March 9, 1869, U.S. Senator William G. Brownlow of Tenn. had written to USG. "Hon David A. Nunn, a Member of the 40th Congress from the Western District of Tennessee, is an applicant for the appointment of Minister to Brazil. Having known him for many years I can cordially, *heartily* endorse his application. Since I have known him he has had my entire confidence and unabated esteem. In the private & public relations of life he is reliable. Mr. Nunn is an able lawyer, a gentleman of Excellent private character and fully qualified for the duties of the responsible office which he seeks. Few men in Tennessee have rendered greater service to, or made greater sacrifices for the Union Cause, than Mr. Nunn.—An original Unionist in a disloyal section, he has been an active friend of the Government, and the target of the Shafts of its enemies. For his vote as a Member of the 40th Congress in favor of the Impeachment of Andrew Johnson, he has been the special object of Rebel hatred and persecution. His appointment as Minister to Brazil would be hailed with satisfaction by the entire Republican Party of Tennessee. He would fill the office with credit and fidelity to the Government." LS, DNA, RG 59, Letters of Application and Recommendation. On April 20, USG nominated David A. Nunn as minister to Ecuador.

On Dec. 18, 1868, William H. Wadsworth, Maysville, Ky., wrote to USG. "It gives me great pleasure to introduce to you the bearer, E. Rumsey Wing, of Louisville, Ky. I assure you he is held in very great estimation by the Unionism of our State; not only for gallant Services in the Army, during the war, but since, for fidelity to, & eloquent advocacy of the cause for which he fought. His merit is very considerable in my eyes, I beg you to believe, since I have ventured to introduce him. I do not think you number amongst yr friends in Kentucky a worthier gentleman." ALS, *ibid.* While visiting Maysville in early July, USG, introduced by Wadsworth, said: "Gentlemen: I am very glad to see you, but you must not expect any speech from me. I leave that with my old schoolmate, Mr. Wadsworth." *New York Tribune,* July 11, 1868. See *Memoirs,* I, 25.

On May 10, 1869, Orville E. Babcock wrote to E. Rumsey Wing. "The President directs me to acknowledge the receipt of your note (on a card) and to say that the person appointed to *Ecuador* will accept. That an appointment was made to Nicaragua, but when it was discovered that the present incumbent was one that they did not wish to remove, his appointment was transferred to another place.—That the present incumbents of Turkey, Peru & Chili are men that the Administration does not wish to remove—The President expects the appointments to Chili and Peru will be vacant within a year by the voluntary retirement of the present ministers" Copies, DLC-USG, II, 1, 4. On Nov. 13, W. A. Bullitt *et al.,* Louisville, telegraphed to USG. "We re[s]pe[c]tfully ask that any mission to be accredited to Kentucky be bestowed upon E Rumsey Wing of L[o]ui[svi]ll[e] Ky as a matter of right and justice to Mr Wing and to the Republicans of Kentucky" Telegram received (at 2:00 P.M.), DNA, RG 107, Telegrams Collected (Bound). On Dec. 6, USG nominated Wing to succeed Nunn. On Jan. 9 and Sept. 3, 1873, Wing, Quito, wrote to USG. "*Personal . . .* I have just learned what leads me to suppose that the current report of my intended resignation, may have reached you. Many reasons conspire to render my resignation impracticable, and had decided me to the contrary. My knowledge of the language, people, and customs superadded to my acquaintance with the many schemes of internal & material improvement pending for the year, make me feel that my continued stay here is a matter of real necessity in a national and commercial point of view,—as I do not think that a man new to the country, could by any means compete with the European agents in securing the same advantages for our countrymen, that I am assured of doing. I may frankly say, that I have obtained a marked popularity here and can hold our own both with the people and government. If Congress will carry out your wise suggestion relative to an 'American steam Line' on this coast, the great proportion of the traffic of Ecuador, will, I am convinced, seek American markets. All of our countrymen here resident urge me to remain. When I came to this post, there was not a solitary American in Government employ, whereas today, with one or two exceptions the engineers, mechanics, and skilled workmen of all types, are Americans. I hope likewise to see all the great material improvements eventually committed to American hands. The first projected railroad is already under American supervision. Personally my health has slightly improved, though I am still unable to resume the active practice of my profession. Pecuniary misfortune lately fallen upon my family, has also made the education of my young brothers a charge upon myself. I did not come to Ecuador until late in the term, and have not yet completed three years here. I have been placed at great expense, in getting finally settled, and have only recently secured a good house permanently. . . ." "I have the honour to request your consideration of my application for the vacant mission to China." ALS, *ibid.,* RG 59, Letters of Application and Recommendation. Related papers are *ibid.*

1. Born in Ky., James H. Embry practiced law in Nashville and befriended Andrew Johnson; during the Civil War, he served as judge, Madison County, Ky. On June 24, 1869, Horace Porter wrote to Moses H. Grinnell, collector of customs, New York City. "The President has been informed by Judge Embry of Kentucky, that his cousin Mr. J. O. Embry has had his papers on file in your office for some time, applying for a position in the Custom House. He is one of the most reliable Union men of the State, and comes from the 8th district which gives a handsome Union majority. The President would be glad to see him obtain a position if it be convenient for you to appoint him." Copies, DLC-USG, II, 1, 4. Grinnell employed J. O. Embry as a clerk. On May 5, USG had removed James H. Embry's father, Bowling Embry, as postmaster, Nashville.

To Jacob D. Cox

Washington. D. C. Nov. 7th *1869*

Hon. J. D. Cox;
Sec. of the Int.
Sir:

Gov. Morton has called in relation to the appointment of Mr. Burson to the vacant directorship on the P R. R. He says he has no connection with the McGarrahan claim[1] further than the loaning of some money, two years ago, but a small amount ~~and~~ which does not the Governor thinks practically interest him in the matter. I think the appointment had better be made before applications becom too numerous.

Very respectfully,
your obt. svt.
U. S. Grant

ALS, DNA, RG 48, Appointment Div., Letters Received. On Oct. 29, 1869, U.S. Senator Oliver P. Morton of Ind., Indianapolis, had telegraphed to USG. "Learning that Judge L Williams of Indiana has resigned his position as Director of the Union Pacific road I earnestly recommend for the place John W. Burson of Muncie Indiana   He is an experienced railroad man of excellent capacity, a successful banker & sterling republican   a better appointment could not be made" Telegram received (at 2:30 P.M.), *ibid.* On Nov. 2, Judge Walter Q. Gresham *et al.*, Indianapolis, telegraphed to USG on the same subject. Telegram received (at 11:00 A.M.), *ibid.*, RG 107, Telegrams Collected (Bound). On March 2, 1870, Morton, Washington, D. C., wrote to USG. "My attention has just been called to the fact that the Commission to John W. Burson of Indiana as Director of the Union Pacific road was only to fill the unexpired term of Mr Williams who had resigned, and will expire in a few days. I respectfully ask his reappointment for the next term. No more responsible or competent man can be found for the place in my opinion." ALS, *ibid*., RG 48, Appointment Div., Letters Received. On the same day, Horace Porter endorsed this letter. "The Secretary of the Interior will make the appointment as asked for by the within letter of Senator Morton." ES, *ibid*. On Sept. 1, John W. Burson, Muncie, wrote to USG. "Other duties demand so much of my time, that I cannot give the attention requisite to the position with which you honored me, as one of the Directors of the Union Pacific Rail Road, that in justice to the government I would ask you to please accept my resignation." LS, *ibid*. Morton wrote an undated letter to USG. "I forgot this morning to present the resignation of Mr Burson as Director of the Union Pacific Road, about which I spoke to you several days, ago. I suggested for particulars reasons there should be nothing published now about the resignation, and no appointment made to fill the vacancy until towards spring. I beg leave to recommend for the appointment to fill the vacancy John. S. C. Harrison of Indianapolis, a grandson of Ex President Harrison, a Banker, and a thoroughgoing and influential Republican." ALS, *ibid*. On Feb. 23, 1872, Jan. 26, 1873, Feb. 3, 1874, and Jan. 18, 1875, Morton wrote to USG recommending the reappointment of John C. S. Harrison. LS (3) and ALS, *ibid*.

1. See letter to Jacob D. Cox, Aug. 22, 1870.

To Charles W. Ford

————

Washington. D. C. Nov. 12th *1869*

DEAR FORD,

Knowing how little you have to do, having nothing upon your hands but to collect the revenue[1] in your district, run a one horse Express Co, and a few little matters of that sort; besides your being a bachiler who has no rights that a married man need respect, I want to trouble you a little.

Last March I rec'd $65,000 00 for my house and furnature in this city. I have not invested but $21,000 00 of the money permanently. In a few years I must look to a private income for my support. I have thought, if a good opportunity presented, I would like to invest in good central improved property in St. Louis. I can pay $25,000 00 down and a balance as high as $20,000 00 pr. annum thereafter. To do this I have a private income of say $8,000 00 pr. annum besides what would be brought in by the property purchased, and have some money maturing, and bonds and stocks that I could sell enough of to make up any deficiency. I do not want to buy vacant land nor dwelling houses. If you see or hear of any such property will you write to me.

Please present my kindest regards to Benton and other friends.

Yours Truly

U. S. GRANT

P. S. Since writing the within I am in receipt of yours enclosing your account against me.

Please find check for the amt. and believe me under many obligations to you for your kindness.

U. S. G.

ALS, DLC-USG. See letter to Charles W. Ford, Jan. 3, 1870.

1. On Jan. 29, 1869, Bvt. Brig. Gen. Frederick T. Dent wrote to Charles W. Ford. "I have delayed answering your letter for a particular reason I wanted to sound, and I now feel I ought to say you will be disappointed in relation to the office of Naval officer at N Y I feel confident you can have the collectorship of the Port of St Louis or Post office there—or Collector of Internal revenue or Assessor of same Mrs G told me that you would be disappnted in relation to Naval officer at N Y—and felt sure you would get whatever you asked for at St Louis—" ALS, DLC-USG. On March 31, USG nominated Ford as collector of Internal Revenue, 1st District, Mo. On March 8, Ford, St. Louis, wrote to USG. "In conversation with Judge Treat today,—I learn that the late Atty Genl Evarts, directed Genl Noble U S Atty here—to enter a discontinuance in the cases of Dan Able, E B Brown & others indicted for violation of Rev. Laws—the facts of which you already know. It appears—this cannot be done before the first of next month, when the court will sit, as it has to be done in *open court*, Now then—suppose the new atty Genl sends an order Countermanding the order sent by Mr Evarts. This leavs, the matter in Court—and these men will be compelled to come up and defend themselves as best they can—It seems a great pity that these men should go unwhipped of justice—when the evidence is so strong against them—" ALS, DNA, RG 60, Letters from the President.

To Lamson & Goodnow Company

Washington, D. C. Nov. 17th *1869.*

SIRS:

At the hand of B. F. Pond, Eq I am this day in receipt of the beautifully wrought set of cutlery, the result of the skill of the workmen of the "Lamson & Goodnow Manufacturing Company," and the gift of the workmen to me.

It affords me special pleasure to see American Manufacturies succeed in making those thing which are generally articles of import. The specimens of cutlery sent me affords such evidence in one line of Manufactury at least. I accept your present then with pleasure because it is American in workmanship; because it is from the hands of the workman that I received it, and because of the very flattering assurances which accompany it.

> I have the honor to be,
> with great respect,
> your obt. svt.
> U. S. GRANT

To WORKMEN LAMSON & GOODNOW'S MANUFACTURING CO.
OF SHELBURNE FALLS MASS.

ALS (facsimile), *Ulysses S. Grant's Letter to the Workmen of Lamson & Goodnow Manufacturing Company* . . . (Shelburne Falls, 1962). On Nov. 17, 1869, B. F. Pond presented the gift to USG. "I have come sir in the name and at the request of the workmen employed in the factories of the 'Lamson and Goodnow Manufacturing Company' of Shelburne Falls, Mass. to present you with a testimonial of their respect and esteem. . . ." *Ibid.* Much of the cutlery, a sixty-two-piece set with ivory and mother-of-pearl handles, is now in the Smithsonian Institution. See *New York Times*, Sept. 28, 1869.

Speech

[*Nov. 22, 1869*]

GENERAL: If any proof were wanting of the unfounded character of the prejudice which, until recently, pervaded at least parts of this country against the race from which you are sprung, it might be found in the high tone and polished style of the remarks which you have just uttered.

That, however, like all similar prejudices, no matter how deeply implanted, must, sooner or later, yield to the force of truth. The throes by which the new birth here was accompanied were, indeed, agonizing, and their effects, even now, are scarcely over.

Provident statesmen, however, have neglected no fit opportunity for sanctioning and securing by law those privileges for your kinsmen which have been the inevitable and natural result of our great civil convulsion. Among them is their right to employment abroad, as well as at home, in the public service—a right which, as you say, has been acknowledged by the appointment of one of the formerly proscribed race to represent the United States in Hayti.

I congratulate myself for this occasion to render homage to the change of public sentiment adverted to, by receiving you, as I cordially do, as the first Envoy Extraordinary and Minister Plenipotentiary from that Republic.

Washington Chronicle, Nov. 23, 1869. On Nov. 22, 1869, Alexander Tate, Haitian minister, addressed USG. "MR. PRESIDENT: I have the honor to deliver to your Excellency the letter by which I am accredited near you in the quality of Minister Plenipotentiary and Envoy Extraordinary of the Government of Hayti. The great and noble progress which humanity has realized in these latter times in this hemisphere—especially due to the laborious and always constant efforts of American philanthropy—the luminous convictions, and the indomitable energy with which your illustrious predecessor, Abraham Lincoln, and the present Administration have consecrated that progress in the fundamental law of this great people of the United States and in its policy, renders it, now and hereafter, more obligatory still and more particularly agreeable, for the Republic of Hayti, than for the other nations of the earth, to be represented near the Government of Washington. The high philanthropy and the sentiment of just reparation toward a race heretofore oppressed in this same country; those noble principles which have determined your Administration, Mr. President, to make choice of a man of that race to represent the great and powerful Republic of the United States at the Republic of Hayti, have awakened in the hearts of all Haytiens—jealous of the progress and of the ultimate elevation of their race—a just feeling of admiration and of gratitude. President Salnave, as the representative of the nation, has charged me to express to your Excellency how much he has been gratified at this mark of esteem and consideration given to our race. He augurs from that the finest hope of the extension of those connections and reciprocity of favor and sympathy which will hereafter exist between the two countries. For my part, Mr. President, I congratulate myself, and am proud that Providence has so arranged events, that the choice of President Salnave has fallen upon me to be the interpreter of sentiments, which I so deeply share toward the people of the United States in general and your administration in particular. You may be assured, Mr. President, that my efforts in the appointment which I have the honor to fill near your Government, will always tend to affirm and consolidate the good harmony which so happily already exists between the Government of the United States and that of the Republic of Hayti." *Ibid.* On Oct. 30, President Sylvain Salnave of Haiti had written a letter of credence for Tate to USG. ALS (in French—marked as received on Nov. 22), DNA, RG 59, Notes from the Haitian Legation.

On March 3, Gideon H. Hollister, U.S. minister, Port-au-Prince, wrote to Bvt. Brig. Gen. Adam Badeau. "Will you do me the favor of asking the President to allow me to remain here as Minister Resident for two or three years. The rebellion has been very expensive to me as I have been obliged to shelter feed & in some instances clothe two hundred & fifty political refugees for several months. Affairs here are very unsettled still but I think Salnave will succeed in the end. What a grand time our friend Booth is having at his new Theatre! . . ." ALS, DLC-Hamilton Fish. On April 10, Salnave wrote to USG congratulating him on his election and praising Hollister. ALS (in French), DNA, RG 59, Notes from the Haitian Legation. On March 12, Thomas Webster, Philadelphia, wrote to USG. "I have the honor to respectfully urge the appointment of Professor Ebenezer D. Bassett, of this city to the Haytien Mission. Professor Bassett is a highly educated colored man and, for years, has been the chief of the faculty of the Philadelphia Colored High School. Beside being conspicuous for natural force of character and intellectual attainments, he is distinguished for probity and patriotism—for independence and for modesty. I beg leave respectfully to refer specifically to a service he rendered the country. In 1863, when the free colored people of this city, and of the north generally were indifferent, sullen, or adverse to the organization of colored troops, and were about to agitate against the measure, because the pay of the colored soldier was inferior to the pay of the white soldier, and because no colored man could rise to be an officer, no matter how meritorious he might be, the Supervisory Committee for Recruiting Colored Troops were able, by means of Mr Bassett's large influence and by his active and persistent efforts, to overcome this prejudice. My position of chairman of the aforesaid committee enables me to speak of his services with knowledge. It was due mainly to his efforts in co-operation with those of Mr Frederick Douglass, that the committee was able to induce the colored clergy and the leading colored men to urge the colored people to enlist and to create the enthusiasm among them which gave the country thirteen regiments from this city—an evidence of devotion on the part of the colored which popularised the great measure with the people at large and greatly assisted in lessening the prejudice of centuries against the negro race." ALS, *ibid.*, Letters of Application and Recommendation. On March 17, Ebenezer D. Bassett, "Principal and Professor of the Classics and Mathematics in the Colored High School, Philadelphia," wrote to USG. "I have the honor respectfully to represent, that, at the urgent solicitations of many discreet and influential friends, both of my own (the colored) race and of the white race, I have made application to be appointed Minister Resident and Consul General at Hayti, and have filed my memorial and its accompanying recommendations in the Department of State. I respectfully trust, that Your Excellency may not deem it improper in me, to refer to these documents, and, further, to hope that Your Excellency may yourself examine them. They will show that they are offered in support of my application by the leading men of my own race in this country, and by distinguished gentlemen in different States of our Union, whose candor, ability and patriotism, command the confidence and esteem of the Nation. More particularly, these papers will show that I am a colored man, born and educated in New England—partly at Yale College, numerous members of the faculty of which institution have cordially joined in my application; that I have labored with gratifying success in this city for fourteen years, to train, discipline and elevate my own race morally and intellectually; that I enjoy an unchallenged character for probity and patriotism, and have the respect and esteem of this community, besides the confidence and good wishes of many leading men, divines, statesmen and others, of different portions of our country. Perhaps Your Excellency will also permit me to state, that I am urged by prominent republicans of this and other states, for this Mission, as a *representative colored man* fitted for the position; and my appointment, or the appointment of some other proper person of my race, would be hailed by them, especially by recently enfranchised colored citizens, as a marked recognition of *our* new condition in the Republic and an auspicious token of our great future. It is in this light, that I would most frankly ask Your Excellency to *first* consider my application, and to then scrutinize the special evidences of my character, fitness and services as they are revealed by the documents herein referred to. I sincerely trust, that I may not be considered egotistical in what I have said, or in stating that many of my testimonials were tendered to me unsolicited, and that numerous other recommendations of a similar character are freely proffered to me by earnest, able, influential republicans. I take great pleasure in referring Your Excellency, by special permission in reference to this application, to George H. Stuart, Esq., of this city." ALS, *ibid.*

On March 18, George B. Vashon, Washington, D. C., wrote to USG. "I have the honor to solicit hereby, that I be nominated to the Senate by you for the Haytian mission, in the event of a vacancy occurring in that office. In taking this step, I am influenced by the hope, that, in the event of its being deemed advisable to have this country represented in Hayti by a colored man, I may not be found lacking in qualifications, either natural or acquired, to serve as its accredited agent, in such a manner as may best tend to sustain its dignity and subserve its interests. A lawyer by profession, and honored by an admission to practise in the Supreme Court of the United States, I have made a special study of international law, as well as of the conduct of negotiations, and of the various other matters pertaining to diplomacy. I am, also, somewhat versed in the political and military history of Hayti, its physical and moral statistics, and the genius and character of its people; as I resided in that island for the period of nearly three years, during the latter portion of which I held the professorship of the Greek and English languages in the *Collége Faustin*, the principal national school at Port-au-Prince. This residence, too, enabled me to attain to quite an extended familiarity with the French language and literature. In furtherance of this present application, I respectfully beg leave to submit herewith a few testimonials as to my character and attainments; and, in the hope, that it may meet with your favorable consideration, . . ." ALS, *ibid.* In an undated petition, John M. Langston *et al.* wrote to USG recommending Vashon for judge of the police court, Washington, D. C. DS (16 signatures), *ibid.*, RG 60, Records Relating to Appointments. George T. Downing and F. G. Barbadoes, National Executive Committee of Colored Men, favorably endorsed this petition. ES, *ibid.*

On March 19, A. W. Henson, Cincinnati, wrote to USG. "As few things of consequence are gained without asking, and as one is not made poorer nor more unworthy by asking, even though his request is not granted, I wish to ~~pr~~ make the following brief statement; For the last sixteen years saving one year in which I served as one of my Country's Defenders, I have been engaged in schoolteaching. At present I am the prin, of one of the Col'd Dist Schools. I have not the fortune to have my claims urgred by Senators, ~~Representa~~use Representatives, nor Governors; therefore I must 'paddle my own canoe'. I am a colored man, and I ~~wo~~ would be pleased to represent our Country ~~on~~ in 'Hayti' If desired I can give testimonials of character fitness &c from Distinguished men of color ~~such~~ among whom I might mention Bishops Dan'l A. Payne D. D. Wm P. Quinn & Jas A Shorter two of whom (P. & Q) have known me from my youth. Hoping that you may see your way clear to recommend me for Minister to Hayti, . . . This is not a long letter; please read it" ALS, *ibid.*, RG 59, Letters of Application and Recommendation. Bassett was confirmed as minister and consul general to Haiti on April 16. On Sept. 15, Salnave twice wrote to USG acknowledging the recall of Hollister and the accreditation of Bassett. ALS (in French), *ibid.*, Notes from the Haitian Legation.

On Jan. 9, 1870, President Nissage Saget of Haiti wrote to USG recalling Tate. ALS (in French), *ibid.* Probably on Feb. 1, Tate wrote to USG declining to attend a White House state dinner for the diplomatic corps on account of ". . . the mournful condition in which they have just been placed by the late announcement this morning of the execution, in Hayti, of the Chief whose Government they here represent, . . ." *Washington Chronicle*, Feb. 2, 1870. Salnave had been executed on Jan. 15. On Feb. 10, Orville E. Babcock wrote to Secretary of State Hamilton Fish. "I am directed by the President to inform you that the arrangement for Mr. Tate at 12 o'clock tomorrow will be perfectly agreeable." LS, DNA, RG 59, Miscellaneous Letters. Tate took his leave on Feb. 11. See Rayford W. Logan, *The Diplomatic Relations of the United States with Haiti, 1776–1891* (Chapel Hill, 1941), pp. 332–44.

On March 21, Saget wrote to USG a letter of credence for Stephen Preston. ALS (in French—marked as received on April 22), DNA, RG 59, Notes from the Haitian Legation. On April 22, Preston addressed USG. "I have the honor to present to Your Excellency my credential letter, as Minister Resident of the Governement of the Republic of Haiti to your Governement. Général N. Saget who has been elected constitutionally as President of the Republic has commissioned me to impress on Your Excellency his admiration for your self & country & his desires that the cordial relations which has existed between the two countries, the two Eldest republics of America, should continue & increase to our mutual benefit. . . . I shall report to my Governement the good fortune I had to witness in NewYork the peacefull jubilee of the colored men of this country, held in honor of the amendement of the United States Constitution, by which abou[t] Eight Millions of *Parias*, the greatest part slaves a short time ago, have become Citizens, Citizens of the Great Model Republic! . . ." AD (in both French and English), *ibid.* USG responded. "Mr. Preston: I thank you for the good wishes which, on behalf the President of Hayti, you have expressed for me personally and for the country of which I am the Chief Magistrate. So far as I am aware there is no reason why the existing friendly relations between the United States and Hayti should not continue and become strengthened. It is hoped that your anticipations of the advantages to be expected by your country from the policy of its Government, which you advocate, may be fully realized. So far as a stranger may be capable of judging that policy seems to show a wise forbearance and foresight. It is natural that recent events in this country should not only be especially interesting to yours, but that one of their most important results in political freedom and equality to that numerous race here, which composes the far greater part of the people of Hayti, should of itself create a sentiment of reciprocal good will, which I trust may be perpetual." *Washington Chronicle*, April 23, 1870.

On July 25, John Bell Hepburn, Port-au-Prince, wrote to USG. "I must humbly request that you will permit me—a mulatto and native of Virginia, sixty four years old and thirty five years absent from my native country—to address a few lines to your Excellency, in admiration of your person and exalted character—for the great deeds in which you are the concentrated power and firm mover, which have redounded to the equalization of rights and privileges to a race hitherto downtrodden and despised. Although separated from your Excellency by geographical distance and clime, still I ever labour to inform myself of all that is transpiring and being done in my native country, as regards the welfare of its inhabitants and more especially that portion which has been so long under the ban of contumely and opprobrium; but now, thanks to an Almighty Power, thanks to your Excellency, thanks to the immortal Lincoln, thanks to the noble coadjutors, both living and dead, who have so nobly brought about the great Magna Charta of Freedom and Equality, by the covenant of the 15th amen[dme]nt, for which you so nobly ask the conservation and by the am[end]-ment of Laws for its' observance in all time to come. I see, Noble President, that your wide spread Philanthropy does not confine itself to the Americo-Anglo-African, but that your benevolent heart extends its' paternal regards to other peoples and to other climes, and that you have offered a helping hand to alleviate the sorrows, woes and lamentations of the Dominican people. O! how shall I rank you on Glory's page? Millions yet unborn will be taught to lisp your Name and revere your Memory as an American. I regret to state to your Excellency that the United States Officials, as well as certain American Merchants in Hayti, have not comprehended the interests of their country by not having ingratiated themselves with the most respectable and intelligent portion of this part of the island. During [the] past three years they have not been wise, by not observing that a state of things, as under the preceding ruler,—Salnave in any case, could not have lasted long, or any of that Chief's promises could have been relied on. I have ever lived an exemplary life for thirty five years that I have been in Hayti,—doing no injury of the slightest nature to any one, but known to be peaceful, inoffensive, laborious and enterprising in my business. However, under the late Ruler, there was no consideration for all this and on the 5th of May 1868, at 8 P. M. my dwelling and store were assailed by an armed band of soldiers, crying 'Long live Salnave.'—A Minnie Rifle was fired through my door, into my store, the ball passed through my body and I was picked up the next morning and carried to the American Consulate where I laid on my back for many months. While yet in this sad and dangerous condition I had moveable property destroyed, by order of Salnave's government, to the value of Sixty thousand Dollars gold, and this in the very presence of Mr Hollister, U. S. Minister here,—who even promised to do something for me, but never did—and up to this day I have not been paid [or] indemnified for my losses, notwithstanding a decree was issued by Salnave's government that I was to be paid. I am sorry also to inform your Excellency that for some cause unknown to me the U. S. Minister paid more attention to Salnave's business than to that of american citizens, so much so that when he was recalled by his Government, he accepted the situation as Minister of Salnave's government to Washington, but Salnave's adviser's would not sanction the nomination. This is the second time that I have had the honor of addressing myself to the President of the U. S.— once to the immortal Lincoln and now to your Excellency—, and I must also humbly request of your Excellency to forgive this intrusion on your precious time, but as a Christian Father & Friend and protector of the oppressed, I lay my grievance at your feet and solicit your intercession for redress. In the nature of things I may never have the honor, the [s]atisfaction, to see your Excellency, but permit me to assure your Excellency that I will never cease to pray to Almighty God to bless you and to preserve your life and that of your family, and that you may long live to see the practicable demonstrations of your comprehensive views and enlarged ideas, for the welfare of the american continent and its inhabita[nts.] Indulging in the hope that this will meet your Exce[llen]cy['s] serious consideration, . . ." ALS, DNA, RG 59, Miscellaneous Letters. On Oct. 12, Hepburn wrote a similar letter to USG. ALS, *ibid.* Hepburn's letter to President Abraham Lincoln, May 7, 1862, is in DLC-Robert T. Lincoln.

On Nov. 2, 1870, Ed. Horton, Port-au-Prince, wrote to USG. "One of your citizens, unknown to you compel by necessity to make myself known to you by the present, more especially Since the 15th amandement of the constitution for which article I thank God for, and the Ex-President Abraham Licoln for, yourself and all that laboured for Such a just cause both the living and the dead; millions unborn will be taught to give thanks to all to whom it may concerns for having accept Our rights and merits. I was born eight miles from Plimouth (North Carolina) in 1825, I am now forty five years of age, my mother and father Still are living in Plimouth (North-Carolina) there is eleven years Since I leaft my native home and are living in Port-au-Prince (Capital of Hayti).—Finding my advantages favorable and prosperos from the time I came to this country up to 1869, I ask of the Government of Hayti of the Ex-President Sylvin Salnave a pasport to live Port-au-Prince and to go down to the cost, to Bainet, a Small village, to buy Some coffee and a cargo of logwood which pasport was granted to me by the Said Government—I want down and brought the quantity of produce namely 65 bags of Coffee and 248000# of logwood which amounted to the Sum of Seven thousand for hundred and forty eight american american dollars, felling myself justify in So doing, knowing that it was a leagle consent of the Government of Hayti and bearing in mind the Same time that there is a treatee betwen my Government and the Government of Hayti that record me that priveledge and protection to do So.—After having bought and paid the Said amount of the Said quantity of coffee and logwood and before I had time to export it, the Government of the President Sylvin Salnave failed and the Government of the President Nissage Saget came in power, and his officers came down to Bainet and Seized my coffee and logwood, I myself knowing that I was not guilty of nothing that concers the government, for I never in my life meddle into the politics of the Country during the 11 years one way or the other; I go to those officers and ask of them for what cause or what have I done to make them Seize my coffee and logwood Général Lis (haytian General) replied: because you are a white man (He calls me white, because I will not consent to became a Soldier and Serve his Country. My Excellence, President, I am Sorry to have to disturb you and to call on you for healp from my Government, but as I cannot do ortherwise than to call upon you for healp or the benefit of my eleven years labours will be lost.—Seeing this to be the only Service for we american citizens that has undergone lately heavy and great losses amidst the abundance of the aclaim made by american citizen, to you, President I pray you to except of mine, though Small, in the name of justice and right, having the high honor to Salute you most respectfully waiting patiently for the return answer according to your jugment and authority. . . . P. S. I have laid the demand of my losses before the Government of Hayti and have waited for an answer from him for the last Six months and he refuses to enter into any Settlement Whatever, I am not able, President, to loose it and if you want more understanding upon the matter, I have good witnesses both of american and haytian citizen." ALS, DNA, RG 59, Miscellaneous Letters.

On Dec. 20, Henry Allen, Port-au-Prince, wrote to USG. "Compel by necessity to call upon your Excellency to my healp—I Henry—Allen, a citizen of the United States, born in Cecel-Conty (Maryland) in March 1800, raised to a man, marred and became father of two children in the same place.—I left home in September 1824 to find a better living, leving my father and mother behind me with nine children myself making the tenth, My father is now living at the Same place were I was born and is about one hundred years of age, I came to Port au Prince (Hayti) were I reseded for 46 years and have followed the Wheels-Wright's buisness with Success, I have brought property and build a large two Stories house of two appartments Six rooms each, a low house 24 by 28, a large work-Shop and propotional increase of necessaries of life, furniture and all that pertained to house keeping, carts, Wheels and tools for the Wheels-Wright buisness, but the 3rd of June 1869 all was burnt and pilaged by Orders of the Haytien-Government and I leaft peniless.—My Excellence and You Members of Congress, under all Considerations, my unjust losses are justely esteemed at $20.000 american Gold.—In verture of the treatie made by the Government of the United States and the haytien Government to garantee all Strangers in Hayti of their just losses and the 15th amandment of the Constitution of the United-States, these two things combine togarther induces me to hope for Success. Among the many petetions that have been already addressed to you, please exapt of this although imperfectly composed, I hope it will be accepted for its merits. Whatever further information may be required will be readely responded to on demand. Admest the abondance of the reclaim made by american citizens to the Government of the United-States, I pray you to except of mine, though Small, in the name of Justice an Right . . ." LS, *ibid*.

To David Butler

Washington D. C. Nov 23. 1869

SIR:

In view of the fact that the next session of the legislature of Nebraska does not occur until the year 1871, and that it will therefore not have an opportunity of taking action upon the ratification of the fifteenth amendment to the Constitution until that time, I

would respectfully suggest that you consider the propriety of con-
vening the legislature in extra session for this purpose, and if the
proposition should meet with your views, I request that a proclamation be issued to that effect at as early a period as you may deem
expedient.

I am induced to write you upon this subject from the earnest
desire I have to see a question of such great national importance
brought to an early settlement, in order that it may no longer remain an open issue, and a subject of agitation before the people.

Very respectfully
U S GRANT.

TO HIS EXCELLENCY DAVID BUTLER
GOVERNOR OF NEBRASKA
OMAHA NEBRASKA

Copy, DLC-USG, II, 1. On Feb. 17, 1870, Governor David Butler of Neb. telegraphed to USG. "Nebraska legislature met two 2 P. M. today ratified fifteenth
15th amendment at four 4 only five 5 votes against One 1 in Senate four 4 in
house," Telegram received (on Feb. 18, 11:20 P.M.), DNA, RG 107, Telegrams Collected (Bound). See letter to Congress, March 30, 1870; *HMD*, 41-
2-73.

On Dec. 9, 1869, USG wrote to the House. "I transmit a report from the
Secretary of State in answer to a resolution of the House of Representatives
of yesterday, asking to be informed what State legislatures have ratified the
proposed fifteenth amendment of the Constitution of the United States." Copies,
DNA, RG 59, General Records; *ibid.*, RG 130, Messages to Congress. On the
same day, Secretary of State Hamilton Fish had written to USG providing the
information. Copy, *ibid.*, RG 59, General Records. See *HED*, 41-2-15. On Dec.
15, Fish wrote to USG stating that Ala. had ratified the Fifteenth Amendment.
Copy, DNA, RG 59, General Records. On the same day, USG transmitted this
information to the House. Copies, *ibid.*; *ibid.*, RG 130, Messages to Congress.
See *HED*, 41-2-26.

To Edwards Pierrepont

[Dec. 3, 1869]

Your letter saying that it was understood that Judge Woodruff's age would exclude him from the appointment of Circuit
Judge is received. As I understand, the Judge is just sixty, and of

robust constitution and vigorous intellect. He may not be appointed, but if he is not it will be from other considerations. I say to you in confidence that if I was to make the appointment to-day, Judge W. would receive it . . . I would be pleased to hear any thing you have to say on the subject . . .

Charles Hamilton Auction, Oct. 8, 1964, no. 79. On Nov. 1 and 27, 1869, Edwards Pierrepont, U.S. attorney, New York City, had written to Attorney Gen. Ebenezer R. Hoar. "The enclosed should have been sent in another of this date— Please have it placed with the other—I wish to write you a few lines upon the subject of the Circuit Judge—Judge Johnson and Judge Woodruff, as you told me, were favorably considered—I know them both—they are both well fitted for the place—I, in common with most of the New York Bar, prefer Judge Woodruff for the following reasons—He is a resident of this City. & Judge Johnson is a resident of Utica, where he has retired upon a fortune left by his late father. The *business* of the Circuit is mainly here—Habeas Corpus, Injunction—Attachmt &c often; *very often*, require prompt action in New York, & Utica is quite as far off as Washington & in winter more distant, in point of time. Judge Woodruff is a man of immense energy & vigor   He is *sixty years old*—no more—Upon this point I am advised, *carefully*—Judge Woodruff (as our friend Evarts will tell you) is experienced as a Judge, very industrious & able & will be generally acceptable—If Judge Johnson li[ve]d here & would go earnestly to work he would be an excellent man for the place—" "My reasons for preferring Woodruff to Johnson, I gave you in the only letter which I have written upon the subject, and which I addressed to you some weeks since. The objection to Woodruff's age had not occurred to me, as he is full of vigor and very industrious: when you suggested that past sixty was rather advanced, and that forty-five was more desirable, I felt the force of the suggestions, but I still think that Woodruff would last very many years, and that it would be far better to have him with his years, than any one, whom years would not improve him—I learned from the President last Saturday, that Woodruff and Benedict were both *strongly* pressed, and that the pressure was likely to give the place to some third man. . . ." ALS and LS, DNA, RG 46, Papers Pertaining to Executive Nominations. Related papers are *ibid.* On Dec. 4, Saturday, Pierrepont telegraphed to USG. "Shall surely see You on Monday evening, the precise hour depends upon the train" Telegram received (at 2:20 P.M.), *ibid.*, RG 107, Telegrams Collected (Bound). On Dec. 8, USG nominated Lewis B. Woodruff as judge, 2nd Circuit.

On May 5, 1870, Woodruff, New York City, wrote to USG. "I am informed that a vacancy is about to occur in the office of Attorney of the U. S. in the Southern District of New York. My regard for Judge Pierrepont induces me first to express my regret that he should desire to relinquish the office. Next I hope I shall not be deemed intrusive if to other recommendations of E. Delafield Smith, Esq., as his successor, I add my own. . . ." Copies, DLC-Benjamin F. Butler; DLC-Hamilton Fish. On May 18, Horace Greeley, New York City, wrote to USG. "Judge Pierrepont having resolved to resigne the post of District Attorney for this district, I venture to suggest the name of E. Delafield Smith, Esq., for his successor. Mr. Smith is still young, is widely popular, and has achieved an eminent standing in his profession. Few surpass him in industry or attainments none in the number of their devoted friends. I respectfully commend him to your favorable regard." Copy, DLC-Benjamin F. Butler. Similar letters are *ibid*. On July 1, USG nominated Noah Davis to replace Pierrepont.

Annual Message

[*Dec. 6, 1869*]

FELLOW CITIZENS OF THE SENATE AND
HOUSE OF REPRESENTAVES.

In coming before you for the first time, ~~it~~as Chief Magistrate of this great Nation, it is with gratitude to the Giver of all good for the many blessings we enjoy. We are blessed with peace at home and are without tangling alliance abroad to forebode trouble. We are blessed with a territory unequaled in fertility, ~~with a population of forty millions of free people, all speaking one language, with equal rights to struggle for fame, fortune, or whatever else each in his place may regard as the greatest personal blessing. We are blessed with facilities for all to acquire an education. We have been blessed with abundant crops~~ of an ~~extent~~ area equal to the abundant support of a population of ~~F~~five hundred ~~people~~ million of people; With abundant crops: with a varie~~d~~ty of climate suited to the production of every ~~variety~~ specie of ~~production~~ earths riches, and to suit~~s~~ the habits, tastes and requirements of every living thing; abounding in every variety of useful mineral ~~and~~ in quantities sufficient to supply the world for many generations: with a population of forty Million of free people, all speaking one language: with facilities for every mortal to acquire an education: with institutions closing ~~fame~~ to none the avenues to ~~any~~ fame or any blessing that may be coveted: with freedom of the pulpit, the press, and the school; with a revenue flowing into the National Treasury beyond the requirements of the government ~~t~~These blessings, and countless ~~more~~ others, are entrusted to your care and m~~y~~ine ~~care, for the present,~~ for safe keeping~~s~~ for the brief period of our tenure of office. In a short time ~~at furthes~~ we must ~~all return~~ each of us return to the ranks of the people who have confered upon us our honors, to account to them for our stewardships ~~whilst we have been public servants~~. I earnestly desire that neither you nor I will be condemned by a free and enlightened constituency, nor by our own consciences. (Happily harmony is being rapidly restored w within our own borders.) Manufactoris, hitherto unknown in our country, are springing up in all sections producing a national independence unequaled ~~in the~~ by any other power. With a country extending from the Atlantic to the Pacific, and embracing in its limits almost from the Tropic to the Frigid zone, ~~in its territory, and~~ an industrious, free and educated people of Forty Million, all speaking one language, gratitude for such blessings should be ~~felt by~~ a common feeling.

Energing from a rebellion of gigantic magnitude, (aided by the sympathies and assistance of nations with which we were at peace,) eleven states of the Union were, four years ago, left without legal state governments. A National debt ~~was contracted~~ of great apparent magnitude was contracted; American Commerce was almost driven from the seas; ~~and~~ the industry of one half of the country was ~~changed~~ taken from the controll of the capitalist and placed where all labor rightfully belongs, in the keeping of those who bestow it. The work of restoring state governments, loyal to the Union, of protecting and fostering free labor, and providing means for paying the interest on the public debt, has received ample attention from ~~Congres.~~ you. Although ~~their~~ your efforts have not met with the sucsess, in all particulars, that might have been expected, yet, on the whole, they have been more sucsessful than could have been reasonably ~~expected.~~ anticipated. ~~Eight~~ Seven of the states which passed ordnances of secession ~~(including West Va)~~ have been fully restored to their places in the Union; ~~the ninth, Georgia, it is confidently hoped will, on the assembling of its Legislature in January next, take such action, guided by the decission of the Supreme Court of the state, as will insure her admission to representation in Congress.~~

Georgia

The ~~State of Georgia~~ eighth, Georgia, held an election at which ~~they~~ she ratified ~~their~~ her Constitution, elected ~~members~~ members of Congress, a Governor & Lt. Governor, a state legislature, and all other officers required of them to elect. The Governor and Lt. Governor were duly instaled, and the legislature met and performed all the acts then required of them by the re-construction acts of Congress. Subsequently however, in violation of their ratified constitution, (as since decided by the Supreme Court of the State) they unseated the colored members of the legislature, and admitted to seats, ~~it is believed~~, some members who are disqualified by the 3d ~~Section~~ clause of the Fourteenth Article to the Constitution, an article which they themselves had ~~just~~ contributed to the ratifiedcation of. Under these circumstances I would submit to you whether it would not be wise, without delay, to enact a law authorizing the Governor of Georgia to convene the members originally elected to the legislature; the members to take the oath prescribed by law, none to be admitted who are ineligible under the Third Clause of the Fourteenth Amendment, and admit their Senators and representatives ~~elected~~ when this is done.

The ~~labor~~ freedmen, under the protection which they have received, are making rapid progress in learning, and no complaints are heard of lack of industry ~~in them~~ on their part where they receive fair remuneration for their labor.—The means provided for paying the interest on the public debt, with all other expenses of government, are more than ample. The ~~revival~~ loss of our Commerce is the only result of the late rebellion which has not received efficient attention from Congress. To this subject I call ~~the~~ your earnest attention, ~~of Congress~~. I will not now suggest plans by which this object ~~can~~ may be effected but will, if necessary, make it the subject of a special message during the session of Congress.

~~On the~~   ~~of April, Congress passed a joint resolution, as follows~~. . . . At the March term Congress, by joint resolution, authorized the Executive to order elections in the states of Va, Miss, & Texas, to submit to them the constitutions which each ~~of~~

~~these states~~ had previously, in convention, framed, and to submit the constitutions ~~to be voted upon~~ either entire, or in separate parts, at the discretion of the Executive. Under this authority elections were called ~~in the States of Virginia, Mississippi & Texas~~. In ~~the former of these states~~ Va[1] the election took place on the   of   ; the Governor and Lt. Governor elected have been installed, the legislature met and did all required by this resolution and all the reconstruction acts of Congress, and abstained from all doubtful authority. I recommend that her Senators and representatives be promptly admitted and that the state be fully restored to its ~~independence~~ place in the ~~Union.~~ family of states. Elections were called in Mississippi and Texas to commence on the 30th of November 1869, and to last two days in Miss. and four days in Texas. ~~It is hoped that the result in both these states will be favorable and that the action of their legislatures, when they meet, will insure the speedy admission of their representatives to seats in the Councils of the Nation.~~ The elections have taken place, but the result is not known.[2] It is ~~to be~~ hoped that the Acts of the legislature of these states will be such, when they meet, as to receive your approval and thus close the work of reconstruction.

Among the evils growing out of the rebellion, and not yet refered to, is that of an irredeemable currency. It is an evil which ~~should~~ I hope will receive your most earnest attention. It is a duty, and one of the highest duties, of government, ~~to return to a specie basis,~~ [to] secure to the citizen a medium of exchange of fixed, unvarying value. This implies a return to a specie basis, and no substitute for it can be devised. It should be commenced now and reached at the earlyest practicable moment consistent with a fair regard to the interests of the debtor class. Immediate resumption, if practicable, would not be desirable. It would compel the debtor class to pay, beyound their contracts, the premium on gold at the date of their purchase, and would ~~produce~~ bring bankruptcy and ruin ~~over the country~~ to thousands. Fluctuations ~~too~~ however in the paper value of the measure of all values, *gold*, is detrimental to the interests of trades. ~~and~~ It makes the ~~merchant~~ man of business an involuntary gambler. In all sales where future payment is to be made both parties speculate as to what ~~then~~ will be the value of the currency to be paid and received. ~~I then~~ I earnestly recommend to you then such legislation as will insure a gradual return to specie payments, and an immediate stop to fluctuation in the value of currency.—The methods to secure the former of these results are as numerous as are the speculators on political economy. ~~t~~To secure the latter I see but one way, and that is to authorize the Treasury to redeem its own paper, at a fixed price, whenever presented, and to withhold ~~all~~ from circulation all currency so redeemed ~~unless bought~~ until ~~bought with~~ sold again for gold. ~~from the treasury.~~

The vast resources of the nation, both developed and undeveloped, ought to make our credit the best ~~of any nation~~ on earth. With a less burthen of taxation than the citizen has endured for six years, the entire public debt could be paid in ten years. But it is not desirable that the people should be taxed to pay it in that time. Year by year the ability to pay increases in a rapid ration. The burden of interest though ought to be reduced as rapidly as it can be done without violation of contract. ~~On~~ The public debt ~~was contracted from the years 1862 to 1868 b by the issue of~~ and is represented, ~~in~~ in great part, by bonds having from five to twenty, and ten to forty years to run, bearing interest at the rate of 6 pr. ct. and 5 pr. respectively. ~~leaving i~~It ~~a~~is optional with the government to pay these bonds at any time after the expiration of the least time mentioned upon their face. The time has expired when Millions of them may be taken up, and is rapidly approaching when all may be. It is believed that all which are now due might be replaced by bonds bearing a rate of interest not exceeding 4½ pr ct. and as rapidly as the remainder become due that they may be replaced in the same way. ~~by~~ To accomplish this it may be necessary to authoriz~~ing~~e the interest to be paid at either of three or four of the money Centers ~~in~~ of Europe, or ~~New York~~ by any Asst Treas. of the U. S at the option of the holder. ~~and the bonds having from thirty~~ I would ~~to give the new~~ recommend that the new bonds mature thirty to fifty years ~~to run.~~ after date.—I would suggest this subject for the concideration of Congres, and also, simultaneously with this, the propriety of redeeming our currency, as before suggested, ~~and~~ at its market value at the time the law goes into effect increasing the rate at which currency will be bought, and sold, from day to day, or week to week, at the same rate of interest as *that* the government pays ~~interest~~ upon its bonds.

The subject of tariff and Int. taxation will necessarily receive your attention. The revenues of the country are greater than the requirements and may, with safety, be reduced. But, as the funding of the debt in a 4 or 4½ pr. ct. loan would reduce annual current expenses from twenty to thirty millions, ~~per annum, enabling~~ thus justifying a still greater reduction of taxation, I would suggest the postponement of this question until the next meeting of Congress.

It may be advisable to modify taxation and tariff in instances where unjust or burdensome discriminations are made by the present law, but a general revision of the laws regulating this subject I recommend the postponement of for the present   I would also suggest the renewal of the ~~income~~ tax on incomes, ~~for a period of three years the tax to expire in~~, but at ~~the~~ a reduced rate, ~~of~~ say of 3 pr. ct. on all incomes over One thousand dollars, and this tax to expire in three years. At that time it should expire altogether. ~~and~~ I would also suggest that the present law be relieved from its inquisitorial features. With the funding of the National debt, as here suggested, I feel safe in saying that taxes, and tariff upon articles which do not come in competition with our own productions, may be reduced safely from ~~eighty~~ sixty to ~~one hundred~~ eighty millions pr. annum, at once, and may be still further, reduced from year to year, as the resources of the country are developed

The report of the Sec. of the Treasury shows the recipts of the Govt. for the fiscal year ending June 30th 1869 to be 370.943.747 $^{21}/_{100}$ dollars, and the expenditures, including interest, bounties &c. to be 321.490.597. $^{75}/_{100}$ dollars. The estimates for the ensuing year are more favorable to the government, and will, no doubt, show a much larger decrease of the public debt.

~~There is n~~No provision has been made by ~~Congress for using the surplus funds in the Treasury, except to the amount of one per cent of the whole debt, annually, which amount is to go into a sinking fund for the gradual extinction of the debt.~~ The receipts in the Treasury beyond expenditures, have ~~far~~ exceeded the amount necessary to ~~carry out this provision~~ to place to the credit of the sinking fund as provided by law. To lock ~~it up in the~~ up the ~~in the~~ surplus in the Treasury, and withhold it from circulation, would lead to such a contraction of the currency as to cripple trade ~~to such an extent as to~~ and seriously effect the prosperity of the Country. Under these circumstances the Sec. of the Treasury ~~concured~~ and myself heartily concured in the propriety of using all the surplus currency in the Treas. in the purchase of Govt. bonds, thus reducing the interest bearing indebtedness of the Country, and of submitting to Congress the question of the disposition to be made of the bonds so purchased. The amount of bonds now held by the Treas. amounts to about Seventy Millions, ~~exclusive of~~ including those belonging to the sinking fund. I would recommend that the whole ~~of them~~ be placed to the credit of ~~that~~ the sinking fund, ~~and that distinct authority be given for a continuance of the policy of purchasing bonds, in open market, with all surplus that can safely be used in that way.~~

Your attention is respectfully invited to the recommendations of the Sec. of the Treas. for the creation of the offices of Commissioner of Customs Revenues, and Chief Comptroller; for the increase of salaries to certain classes of officials; the substitution of increased National Bank circulation to replace the outstanding Three per cent Certificates; and most especially to his recommendation for the repeal of laws allowing shares of fines, penalties, forfeitures, &c. to officers of the Government or to informers ~~His recommendation to have authorized a new loan to replace the old one~~

The office of Commissioner of Internal Revenue is one of the most arduous and responsible under the government. It falls but little, if any, short, ~~in importance,~~ of a Cabinet position in its importance and responsibilities. I ~~respec~~ would ask for it therefore such legislation as, in your judgement, will place the office upon a footing of dignity commensurate with its importance, and with the character and qualifications of the class of man required to fill it properly.

As the United States is the freest of all ~~governments~~ nations so to its people sympathise with all peoples strugling for liberty and self government. But, while sympathizing, it is due to our honor that we should abstain from enforcing our views upon unwilling nations, ~~or~~ and from taking an interested part, *without invitation*, in the quarrels between different nations, or between nations and their subjects, ~~where we are at~~   Our course should always be in conformity with strict justice and law, international and local. ~~I~~Such has been the policy of the administration in dealing with ~~Spain and one of her colonies~~ these questions.—For more than a years a valuable province of Spain, and a near neighbor of ours, in whom all our people can not help but feel~~ing~~ a deep interest, has been strugling for independence and freedom. Belligerency has not been accorded however because, according to the principles ~~before~~ here innunciated, I have not deemed such a course just. [The People & Government of the United States entertain the same warm feelings & sympathies for the people of Cuba in their pending struggle, that they manifested throughout the previous struggles between Spain & her former Colonies, in behalf of the latter.

But the contest has at no time assumed the conditions which amount to a war, in the sense of International laws, or which have shown the existence of a *defacto*, political organization ~~by~~of the insurgents, sufficient to justify a recognition of belligerency.] To this day we have no evidence that the governmt of *Free Cuba* has a permanent seat of government, a single port ~~under their controll,~~ ~~Admiralty~~ into which to carry prizes; Admiralty, or other courts, to adjudicate prizes or to administer justice, and without ~~some or~~ all, or some of these requisites I have not felt justified in ~~doing otherwise than as has been done~~ recognizing belligerency. The principle is maintained however that this nation is its own judge when to accord belligerency either to a people struggling to free themselves from a government they believe oppressive,[3] or to nations at war with each other.

~~But while sympathizing~~ ~~t~~The United states have no disposition to interfere with the existing relations of Spain to her Colonial possessions on this Continent. They believe that in due time Spain, as well as other European powers will find it their interest in terminating those relations, and establishing their present dependencies as independent powers; members of the family of nations.

These dependencies are no longer regarded as subject to transfer from one European power to another. When the present relation of Colonies ceases they are to become independent powers, exercising the right of choice, and of self controll in the determination of their future condition and relations with other powers.

The United States, in order to put a stop to bloodshed in Cuba and in the interest of a neighboring people, proposed their good offices to put an end to the revolution now existing in Cuba to bring to a termination of the Contest. The offer was informal, and not being accepted by Spain on a basis which we believed could be accepted, by Cuba was withdrawn. It is yet hoped that Spain may find her interest in availing herself of the the good offices proposed in a way advantageous both to Spain and Cuba. of the United States may yet prove advantages for the settlement of this unhappy strife.

The United States, in order to put a stop to bloodshed in Cuba informally tendered their good offices upon a basis that they had reason to believe would be acceptable to Spain—viz: independence of Cuba,—cessation of hostilities by armistice—abolition of slavery—and purchase of the Island by Cuba. The Spanish government replied informally that they would accept the tender, and suggested instead a different basis—the insurgents to lay down their arms—an amnesty to be proclaimed—a vote to be taken on Independence—Independence to be granted by Spain on payment of purchase money or its guarantee by the United States. The United States declined to offer a proposition which the Cubans could not be induced to accept—and, their good offices having been accepted, formally renewed the proposition before made informally. Spain replied that the offer was an embarassing one to her— that she desired the good offices of the United States, and would indicate later when and how they could be used. The United States replied withdrawing their offer of good offices.

A number of illegal expeditions against Cuba have been broken up. It has been the endeavor of the Administration to execute the neutrality laws, in good faith, no matter how unpleasant the task, made so by the sufferings which we have endured by lack of like good faith towards us by other nations.

[On the 26th of March last the United States Schooner "Lizzie Major." was arrested on the high seas, by a Spanish Frigate and two passengers taken from it, and carried as prisoners to Cuba, Representations of these facts were made to the Spanish Government, as soon as official information of them reached Washington, the two passengers were set at liberty and the Spanish Government assured the United States that the Captain of the Frigate in making the capture had acted without law, that he had been reprimanded for the irregularity of his conduct, and that the Spanish authorities in Cuba would not sanction any act that could violate the rights, or treat with disrespect the sovereignty of this nation.]

The question of the Seasure of the ~~Schooner~~ Brig Mary Lowell, at one of the Bahama Islands, by Spanish authorities, is now the subject of Correspondence between this government and that of Spain and Grat Britten

Under the arbitrary laws of ~~Cuba~~ Spain for embargoing and confiscating the property of persons supposed to favor the insurrection several large claims have arisen for illegal and unjust interference with the rights and property of Citizens of the United States. When the decree under which the authorities acted was promulgated ~~this government~~ the sec. of State of the U. S. pointed out to the Spanish Minister that unless enforced with great caution, it might give rise to disputes between American citizens and the Spanish authorities.

The United States have been vigorous and outspoken in their remonstrances against the barberous and cruel way of conducting the war,—especially against the shooting of prisoners of war, taken with arms in their hands, without trial and conviction. Our remonstrances have been coupled with a demand for indemnity to the families of Speakman & Wyeth,[4] two American citizens who were shot, without trial, for being concerned in an expedition of which they declared and were probably prepared to prove their innocence.

Admiral Hoff was sent to investigate into these cases and reports them to be cases of cruel murder on the part of the Spanish authorities. As yet no satisfactory response has been made to our demands. The Spanish government deny their responsibility in in the case of Speakman and say nothing as to Wyeth. These executions were made by troops under the command of Count Valmaseda. In May last he issued a proclamation for carrying on the war without quarter or mercy. Protests were made against the cruelty of this proclamation.

The Captain General of Cuba ~~also, about the same time~~, issued a proclamation ~~directing~~ authorizing search to be made of vessels on the high seas. Immediate remonstrance was made against this, whereupon the Capt. Gn. issued a new proclamation limiting the right of search to vessels of the United States so far as authorized under the treaty of 1795. The Spanish Ministers attention was called to the fact that this was a belligerent right, and enquir~~ed~~y made whether a state of war existed between Spain and Cuba. The claim to the right of search was then abandoned.

I have always felt that the most intimate relations should be cultivated between the Republic of the United States and all *independent* nations on this continent. It may be well worth concidering whether new treaties between us and them may not be profitably entered into to secure more intimate relations, friendly, commercial and otherwise.

The subject of an interoceanic canal, to connect the Atlantic & Pacific, through the Isthmus of Darien, is one which Commerce is much interested in. Instructions have been given to our Minister to the Republic of the United States of Columbia to try to obtain authority for this government to make a survey to determine the practicability of such an undertaking, and charter for the ~~work if it be practicable~~, right of way to build such a work if the survey proves it to be practicable.

~~In compliance with agreement between the United States government and that of Peru to send a mixed commission to Lima~~

In order to comply with the agreement of the United States as to a mixed Commission at Lima for the adjustment of claims, it became necessary to send a Commissioner and Secretary to Lima in August last. No appropriation having been made by Congress, for this purpose, it is now asked that one be made covering the past and future expenses of the Commissions.

The good offices of the United States to bring about a peace between Spain and the South American Republics with which she is at war, having been accepted by Spain, Peru & Chili, a Congress has been invited to be held in Washington the coming Winter.

A grant has been given to Europeans of an exclusive right of transit over the territory of Nicaragua, to which Costa Rica has given its assent, which, it is alleged, conflicts with vested rights of citizens of the United States. The Department of State has now this subject under consideration.

The Minister of Peru having made representations that there was a state of War between Peru and Spain, and that Spain was constructing in and near New York thirty gunboats which might be used by spain in such a way as to relieve the Naval force at Cuba so as to operate against Peru, orders were given to prevent their departure. No further steps having been taken by the representative of the Peruvian Government to prevent the departure of these vessels, and not feeling authorized to detain the property of a Nation with which we are at peace, on a mere Executive order, the matter has been refered to the courts to decide.[5]

The conduct of the war between the Allies and the Republic of Paraguay has made the intercourse with that country so difficult that it has been deemed advisable to withdraw our representative from there.

[Toward the close of the last Administration a Convention was signed at London for the settlement of all outstanding claims between Great Britain and the United States, which failed to receive the advice and consent of the Senate to its ratification. The time and the circumstances attending the negotiation of that treaty, were unfavorable to its acceptance by the People of the United States and its provisions were wholly inadequate for a settlement of the grave wrongs that had been sustained by this Government as well as by its citizens. The injuries resulting to the United States by reason of the course adopted by Great Britain during out late Civil War, in the increased rates of Insurance,—in the diminution of exports and imports, and other obstructions to domestic industry and production—in its effect upon the foreign commerce of the country—in the decrease and transfer to Great Britain of its commercial marine,—in the prolongation of the War and the increased cost (both in treasure and in lives) of its suppression,—could not be adjusted and satisfied as ordinary Commercial claims, which continually arise between Commercial nations; and yet the Convention treated them simply as such ordinary claims, from which they differ more widely in the gravity of their character than in the magnitude of their amount—great even as is that difference.—not a word was found and not an inference could be drawn from the Treaty to remove the sense of the unfriendliness of the course of Great Britain, in our struggle for existence which had so deeply & universally impressed itself upon the People of this Country.

Believing that a Convention thus misconceived in its scope, and inadequate in its provision would not have produced the hearty cordial settlement of pending questions which alone is consistent with the relations which I desire to have firmly established between the United States and Great Britain, I regarded the action of the Senate in rejecting the treaty to have been ~~merely~~ wisely taken in the interest of peace, and as a necessary step in the direction of a perfect and cordial friendship between the two Countries. A sensitive People, conscious of their power, are more at ease under a great wrong wholly unatoned, than under the restraint of a settlement which satisfies neither their ~~pride~~] sense of Justice [nor their ~~great~~ grave *sense* of the grievance they have endured. The rejection of the Treaty was followed by a state of public feeling on both sides, which I thought not favorable to an immediate attempt at renewed negotiations; I accordingly instructed the Minister of the United States to Great Britain, and found that my views in this regard were shared by Her Majesty's Ministers. I hope that the time may soon arrive when the two Governments can approach the solution of this momentous question, in a spirit and with an appreciation of what is due to the rights, dignity and honor of each and with the determination not only to remove the causes of complaint in the past, but to lay the foundation of a broad principle of public laws, which will prevent future differences and tend to firm and continued peace and friendship.]

This is now the only grave question which the United States has with any foreign nation.

Mr. Motley was early instructed to say to Lord Clarendon that the action of the Senate in the rejection of the Johnson-Clarendon convention, since it made no adequate provision for determining the principles at issue between the two countries, and absolutely no provision for the adjudication of the grievances which the United States had suffered is heartily approved by the Administration. He was further instructed to say that it was not thought wise to re-open negociations on the subject, in the then excited state of the public mind; but that after a short interval, when the matter could be reviewed more calmly, that the subject might be discussed with a greater hope of arriving at an amicable result. To the wisdom of these views Mr. Motley understood Lord Clarendon to assent. Since then the British Government have been made acquainted with the manner in which this Government ~~viewed~~ views the grievances which it, and its citizens; have suffered at the hands of Great Britan and British subjects upon the high seas during the rebellion. Her Majesties government has ~~also~~ been invited to conduct negotiations at Washington for a settlement in case that, on their full comprehension of the grievances of which we complain, they desire to meet this Government in a sincere effort to amicably provide for a proper settlement of our National and individual wrongs. ~~Should~~ Should an early settlement of this question not be reached it will then become a question for this government to consider whether our own Congress should not provide the means for paying what are known as the "Alabama" claims to our own citizens.

~~At the last session of Congress a resolution passed the lower house authorizing, or directing, the Sec. of State to negociate a treaty for reciprocal trade between the United States and the provinces of Great Britten, on this Continent; It did not pass the~~

~~Senate to be submitted to Congress at this session for ratification or rejection. It did not pass the Senate hence no such treaty has been entertained~~ entered into.

The question of renewing our treaty for reciprocal trade between the United States and the British possessions, on this Continent, has not been favorably considered ~~I respectfully recommend that this be not further entertained.~~ by the administration. The advantages of ~~reciprocal trade~~ such a treaty ~~are~~ would be all-most ~~onesided~~ wholly in favor of the British producer. Except possibly ~~with~~ a few people engaged in the trade between the two sections no citizen of the United States would be benefited by reciprocity Our internal taxation would prove a protection to the British producer almost equal to the protection which ~~home~~ our manufacturers now receive from the tariff. Some arrangement ~~for the interchange of products between the United States and the dDominion of Canada may be desirable, but~~ however for the regulation of commersial intercourse between the Uniteds States and the dominion of Canada may be desirable, but I do not understand this to mean reciprocity.[6]

I would not be understood as advocating a prohibitory, or even a high protective, tariff; but I do advocate a tariff which will ~~enable our own manufacturers to compete with the foreign~~ give the greatest revenue to the country, and enable American manufacturers to compete with the foreign, without reducing the wages of the laborer to European prices. When production of any given article equals consumption competition will reduce its price to the lowest at which ~~it~~ can be produced. Cheap goods, and the ability to pay for them, means home production, and exports, ~~equal~~ exclusive of specie, equal to imports. Young nations must give partial protection to secure this.

The commission for adjusting the claims of the Hudson's Bay & Puguet Sound Agricultural Co upon the United States has terminated its labors. The award of Six hundred & fifty thousand dollars has been made and all rights and titles of the company, on the territory of the United States ~~is~~ extinguished, ~~The~~ and deeds ~~will soon~~

be delivered. An appropriation by Congress to meet this sum is asked.

The commission for determining the Northwestern land boundary between the Uniteds States and the British possissions, under the treaty of 1856, have completed their labors and the commission has been dissolved.

[In obedience to the recommendation of Congress a proposition was early made to the British Government to abolish the Mixed Courts created under the Treaty of April 7. 1862 for the Suppression of the Slave trade—The subject is still under negotiation.

It having come to my knowledge that a corporate company, organized under British laws proposed to land upon the shores of the United States and to operate there a submarine Cable under a concession from His Majesty the Emperor of the French of an exclusive right for 20 years of telegraphic communication between the shores of France and the United States with the very objectionable feature of subjecting all messages conveyed thereby to the scrutiny and control of the French Government; I caused the French and British Legations at Washington to be made acquainted with the probable policy of Congress on this subject, as foreshadowed by the Bill which passed the Senate in March last—This drew from the representatives of the Company an agreement to accept as the basis of their operations the provisions of that Bill, or of such other enactment on the subject as may be passed during the approaching session of Congress, and also to use their influence to secure from the French Government a modification of their concession so as to permit the landing upon French soil of any cable belonging to any Company incorporated by the authority of the United States or of any state in the Union, and on their part not to approve oppose the establishment of any such cable. In consideration of this agreement I directed the withdrawal of all opposition by the United States authorities to the landing of the Cable and to working it until the meeting of Congress. I regret to say that there has been no modification made in the Company's concession, nor, so far as I can learn, have they attempted to secure one. Their concession excludes the capital and the citizens of the United States from competition upon the shores of France. I recommend legislation to protect the rights of citizens of the United States, as well as the dignity and sovereignty of the nation against such an assumption. I shall also endeavor to secure by negotiation, an abandonment of the principle of monopolies in ocean telegraphic cables.]

Copies of this correspondence isare herewith accompanying.

[The unsettled political condition of other Countries less fortunate than our own sometimes induces their citizens to come to the United States for the sole purpose of becoming naturalized. Having secured this, they return to their native country, and reside there without disclosing their change of allegianse. They accept official positions of trust or honor which can only be held by citizens of their native land, they journey under passports describing them as such citizens, and it is only when civil discord, after perhaps years of quiet, threatens their persons or their property, or when their native state drafts them into its military service, that the fact of their Cchange of allegiance is made known.

They reside permanently away from the United States, they contribute nothing to its revenues, they avoid the duties of its citizenship and they only make themselves known by a claim of protection. I have directed the diplomatic and consular offices of the United States to scrutinize carefully all such claims of protection. The citizen of the United States, whether native or adopted, who discharges his duty to his country, is entitled to its complete protection. While I have a voice in the direction of affairs, I shall not consent to imperil this sacred right, by conferring it upon fictitious or fraudulent claimants.]

On the accession of the present Administration, it was found that the Minister for North Germany had made propositions for the negociation of a convention for the protection of Imigrants passengers, to which no response had been given. It was, by this Administration, concluded that, to be effectivetual, all the maratime powers engaged in the trade should should join in such a measure. Invitations have been extended to the Cabinets of London, Paris, Florence, Berlin, Brussels, The Hague, Copenhagen and Stockholm to empower their representatives at Washington to simultaneously enter into negociations, and to conclude with the United States conventions, identical in form, making uniform regulations as to the construction of the parts of vessels to be devoted to the use of emigrant passengers, as to the quality and quantity of food, as to the medical treatment of the sick, and as to the things to be observed during the voyage in order to secure ventilation, to promote health, to prevent intrusion, and to protect the females, and providing for the establishment of tribunals in the several countries for enforcing such regulations by summary process.

Your attention is respectfully called to the law regulating the tariff on Russian hemp, and to enquire whether, in fixing the charges on Russian hemp higher than they are fixed upon Manilla, is not a violation of our treaty with Russia placing her products on the same footing with those of the most favored nations?

In consequence of lack of an early appropriation of the money to pay Russia the price agreed upon, by treaty, for the purchase of Alaska there was a delay of payment of about two months after it was done. The Russian Govt. now makes a demand for interest, at the rate of 6 pr. ct. pr. annum, on the amount of the purchase money during the delay. An appropriation is asked to meet this interest.

The translation of the 4 Articles of the Treaty of 1850, between the United States & Turkey, which was, at the time of the conclusion of the treaty, submitted to the Senate, and approved by them, contains the provision that citizens of the United States, in Turkey, shall not be arrested by the local authorities, but they shall be tried by their Minister or Consul. It now appears from the separate examination of four competant persons in Constantinople that the original of this Treaty in Turkish does not contain this provision. What action should be taken in a case of this kind is submitted for your consideration.[7]

Our manufactories are developeing increasing with a wonderful rapidity under the protection which they now receive. With the improvements in Machinery ~~now going on~~, already effected and still increasing, making machinery take the place of skilled labor to a very large extent, our imports ~~must fall~~ of many articles must fall off largely within a very few years. Fortunately too these manufactories are not confined to one locality ~~so much~~ as formerly, and, it is to be hope, will become more and more diffused making the interest in them equal in all sections. They give employment, and support, to tens of thousands of people, at home, and retain with us the means which otherwise would be shipped abroad. The extension of rail-roads in Europe, and the East, is bringing into competition with our agricultural products like products from other Countries. Self interest if not self preservation ~~makes~~ therefore dictates caution against disturbing any industrial interest of the Country. ~~Int the future we will have to look more to our immediate neighbors, in the tropics, to take more of and to to take more of our surplus.~~ teaches us also the necessity of looking to other markets for the sale of our surplus. Our neighbors south of us, also China and Japan should receive our special attention   It will be the endeavor of the Administration to cultivate such relations with all these nations as to ~~secure better~~ entitle us to their confidence, and make it their as well as our interest to establish better Commercial relations. ~~with them.~~

Through the agency of a more enlightened policy than heretofore pursued towards China, largely due to ~~an American citizen~~ the sagacity and efforts of one of our own distinguished citizens, the world is about to commence largely increased relations with that ~~hitherto exclusive~~ populous, and hitherto exclusive nation. As the United [*States*] have been the initiaters ~~of~~in this new policy, so too they should be the most earnest in ~~giving it a fair trial~~ shewing their good faith in making it a success.

In this connection I advise such legislation as will forever preclude the enslavement of their people, upon our soil, under the name of Coolies; and also prevent Americal vessels from engaging ~~fr~~ in the transportation of of "Coolies" to any country tolerating the system. ~~As a begining, and t~~To shew ~~our appreciation of the importance of the Chinese nation among the family of nations,~~ I would also recommend that the Mission to that country be raised to one of the first class.

On assuming the responsible duties of Chief Magistrate of this Great Nation it was with a conviction that three things were essentia[l] to our peace, prosperity and fullest developement. First among these is strict integrity in fulfilling all our obligations. Second; to secure protection to the person and property of the citizen of the United States, in each and every portion of our common country; wherever he may choose to move, without reference to original Nationality, religion color or politics, demanding of him only obedience to the laws, and proper respect for the rights of others. Third; union of all the states, (with equal rights,) indestructible by any constitutional means.

To secure the first of these Congress has taken two essential steps; first, by declaring, by Joint Resolution, that the public debt shall be paid, principle & interest, in coin, and second, by providing the means for paying. Providing the means however could not secure the object ~~attained~~ desired, without a proper administration of the laws for the collection of the revenues, and an economical disbursement of them. To this subject the administration has most earnestly addressed itself, with results, I hope, satisfactory to the country. There has been no hesitation in changing officials to secure an efficient execution of the laws, sometimes to where, in a party sence, bad political results were likely to follow, nor hesitation in sustaining efficient official against remonstrances wholly political.

It may be well to mention here the embarrassment possible to arise from leaving on the Statutes books the amended Tenure of Office bill, and to earnestly recommend ~~its~~ their total repeal. It could not have been the intention of the framers of the Constitution when providing that appointments made by the President should receive the concent of the Senate, that the latter should have the power to retain in office persons, placed there by federal appointment, against the will of the President? The law is inconsistent with a faithful and efficient administration of the Government. What faith could an Executive put in officials forced upon him, and those too who he had ~~removed~~ suspended for reason? How would such ~~an~~ officials be likely to serve an Administration that they knew did not trust th~~i~~em?

~~The second of~~ The only recommendations for legislation I ~~can think of~~ have to make to secure this first requisite to our growth and prosperity, have already been ~~recommended~~ made. It is to insure a gradual return to specie payments and to give an immediate fixed specie value to our currency.

For the second; time, and a firm but humane administration of ~~the~~ existing laws, (amended from time to time as they may prove ineffective, or harsh and unnecessary,) is probably all that is required. It may be well however to consider the propriety of removing in whole, or in part, all disabilities imposed by the Fourteenth Article of the Constitution.

The third cannot be attained by special legislation, but must be regarded as fixed by the Constitution itself, and gradually acquiesced in ~~as the passed is forgotten.~~ by force of public opinion.

From the foundation of the Government to the present the management of the original inhabitants of this Continent, the indian, has been one of embarrassment, and expense, and has been attended with continuous ~~wars, murders and~~ rober~~y~~ies murders and wars. From my own experience upon the frontiers, and in indian countries, I do not hold either legislation, or the conduct of the whites who come most in contact with the indian, blameless for these hostilities. The past however can not be undone, and the question must be met as we now find it. I attempted a new policy towards these wards of the Nation, ~~for~~ (they cannot be regarded in any other light than as wards,) with fair results, ~~I believe,~~ so far as tried, and I hope to be attended ultimately with great success. ~~if persisted in.~~ The Society of Friends are well known as having succeeding in living in peace with the indian in the early settlement of Pa. while their White neighbors of other sects, in other sections, did not do so. They are also known for their opposition to all strife, violence and war, and are generally noted for their strict integrity and fair dealings. These considerations induced me to give the management of a few reservations of Indians to them,

~~Their management~~ has ~~not~~ ~~dis~~ and to throw the burden of selection of Agents upon the Society itself. The result has ~~been~~ proven most satisfactory. ~~and~~ It will be found more fully set forth in the report of the Commissioner of Indian Affairs. For Superintendents ~~of~~ and Agts. of Indians, not on reservations, Officers of the Army were selected. The reasons for this are numerous. When Indian Agents are sent there; or near there, troops must be also. The Agent and commanders of troops are independent of each other, and ~~some~~ are subject to orders from different departments of the government. The Army officer holds a position for life; the Agt. one at the will of the President. The former is personally interested in living at peace with the indian, and in establishing a permanent peace to the end that some portion of his life may be spent with in the limits of civilisation and society. The latter has no such personal interest. Another reason is an economic one; and still another is, the hold which the government has upon a life officer, ~~which they have not upon one appointed for a limited time~~, it has to secure a faithful discharge of duties in carrying out a given policy.

The building of rail-roads and the access thereby given to all the agricultural and mineral regions of the country is rapidly bringing civilized settlements in contact with all the tribes of indians. No matter what ought to be the relations between such settlements and the aborigines, the fact is they do not get on together, and one or the other has to give way in the end. A system which looks to the extinction of a race is too abhorant for a Nation to indulge in without entailing upon the wrath of all ~~civilized~~ Christendom, and without engendering in the Citizen a disregard for human life, and the rights of others, dangerous to society. I see no remedy for this except in placing all the indians on large reservation, as rapidly as it can be done, and giving them absolute protection there. As rapidly as they are fitted for it they should be induced to take their lands in severalty and should be induced to set up territorial governments for their own protection. For fuller details on this subject I call your special attention to the reports of the Secretary of the Interior and the Commissioner of Indian Affairs.

The report of the Sec. of War shews the expenditures

of the War Dept. for the year ending June 30th 1869, to be $80.644.042.^{76}/100 of which $23.882.310.^{6}/100 went for the payment of debts contracted in the war, and is not chargable to current Army expenses. His estimate of $34.531.031.30 for the expenses of the Army for next fiscal year is as low as it is believed can be relied on. The estimates of Bureau officers have been carefully scrutinized and reduced whereever it has been deemed practicable. If however the condition of the country should be such, by the begining of the next fiscal year, as to admit of a greater consentation of troops, the appropriation asked for will not be expended.

The appropriations estimated for for River & Harbor improvement, and for Fortifications, is submitted separately. Whatever amount Congress may deem proper to appropriate for these purposes will be expended.—The ~~forts~~ recommendedation ~~by~~ of the General of the Army that appropriations be made for the ~~F~~forts at Portland, ~~Me.~~ Boston, ~~Mass.~~ New York, Philadelphia, New Orleans and San Francisco, if for none other, is concurred in. I also ask your special attention to the recommendation of Gen. Thomas for ~~protection~~ the sale of the Seal Islands of St. Paul and St. George, Alaska Territory, and suggest that it either be complied with, or that there be legislation for the protection of the Seal fisheries, ~~and to produce a~~ A revenue should be derived from them.

The report of the Sec. of War, accompanying this, contains a synopsis of the reports of the Heads of Bureaus, of the Commanders of Military Divisions and of the Districts of Virginia, Mississippi and Texas, and the report ~~report~~ of the General of the Army in full. The recommendations therein contained have been well considered, and are submitted for your action. I will however call special attention to the recommendation of the Chief of Ordnance for the sale of Arsenals, and lands no longer of use to the government; ~~and~~ also the recommendation of the ~~General of the Army~~ Sec. of War that the Act of March 3d 1869, prohibiting promotions and appointments in the staff Corps of the Army, be repealed. The extent of country to be garrisoned, and the number of Military posts to be occupied, is the same with a reduced Army that it is with a large one. The number of Staff officers required is more dependent upon the latter than the former condition.

The report of the Sec. of the Navy, accompanying this, shows the condition of the Navy when the Administration came into office, and the improvements made since. Strenuous efforts have been made to place as many vessels, "in Commission," or render them fit for service if required, as possible, and to substitute the Sail for steam whilst ~~on ordinary duty~~, cruising, thus materially reducing the expenses of the Navy while adding greatly to its efficiency. Looking to our future I recommend a liberal, though not extraviagant, policy towards this branch of the public service.

The report of the PostMaster General furnishes a clear and comprehensive exhibit of the operations of the postal service, and the finantial condition of the Post Office Department.

The ordinary postal revenues for the year ending June 30th 1869, amounted to $18.344.510 72 ~~dollars~~, and the expenditures to $23.698.131 50 showing an excess of expenditures, over receipts, of $5.353.620.78. The excess of expenditures over receipts for the previous year amounted to $6.437.991.85

The increase of revenues for 1869 over those of 1868 was $2.051.909.92, and the increase of expenditures was $967.538.85. The increased revenue in 1869 exceeded the increased revenue in 1868 by $996.335.99; and the increased expenditure in 1869 was $2.527.570.34 less than the increased expenditure in 1868; showing by comparison this gratifying ~~result~~ feature of improvement, that while the increase of expenditures over the increase of receipts in 1868 was $2.439.535.26, the increase of receipts over the increase of expenditures in 1869 was $1.084.371.07.

Your attention is respectfully called to the recommendations made by the PostMaster General for authority to change the rate of compensation to the main trunk rail-road lines, for their services in carrying the mails; for having executed post-route maps; for reorganizing and increasing the efficiency of the Special Agency service; for increase of Mail service on the Pacific, and for establishing Mail service, under the flag of the Union, on the Atlantic;

and most specially do I call your attention to his recommendation for the total abolition of the franking privilege. It is an abuse which no one receives an advantage from, and it reduces the receipts ~~to the~~ for postal service from 25 to 30 per cent, and largely increases the service to be performed. The method by which postage ~~should be returned~~ should be paid upon public matter, is set forth fully in the report of the PostMaster General.

The report of the Secretary of the Interior, shows the quantity of public lands disposed of during the year ending June 30th, 1869, was 7.666.151.97 acres, exceeding that of the preceding year by 1.010.409. acres. Of this amount 2.899.544. acres were sold for cash, and 2.737.365 acres entered under the homestead laws.

The remainder was granted to aid in the construction of works of internal improvement, approved to the states as swamp lands, and located with wareants and scrip.

The cash receipts from all sources were $4.472.886.28, exceeding those of the preceding year $2.840.140.38,

During the last fiscal year 23.196 names were added to the pension rolls, and 4876 dropped therefrom, leaving at its close 187.963. The amount paid to pensioners, including the compensation of disbursing agents, was $28.422.884.08, an increase of $4.411.902.09 on that of the previous year.

The munificence of Congress has been conspicuously manifested in their legislation for the soldiers and sailors who suffered, and the relatives of those who perished, in the recent struggle to maintain "that unity of government which makes us one people." The additions to the pension rolls of each ~~succeeding~~sive year since the conclusion of hostilities result in a great degree from the repeated amendment of the act of 14th of July 1862, which extend its provisions to cases not falling within its original scope. The large outlay which is thus occasioned is further increased by the more liberal allowance bestowed since that date upon those who in the line of duty were wholly or permanently disabled. Public opinion has given an emphatic sanction to these measures of Congress, and it will be conceded that no part of our public burdens is more cheerfully borne, than that which is imposed by this branch of the service. Its necessities for the next fiscal year will, in addition to the amount justly chargeable to the Naval pension fund, require an appropriation of $30.000.000.

[During the year ending 30 September 1869, the Patent Office issued 13762 patents, and its receipts were $686,388.62, being $213,926.02 more than the expenditures.]

I would respectfully call your attention to the recommendation of the sec. of the Interior for uniting the the duties of supervising the education of Freedmen with the other duties devolving upon the Commissioner of Education.

If it is the desire of Congress to make the sCensus, which must be taken during the year 1870, more complete and perfect than heretofore I would suggest early action upon any plan that may be agreed upon. As Congress, at the last session, appointed a Committee to take into consideration such measures as might be deemed proper in reference to the Census, and to report a plan, I desist from saying more.

I would recommend to your favorable consideration the claims of the Agricultural Bureau for aliberal appropriation. In a country so diversified in climate and soil as our, and with a population so largely dependent upon agriculture, the benefits that can be confered by properly fostering this bureau are incalculable.

I desire respectfully to call the attention of Congress to the inadequate salaries of a number of the most important officers of Government. In this message I will not innumerate them but will specify only the Justices of the Supreme Court. No change has been made in their salaries for fifteen years. Within that time the labors of the court have largely increased, and the expenses of living in Washington have at least doubled. During the same time Congress has twice found it necessary to increase largely the compensation of its own Members; and the duty which it owes to another department of the Goverment, deserves, and will undoubtedly receive, its due consideration.

There are many subjects not alluded to in this message which might with propriety be introduced, but I abstain, believing that your patriotism and statesmanship will suggest ~~such legislation~~ the topics and legislae~~t~~ion most condusive to the interests of the whole people. On my part I promise a rigid adherence to the laws, and their strict ~~enforcement~~ enforcement.

ADf (bracketed material not in USG's hand), DLC-USG, III. On Dec. 6, 1869, USG submitted the final version to Congress. DS, DNA, RG 46, Annual Messages.

On Nov. 12, Secretary of State Hamilton Fish had written in his diary: "After the Cabinet adjourned the Prsdt requested me to remain—he said he had made a rough draft of a part of his Message—had been interrupted frequently, but wished to read me what he had written—after reading several pages Cresswell came in—he discontinued reading—& replaced the sheets in his drawer—remarking that he 'need not detain me any longer at present' 'another time will do as well—no need of immediate hurry'—He had read as far as to suggest a plan for resumption, viz, first to replace the loans at lower rates of interest—& then to establish the rate at which the Treasury will either buy or sell gold for greenbacks or in other words, redeem or reissue greenbacks, in or for gold—this rate was established to be advanced at a rate of interest equal to that at which the loans shall be placed, until the same came to par—" DLC-Hamilton Fish. On Nov. 15, Fish recorded: "The President requesting me to remain says he was interrupted, in reading his Message the other day—& proceeds to read the remainder of what he has written—it is a rough draft & will require considerable alteration—He recommends the renewal of the income tax for three years, reducing the rate of tax to three percent—I express doubt as to the propriety of the recommendation—the tax is very unpopular—but if continued it should be relieved of its inquisitorial character, & the publicity given to private affairs—he makes a note for the purpose of such alteration—He recommends no alteration in the tariff or tax laws for a year—to allow time to see the effect of the reduction of expenditures by reason of the placing of the loans at a lower rate of interest—Alludes to the Cuban question—the sympathy felt for them, but no justification for recognition of belligerency has arisen—asserts the right to recognize belligerency—&c speaks of the Isthmus Canal—I suggest that the question of the French Cable—some others may need to be referred to—He does not remember the particulars of the Cable question sufficiently to treat it—I am to prepare a memorandum on that & some other points." *Ibid.* On Nov. 22, Fish noted that the "President read to us his Message as far as written—I had previously presented to him an abstract of the foreign affairs, transacted & pending I leave with him a proposed passage for the Message relating to the Alabama Claims, & other questions with Great Britain—" *Ibid.* The next day, USG again read a portion of his draft to the cabinet. On Nov. 26, Fish recorded: "*President* mentions to me that he had adopted entirely, a large part of what I had submitted to him for consideration for his message—& had condensed some other portions—I hand him, & read to him, a paragraph on the French telegraph Cable—which he says he will adopt—. . . *Cox* suggests that the passage in Presidents Message respecting reciprocity might be changed in phraseology so as to be conciliatory to the Canadians—" *Ibid.* On Nov. 27, Fish wrote: "*President*—handed him memo for Message, on the subject of Emigrant Passengers—Abuse of Naturalization papers—Lizzie Major—Mary Lowell—Cuban

Belligerency & the relation of the European Colonial Possessions to the Pan. States—(that they are no longer subject to transfer by one European power to another, but when the Existing relation ceases they are to be free to establish their own [condition], & relations with other powers)—left with him also Copy of House Resolution about Canadian Commercial Intercourse—He modifies his previous statement in the Message respecting 'Reciprocity'—& as also some other, less important passages—& adopts what I propose on the other subjects liable to 'modification of language'—Expressing himself particularly pleased with what I presented on Naturalization Cuban Belligerency—& Colonial possessions—this latter if adopted will be an advance upon the 'Monroe doctrine—the natural growth of 46 or 47 years—!" *Ibid.* On Nov. 29, Fish noted that "the Prsdt had embodied in his Message, in addition to the passages I had submitted to him, much more on the subject of the Alabama Claims, which from Badeaus description I infered, & ~~as this will~~ had been transcribed from the Abstract of business of the Department which was prepared for his information some time since—I thereupon remarked that I was not aware whether I had not seen the whole of the Message relating to the business of my department, & possibly this despatch from Sickles may have some bearing—He says he had taken, as I had prepared it, the sheets which I had given him—& had made up the rest from the Abstract recd from my office—having generally copied the very language—I remark that much of that was only intended for his own information, & would not be appropriate for a message—Judge Hoar remarked that his idea of the communication to be made by Message, was that it should be general—& not enter into detail unless imperatively decided—The Prest—says he can very easily strike it out—that what he has thus copied makes several pages of his writing— He will read the Message to the Cabinet tomorrow—throughout—" *Ibid.* On Nov. 30, Fish recorded: "Prsdt—requests me to remain, will not read the whole message to the to the Cabinet—will not detain them—but wishes to read to me that part relating to the business of the State Department, & Foreign Affairs— which he does—he strikes out several pages—including much of detail of negociation & of instruction which I express the opinion is not proper to ma[ke] public— much remains that might be slightly modified in expression—but on the whole I am well content with the changes—" *Ibid.*

1. On Dec. 7, U.S. Senator-elect John W. Johnston of Va. *et al.* met with USG. "Mr. President, on behalf of the Congressional delegation, my colleague and self, the Legislature and people of Virginia, I am deputed to tender you our heartfelt thanks and appreciation of yourself for the recommendations made by you in your message to Congress last spring in regard to a vote by the people on different sections of the State constitution; also for your recommendation to Congress in your annual message yesterday for the prompt admission of Virginia's Senators and Representatives to Congress, and her recognition as a State. I am sure in that your policy will not only forevermore insure the State to the Union, but will tend to the speedy restoration of quiet and prosperity to the State." *Washington Chronicle*, Dec. 9, 1869. USG replied: "I hope to see Virginia soon back in the Union, and shall be very much delighted to announce the event officially to the people of the country." *Ibid.*

2. On Oct. 8, Bvt. Maj. Gen. Adelbert Ames, provisional governor, Jackson, Miss., telegraphed to USG. "By papers I see a telegram has been sent you wherein I am quoted to the effect that I will not give a fair election   The state-

ment is without truth" Telegram received (at 4:00 P.M.), DNA, RG 107, Telegrams Collected (Bound). On Dec. 2 and 3, Ames telegraphed to Horace Porter. "The only twelve (12) counties heard from show a republican gain of almost eight thousand (8000) the Democratic majority last year was seven thousand six hundred (7600) returns unofficial & imperfect" "The majority of the republicans exceeds all expectation victory complete" Telegrams received (at 12:40 P.M. and 12:10 P.M.), *ibid.*

3. On Jan. 31, 1870, Horace Greeley *et al.*, New York City, wrote to USG. "We have the honor of presenting to you the following Preamble and Resolutions, unanimously adopted by a Mass meeting of American citizens held at the Cooper Institute in this city the 19th inst. 'Whereas, the Monroe doctrine, that European monarchies ought not to be allowed to extend their acquisitions of territory and political power in the American hemisphere, has become the fixed policy of the Republic; and Whereas, The proximity in such possessions of those monarchies has proved dangerous to our peace and safety; and Whereas, We hold, with our fathers of 1776, that Governments are instituted for the benefit of the governed, "the rule of the people by the people, for the people"; therefore, Resolved, By the people of New York, without distinction of party, in mass meeting assembled, that the people of the United States sympathize with the people of Cuba, who have been for more than a year carrying on war against Spain in vindication of the inalienable right of self-government. Resolved, That the time has come, in the language of President Grant's Message, "to accord the right of belligerency to a people struggling to free themselves from a Government they believe to be oppressive." Resolved, That our representatives, the President, the Senate, and the House of Representatives of the United States, be requested to proclaim, in legal form, the existence of a state of belligerency between the Cuban patriots and the Spanish nation. Resolved, That a copy of these resolutions, signed by the officers of this meeting, be sent to the President and the Speakers of the Senate and House of Representatives of the United States, and that their publication in all the journals of the Republic be respectfully asked.' " DS, DLC-Horace Greeley.

4. Spanish firing squads in Cuba executed Charles Speakman (June 17, 1869) and Albert Wyeth (June 21). See *HED*, 41-2-160, pp. 98–99; *SED*, 41-2-7, pp. 32–49. On July 3, Porter wrote to Secretary of the Navy George M. Robeson. "The Secretary of State will forward to you to day a communication from our Consul General in Cuba dated June 24th 1869: The President requests that you will transmit a copy to the Naval Officer commanding the West Indies Squadron with instructions to send a vessel to the locality named with orders to make a thorough investigation of the circumstances." LS, DNA, RG 45, Letters Received from the President. On the same day, J. C. Bancroft Davis, asst. secretary of state, recorded: "By directions of the President, I asked the spanish minister to call at my house this evening to read to him Mr Plumb's dispatch No 49 and its enclosure. I read He came about 9 o'clock. I read to him the dispatch, saying to him that it was by the order of the President: and that a vessel of war was to be sent at once to Santiago de Cuba to inquire into the facts—that I had seen Admiral Porter and that probably Admiral Hoff himself would go. I then said that it appeared by Plumb's dispatches that the same state of things existed in other parts of the Island—that the volunteers seemed elsewhere to have overcome the Spanish authorities so that they were unable to preserve the peace, and I read to him parts of Mr Plumbs dispatches Nos 44 &

46. He replied that it as to the Santiago de Cuba case it was a misfortune—but the man was dead & what could he do. He would write his government & get authority to pay the family & would telegraph the Captain General to aid Admiral Hoff in his investigation. He had seen a statement of the case in the New York papers in which it was asserted that the man was taken with arms in his hands. I replied that the President expressly desired me to say that as to men taken with arms in their hands against Spain, the govt could did not interfere whatever they might think of so summary a proceeding, but that he thought this was a case where common humanity required a delay long enough to give the man time to substantiate his case by proof if he could. He said he supposed the Govt would not interfere on behalf of those taken with arms in their hands. They were citizens of no country. He then expressed in those terms his disgust at the 'nasty Cuban question'. He thought the Rebellion would be speedily put down—'but what then'. 'If they want independence they can have it'. They dont know what they do want—Except that 'they want to keep slavery, that which we want to abolish'. I told him the desire of the Presdt was to keep this govt out of it, but that our commercial & personal relations with Cuba were so great that it was difficult to do it. We had within the last week broken up an expedition, when it was clear there were many persons in the country sympathising with it. He said 'what are you going to do with those men?' I replied 'the leaders will undoubtedly be indicted—especially the men who have broken faith, but as for the men, I think they it will be better to let them go than to try to convict them. Dont you?' He answered. 'Certainly, Certainly, that is [. . . . .]politique—' I then said we had another difficulty to contend with—the fevers raging in those waters and seriously impairing the strength of our navy by forcing us to bring our vessels home. He said, why dont you send your men to the Havana hGovt hospitals. They will find Doctors there that understand the fever. Your doctors dont understand it & the men die. I will telegraph the authorities at Havana to admit your seamen to the hospital. I thanked him for this and the interview terminated." Fish diary, DLC-Hamilton Fish. On July 6, Robeson wrote to Fish. "Under date of 3d inst., the President informed this Department that you would forward to it a communication from our Consul General in Cuba, and requested that a copy should be transmitted to the Commander of the North Atlantic Squadron. The Department begs leave to call your attention to the fact that no letter has yet been received from the State Department   Rear Admiral Hoff has telegraphed to this Department that in obedience to orders received by telegraph he would proceed immediately in company with the Monitor 'Centaur' to Santiago de Cuba to investigate the circumstances attending the reported murder of an American citizen at that place." Copy, DNA, RG 45, Letters Sent to the President.

5. On Nov. 15, Fish wrote in his diary: "Prsdt spoke of the GunBoats—would wish that they could be submitted to judicial proceedings   does not wish them to sail at present, & feels the inconvenience of holding—I am to see Cushing, & try to arrange that the Peruvian Minister, or someone in that interest, file information against them" DLC-Hamilton Fish. On Nov. 26 and Dec. 7, Fish recorded: "Attend President on Summons—Judge Pierrepont—Secr of the Navy present—Question of the Spanish GunBoats under consideration—proposition to libel them discussed   It seems agreed that they cannot be held,—that the Court will discharge them—The question of a 'sham' proceeding is discussed—Pierrepont points out the unreality of the proceedings—I object to all

such attempts to assume a position with~~out~~ an ~~appearance~~ appearance of earnestness, but none in reality—That if the case is thrown into the Courts, I think
we should say to the Court that the Government desires to interpose no delay,
but hopes the Court will dispose of the case as soon as its convenience will permit—That the attitude of the two Governments (Spain, Peru) has changed with
regard to the question of belligerency—that we detained the two Peruvian
Ministers, for six months, at the request of Spain, who alledged a state of war
with Peru—they were finally allowed to sail with the consent of the Spanish
Govt & under conditions &c—That we have offered to Mediate between Spain &
Peru—thus recognizing a state if not of War, of interrupted relations   President
& Robeson at first depart from the view that we expedite the proceedings—I allude to the possible claim for damage, by detention—the risk to which the vessels are subjected—the position in which we shall stand before the World, appearing to litigate & to delay, & thus defeated in our own Courts & also the
still more punitive, in case of fire, either accidental or incendiary, while the
vessels are thus held—whatever the facts we shall be charged by m[en] believed
to be in collusion with the Accident—President decides that Pierrepont libel the
vessels & state to the Court that the U. S desires no delay longer than to enable
the Court to decide the question of laws &c—" "Before the Cabinet met, the
President called me into the Secretarys room, where Pierrepont was—P—asked
about the Spanish Gun boats—says they cannot be detained—he can postpone
the release—or expedite it—I tell him that it is the policy of the government to
be rid of them—& the sooner it can be properly done the better—. . . Pierrepont
says he can either delay or hasten decision   Can have a special Admiralty term
set for 20 Decr   I express the opinion that it had better be decided before
then—. . ." *Ibid.* On Dec. 10, Judge Samuel Blatchford, U.S. District Court,
ordered the gunboats released. *New York Times*, Dec. 11, 1869. On Dec. 13,
Fish wrote in his diary: "A note from Genl Porter, requests me to call at the
Presidents at noon—Prest has sent for me to hear Mr Loury of Ky—on the
Cuban question & Gun Boats—Mr L—, reads affidavits of Dr Tinker, Mr Al-
dama, & another Cuban, to shew that a State of war Exists—& that there is a
Govt of the Revolutionary party—produces a Map with the greater part of the
Island colored blue, to represent the possession & control of territory by the
Insurgents—after reading these affts &c he argues in favor of libelling the Gun
Boats on the strength of the Expression in the Neutrality Act . . . President,
does not think the state of War &c exists   the only point that has impressed
him, is that made with regard to 'colony district or people'—He expresses the
opinion that the GunBoats cannot reach Cuba—& strong sympathy with the
Cubans—does not think Spain will regain the Control of the Island—but the
Cubans are inefficient, & have done little for themselves—Come here in large
numbers & make trouble for us—did not know the boats wd be released so soon—
thought the case w'not turn up before 20th—had not before heard the point about
'Colony &c—after about two hours, Loury left—the President desiring him to
see Atty Genl—who is 'the Law advis[or] of the Govt—to present this question
about 'Colony &c to him—I told the President it had been consid[ered] & Judge
Hoar did not think it had any bearing on the case—Mr Loury stated that Evarts,
John K Porter & *Pierrepont*, had given opinions in favor of that view . . ." DLC-
Hamilton Fish. On Dec. 20, George Francis Train, New York City, telegraphed
to USG. "By releasing the Spanish gunboats you have made England a present
of the Alabama claims—There is treason in the cabinet"   Telegram received
(at 3:30 P.M.), DNA, RG 107, Telegrams Collected (Bound).

6. On Dec. 22, Fish wrote to USG. "The Secretary of State to whom was referred the Resolution of the Senate, of the 8th instant, requesting the President, if in his judgment not incompatible with the public interest, to inform the Senate 'whether since the last Session of Congress, any negotiations have taken place or been proposed, between this Government and the Government of Great Britain and Ireland in respect to a Reciprocity Treaty or Reciprocity Laws on the subject of trade and commerce between the United States and the Dominion of Canada, and that, if consistent with the public service, he communicate to the Senate any correspondence that may have taken place since the last session of Congress on that subject, between the Executive and the Government of Great Britain and Ireland, or that of the Dominion of Canada,' has the honor to state that neither correspondence nor negotiation upon the questions referred to, has been entered into; and that the conversations in relation thereto which have been held, were too informal to be made the subject of an official report." LS, *ibid.*, RG 46, Presidential Messages. On the same day, USG wrote to the Senate. "I transmit to the Senate, in answer to their resolution of the 8th instant, a report from the Secretary of State." DS, *ibid.* See *SED*, 41-2-19.

7. On Dec. 7, USG wrote to the Senate. "I transmit to the Senate a copy of a correspondence, a list of which is hereto annexed, between the Secretary of State and the Minister Resident of the United States at Constantinople, and invite its consideration of the question as to the correct meaning of the 4th Article of the Treaty of 1830 between the United States and Turkey." DS, DNA, RG 46, Presidential Messages, Foreign Relations, Turkey. The enclosures are *ibid.*

To William W. Belknap

Washington. D. C. Dec. 9th *1869.*

Hon. W. W. Belknap;
Sec. of War:
Sir:

Mr. W. E. Dodge, of New York City, will call on you in behalf of himself and others of New York City, interested in the main trunk railroad line in Texas. Gn. Reynolds, ~~it seems,~~ has issued an order affecting the interest of the road which it seems to me, from the statement of Mr. Dodge, in whos statements I place every reliance, ought to be suspended until the meeting of the Legislature of Texas.

Please see Mr. Dodge and if you agree with me telegraph Gen. Reynolds advising suspension of his order.

Respectfully &c,
U. S. Grant

ALS, DNA, RG 94, Letters Received, 507D 1869.

Speech

[Dec. 11, 1869]

GENTLEMEN: I am gratified to receive this delegation, as I have watched the proceedings of your Convention with great attention. I have done all I could to advance the best interests of the citizens of our country, without regard to color, and I shall endeavor to do in the future what I have done in the past. I hope that the measures you have inaugurated will result in the securement of your best aims.

New York Tribune, Dec. 13, 1869. A variant of the Associated Press text also appeared. "I am very glad to meet a delegation from the working men of the country. I heartily sympathize with the movements now generally in progress to secure their rights. If they move in the right direction, and organize properly, they are strong enough to enforce all their just demands. So far as in my power I will endeavor to secure ample protection for them, and for all classes. The time has passed when the persons or property of citizens can be endangered by their loyalty to the Government." Washington Chronicle, Dec. 13, 1869. On Dec. 11, 1869, N. C. legislator James H. Harris had addressed USG. "MR. PRESIDENT: In accordance with a resolution passed by the National Labor Convention, just held in this city, composed mostly of colored men, representing the sentiments and views of the colored citizens of this great nation, I am here, Sir, to tender you the congratulation of that body, and the thanks of the colored men for the impartial and just manner in which you have administered the affairs of the country. Especially do we see this in your recognition of the claims of the negro in appointing black men to offices of great responsibility and trust, not because they were black, but in recognition of the fact that they are a part of the body politic. . . . Sir, in your administration we see a practical carrying out of the fundamental principles upon which the Government and the Republican party were founded, namely, liberty, humanity, equality, and justice. In conclusion, permit me again to thank you, in the name of the colored bone and sinew of the land, which stands ready to defend you and the country." New York Tribune, Dec. 13, 1869. Rev. J. Sella Martin of Mass. also spoke. "MR. PRESIDENT: One great subject of interest during our deliberations was the securing of land for the laborers of the South, so that they may become permanent settlers and independent citizens. There are 8,000,000 of acres of land that may be used by Congress to secure those results, and we desire to secure your influence to prevent any renewal of the lapsed land grants to railways and corporations to the detriment of actual settlers." Ibid. See W. E. B. DuBois, Black Reconstruction in America (New York, 1935; reprinted, 1962), pp. 361–66; Philip S. Foner, Organized Labor and the Black Worker, 1619–1973 (New York, 1974), pp. 30–34.

To Alexander R. Shepherd

Washington D. C. Dec 11. 1869

SIR:

I am in receipt of your communication of the 10th inst, requesting me to designate a horse from which the artist may model the equestrian statue[1] to be placed on the terrace of the South front of the Treasury building, In reply I have to say that I think the most appropriate horse for the purpose is one now in my possession named "Cincinnati."

Very truly yours
U S GRANT.

ALEX. R. SHEPHERD SECRETARY,
GRANT STATUE COMMITTEE

Copy, DLC-USG, II, 1. Alexander R. Shepherd, born in 1835, operated a successful plumbing business in Washington, D. C., and owned an interest in the *Washington Star.* Active in civic affairs, he served as president of the common council in 1862 and received an appointment to the levy court in 1867. On Nov. 8, 1869, Crosby S. Noyes, editor, *Washington Star,* and William J. Murtagh, publisher, *Washington National Republican,* wrote to USG. "The undersigned would respectfully ask of you the re-appointment of our fellow citizen Mr Alexander R. Shepherd to be a member of the Levy Court for this county on the expiration of his present term 15th Dec next. Mr Shepherd stands among our first citizens in energy, integrity, and public spirit, and no man in the county is capable of giving more intelligent, active service to the public in this position than he. He is a large property holder, both in the city and the county and no one individual has done more than he to build up the city and improve the county. Throughout his career his name has been identified with every good work or improvement brought forward for the public benefit and we are satisfied that if the people of the county could be consulted they would with almost entire unanimity ask his retention in his position in the Levy Court. In a party point of view Mr Shepherd has been a sound consistent Republican and throughout the late war his means and his active personal services were given without stint in behalf of the Union cause We know of no man who could successfully or acceptably replace him in the Levy Court and would most earnestly urge his re-appointment." LS, DNA, RG 60, Records Relating to Appointments. A petition recommending Shepherd is *ibid.* On Dec. 27, Shepherd *et al.* wrote to USG. "The undersigned, members of the Levy Court, respectfully represent that there is much need of a Justice of the Peace to be located at or near the village of Brightwood, and also one at or near Tenalleytown, and they therefore beg to recommend Benjamin D. Carpenter and Clement A. Peck, residents, respectively of the localities above-mentioned—as suitable persons for appointment to the office named." DS (9 signatures), *ibid.*

1. The model for a statue of USG by Joseph A. Bailly, Philadelphia, had been exhibited in the office of U.S. Treasurer Francis E. Spinner. See *Washington Chronicle*, April 7, 1869. On Oct. 21, 1870, Orville E. Babcock wrote to Alfred B. Mullett. "The President says he will be ready to sit for Mr Bailly, on Monday morning, about 9. am. So please have things ready to make the most of the time, Mr B. will appreciate this economy of time" ALS, DLC-USG, 1B. See *Washington Star*, Nov. 11, 1870.

To Robert C. Grier

———

Executive Mansion
December 15, 1869.

TO THE HONORABLE ROBERT C. GRIER,
SIR,

Your letter dated December 11, 1869, containing the tender of the resignation of your office of Associate Justice of the Supreme Court of the United States, to take effect on the first day of February next, has been received by me to-day, and your resignation is accordingly accepted to take effect on that date.

I sincerely regret the increasing physical infirmities which induce you to retire from the bench, and with the assurance of my personal sympathy and respect desire also to express my sense of the ability and uprightness with which your judicial duties have been performed. In looking upon your long and honorable career in the public service, it must be especially gratifying to yourself to remember, as it is my agreeable duty and privilege on this occasion thus distinctly to recognize, the great service which you were able to render to your country in the darkest hours of her history by the vigor and patriotic firmness with which you upheld the just powers of the Government, and vindicated the right of the nation under the Constitution to maintain its own existence. With the hope that your retirement may be cheered by the knowledge of public gratitude as well as by private affection

I remain
Very respectfully yours
U. S. GRANT

LS, Dickinson College, Carlisle, Pa. Robert C. Grier, born in 1794 in Cumberland County, Pa., graduated from Dickinson College in 1812 and began to practice law in 1817. In 1846, President James K. Polk appointed him to the U.S. Supreme Court. See letter to Ellen H. Stanton, Jan. 3, 1870.

On April 14, 1869, Samuel F. Miller, U.S. Supreme Court, had written to USG. "As one of the very few members of the Supreme Court, whose feelings have been and now are, in accord with the great political party which elected you, and who also desires the success of your administration, I feel no little solicitude that the selection you shall make for the additional member of that court under the law of the last session, shall be a wise one. As I have given the matter much thought I venture to make one or two suggestions. All the eight judges now constituting that court, are residents and citizens of states north of Mason & Dixons line. This presents a strong reason, when taken in connection with a proper ~~to~~ purpose to show the reconstructed rebel states that they shall have fair play in the future, why the next Judge of that court should be selected from one of those states; if a man can be found fully suitable for the position   I know that there are able lawyers there, who residing there at the outbreak of the rebellion, have resisted it with all their power, and at great personal sacrifice. But I must confess my fears that so thoroughly were all the best lawyers of that region, whether whigs or democrats before the rebellion, indoctrinated with the narrow and strict construction of the federal constitution, which enfeebles the federal powers and enlarges those of the states, that no one of sufficient ability can be found among the old resident lawyers there, who would not, when his conscience was appealed to on the bench, bring to that great court the very doctrines which have caused us so much trouble, and which may yet be appealed to, and are now every day, to overthrow the legislation of the last eight years. I therefore recommend for the place Hon. H. Clay Caldwell of Little Rock, at present Judge of the District Court of United States. Judge Caldwell is about thirty five or forty years old. He is as able a man and as sound a lawyer, as I with all my acquaintance know in the South. He practiced law many years in my circuit in Iowa, of which State he has been a prominent legislator, and influential man. He entered !Little Rock in 1863 at the head of his Regiment, and was appointed Judge of the United States Court there by Mr Lincoln. He has resided there ever since with his family, now nearly six years, in his own house. He is the pride of the loyal men of the State, and even the rebels and democrats admit his ability and integrity, and would be pleased at his appointment. He is a thorough unadulterated Republican, and will make if appointed, a Judge of whom you will be proud, long after you have retired into private life. I take the liberty of saying that I belive I am as familiar with the bar of the South and West, as any one with whom you are likely to advise, and that I know of no abler or purer man, or a more capable and industrious Judge than Judge Caldwell, and no one whom if I were President, I would sooner appoint. Be pleased to excuse the the length of this letter and the freedom of its expressions. I hope you will not consider it a mere formal recommendation, for it proceeds from an anxiety which I do not doubt you share, that the appointment that the appointment shall be the very best that can be made for the public service." ALS, DNA, RG 60, Applications and Recommendations. Letters to USG, and related papers, recommending for the U.S. Supreme Court Henry C. Caldwell of Ark., David C. Humphreys of Ala., William W. Howe of La., William Marvin of Fla., and Judge Advocate Gen. Joseph Holt are *ibid.* Papers relating to David

K. Cartter of Washington, D. C., are *ibid.*; DLC-Cartter Family. Correspondence to USG anticipating the retirement of Samuel Nelson, U.S. Supreme Court, and recommending Ward Hunt of N. Y., are in DNA, RG 60, Applications and Recommendations.

On Dec. 14, USG nominated Attorney Gen. Ebenezer R. Hoar to fill a restored ninth seat on the U.S. Supreme Court. On Dec. 22, the Senate tabled the nomination. On Dec. 23, Edwin D. Morgan, New York City, wrote to USG. "I am very sorry Mr Hoar was not confirmed as a Justice of the Supreme court. In such hands as his and Stantons, the country would have felt great Security. Hoar is a fit man for the place and if he had had a little more experience in intercourse with Senators, I think he would have fared better in the Senate. It seems to me proable that you will turn your attention to some man in the South. John J. Speed is not a great man, but he is a good man. I think he would do as a judge, perhaps, better than as Atty General. Of one thing, we could all be sure in his case, as much as in Mr Stanton or Mr Hoar he would never give a copperhead decision. Pardon my Suggestions . . ." ALS, DLC-USG, 1B. On Dec. 25, Hoar, Concord, Mass., wrote to Secretary of the Interior Jacob D. Cox. "Let me say in the first place that to receive such a letter as yours, written by a man who has known the whole of my principles, purposes and conduct in public affairs for the last ten months, is an ample compensation for whatever indignity the majority of the Senate are capable of offering. Your message from the President is very gratifying, and in entire accordance with my own wishes and purposes. In anticipation of such an event as has occurred, I said to him before I left Washington, that I hoped, in deciding what he ought to do, he would leave wholly out of view every thing personal to myself; that I had neither wishes nor desires connected with public life, and was not afraid that any body would find it in his power to do me any permanent injury; and that I should trust that he would take the course which would be the best for the dignity, harmony, and success of his administration. I do not like to advise in a matter with which I am so much involved—and my advice would not be likely to be of much value—But as it looks to me, this is a matter which concerns the President much more deeply than it does the particular subject of the operation. It is a coalition between the democrats & the carpet-baggers, to determine just how soon and to what extent the rebel states shall be placed on the same footing with the rest, in sharing all the places of honor and trust in the Government—and the occasion has been seized by the men who feel indignant that they could not dictate the selection of CIRCUIT JUDGES, and who have been so long accustomed to wield the whole executive power of the government under Johnson, to strike a blow at the whole constitutional authority of the President—Under the last administration all nominations had come to be a mere matter of bargain; and Senators would agree that they would have one friend of Johnson's confirmed, provided he would nominate one, two, or three men of their selection for other places. It is not easy for men who have been accustomed to such methods, to entertain the idea that the people have elected a very different kind of man for President, and with a view to a very different kind of administration. The question must be met at some time—and though I do not expect to enjoy it, probably no one else would be likely to enjoy it any more; and the place of football in the game seems to have providentially fallen to my share. I do not see that the President can withdraw the nomination—unless he becomes satisfied that it was an improper one—I should prefer to have a square vote of rejection, and with the yeas and nays upon it, if I have friends enough in the Senate to call for them—and shall make them as public as possible—There will be no flinching on my part—If any Senators have voted, or shall vote, upon considerations merely personal, I can only hope that they may live to regret it—not from any harm it will do them, but from a changed opinion. But for those gentlemen who mean to parcel out the offices, or else have a break with the President, I have a pretty decided conviction that they have mistaken their man in him, as well as mistaken what the people expect of him. At any rate they have not in the least mistaken their man in me. I am willing that you should use what I have written at your discretion—and should like to have the President know it. I enclose a letter that I have just received, as a specimen of a considerable number from various quarters—and shorter as well as less personal—than most of them—It is from Sam Bowles, the editor of a paper of large circulation in Western N. England, and a friend of Colfax—to whom I thought some of sending it—But though I should like well enough to have him see it, I concluded to say nothing to any one unless in reply to them. I think I shall stay at home unless something occurs to make it expedient for me to be in Washington sooner, until Monday the 3d of January—and then ~to~ resume operations with you as serenely as if nothing had happened—I hope the President will *say* nothing about his future intentions at present—'It is a very pretty quarrel as it stands;' and I think I see *his* road out of it very clear. . . ." ALS, Cox Papers, Oberlin College, Oberlin, Ohio.

On Jan. 7, 1870, Secretary of State Hamilton Fish recorded in his diary: "Judge Hoar left the Cabinet—& Cox took the occasion to bring up his pending nomination—says it is important to know what the position of the Administration is to be with regard to it—whether we are to say that the President desires his confirmation &c &c—President says, very emphatically, that he does desire it, & has so said has had conversations this morning with several Senators—Robeson suggests that the power of the Administration may be brought to bear upon the Senators opposing the confirmation—I express my agreement that this should be done—& that they be made to understand that the Administration will not be granting favors to those who are opposing its policy, or its nominations—The position of several Senators with regard to Hoar's nomination, is described among them Sawyer of S—C—& Spencer of Alabama—in consequence of what was said about Sawyer, that I proposed to withhold the nomination of Delaney as Minister to Liberia—The President expresses a willingness to withhold political patronage from those recommended by Senators & others [in] opposition to the policy or attitude of the Administration" DLC-Hamilton Fish. See Allan Nevins, *Hamilton Fish: The Inner History of the Grant Administration* (New York, 1936), pp. 303–5.

On Jan. 8, U.S. Senator Charles D. Drake of Mo. wrote to USG. "It has occurred to me that possibly the letter I took the liberty of addressing you some days since in relation to the Supreme Judgeship, might have produced upon your mind the impression that I wished the nomination of Judge Hoar not to be pressed, or, if pressed, to fail; but such was not my purpose. That letter was written under the supposition that that nomination might be withdrawn; which, from indications since, would seem not to be intended. If the nomination should come to a vote, I expect to vote for its confirmation." ALS, MoSHi.

On Feb. 3, the Senate rejected Hoar's nomination. On Feb. 7, USG nominated Joseph P. Bradley and William Strong to the U.S. Supreme Court. On

March 31, 1869, Grier had written to USG. "I understand that a bill has passed or is about to pass Congress providing for the appointment of nine new Circuit Judges. Presuming that the result of my observation of the men practising in the 3rd Circuit may be of some value to you in making your selection, I take the liberty of stating to you that Mr. Joseph P. Bradley of Newark N. J. seems to me to be very thoroughly fitted for one of those Judgeships. He is an accomplished and sound lawyer—and is especially conversant with matters of Federal Law coming before the Courts of the United States. He would make a most excellent Judge." Charles Fairman, "Mr. Justice Bradley's Appointment to the Supreme Court and the Legal Tender Cases," *Harvard Law Review*, 54 (April, 1941), 998. On Nov. 16, Frederick T. Frelinghuysen, Newark, wrote to USG. "Mr. Joseph P. Bradley of this city by reason of his peculiar qualifications for high judicial position has been recommended by the Judges of all our Superior courts, and by the members of the bar of our state, without distinction of party, for appointment to the Circuit Judgeship (recently created) of this judicial district—I do not write, so much, to say that I concur in this recommendation, as to say that I have for years been intimately acquainted with Mr Bradleys attainments as a lawyer and that by reason of his being so well based & founded in the great principles of law, a position on the bench of the Supreme Court would be for him even more appropriate & fitting than the Circuit Judgeship—As the Justices of the Supreme Court, before whom Mr. Bradley has frequently made arguments are familiar with his qualifications, I do not doubt that they would verify what I have said of him—" ALS, New Jersey Historical Society, Newark, N. J.

On Dec. 13, Strong, Philadelphia, telegraphed to USG. "I will do myself the honor of calling upon you tomorrow morning" Telegram received (at 1:20 P.M.), DNA, RG 107, Telegrams Collected (Bound). On Jan. 1, 1870, Judge William McKennan, U.S. Circuit Court, Washington, Pa., wrote to USG. "As a matter of delicacy I do not wish ostensibly to take part in reference to the appointment of Judge Greer's successor, but I cannot withold a word in regard to Judge Strong—I have known him thoroughly for many years—As a lawyer he attained a high rank, as a Judge, he gave evidence of mental and moral qualities which gained for him the admiration and secured for Hhim the confidence of men of all parties—As a man he has always been without reproach—You will perhaps remember what I said to you on our way from Pittsburgh here as to the scene in the Supreme Court room at Pittsburgh, when the Judges delivered their opinions in the case involving the Constitutionality of the Enlistment or draft law—The manner and deportment of Judge Strong made an impression upon me that is still vivid—No man ever exhibited more admirable firmness, fearlessness and patriotism than he did on that occasion, and to him we are mor[e] indebted than to any one else for averting outbreak[s] and collisions, for which many of the people we[re] ripe, and which must have caused the mos[t] serious embarrassments—For this alone he is entitled to the most conspicuous recognition—But he is besides peculiarly fitted for the ben[ch] of the Supreme Court, and so generally is thi[s] conceded, that, in Penna. at least, it seems to be taken for granted that you have made [up] your mind to appoint him. His nomination would be received with the same general a[p]proval which followed the appointment of Stanton—And, in view of my official association with the appointee, to no one would it be more gratifying . . ." ALS, *ibid.*, RG 60, Applications and Recommendations. Additional letters recommending Strong are *ibid.*

On Feb. 11, Bradley, Newark, wrote to USG. "The honor of being nominated by you to the bench of the Supreme Court is so highly appreciated by me, that you must permit me to express my acknowledgements. I feel the responsibility of the position, should your selection be approved by the Senate. The questions that come before the Supreme Court are so grave and vital to the Country and its institutions that it seems to me a man must have an unusual share of self confidence not to feel great diffidence in taking part in its decisions. It is possible that the Senate will fail to confirm the nomination; and if so, I can only say that many persons can be found much better qualified than myself for the position—" ALS, USG 3. In an undated letter, Strong wrote to USG. "I cannot refrain from sending you a line to express in some feeble degree my sense of the great obligation you have conferred upon me, by nominating me for an Associate Justice of the Supreme Court. You have done me great honor. I shall ever gratefully remember your kindness. A seat in the Supreme Court would satisfy all my ambition; except ambition to discharge its duties well. Please accept my thanks." ALS, Free Library of Philadelphia, Philadelphia, Pa. See Fairman, "Mr. Justice Bradley's Appointment," 977–1034; *ibid.*, 54 (May, 1941), 1128–55; Sidney Ratner, "Was the Supreme Court Packed by President Grant?" *Political Science Quarterly*, L, 3 (Sept., 1935), 343–58.

To William W. Smith

Washington, D, C,
Dec. 15th 1869,

DEAR SMITH:

Julia has been talking for the last two weeks of writing to Emma and you to come on to spend the Christmass Holidays[1] with us. She has not done so however, and now wants me to write it, and say that we hope you will be able to come some time next week. I think you can spend two days here as pleasantly as elswhere.

Please present my kind regards to Mr. McKennan and family.

Yours Truly

U. S. GRANT

ALS, Washington County Historical Society, Washington, Pa. On Dec. 18, 1869, USG telegraphed to William W. Smith, Washington, Pa. "Can you not come so as to be here Christmass dDay?" ALS (telegram sent), Alice L. Bates, Los Angeles, Calif.; telegram received, Washington County Historical Society. On Dec. 20, Monday, Smith telegraphed to USG. "Your telegram is just received Father is in Philadelphia & expects to return on Saturday and we to leave here on monday for Washington if he should return sooner will start this week and telegraph you" Telegram received (at 12:15 P.M.), DNA, RG 107, Telegrams Collected (Bound). On Dec. 21, Smith telegraphed to USG. "We hope to arrive in Washington Friday morning" Telegram received (at 10:00 A.M.), *ibid.* On Dec. 22, Smith, Wheeling, West Va., telegraphed to USG. "Will leave here on six oclock train which arrives in Washington one oclock tomorrow" Telegram received (at noon), *ibid.* On Dec. 24, Smith, Sir Johns Run, West Va., telegraphed to USG. "We were detained by a wreck Will not get to Washington till twenty minutes past six (6)" Telegram received (at 11:30 A.M.), *ibid.*

1. Sending an engraved invitation, USG invited Adam Badeau to the White House for Christmas dinner. Robert F. Batchelder, Catalog 42 [1983], no. 330.

To David Van Nostrand

DEAR SIR:

Please accept my thanks for the following works which you were kind enough to send me: "Barnes Submarine Warfare", "Gen. Foster's Submarine Blasting", "Maj. Head's new system of Fortification" and "Maj Arnolds Cavalry Horses";[1] also two copies of the second volume of Col. Ferd. Lecomte's work.[2]

They are all of peculiar interest to the student, and will make a valuable acquisition to my military library.

I am very truly yours
U. S. GRANT

EXECUTIVE MANSION.
Dec. 15th 1869
D. VAN NOSTRAND ESQ.
NEW YORK—

LS, Ford Collection, NN. David Van Nostrand, born in New York City in 1811, was a bookseller and publisher who specialized in military manuals and histories as well as scientific and technical works. On July 28, 1870, USG, Long Branch, wrote to Van Nostrand. "Received of D._____ Van Nostrand two hundred and fifty dollars, dividend on stock of Michigan Central Iron company $250,00" DS, NNP.

1. In 1869, Van Nostrand had published John S. Barnes, *Submarine Warfare, Offensive and Defensive,* . . . ; John G. Foster, *Submarine Blasting in Boston Harbor,* . . . ; George E. Head, *An Essay on a New System of Fortification*; Abraham K. Arnold, *Notes on Horses for Cavalry Service.*
2. Ferdinand Lecomte had written two multi-volume works, *Guerre de la*

Sécession . . . , 3 vols. (Paris, 1866–67) and *Guerre de la Prusse et de l'Italie Contre l'Autriche* . . . , 2 vols. (Paris, 1868).

To Lt. Gen. Philip H. Sheridan

Washington, D. C. Dec. 16th *1869*

[GEN. P. H. SHERIDAN
INDIENAPOLIS IND]

I regret my inability to be present with the Society of the Army of the Cumberland at their annual meeting; and also my non-acknowledgement [by letter] of the invitation which was duly received. Not being able to answer upon receipt the matter escaped my memory, under the pressure of public business, until I saw notices of your meeting. I hope the society may have many pleasant reunions, and that the time of some of them may be so selected as to enable me to attend ~~them~~. Please receive my hearty congratulations for the choice of President made by the Society.[1]

U. S. GRANT

ALS, James M. Victor, Broadview, Ill. On Dec. 15, 1869, the Society of the Army of the Cumberland met in Indianapolis. In the absence of Maj. Gen. George H. Thomas, Lt. Gen. Philip H. Sheridan served as presiding officer. On Dec. 16, Walter Q. Gresham and Benjamin J. Spooner, Indianapolis, telegraphed to USG. "Think you ought to say something by telegraph to society of the army of the Cumberland Now in session here   They say you have not replied to their invitation"   Telegram received (at 9:10 A.M.), DNA, RG 107, Telegrams Collected (Bound).

1. Final sentence replaced by another, with interlineations not in USG's hand. "Please accept my hearty congratulations for the honor the Society has conferred upon you in the choice of a Presedent."

To Elihu B. Washburne

Washington, D. C. Dec. 17th *1869*

DEAR WASHBURNE;

It is not the presure of business so much as the pressure of callers that prevents my writing oftener. I hear from you however often through the notes which you give from time to time to persons coming to the United States, and through the State Dept.— Every thing seems to be progressing well in the United States. Our currency is increasing in value; repudiators meet with no favor, and on the whole I think a very healthy political feeling is springing up in the country. Congress has assembled apparently feeling well. Generally they have accepted the recommendations contained in my message. Of course you will find people to differ with this or that view, but, on the whole, it may be said to be acceptable, as a whole, to the majority. You read the papers from here however and can judge for yourself upon these matters.

My family are all well and join me in love and regards to Mrs. Washburne and the children. Sometimes I feel tempted to set an example to my successors in office by taking a vacation in the recess of Congress and spending it in Europe. I probably will not do so, but I have often contemplated it.

Yours Truly
U. S. GRANT

ALS, MHi. On Nov. 22 and 26, 1869, Elihu B. Washburne, Paris, had written to USG. "I have given the Rev. Père Hyacinthe a letter of introduction to Gov. Fish, suggesting that he would be glad of an introduction to you when he shall visit Washington, if it shall be agreeable to you. I have known much of Father Hyacinthe since I have been in Paris and I have a profound admiration for his character. I honor him for his virtues, for his piety, for his courage and his eloquence. I am certain you and your family would be glad to know so distinguished a man. He has a great admiration for you and says he wants to shake the hand of that illustrious man who has borne such a part in breaking the shackles of four millions of slaves. I wrote Gov. Fish about my visit to the Emperor at his Palace at Compiègne, some sixty miles from Paris, and at the request of his majesty I sent his friendly salutations to you thro [the] Secretary. It is possible you may feel interest enough in the matter to read my despatch to the State Dept. I believe all the Senators and Representatives who have been in Europe this season have left for home except Gov. Fenton and Genl Banks. The latter has been to the opening of the Suez Canal. The former is now here and I see a good dea[l] of him. He speaks in the warmest terms of you personally and of his faith in the success of your administration. I am certain that in the long run you will find the Senator all I represented him to you. I will not trouble you with a long letter for I am quite certain you have no time to think of me so far out of the way and one who has become of so little account as I have." "I have the honor to send to you, through the Department of State, two copies 'Etudes Pratiques sur la Question d'Orient' and, at the request of the author of the work, to ask your acceptance of the same." ALS (press) and LS (press), DLC-Elihu B.

Washburne. On Dec. 8, Washburne twice wrote to USG. "Mr. Burch asks me to send the enclosed letter to you. There may be something in his suggestions worthy of consideration, and I think you had better pass the letter over to Gov. Boutwell. Europe is more and more amazed at the achievements of your administration in reducing the debt. Now if you can only keep down expenses to a low figure it will redound still more to the credit of the Government. Beseech members of Congress not to vote away one dollar more of the public money than is absolutely necessary, and if they do, just give them the benefit of an honest veto." "This will be handed you by my friend, the Hon. Walter S. Gurnee, formerly of Chicago, but more recently of N. Y. Mr. G. has resided a good deal abroad and has recently been residing in Paris, with his family. He is a gentleman of intelligence, cultivation and wealth, and particularly well posted in matters abroad and in our financial matters.—As he about returning to America, and will visit Washington, I take great pleasure in giving him this letter to you. He can tell you about matters in Paris and about me more than I can write you, and as he is my friend I am quite certain you will be glad to see him." ALS (press), *ibid.*; ALS, USG 3.

To Senate

TO THE SENATE OF THE UNITED STATES:

I hereby request the return of such part of my message of Dec. 9th,[1] in response to Senate resolution of Dec. 6th. requesting the reports of the Military Commanders of the District of which Georgia is a part,—to wit: an anonymous letter purporting to be from "a Georgia woman". By accident the paper got with those called for by the resolution, instead of in the waste-basket where it was intended it should go.

U. S. GRANT

EXECUTIVE MANSION.
WASHINGTON, D. C.
DEC. 20, 1869

DS, DNA, RG 46, Annual Messages. On Dec. 6, 1869, "a Georgia woman," Washington, D. C., had written to U.S. Representative Benjamin F. Butler of Mass. "Listen to the appeal of a Georgia woman—who speaks for Georgia when the voices of her men ~~are~~ have to be silent—I have just read Gov Bullocks indictment against the people of Geo I hear he is ~~present~~ in this city to present & enforce his demands on Congress—. . ." AL, *ibid.*, RG 94, Letters Received, 1156S 1869.

1. On Dec. 9, USG had written to the Senate. "In compliance with the resolution of the Senate of the 6th inst. requesting reports of Military Com-

mander of the District of which Georgia is a part, in regard to the political and civil condition of that State—the accompanying papers are submitted." DS, *ibid.*, RG 46, Annual Messages. The enclosures are *ibid.* and in *SED*, 41-2-3. See letter to Senate, Feb. 11, 1870.

To Senate

To THE SENATE OF THE UNITED STATES.

In compliance with the request of the Senate, I send to them the papers in my possession relating to the persons nominated as Circuit Judges of all the Circuits except the first. There are none in my possession relating to the person nominated in that Circuit.

U. S. GRANT

WASHINGTON, DEC. 21, 1869.

DS, DNA, RG 46, Papers Pertaining to Nominations. See *Senate Executive Journal*, XVII, 322–23.

On April 10, 1869, USG signed a bill increasing the number of Supreme Court justices from seven to nine and revising their circuit court duties, creating a circuit judge for each of the nine judicial circuits, and providing for the retirement of federal judges, all provisions taking effect on Dec. 6. On April 8, U.S. Representative Robert C. Schenck of Ohio had spoken during debate on the bill: "As I understand the matter before the House there are but two material amendments proposed by the Senate to the amendments of the House. The rest are verbal. One of those material amendments proposes that these appointments of judges shall not take place until December next. That I think is a decided improvement on the House proposition. All through this city there are handed around at this time papers to be signed recommending some one for Supreme judge or for circuit judge. Chaffering goes on; bargains are made. 'I will go for your collector or assessor if you will go for my judge.' Now, I do not want judges appointed at this time and in the midst of such scenes as that. I think it would be better to wait until next December. In the mean time let the merits of prominent individuals in the different circuits be discussed, and let the bar of the country and the people of the country concentrate some public opinion upon particular men, and the selections will be more judiciously made by all the parties upon whom the power of selection rests than they would be if they were appointed now in the midst of that mass of appointments being made for various other offices not half as important as judicial offices. . . ." *CG*, 41-1, 649. See *U.S. Statutes at Large*, XIV, 209; *ibid.*, XVI, 44–45; Charles Fairman, *Reconstruction and Reunion, 1864–88* (New York and London, 1971), I, 487–88, 559–60.

On Nov. 12, John A. Bolles, solicitor and judge advocate, U.S. Navy, wrote to USG. "*Personal* . . . I respectfully ask you to appoint me Circuit Judge of the

U. S. under the Act of Apl 10. 1869. for the 1st Circuit. My residence is in Massachusetts, in that Circuit. I have been a member of the Boston Bar ever since April, 1833. At the beginning of the rebellion, I left my law practice, & went into the military service, & served on Genl Dix's staff to the end of the war. Since that time I have been Solicitor & Naval Judge Advocate General. My age indisposes me to go back to the conflicts of the Bar, & I respectfully hope that you know me to be qualified for the judicial appointment which I now ask, & I am sure that you know me to be your true & earnest political & personal friend." ALS, OFH. On June 22, 1870, Bolles twice wrote to USG requesting an appointment to the D. C. Supreme Court. ALS, DNA, RG 60, Records Relating to Appointments. On Dec. 8, 1869, USG nominated George F. Shepley as judge, 1st Circuit. See *PUSG*, 12, 120; *ibid.*, 18, 123–24.

On May 12, William E. Dodge, New York City, wrote to USG. "It has been my purpose to avoid intruding upon you my desires in regard to any appointments and have thus far refused the numerous applications for letters to you in their behalf—but having heard that Ex. Senator Foster has been named by many friends in Connt for the position of Judge of the 2d district Circuit Court. I am very anxious that he should receive the appointment as I am sure no man in the State is better fitted for the office—I have known him intimately for many years and have the highest respect for his ability and high moral & religious character and am confident that his appointment would give great satisfaction to our friends in the district, and as a native of Connt I should be proud to see such a man in the position." ALS, NHi. On Oct. 20, John H. Hubbard, Litchfield, Conn., wrote to USG. "Pardon me for saying, that in my judgment no better man can be found for the position of Judge for the District comprising the states of New York, Connecticut, and Vermont, than Ex. Senator Foster, of Norwich Conn. I believe his appointment would give perfect satisfaction to the people of the District, and I hope it may be made. I was a member of the 38th and of the 39th Congress and was then, as now, a Republican of the radical type. I beg leave also to say, that this paper has not been solicited by Mr Foster, or by any one of his friends, but is most respectfully submitted of my own free will and choice, without solicitation from any one. I regard Mr Foster as most eminently qualified for the place before named." ALS, OFH. On Nov. 19, Governor Marshall Jewell of Conn. wrote to USG urging the same appointment. ALS, CtY. On Nov. 5, Miller, Peet, and Opdyke, attorneys, New York City, had written to USG. "A long acquaintance socially & professionally with Hon C. L Benedict U S Dist Judge enables us to recommend him for appointment a U S. Circuit Judge for this Circuit—His Experience & learning in the peculiar class of cases brought before that court is second to ~~non~~that of none at our Bar and his character & integrity equally fit him for so responsible a position. We believe we express the wish of the Bar of this state when we suggest his appointment to the honorable position we have mentioned" LS, NHi. On Nov. 22, John M. Parker, N. Y. Supreme Court, Oswego, wrote to USG. "I have been long acquainted with the Honorable Ira Harris, late a Justice of the Supreme court of this State. His capacity & fitness for the office of Judge were eminently illustrated by the ability & integrity with which he filled that office—I have no hesitation in saying that his qualifications for the office of Circuit Judge of the United States are of the very highest order—" ALS, NIC. Additional letters of recommendation are *ibid*. On Nov. 27, John H. Reynolds, Albany, N. Y., wrote to USG recommending Ira Harris. ALS, NNP. On Dec. 8, USG nominated Lewis B. Woodruff as judge, 2nd Circuit. See letter to Edwards Pierrepont, Dec. 3, 1869.

In 1869, U.S. Representative James S. Negley of Pa. *et al.* petitioned USG. "We very earnestly recommend to your Excellency the appointment of the Hon. Samuel A. Purviance of Pittsburgh, Penna. for the Office of circuit Judge of the circuit composed of Pennsylvania and New Jersey. Mr Purviance is a gentleman of high legal attainments is regarded one of the best lawyers in Penna. a gentleman of strict integrity, and is greatly esteemed for exemplary moral deportment, and excellent social qualities. He has filled many important positions in his Native state Pennsylvania, and with credit to himself and entire satisfaction to his constituents. Mr Purviance was a member of the Convention for revision of the Constitution of Pennsylvania—a member of the Legislature of the state—twice elected to Congress—and subsequently Attorney General of the state As a Republican, honestly embracing the principles of the party, and ably advocating them in every important canvass since the organization of the party, he ranks amoung the most conspicuous as an able effective speaker; and in no canvasse was he more ardent and untiring in his efforts thatn in the campaigns of 1860. 64. &. 1868. We feel assured that his appointment would give very general satisfaction as one eminently fit to be made." DS (8 signatures), NNP. About the same date, William Strong *et al.* petitioned USG. "The undersigned, members of the Bar of Philadelphia, have learned that it is probable that the name of the *Hon. Joseph Allison*, now President Judge of the Court of Common Pleas of that city, will be presented to your Excellency for the appointment of Judge of the Circuit Court of the United States, under the recent Act of Congress to amend the Judicial System of the Union. Under these circumstances, it gives us great pleasure to express our opinion of the high qualifications of Judge Allison for the position, from his legal ability, the firmness and integrity with which he has discharged the duties of his present post for seventeen years, his moral and religious character, and his unswerving loyalty. For these reasons we feel convinced that his appointment would give universal satisfaction." DS (37 signatures), DLC-Pennsylvania Miscellaneous. On Dec. 8, USG nominated William McKennan as judge, 3rd Circuit. See letter to William W. Smith, Sept. 25, 1868.

On March 12, 1869, U.S. Senator Waitman T. Willey of West Va. wrote to USG. "Hon. T. W. Harrison, of West Va, informs me that he will be an applicant for the appointment of Justice under the Judiciary Act now pending before congress, in the circuit where he resides. Mr. H. is now the presiding Judge of one the circuit courts of West Va, where he has served for many years with distinction, and with satisfaction to the people whom he has served, and is, in every respect a gentleman of the highest character and standing, and as such I commend him to your favorable consideration." ALS, OFH. Endorsements by U.S. Representative James C. McGrew of West Va. *et al.* are appended to the letter. On May 24, Samuel Shellabarger, New York City, wrote to USG recommending Benjamin Stanton's appointment as judge, 4th Circuit. ALS, *ibid.* On Oct. 21, Edwards Pierrepont, U.S. attorney, New York City, wrote to USG and Attorney Gen. Ebenezer R. Hoar. "Hon. Edward C. Carrington the District Atty at Washington desires the Office of Circuit Judge in the circuit comprising his native State Va. & other States—I first made Mr Carringtons acquaintance in the Surratt trial at a part of which Gen. Grant was present—I found Mr Carrington a most high-toned courteous gentleman a very laborious & earnest lawyer a most loyal man from the very core—He deserves honors and recognition from this Govermt. I have made it a rule, from which I have not varied, to press no man for a particular place, but to leave the appointing power to do what it thinks fit after learning any facts which I may be able to communicate—It gives me great pleasure to speak of the high qualities which I have ever found in General Carrington and it will much gratify me to learn that General Carrington receives the very high consideration of this Govermt in relation to any place to which he may aspire" ALS, CtY. USG also received letters from Judge Advocate Gen. Joseph Holt (OFH, Oct. 22), Edward Lander (*ibid.*, Nov. 10), Alexander H. H. Stuart (ViU, Nov. 13), and John H. Johnson (Duke University, Durham, N. C., Nov. 18) recommending Edward C. Carrington. On Nov. 9, Willey, Morgantown, wrote to USG recommending Edwin Maxwell as judge, 4th Circuit, and on Jan. 17, 1870, Willey *et al.*, Washington, D. C., wrote to USG recommending George Loomis for the same position. ALS, OFH; LS (4 signatures), DNA, RG 60, Applications and Recommendations. On Oct. 25, 1869, U.S. Senator Jacob M. Howard of Mich., Detroit, had written to USG. "I understand that Hon H H. Wells of Richmond, formerly gov. of Va, is a candidate for Circuit judge for the circuit comprising Maryland Virginia & W. Virginia under the recent act of Cong. that takes effect in Decr next. Mr. W. was long a practicing attorney & counsellor & a member of the Detroit bar, and as such I have been intimately acquainted with him. He is an able lawyer & a man of the strictest integrity and in my opinion a very fit selection for the place, and I take the liberty sincerely and earnestly to recommend his appointment" ALS, *ibid.*, Records Relating to Appointments. On Oct. 30, U.S. Representative Oakes Ames of Mass., North Easton, wrote to USG. "Allow me to present the name of Gov H. H Wells to your consideration for the position U. S. Circuit Judge for the Circuit of Md—Va North & South Carolina I have known Mr Wells for several years and have had business connections with him and have found him to be an able good Lawyer and a high minded honorable man: and beleive he would honor the position—and reflect credit on you for the appointment" ALS, *ibid.* On Nov. 3, Bvt. Maj. Gen. Edward R. S. Canby, Richmond, wrote to USG. "While on duty in Washington several years ago the nature of my duties established an official although indirect relation with the Hono H. H. Wells then in the military service of the United States and stationed at Alexandria, which gave me the means of determining the manner in which his official duties were performed and of forming an estimate of his character and ability, and for some months past the nature of our official relations has been such as to test fully the correctness of the estimate previously formed and to acquire a fuller knowledge of his general and professional attainments. These opportunities of official and personal observations enable me to speak confidently of his high personal character, great professional ability and of that order of mind and of training which qualif him eminently for judicial positions." ALS, *ibid.* Additional letters recommending Henry H. Wells as U.S. circuit judge are *ibid.* On May 6, 1870, USG nominated Wells as U.S. attorney, District of Va. On July 5, 1869, U.S. Representative John Cessna of Pa., Bedford, had written to USG. "I take great pleasure in bearing testimony to the integrity—ability, learning and fidelity of Hon Geo. A. Pearree of Maryland— Judge P. will be urged by his friends as a suitable person for the position of Judge of the U. S. Circuit Court for the fourth District—He was one of the few Border State men who were true to our cause during the late struggle—is now a sound & reliable Republican and a gentleman of good moral character & high social position—" ALS, *ibid.*, Applications and Recommendations, Circuit Judges. On Aug. 27, Governor Oden Bowie of Md. wrote to USG. "Desirous that our State may receive the appointment to the Judgeship of the Fourth Judicial Circuit and knowing the peculiar fitness of Judge Pearce for the position I venture to express the hope that Your Excellency may see fit to appoint him." ALS, *ibid.* Related papers are *ibid.* On Nov. 20, Grayson Eichelberger, Frederick, Md., wrote to USG. "I have just learned that the charge of indifference to the republican cause has by some one been preferred against Judge Pearre. In refutation of any such charge, I beg to state that as soon as the present party came into power in this State, numerous suits were instituted in this county by rebels and rebel sympathisers against the Union judges of election for refusing to permit them to vote. In so doing, the Union Judges of election but complied with the provisions of our then existing Constitution & of our State laws upon that subject. So strong & so much biasseed were the feelings of our Circuit Court judges that we could expect nothing from them. I was of counsel for the Judges of election, but was too much indisposed at the time the cases came up for trial to take an active part in the argument of the cases. Judge Pearre, happening to be here on a visit at the time, tried the first case for me at my request and though we had no expectation of a favorable decision of the law involved by the Court, still so powerful was Judge's Pearre's argument in the case & such was it's effect upon the Democrats, that it forced a withdrawal of all the remaining suits, though the one tried was by the Court decided against the Election Judges. His Effort was a labor of love. I can state further that, at the request of the party, he came down here & made the most powerful and effective effort in favor of your election & of the principles of the Republican party that I heard any were during the Canvass." ALS, *ibid.* On Dec. 8, USG nominated George A. Pearre as judge, 4th Circuit; the Senate twice tabled this nomination. On April 6, 1870, USG withdrew Pearre and nominated Hugh L. Bond. See *Calendar*, Feb. 3, 1869.

On March 20, 1869, Myra Clark Gaines, Washington, D. C., wrote to USG. "I am informed, that the 'Judiciary Bill' will soon pass. It is very important to me, as well, as to a great portion of the community of New Orleans, that a disinterested Judge, should be appointed, for that Circuit: Permit me to suggest the name of Judge J. Smith, Whittaker. He iswas a zealous Republican, an earnest supporter of your election, and is acknowledged by the Bar, of New Orleans, and elsewhere, as as a man, combining rare legal ability, integrity of character, and with all the qualities of a refined gentleman." ALS, DNA, RG 60, Records Relating to Appointments. Related papers are *ibid.* On March 31, U.S. Representative George W. McCrary of Ind. wrote to USG. "I have known Hon. E. Jeffords now of the High Court of appeals of Mississippi for a number of years, and am fully prepared to join with others in recommending his appointment as judge of the Circuit Court of the United States for The Fifth Circuit, in the event of the final passage of the pending Bill for the re organization of the Judicial system of the United States. Judge Jeffords resided in the same City with myself for a number of years prior to the outbreak of the rebellion, and we practiced law in the same Courts. He is a ripe scholar,—an excellent lawyer, and a ~~thorough~~loyal and patriotic citizen. He is entirely devoted to the law and if appointed to the position named he would I am sure make it the aim of his life to, fill it with honor to himself and advantage to the Country" ALS, OFH. U.S. Representatives Francis W. Palmer and William Smyth of Iowa favorably endorsed this letter. AES, *ibid.* On April 9, U.S. Senator Willard Warner of Ala. *et al.* petitioned USG. "The undersigned respectfully but most earnestly recommend to you for appointment as United States Circuit Judge for the fifth Judicial Circuit Judge William B. Woods of Alabama. Judge Woods graduated at Yale College in the Class of 1845, was admitted to the bar of Ohio in 1847 and was engaged in the active practice of law from that time until the outbreak of the war when he entered the Union Army as Lt. Colonel of the 76th Reg. O. V. I. serving throughout the entire War with distinguished skill and gallantry, and was promoted on the recommendation of Gen. W. T. Sherman to the rank of Brigadier and Brevet Major General. At the close of the war in 1865 he settled in Alabama and invested all of his property there, of which state he has since been a continued resident. In 1868 he was elected Chancellor of the Middle Division of Alabama, which position he now holds ~~with~~ to the great satisfaction of the bar and people of Alabama and with distinguished credit to himself. He is a man of great ability, of incorruptible integrity, of untiring industry and fine culture and is in every way admirably fitted for judicial position" DS (8 signatures), DNA, RG 46, Papers Pertaining to Certain Nominations. On the same day, Columbus Delano, commissioner of Internal Revenue, wrote to USG. "General William D Woods of Alabama will apply for a Judgeship under the recent bill increasing the bench of the United States Court. Gen'l Woods is now one of the Chancellors of the State of Alabama. He was in the army under your command until you reached Chattanooga. He subsequently accompanied Gen'l Sherman to the close of the war. I have known him many years, having lived within a few miles of him. He is a gentleman of intelligence, great ability and is a sound lawyer and I sincerely hope you may find it consistent with your duty to give him the appointment he seeks. I do not intend to make recommendations outside of my own department, but my long acquaintence with & high appreciation of Gen'l Woods induces me to deviate in this instance & this must be my apology for intruding my opinions in his favor." ALS, *ibid.* Also on the same day, Governor Rutherford B. Hayes of Ohio wrote to USG. "I am informed that Gen Wm B Woods, now one of the Chancellors of the State of Alabama, will be named for appointment as United States Circuit Judge under the new Judiciary Act, for his Circuit. I am personally acquainted with Gen Woods and know the reputation he bore in Ohio before the War as a lawyer and as a public man. He is a learned, able and sound lawyer—a gentleman of integrity and talents of a high order, educated and accomplished, and with a reputation in all respects suited to the high office for which I take pleasure in recommending him—" ALS, *ibid.* On April 10, James F. Wilson, Washington, D. C., wrote to USG. "I am informed that Hon. W. B. Woods, of Alabama, will be urged upon you for appointment to the position of U. S. Circuit Judge, for the fifth circuit, under the act recently passed by Congress. This information is a cause of great satisfaction to me; for I not only know Mr. Woods well, and from my boyhood; but also most thankfully recollect his kind favors to me, when, as the occupant of a workshop, I was struggling to reach the profession of the Law. Kindly he led me along, and most gratefully I remember his good offices. These things are not reasons sufficient to support an appointment of Mr. Woods to a circui[t judge]ship; but they are indices to my knowlege of his fi[tness] for the place. The close relations which they indicate, leading to a careful observance of his subsequent career, entitle me to speak of him as few other men may speak. I have watched him with interest, and honored him with pleasure. At the bar, in the field of politics, and in the military service of the country during the recent rebellion, he has been successful. At the close of the rebellion he settled in Alabama; has been honored with a place on the Bench of that state. His appointment to the circuit court of the fifth c[ir]cuit will not be a mistake, and I pray you to make it, and this prayer is not merely for the advantage of Mr. Woods, but more for the good of the public service." ALS, *ibid.* On April 14, U.S. Senator John Sherman of Ohio wrote to USG. "I have personally known Gen: Wm B: Woods of Alabama for over 20 years—and can bear my testimony to his ability as a lawyer—his services as a soldier—and the excellent qualifications he possesses for high Judicial Office—He was well trained as a lawyer and practiced his profession until the beginning of the War—when he was the Democratic Speaker of the Ohio House of Representatives—He promptly entered the military service raising his own command—and served through the war with high credit—He then took his part in the reconstruction of Alabama where he removed his family purchased property—and became a Chancellor—I should not hesitate to appoint him to the highest Judicial office in the South—" ALS, *ibid.* Related papers are *ibid.* On Dec. 8, USG nominated William B. Woods as judge, 5th Circuit.

On Nov. 30, Howard and U.S. Representative Thomas Ferry of Mich., Detroit, telegraphed to USG. "Dont make any appointments of circuit or District Judge for Michigan until you have heard from her delagation   This is important to us" Telegram received (at 2:10 P.M.), *ibid.*, RG 107, Telegrams Collected (Bound). On the same day, Governor Henry P. Baldwin of Mich., Detroit, telegraphed to USG. "I join in the request of Messrs Howard and Ferry for postponement of appointment of Circuit & District Judges, our congressional delegation are a unit for this" Telegram received (on Dec. 1, 9:15 A.M.), *ibid.* On Nov. 29, Judge Ross Wilkins, Detroit, wrote to USG. "I most cordially recommend the appointment of the Honorable Solomon L. Withey as circuit Judge for the Sixth Judicial Circuit. I have known Judge Withey for many years, and since his appointment as District Judge for the Western District of Michigan I have had opportunity to become intimately acquainted with his qualifications for the discharge of Judicial duties. He has assisted me in holding my terms on two occasions, and in my judgment, both his learning his fairness and impartiality most emminently qualify him for the place named. I speak advisedly when I say that I am fully satisfied that his appointment will give great satisfaction to the people of Michigan. Pardon me for urging the appointment, but trusting to our long continued acquaintance I have ventured to do so knowing that that you could properly appreciate my motives. My age and infirmities will soon compel me to retire from the Bench no longer to mingle in the active business of life, and I should be exceedingly gratified to feel in the appointment of Judge Withey, that our old friendship was remembered by you." LS, *ibid.*, RG 46, Papers Pertaining to Nominations. On Dec. 11, Howard, Washington, D. C., wrote to USG. "I send you enclosed a letter of the Governor of Michigan recommending the appointment of Solomon L. Withey as Circuit Judge of the 6th Circuit. As I have heretofore expressed myself, I fully concur in this recommendation. Judge Withy is a very able & excellent Judge—a true republican, whose opinions are *fully & unhesitatingly* in accordance with the legislation of Congress on the subject of *reconstruction.* You need not doubt this. I know the man. He is an able jurist.—an honest man—an accomplished gentleman and a thorough, unflinching republican & supporter of your administration.—In my opinion, *a better appointment cannot be made*." ALS, *ibid*. On Dec. 3, Baldwin had written to USG. "I would respectfully place before you the names of Hon Solomon L. Withey, the present Judge of the United States District Court—in the Western District of Michigan, as a proper person to be appointed Judge of the Sixth Judicial Circuit of the United States. Judge Withey has long been a resident of Michigan, and as a member of the Bar, of the State Senate, and of the State Constitutional Convention, as well as a citizen, has deservedly occupied a very high position. He has been the Judge of the Western District of the State—from its organization; in addition to holding Court in his own District, he has held terms for his brother Judges in the Eastern District of Michigan, and in the Northern District of Ohio, in all of which he has given the highest satisfaction. Judge Withey is a man of great purity of character and of sterling worth. In my judgment but few men—are in all respects—as well fitted for the place as Judge Withey: I most sincerely hope the appointment will be conferred upon him" ALS, *ibid*. On Dec. 8, USG nominated George H. Yeaman as judge, 6th Circuit; on Dec. 17, USG withdrew Yeaman and nominated Solomon L. Withey. On Jan. 10, 1870, USG nominated Halmer H. Emmons of Mich. in place of Withey, who declined the judgeship. See letter to Mary Grant Cramer, March 31, 1869.

On July 12, 1869, Walter Q. Gresham, New Albany, Ind., wrote to USG. "The name of Hon H. C. Newcomb of Indianapolis will be presented at the proper time for the office of Judge of the Circut Court of the US for the 7 Circut. Mr N has a strong vigorous and well trained intellect—He is a profound lawyer, and has sustained himsf as one of the leading attorneys of the Indianapolis bar, for many years—His character is spotless, and there are, in my opinon, few men so well qualified for the Bench—" ALS, CSmH. On Nov. 6, U.S. Representative John Coburn of Ind., Indianapolis, wrote to USG. "I have the honor to recommend the Hon Horatio C. Newcomb of this city for the office of Judge of the Circuit Court of the United States for the Circuit Composed of the States of Indiana Illinois & Wisconsin. Mr Newcomb is well qualified for the position. His standing as a lawyer is high, and as a citizen his purity and uprightness of character are proverbial. His sound sense, coolness, and honesty of purpose peculiarly fit him for the position. He is in the prime of life and amply able to perform the laborious duties of the office. If the question of locality should have any influence, permit me to say, that as between our State and Illinois the latter has already a Supreme Judge in the person of Judge Davis—But be that as it may I am confident Mr Newcomb's qualifications are quite equal to those of any jurist named for the place—Hoping sincerely that you may find it proper to appoint him . . ." ALS, NNP. On March 24, 1871, USG appointed Horatio C. Newcomb as asst. secretary of the interior. On March 29, Newcomb, Indianapolis, wrote to USG declining the appointment. ALS, DNA, RG 48, Appointment Div., Letters Received. On Sept. 4, 1869, Judge Robert C. Gregory, Ind. Supreme Court, *et al.*, Indianapolis, had petitioned USG. "The undersigned cordially and earnestly recommend the appointment of Hon. Jehu T. Elliott as Circuit Judge for this circuit. We know him intimately—some of us have known him for a quarter of a century, and we are able unhesitatingly to say that he is a lawyer of great learning and a pure and upright Judge who would honor the position, and whose appointment would in our opinion give satisfac to the bar and the people" LS,

InHi. On March 26, David Davis, U.S. Supreme Court, had written to USG. "In view of the probable passage of the bill to reorganize the Federal Judicial System, and the interest felt by the bench and bar of the Country in the Selection of judges, I have thought it would not be considered improper for me to say a word in reference to the appointment of the Circuit Judge for the Seventh Circuit. The States of Illinois, Indiana, and Wisconsin compose that Circuit, and Courts are held in four places, Chicago, Springfield, Indianapolis and Milwaukee. There is no difficulty, with the present judicial force, to dispose of the business in all the districts, but the northern District of Illinois, which embraces Chicago. *There* the business has accumulated, and the District Judge is overworked, and requires more assistance than I can give him, consistently with the proper discharge of my duties at Washington. I assume, therefore, that the new Circuit Judge should be a resident of Chicago. In my opinion, there is no one better qualified to fill this position than Judge Thomas Drummond, the present District Judge at that place—I think he is recognized by the profession throughout the Country, as one of the best judicial officers in it, and I believe him equal to any judicial position. Having been associates with Judge Drummond a great deal in the trial of causes, for the last six years, I can bear testimony to his integrity, industry, courage and capacity. His capacity is illustrated by the fact, that his decisions are rarely reversed, as the records of the Supreme Court will Show. His temper is good, and deportment to the bar unexceptionable, and no one ever filled a judicial position with a higher sense of its importance, or discharged its duties more conscientiously. I think the appointment of Judge Drummond would be desired by the bar of Illinois, and would be acceptable to the bar of the other States. Judge Drummond, from his long judicial life, necessarily, is outside of active politics, and cannot be expeted to secure much political influence. I have, therefore, Mr President, felt it my duty, and esteemed it a privilege to bear testimony to his worth and services—Hoping that it may comport with your views of public duty, to appoint him, (should the bill now before congress become a law) Circuit Judge for the Seventh Circuit." ALS, DNA, RG 46, Papers Pertaining to Nominations. USG noted at the foot of this letter: "Atty Gn." AE, *ibid.* On April 1, Horace White, editor, *Chicago Tribune,* wrote to USG. "I am impelled by a sense of duty to address you on the subject of the appointment of a Judge of the U. S. Circuit Court for this circuit under the new Law. I believe you are personally acquainted with Judge Drummond. His long & toilsome service, his impartiality, integrity, firmness & wisdom are known to you. If there be a just Judge this side the Kingdom of Heaven Thomas Drummond is one. He is entitled by the rules of promotion to the new place if I am not mistaken. At all events he is entitled to it by his eminence as a jurist & I do hope you will embrace this opportunity to secure the services of so noble & trustworthy a man in the elevated position which you are soon to fill by appointment; & at the same time to confer upon him a benefit, for he poor, & I imagine he finds it difficult to make both ends meet, out of the pitiful compensation which he now receives. I may add that what I have written above expresses the universal wish of this community so far as I can ascertain." ALS, *ibid.* On April 6, Elihu B. Washburne endorsed a letter of the same day from R. H. McClellan, Galena, to USG. "Mr. McClellan and other old friends of Judge Drummond here desire this letter brought to the attention of the President. I can endorse all that is said of Judge D. There is no Judge in the country more able just and incorruptible than Drummond. We all expected Lincoln would have appointed him Judge Supreme Court when he appointed Davis." AES, *ibid.* Related papers are *ibid.* On Dec. 8, USG nominated Thomas Drummond as judge, 7th Circuit.

On April 23, Governor Joseph W. McClurg of Mo. wrote to USG. "Permit me to say this is written in *all earnestness.* I assure you it is not from feelings of mere courtesy for a personal friend, but with a sincere desire for the public good, while at the same time a valuable public servant may have his services and his abilities recognized. I recommend the Hon. *Benjamin F Loan*, of this state, for appointment for Judge of the 8th U. S. Judicial Circuit. An intimate personal and political acquaintance for six years enables me to recommend him with the utmost confidence; because he is an experienced lawyer of acknowledged ability; because his character for moral honesty and political integrity is unimpeached and unimpeachable; because Missouri should be recognized and through one who did so much to hold her to her moorings in the Union and to place her in her present proud position. I am so desirous of General Loan's appointment that I am willing to let it answer for all other requests from me during your first administration, while I am satisfied it would be deserved and render general satisfaction." ALS, MoSHi. On Nov. 10, U.S. Senator John M. Thayer of Neb., Omaha, wrote to USG. "I earnestly recommend the appointment of the Hon. *Benj. F. Loan* of Mo. to the Circuit Judgeship of this Circuit. Gen. Loan is an able lawyer,—of very high standing in his profession,—an uncompromising Republican,—of liberal views, and who is imbued with the true spirit of Republicanism and of progress. I believe his appointment will give entire satisfaction. I shall be extremely gratified if he shall receive your favorable consideration in this matter." ALS, PHi. On July 12, Wilson, Fairfield, Iowa, had written to USG. "The name of Hon. John F. Dillon of this State will be presented to you with a view to his appointment to the position of Judge of this Circuit under the recent act of Congress reorganzing the judicial system. The purpose of this letter is to urge upon you *most earnestly* the appointment of Mr. Dillon. You may look this Circuit over and find no more competent man for the position. Mr. Dillon is a member of the Supreme Court of this State, and is one of the most acceptable Judges we have ever had on our bench. In every respect is he qualified for the position to which his appointment is asked. Every element in his character involved in the position we ask for him is above reproach." ALS, DNA, RG 46, Papers Pertaining to Nominations. On Sept. 20, U.S. Senator Matthew H. Carpenter of Wis., Milwaukee, wrote to USG. "It affords me great pleasure to say that I am well acquainted with Chief Justice Dillon of Iowa, and that his standing professionally and judicially is second to no mans in the North West. He is an agreeable gentleman, a ripe scholar, a good lawyer and an upright judge. I believe his appointment, as judge of the Circuit Court of the United States for the Circuit of which Iowa forms a part, would be acceptable to the people of the whole circuit, specially gratifying to the people of Iowa, *and exceedingly honorable to the government.*" ALS, *ibid.* On Oct. 4, Grenville M. Dodge, Council Bluffs, Iowa, wrote to USG. "Judge J. F. Dillon of the Supreme Court of Iowa is an applicant for the position of U. S. Circuit Judge for the District composed of Iowa Mo—Ark—Minnesota Neb—&c His very superior fitness and qualifications for the position, his life long devotion to the profession and the Law are fully attested by the very strong endorsements he he has from the *Bench & Bar.* I have known Judge Dillon *personally for fifteen years* and I can speak most unhesitatingly of the high estimation he is held in our State. . . ." ALS, *ibid*. On Nov. 17, Charles W. Ford, collector of customs, St. Louis, wrote to USG. "An effort is being made in Iowa & Missouri, by the Bar, and all good people generally, to secure the appointment of Jno F Dillon of Davenport—as the Judge for this District I have not the pleasure to know Mr Dillon, personally, but many of my personal friends here, in whom both you & I have confidence, do know him—and all represent him as a man of most excellent character, an accomplished lawyer, devoted to his profession & well qualified for the position I believe his appointment would give satisfaction to the country & meet the approbation of all good men who desire to see the laws impartially administered" ALS, *ibid*. On Nov. 27, U.S. Senator Thomas W. Tipton of Neb. wrote to USG. "So many Lawyers and Judges of Nebraska are anxious for the appointment of Judge Dillon of Iowa as circuit Judge for the Dist including the states of Neb, Iowa &c, that I feel free to say that if nominated by the President I will vote for the confirmation with great pleasure—" ALS, *ibid*. On the same day, Alton R. Easton, St. Louis, wrote to USG. "From the representations of many of the most prominant persons of the legal profession and others here, in regard to the selection of U. S Judge, under the new Law, for the District embracing Missouri and other States; I have no hesitation in saying, that, the Hon John F. Dillon Chief Justice of the Supreme Court of Iowa, is the proper person for the position, and that his appointment will give general satisfaction—Many of your freinds here, who have expressed an opinion on this subject, will be much gratified at this selection." ALS, *ibid*. On Dec. 6, U.S. Senator Edmund G. Ross of Kan. wrote to USG. "I have the honor to state that I am in receipt of a large number of letters from prominent & influential members of the Bench & the Bar of the State of Kansas, asking the appointment of Hon J T Dillon to the judgeship of that District I have also the honor to endorse their request" ALS, *ibid*. On Dec. 9, Dodge telegraphed to USG. "We feel great interest in the appointment of Judge for this District Let me assure you that the appointment of Judge Dillon will be considered throughout the District as the best that can be made" Telegram received (at 1:10 P.M.), *ibid*.; (press) *ibid*., RG 107, Telegrams Collected (Bound). On Dec. 2, John B. Sanborn, Washington, D. C., had written to USG. "I have [the] honor respectfully to submit the follow[ing] recommendations for my appointme[nt] to the office of Circuit Judge . . . These letters are from Judges before wh[om] I practiced before the war. aAs I have no[t] been in practice in Minnesota since, I have not asked for recommendatio[ns] from the present judges. My political principles have always been republican and I have not sought [po]litical endorsements. If any Judicial appointment can be conferred upon me it will be gratefully accepted w[ith] the determined purpose to discharg[e] theits duties of the office faithfully." ALS, NNP. U.S. Senator Alexander Ramsey of Minn. endorsed this letter. "In transmitting the inclosed papers of Gnl. J. B. Sanborn I bear testimony, to his legal capacity, republican principles, and great fitness for the place position he seeks and should not the appointment be conferred upon the Hon. Gordon E. Cole whom I have heretofor, with others prsented for this Judgship I would cherfully recommd Gnl. Sanborn therefor." AES, *ibid*. On Dec. 9, USG nominated John F. Dillon as judge, 8th Circuit.

On April 21, Joseph B. Crockett, Silas W. Sanderson, Royal T. Sprague, and Augustus L. Rhodes, San Francisco, wrote to USG. "The undersigned, Justices of the Supreme Court of the State of California, beg leave respectfully, to present for your consideration, the name of our associate, the Hon Lorenzo Sawyer, chief Justice of the Supreme Court of this State, for the office of Circuit Judge of the United States, for this coast, under the Act for reorganizing the Judicial department of the government—. . ." DS, DNA, RG 46, Papers Pertaining to Nominations. On Dec. 3, Hayes wrote to USG. "A friend, in whose statements I rely, assures me that Hon Lorenzo Sawyer of California is an able lawyer, a man of spotless integrity and a judge of high reputation. He is a Native of the same County with myself and in the belief that he is qualified I would be gratified to hear of his appointment as U S Circuit Judge." ALS, *ibid*. On Dec. 6, U.S. Representative Thomas Fitch of Nev. wrote to USG. "If Hon C J Hillyer cannot receive the appointment of U S Circuit Judge for the Pacific coast, then I respectfully request the appointment of Judge Sawyer of California and beg leave to say that his selection for the place would be more satisfactory to the people of Nevada than that of any other gentleman named in connection with the position" ALS, *ibid*. Related papers are *ibid*. On Dec. 8, USG nominated Lorenzo Sawyer as judge, 9th Circuit.

To John P. Newman

EXECUTIVE MANSION, DEC. 24, 1869.

Dear Doctor: Please find enclosed my check for $100, for distribution among the poor, and don't forget "The Ragged Schools" on the Island.

Yours truly,

U. S. GRANT.

Frank A. Burr, *Life and Deeds of General U. S. Grant*, . . . (Philadelphia, 1885), p. 44. About the same time, USG wrote an undated note to John P. Newman, Metropolitan Methodist Episcopal Church, Washington, D. C. "Please give $10 to the blind man and $10 to the soldier's widow." *Ibid*. On Dec. 25, 1869, Newman wrote to A. K. Browne, Washington Association for the Improvement of the Condition of the Poor. "President Grant has placed in my hand, as his pastor, one hundred dollars for the use of the poor, and I herein inclose the same to you for distribution through your Association, which I consider worthy of all confidence." *Washington Chronicle*, Dec. 27, 1869.

An unaddressed circular was copied as a letter of Nov. 25 from Julia Dent Grant. "It is the wish of the Ladies in Washington, to celebrate the liquidation of our church debt in a suitable manner. We have therefore determined to hold our Jubilee in the Metropolitan church on Christmas Eve. It is our purpose to have President Grant with us on that occasion; and as he is one of the trustees of the church we propose to present to him the Fifty thousand dollars. for the Metropolitan. in behalf of you & the other ladies who have aided in this good work. You will therefore, without fail, please report the amount you have collected by December 23rd 1869 and remit the same by draft on New York to our pastor, The Rev Dr J P. Newman. which will be duly acknowledged in our church papers. And we shall be pleased to have you with us on that interesting occasion." Yates Papers, IHi; DLC-John P. Newman. See *PUSG*, 16, 347–48.

Memorandum

[*1869–1870*]

Reasons why San Domingo should be annexed to the United States.

It is an island of unequaled fertility. It contains an area (that part of it known as ~~S~~the republic of San Domingo) of 20.000 square miles, or 12,800.000 acres. One half of this is now covered with the most valuable timbers known to commerce; at an elevation above the diseases incident to a tropical climate, and is capable of producing, when cleared of the native forrest, 1500 lbs. of coffee pr. acre. The valleys and low lands are of great productiveness, the sugar cane requiring re-setting only once in twenty years, and producing, [to the acre] with much less labor, nearly double [that] of the best sugar lands of La. to the acre. Tobacco, tropical fruits, dyes, and all the imports of the equatorial region, can be produced on these lands.—San Domingo is the gate to the Carib[b]ean Sea, and in the line of transit to the Isthmus of Darien, destined at no distant day to be the line of transit of half the commerce of the world. It has but a sparce population and that in entire sympathy with our institutions, anxious to join their fortunes to ours; industrious, if made to feel that the products of their industry is to be protected; & tollrent as to the religious, or political views of their neighbors. Caste has no foothold in San Domingo. It is capable of supporting the entire colored population of the United States, should it choose to emigrate. The present difficulty, ~~though sensless, to~~ in bringing all parts of the United States to a happy unity and love of country grows out of the prejudice to color. The prejudice is a sensless one, but it exists. The colored man cannot be spared until his place is supplied, but with a refuge like San Domingo his worth here would soon be discovered, and he would soon receive such recognition as to induce him to stay: or if Providence designed that the two races should not live to-gether he would find a home in the Antillas.

A glance at the map will show that England has now a cordon of islands extending from southern Florida to [the] East of the Island of Cuba, with Jamaca, and Grand Cayman south of that island, and a ~~succession of~~ foothold upon the main land in ~~e~~Central America, thus commanding [on both sides of Cuba] the entrance to the Gulf of Mexico, both sides of Cuba, a gulf which borders upon so large a part of the territory of the United States. Again she has a succession of islands runing from [the] East of St. Thomas to South America, with another foothold upon the main land, British Guiana, thus nearly surrounding the Caribean Sea. The coasting trade of the United States, between the Atlantic seaboard and all ports ~~w~~West, and ~~s~~South west of the Cape of Florida, has now to pass through forign waters. In case of war between ~~Great Bri~~ England and the United States, New York and New Orleans would be as much severed as would be New York and Calais, France.

Our imports of tropical products, ~~exceed~~ and products of slave labor, exceed our exports to the countr~~y~~ies producing them more than the balance of trade against the United States.

San Domingo can produce the sugar, coffee, tobacco, chocolate and tropical fruits for a population of 50.000.000 ~~mill~~ of people. Coffee and sugar there can be produced, with free labor, at but little more cost pr. lb. than wheat is now produced in our great North West. With the acquisition of San Domingo the two great necessities in every family, sugar and Coffee, would be cheapened near one half.

San Domingo is weak and must go some where for protection. Is the United States willing that she should go elsewhere than to ~~the~~ herself [seek protection from a foreign power]? Such a confession would be to abandon our oft repeated "Monroe doctrine."

San Domingo in the hands of the United States would make slave labor unprofitable and would soon extinguish that hated system of enforced labor. To-day the United States is the largest supporter of that that institution. More than 70 pr ct. of the exports of Cuba, and a large percentage of the exports of Brazil, are to the United States. Upon every pound we receive from them an export duty is charged to support slavery and Monarchy. A prohibitory duty, almost, is placed upon what we have to sell. Get San Domingo and this will all be changed.

San Domingo from its exposeure to the trade winds, and its elevation is, in large part, free from the diseases of the tropics. It is nearer New York City, and all the North Atlantic Sea ports, than any American Sea port in the Gulf of Mexico. It can be reached without passing through the waters of a foreign country. In case of a Maratime War it would give us a foothold in the West Indias of inestimable value. Its acquisition is carrying out Manifest destiny. It is a step towards claring Europe all European flags from this Continent. Can any one favor rejecting so valuable a gift who voted $7.200.000 for the icebergs of Alasca?

ADf (bracketed material not in USG's hand), DLC-USG, III.

To Charles W. Ford

Washington. D. C. Jan. 3d *18*670.

DEAR FORD:

I am in receipt of your last letter enclosing plat of house and grounds for sale by Leffingwell.[1] The property is more than I could expect to pay for; hence is out of my reach. Out of all of the other lots you sent to me there were two that I thought possibly I might consider, one of them on 3d Street, below Chesnut, price $18,000 00. The other above Chesnut, offered by Priest[2] I believe, price $30.000 00   These amounts I could manage easily paying about one half down and the balance in one and two years. I do not know however but it may prove quite as well to wait a while before purchasing. The tendency seems to me to be down as we approach specie payments.—Was is not that several people are

now waiting to talk to me I would get out the plats so as to dis-
cribe to you the two pieces I allude to on 3d street so that you
might, at your leasure, look at them.

Yours Truly
U. S. GRANT

ALS, IHi. See letter to Charles W. Ford, Nov. 12, 1869.

1. On Aug. 18, 1875, Hiram W. Leffingwell, St. Louis real estate agent,
wrote to USG. "I respectfully make application for the position of U. S. Marshal
of this district in case change is meditated. I have resided in this state since
1838, am thoroughly acquainted with the requirements and duties of the office,
having had five years experience as first deputy, am and have been a 'square toed'
Republican of the old school, belong to no *clique*, and have no friends to shield
or enemies to punish. If it should be your pleasure to bestow the responsibilities
upon me, I will conscientiously discharge the duties solely to the public good.
I have the honor to refer to a few gentlemen of known party fealty and high
standing as citizens: Many could be obtained if necessary." ALS, DNA, RG 60,
Records Relating to Appointments. On Sept. 21, Gen. William T. Sherman,
St. Louis, wrote to USG. "I have just been asked to sign a petition in behalf of
Mr Leffingwell of this city for the appointmt of U. S. Marshal for this District.
I have cast my Eye on the long list of signatures and recognise the names of all
or nearly all Our Mutual Friends, but still Petition. But I have known Mr Leffingwell so long and so favorably, that I cannot withhold some Expression of
confidence. I was interested in a large business here more than twenty years
ago, which was managed by Mr Leffingwell, so skilfully and so Entirely to the
satisfaction of all the parties concerned, that I have no hesitation in presenting
his name to you, as worthy of your personal & official consideration." ALS, *ibid.*
The petition and numerous other letters addressed to USG concerning Leffingwell are *ibid.* On Dec. 15, USG nominated Leffingwell as marshal, Eastern District, Mo.

2. John G. Priest, St. Louis real estate agent.

To Ellen H. Stanton

———

Washington, D. C. Jan.y 3 18670

MRS. E. M. STANTON;
DEAR MADAM;

I have caused to be issued, and send herewith, a Commission
as Justice of the Supreme Court for your much lamented husband.[1]

In forwarding this to you I am at a loss to find words expressive of my sympathy for you in your great affliction, and of the estimation I placed upon the ability, integrity, patriotism and services of him whom a nation joins you in mourning the loss of.[2]

With great respect
your obt. svt.
U. S. GRANT

ALS, DLC-Edwin M. Stanton. Ellen M. Hutchison of Pittsburgh had married Edwin M. Stanton, a widower, on June 25, 1856. See letter to Robert C. Grier, Dec. 15, 1869.

On June 23, 1869, Edwards Pierrepont, U.S. attorney, New York City, had written to Stanton. "I wished to have written on Monday but was so crowded with engagements that I *could not*. I saw the President on Friday & took a long drive with him alone & on Sunday I was invited to dine with him at 3 oclok at Mr Stewarts quite privately & I saw much of him there—The particular thing which I wish to write is this, he spoke several times of you with *marked* favor— and after dinner Mrs Grant talked with me for a long time privately, & *kept speaking* of you in the highest terms of praise the *very highest*—saying how much was due to you & that the General had made a mistake in not giving you a place of the highest grade &c. & that it ought to be done now &c.—This was repeated over & over by her in a way so marked & so unusual that I, of course, know it had some especial purpose being as it was, directed to me, when our relations were by her so well known—Our conversation lasted at least three quarters of an hour & was entirely out of hearing of the others, quite excited their curiosity from its length & earnestness and has some specific meaning. It was *very* marked, & *very emphatic*—My best regards to Mrs Stanton & to all the family" ALS, DLC-Edwin M. Stanton.

On Oct. 26 and Nov. 3, Stanton, Washington, D. C., wrote to Bishop Matthew Simpson. "Private & Confidential . . . You have been aware of my infirm health during the past year, and will be glad to know that by relaxation from labor, & travel it has very much improved so as to encourage hopes that it may be fully restored to enable me to enjoy some years longer of usefulness. But this may depend upon how I am employed. When I left my private pursuits for the public interest I had the best professional practice in the United States, was rapidly accumulating wealth, & living at ease. My expenses above my salary exhausted my surplus resources and with years advanced, and diminished strength I must toil for my living. There is a vacancy on the Supreme Bench for which I have adequate physical power, & so far as I can judge of my intellect, its powers are as acute & vigorous as at any period of my life—and perhaps more so. General Grant in justice to the Country, to himself & to me, ought to give *me* that appointment: So far as relates to himself not all his friends in the United States, upheld & advanced him as firmly & successfully during the war as I did in my official acts. There is no man who would uphold the principles of the war on which his usefulness & fame must *rest*, with more or equal vigor from the Bench. The Bench has now a great part to play in history during his administration, and upon no experienced resolute jurist, can he rely with greater confidence. My appointment would gratify the great mass of republicans, & rally them around Grant—it would be considered as disinterested, unpurchased, and a sure proof of the Presidents loyal determinations. My residence here in the District is also a reccommendation being free from Geographical discriminations. I have said *nothing to General Grant* on the subject and *shall not*—but I would be glad to have *you* talk with him fully & freely and report to me his views on this question. To me it may in considerable degree be a question of life—it certainly is of health, for I must go to the Bench or Bar. His name & fortune he owed at a critical moment to me. He can preserve me to my family under Providence. I have communicated to you more fully than ever before to mortal man, & in confidence you will do what seems right of which you are a better judge than I am. Hoping to see or hear from you soon . . ." "I am under much obligation for your note received this morning. When I heard that your daughter & her husband were to start so soon for Europe it caused me much regret to have troubled you with any affair of my own, but I hope it gave you no inconvenience. The result of your conference is very plain to me, and gives me no surprise, being what I had expected, and I am quite sure that you will conform to my wish that the matter be strictly confidential and confined to your own bosom. In regard to Childs—who for several years has been an active bitter enemy of mine because of my annulling a bargain between him & Genl Cameron which I disapproved—he doubtless *knows* the Presidents purpose, and my health is made an evasive excuse by Childs for a predetermined purpose; influenced by quite [d]ifferent consideration from that assigned. I shall take no step in the matter, and no allusion to it has ever been made except in my letter to you. So far as my health is concerned it is in the hands of Providence, and as respects Genl Grant he will be influenced by his judgment as to his own interest. . . ." ALS, InFtwL.

On Dec. 16, Vice President Schuyler Colfax *et al.* wrote to USG. "We have the honor to recommend the Hon. Edwin M. Stanton of Pensylvania, for appointment as associate justice of the Supreme Court of the United States, in place of Mr Justice Grier who it is understood has resigned or is about to resign his seat on that Bench. The eminent qualification of Mr Stanton for this position, and the great obligation which in our opinion this country is under to him, speak more loudly in his favor than we can; so we content ourselves with mere recommendation, and we most ardently hope that he may be so appointed." DS (39 signatures), Louisiana State University, Baton Rouge, La. On Dec. 18, Speaker of the House James G. Blaine *et al.* wrote to USG recommending Stanton. DS (118 signatures), DLC-Edwin M. Stanton. On Dec. 19, USG visited Stanton and presented a card to Ellen H. Stanton. "Mrs. Judge Stanton, with compliments of Gen. U. S. Grant." Benjamin P. Thomas and Harold M. Hyman, *Stanton: The Life and Times of Lincoln's Secretary of War* (New York, 1962), pp. 635–36. On Dec. 20, USG nominated Stanton to replace Grier.

Also on Dec. 20, William Dennison, New York City, telegraphed to USG. "A thousand thanks for Your appointment of Ex Secretary Stanton to the Supreme Bench. The whole country will heartily approve the appointment" Telegram received (at 10:20 A.M.), DNA, RG 107, Telegrams Collected (Bound). On the same day, Edwin D. Morgan, New York City, telegraphed to USG. "Every real friend of the administration is grateful by the appointment of Edwin M Stanton to the bench of the Supreme Court, I congratulate you upon the appointment" Telegram received (at 1:25 P.M.), *ibid.* On Dec. 21, Stanton wrote to USG. "I beg you to accept my thanks for your nomination of me as one of the Justices of the Supreme Court of the United States. It is the only public office I ever desired, and I accept it with great pleasure. The appointment affords me the more pleasure as coming from you with whom for several years I have had personal official relations such as seldom exist among men. It will be my aim so long as health and life permit to perform the solemn duties of the office to which you have appointed me with diligence impartiality and integrity." Copy, Louisiana State University, Baton Rouge, La.

1. On Dec. 24, USG wrote to all dept. heads. "The painful duty devolves upon the President of announcing to the people of the United States the death of one of its most distinguished citizens and faithful public servants, the Hon. Edwin M. Stanton, which occurred in this city at an early hour this morning. He was distinguished in the councils of the nation during the entire period of its recent struggle for national existence; first, as Attorney General; then, as Secretary of War. He was unceasing in his labors, earnest and fearless in the assumpsion of responsibilities necessary to his country's success, respected by all good men and feared by wrong doers. In his death the Bar, the Bench, and the nation sustain a great loss which will be mourned by all. As a mark of respect to his memory, it is ordered that the Executive Mansion, and the several departments at Washington be draped in mourning, and that all business be suspended on the day of the funeral." LS, DNA, RG 45, Letters Received from the President; *ibid.*, RG 56, Letters from Executive Officers; *ibid.*, RG 59, Miscellaneous Letters; *ibid.*, RG 60, Letters from the President; *ibid.*, RG 107, Letters Received from Bureaus.

2. On June 6, 1870, U.S. Representative Samuel Hooper of Mass. wrote to Secretary of State Hamilton Fish. "I have received through the Honble Z. Chandler your check for One Thousand Dollars, endorsed to my order, as Treasurer, for payment of General Grant's Subscription to the 'Stanton Fund,' and I shall observe the request contained in your note inclosing the check to Mr Chandler." ALS, DLC-Hamilton Fish.

To George S. Boutwell

Washington. D. C. Jan. 14th *1870*

HON. G. S. BOUTWELL,
SEC. OF THE TREAS.
DEAR SIR:

This will introduce to you Mr J. P. Tweed, an old merchant of Cincinnati with whom I have been acquainted, and our families intimate, from my childhood. Mr. Tweed has business before the Dept which he will explain the merits of which however I know nothing. I can say for Mr. though that he has always sustained a high character.

Respectfully &c.
U. S. GRANT

ALS, Williams College, Williamstown, Mass.

Speech

———

[Jan. 15, 1870]

Mr. Minister, I am pleased to receive you as the representative of the sovereign of a country so interesting to the United States as the kingdom of Hawaii. His desire to strengthen the friendly understanding between the two countries is cordially reciprocated by me.

I am well aware of those intimate business and personal relations to which you refer, and have every disposition to strengthen them by such further treaty stipulations as may be supposed to be advantageous or necessary. It is hoped that your official residence here may contribute to this result.

Washington Chronicle, Jan. 17, 1870. USG spoke on Jan. 15, 1870, in response to remarks made by Elisha H. Allen, Hawaiian minister. "I have the honor to present to you, my letters of credence from His Majesty, The King of the Hawaiian Islands. He especially instructed me to express to the President His earnest desire that the friendly relations which have always existed between the Government of the United States and His own, should be perpetuated and strengthened. You are aware, Mr President, that the people of the United States, residing in the Hawaiian Kingdom are more numerous than all other foreigners there, and that they have important interests in ~~trade~~, ~~in~~ agriculture, navigation and commerce. They have largely contributed to build up a commerce with the United States, which may be increased to the benefit of both countries.—The productions of the one are in the main unlike those of the other, and hence all reasonable facilities for an interchange will be mutually advantageous. In view of the geographical position of the Islands, which afford a central, and safe resort for shipping, and of the commercial relations with the United States, some further treaty stipulations are regarded as desirable, and highly important. The King desires to adopt the most liberal policy, and He feels assured, from the past intercourse with the Government of the United

States, that the same spirit will mark its course in the future—" AD, DLC-Elisha H. Allen.

On Dec. 6, 1869, USG had written to the Senate. "I submit to the Senate for its consideration with a view to ratification a Convention between the United States and His Hawaiian Majesty, signed in this city on the eighth day of May last, providing for the extension of the term for the exchange of the ratifications of the Convention for commercial reciprocity between the same parties, signed on the twenty-first day of May, 1867." DS, DNA, RG 46, Presidential Messages, Foreign Relations, Hawaii. Related papers are *ibid.*; *ibid.*, RG 59, Notes from the Hawaiian Legation. On June 2, 1870, the U.S. Senate rejected the treaty negotiated in 1867 between the U.S. and the Kingdom of Hawaii enumerating goods admitted free of duty from each country. Fear of diminished U.S. revenue, claims of undue benefit to Calif. sugar refiners, and concern that commercial reciprocity would make U.S. annexation of Hawaii more difficult contributed to the vote. See Merze Tate, *Hawaii: Reciprocity or Annexation* (East Lansing, 1968), pp. 52–83.

On Sept. 27, Zephaniah S. Spalding, Washington, D. C., wrote to USG. "I have the honor to submit to the President of the United States that for the past three years I have resided upon the Hawaiian Islands, acting in the capacities of special agent, Chargé d'Affaires, and U. S. Consul for the port of Honolulu, and that I have lately returned from that country—That during such period I have made myself acquainted with the people, government, and resources of the Hawaiian Kingdom, and have had the means of enjoying in a more than ordinary degree the confidence of the King and his Ministry. I am from my own knowledge, and from personal interviews with those in power, warranted in saying that the Hawaiian Government entertains the highest respect for the Government of the United States, and desires closer relations with this country by means of a reciprocal commercial treaty; and that His Majesty and his Ministers 'are willing to meet all the views of the United States regarding such a treaty, which they regard of great mutual importance to both countries—' I have the honor to be fully possessed of the views of His Majesty's Minister of Foreign Relations on the subject, and am able to say that 'His Majesty's Government are and will be ready to make any reasonable concessions which will draw more closely the interests of both countries—' I therefore have the honor to submit the following basis for a reciprocal treaty between the Hawaiian Islands and the United States, the main features of which I am assured will be sanctioned and agreed to by the Hawaiian Government. 1st The United States to admit free of duty Sugar, not above Number 16, Dutch Standard in color, and such other articles as may be agreed upon, all to be products of the Hawaiian Islands—2nd The Hawaiian Islands to admit free of duty such articles as may be agreed upon, and to be the general products of the United States, with the exception perhaps of Spirits—3rd The Hawaiian Government to grant or lease to the Government of the United States, or their representative, for the term of ninety nine years, at a nominal rental, sufficient land and water privileges upon the Island of Oahu near the port of Honolulu to enable the said U. S. Government to establish a Naval Depot, with all the necessary buildings, docks, wharves, storehouses &c &c, which shall at all times be free to and under the control of the said United States Government, or their representative, and which the Hawaiian Government will protect and defend to the extent of their ability— I am justified in further saying that the Hawaiian Government will agree that like privileges shall be granted to no other country, and also that the United States may protect and defend their own property whenever the Hawaiian Government shall fail to do so—In order to carry out the idea hastily sketched in the foregoing, I have the honor to tender to the President of the United States my personal services, in such manner and capacity as may be deemed best and proper, and for the interest of the United States—" ALS, DNA, RG 59, Despatches from U.S. Consuls in Honolulu. Related papers are *ibid.*

On March 8, 1869, Jacob Ammen, Lockland, Ohio, had written to USG. "Permit me to call your attention to Brig. Gen. H. P. Van Cleve, a graduate of the U. S. Mil. Academy of the class 1831, and whose record during the rebellion is familiar to you—He is desirous of representing the Government in a diplomatic capacity at Honolulu—His merits as a gentleman, and his qualifications for the position are so well known to you, as to insure your favorable consideration of his application." ALS, *ibid.*, Letters of Application and Recommendation. On April 16, Governor William R. Marshall of Minn. telegraphed to USG. "I hope you will appoint Genl Van Cleve commissioner to Sandwich Islands now that McCook is provided for, I ask it in behalf of the soldiers of Minnesota" Telegram received (at 11:30 A.M.), *ibid.*; (press) *ibid.*, RG 107, Telegrams Collected (Bound). See *PUSG*, 18, 577. On March 2, 1871, USG nominated Horatio P. Van Cleve as postmaster, St. Anthony's Falls.

In [*March, 1869*], U.S. Senator Thomas W. Osborn of Fla. *et al.* petitioned [USG]. "The undersigned Senators and Representatives in Congress beg leave most respectfully but earnestly to recommend Hon A. S Welch for the appointment of Minister Resident of the Hawaiian Islands—We are fully satisfied of the high character and competency of Mr Welch for the place and we urge his appointment not only on that account but because of the very efficient and signal service that he has rendered the country in the work of Reconstructionng his adopted State. His term in the United States Senate ends on the 4th of March 1869, and we earnestly hope that he may receive the place he now asks for from the hands of the President." DS (30 signatures), DNA, RG 59, Letters of Application and Recommendation.

On May 4, U.S. Senators Alexander McDonald and Benjamin F. Rice of Ark. wrote to USG. "Failing to see you and being extremely anxious about the appointment of James M. Johnson for Minister to the Sandwich Islands we thought it proper to make known his Claims he is an old Citizen of our state always a loyal man twice Elected to Congress a Colonel in our army during the War and now Leut Governor of our state and Eminently fitted for this position—And only our extreme desire to have Some representation induces us to yield him for any position outside of our state. he is a man so well known and one so satisfactory as to make no questions about his Confirmation and satisfies all opposition in our own delegation" LS, *ibid.* On May 7, McDonald wrote to USG. "My Colleague and Myself have Called several days in the last three days but owing to the pressure have been unable to see you—We are Exceeding Anxious in referance to an appointment of Minister to the Sandwich Islands J. M. Johnson . . ." ALS, *ibid.* On June 3, Governor Powell Clayton of Ark. *et al.* telegraphed to USG. "We earnestly ask as an especial favor the appointment of James M Johnson as minister to the Hawaiian Islands, He is competent and deserving, his appointment would give great satisfaction, he has always been loyal, raised and commanded a regiment of arkansas troops during the war, elected to congress under the Murphy Government, is now Lt Governor of this state" Telegram received (on June 4, 9:00 A.M.), *ibid.*; (press) *ibid.*, RG 107, Telegrams Collected (Bound).

On May 11, Joseph R. Hawley, Hartford, wrote to USG. "I beg leave to recommend to you for appointment as Minister Resident at The Hawaiian Islands, *Elias Perkins*, a native and for many years a resident of New London in this State. Mr. Perkins was for many years a merchant in the whaling business at that port. He was for five years in mercantile business at Honolulu, and after a residence of three years at home, he was appointed by President Lincoln Consul at Lahaina, which appointment he held six years, and until removed a month or two ago. About a year ago, Mr. McCook, the minister, brought Mr. Perkins from Lahaina to Honolulu to take charge of the consulate at the latter place, which was involved in some difficulties. Mr. McCook, desiring to return to the States, obtained leave from the Department to place matters in the hands of Mr. Perkins as Chargé d'Affairs, and the duties of that position Mr. Perkins discharged for several months. He is altogether 'honest, faithful and capable'. With all the business at the Sandwich Islands that pertains to shipping and especially the whaling interest Mr. Perkins is thoroughly familiar. He has a very extensive acquaintance ~~with~~ throughout the Kingdom. He has the full confidence of the King and his cabinet. I am very sure that if the representative of the Hawaiian Kingdom were asked in confidence he would feel authorized to say that no appointment would be more gratifying to the King. Mr. Perkins is a staunch American and a thorough Republican. *Eleven* of the brothers and cousins of the family were *officers* in our army during the late war. . . ." ALS, *ibid.*, RG 59, Letters of Application and Recommendation. Related papers are *ibid.*

On May 14, Walter L. Graham, Butler, Pa., wrote to USG. "I am not one of those persons who incessantly bore for position But I feel as though you should know some facts—I was a member of the Chicaugo Convention of 1860 and was the first man from Pennsylvania to support Abraham Lincoln for President and did so with Earnestness and success yet by some means I was entirely overlooked during his administration although a large proportion of that Convention received Foreign appointments under his administration I recd nothing—I have with as much zeal advocated your Elevation to the same position although not a member of the Convention that nominated your—And if you Can make my services profitable to you and the Government I will offer them as Minister to the Hiwaian Islands—I am personally acquainted with Mr Harris the Minister of finance under the King of those islands and could I am sure be of service to this Government I would refer you to A. G. Curtin or Simon Cameron of this State" ALS, *ibid.*

On March 23, McDonald and Rice wrote to Secretary of the Treasury George S. Boutwell. "our delegation having entire Confidence in the ability and integrity of Hon H. A. Millen of our state, from a long personal acquaintance unhesitatingly recommend him for the position of Auditor or Comptroller in your Department beleiving him well qualified a true man and one who has served his party & his Country faithfully a Gentleman of fine address and much Experience—his appointment would place our delegation under obligations of more than an ordinary character" LS, *ibid.* Related papers are *ibid.* On April 20, Lucien J. Barnes, Washington, D. C., wrote to Horace Porter. "I ask one favor for the good of the country. Henry A. Millen of Arkansas was nominated last Saturday as Minister Resident at the Sandwich Islands. He is incompetent.

He was not an applicant for that or any other foreign appointment. I ask that The President withdraw his name, and consider the names & recommendations of Arkansas men now on file at the State Department for foreign appointments. So far as I know them they are those of St John—Hutchinson and myself besides Mr. Simms who has been appointed Consul to Prescott. If I did not do as much for General Grants election to the Presidency as all three of them together I will withdraw from the contest. Please present this to His Excellency today . . . P. S. I have just been informed that the Committee on Foreign Relations reported against Mr. Millen yesterday." ALS, *ibid*. On April 17, USG nominated Henry A. Millen as minister to Hawaii but withdrew the nomination on April 21.

On March 19, 1873, George E. Ellis, Boston, wrote to Secretary of State Hamilton Fish. "You may remember that about four years ago, I wrote to you in behalf of Mr. Henry A. Pierce of this City, as an applicant for the Commissionership of the United States at the Sandwich Islands. Mrs. Pierce has just called on me soliciting me again to do what is in my power in her husband's service. She says that efforts are making by another applicant for his Office to dislodge him. She also brings me a letter to her from Mr. Charles Brewer, one of the most honored Merchants of this City, long a resident at, & still connected with the Islands—a gentleman whom I have personally known & esteemed for more than thirty years. From his note to Mrs. Pierce, I make the following Extract. 'Dr. McGrew of Honolulu I hear is in Washington, & seeking to route Mr. P. from his Office for himself. He is *totally* unfit for the Office, being a *violent* & *very passionate* man, & has been an enemy of Mr. Pierce's the past three years.' . . ." ALS, *ibid*. On Dec. 6, 1869, USG had nominated Henry A. Peirce as minister to Hawaii. For John S. McGrew, see letter to Hamilton Fish, Sept. 3, 1869.

On March 31, Wesley Newcomb, Ithaca, N. Y., had written to USG. "I have been requested to give my views, and observations upon the present and prospective condition of the Sandwich Islands; and the circumstances that will in a great degree determine the future of the Kingdom.—1st The native race is rapidly decreasing in numbers, and with the recent introduction of *Leprosy* added to other well known causes will farther increase the percentage of mortality. 2d The present King, Kamehameha Vth will scarcely continue to rule over his people for any great length of time; and at the time of his death will come the struggle among powerful nations to obtain control of the Islands. 3d This will probably be as at Tahiti under the name of a *Protectorate* if *Europæan* influence is in the ascendant; but if American management secures the friendship of the Chiefs & the people then the Islands will become a territory of the United States. 4th To accomplish this last named object will require the appointment of persons of standing, influence & above all of *temperate habits*; and an acquaintance with *native character*, to the position of representatives of our Country. We have already suffered much in the estimation of the Govt of Hawaii by inexperdenced and dissolute consuls and other officials. 5th In the whole circle of my extended acquaintance I know of no man so well adapted to meet all the requirements named, as *Chas Bunker Esqr*, for some years a resident of the Islands, having at the same time an extensive circle of California friends; one posted on the affairs of the Hawaiian Govt and a personal friend of Kamehameha 5th and at the same time having the confidence of Kaio, Kanaina & other high Chieftains.—As Consul to Honolulu he would carry the weight of character, with great legal attainments and suavity of manner into all his associations, and give dignity to the position and honor to the Goverment. Whoever may be appointed to the place, let him be a first class man and not a hackneyed Politician broken down at home & despised abroad. Having resided five years upon the Island of Oahu where I hold some property to be affected favorably or adversely by the appointment of officials, and having for 20 years been in constant correspondence with Honolulu I may be excused for expressing my views of the condition of the Hawaiian Govt without the charge of obtrusiveness.—I may add, that I need not endorse the Patriotism of Mr. Bunker—He was neither a *Rebel* nor what is worse a sneaking *Copperhead* during the War, but a true, active & consistant Union man." ALS, *ibid.* On April 9, Ralph Waldo Emerson, Concord, Mass., wrote to Attorney Gen. Ebenezer R. Hoar. "Charles Bunker Esq. an old classmate of mine at Cambridge, graduated in 1821, a native of Nantucket, a lawyer, & for several years United States Consul at Honolulu, desires to return to the Sandwich Islands in the same capacity as consul. Mr Bunker is known to me as an intelligent & amiable gentleman of correct life, for many years past a resident of Roxbury. He brings good vouchers of his social & political rectitude from Rev. Dr Putnam, Hon. A. H. Rice, late Governor Andrew, & others. I am assured also, that, during his residence at Honolulu, he enjoyed the strong good will of the King of the Sandwich Islands; & of Mr Wylie his Minister of Foreign Affairs; & was by this gentleman proposed as Judge of the Supreme Court of Hawaii,—though not confirmed because of his (Mr B.'s) absence. His appointment to the office of Consul is strongly urged by Dr W. Newcomb, of Cornell University, resident for five years, & still an owner of property, in Oahu,—in a paper testifying to the need of sending to to that country as officials persons of correct moral character & wholesome influence—men acquainted with the natives & respected by them,—in view of the impending changes in the islands on the event of the death of the king. If the appointment of this Officer comes in any manner under your action, I believe thus much may be safely said on Mr Bunker's behalf." ALS, *ibid.* Related papers are *ibid.*

On April 15, Barnes, Washington, D. C., wrote to USG. "I have the honor to apply for the appointment of Consul at Honolulu, Sandwich Islands and in this connection ask the consideration of recommendations filed with my application of March 10th last; for the Consulate at Havre, France. I was born in Livingston County NewYork in 1839 but for the past twenty years have resided successively in Michigan, Illinois, Missouri and Arkansas. I entered the service in the late war—in 1861 as a First Lieutenant of the 1st Mo. Light Artillery (Col. Frank P. Blair Jr.) and left the servise in May 1864 by acceptance of my resignation by Maj. Genl. Rosecrans. For the past five years a resident of Arkansas I have been an active participant in the efforts to reconstruct that state, and in the last canvass did as much as perhaps any man in the State for the success of the Republican ticket, knowing at the same time, that assassination was to be the only reward to many (perhaps myself) for such labors. After several members of the Legislature had been shot, I went outside of my own county and canvassed several counties with Hon. Thomas Boles member from the 3rd Arkansas District, riding on horseback, by day and by night in sunshine and drenching rainstorms, speaking in each county and encouraging our voters by fearlessly defending our cause in the presence of armed crowds of our opponents. The election returns will bear me out in the assertion that by these very efforts the State was saved from falling (Georgia like) into the hands of the 'Democracy. From various causes the five electors chosen by the people were disqualified from casting the vote of the State for President and Vice President, and as a partial recognition of my services during th[e] canvass the Legislature unanimously elected me at the head of the Arkansas Electoral College and my colleagues afterwards appointed me as messenger to bring the vote of the state to the Capitol. . . ." ALS, *ibid.* Related papers are *ibid.* See *PUSG*, 17, 249.

On May 12, A. T. Maupin, Staunton, Va., wrote to USG. "I beg you to excuse me for again tresspassing upon your time and patience Before leaving Washington, I was induced by several friends to apply to the Secretary of State for the Consulship to Honolulu. . . . And now, after sacrificing my property, my friends and losing social position, rather than betray my government, or sacrifice my principles, to be *repudiated* by that government, & the party I have served at such fearful cost, is humililating beyond descriptions and in the name of justice, and right, I appeal to you not to do it." ALS, DNA, RG 59, Letters of Application and Recommendation. On April 14, Thomas Kline, Waynesboro, Va., had written to U.S. Senator Charles Sumner of Mass. "I have learned that There is Two or Three applicants for The position of Post master at Staunton Va and that President Grant has nominated Mr Edward Sears for That position. . . . Mr Maupin The present encumbent is a *Rascal*—he was a deserter from The Confederate Army to avoid Court Martial for Conduct unbecoming An officer & for Shooting off his finger to escape a battle. He has been guilty of Very *mean* things since he was appointed Post master at Staunton Va, some time in 1865, and up until after Prest Grants election he was a Seymour & Blair man. . . ." ALS, *ibid.*, RG 46, Papers Pertaining to Executive Nominations. Related papers are *ibid.* On March 31, USG had nominated Edward H. Sears as postmaster, Staunton; the Senate confirmed him on Dec. 21.

On May 7, Henry F. Hitch, New York City, wrote to Fish. "As a member of the only American house in Pernambuco Brazil, and one of the oldest in the Empire, I take the liberty of addressing you, in order to bear testimony, for myself and my partners, to the untiring zeal and most honorable record of Mr Thomas Adamson jr United States Consul at Pernambuco for the last seven years and a half. Mr Adamson was sent to Pernambuco by Mr Lincoln and arrived there at a time when the enemies of our Country were most active and when the strongest prejudice existed against us; all the sympathy was for the Rebels and news of their successes was received with exultation. During the raid of the Florida & Alabama on the Brazil Coast Mr Adamson's position was a most difficult and delicate one and he was as true as steel to the best interests of our Country, and by his strong representations and protests prevented the continuance of the use of the Island of Fernando de Noronha, and the port of Pernambuco as points of departure for the Rebel cruisers ~~Through the~~ Owing to the destruction of numerous American vessels on the Coast a very large number of Seamen were thrown on Mr Adamsons hands and I need only refer to the records of the Department for corroboration when I say that all the business connected with the maintenance and forwarding home of the men was carried out not only with great ability and the most zealous care for the welfare of his destrained Countrymen, but with rare economy to the Government. . . ." ALS, *ibid.*, RG 59, Letters of Application and Recommendation. On June 1, Caleb N. Taylor, Bristol, Pa., wrote to USG. "In behalf of many of my constituents to he is well and most favorably known I respectfully recommend that you will be pleased to appoint Thomas Adamson Jr of Phila. Consul of the U. S. at Honolulu.

From the favorable representations made to me by my constituents I have no reason to doubt but that the interests of the Government will be promoted by his appointment as asked for." ALS, *ibid.* Related papers are *ibid.* On the same day, USG suspended Thomas Adamson, Jr., as consul, Pernambuco, naming Samuel G. Moffett in his place; on Dec. 6, USG nominated Adamson as consul, Honolulu.

On Oct. 27, 1870, Joseph B. Atherton, Boston, wrote to USG. "Observing in some of the Boston & N. Y. newspapers, the account of the unpleasant affair at Honolulu between the U. S. Consul, Mr Adamson, & Commodore Truxton of the U. S. Navy & still later a notice of the displacement of the said consul, has led the writer to risk a few lines to you in favor & commendation of Mr Adamson, in hopes that they may have a little weight & perchance help save him from removal. The writer, an American citizen, tho on a visit here at the present time, is a resident Merchant of Honolulu & connected with one of the oldest firms on the Hawaiian Islands, & a signer of the petition for the confirmation of Mr Adamson as U. S Consul at Honolulu to the U. S. Senate in May last. Without knowing the real facts of the late disturbance, I am led to believe from what I know of Mr Adamson, that if he erred, it must have been rather from ignorance, or from a belief that he was doing right; than from any intentional insult to the Hawaiian Government. Mr Adamson may not have suited the Masters & Owners of whaleships, because he last year gave the Sailor a little more that they thought their due, or those few merchants who do the business of the whalers; but the writer believes the large majority of American Merchants & residents of Honolulu are or were in May last very much satisfied with him as Consul, & that the Consulate & Hospital attached to it were never more economically managed than under his management. . . ." ALS, *ibid.* Following the death of Queen Kalama, Adamson failed to lower the consulate flag to half mast. On Sept. 21, when Commander William T. Truxtun, *U.S.S. Jamestown*, ordered marines to lower the flag, Adamson resisted. See *New York Tribune*, Oct. 12, 1870; letter to Zachariah Chandler, Sept. 22, 1870. On Feb. 2, 1871, USG appointed Adamson as consul, Melbourne; on June 17, 1874, as consul gen.

On July 19, 1870, U.S. Representative Aaron A. Sargent of Calif. and U.S. Senator William M. Stewart of Nev. had written to USG. "The undersigned respectfully recommend James R. Hardenburgh of California as Consul at Honolulu. He is eminently fit for the position, and we believe we express the wish of the entire Pacific delegation." LS, DNA, RG 59, Letters of Application and Recommendation. On Jan. 9, 1871, USG nominated James R. Hardenbergh as surveyor gen., Calif.

To Jesse Root Grant

———

Washington. D. C. Jan. 15th *1870*

DEAR FATHER:

Your letter asking the appointment of Mr. Day as PostMaster is received. The postMaster General showed me a similar letter

from you to him some days ago and I declined making the nomination until the Member of Congress from that district was consulted. The postMaster Gn. will say to the M. C. that you are very
anxious for the apt. to go to Mr. Day.

We are all very well.

Yours Truly
U. S. GRANT

ALS, James F. Ruddy, Rancho Mirage, Calif.
      On Feb. 6, 1866, President Andrew Johnson nominated Jesse Root Grant
as postmaster, Covington, Ky. On Feb. 9, 1870, USG nominated Jesse Grant
to continue in that office after his term expired. On March 2, the nomination
was confirmed. On the same day, USG signed the commission. DS, DLC-
Jeremiah T. Lockwood.
      On April 3, 1869, R. Tarvin Baker et al., Newport, Ky., wrote to USG.
"We protest against appointment of Wynings as postmaster He is not citizen
of our place We are satisfied with Terrell and desire his continuance. Newport
is the only city in the state that went for Grant and who fought for him feel
that we ought to be heard." Telegram received (at 6:30 P.M.), DNA, RG 107,
Telegrams Collected (Bound). On March 31, USG had nominated Benjamin
L. Winans as postmaster, Newport, in place of William G. Terrell. On March
23, Terrell, Cincinnati, had telegraphed to USG. "I learn that your father is
under the impression that I once in his presence avowed my intention to resign
in the event of your election. This is a grave misapprehension, on the contrary
I repeatedly & publicly declared I should resign in case of a democratic administration refusing to retain office under the sole benefit of office tenure act
Colonel Jones our representative knows this" Telegram received (at 2:10 P.M.),
ibid.

To Benjamin F. Butler

Personal   *Washington, D. C.* Jany. 24th *18670.*

SIR:

Your personal letter of Jany. 22d 1870. came to me Saturday.[1]
Mr. Dawes did call on me some weeks ago and during the interview he told me the appropriations asked for exceeded those given
to Mr. Johnson for the last year of his administration by twenty-
nine millions.—To which I expressed much surprise. I did not
then suppose his statement included the number of errors made in
his speech.[2]

I did not understand from his remark that he intended to make an open attack, but supposed he would consult with the different Cabinet officers on this matter.

Yours truly
U. S. GRANT

HON. B. F. BUTLER.
HOUSE OF REPRESENTATIVES.

LS, DLC-Benjamin F. Butler.

    1. The same day.
    2. On Jan. 18, 1870, U.S. Representative Henry L. Dawes of Mass., chairman, Committee on Appropriations, speaking in opposition to a bill to enlarge the Philadelphia Navy Yard at League Island, criticized USG's appropriation requests as extravagant. On Jan. 25, Secretary of State Hamilton Fish noted in his diary. "Dawes' recent speech was talked of—The President is very indignant—'hopes the Democrats will take him as a Candidate for Congress'—Boutwell thinks he will carry many Republicans with him—(Boutwell is always timid & cautious)—" DLC-Hamilton Fish. On Jan. 26, U.S. Representative Benjamin F. Butler of Mass. defended USG's policies. *CG*, 41–2, 795–804. On Jan. 27, Dawes responded. ". . . I went to the President and I laid these estimates before him, and these differences between this year and the next. . . . He talked with me of economy, and the best means of securing it. He said that his influence would be exerted to the utmost to bring down these estimates. He said that he had made a personal examination of the estimates for the War Department, and knowing the necessities of that Department better than those of any other, he thought these estimates were cut down as low as they possibly could be. . . ." *Ibid. (Appendix)*, 72–79.

To Mrs. John A. Dahlgren

    The President & Mrs. Grant regret that they cannot accept Mrs. Dahlgren invitation to meet Prince Arthur at the Navy Yard on Wednsday next. They expect company on the afternoon of that day, and will have guests at dinner in the evening.

WASHINGTON D. C.
JAN.Y 24TH 1870.

AL, DLC-John A. Dahlgren. As a matter of presidential protocol, USG resisted pressure to call upon Queen Victoria's twenty-year-old son Prince Arthur. Instead, USG received Prince Arthur at the White House, held a dinner for him, and attended a ball in his honor. See Hamilton Fish diary, Jan. 6–8, 24, 26, 1870, DLC-Hamilton Fish; *New York Times*, Jan. 22–28, 1870.

To Elihu B. Washburne

Washington, D, C,
Jan.y 28th 1870.

Dear Washburne:

I received your interesting personal letter a day or two ago and snatch a few moments to answer it. In reality I have no quiet time in which to write letters; scarsely to read the current news of the day. The continuous press of people continues yet about as it was last Spring.

You will see by the papers that the ratification of the Fifteenth Amendment is assured! With this question out of politics, and reconstruction completed, I hope to see such good feeling in Congress as to secure rapid legislation and an early adjournment. My peace is when Congress is not in session.—My family are all well and wish to be remembered to Mrs. Washburne, the children and yourself. The Emperor has been kind enough to send me pleasant messages several times which please say to him have been duly received and are highly appreciated. Please convey to him my best wishes for a continuance of his good health, and the happiness and prosperity of the people over whom he has been called to rule. It has been the desire of my life to visit Europe, and particularly France, but so far I have been too busy. If spared to get through my present office I shall take a year or two to visit those parts of the world I have not yet seen.—I hope there will be no objection to Jones[1] confirmation, and was it not for your fears, and his, on the subject I should never have dreamed that there was opposition. I have talked to no Senator who expressed opposition.

Yours Truly
U. S. Grant

ALS, IHi. On Feb. 17, 1870, Elihu B. Washburne wrote to USG. "I duly received your letter of the 28th ult. I went down to the Tuileries yesterday and delivered your message to the Emperor, in person. He received me very cordially, as he always does, and expressed himself as much gratified in hearing from you and desired me to express to you his cordial thanks for your kind wishes. When I spoke of your wish to visit France when out of your present office he said it would afford him the greatest pleasure to welcome you to Paris, but that if you did not propose coming till out of your *present office*, he thought it would be some time before he saw you, for he took it for granted you would be re-elected. He made many inquiries about our country, particularly in regard to the Red River troubles and the Mormons. In fact, he has enquired about the Mormons several times and he has seemed greatly interested in the solution of that question. He had the most erroneous idea of things in the Mormon country till I explained to him. You may see a great many sensational despatches in the newspapers about the disturbances in Paris, and one might be led to think that we are on the eve of a grand revolution. Far from that. It is the opinion of all the best informed men here, with whom I talk, that the Government has never been stronger than at the present time. Whatever may be said to the contrary the new Parliamentary regime is a success. Yet with this mercurial and changeable people, nobody can tell how long it will stand. The new ministry is a very strong one. The members of it are liberal men, men of ability, high character [a]nd three or four of them of great [w]ealth, and have a stake in the permanence of the Government. I note what you say about Jones's confirmation. I wish it would happen that he might be confirmed without further delay, as he is very uneasy. You know how glad I shall always be to get a line from [yo]u but I know how your time is taken [u]p and how difficult it is to snatch [e]ven a moment from your public duties. My wife joins in kindest regards to your self and family." ALS (press), DLC-Elihu B. Washburne.

On Jan. 7, Washburne had written to USG. "In the first place, I wish you and yours 'happy New Year,' in which I am most cordially joined by my whole household. In the second place, I thank you for your favor of the 17th ult. You can well appreciate the interest I feel in all that is going on at 'home' and how gratified I am to have a word from you occasionally. So far as I can judge things are going well. I was delighted with your message, as everybody here has been. I have read all the reports of your cabinet officers and I consider them very able as they are very satisfactory and most creditable to your administration. The one thing in which I take the most pride is the splendid financial success of your administration which is shown by the constant appreciation of our credit abroad. I was rejoiced at your recommendation in regard to Georgia as well as at the action of Congress in the matter. I cannot account for the action of the Senate in regard to Hoar. He is just the man for the Supreme Bench and I hope you wont withdraw his name, but let the Senate take the responsibility of rejecting him. If you yield to the clamor to nominate a southern man, ten to one you will be sold out in the end. See how Lincoln came out in his appointments of Supreme Judges. I was so glad you appointed poor Stanton. I only wish he could have lived and had his health. He would have put some *red* blood into that court   I need not say how delighted I was with the appointment of Drummond. Now if you could put old Ben Sheldon in his place as District Judge, you would entitle yourself to the gratitude of all good men in Illinois. That would be almost *too good* to think of.—The appointment of Sawyer was capital. I was glad you withdrew Yeaman. The Maryland man I know nothing of, but I am a *little* afraid. We are getting along here very well, though Mrs. W. does not get strength very fast. The children are all well and like Paris. I am improving under the treatment of Dr. Brown-Sequard. Genl Washburn writes that Mr. Dent laughed at the report of my dancing at Compiègne. Instead of a simple quadrille of ten minutes, the burlesque account put me in for two hours at a 'breakdown', whereat all the papers at home blackguard me. If they would only accuse me of rob-

bing the people by speculating in gold and bonds I could stand it, but to be
accused of kicking up my heels for two hours in the Emperors palace is too
much for poor human nature!! I saw the Emperor on New Year's when the
Diplomatic Corps called on him. He enquired kindly for you and said he wished
I would give you his compliments of the Season when I wrote to you. This is the
second time he has sent that message, the first of which I communicated through
Gov. Fish. Whatever may be the real feelings of His Majesty towards our country, it is evident he has a very high regard for you personally. Should you
deem it proper to return the compiments of the season to him, I should be very
happy to present them. I have written the Gov. a long despatch to-day in regard
to the revolution we have been passing through here. Perhaps you might be interested in it. Didn't I laugh when I read the account of how poor little Mungen
brought his Copperhead friends to the Confessional on the repudiation question.
Mrs. W. joins me in the kindest regards to yourself wife and children." ALS
(press), *ibid*. See letter to Elihu B. Washburne, Dec. 17, 1869.

1. On Dec. 27, 1869, Washburne had written to USG. "I am greatly
alarmed this morning by seeing in a Washington despatch in a N. Y. paper of
the 15th inst. that the Senate Committee on Foreign Relations would report
adversely on Jones's Confirmation. I can hardly conceive that possible, for there
is certainly no good reason for such action. Mr J. was nominated for a vacancy
and therefore nobody was turned out to make room for him. And then again, he
makes a most creditable minister and has obtained the respect of the court and
of his colleagues of the Diplomatic Corps.—What reason on earth there can be
for rejecting him I cannot conceive, unless it is considered desirable to strike
at you, knowing that he has ever been one of your most devoted friends and always a most earnest and efficient republican. Few men in the last Canvass did
more effectual work than Jones and Gov. Morton, who is on the Committee of
Foreign Relations, knows that Indiana was saved to us last October, a year ago,
by the efforts he made. I wish you could see some members of the Committee
and tell them what I have written you in relation to the manner in which Mr.
Jones is discharging his duties. Mr. Sumner, Mr. Patterson and Gov. Morton
ought to take my word. I dont recollect the other members. To reject Jones on
account of unfitness for the position would be considered somewhat ludicrous
when we take into account that the Senate confirmed Watts to a first class mission, that of Vienna. Jones is vastly superior to Watts. Chandler, Ramsay and
Fenton have all been at Brussels this past summer and will back up what I have
said. I write earnestly in this matter, because I feel a great interest. The rejection would be a cruel blow and no public interest can be subserved. I am certain
that the Committee or the Senate will not do such an act of injustice. We are all
quite well. With the Compliments of the Season for yourself and family, . . ."
ALS (press), DLC-Elihu B. Washburne.

On March 29, Orville E. Babcock had written to Attorney Gen. Ebenezer
R. Hoar. "The President directs me to request that you send per bearer a nomi-
nation for Benjamin H. Campbell to be U. S. Marshal for the Northern Dist of
Ills. vice J. R Jones resigned." LS, DNA, RG 60, Records Relating to Appoint-
ments. On March 30, a newspaper reported: "President Grant yesterday sent to
the Senate the name of B. H. Campbell, of Galena, for Marshal of the Northern
District of Illinois—the position now held by his brother-in-law, Hon. J. R.
Jones. . . . Politically, Mr. Campbell was formerly a Whig, and since the de-

cease of that party, has been an uncompromising Republican, although neither an office-seeker nor an active politician. He is a father-in-law to Gen. Babcock, of Gen. Grant's Staff, and has, for some years, been on terms of intimacy with General Grant. We learn that the subject of his appointment was never mentioned between the President and Mr. Campbell, and that the office has been tendered to the latter with out the slightest solicitation on his part." Clipping, J. Russell Jones Scrapbook, ICHi.

On April 5, J. Russell Jones, Chicago, telegraphed to Babcock. "There is a telegram in town saying my destination is changed to Switzerland, I very much hope this is not true as I greatly prefer Belgium." Telegram received (at 8:35 A.M.), DNA, RG 107, Telegrams Collected (Bound). On April 12, USG nominated Jones as minister to Belgium; on April 22, the Senate tabled this nomination. On the same day, Jones telegraphed to Babcock. "There must certainly be a screw loose somewhere, Have you seen Trumbull?" Telegram received (at 11:00 A.M.), *ibid.* On June 1, USG gave Jones a recess appointment. Renominated on Dec. 6, Jones was confirmed on March 15, 1870. See *PUSG*, 7, 410–11; George R. Jones, *Joseph Russell Jones* (Chicago, 1964), pp. 47–61.

To Senate

————

To the Senate of the United States:

In reply to the resolutions of the Senate of the 28 inst. requesting the return of the notifications, dated the 22d inst., of the confirmation of G. C. Wharton[1] to be U. S. Attorney for the Western Dist. of Ky. and L. B. Eaton[2] to be U. S. Marshal for the Western Dist. of Tenn., I have to state that on the 24th inst. commissions for these officers were signed and sent from this office.

If, however, reasons exist why these officers should not have been confirmed, the same reasons would apply why they should not be retained. I would be pleased to hear and consider any information the Senate have to present on the subject.

U. S. GRANT

EXECUTIVE MANSION
JANY 31ST 1870

DS, DNA, RG 46, Papers Pertaining to Nominations. On Jan. 31, 1870, Secretary of State Hamilton Fish wrote to USG. "The Secretary of State, to whom has been referred two Resolutions of the Senate passed in Executive Session on the 28th instant, requesting the President of the United States to return to the Senate its resolutions advising and consenting to the appointments of Lucien B.

Eaton, and Gabriel C. Wharton, the former as Marshal of the United States for the western District of Tennessee and the latter as Attorney of the United States for the District of Kentucky, has the honor to lay before the President the resolutions of confirmation referred to. It will be observed that they contain other confirmations than those of Messrs. Eaton and Wharton and their return to the Department of State with these names omitted will be necessary, in order to show the authority upon which commissions have been issued to the several parties, besides the two specified, whose names are embraced in the resolutions." Copy, *ibid.*, RG 59, General Records. On Feb. 11, Fish wrote to Orville E. Babcock. "I have to inform you that the Commissions of Gabriel C. Wharton, as United States Attorney for the District of Kentucky, and L. B. Eaton Marshal of the United States for the Western District of Tennessee, are in this Department" Copy, *ibid.*, Domestic Letters. On Feb. 12, Babcock wrote to Fish. "The President directs me to return to the State Dept. the enclosed papers and say that he desires the commissions issued to G. C. Wharton and L. B. Eaton." Copy, DLC-USG, II, 1. See *Senate Executive Journal,* XVII, 354, 355.

1. On Dec. 18, 1869, Benjamin H. Bristow, U.S. attorney, Louisville, had written to USG. "I have the honor to tender my resignation of the office of Attorney of the United States in and for the District of Kentucky, to take effect on such day as your Excellency may designate not later than the first of January proximo. In retiring from official Connection with your Administration I desire to express my sincere gratitude for the personal and official kindness uniformly extended to me by the Heads of the various Executive Departments of the Government" ALS, DNA, RG 60, Records Relating to Appointments. On Dec. 22, USG endorsed this letter. "The Atty. Gn. will please send the nomination of Gabriel C. Wharton to fill the vacancy occasioned by Col. Bristow's resignation. I would like to fill this vacancy to-day to avoid the pressure that will be brought for various candidates." AES, *ibid.* On the same day, Noah H. Swayne, U.S. Supreme Court, wrote to USG. "Col. B. H. Bristowe the U S Atty for the District of Kentucky has [resign]ed. Judge Ballard myself and others have recommended *Col. Wharton,* the present Assist. Atty, to fill the vacancy. I know him to be worthy meritorious & competent. Judge Hoare being absent I have advised Col Wharton to call on you. I would call with him, but that I am to hear a case from Florida this morning and can not spare the time   It is desireable that the appointment should be made as Early as you feel prepared to act upon the subject." ALS, *ibid.* Related papers are *ibid.* On the same day, USG nominated Gabriel C. Wharton, former lt. col., 10th Ky., as U.S. attorney, District of Ky.

2. On March 2, W. T. Poston *et al.,* Memphis, wrote to USG. "I take pleasure in endorsing Col. L. B. Eaton, of the Memphis Post, as well qualified in every respect to discharge the duties of United States Marshal of the District of West Tennessee, and consider it my duty to urge his appointment, as a recognition of his the invaluable Services rendered to the party and the Country by the Post, and to relieve its Editors—General Eaton and Col Eaton—in a measure, of the debt which they have incurred in their persevering struggle to maintain it   In my humble opinion you can, by no other appointment, so suEfficiently serve the Republican party of West Tennessee, and I might add, of Arkansas and North Mississippi   I make this recommendation with the more pleasure as the position is at present disgraced by an untrustworthy officer,—a chronic office-Seeker and an unprincipled politician" LS, *ibid.* On Dec. 18, U.S. Repre-

sentative Isaac R. Hawkins of Tenn. and David A. Nunn wrote to USG. "we have the honor to submit herewith, for your information, an authenticated copy of the papers relating to the defal-cation of L. B. Eaton while clerk of the Municipal court at Memphis, refered to in our interview on the 15th inst. . . ." LS, *ibid*. U.S. Representatives Roderick R. Butler and William B. Stokes of Tenn. favorably endorsed this letter. ES, *ibid*. Related papers are *ibid*. On Dec. 6, USG nominated Lucien B. Eaton, former capt., 65th Ohio, and associate editor, *Memphis Post*, as marshal, Western District, Tenn.

To Senate

————

TO THE SENATE OF THE UNITED STATES.

I transmit to the Senate, in compliance with its resolution of the 31st ultimo, a report from the Secretary of State, communicating information in relation to the action of the legislature of the state of Mississippi on the proposed fifteenth amendment to the Constitution of the United States.

U. S. GRANT

WASHINGTON,
FEBRUARY 1. 1870.

DS, DNA, RG 46, President's Messages. On Feb. 1, 1870, Secretary of State Hamilton Fish wrote to USG providing the information. LS, *ibid*. On Jan. 25, Bvt. Maj. Gen. Adelbert Ames, provisional governor, Jackson, Miss., had written to USG. "I have the honor to transmit the constitution of the State of Mississippi as adopted at the election held on the 30th of Nov and 1st Dec 1869." ALS, *ibid*., RG 59, Miscellaneous Letters. See *SED*, 41-2-30.

On Jan. 18, Ames had telegraphed to Horace Porter. "Have been elected to the senate without being relieved from command here. Can I have a telegraphic order to proceed to Washington" Telegram received, DNA, RG 107, Telegrams Collected (Bound). On Jan. 19, Porter wrote to Ames. "I have just recv'd your telegram and after consultation with Belknap telegraphed you to apply to Sherman officially. Sherman has pitched into both you and me in regard to communicating directly, and we thought it would be much better to wait till your application comes up officially. There will be no trouble about your request being granted I shall explain more fully when we meet I congratulate you most heartily on the very great honor that has been conferred on you. It *is* an honor which no one can dispute The President says you have taken the best course to come to Washington to decide the matter" ALS, ICU.

To Paul N. Spofford

———

Washington. D. C. Feb.y 2d 18~~6~~70

P. N. SPOFFORD, ESQ,
29 BROADWAY NEW YORK CITY:
DEAR SIR:

Your letter enclosing one from Mr Wm G. Haskell,[1] Attorney for Mrs. Rawlins, is received. In reply to the enquiry made in your letter I enclose you a copy of a letter from Mr. Grennell stating the views of some of the subscribers to the Rawlins Fund as to how it should be disposed of. I heartily concur in these views. Gen. Rawlins left three young children[2] almost wholly unprovided for, and a widow who is not the mother of either of the children. I think it would be bad policy not to protect the children in their just share of the bounteous liberality of yourself and the other subscribers to the fund for their relief.

With great respect,
your obt. svt.
U. S. GRANT

P. S. My understanding from the enclosed instructions is that Mrs. Rawlins is an equal heir, during widowhood, with each of the children, and not with the whole of them, as might be infered from the phraseology. My great desire however is to find exactly what the donors do wish and to carry out that wish fully.

U. S. GRANT

ALS, William N. Dearborn, Nashville, Tenn. Paul N. Spofford, born about 1822 in New York City, engineer in chief of N. Y. under Governors John Young and Hamilton Fish, charter member of the Union League Club, was associated with his father's commercial firm of Spofford, Tileston, & Co. On Feb. 5, 1870, Moses H. Grinnell, Spofford, and other subscribers to a trust fund established to benefit the survivors of John A. Rawlins wrote to USG. "We suppose that it will facilitate and, in a measure, lessen the labor which you have been good enough to undertake in respect to the fund which we, together, have subscribed for the benefit of the family of the late General John A. Rawlins if we should make an explicit declaration of the purposes for which it is placed in your hands. We beg therefore to state that it is placed in your hands upon the following trusts, to continue until the youngest surviving of the two younger children of General Rawlins now living shall attain the age of twenty one years, that is to say in trust: First To invest it according to your own discretion in such securities or

property as you may approve, and to change such investments from time to time
as your own judgment may dictate   Second. To collect and receive its income
as it shall accrue and to pay over one quarter of it, periodically to General
Rawlins' widow during the continuance of the trusts, or so long as she shall
remain his widow unmarried to any other person, and to apply the remaining
three quarters of such income (or if the widow should die during the continuance
of the trusts, or should marry again, then, from the time of her death or re-
marriage to apply the whole of such income) to the use of General Rawlins'
three children in such manner as you may consider most expedient in order to
promote their maintenance and education. . . . Third. When the youngest surviving of the two younger children of General Rawlins, now living, shall attain
the age of twenty one years, or, if neither of them shall live to attain that age;
then, upon the decease of the last survivor of them, to divide and distribute the
capital of the said fund as follows (1) If the widow of General Rawlins shall
then be living, and shall not have married again, by paying over to her one
fourth part of such fund, so that she may thenceforth hold it to her own use
absolutely, and (2) by paying over the entire remainder of *the* said fund together with its accumulations (or if the widow of General Rawlins shall have
married again or shall have departed this life, by paying over the whole of the
said fund with its accumulations) to the said three children in equal proportions,
so that each of them may thenceforth hold his or her share of it to his or her
own use absolutely. . . . Fourth. As you know the children of General Rawlins
are the children of a former marriage, and, inasmuch therefore as circumstances might arise which would induce his widow to relinquish their guardian-
ship, it is to be understood that if any such event should occur, you are to be at
liberty in your discretion at any time during the continuance of the trusts, to
pay over to her, in lieu of the provision above made for her benefit, such a proportion of the said fund, not exceeding one quarter of it, as you may consider
just and proper, and the aforegoing provisions are declared to be subject to the
exercise of the power and discretion on your part in this article expressed. Fifth.
If the duties devolving upon you in connection with the management and disposition of this fund shall at any time become onerous, or if you should for any
cause desire to resign your trust, it is understood that you are to be at liberty to
do so and in that event to appoint a successor in your place who shall be clothed
with the same rights and powers as are hereby conferred upon you." DS, USG 3.

On Sept. 7, 1869, 3:00 P.M., USG sent an unaddressed telegram. "Put me
down for $1,000 for the widow of General Rawlins." *New York World*, Sept. 8,
1869. See *ibid.*, Sept. 11–13, 1869. On Nov. 27, Col. Daniel Butterfield, New
York City, sent to USG a check for $1,000. DS, USG 3. On the same day, USG
wrote a receipt. "Received at the hand of Genl Butterfield Ten Dollars—being
the subscription of W. F. Wheeler—Helena M. T. to the Rawlins Fund—" DS,
Historical Society of Montana, Helena, Mont. See letters to Mary E. Rawlins,
[*Sept. 6, 1869*], Feb. 13, 1871.

1. William G. Haskell, pastor, First Universalist Church, Danbury, Conn.,
preached a *Memorial Sermon on the Life and Death of Gen. John Aaron Rawlins*, . . . (Danbury, 1869).

2. James B., born 1856; Jennie S., born 1858; Emily S., born 1860. Three
children born to Mary Rawlins predeceased their father. *Ibid.* See letters to
William D. Rawlins, June 22, July 30, 1872, June 18, 1873; *Report of the Pro-*

ceedings of The Society of the Army of the Tennessee at the Thirty-First Meeting . . . (Cincinnati, 1900), p. 56; New York Times, June 22, 1941.

Executive Order

Washington. D. C.
February 4th, 1870.

Under and in pursuance of the authority vested in me by the provisions of the second Section of the Act of Congress approved on the 27th day of July, 1868, entitled "An act to extend the laws of the United States relating to Customs, Commerce and Navigation, over the Territory ceded to the United States by Russia, to establish a collection district therein, and for other purposes", the importation of distilled spirits into and within the District of Alaska is hereby prohibited, and the importation and use of fire-arms and ammunition into and within the Islands of Saint Paul and Saint George, in said District, are also hereby prohibited, under the pains and penalties of law.

U. S. GRANT
President.

DS, DNA, RG 36, Special Agents Div., Alaska File. Misdated Feb. 8, 1870, in *HED*, 44-1-135. On Sept. 9, 1870, and Feb. 29, 1872, USG amended this order. "So much of executive order of February 4, 1870, as prohibits the importation and use of fire-arms and ammunition into and within the Islands of Saint Paul and Saint George, Alaska, is hereby modified so as to permit the Alaska Commercial Company to take a limited quantity of fire-arms and ammunition to said islands, subject to the directions of the revenue officers there and such regulations as the Secretary of the Treasury may prescribe." "So much of Executive Order of February 4, 1870, as prohibits the importation and use of distilled spirits into and within the Territory of Alaska, is hereby modified so as to permit wine to be shipped to said Territory for use in the communion services of the Russian churches, subject to such regulations as the Secretary of the Treasury may prescribe." *Ibid.*, 44-1-83, pp. 29, 72. On July 3, 1875, USG approved instructions forbidding the importation of breech-loading rifles and ammunition into Alaska Territory. *HRC*, 50-2-3883, pp. 278–79.

To Senate

To the Senate of the United States.

For the reasons stated in the accompanying communication from the Secretary of the Interior, I respectfully request to withdraw the Treaties hereinafter mentioned which are now pending before the Senate.

1st. Treaty concluded with the Great and Little Osages May 27th 1868.

2nd Treaty concluded with the Sac and Fox of the Missouri, and Iowa, tribe of Indians February 11th 1869.

3rd Treaty concluded with the Ottoe and Missouria Indians Feb'y 13th 1869.

4th Treaty concluded with the Kansas or Kaw Indians March 13. 1869.[1]

U. S. Grant

Executive Mansion
February 4th 1870

DS, DNA, RG 46, Presidential Messages, Indian Relations. On Feb. 4, 1870, Secretary of the Interior Jacob D. Cox wrote to USG. "I have the honor to invite your attention to sundry Indian Treaties now pending before the Senate, and to submit for your consideration the propriety of requesting that body to return them to you. . . . The proper Indian Superintendent was instructed to ascertain the views and wishes of the Great and Little Osages in regard to the stipulations of the first mentioned Treaty. He represents that a majority of them prefer that it should not be ratified. The instrument provides for the relinquishment of a large and valuable tract of land in Southern Kansas and its transfer to a Railroad Company. He likewise reports that the Chiefs, Head men and Members of the tribes, parties to the second Treaty, earnestly protest against its ratification and state that the consideration named therein for which their lands are to be sold to a Railroad Company is less than one half of their market value. With regard to the third Treaty, the Ottoes and Missourias, the Superintendent reports that the lands proposed to be ceded are rated far below their real value. The Treaty with the Kansas or Kaw Indians, contains a provision for the sale of their lands to a Railroad Company, and this alone furnishes, in my opinion, an insurmountable objection to it. Attention was invited to this feature, when the treaty was submitted. The possessory rights of the Indians should only be extinguished in favor of the United States, and the land to which such rights had attached should, thenceforth, be subject to the laws regulating the disposal of the public domain, including those which provide for homestead settlements and pre-emption entries, unless in case of tracts and reservations of exceptional value, sales can be made in small parcels to actual settlers at the present worth of the land. The policy of selling, by virtue of an Indian treaty stipulation, immense bodies of land to a corporation, is of comparatively recent origin. It seriously retards their settlement and cultivation, and should not, I submit, be hereafter sanctioned by that branch of the Government, which is clothed with the power of making treaties. In the case of the Kaw Reservation, I have hesitancy in making a recommendation, because the treaty before the Senate was concluded under circumstances which gave that body a more direct part in the negotiation than is common; but it is an indisputable fact, that the reservation could not be rightfully appraised at less than two dollars and a half per acre for the whole, when the treaty was signed, and the better opinion now is that the average present value is even above five dollars per acre. I can see no just reason, therefore, for making an exception in my recommendation as to this treaty, and include it in the class which I regard as contrary to public policy and inconsistent with justice to the Indian tribes." LS, *ibid.*

On Feb. 12, U.S. Senator Edmund G. Ross of Kan. wrote to USG. "I have the honor to call your attention to certain statements contained in the letter of the Secretary of the Interior of the 4th inst, recommending the withdrawal of certain Indian Treaties, & transmitted by you to the Senate on the same day, with a Message withdrawing the Treaties named therein. In that communication the secretary says: 'The proper Indian superintendent was instructed to ascertain the views and wishes of the Great and Little Osages in regard to the stipulations of the first-mentioned treaty. He represents that a majority of them prefer that it should not be ratified. The instrument provides for the relinquishment of a large and valuable tract of land in Southern Kansas and its transfer to a railroad company.' If you will take the trouble to refer to the communication of the Indian Superintendent, upon which the statement of the Secretary is based, you will see that the reason why the larger portion preferred that the Treaty should not be ratified, was, to use the Superintendent's words, 'more from a feeling that by the terms of the Treaty they do not receive so much for their land as they think they ought to, than from any improper influences brought to bear upon them by the Commissioners' That appears to be the only objection they had to the ratification, & that it was the only matter in the Treaty which interested them at all, is shown by a subsequent statement in the same communication, that 'they state, however, that whether their pending Treaty be ratified or not, they are anxious to sell their lands, & remove to the Indian Territory.' Instead of the Treaty providing for the sale of the Reservation to *a* Railroad Company, it provides for its sale to *six* corporations, no one of which is permitted to purchase more than five-sixteenths of the whole, & in every instance the permission to purchase is accompanied with conditions & restrictions which compel the construction of a corresponding number of miles of Railroad before any benefits from the purchase are secured, & in every instance the maximum price of the lands is fixed—the corporations get title to not an acre till their roads are completed, & then are required to sell every acre in five years thereafter, or in default, the unsold residue reverts to the U.snited States. In addition, the Treaty guarantees to the twenty thousand settlers now on those lands their homes at $1.25 per acre—pays, or should be made to pay to the Indian all he should ask for it—that the unoccupied residue must be appraised, & held open to settlement & purchase at the appraised value until the roads are completed—that every 16th section shall be donated to the school fund of the State—that the most valuable acre of timbered or watered land on it shall not be held for more $7.50 pr acre, or the best acre of prairie land for more than $5.00, or the best acre of prairie land more than ten miles from a Railroad for more than $2.50 pr acre   These are the leading features of the Osage, as also of the Kaw Treaty, as they have lain upon the Senate table, with the endorsement of the Committee on Indian Affairs, since the last session of Congress. With regard to the price proposed to be paid, under these Treaties, in view of the fact that they have appreciated in value during the two years that have elapsed since they were signed, I presume no objection would be made to a reasonable increase   As to the Treaties with the Sacs or Foxes of Missouri, & the Ottoes & Missourias, the only objection urged by the Secretary, is the price to be paid the Indians, which I presume can be satisfactorily adjusted When it is remembered that the ratification of these Treaties will secure to our State ~~700~~ the construction of 700 miles of Railroad more than we now have, it is not strange that our people should be anxious for their ratification, or that I should urge it zealously in their behalf. I wish to call your attention to the fact That ~~T~~the people of the prairie states of the West are dependant solely upon Railroads for their facilities of trade, & for a market, & ~~they~~ those states could never have been considerably settled, but for the confident expectation of securing them, sooner or later. That ~~T~~the people of those new states have not the means to build these roads, & can secure it from others only by a pledge of lands in liberal quantities   That It is only this liberal encouragement to the construction of Railroads that has given to those states the prosperity they enjoy, & but for this aid, many millions of acres of their lands, now under prosperous cultivation, would have remained to this day untouched by the plow, & the sites of many of their beautiful cities would have been yet in wilderness & bare prairie. Every man living in & identified with the West, realizes these facts. That ~~T~~these lands lie in our state, & have for years impeded the developement of our agricultural & commercial interests. They have largely diminished the grants of land intended to be given in aid of the construction of important Railroad lines, & we think it not unreasonable to ask that they should now be permitted to purchase them under the perfect guarantees of these Treaties, & thus indemnify themselves for that diminution. I may add that by a law of Congress passed March 3d 1863, the Congress authorized the President to conclude treaties with the several Indian tribes then in Kansas, providing for the extinction of their titles; & their removal without the state. May it not be considered that the faith of the Government was thereby pledged to the State of Kansas for the removal of those Indians, & the opening of their lands to settlement. Kansas now respectfully asks the Government to fulfill that pledge, & inasmuch as the ratification of these treaties will accomplish those objects, & in addition secure very great commercial advantages to the State, without compromising the rights or interests of any parties, in any manner whatever, but rather promote the interests of all, I very earnestly request that the Treaties withdrawn by your communication of the 4th inst, be returned to the Senate, with such suggestions of modification as in your judgment may seem proper & just. I have the honor to transmit herewith, a series of resolutions recently passed by the Legislature of Kansas on this subject." ALS (first quoted passage is a clipped and pasted printed extract), DNA, RG 75, Letters Received, Central Superintendency. Related papers are *ibid.*

1. On April 5, 1869, Cox had written to USG. "I have the honor to transmit certain articles of agreement made and concluded at the Kaw Indian agency Kansas on the 13th ultimo between the commissioners on the part of the United States, and certain chiefs or head-men of the Kansas or Kaw tribe of Indians on behalf of said tribe. In connection therewith, I invite your attention to the accompanying copy of a letter from the Commissioner of Indian Affairs, and of the report of agent Stover and Wm R. Irwin Esq., commissioners on the part of the United States. These papers furnish full explanations of the circumstances which led to the conclusion of the treaty. It seems that, pursuant to the suggestion of the Senate Committee on Indian Affairs, negotiations were commenced during the term of my immediate predecessor, and the stipulations are substantially in accordance the views of that Committee. I forbear commending the treaty to your favorable consideration, as some of its stipulations are, in my opinion, not conducive to the interests of settlers upon the public lands." LS, *ibid.*, RG 46, Presidential Messages, Indian Relations. On April 6, USG wrote to the Senate. "I transmit herewith for the Constitutional action of the Senate certain articles of agreement made and concluded at the Kaw Indian agency Kansas on the 13th ultimo between the Commissioners on the part of the United States, & certain chiefs or head men of the Kansas or Kaw tribe of Indians on behalf of said tribe, together with a letter from the Secretary of the Interior to which attention is invited." LS, *ibid.* Related papers are *ibid.*

To Senate

TO THE SENATE OF THE UNITED STATES:

In reply to the resolution of the Senate of the 4th. instant, requesting information in regard to the proceedings had in the state of Georgia in pursuance of the recent Act of Congress entitled "An Act to promote the reconstruction of the state of Georgia," and in relation to the organization of the legislature of that state since the passage of that act, I herewith transmit the report of the Secretary of War, to whom the resolution was referred.

U. S. GRANT

EXECUTIVE MANSION
WASHINGTON, D. C.
FEBRUARY 11TH 1870.

DS, DNA, RG 46, Presidential Messages. See *SED*, 41-2-41.

On Dec. 22, 1869, USG had signed "AN ACT to promote the reconstruction of the State of Georgia." Copy (printed), DNA, RG 94, Letters Received, 1156S 1869. On Dec. 23, Bvt. Maj. Gen. Alfred H. Terry, Atlanta, telegraphed to Gen. William T. Sherman. "I have received a telegram from Governor Bullock stating that he and others have urged upon The President my assignment to the command of Georgia as a Military District I beg that this may not be done. The matter will be decided tonight" Telegram received (at 7:30 P.M.), *ibid.*; copies (2), *ibid.* On Dec. 24, Secretary of War William W. Belknap wrote to Sherman. "The President desires that the order as to Georgia be issued. It need not be delayed longer" AL (initialed), DLC-William T. Sherman. On the same day, Sherman drafted General Orders No. 83. "Bt Maj. General A H Terry, in addition to his duties as Commander of the Dept of the South, is by order of the President of the U. S. appointed to exercise the duties of Comdg Gnl of the District of Georgia, as defined by the Act of Congress approved Dec 22d 1869." ADf (initialed), DNA, RG 94, Letters Received, 1156S 1869; copy (printed), *ibid.* Related documents are *ibid.*

On Jan. 3, 1870, Nelson Tift, Albany, Ga., wrote to USG. "I enclose a printed copy of my letter 'To the Legislature the Press & People of Georgia' and beg to call your attention to the construction which I have placed upon the Act of Congress 'To promote the reconstruction of the state of Georgia' and which I beleive is in accordance with your own views. I do this because Governor Bullock has assumed the title of Provisional Governor,—which is not authorized by the Act of Congress,—and intends to usurp authority over the legislature & people, and expects to be supported in his illegal & tyranical course by yourself as President & the Military under your command. The people of Georgia are at your mercy & expect your protection." ALS, *ibid.*, 1155S 1869. The enclosure and related documents are *ibid.*

On Jan. 11, Terry telegraphed to Sherman. "The Senate of Georgia has been organized I am informed persons who took the oath in that body are disqualified The House of Representatives is partialy sworn. I am informed that nine (9) disqualified persons have already taken the oath. It is expected that others will do so One of the Senators who took the oath stated night before last that he believed himself disqualified, but that his people expected him to take the oath. an immense pressure has been brough to bear on disqualified persons to induce or compel them to take the oath. Money has been raised to defend them in case of prosecution. am I authorized as Military Commander Under the reconstruction acts and under section *one* (1) and *five* (5) of the act of *December* 22d 1869 to investigate the questions of eligibility & determine for the time being the right of these persons to seats or must the taking of the oath ~~for~~ be considered conclusive It is very important that any action which may be taken should be taken at once Please answer." Telegram received (on Jan. 12, 11:40 A.M.), *ibid.*; copy, *ibid.* On Jan. 12, Sherman telegraphed to Terry. "Your despatch of this moring was shown the President & Secretary of War, and the result is in these words. 'Exercise your own discretion. If a flagrant case arises, when a disqualified person proposes to take the oath, investigate the question of Eligibility, and determine for the time being his Right." ALS (telegram sent), *ibid.*; copies (2), *ibid.* On Jan. 13, Terry telegraphed to Sherman. "Your despatch received. Nearly all have taken the oath under your despatch. I am investigating their cases. Am I right?" Copies (3—one marked as received at 3:00 P.M.), *ibid.* On the same day, Terry twice telegraphed to USG. "The Governor's interference consists in adjourment of the House in order to hear from Washington relative to disqualified persons under Genl. Sherman's despatch. I have ordered an investigation as to eligibility. I think it would be unfortunate to countermand my action." "The trouble arises from the union of a few Republicans with the Democrats. Their pretext is that the Governor is dishonest and has stolen funds of the state. I believe the charges unfounded and I think they are governed by other motives." Copies (2 of the first), *ibid.* On Jan. 14, Sherman telegraphed to Terry. "I have shown the President your despatch of January 13, and he says you are acting all right." ALS (telegram sent), *ibid.*; copies (2), *ibid.* On the same day, Terry telegraphed to Sherman. "I send the following facts. One senator took the oath on Monday. He has applied to withdraw it saying that he took it under a misapprehension. He was a judge before the War and admits that he gave aid and comfort. He says that party pressure was too strong for him to resist. The Committee of the House at the first session report only three members disqualified but I have seen the applications recently made of sixteen (16) of them for relief from disability theirus admitting their ineligibility. The fight is being made by Republicans who at the former session united with Democrats to elect senators. They wish to prevent a new election and now join with the democrats in the effort to control the organization of the House so that ineligible members may not be unseated. I think the fairest way for all parties is to determine before the organization who are entitled to sit and let them organize. My action is not to favor either side in their contests but only to prevent disqualified persons from getting into the Legislature. I understand it to be decided that I have the authority to do this under the Reconstruction Acts and if so I think my duty to exercise it. Please show this to the President as being partly in answer to his despatch." Copies (2), *ibid.*

On Jan. 20, Nedom L. Angier, Ga. treasurer, Washington, D. C., wrote to USG. "Knowing your great desire and determination to have the laws fully executed, and having full confidence that you will allow no infraction of the Laws where it is in your power to prevent, I most respectfully ask to be allowed to make some quotations and deductions therefrom for your consideration. Section 2 of 'an Act to promote the reconstruction of the State of Georgia.' *requires each and every member to take the oath or oaths required by the Constitution of Georgia.* Article 3. Section 4. Paragraph 10. of the Constitution of Georgia requires evry Senator or Representative, before taking his seat to take an oath to support the Constitution of the United States and of the State of Georgia. Article 4 Section 1 Paragraph 1. The Executive power shall be vested in a Governor who shall hold his office during the term of four years. Article 4 Section 2 Paregraph. 8. There shall be a Secretary of State, a Comptroller General, a Treasurer and a Surveyor General, elected by the General Assembly and they *shall hold their offices for the like period as the Governor.* These last having been elected before the colored members were expelled and without the votes of the three members, who were, by the Committee, reported inelligible, are by the Constitution of Georgia, *which each member swears to support, entitled to hold their offices four years* 'or a like ~~time~~ period *as the Governor.*' And I earnestly and most respectfully call upon you Mr. President, in full confidence, that you will see that neither Governor Bullock or the General Assembly of Georgia is allowed to violate these provisions of the Constitution, and the Act to promote the reconstruction of the State of Georgia. Section 4 of Said last named Act, authorizes each House after they have qualified, to reorganize said Senate and House of Representatives, respectively, by the election and qualification of the proper officers of each House.' But the Act gives them no power to go any further back, and I again look to you Mr President in the same spirit and confidence to confirm all concerned, strictly to the provisions of the Act, that the past acts and legislation may Stand, and save Georgia from being thrown into a wild state of excitement and trouble. The State, in her legislation since the New Constitution was adopted and approved, has endorsed some Railroad bonds, and pledged her endorsement to others, which have gone forward and spent large amounts of money to develope the State and add to her wealth and prosperity by reason of those pledges. Besides these, she has committed herself in various other ways, and by a vast number of acts, now having the force of Salutary Law, and no one can tell the amount of injury that might accrue by going beyond the provisions of the Bill, and tearing evry thing up or tearing evrything loose. It is absolutely necessary to hold what wholesome restraints we have, and go forward and make all the improvement we can. To you we look mMost Worthy President, in the fullest confidence to curb any reckless disregard of law—to steady the restless passions and evil propensities that foment discord and mischief; and to give peace and prosperity to all portions of our beloved Country. . . . Jany 21. Failing in my efforts for an interview with you yesterday, I beg to be allowed to present other matter for your consideration. The law requires the nett earnings of the Western and Atlantic Railroad, (which road belongs to the states,) to be paid into the State Treasury monthly. The payment for the month of September is the last that has been recieved up to my leaving on the 15th inst. Gov. Bullock is the chief officer of the road. Former Administrations paid into the State Treasury, of nett earnings of said road, from 30. to 50 Thousand Dollars monthly. Certain amounts are known to have been paid, or loaned to individuals in no way connected with the road, in palpable violation of law, supposed to be for, or in the interest of, the Governor to secure influence. Democrats, or rather I should say '*Bullock democrats*,' who sustain him but abuse you and your policy were the sharers. Propositions, are said to have been made to some members, who have taken the oath, to have them pardoned if they will withdraw it and join the extreme, plundering wing. The Governor and his adherents claim that the General Assembly, when organized, can oust all the State House Officers before their term expires; not by impeachment, but by having a new election. The same is claimed in relation to Judges, in fact of evry thing that has been done. Hence his great anxiety, & determination law or no law, to have a majority in each House. Should he get a majority our only hope is you our most Worthy President, and we look to you with full confidence, knowing as we do your regard and reverance for the Law, to give such instructions as shall thwart this wicked, lawless, and to the people of Georgia, injurious, destructive scheme. In your arm is power, and the more you exercise that power for good, the more will you be loved. The honest moderate republicans and honest moderate democrats would coalesce if allowed to organize and defeat the Governors plans for corruption and plunder, and unmask his frauds in the use of the State's funds. So far as I am concerned I can take the Test, or what is sometimes called the 'Iron Clad Oath,' and I have ever given you my willing, earnest, hearty support. And sustained all the Congressional plans of reconstruction but I will not compound with fraud for the sake of Governor Bullock's influence or friendship. Pardon me for trespassing so much upon your time and believe me your sincere friend, . . ." ALS, USG 3.

On Jan. 22, Sherman telegraphed to Terry. "Capt. Telford arrived last night, and I sent all your papers through the President to the Attorney General. I have just come from a Consultation with the President, Secretary of War and Attorney General, who has examined all the papers; and has given his opinion in writing a copy of which I send you by the Wires, and another by Mail. I advise you to let the Legislature organise on Monday, decide all questions as they arise, and dont depend on us here to determine absolutely the questions of doubt, for the Attorney General thinks you are the only power other than that reserved to itself by Congress." ALS (telegram sent), DNA, RG 94, Letters Received, 1155S 1869. On the same day, Attorney Gen. Ebenezer R. Hoar had written an opinion. "It seems to me that the military commander in Georgia is to exercise his own best judgment upon all the questions arising in relation to the organization of the legislature of Georgia; and is not subject to the direction of any other officer. The questions are very difficult, and some of them hardly admit of a solution that can be pronounced certainly correct—I can only say that I have not been able to conclude that any other course is more probably the right one than that which Gen. Terry indicates as the tendency of his own opinion. I think that the admission of a person receiving the next highest number of votes to a seat on the ground that the person receiving the highest number is ineligible, should only apply to cases where the latter was absolutely and clearly ineligible at the time of the election, so that the voter is presumed to have intended to throw away or trifle with his vote—as if, for example, he had voted for a woman when only men were competent, to hold the offices,—but has no application to the case where the person receiving the highest number of votes fails to qualify after the election, as by refusing or neglecting to take a required official oath—or where his disabilities might be removed by Congress—The voter may vote for a man who *may* be qualified, without subjecting himself to the consequence of having his vote disregarded. But on this point, as on others, Gen. Terry is required to exercise his own judgment—" ADS, *ibid.* See *SED,* 41-2-31; Hamilton Fish diary, Jan. 21, DLC-Hamilton Fish.

On Jan. 31, Terry twice telegraphed to Sherman. "I am doing my best to prevent any changes in senators or other officers formerly elected. Bullock does not wish to be elected senator and I doubt whether Blodgett does. But Bullock holds that the former elections were illegal because the Legislature was illegally organized at the outset b̶y̶ by the admission of persons who are now shown to have been ineligible and in this I think he is right. If it is the wish of the President that matters should stand as they are Bullock will consent to a new election or reappointment of all those elected before. He wishes to understand clearly what are the views of the administration and to those he will conform. Perhaps the President may see fit to express his views by a telegram" "Since sending my despatch of this afternoon I have thought that it would be very desirable that I should go to Washington for the purpose of saying to you things that I can hardly say either by telegram or letter—After a free conference with you and obtaining in full your views and those of the administration I think that I can shape things here as you desire. Please answer before noon to-day." Copies (2), DNA, RG 94, Letters Received, 1155S 1869. On Feb. 1, USG endorsed this telegram. "Direct Gn. Terry to come to Washington." AES, *ibid.* On the same day, USG endorsed the earlier telegram. "If Gn. Terry comes to Washingto[n] it will not be necessary to give any answer to this despatch by telegraph." AES, *ibid.*

On Feb. 9, A. Alpeora Bradley, Ga. senator, *et al.* telegraphed to USG. "Please answer quickly Yes or no Should we vote for Senators before repealing the black Code of Georgia." Telegram received (at 11:00 A.M.), *ibid.*, RG 107, Telegrams Collected (Bound). On the same day, Horace Porter telegraphed to

Bradley. "President has received your dispatch—He cannot advise you. Prefers that you use your own discretion" Copy, DLC-USG, II, 1.

To Senate

———

To the Senate of the United States:

The papers in the case of Commander Jonathan Young, of the U. S. Navy, show:

That when the Naval promotions were made in [1866], the name of Commander Jonathan Young was not included among them, and he was passed over while Commander George W. Young was not passed over. That among other testimonials, is one from Vice Admiral D. D. Porter, stating, "that Commander Jonathan Young was passed over by mistake, that he was recommended for promotion, while Commander George W. Young was not recommended for promotion, and by some singular mistake, the latter was promoted, while the former was passed over".

That eminent Officers, formerly *junior* to Commander Young, but promoted over his head, desire his restoration to his former position, because they consider such restoration due to his character, ability and services.

In view therefore of these facts and of the general good standing of Commander Jonathan Young and of his gallant and efficient services during the war, and to remedy, so far as is now possible, what is believed to have been a clerical error of the Department, which has worked to his injury, the Department now recommends that he be restored to his original standing upon the Navy. list:

For these reasons, I nominate, Commander Jonathan Young, to be restored to his original position, to take rank from the 25th July 1866 and next after Commander Wm T. Truxtun.

U. S. GRANT

WASHINGTON CITY
11TH FEBRUARY 1870.

DS, DNA, RG 46, Executive Nominations. On Feb. 11, 1870, Secretary of the Navy George M. Robeson wrote to USG. "I have the honor to submit, herewith, a nomination of Commander Jonathan Young, for restoration to his original position in the Navy, for the reasons set forth in the Nomination." Copy, DNA, RG 45, Letters Sent to the President. Jonathan Young was confirmed as commander on March 25 to rank from July 25, 1866.

To Edward Cromwell

———

Washington D. C. Feb 16. 1870

EDWARD CROMWELL, (ESQ) CHAIRMAN &c.
NEW YORK CITY, N. Y.
SIR:

I am in receipt of your letter of Feb 11th. announcing the calling of a meeting to urge state legislation for a *home* for the maimed and disabled veterans who defended our country in her hour of need. I regret that my duties will not permit my accepting the invitation to be present on the occasion

The object is one that appeals to the heart of every one who sympathised and acted in the preservation of our great republic.— I hope your meeting will be very successful and that not only will N. Y. provide for her heroes, but that each state, that has not already done so, will give the just aid to the band of deserving men, and also provide for the orphans of those who gave their lives to preserve the life of their government.

Yours truly
U. S. GRANT

Copy, DLC-USG, II, 1. Edward Cromwell, prominent New York City produce merchant, solicited this letter, read to a large audience at Cooper Institute, later addressed by Gen. William T. Sherman. *New York Times*, Feb. 22, 1870. See *ibid.*, Feb. 1, 1908.

To Elihu B. Washburne

Washington. D. C. Feb.y 17th *18670*

HON. E. B. WASHBURNE. MINISTER &c.
PARIS, FRANCE;
DEAR SIR:

This will introduce to you Mrs. B. Holliday, the wife of an *old friend* of *mine*, who is about visiting Europe on a tour of pleasure. Any attention shown Mrs. H. will be duly appreciated by her and myself.

Yours Truly
U. S. GRANT

ALS, IHi. Notley Ann Calvert, born in 1824 in Ky. and raised in Weston, Mo., married Ben Holladay on Dec. 31, 1839. On Feb. 17, 1870, USG wrote a similar letter introducing Mrs. Holladay to John Lothrop Motley, U.S. minister, London. Copy, DLC-USG, II, 1.

In an undated letter, probably written in April, 1869, USG wrote to Elihu B. Washburne introducing "Mrs. Caroline E. Benton of Phil., who goes to France with her family on the same vessel as yourself. You will find them very pleasant people indeed. Wishing you a very pleasant voyage, . . ." LS, IHi. On May 15, USG wrote a letter of introduction for Mrs. James W. Paul, Philadelphia. Copies, DLC-USG, II, 1, 4. On Sept. 24, USG wrote to "Ministers, Consuls and Diplomatic Agents representing the United States in foreign Countries." "This letter will introduce to you the bearer Mr. G. W Fishback of St Louis, one of the Editors and proprietors of the Missouri Democrat,' and one of our most influential citizens, who is about to travel abroad for pleasure. Mr. Fishback has been an intimate personal friend of mine for many years and I take great pleasure in commending him to you, and bespeaking for him such attentions as it may be in your power to extend to him during his sojourn in your vicinity.—" Copies, *ibid.*

On Feb. 7, 1870, USG wrote a letter of introduction for "J. M. Richards, Prest. of the Chicago, Ill. Board of Trade, . . ." Copies, *ibid.*, II, 1; DLC-Caleb Cushing. On May 18, USG wrote identical letters to Washburne and J. Russell Jones, U.S. minister, Brussels. "Allow me to introduce to you Miss Fannie E. Dunn, daughter of Gen. W. McK. Dunn, U. S. A. Miss. Dunn is traveling in Europe with Judge Erskine of Ga. who can give you an interesting account of matters in the Southern States. Any attention you may be pleased to extend to the party will be fully appreciated by them . . ." Copy, DLC-USG, II, 1. On May 19, USG wrote to Washburne. "I take pleasure in introducing to you Gen. Robt. B. Potter of Philadelphia, who with his family visits Europe on a tour of business and pleasure. I need not tell you of his distinguished services during the war for you will remember him at Petersburg during the last campaign against the rebels. I bespeak for them any attention you may be able to bestow, all of which will be duly appreciated. With kind regards for Mrs W. and yourself . . ." Copy, *ibid.* On May 19 and 20, USG wrote similar letters to Jones and Motley. Copies, *ibid.* On June 4, USG wrote to George P. Marsh, U.S. minister, Florence, introducing Miss Constance Kinney, Washington, D. C. Copy, *ibid.* On June 13, USG wrote to Anton C. Hesing, *Illinois Staats Zeitung*, Chicago. "Your friend Mr Judd Representative from the 1st Cong. Dist. of Illinois informs me that you are about to visit your native land,—Germany. Your position and services in the cause of freedom and the respect I have for you prompts me to commend you to the consideration of our Diplomatic and consular Representatives abroad. Wishing you a pleasant voyage and a safe return to this the country of your adoption . . ." Copy, *ibid.*

On June 22, USG wrote to Washburne introducing "Mr. John C. Benton, son of my friend M. M. Benton of Covington, Ky. He goes to Paris to pursue the study of law and the languages, and I bespeak for him during his sojourn in your city such courtesies as it may be in your power to extend." Copy, *ibid.* USG wrote introducing Stephen S. L'Hommedieu, Cincinnati, on June 27 (copy, *ibid.*); James F. D. Lanier, New York City, on June 30 (LS, IHi). On July 14, USG wrote a letter of introduction. ". . . Dr. F. S. deHaas, of the M. E. Church, formerly of this city but now of Cincinnati, Ohio. The Dr. is an acquaintance of mine, for whom I can vouch. Any attention which he may receive will be duly appreciated by him and me" Doris Harris Catalogue 1, [1966], no. 37. USG wrote introducing S. Norment, Washington, D. C., on June 6 (copy, DLC-USG, II, 1); Daniel Butterfield, on July 18 (copy, *ibid.*). On July 22, USG, Long Branch, wrote a note. "This will introduce my young friend Willie Hillyer of New York City to representatives of this Gov't abroad Attentions shown him will be duly appreciated by myself as well as the recipient of them Master Hillyer though young visits Europe for the first time, alone and may be much benefitted by kindness from his seniors in years, as well as in experience abroad" Copy, Hillyer Papers, ViU. On Dec. 12, 1871, USG wrote identical letters to Washburne and Jones introducing "Mrs: M McCook, Baldwin, Sister of Genl: A. M. D McCook—. . ." Copy, DLC-USG, II, 1.

On April 12, 1873, USG wrote to Washburne. "Madam Hardy and Madam Hoy, citizens of the United States, and Sisters of the Sacred Heart, are now in Paris. Should any occasion arise where they may require it, I have to request that you will be kind enough to extend to them such aid and assistance as may be in your power." Copy, *ibid.*, II, 2. On May 5, USG, Chicago, wrote to Washburne. "The bearer of this, Mrs Hewitt (with her daughter) visits Europe on a tour of pleasure. Mrs Hewitt is an old friend of Mrs Grant and mine, I bespeak for her and, her daughter, such courtesies as you can and do bestow upon such worthy American citizens With kind regards to your family" LS, IHi. USG, Long Branch, wrote to Washburne introducing William B. Dinsmore, New York City, on July 20 (LS, *ibid.*); Orestes Cleveland, Jr., on Feb. 13, 1874 (copy, DLC-USG, II, 2); Dr. George H. Mitchell, New York City, on July 2 (LS, IHi).

On July 7, 1876, USG wrote to Washburne introducing "Mrs. Ames of St. Louis, who purposes passing several years in Europe. I take pleasure in introducing her to you as a friend of my family and a lady of refinement as well as worth. . . ." LS, *ibid.* On the same day, USG wrote an identical letter to Edwards Pierrepont, U.S. minister, London. Copy, DLC-USG, II, 3.

To John Bigelow

———

Washington, D C. Feb.y 19th *18670*

DEAR SIR:

Your letter of the 15th inst. is received, and I very much regret the interpretation it gives of the letter to which it is a reply. I have probably five hundred applications for ten cadet appointments at my disposal. These appointments are made, by law, One year before the admission of the appointee. When personal application is made I uniformly make to the applicant, verbally, the reply which I made you in writing. In all other cases the applications and recommendations are filed with the Inspector General of the Military Academy and no response is made. In your case however, knowing you personally as well as by reputation both as representative of this Government abroad and as a distinguished writer at home, I thought it due to you to answer your application for a Cadetship for your son, both to relieve any suspense you might be in and to enable you to make application to the Member of Congress representing your district should you desire to do so.

I assure you no reflection was intended, but quite the reverse.

I am, with great respect,
your obt. svt.
U. S. GRANT

HON. JOHN BIGELOW
HIGHLAND FALLS, N. Y.

ALS (facsimile), John Bigelow, *Retrospections of an Active Life* (Garden City, N. Y., 1913), IV, 346–47. On Feb. 7, 1870, USG had written to John Bigelow. "Your letter forwarding an application of your son for an appointment at large as cadet at West Point reached me in due time. In reply I have to say that while it would afford me pleasure to appoint your son, yet I feel it my duty to give these appointments to the sons of officers of the Army and Navy, (these branches of the government having no representation in Congress)—or the sons of volunteers who fell during the rebellion, or rendered eminent service during the same trying period. The number of applicants from the above enumerated classes exceed by a great many the number of appointments within my gift." Copy, DLC-USG, II, 1. On Feb. 15, Bigelow wrote to USG. "I have your favor of the 7th inst. in reply to my son's application for a cadet's commission at West Point, in which you inform me that you feel it your duty 'to give these appointments to the sons of officers of the army and navy (those branches of the government having no representation in Congress), or to the sons of volunteers who fell during the Rebellion or rendered eminent service during the same trying period.' Had my son's application been simply denied, I should have had no farther occasion to trouble you with the subject, Mr. President. I should have been constrained to presume that the commissions in question were reserved for more meritorious candidates or such as you so esteemed. You have, however, been pleased to assign reasons for your decisions which I could hardly be expected to pass in silence. In the first place, you justify the new distinction you have made between the civil and military elements of our society upon the ground that the army and navy have no representation in Congress. During the Rebellion, unless I have read its history incorrectly, the army and such officers of the navy as were in American ports were allowed all the privileges of suffrage enjoyed by the rest of the community. On the other hand, during that whole period I was on foreign service, and in that respect at least within the category of unrepresented public servants for whom you inform me that the West Point commissions are to be henceforth specially reserved. It is true I have my vote now, but so have most of those who served in the Rebellion; for most of them, like myself, have quit the public service, and are in the enjoyment of all the privileges of citizenship. As a farther reason for refusing my son's application, Mr. President, you state that you felt it your duty to bestow your West Point patronage upon the sons of volunteers (among others) 'who had fallen in the Rebellion, or who had rendered eminent service during the same trying period.' I cannot suppose, Sir, that you would take advantage of such an occasion, or indeed of any, to treat me with deliberate disrespect. I infer, therefore, that you were not aware, or have forgotten, that during the entire War I held commissions from the State Department which required me to reside in France. Of my services, first as Consul and afterwards as Minister Plenipotentiary for a period of nearly six years, I do not pretend to fix the value; but your note of the 7th inst. makes it proper for me to state that my official conduct from first to last received the unqualified and repeated approval of the government I represented; and I have yet to learn that the final and happy disposition of the momentous questions with which I was charged and towards which I must be presumed to have contributed according to my opportunities, gave anything less than complete satisfaction to the country at large. I shall not claim that any services it was my fortune to render my country, whether as consul or minister or in any other capacity, were 'eminent'; but I do feel at liberty to question the propriety of excluding my son from the Military Academy at West Point upon the ground that the services his father rendered during the Rebellion were too inconsiderable to entitle him to be considered by you, even as a candidate for its privileges. I united in my son's application very reluctantly, Mr. President, and only to satisfy him that I was willing to make what would seem to him a trifling sacrifice to gratify his ambition. You have denied it for reasons which reflect upon my character as a public servant. I am unwilling to attribute to you any such purpose; but whether you did or did not entertain it, it was equally impossible for me to permit such a reflection to pass unchallenged." Bigelow, IV, 344–46.

On Jan. 28, Bigelow had written to USG. "My Eldest Son is extremely anxious to enter the Military Academy at Westpoint. Col. Michie with whom he is studying at presant encourages me to believe that he would sustain himself there creditably I enclose his application together with a letter which Colonel Michie unsolicited, very kindly offered him. If it should prove agreable to you to comply with my sons wishes, I feel confident that he will in no Sense discredit your choice, and that no one would more gratefully appreciate the distinction than he. Permit me to add that I should regard his appointment as a personal kindness to which I could never become insensible. My Son makes his application thus early because the time is at hand when he will have to Shape his Studies with Special reference to the Career he is to follow." LS, DNA, RG 94, Correspondence, USMA. On the same day, John Bigelow, Jr., wrote to USG. "I venture to hope that I may be considered among the candidates for an appointment at large to the United States Military Academy at Westpoint for the year 1871. It would be particularly gratifying to me to receive such a commission at the hands of Your Excellency. I will be 17 years and one month old on the 12th day of June 1871. I have the honor to enclose to you a letter from Colonel Peter S. Michie who is attached to one of the departments of instruction at the Academy and under whose direction I am now pursuing my mathematical studies, from which Your Excellency can judge of the probabilities of my being able to maintain a creditable rank in the Academy. I will only add to his statement that the course of studies at Westpoint is very much to my taste. I sincerely hope it will suit Your Excellency's convenience to entertain this application favorably." ALS, *ibid.* The enclosure is *ibid.* Young Bigelow later received a congressional appointment to USMA, graduating in 1877.

To Ambrose E. Burnside

Washington, D. C. Feb.y 24th 1867 0.

DEAR BURNSIDE;

I understand strenuous efforts are being made in your state to defeat the re-election of Senator Anthony? I hope this may not be so but fear otherwise. Senator Anthony is a gentleman of ability, refinement and character to do honor to his station, and to be the pride of his state. If I knew any thing that I could do to help him I would freely do it. I have not seen the Senator recently, and never spoke to him on this subject, but will try to see him now and ask him if there is any thing for me to do in his behalf.

I write this to you believing you to be a friend of Senator Anthony, and that you have influence to help him. I do not write however for publication but to let you know my feelings in the matter, and to let you use my name, in conversation, in his behalf when you think it can be of any service.

My kindest regards to Mrs Burnside and yourself.

Yours Truly

U. S. GRANT

ALS, New York State Library, Albany, N. Y.

On Feb. 24, 1870, Frederick Lively and Peter Fogg, Boston, telegraphed to USG. "Ask Senator Anthony for My Boston letter sent this week." Telegram received (at 5:00 P.M.), DNA, RG 107, Telegrams Collected (Bound).

To House of Representatives

TO THE HOUSE OF REPRESENTATIVES:

In answer to the resolution of the House of Representatives of the 15th instant, I transmit a report from the Secretary of State upon the subject, and the papers by which it was accompanied.

U. S. GRANT

WASHINGTON,
FEBRUARY, 28TH 1870.

Copies, DNA, RG 59, General Records; *ibid.*, RG 130, Messages to Congress. On Feb. 28, 1870, Secretary of State Hamilton Fish had written to USG transmitting documents concerning the treatment of American citizens (Fenians) imprisoned in Great Britain. Copy, *ibid.*, RG 59, General Records. See *HED*, 41-2-170. On June 20, July 9, 30, 1869, John Savage, Paris, had written to USG concerning this matter. ALS, DNA, RG 59, Miscellaneous Letters. An extract of the first letter is in *HED*, 41-2-170, pp. 38–39. On Feb. 6, 1870, Savage, Fordham, N. Y., wrote to USG. "I had the honor of addressing three letters to you from Paris last Summer, communicating facts developing unparalleled horrors in the treatment of Americans—native and adopted—in British dungeons; and imploring your humane intervention, if not official protest, in behalf of those gallant spirits who had so well served the Cause of Freedom and Justice in the armies of the Union I will not dwell here on the high sense of duty which inspired me to convey to your Excellency those harrowing facts, or enlarge on the belief that the opportunity for such intervention was peculiarly inviting. As the matter is before Congress I will simply proceed to lay before you additional evidence of a most touching nature calculated to show that the result feared—and to prevent which was my hope and desire in writing—has at least in one case been reached; that insanity and probably death has come upon a gallant American citizen-soldier for want of the proper intermediation of the government he helped to preserve; while several others are on the direct path to a similar destiny from the same cause. In my former letters I referred to Captain Underwood OConnell and young McClure who served so well in the Cavalry during the War. The treatment of the former has not been amended; and the systematic inhumanity pursued towards him is rapidly reducing him to idiotcy. . . . Colonel Wm G. Halpin who before the late war was well-known as an Engineer and Surveyor of talent—in connection I think with the City government of Cincinnati; and during the war greatly distinguished himself as an officer of the 10th Ohio regiment—is the only one of the prisoners whose tolerably good health offers any exception to the rule of wretchedness superinduced by ill-treatment. This is attributed to his steady refusal to take any medicine from the prison officials, in view of the terrible effects of the same on his comrades. More than three months ago Colonel Halpin wrote a letter to the Secretary of State of his government at Washington. It was suppressed. More recently, previous to January 1st he wrote a full statement to the same official. It was laid before the Home Secretary of Great Britain Mr Bruce; and is in all probability still before him, as 'They seem determined not to allow him (Colonel Halpin) to communicate with the American Government, seeing from his letters that he establishes his innocence of the violation of any British law.' Halpin also filed four charges against the governor and doctor. Of course never heard from. The case of Colonel (Captain) Rickard Burke (also a brave Union soldier) suggests the pertinacious application of revolting means to a fearful end. Mr. Downing a Member of Parliament who seemed to give a deaf ear to the general outcry against the usage of the State prisoners, specially singled out the case of Rickard Burke for protest in the House of Commons. He said the prisoner was subjected to a species of diet which was in fact a process of 'slow starvation.' The *Irishman* newspaper says that Colonel Burke being an American Citizen, the American Minister interested himself in his behalf, but with what effect is seen in the fact that the unfortunate American victim of slow starvation has been driven mad, and secretly withdrawn from his Chatham jail to perish probably in a madhouse at Woking. . . ." ALS, DNA, RG 59, Miscellaneous Letters. Extracts printed in *HED*, 41-2-170. See *PUSG*, 18, 84. On Feb. 16, Savage wrote to USG. "A European mail arrived since I had the honor of addressing you has brought additional confirmation of the ill-treatment of American citizens in British prisons. By degrees—slow but sure—public opinion in England is compelled to admit the existence of such evils in the system applied to political prisoners in that country as might readily be deemed too un-Christian for belief. It is to be sincerely hoped that the United States government will take advantage of the opportunity thus being created to institute an investigation into the cases of those prisoners at least who like Col. Halpin claim to have broken no neutrality. law, or like Captain OConnell who was arrested before he had a chance to break any law. . . ." ALS, DNA, RG 59, Miscellaneous Letters.

On Feb. 23, Governor Lucius Fairchild of Wis. wrote to USG. "In compliance with the request therein contained, I have the hono[r] to forward to you a copy of a Joint Resolution of the Legislature of the State of Wisconsin approved February 17, 1870 entitled 'Joint Resolution relative to American Citizens confined in Foreign Prisons'" LS, *ibid*. The enclosure is *ibid*.

On April 12, 1869, Fish wrote to USG. "The Secretary of State, to whom was referred a paper entitled, 'Proceedings of certain citizens of Cincinnati,' bearing date the 22d of last month, relative to the case of William G. Halpine, and requesting that measures be adopted with a view to his release,' has the honor, pursuant to the President's order, to report: It appears from a despatch of the United States Consul at Dublin to this Department of the 15th of November 1867, that William G. Halpin was convicted of treason felony against the British Government and was sentenced to fifteen years penal servitude. In an instruction of the 16th of of July last, Mr Seward directed Mr Moran, then Chargé d'Affaires at London, to use his good offices towards obtaining the release of Colonel Halpin. Another instruction relative to the same case was addressed by Mr Seward to Mr Johnson, under date of the 23d of September last. Nothing else in regard to it appears to be on record or on file. Messrs Warren and Costello who are understood to have been convicted of the same offence as Colonel Halpin, were a short time since released, partly at least through the good offices of Mr Johnson. Unfortunately, however, they had scarcely been discharged when on certain occasions in Ireland they made speeches which were reported in the newspapers and which from expressions contained in them, gave great offence to the British public and, as appears by a despatch of Mr Johnson of the 24th ultimo, to the British Government itself. Mr Johnson consequently expresses a doubt whether any more discharges in such cases will be ordered, at least for some time. Another instruction in the case of Colonel Halpin will, however, be addressed to him." Copy, *ibid.*, General Records. The Cincinnati proceedings of March 22 are *ibid.*, Miscellaneous Letters.

In July, 1870, U.S. Representative John A. Bingham of Ohio *et al.* wrote to USG. "Late Lt. Col. Wm G. Halpin served for three years in the war for the Union. he is a citizen of the United States and of the State of Ohio. On the 4th day of July 1867 as he was returning from Liverpool England to America on the Steamer City of Paris with our flag at her bow, when off Queenstown Ireland the steamer was boarded by Brittish officers and he was arrested on suspicion of connection with the then recent insurrection in Ireland. . . . Waiving for the present all questions of American rights under the laws of nations we appeal to you, in the name of humanity, to extend your good offices to secure his release. Certainly the prompt, vigorous and successful action of our government in sheilding the Canada border should assure a most favorable hearing for any proposition you may deem proper in this case." DS (31 signatures), *ibid.* On Jan. 26, 1871, Jeremiah O'Donovan Rossa, New York City, wrote to USG. "I am one of the Irishmen banished from the British dominions, and having left after me in prison one in whom your government seemed to be interested I address you now on his behalf General William G. Halpin is the person. One of the Conditions of release presented to him for his acceptance was that he would not claim the exercise of any legal right in England or Ireland during the next twelve years. I heard him say that this clause was introduced for the purpose of preventing him from prosecuting the witnesses in his case who committed perjury. If any question arises between your government and the English regarding Mr Halpins detention in prison, I wish you to understand that he does not refuse 'to leave the Country' but he refuses to sign an acceptance of conditions which would preclude him from doing what he says he will do, if ever he leaves prison. As I am writing to you on my friends case, I will lay before you another matter which concerns myself. I was living in this Country some seven or eight years ago and wishing to become naturalized, I swore allegiance to the American government and renounced allegiance to others, a fact which the accompanying certificate will attest. In 1863 I entered into partnership in New York with one Denis ODonovan. This business partnership continued up to my arrest in Ireland in 1865, as may be seen by the record of importations in the Custom House books. I was in America in July 1865, but was made a prisoner in Ireland a few months after by the English, and have been in prison since. I have been at the naturalization office today to know, if under such circumstances, there would be any barrier to my citizenship. I am told there is, and that I can see Judge Brady tomorrow. I hope you will not consider me out of order in stating this matter, and seeking from the guardian of the ~~United States~~ Country his decision thereupon" ALS, *ibid*. Related papers are *ibid*.

On Jan. 30, 1872, USG wrote to the House of Representatives. "In answer to a Resolution of the House of Representatives of the 15th instant, calling for certain correspondence relating to the release of the Fenian prisoner Wm G. Halpine, I transmit herewith a report of the Secretary of State." Copy, *ibid*., Reports to the President and Congress; *ibid*., RG 130, Messages to Congress. On the same day, Fish had written to USG. "The Secretary of State to whom was referred the resolution of the House of Representatives, . . . respectfully reports that there is no unpublished correspondence between the British Government and our own relating to the release of the Fenian prisoner, Wm G. Halpine." Copy, *ibid*., RG 59, Reports to the President and Congress. See *HED*, 40-3-1, part 1, pp. 323–27, 341–42, 352–54; *ibid*., 42-2-114; *New York Times*, June 30, 1915; O'Donovan Rossa, *Irish Rebels in English Prisons: A Record of Prison Life* (New York, 1882), 300–16, 417–38.

To Senate

———

To THE SENATE OF THE UNITED STATES:

Herewith I have the honor to transmit a communication from the Secretary of the Interior relative to the obligation of Congress to make the necessary appropriations to carry out the Indian treaties made by, what is known as, the "Peace Commission" of 1867.

The history of those treaties, and the consequences of non-compliance with them by the Government, are so clearly set forth in this statement that I deem it better to communicate it, in full, than to ask the necessary appropriation in a shorter statement of the reasons for it. I earnestly desire that if an Indian war becomes inevitable the government of the United States at least should not be responsible for it.[1] Pains will be taken, and force used if necessary, to prevent the departure of the expeditions[2] referred to by the Secretary of the Interior.

U. S. GRANT

EXECUTIVE MANSION
MARCH 8 1870

DS, DNA, RG 46, Presidential Messages. The enclosure is *ibid*. See *SED*, 41-2-57; *HED*, 41-2-185. On March 17, 1870, "Iowa," McGregor, Iowa, wrote to USG. "Having observed in today's Papers a notice of a meeting between yourself and some members of the society of Friends (Quakes) it suggested a few thoughts whereby the difficulty might be removed which I have not seen in print, and may not have occurred to you and those having particular charge of this business. Some of our prominant millitray Officers have suggested extermination as the only cure for the evil, as it now exists, but this is inhuman and unchristian, 'tis true they are wild and Savage, and even treacherous, but we have done much to make them so. We have pushed them back from their own lands, have allowed them to be swindled by dishonest agents &c; this we all know, but now the cure. I would propose that the Government pass a Law that each County in the United States—have apportioned to them an equal number of the Indians—*in families as they exist*, which they shall provide for, or assist those who will try and do something to make a living—the children to be compelled to be sent to schools, and when of proper age to be apprenticed to some trade or profession, suitable to their talents or preferences, all this can be at but little cost to each county as there would be but few *for each* to care for about 10 to each co. and in but a few years, the old people will have passed away, and the children will have become civilized and useful citizens, by this arrangement the tribes will be broken up and divided, and no opportunity to form Bands for evil, in one half a century all traces of the Indian will be lost, our credit for humanity will be maintained, and will be a great Saving of Expense to the Government by doing away with armies to guard, and no appropriations or indemnties called for. These are crude suggestions but if they meet your approbations, can be put into proper form by those who understand these thing better than Your humble servant." AL, DNA, RG 75, Letters Received, Miscellaneous.

1. On Feb. 19, USG wrote to the Senate. "In reply to the Resolution of the Senate of the 11th instant, requesting 'any information which may have been received by the Government of the recently reported engagement of Col. Baker with the Indians, with copies of all orders which led to the same'; I transmit a Report from the Secretary of War, to whom the Resolution was referred." DS, *ibid*., RG 46, Presidential Messages. Related papers are *ibid*. See *SED*, 41-2-49. On March 7, Gen. William T. Sherman wrote to Lt. Gen. Philip H. Sheridan. "I enclose you a couple of slips from the Morning Chronicle of yesterday and to day, to show you that your communications have been given to the public, and what the first impressions are. The Peigans were attacked on the application of Gen. Sully, and the Interior Department, and that these should now be shocked at the result of their own requisitions, and endeavor to cast blame on you and Col Baker is unfair. Gen. Sully by communicating by telegraph for the use of

Mr. Colyer did an unofficerlike and wrong act, and this will in the end stand to his discredit. Gen. Schofield is now here, summoned before the Mil. Committee to give testimony about the sales of Cadets warrants during the time he was Secy. of War. He expects to get through to day or tomorrow, and will at once return to his Post at St. L[o]uis. I have just returned from the President, where I went with Gen. Schofield to pay his respects—and the President said he wanted to talk to me about increasing the military force in Utah, not so much on account of the Gentiles as of the recreant Mormons, who are appealing for protection in the event of their defection from Brigham Young. He wants a post established in Southern Utah, and some Cavalry also to be sent to the Territory. I suppose there would be no trouble in adding a couple companies of Infantry, and a Squadron of Cavalry to the troops now there. He also spoke of Pembina with reference to any complications likely to arise from the Revolution or insurrection of the Winnepeg Colony. I told him it would be a matter of cost to build a Post, say $50,000, for two companies at Pembina, and the breaking up probably of the Posts of Ripley and Abercrombie. He answered that the cost would be no objection. Before positive orders are issued I wish you would consult the Dept. Commanders, and let me know their views, as well as your own. The time is approaching for making the preliminary preparations, as I suppose all materials will have to be hauled from St Cloud." Copies, DNA, RG 94, Letters Received, I106 1869; *ibid.*, Letters Sent. On March 28, Sherman wrote to Sheridan. "Your despatches embracing Col Bakers report are received and have been shown to the Secretary of War & the President, and full copies filed with the Secretary of the Interior. You may assure Col Baker that no amount of Clamor has shaken our Confidence in him and his officers—and that if any responsible parties will father the Reports that have been so extensively published we will give him the benefit of an Official Investigation. An abstract will be given the Press—omitting the names of Sully & Pease." ALS, *ibid.*, RG 94, Letters Received, I106 1869.

2. On March 31, Secretary of the Interior Jacob D. Cox wrote to USG. "I have the honor to inform you, that a copy of the correspondence in relation to a contemplated 'Expedition to the Big Horn Mountain country,' to which your attention was invited by a letter from Governor Campbell of Wyoming territory, has been, this day, communicated to the Secretary of War for his information." LS, OFH. The letter of March 23 from Governor John A. Campbell of Wyoming Territory to USG is printed in *SED*, 41-2-89, pp. 5, 16. On May 23, USG wrote to the Senate. "In response to your resolution of the 12th: instant, requesting information 'in relation to an organized band of persons at Cheyenne in the Territory of Wyoming or vicinity, the number, and designs of such persons,' I transmit herewith the reports of the Secretary of War and Secretary of the Interior to whom the resolution was referred." DS, DNA, RG 46, Presidential Messages. The enclosures are *ibid.* Additional papers are *ibid.*, RG 94, Letters Received, 207A 1870. See *SED*, 41-2-89.

To Gen. William T. Sherman

Washington D. C. March 10th *1870*

DEAR GEN.

Enclosed I send you check for $154 81/100   The charge for laying water pipe should be paid by me. I think there must be yet one or two more instalment to pay. If you have the opportunity to find out, and will let me know, I will pay it all up at once. Perhaps I should not trouble you with this but find out for my self, which I will d[o] soon.

AL (signature clipped), DLC-William T. Sherman. See letter to Lt. Gen. William T. Sherman, Jan. 5, 1869.

To Senate

TO THE SENATE OF THE UNITED STATES:

I would respectfully call your attention to a treaty now before you for the acquisition of the Republic of St. Domingo,[1] entered into between the agents of the two governments on the 29th. of November, 1869., and by its terms to be finally acted upon by the people of St. Domingo and the Senate of the United States within four months from the date of signing the treaty. The time for action expires on the 29th. instant, a fact to which I desire expressly to call your attention. I would also direct your notice to the fact that the government of St. Domingo has no agent in the United States who is authorized to extend the time for further deliberation upon its merits.

The people of St. Domingo have already, so far as their action can go, ratified the treaty and I express the earnest wish that you will not permit it to expire by limitation. I also entertain the sincere hope that your action may be favorable to the ratification of the treaty.

U. S. GRANT

EXECUTIVE MANSION.
WASHINGTON, D. C.
MARCH 14. 1870.

DS, DNA, RG 46, Presidential Messages, Foreign Relations, Dominican Republic. On March 15, 1870, Secretary of State Hamilton Fish recorded in his diary. "The Prsdt mentioned having sent a message to the Senate yesterday on the subject of the San Domingo treaty—I had heard of it last Evng—from Sumner who said it excited a great deal of Comment—I remarked, pleasantly—Well Mr President, I suppose I am to regard the sending a Message on such a subject peculiarly belonging to my Department ~~as a~~ without notice to or consultation with me, as a want of confidence in my ~~Dept~~administration of the Dept—He seemed somewhat startled, & replied Oh no—I ought to have sent it through you, or to have consulted you—but the time for ratifying the Treaty was drawing to a close & the Committee in the Senate was keeping it back.' I thought that wrong, & sketched in pencil a message & told Genl Porter to send it to you. He said that was not necessary or usual, & without thought ~~he~~ I allowed it to be copied, & sent—He then Added but I ought to have sent it through your Department'—" DLC-Hamilton Fish. See *SED*, 41-3-17; letter to Hamilton Fish, March 22, 1870.

On March 31, Spofford, Tileston, and Co. telegraphed to USG. "Coen with full authority to extend time from S Domingo goes to Washington tonight c/o you d[i]r[e]ct Tybee detained until tomorrow answer immedy" Telegram received, DNA, RG 107, Telegrams Collected (Bound). See *SED*, 41-3-17, p. 97; Allan Nevins, *Hamilton Fish: The Inner History of the Grant Administration* (New York, 1936), pp. 255–56, 325. On April 5, USG submitted to the House of Representatives a report by Fish denying a request for information regarding the Santo Domingo treaty. Copies, DNA, RG 59, General Records; *ibid.*, RG 130, Messages to Congress. The enclosure is *ibid.* See *HED*, 41-2-237.

On March 25, USG wrote to the Senate. "In reply to a Senate resolution of the 24th inst. requesting to be furnished with a report, written by Captain Selfridge, upon the resources and condition of things in the Dominican Republic, I have to state that no such report has been received." DS, DNA, RG 46, Presidential Messages, Foreign Relations, Dominican Republic. On the same day, Admiral David D. Porter wrote to USG. "I have the honor to return herewith Senate Resolution dated the 24th instant, referred by you to this Department, and to transmit the accompanying copy of a report made by Lieut. Commander Thomas O. Selfridge on the 14th of July, 1869, upon the political condition of the Republic of Hayti, which is supposed to be the report referred to in the Resolution." Copy, *ibid.*, RG 45, Letters Sent to the President. See *What Finer Tradition: The Memoirs of Thomas O. Selfridge, Jr., Rear Admiral, U. S. N.* (Columbia, S. C., 1987), pp. 150–51. On June 17, USG wrote to the Senate. "In answer to the resolution of the Senate, of the 8th instant, requesting the President 'to communicate in confidence the instructions of the Navy Department to the Navy Officers in command on the coast of Dominica and Haiti, and the reports of such officers to the Navy Department from the commencement of the negotiation of the treaty with Dominica,'—I herewith transmit the papers received from the Secretary of the Navy, to whom the resolution was referred." DS, DNA, RG 46, Presidential Messages, Foreign Relations, Dominican Republic. The enclosures are *ibid.*

1. On Dec. 21, 1869, Fish recorded in his diary. "President tells me that Genl Babcock has returned—& has brought with him the Treaty for Annexation & also for the lease of Samana Bay. Babcock reads me the Annexation treaty—

He took possession of Samana hoisting the American flag & leaving two Enlisted men in charge—A war vessel to look in from time to time—a general feeling in favor of annexation—At Presidents request read the Annexation treaty to Cabinet—Secrecy with regard to it, enjoined until NewYear—The Samana Bay treaty may be referred to, & the public led to suppose that is the only treaty, until after the end of the year. this is on account of the agreement or contract of loan with Hartmont by the terms of which the money must all be paid to the Dominican Govt—before 6th January—Baez has promised Babcock, if it be not paid during the present year, not to receive it, & to declare the Contract void— Should the prospect of Annexation become known, they would send the money down at once—" DLC-Hamilton Fish. On Jan. 10, 1870, USG twice wrote to the Senate. "I transmit to the Senate for consideration with a view to its ratification, a Treaty for the annexation of the Dominican Republic to the United States, signed by the Plenipotentiaries of the parties on the 29th of November, last." "I transmit to the Senate for consideration with a view to its ratification, a Convention between the United States and the Dominican Republic for a lease to the former of the Bay and Peninsula of Samana." DS, DNA, RG 46, Presidential Messages, Foreign Relations, Dominican Republic. The enclosures are *ibid.* See *SED*, 41-3-17, pp. 98–102. On Jan. 15, Fish noted in his dairy. "President refers to the S. Domingo Annexation treaty, & remarks that it has not attracted as much attention or excitement as he had anticipated—The sentimen[t] in its favor is not as strong as he expected—" DLC-Hamilton Fish.

To Hamilton Fish

Washington D. C. March 22d *1870*

HON. H. FISH:
SEC. OF STATE,
DEAR SIR:

I forgot to mention in Cabinet a matter which I intendd to say to you to-day. A few days since you mentioned a project proposed by Senator Sumner in regard to the St. Domingo treaty. The proposition was to have the treaty recommitted to the Committee on Foreign Relations, and ask for extension of time &c.— What I wanted to say was that we decline saying to Mr. Sumner anything whatever as to what the Administration is willing to do, or would like to have done, in regard to the management of that treaty. He is an enemy of the treaty; will kill it to-morrow if he can, and only favors delay probably to better secure its defeat. I do not think it good policy to trust the enemies of a measure to manage it

for, (and to speak in behalf of), its friends. There are several devoted friends of the treaty who will manage it in the Senate if no
one is authorized to speak for the Administration.

I wanted to say this for fear you might admit to Mr. Sumner
that his proposition was a good one, ~~which~~ and that, if you should
do so, he would be very likely to use ~~int~~ in support of delay.

Yours Truly
U. S. GRANT

ALS, DLC-Hamilton Fish. On March 30, 1870, Secretary of State Hamilton Fish
recorded in his diary that USG "requests me not to communicate to Sumner any
confidential, or important information received at the Dept—that he is 'probably
without knowing it, unfair & not accurate' in his representation of what he
receives from the Dept—that he has represented me as opposed to the San
Domingo treaty, & otherwise misrepresented the Administration, & its views—"
Ibid.

Special Message

———

To *the Senate and House* of *Representatives*:

In the Executive Message of December 6th 1869, to Congress,
the importance of taking steps to revive our drooping Merchant
Marine was urged, and a special message promised at a future day,
during the present session, recommending more specifically plans
to accomplish this result. Now that the committee of the House of
Representatives intrusted with the labor of ascertaining "the cause
of the decline of American commerce" has completed its work and
submitted its report to the Legislative branch of the government,
I deem this a fitting time to execute that promise.

The very able, calm and exhaustive report of the committee
points out the grave wrongs which have produced the decline in
our commerce. It is a national humiliation that we are now compelled to pay, from twenty to thirty millions of dollars annually,
(exclusive of passage monay which we should share with vessels of
other nations) to foreigners for doing the work which should be
done by American vessels, American built, American owned and

American manned. This is a direct drain upon the resources of the country of just so much money, equal to casting it into the sea, so far as this nation is concerned.

A nation of the vast and ever increasing interior resources of the United States, extending as it does from one to the other of the great oceans of the world; with an industrious, intelligent, energetic population, must, one day, possess its full share of the commerce of these oceans, no matter what the cost. Delay will only increase this cost and enhance the difficulty of attaining the result. I therefore put in an earnest plea for early action in this matter, in a way to secure the desired increase of American commerce. The advanced period of the year, and the fact that no contracts for ship building will probably be entered into until this question is settled by Congress, and the further fact that, if there should be much delay, all large vessels contracted for this year will fail of completion before winter sets in, and will therefore be carried over for another year; induces me to request your early consideration of this subject. I regard it of such grave importance, effecting every interest of the country to so great an extent, that any method which will gain the end will secure a rich national blessing. Building ships and navigating them, utilizes vast capital at home; it employs thousands of workmen in their construction and manning; it creates a home market for the products of the farm and the shop; it diminishes the balance of trade against us precisely to the extent of freights and passage money paid to American vessels, and gives us a supremacy upon the seas of inestimable value in case of foreign war. Our Navy at the commencement of the late war consisted of less than 100 vessels of about 150.000 tons and a force of about 8000 men.

We drew from the merchant marine—which had cost the Government nothing, but which had been a source of national wealth—600 vessels, exceeding one million tons, and about 70.000 men to aid in the suppression of the rebellion. This statement demonstrates the value of the merchant marine, as a means of national defence, in time of need. The committee on the causes of the reduction of American tonnage after tracing the causes of its decline,

submit two bills which, if adopted, they believe will restore to the
nation its Maritime power. Their report shows with great minute-
ness the actual and comparative American tonnage at the time of
its greatest prosperity; the actual and comparative decline since,
together with the causes, and exhibits all other statistics of material
interest in reference to the subject. As the report is before Congress
I will not recapitulate any of its statistics, but refer only to the
methods recommended by the Committee, to give back to us our
lost commerce.

As a general rule, when it can be adopted, I believe a direct
money subsidy is less liable to abuse than an indirect aid given to
the same enterprise. In this case however my opinion is that, subsidies while they may be given to specified lines of steamers, or
other vessels, should not be exclusively adopted, but, in addition to
subsidizing very desirable lines of ocean traffic, a general assistance
should be given, in an effective way. I therefore commend to your
favorable consideration the two bills proposed by the Committee
and referred to in this message.

U. S. GRANT

EXECUTIVE MANSION
MARCH 23D 1870

DS, DNA, RG 46, Annual Messages. Printed in *SED*, 41-2-70.

Speech

[*March 25, 1870*][1]

DOCTOR FLORES: I congratulate myself that it has devolved
upon me to welcome you again as the diplomatic representative of
Ecuador in the United States. The comprehensive way in which
you speak of our country shows that you were an intelligent observer when you were first here, and that you continue to take so
kind an interest in our career, that your abode with us cannot fail
to be acceptable.

The special occasion upon which you come is to us somewhat

novel. The cause of peace and good will, however, between kindred nations is one which must always be dear to us as their common friend, and we will endeavor, impartially to discharge the trust which has been conferred upon us with reference to that high object. The enlightened course which you have heretofore pursued in regard to it affords an earnest that your future endeavors in that direction will be guided by the same intelligence and zeal, and affords grounds, also, for confidence that they may be crowned with success.

Washington Chronicle, March 26, 1870. USG spoke in response to remarks by Dr. Antonio Flores, minister from Ecuador. "MR. PRESIDENT: I am once more accredited, after a lapse of nearly ten years, to the first republic, to this great nation, from which the world receives not only wheat, cotton, and gold, but what is still more valuable, the rare example of liberty without anarchy, and of order without despotism. . . ." *Ibid*.

1. On March 23, 1870, Secretary of State Hamilton Fish had written to USG. "Doctor Antonio Flores, the new Minister from Ecuador, was here to day and informally asked for the appointment of a time to present his credentials to you. I said in reply that you would probably receive him a little before twelve o'clock on Friday next, the 25th instant. If, therefore, it should not be inconvenient to you, he will then accompany me to the Executive Mansion." LS, OFH.

To William Elrod

Washington, D, C,
March 27th/70

DEAR ELROD:

As it is now getting to be about time to commence Spring work I will state a few things I want done on the farm. I want you to continue getting out grapes until as much of the field in front of the house as is suited to that purpose is filled up. I would not put out many this year, and would be careful that all that you do set out are well done. I would not rent a foot of land nor permit a tenant on the place except it be some one who you want to hire to work. The place bought from Mrs. Orr[1] I would keep to be occupied by an experienced grape grower when the yeald is sufficient to warrant hiring such a man.

The house on the southside of the creek, on the Orr land, I would pull down and throw all the land on that side of the creek into one pasture.—All male calves hereafter I would sell for veal and put the money, if you can spare it, into cows or young heiffers.— I presume, from not hearing on the subject, that you will have a fruit crop this year? If so would it not be profitable to sell to Hucksters and let them take ~~them~~ it away, or you deliver in bulk?

When you write give me an account of stock. The horse I am raising for the farm is but two years old and I expect to keep him here for the balance of my term of office. I have the promise of a very fine one in Wisconsin however which I may be able to send earlyer.

Yours Truly
U. S. GRANT

ALS, LeRoy H. Fischer, Stillwater, Okla.

1. Ann Jane Orr. On April 5, 1869, Charles W. Ford, St. Louis, had telegraphed to USG. "Shall I advance Elrod two thousand 2000 dollars to pay for the widows Orrs place—eight acres   Answer"   Telegram received (at 1:50 P.M.), DNA, RG 107, Telegrams Collected (Bound). On April 6, Ford telegraphed to USG. "I have drawn on you today for two thousand and five ($2005) dollars and have also written you"   Telegram received (at 12:30 P.M.), *ibid.*

To Frances K. Thomas

Washington, D. C.
March 29, 1870,

MRS. GEO. H. THOMAS,
SAN FRANCISCO, CAL.

It is with heartfelt sympathy for you, the Army and the Nation that I send to you my condolence in the hour of your great bereavement. No eulogy of mine can add to the nation's knowledge of the goodness, fame and virtues of your deceased husband nor of the loss sustained by a grateful people in his death

U. S. GRANT

Copy, DLC-USG, II, 5. On Nov. 7, 1852, Bvt. Maj. George H. Thomas married
Frances L. Kellogg of Troy, N. Y. On March 28, 1870, Maj. Gen. Thomas died
in San Francisco. On March 29, Gen. William T. Sherman telegraphed to Mrs.
Thomas. "Notice of the death of General Thomas has fallen on us as a thunder-
bolt from the clear sky. I have shown the telegram to the President who will
transmit his assurances of sympathy and condolence. I will do all I can to manifest the feeling of the Whole Army at this to us great loss. I have given the
necessary authority for the transfer to Troy NewYork, where I will meet you,
meantime accept the sympathy of one of his oldest friends, and classmates, one
who honored him in life and. now reveres his Memory," ALS (telegram sent),
DNA, RG 94, Letters Received, 216A 1870.

On March 31, William McMichael, Philadelphia, wrote to USG. "On behalf
of the Committee having the matter in charge, I respectfully invite you to attend a meeting to be held at the Academy of Music, in this City, on Monday next
April 4th 1870 at 8 O'Clock P. M to take suitable action in reference to the
death of the lamented Major General George H. Thomas. Our various military
and civic associations and citizens generally will assemble to give expression to
the Sincere and universal sorrow which the death of this eminent soldier and
patriot has caused, and it would be a source of pride and gratification, not only
to the large body of soldiers here who formerly served under your command, but
also to all our citizens, if you would honor the occasion with your presence."
ALS, OFH. On April 5, USG wrote to McMichael. "I regret that my public
duties will prevent my ~~performing~~ attending the meeting you so kindly invite
me to attend. The object of the meeting is one that all loyal hearts will join—
In the death of Genl Thomas—the ~~country~~ Republic ~~lossesses~~ one of ~~her~~ its
bravest and purest defenders—I am sure the good people of your City will show
his memory all honor." Df, *ibid.*; copy, DLC-USG, II, 1. On April 8, USG attended Thomas's funeral in Troy. See *New York Times*, April 8, 9, 1870. On
April 16, Governor Rutherford B. Hayes of Ohio wrote to USG. "I have the
honor to transmit herewith a copy of Senate Joint Resolution No 6 'relative to
the decease of Major General George H. Thomas,' adopted April 14, 1870" LS,
DNA, RG 94, Letters Received, 216A 1870. The enclosure and a similar resolution from the N. Y. legislature are *ibid.*

On April 13, Maj. Gen. Winfield S. Hancock, St. Louis, had telegraphed to
Sherman. "If my rank will not entitle me to a division and the changes in Department are such as to make it practicable I would prefer this station   I leave
at once for St Paul." Telegram received (at 5:40 P.M.), *ibid.*, Letters Received,
147H 1869; copy, *ibid.* On April 14, Horace Porter endorsed this telegram.
"Respectfully returned to Gen. Sherman. The President says he has seen you
himself in reference to this matter" AES, *ibid.* On April 14, Sherman wrote to
Hancock, St. Paul. "I have laid your dispatch of the 13th from St. Louis, before
the President, who authorizes me to say that your wishes and claims for the
succession to the command of the Military Division of the Pacific made vacant
by Genl Thomas' death were ~~fully~~ fairly considered. And also your preference
for the Department of the Missouri in case of a change in its commander, were
also known to him, but he has ordered otherwise. The President authorizes me
to say to you that it belongs to his office to select the Comm'dg. Genls. of Divisions and Depts. and that the relations you chose to assume toward him officially and privately, absolve him from regarding your personal preferences.

The order announcing these changes will be made public in a very few days, and they will not touch the Department of Dakota or Mil Div of the Mo." Copies, *ibid.*; *ibid.*, Letters Sent. On April 27, Hancock wrote to Sherman. "Your letter has been received detailing the reasons the President gives why my claims to a more important command should not be regarded. I intended by my dispatch, to ask for a Division if the existing Divisions were all continued; otherwise, for the Department of Missouri, if changes made it practicable—Not as a favor, but as a a claim to a command to which I thought my rank entitled me. As the President leads me to believe that because I have not his personal sympathies, my preferences for command will not be regarded—notwithstanding my rank, I shall not again open the subject; but will add in conclusion, that I think it is an unfortunate precedent to establish that Military rank in time of peace especially, in the assignment of General Officers to command of Divisions and Departments, shall not have that consideration hitherto accorded to it." ALS, *ibid.*, Letters Received, 147H 1869. Related papers are in DLC-William T. Sherman. See also *Correspondence Between General W. T. Sherman, U. S. Army, and Major General W. S. Hancock U. S. Army* (St. Paul, 1871), discussing allegations that Hancock, angered by his removal from command in La., had refused to speak to USG in Washington.

To Congress

To THE SENATE AND HOUSE OF REPRESENTATIVES

It is unusual to notify the two houses of Congress, by message, of the ~~of~~promulgation, by proclamation of the Sec. of State, of the ratification of a Constitutional Amendment. In view however of the vast importance of the 15th Amendment to the Constitution, this day declared a part of that revered instrument, I deem a departure from the usual custom justifiable. A measure which makes at once ~~f~~Four Millions of people heretofore declared by the highest tribunal in the land, not citizens of the United States, nor eligible to become so, ~~and vaguely intimating that the Black man had no rights which the White man was bound to respect, full and equal citizens, before the law, having the right to vote and be voted~~ voters in every part of the land, the right not to be abridged by any state, is indeed a measure of grander importance than any other one act of the kind from the foundation of ~~of~~our free government to the present day.

Institutions like ours, where [in which] all power is derived directly from the people, must depend measurably [mainly] upon the intelligence, patriotism and industry of these people. I call the attention therefore of the newly enfranchised race to the importance of their striving in every honorable manner to make themselves worthy of their new privileges. To the race more favored heretofore by our laws I would say withhold no legal privilege of advancement to the new citizen. The framers of our Constitution firmly believed that a Republican government could not endure without intelligence and education gennerally diffused among the people. The "fFather of his Country" in his farewell address uses this language. "Promote then, as a matter of primary importance, institutions for the general diffusion of knowledge. In proportion as the structure of a government gives force to public opinion, it is essential that public opinion should be enlightened" In his first annual message to Congress the same views are forcibly put [presented], and are again urged in his eighth message.

~~Again~~ I repeat that the adoption of the 15th Amendment to the Constitution completes the greatest civil change, and constitutes the most important event that has occurred, since the nation came into life. The change will be beneficial in proportion to the heed that is given to the urgent recommendations of Washington. If these recommendations were important then, with a population of but a few Millions, how much more important now, with a population of Forty Millions, and increasing in a rapid ratio?

I would therefore call upon Congress to take all the means within their Constitutional powers, to promote and encourage popular education throughout the Country; and upon the people every where, to see to it that all who possess and exercise political rights, shall have the opportunity to acquire the knowledge which will make their share in the government a blessing and not a danger—By such means only can the benefits contemplated by this Amendment to the Constitution be secured.

[EXECUTIVE MANSION
MARCH 30 1870]

ADf (bracketed material not in USG's hand), DLC-USG, III. On March 30, 1870, USG submitted the final version. DS, DNA, RG 46, Presidential Messages. See *SED*, 41-2-74. On March 31, James M. Scovel, Camden, N. J., telegraphed to USG. "The Proclamation of Enfranchisement fixes your place forever in history beside the author of the Proclamation of Emancipation" Telegram received, DNA, RG 107, Telegrams Collected (Bound).

On Feb. 24, Governor-elect Edmund J. Davis of Tex. had written to USG. "The Legislature of this State at its recent Session has adopted the 14th and 15th Amendments with great unanimity, and has in other respects shewn a disposition in good faith, and with alacrity to follow the requirements of Congress in the matter of reconstruction. It has elected Senators of excellent personal character, and in Sentiment fully in accord with the majority in Congress. Under the circumstances I think the process of reconstruction may safely be expedited by the prompt admission of this State. But while this should be done without delay, I do not think it advisable to immediately withdraw the U. S. troops from the State. I have to request that this be done gradually and by concert with the State authorities as soon as the new organization is prepared to maintain public order, which I trust will not be long hence. In connection with this matter, I believe our Senators and Representatives in Congress, will coincide with me, in requesting that General J. J. Reynolds, be left in Command here. As you will perceive from the resolutions of the Legislature transmitted (in another enclosure) in relation to that officer, the members of that Body have a high appreciation of his services and integrity, and in this opinion I fully agree. While it is advisable to retain U. S. troops in the interior, for the present; the frontier calls for considerable addition to the military force for the protection of the Settlers, or else the adoption of some new policy that will put an end to the harrassing warfare that has disturbed the borders of Texas since annexation. I believe it has been suggested by the military authorities of the United States, that the Territory of Texas, known as the 'Pan-Handle', be added to the Indian Territory, as a reservation for those Savages which infest Texas. Some such measure, or a war of extermination seems necessary to secure permanent peace here, and relieve the Government of the great expense attending the maintenance of large bodies of troops on our frontier. With the reestablishment and maintenance of law and order, promptly and permanently—as we hope—the suppression of Indian depredations, and the encouragement of a system of Internal Improvements that will directly connect our State with the rest of the Union, we have reason to anticipate that our State with its cheap and fertile lands will offer a tempting field to immigrants from the older States and from Europe. We invite them to a free occupancy of our vacant territory, and propose to make them secure in life and property. Asking your kind cooperation in securing the early reconstruction of our State, and your valuable assistance in carrying out the purposes above indicated—. . ." ALS, *ibid.*, Letters Received from Bureaus.

On March 7, Secretary of State Hamilton Fish wrote in his diary. "Took to the President the report in answer to the Senate resolution calling for information as to the States which have ratified the 15th Amendment—He thinks it best not to send it in to day—I call attention to the mode of reply—not committing the Dept to the recognition of any particular State (Georgia) nor expressing opinion as to the effect of any resolution—He still decides to withhold it.—directs me to leave it with Genl Porter—he does not sign the Message to the Senate—I leave the papers with Porter—On my suggestion he directs a telegram to be sent by the War Dept to Genl Reynolds (in Texas) inquiring whether the Resolutions— of Texas, ratifying the 15th Amendmt have been forwarded—if not directing that they be forwarded—In this connection I here note that one day last week when going up to the Presidents Room, I found old Mr Dent, sitting by the windows in the lower Hall, at the White House—I was passing, having bid him 'good morning' he stopped me & asked 'have you got it yet?' I asked 'got what?' hesitating with the infirmity of memory: he said—'Oh—what is it? you know—I mean the 15th Amendment—the Texas resolutions'—On answering 'No—not yet'—he replied with a significant chuckle, & laugh 'No—and you won't get it—'—" DLC-Hamilton Fish.

On the same day, Orville E. Babcock wrote to Secretary of War William W. Belknap. "The President will be pleased to have you telegraph to Gen. Reynolds, Austin, Texas., and ask him if the action of the Texas legislature on the amendments to the Constitution has been forwarded to Washington. If it has not, ask him to have it sent at once." LS, DNA, RG 94, Letters Received, 253M 1870. Related papers are *ibid.* On March 15, USG wrote to the Senate. "I transmit a report from the Secretary of State, in answer to a resolution of the Senate of the 3d instant, asking to be informed what States have ratified the amendment known as the Fifteenth Amendment to the Constitution of the United States so far as official notice thereof has been transmitted to the Department of State, and that information from time to time may be communicated to that body as soon as practicable of such ratification hereafter by any State." DS, *ibid.*, RG 46, Presidential Messages. The enclosure is *ibid.* See *SED*, 41-2-63.

On the same day, Fish wrote that USG "read a draft of another Message which he proposes to send so soon as the proclamation be issued announcing the adoption of the 15 Amendment—recommending a general Amnesty & Pardon to all engaged in the Rebellion—Boutwell, Robeson, & I object to the word 'Pardon'—I suggest whether he would not except from the Amnesty those who were in Congress & left their Seats at the outbreak of the Rebellion, & the higher grade of Officers in the Army & Navy—The general opinion seemed to be that there should be no exceptions. Boutwell thought it should be extended to all who by some affirmative act declare themselves desirous to avail of it, & determined hereafter to abide by the laws &c—& this was the conclusion to which all finally arrived—" DLC-Hamilton Fish.

To John Sherman

Washington D, C,
March 30th 1870.

HON. J. SHERMAN: U. S. S.
DEAR SIR:

Your note of this date just rec'd. Presuming that no vote will be reached to-day on the Dominican treaty, I will take no steps in the matter before to-morrow, unless further advised of the necessity of so doing. I regret the failure of a favorable vote on your motion.[1]

Truly yours
U. S. GRANT

ALS, DLC-John Sherman. During an interview on March 29, 1870, USG had discussed the advantages of annexing Santo Domingo. "A government as extensive and populous as the United States consumes many things that grow only in the tropics. The population of the country is rapidly increasing, and, as a natural result, the consumption of tropical productions becomes larger in proportion. We talk about the balance of trade being against us in Europe. This is an error. The United States consumes about $75,000,000 worth of sugar in a year. This is almost entirely a drain upon the wealth of the country. It is true bills are drawn on Europe, but chiefly to pay balances against us in the tropics. The balance against us in Brazil alone is over $20,000,000, and proportionately the same is the case in all the tropical countries with which we have commercial transactions. This being the incontrovertible fact, it certainly is a most desirable step to acquire a country where American capital, labor and enterprise could be employed in raising sugar, coffee and other tropical growths for American consumption. . . . This whole question I resolve under four heads. First, the United States requires such a possession as St. Domingo in an agricultural point of view, for the reasons I have already stated. Second, the laws of Porto Rico and Cuba are inimical to American commerce. There is no reason why American manufactures and provisions, such as we are able to compete in, should not go to those islands. As I say their laws are hostile to the interests of this country— they are a check upon American commerce. I wish most earnestly to see commerce revived. A strong foothold in the West Indies would very soon regulate this. Third, the country has become so immense in its proportions, that it requires outposts. Our vulnerable point is the Gulf. Before it is too late we should plant ourselves there. This will be a guard against aggression from foreign sources and will consolidate the power of resistance by this country. The last reason is, without such a foothold, in event of a struggle the enemies of the United States would rendezvous in the Gulf and the whole power of the nation might be called upon to concentrate against a danger which by timely action could have been averted. . . . how can we tell what moment there might be a demand for action in these very waters? It is the part of prudence to be always prepared for every emergency." *New York Herald*, March 30, 1870.

1. On March 28, U.S. Senator John Sherman of Ohio had introduced a resolution. ". . . That the further consideration of the treaty of annexation with the Dominican Republic be postponed until the 1st day of May next, and that the President be requested to appoint three commissioners, with authority to proceed to said Republic and to collect full information as to the resources and condition of said Republic, and especially as to their public debt and public lands, and to negotiate such modifications of the seventh article of said treaty as will definitely fix the amount of the liability of the United States under the said article, and the application of the money to be paid by the United States under said treaty." *Senate Executive Journal*, XVII, 410–11. No action followed. On April 4, Secretary of State Hamilton Fish wrote in his diary. "President

called at my house in the Evening—He has abandoned the idea of sending Commissioners to San Domingo, at present—Says the Treaty will be discussed in the public papers, more earnestly than it has been—senator Morrill of Maine this morning urged that the President should not press the treaty—says it has no 'earnest' friends in the Senate—that the weight of Argument & fact is against it—I mentioned this to the President—" DLC-Hamilton Fish. See letter to Oliver P. Morton, Dec. 9, 1870.

To Senate

To the Senate of the United States.

I transmit, for consideration with a view to its ratification, a Treaty between the United States and the United States of Colombia, for the construction of an Interoceanic canal across the Isthmus of Panama and Darien,[1] signed at Bogota on the twenty-sixth of January last.

A copy of a despatch of the 1st ultimo to the Secretary of State from General Hurlbut, the United States Minister at Bogota, relative to the treaty, is also transmitted for the information of the Senate.

U. S. Grant

Washington, 31 March 1870.

DS, DNA, RG 46, Presidential Messages, Foreign Relations, Colombia. The enclosures are *ibid*. See *SED*, 46-2-112, pp. 38–45.

On Sept. 4, 1869, USG had authorized Stephen A. Hurlbut "to conclude and sign with the government of Colombia a Convention on the subject of a ship canal between the Atlantic & Pacific Oceans, . . ." DS, Mr. and Mrs. Philip D. Sang, River Forest, Ill. On Jan. 4, 1870, Secretary of State Hamilton Fish wrote in his diary. "Hurlburt's hope of a successful negociation of a treaty with Colombia, for a Canal concession, & the declaration of the Columbian Minister (Acosta) on Thursday last, of the disposition of his Goverment, to ratify the Treaty, were stated—President thinks the Canal can be completed within five years—" DLC-Hamilton Fish.

On Jan. 5, Secretary of the Navy George M. Robeson wrote to USG. "I have the honor to request that you will issue your order directing the Secretary of War to transfer to the Navy Department, to be expended under the direction of the Secretary of the Navy, the sum of $40,000, which this Department has ascertained to be standing, unexpended, on the books of the Engineer department of the U. S. army, to the credit of an appropriation for the survey of the Isthmus of Darien. The expedition is ready to sail, and only is detained by the want of certain necessary articles which cannot be purchased from any other fund." Copy,

DNA, RG 45, Letters Sent to the President. On Jan. 21, USG wrote to the House of Representatives. "In answer to the resolution passed by the House of Representatives on the 17th instant requesting to be informed 'under what act of Congress or by other authority appropriations for the Navy are diverted to the survey of the Isthmus of Darien'—I transmit a report by the Secretary of the Navy, to whom the resolution was referred." Copy, *ibid.*, RG 130, Messages to Congress. On Jan. 20, Robeson had reported to USG that "No appropriations for the Navy have been directed to the survey of the Isthmus of Darien. . . ." Copy, *ibid.*, RG 45, Letters Sent to the President. See *HED*, 41-2-81.

On March 3, Secretary of War William W. Belknap wrote to USG. "On January 15 1870, I received a communication from Hon. George M. Robeson, Secretary of the Navy, requesting me to cause a requisition to be issued in favor of Past asst. Paymaster J. Porter Loomis, of the U. S. Steamer Nipsic, Navy Yard, New York, for the sum of Eight thousand (8000) dollars in coin, to be charged to the appropriation for the Darien Expedition, and on January 18 /70 in compliance with your directions and instructions a requisition ~~a requisition~~ for the above amount was issued. The section of the act of July 28th, 1866 which makes the appropriation above referred to, is as follows:—'To provide for a survey of the Isthmus of Darien, under the direction of the War Dept, with a view to the construction of a ship-canal in accordance with the report of the Superintendent of the Naval Observatory to the Navy Dept., forty thousand dollars.'—(Sec 1., Chap. 296, 14 Stat. p. 311.) On a close examination of that paragraph it seems clear that the amount thus appropriated can legally be expended only for work done and services performed by and under the direction of the Secretary of War; that the survey referred to must be conducted under his superintending management and administrative direction and that said amount cannot lawfully be expended by the Secretary of the Navy or its expenditure be authorized by him and that consequently the Secretary of the Navy is not entitled to make requisition for the same upon the Secretary of War. This being the case, it is the duty of the Navy Dept. to cause to be refunded to the appropriation for 'Surveying Isthmus of Darien for a Ship Canal,' the amount of eight thousand (8000) dollars in coin issued to Passed assistant Paymaster Loomis, and a request has therefore been made to the Secretary of the Navy to that effect." Copies, DNA, RG 107, Letters Sent; *ibid.*, Letters Received from Bureaus. Related papers are *ibid.*

On Dec. 6, USG wrote to the Senate. "Referring to my message of the 1st February last, transmitting to the Senate for its consideration, with a view to ratification a treaty between the U. S. and the United States of Colombia for the construction of an inter-oceanic canal across the Isthmus of Darien, signed at Bogota on the 26th of January last, I herewith submit correspondence on the subject between the Secretary of State and the Minister of the United States at Bogota, a list of which is hereto appended." Copies, *ibid.*, RG 59, General Records; *ibid.*, RG 130, Messages to Congress. USG referred to his message of March 31. The enclosures are printed in *SED*, 46-2-112, pp. 46–84.

1. On March 8, Orville E. Babcock wrote to Charles W. Jenks, editor, *The Bureau*, Chicago. "I am directed by the President to inform you that he received the copies of the 'Bureau' and your letter of the 15th of February, and to inform you that he perused with satisfaction your article upon the great enterprise of a Ship Canal across the Isthmus of Darien. He wishes wishes me to thank you

for the kind sentiments expressed in your letter." Copy, DLC-USG, II, 1. On
April 25, Jenks wrote to USG. "You will pardon my voluminousness and peruse
this, and I will promise not further to weary you in the matter, There are three
things I wanted accomplished by your administration The Darien Canal—The
opening of the Arctic Sea. The Establishment of Posts of Meteorological observation. The latter, has been done, and it will save Chicago alone a million annually—The other two must come. The Darien Canal matter is being investigated—and the Arctic matter, you now have for decision. In this last, as in all
the others, I have no personal motive or end to gratify, only, that now when for
the first time, our *Government* has taken up the subject, I do pray that we may
not follow in the rut of all other European and American explorations—A skillful
and scientific officer of our own Navy has opened the way by a carefully prepared
hypotheis, the result of thirty years of observation & study—I have almost daily
new evidence of its truthfulness—from old seamen, who were often in the open
gateways to the Pole, but having no charts of the latitude dared not go out of
their course, in exploration—I have never met Cap Bent, but upon my return
from Washington last week, I wrote him of the disgraceful squabbles of Cap
Hale & Dr Hayes, at W, (neither of whom are men of scence or seamen) and
this a. m. I recd the letter herewith, Some of the suggestions are so pertinent,
I send the letter for your perusal, Cap Bent has no aspirations for the service
himself, but he does wish, and it seems to me most properly that a test should
be made of his hypothesis—I also enclose you a photogh he sent me, it is an
honest, intelligent face, and commends itself to all—Let me pray you, consider
his claims, which to every seaman & naval officer to whom I ever have committed
them, has gained their hearty endorsement. You need not trouble yourself to
return any of the enclosed, but if they shall aid you in the solution of this interesting question, I shall only be too happy to have been able to serve you & my
Country" ALS, DNA, RG 107, Letters Received from Bureaus. The enclosed
letter of April 23 from Silas Bent, St. Louis, to Jenks is *ibid.*

Speech

[*April 1, 1870*]

Sir: I can assure those present that there has been no event
since the close of the war in which I have felt so deep an interest
as that of the ratification of the fifteenth amendment to the Constitution by three-fourths of the States of the Union. I have felt the
greatest anxiety ever since I have been in this house to know that
that was to be secured. It looked to me as the realization of the
Declaration of Independence. I can not say near so much on this
subject as I would like to, not being accustomed to public speaking, but I thank you very much for your presence this evening.

Washington Chronicle, April 2, 1870. USG addressed Republicans from the First Ward, Washington, D. C., outside the White House. Before speaking, USG told reporters: "Gentlemen. It will not be necessary to use much paper in relating what I have to say. You can easily remember it." *Washington National Republican*, April 2, 1870.

On April 9, 1870, Charles R. Douglass, son of Frederick Douglass, Washington, wrote to USG. "I have the honor to request, in behalf of the Committee of Arrangements for the purpose of celebrating the ratification of the Fifteenth amendment, and the eighth anniversary of the Emancipation in the District of Columbia, that the Colored employees of the several Departments of the government be allowed leave of absence on Wednesday next, (13th instant,) for the purpose of participating in said celebration." Copies, DNA, RG 60, Letters from the President; *ibid.*, RG 107, Letters Received from Bureaus. On April 15, the Boys in Blue *et al.* sponsored a torchlight procession in honor of the Fifteenth Amendment and to support territorial government for D. C. At the White House, USG spoke to the crowd: "I could not say anything more to those assembled here to-night to convince them I have desired this amendment than what I have said already. All that I can add is that I hope that those who have received the franchise will prove themselves worthy of it: and to those who have always possessed it that if I had not have had that confidence in them which I have I should not have been so anxious for it." *Washington Chronicle*, April 16, 1870. Variant text in *Washington National Republican*, April 16, 1870.

On June 24, Secretary of State Hamilton Fish recorded in his diary. "Presented to Prsdt—the Address of 'the British & Foreign Anti Slavery Socy & other friends of Freedom' on the Adoption of the 15—Amendment—" DLC-Hamilton Fish. The undated document is in DNA, RG 59, Miscellaneous Letters.

To Charles W. Ford

Washington, D, C,
Apl. 7th 1870

DEAR FORD:

I must trouble you again to attend to some private business for me. There is an old gentleman by the name of Carlin,[1] formerly of Carondelet but now of New Orleans, who owns about 47 arpents of the land which Mr. Wrenshall Dent[2] is now serving for. Mr. Carlin is here at present and is anxious to compromise so far as his land is concerned. His proposition is to sell for One hundred dollars per arpent. I am perfectly willing to pay that amount if that and the Dent titles make one clear, indisputable title. Mr. Carlin goes to St Louis next week and will call on Mr. Saml Glover,[3] Dent's lawyer, who I promised, with you, should be prepared to give him my answer. Now what I want to ask you to do is to see Glover and ascertain from him whether Carlin's title, with the other, makes the whole perfect and if so for him to say to Mr. Carlin when he calls that I will accept his proposition and send him to you for settlement.

If Mr. C. requires the money immediately you can draw on me for the amt. at three days sight. I would prefer however about sixty days time if that is just as agreeable.

Yours Truly
U. S. Grant

ALS, DLC-USG. On April 6, 1870, Frederick T. Dent had written to Charles W. Ford. "Your letter is received. I went myself with McDonald to Delano and had Wren Fielding appointed a StoreKeeper—try him if he does not do remove him—McGuire is not our Lawyer. Grover & Shepley have charge of the case—Carlean wants to compromise it is to late" ALS, *ibid.* On March 26, Julia Dent Grant had written to Ford. "Mr W D. Fielding is very anxious to obtain employment in some department in St Louis If you can assist him in any way I shall be oblige to you" ALS, *ibid.* See *PUSG*, 18, 571.

On April 25, USG twice telegraphed to Ford. "did you receive a letter from me about two 2 weeks since" "Your letter of twenty third received the Carlin purchase will not stop suit so far as the remainder of the property is Concerned would like however to Compromise all on any other of it on same terms money ready for M C at three 3 days sight" Telegrams received (at 9:37 A.M. and 11:32 A.M.), DLC-USG. See letter to Charles W. Ford, May 5, 1870.

1. On Sept. 29, 1859, Delphy and Mary Carlin, Brooklyn, had sold to Alexander J. P. Garesché, St. Louis, ". . . the undivided half of the northern half of lot No one in the commons of the Town of Carondelet South of the river des Pères, . . ." DS, USG 3.

2. George Wrenshall Dent, USG's brother-in-law. On Nov. 26, 1869, James W. Denver, Washington, D. C., had written to USG. "The enclosed letter was received here during my absence and was mislaid, which accounts for my apparent neglect in forwarding it to you as requested by the writer, Mr. Nickerson of Cal. whom I think you know very well. I dont know that I ought to say any thing about such matters, but I cannot forego the opportunity of expressing the warm personal friendship I entertain for G. W. Dent and the expression of the hope that you will find it in your power to give him the appointment sought for, or any other that may suit him. I am sure he is well qualified and I know there is not a more honorable, honest or upright man to be found in the country. Trusting that you may be able to give him the place . . ." ALS, DNA, RG 56, Appraiser of Customs Applications. Denver enclosed a letter to USG of Oct. 18 from Benjamin R. Nickerson, Republican State Central Committee, San Francisco, recommending George W. Dent for collector of customs. On March 21, 1870, Timothy G. Phelps, collector of customs, San Francisco, wrote to USG. "I am about to suggest a matter of Some delicacy, but I feel a farmer may talk

frankly with a Soldier, without danger of being misunderstood I refer to a position for Mr Geo W Dent I Served in the State Senate with Mr Dent for two years, and in the time learned to like, very much, the man, for his gentlemanly deportment, his abilities, and his Sterling integrity Mr Dent like too many old Californians has been, to Some extent, unfortunate, and is now comparatively a poor man. I do not doubt your desire to Serve him, as you must know his worth . . ." ALS, *ibid.* On May 13, USG nominated Dent as appraiser of merchandise, San Francisco.

3. Samuel T. Glover, St. Louis attorney, was in partnership with John R. Shepley.

To Roscoe Conkling

Washington D. C. Apl. 12th *1870*

HON. ROSCOE CONKLING, U. S. S.

DEAR SIR:

The P. M. Gn. has not returned, hence will be no change in Albany post office[1] to-day.—Mr. Grinnell[2] has not arrived.

Truly yours,

U. S. GRANT

ALS, DLC-Roscoe Conkling.

1. On March 18, 1869, J. P. Sandel, Albany, N. Y., telegraphed to USG. "Please appoint me postmaster at our town I lent you some money you know" Telegram received (on March 19, 8:45 P.M.), DNA, RG 107, Telegrams Collected (Bound). On April 19, Truman G. Younglove, Albany, telegraphed to USG. "My convictions are decidedly that political interests in this city will be best subserved by the appointment of D. H. Mills Post Master, I hope he will be He is always efficient and reliable" Telegram received (at 7:00 P.M.), *ibid.* On April 20, USG nominated Morgan L. Filkins as postmaster, Albany. On July 19, 1870, USG suspended Filkins's appointment and designated John F. Smyth to replace him.

2. On April 10, Thurlow Weed, New York City, had written to USG. "It is a long time since I have had the pleasure of communicating with you—during that time my health has been greatly impaired—but I am glad to say that it is now somewhat improved—Although I have been compelled to withdraw from my life-long activity in politics, yet I have not failed to observe with more satisfaction than I can well express your wise, patriotic & successful administration of the government to which the nation appreciating your elevated character called you I have been especially desirous of telling you how gratified I was at the selection you made for collector of New York—Mr: Grinnell is & for many years has been my intimate friend, and his appointment was a well deserved tribute to his high character for ability and integrity, and one that insured to the government an honest, faithful & intelligent discharge of the duties of the

office—I need not tell you of his personal & political popularity throughout the State, nor of his devotion to you personally, nor how true he has ever been to the principles of our party—No one has contributed more of time & money to secure its success and triumph—I did not solicit his appointment because I knew his claims could not fail to be deemed paramount at Washington. Hoping & believing that he will continue to give entire satisfaction to you & to The Department . . ." LS, OFH. On April 15, "The Special Committee of the German Republican Central Committee," New York City, wrote to USG recommending Alfred Pleasonton as collector of customs, New York City. DS (4 signatures), DNA, RG 56, Collector of Customs Applications. Letters recommending William H. Robertson are *ibid.* On April 20, Secretary of State Hamilton Fish wrote in his diary that USG "says Grinnell was twice reques[ted] to resign: but, instead of that, he comes on here & makes intercession to be retained—Says he is very inefficient, & has made new regulations very offensive to the Merchants & tradesmen—Instances the Carting Contract which is '[a] job,' that Boutwell intends to overrule it—I remark that I think he has made a lucky escape in not getting caught with Murphy—He thinks he would no[t be] a good Collector—I say that I think it would have bee[n] an unfortunate appointment, & an unpopular one that Murphy was at the head of one of the three Republican Organizations in NY. that divided & distracted the Republican party—he could not fail to lean to his own associates, & would continue the divisions in the party—that he was a strong Roman Catho[lic] & his appointment would offend the Protestant Irishm[en] who are almost the only Irishmen who vote with us that he is a man of limited Education—& made his money as I am informed, out of Contracts during the War—He says he made it by the rise of real Estate—purchased at the begining of the War—" DLC-Hamilton Fish. On June 14, Thomas D. Anderson, New York City, wrote to USG. "On account of your well known approval of a simple act of justice rendered to any one whose character has been unwarrantably aspersed I feel sure that I need not apologize for my apparent intrusion on your attention—I see by th papers that you have thought of appointing Mr Thomas Murphy to th collectorship of New York and I also see that he has been attacked on account of his religion—He has been represented as a bigoted Roman Catholic and likely to prostitute his office to th purposes of promoting his faith. Now, sir I am a Baptist minister you may judge therefore how much sympathy there is between our religious views. But I spurn any effort to prejudice a man's appointment to office on account of his faith—Mr Murphy— used his influence to help us obtain for our church th lots on which we are now building directly opposite his own residence and offererd us generously a subscriptn this was, when he was candidate for *no* office and when I cd be politically of no service to him   I believe him, from pleasant & frequent neighborly intercourse with him, as pure from th introduction of his religious views into political life as I am myself. May God preserve us from inquiring into a man's faith before we accord to him all th rights of citizenship   Let me add I know nothing of Mr Murphy's political fitness for th position, nor of its bearing on th party. I am not in party politics and have written simply from a sense of justice—I want no publicity given to this but if it can at any time serve you in your impartial appointments you are at liberty to use it." ALS, DNA, RG 56, Collector of Customs Applications. On July 1, USG nominated Thomas Murphy to replace Moses H. Grinnell as collector of customs, and nominated Grinnell as naval officer. See George Rothwell Brown, ed., *Reminiscences of Senator William M. Stewart of*

Nevada (New York and Washington, D. C., 1908), pp. 254–57.

On July 13, Horace Porter wrote to Murphy. "You are about to enter upon the duties of Collr of Customs in N. York. Many persons in seeking office may use the Presidents name or mine in urging their claims. I wish to state to you distinctly, at the outset, that *no one is authorized to do so.* Many friends of mine whom I should be very glad to oblige have importuned me to write you letters in their behalf, but I have persistently refused to add to your present embarrassment by so doing. You will never hear from me on the subject of office. My only desire is to see you so distribute the partronage of your office as to render the most efficient service to the country, and the cause of the Administration." Copy, DLC-USG, II, 1. See *SRC,* 41-3-380. On July 14, Orville E. Babcock wrote to Murphy. "I am in receipt of letters applying for recommendation to you for places in the New York custom-house. I do not wish to embarrass you, or the working of that office in any way, and I have therefore given no such letters, nor shall I do so. I wish you all success, and know that if you are to be responsible for that great office you must appoint your own assistants." *SRC,* 42-2-227, III, 208–9. On Oct. 31, Porter wrote to Murphy. "I am directed by the President to forward to you the marked portion of the enclosed newspaper article. While the President does not for a moment suppose that you ever uttered the language it imputes to you, he deems it well to take this opportunity to say that, if any persons have been employed in the Custom House upon representations that they are his particular friends or favorites he hopes they may be discharged, and that if any persons ever apply for positions under you upon such a pretence he requests that they may not be employed." Copy, DLC-USG, II, 1. See *SRC,* 41-3-380; *SRC,* 42-2-227; letter to Moses H. Grinnell, March 19, 1869.

To Hamilton Fish

———

Washington D. C. Apl. 19th *1870*

DEAR GOVERNOR:

I think it advisable to send in the name of Gen. Badeau for Consul to London at once to avoid the pressure which is certain to come for the rentention of Mr. Morse.[1] He has had considerable time now to tender his resignation in and it has not been sent but letters have been written to friends to save him. Please send the nomination for my signature, and to be sent to the Senate, tomorrow.

Truly yours,
U. S. GRANT

HON. H. FISH,
SEC. OF STATE.

ALS, DLC-Hamilton Fish. On April 12, 1869, USG had nominated Freeman H. Morse as consul gen., London. On April 20, 1870, Secretary of State Hamilton Fish recorded in his diary. "President—sent note (dated 19th) requesting immediate nomination of Badeau vice Morse (Consul General at London)—sent the ~~nom~~ message—In the Evening I dine at the Presidents—the date of his note he says was a mistake He remarks that 'this asking persons to resign, is not what it is cried up to be' that Morse instead of resigning, is havg letters written home to make influence for his retention. Refers to one from a member of his Family to Sumner, whic[h] the latter sent to me—now on file—Others are 'understood' to have been written . . ." DLC-Hamilton Fish. On April 21, USG nominated Adam Badeau as consul gen. at London to replace Morse.

1. Morse, born in 1807 in Bath, Maine, acclaimed ship-carver, Whig and Republican U.S. Representative (1843–45; 1857–61), went to London as consul in 1861.

To Henry C. Bowen

Washington, D. C. Apl. 21st *18~~67~~0*

DEAR SIR:

I have the pleasure to acknowledge the receipt of a copy of the New York Independent, printed on Satten in commemmoration of its Twenty-first birth day, which you have favored me with. The execution is beautiful, and with the binding make it a valuable contribution to any library aside from the intrinsic merit of the reading matter which will have great value when the events of the last ten years come to be looked back upon with almost incredulity that such events could have occured in a Christian country and in a civilized age.

Please accept my thanks for this contribution to my library which, I know, will be prized by my children long after libraries cease to present attraction to me.

Truly yours
U. S. GRANT

To HENRY C. BOWEN
NEW YORK INDEPENDENT

ALS, DLC-USG, 1C. Henry C. Bowen, born in 1813, a silk merchant who, in 1848, cofounded the *New York Independent*, a Congregationalist and antislavery journal. In 1861, he became its sole proprietor and publisher.

To Hamilton Fish

———

Washington D. C. Apl. 25th *1870*

Dear Sir:

I think it advisable, in the present condition of Paragua,[1] that we have at least a nominal representation there. I suggest therefore the nomination of Mr. Stevens[2] to go in to-day.

Truly yours
U. S. Grant

Hon. H. Fish
Sec. of State.

ALS, DLC-Hamilton Fish.

1. From Nov., 1864, until March, 1870, Paraguay fought a bitter and sanguinary war against Brazil, Argentina, and Uruguay.

2. On March 17, 1869, Speaker of the House James G. Blaine wrote to USG. "The undersigned begs leave to recommend the appointment of John L. Stevens of Maine as Commissioner to the Sandwich Islands—By long, devoted & efficient service in the cause of Republican principles, by high character, & by general culture Mr. Stevens is well fitted for the discharge of the duties of the position—" ALS, DNA, RG 59, Letters of Application and Recommendation. On April 13, USG nominated John L. Stevens as consul, Birmingham. On April 27, Blaine wrote to USG again recommending Stevens as minister to Hawaii. ALS, *ibid.* USG endorsed this letter. "Respectfully refered to the Sec. of State." AE (initialed—docketed as May, 1869), *ibid.* Related papers are *ibid.* On March 11, 1870, USG nominated Stevens as minister to Uruguay and, on April 26, simultaneously minister to Paraguay.

To Charles W. Ford

———

Washington D. C. AMay 5th *1870*

Dear Ford:

In my letter to you in regard to the compromise with Carlin for his share of the Carondelet property, now in litigation, I stated that I would compromise on the same terms with any, or all, of the other holders.[1] On reflection I think Dent's lawyer might, if he should try, effect a compromise with all of them on some terms. Suppose you consult with him on this subject, and advise as to the best mode of bringing about such a result. I am willing to extinguish all titles by the payment of a fair amount of money or by a division of the lands in controversy.

Truly Yours

U. S. GRANT

ALS, DLC-USG. See letter to Charles W. Ford, May 9, 1870.

1. On Jan. 18, 1870, Jesse Holladay, North Pacific Transportation Co., San Francisco, had written to "Dear Brother," probably Ben Holladay. ". . . President Grant has written to his Brother in in Law (Mr Dent) here, proposing to purchase my interest in the Segerson lands. He has bot. Burns interest, He can have mine for $200—per arpen, only a portion of my interest is covered by the Dent suit, in which I hear the President is interested, Please state to him my terms would like to know as soon as possible whether he will take it—. . ." ALS, DLC-USG. See letter to Charles W. Ford, June 27, 1870.

To Charles W. Ford

Washington D. C. May 9th *1870*

DEAR FORD,

The day I wrote you in relation to effecting a compromize for the Carondelet property Gen. Dent rec'd. a letter from Mr. Shepley suggesting the same course. I told Gn. Dent to telegraph to Mr. S. that I had written to you that day on the subject, and that you would probably call on him relative to it. My feeling is that Mr. Dent is the rightful owner of the land, but that by his neglect, and obstinacy, he has lost his title to it. If therefore a compromise, on any fare terms, can be effected I think it will be much better than a law suit. I wish you would see Shepley or Glover and ask them their advice and good offices in the matter.

I shall be in St. Louis about July. I think I like the 3d St. Ware House property which you wrote me could be bought for $18.000 00/100 dollars, or less. If you think well of it you may close the sale, on the best terms you can, payment to be made, in full, by the 20th of July. I do not want any deed of trust recorded against the property but cannot pay more than $5000 00 before the time specified. The amount of $5000.00/100 I can pay on call.

I don't see, notwithstanding the positive assurance you gave me to the contrary, that you have changed your condition in life! If you should do so during my Summer vacation I want you to bring your bride to Long Branch, and be my guest, for a week, or as long as you can be still in one place.

Yours Truly
U. S. GRANT

ALS, USG 3. On May 11, 1870, Charles W. Ford, St. Louis, wrote to USG. "Your letter on the subject of compromising the Corondolet claims was duly recd When I closed up with Mr Carlin, he offered his services in effecting any compromises thought hereafter, advisable to make with the various claimants— so; I saw Mr Sheply—the Atty. then found Mr Carlin. but, too late to be of any service—as he left the same day for N. Y. I then saw Mr Maguire, He had seen Calvin Burns—(you know him) and he Burns said he would compromise on the same terms Carlin did had, but, that he had gone in jointly with others to defend & he would see how he could withdraw—He is not very reliable. The cases are set for trial on the 17th Mr Maguire says—the new patent, recently put on record. will kill your claim. He reports Mr Glover as saying the same thing. of which the opposite party are fully aware—The time for a compromise between this & the 17th is so short, that little could be done—Especially—with such advice as is given by the opposing council. & we are now at work to find some good and sufficient reason upon which we can get an adjournment of the trial—If we can succeed in getting a continuance, Mr Maguire and Mr Carlin both think— that compromises can be made. If the matter is urged now, they think it will have a bad effect in getting a continuance—Carlin will be back in the fall— when he will assist in making settlements &c. I will telegraph you the result of a continuance—as soon as the cases are reached—& if Burns desires to sell out before I will arrage it with him. I enclose you the two deeds for the Carlin tract. which are clear of all incumbrances &c, and other papers relating to the same," ALS, *ibid.* On May 13, USG twice telegraphed to Ford. "I accept the compromise proposed in your despatch of this date close it—" "Terms suit me draw three days sight for first payment" Telegrams received (at 12:35 P.M. and 7:05 P.M.), DLC-USG. On May 14, George W. Dent, San Francisco, wrote to USG. "Your letter of 4th Inst has just come to hand advising me of your arrangement with Mr Carlin—Since your letter was written—and while it was on its way to me, I received a letter from my brother Fred to which I responded, and, that you may better understand why I answered his letter in the positive terms conveyed in my letter to him, I make the following extract from his letter: 'Father is fretting about that Carondelet trial—it is to come off soon—We have compromised with Carlin at $100 per acre—this is your part of it, and by paying back the amount and interest and expenses &c you have a clear title to some 45 acres worth $1000 per acre. We will do the same for all the rest if they come up before trial &c'—By the terms of the agreement between Glover & Shepley and myself I agreed to pay them in addition to the $1000 paid a further sum of $5000 upon the favorable determination of the Suit before the Supreme Court of the U. S. *and further*, that should I, in any way compromise with the parties then the whole amount of the obligation ($5000) should be payable. Knowing my brothers disposition to arrive hastily at conclusions, and his, as well as my own inability to raise the necessary amount of funds to comply with the sweeping terms proposed by him, I immediately concluded that it was worse than folly to attempt such a thing, and that it would delay action in the Dist Court in St Louis, and not unlikely damage our case. Had he intimated to me that he had written his letter at your instance and informed me of your proposed kind offices in advancing the money—then my reply would have been entirely different. As it is, I trust this explanation will be understood, and serve to induce you to properly understand the tone of my letter to my brother. I appreciate highly and thank you kindly for your manifest friendship to our family in this matter. Would it not be well to get Mr Ford to ascertain from Messrs Glover & Shepley if, in the event of a compromise before suit, they will release me from the contingent fee of $5000—this was the agreement—but I have signed no obligation to that effect—notwithstanding the bond is not signed my word has passed to them, which I hold as sacred as the bond, were the latter 'signed, sealed and delivered' This is the only obstacle in the way. I apprehend that some of the parties, where they have made substancil improvements, would be lothe to compromise at the price named. Mr Jesse Holladay, (brother of Ben Holladay) who resides here, owns about 100 arpents—only a portion of which is covered by the Cerré and Bolay claims—He offers me *all* at $100 per arpent—⅓ cash, balance in 1 2 & 3 years with 6 pr ct interest. This I consider very reasonable, from the fact that considerable of his property is not included in our surveys and the title good. His interest is with Burns, and is undivided. If you think well of this proposition, and desire to obtain land *out side* of—our claims at $100 per arpent, I would be happy to join you—and make the purchase. Of this please advise me by dispatch or otherwise—If Holladay should be tamperd with by Burnes he may abandon the idea of selling—hence I think it would be well to let me know at an early day. I am thoroughly convinced that this property, Cerre & Bolay tracts of land, with a perfect title will command a good price at the present time, and prospectively I know of no better investment. Your offer to step forward and assume the payment of so large a sum is more than any member of my family could have expected, and as one, I thank you kindly. and promise that you shall not only get your money back with interest, but share largely in what may be made from sales. . . . Love to Father, Sister & family." ALS, USG 3. See letter to Charles W. Ford, May 16, 1870.

To Hamilton Fish

———

Washington D. C. May 11th *1870*

DEAR SIR:

I believe I directed the withholding of the commission of C. B. Thompson, who was confirmed as Post Master of Leroy, N. Y. I now think it better that the commission should be issued, particularly as the M. C.[1] from that district is very anxious about it.

Respectfully &c

U. S. GRANT

HON. H. FISH,
SEC. OF STATE.

ALS, DLC-Hamilton Fish.

    1. U.S. Representative John Fisher of N. Y.

Speech

———

[*May 13, 1870*]

COUNT CORTI: I am happy to receive you as the diplomatic representative of the sovereign of a country interesting to all others claiming to be civilized, and to which all are more or less indebted for means of raising themselves to the scale of nations. The good wishes which you express on behalf of the King of Italy are heartily reciprocated by me and by my countrymen, who ardently wish that the prosperity and happiness of that region may, in the process of time, be more and more augmented and strengthened.

From what we know of your antecedents it is not to be doubted that the wisdom of His Majesty's choice of you, as his Envoy Extraordinary and Minister Plenipotentiary to the United States, will be confirmed by results.

Washington National Republican, May 14, 1870. On May 13, 1870, Count Luigi Corti, minister from Italy, had presented his credentials to USG. His remarks are *ibid*. Corti, born in 1826, had been minister to Sweden and Norway (1864–67) and minister to Spain (1867–70).

To Charles W. Ford

Washington D. C. May 16th 1870

Dear Ford:

Your letter enclosing papers in regard to the Carlin compromise is rec'd. When I wrote to you about the purchase of 3d St. property[1] I was not thinking of the possibility, or probability, of compromising much more. If the whole, or nearly the whole, 550 Arpents is compromised it will be about as much weight as I can carry. If no more is compromised, or but little more, I can still pay for the 3d st. property if you think it a good investment.

I will speak to the Com. of Int. Rev. about McDonald.

Yours Truly

U. S. Grant

ALS, USG 3. On May 30, 1870, Charles W. Ford, St. Louis, wrote to USG. "I have written you several times of late on the subject of the Carondelet Commons matter; also, sent you some deeds by express. The inclosed papers came from Mr. Eaache, [Eunche(?)] and will explain themselves. Saturday last I saw Mr. Burns. He told me that the investigator of titles had his claim in hand and hoped he would soon make a finish of them. As soon as it is done to meet the approbation of Mr. Shepley, he would be ready to carry out his arrangement to sell to you. I told him it would be satisfactory. I was a little surprised at this, as I did not expect he would do it after the decision of Treat. I can only explain it on the ground that he is hard up for money. I wrote you a few days ago about this man McDonald, as supervisor in place of Marr. I inclose you a couple of slips cut from the Leavenworth Commercial. I understand McDonald was in the town of Leavenworth when these articles appeared, but offered no remonstrance or explanation in regard to them. The Democrat here has been McDonald's friend, and, I think, recommended him for the appointment. McKee told me that he called McDonald's attention to these articles and asked what they meant. He answered very coolly that he did not read the newspapers, and they were of no consequence. I fear the honest way they were unanswerable, and the Democrat has dropped him. McKee says he can't defend a man, for such charges as these, who has nothing to say for himself. From all I can hear, I am satisfied McDonald is a bad egg, and that so far as being any credit to your Administration, he is a downright discredit to it. He is entirely without capacity as a business man, and the business community know it, and have no confidence in him whatever. ~~You will pardon me for the interest I take in the matter. I do not want such a man to go about the country representing himself your special and personal friend, when I know, and others, too, that you take no stock in such a character. He is no credit to you or your Administration, but an absolute damage, and I hope, for your sake and ours, you will have him squelched.~~ You will pardon me for the interest I take in the matter, but I hate, and so does all your friends, to see such a man as McDonald traveling through the country as your special champion, and attempting to rule the interests of the internal revenue in such a loud manner—a man that republican papers denounce as being without sense, without truth and common honesty. I tell you this confidentially, having no doubt of its truth. We all hope you will satisfy yourself of the truth of it, if you have any doubts, and do yourself justice and the country a service by squelching him at once." *HMD*, 44-1-186, pp. 100–1 (brackets and cancellations in text). On April 13, 1876, Lucien Eaton, special government counsel, read the retained draft copy to a select committee investigating the Whiskey Ring. See letter to Columbus Delano, Oct. 7, 1869.

1. See letters to Charles W. Ford, Nov. 12, 1869, Jan. 3, 1870.

To Ebenezer R. Hoar

———

Respectfully refered to the Atty. Gen. If any action is called for by the General Govt. it ought to be taken at once. I do not see that it is possible for the U. S. to permit the Union P. R. R. to go into the hands of a receiver, at the dictum of a territorial Judge.

U. S. GRANT

MAY 17TH 1870.

AES, DNA, RG 60, Letters from the President. Written on a letter of May 12, 1870, from U.S. Representative Oakes Ames of Mass., director, Union Pacific Railroad, to USG. "The Union Pacific Railroad Company respectfully represents: That one James W Davis has brought suit in equity against the Company and the United States district court for the Territory of Wyoming, alleging that the Company is indebted to him to the amount of half a million dollars or upwards for ties and timber furnished and delivered on the line of said road for its construction; and praying for an answer, for an accounting and decree for the payment of the amount due, and for a receiver of the railroad of the Company and the sale of its assets to pay the amount. That the suit came on for a preliminary hearing before the court at Cheyenne in said Territory on the 26th of April, 1870, and the court decided that a receiver should be appointed to take possession of the railroad of the Company within the Territory unless the Company should deposit, subject to the order of the court, the sum of five hundred thousand dollars, and the case was adjourned for twenty days to give the Company time to make such deposit. The proposed action of the territorial court is unprecedented, unnecessary, and injurious to the Government for the following reasons: . . . The Company therefore request the intervention of the United States in its behalf; that the United States District Attorney of Wyoming may be instructed to appear in the case and oppose the appointment of a receiver, and to move the acceptance of the bond offered as security, and that such other action may be taken by the Executive as may be necessary to protect the interests of the Government in this great public highway." LS, *ibid.* On May 23, Attorney Gen. Ebenezer R. Hoar endorsed this letter. "Ch J. Howe refused to appoint a receiver—No further action required" AES, *ibid.*

Proclamation

BY THE PRESIDENT OF THE UNITED STATES OF AMERICA,
A PROCLAMATION:

Whereas it has come to my knowledge that sundry illegal military enterprises and expeditions are being set on foot within the territory and jurisdiction of the United States, with a view to carry on the same from such territory and jurisdiction against the people and district of the Dominion of Canada, within the the the Dominions of Her Majesty the Queen of the United Kingdom of Great Britain and Ireland, with whom the United States are at peace,

Now therefore I, Ulysses S. Grant, President of the United States, do hereby admonish all good citizens of the United States and all persons within the territory and jurisdiction of the United States against aiding, countenancing, abetting or taking part in such unlawful proceedings, and I do hereby warn all persons that by committing such illegal acts they will forfeit all right to the protection of the Government or to its interference in their behalf to rescue them from the consequences of their own acts; and I do hereby enjoin all officers in the service of the United States to employ all their lawful authority and power to prevent and defeat the aforesaid unlawful proceedings, and to arrest and bring to justice all persons who may be engaged therein.

In testimony whereof I have hereunto set my hand, and caused the seal of the United States to be affixed. Done at the city of Washington, this twenty-fourth day of May, in the year of our Lord one thousand eight hundred and seventy, and of the Independence of of the United States the ninety-fourth.

U. S. GRANT

DS, DNA, RG 130, Presidential Proclamations. On May 25, 1870, Isaac F. Quinby, U.S. marshal, Rochester, N. Y., telegraphed to Frederick T. Dent.

"Does the President desire me to go to Seat of Fenian trouble in this State." Telegram received (at 10:00 A.M.), *ibid.*, RG 59, Miscellaneous Letters; copy, *ibid.* On the same day, Dent wrote to Secretary of State Hamilton Fish. "The enclosed telegram from Marshall Quinby is just recvd   I submitted it to the President who directed me to send it to you . . . No answer has been sent" ALS, *ibid.* On May 25, Fish recorded in his diary. "Prsdt sends telegram from Quimby, asking if he shall proceed to the Scene of trouble—I go to the White House President ill in bed—See Dent—give him recent telegrams (rcd since those shown the Prsdt yesterday)   he shows to President—returns saying Prsdt sees no reason to send Quimby to frontier—I so telegraph to him" DLC-Hamilton Fish.

On May 26, John Charles Laycock, Philadelphia, wrote to USG. "As one of your constituents I deem it my privilege to address the executive, to whom his constituents delegated the Executive power of the United States—When it appears obvious that tardiness, or Weakness has been exhibited by the Government—If the Proclamation issued by The President had been issued one Week earlier, it would have prevented the outrage of the Irish on the Canadians, under the cognomens of a Raid—*a fenian* Raid—It would have saved numerous lives, and millions of money—Why was it not issued, when for many months it was notorious that illegal organizations were in active operation to Violate the neutrality laws—? Organizations formed to invade, murder, and rob, in Violation of all law, (international, or national—)   When a Government knowing this, is supine—it is criminal, and becomes a coadjutor of the outlaws, and a participant in all their outrages—AND RESPONSIBLE—. . . I have with this exception been a great admirer of your individual career, and of your Cabinet— (as one of the great majority who have been similarly impressed—) and wish to remain so." ALS, DNA, RG 59, Miscellaneous Letters. See Allan Nevins, *Hamilton Fish: The Inner History of the Grant Administration* (New York, 1936), pp. 392–95.

To Senate

To THE SENATE OF THE UNITED STATES:

I have the satisfaction of transmitting to the Senate for consideration with a view to its ratification a Convention between the United States and Her Britannic Majesty,[1] relative to naturalization signed in London the 13th instant.

This Convention is substantially the same as the proctocol on the subject signed by Mr. Reverdy Johnson and Lord Stanley[2] on the 9th of October 1868, and approved by the Senate on the 13th of April 1869.

If the instrument should go into effect it will relieve the parties from a grievance which has hitherto been a cause of frequent annoyance, and sometimes of dangerous irritation.

A copy of Mr Motleys despatch on the subject and of the Act of Parliament of May 12th 1870 are also transmitted

U. S. GRANT.

WASHINGTON, MAY 26TH, 1870.

Copies, DNA, RG 59, General Records; *ibid.*, RG 130, Messages to Congress. A printed copy of USG's letter and enclosures are *ibid.*, RG 46, Presidential Messages, Foreign Relations, Great Britain. On Feb. 27, 1871, USG wrote to the Senate. "I transmit to the Senate, for it's consideration with a view to ratification, a Convention between the United States and Great Britain, concluded at Washington on the 23d instant, supplemental to the Convention between the two countries concluded May 13th 1870, concerning the citizenship of citizens or subjects of either country emigrating to the other. The conclusion of the supplemental Convention now submitted was found to be expedient in view of the stipulation contained in Article II of the before named Convention of May 13th, 1870, that the two Governments should agree upon the manner in which the renunciation, within the periods specified, by naturalized citizens and subjects of either country, of their naturalization, should be effected." DS, *ibid.* The enclosures are *ibid.*

1. On July 13, 1870, USG wrote to the Senate. "In answer to their Resolution of the 8th instant, I transmit to the Senate a Report from the Secretary of State and the papers which accompanied it." DS, *ibid.*, Presidential Messages. The enclosures are *ibid.* See *SED*, 41-2-114.

2. Edward H. Stanley, British foreign secretary, 1866–68.

To Senate

To the Senate of the United States:

I transmit to the Senate for consideration, with a view to its ratification, an Additional Article to the Treaty of the 29th of November, last, for the annexation of the Dominican Republic to the United States, stipulating for an extension of the time for exchanging the ratifications thereof,—signed in this city on the 14th. instant by the plenipotentiaries of the parties.

It was my intention ~~also~~ to have also negociated with the Plenipotentiary of St. Doming, amendments to the treaty ~~of for the~~ of anexation, ~~of the iIsland of St. Doming~~, to obviate objections which may be urged against ~~the present treaty. it~~ the treaty as it is now worded.[1] But on reflection I deem it better to submit to the Senate the propriety of their amending the treaty in such a manner [as follows first] as to fix definitely [specify;] first that the obligations of this govt. shall not exceed the $1.500.000 00/100 stipulated in the treaty: second to determine the manner of appointing the agents to receive and pay out [disburse] the same: third to settle [determine] the class of creditors who shall take precedence in the settlement of their claims: and, finally such other [to insert] amendments as may suggest themselves to the minds of Senators to carry out, in good faith, the [conditions of the] treaty submitted to the Senate of the United States, in January last, according to the spirit ~~in which~~ and intent of that treaty. ~~was negociated.~~ From the best [most reliable] information I can get [obtain] the sum agreed to be paid to St. Domingo [specified in the treaty] will pay every just claim against that [the] republic [of St. Domingo.] and leave a balance sufficint to carry on a territorial govt. until such time as new laws for providing [a territorial] revenue can be enacted and put in force.

I feel an unusual anxiety for the ~~success of the~~ ratification of this treaty because I believe it will redound greatly to the ~~interest~~ glory of the two countr~~y~~ies interested, to civilization, and to the extirpation of the institution of slavery.

The theory [doctrine] promulgated by President Monroe ~~that [any attempt on the part of European powers to "extend their system to any portion of this hemisphere" would be considered by the United States "as dangerous to our peace and safety"]~~ has been adhered to, by all political parties, and now with apparent universal acquiescence, we have declared that no [I now deem it proper to assert the equally important principle that hereafter no] territory on this Continent ~~can~~ shall [be regarded as subject to transfer to a European power.]

T The government of St. Doming has voluntarily sought this alliance [annexation]. It is a weak power, numbering probably less than 120.000 souls, [and yet] possessing one of the richest territories under the Sun, capable of supporting a population of

10.000.000 of people in luxury. I have information, which I believe, reliable that a first class European power stands ready now
to offer $2.000.000 for the possession of Samina Bay. [alone]   If
refused by us with what grace can we say to any [prevent a] foreign
power[2] who may come in for [from attempting to secure] the prize
we refuse, "hands off"?   The people of St. Domingo are not capable of maintaining themselves in their present condition, and must
look for outside support. She [They] yearns for the protection of
our free institutions and laws, our progress and civilization. Let us
give them: and if in good time providence should make it clear that
a Confederation of all the Islands of the Caribian Sea, and Gulf of
Mexico, under a protectorate or other supervision of the United
States should be desirable, there will be nothing in this treaty to
prevent it. such an arrangement. [Shall we refuse them?]

The acquisition of St Doming is desirable because of its geographical position. It commands the entrance to the Caribian sea
and [the] Isthmus transit of Commerce. It possesses the richest soil,
best and most capacious harbors, most salubrious climate and the
greatest abundance of [most valuable] products of the forrest, mine
and soil, for commerce of value of all any of the [West India]
islands. Its possession by us would [will in a few years] build up a
coastwise Commerce of immense magnitude in a few years, which
would will go a great ways far towards towards restoring to us our
[lost] Merchant Marine. It will give to us those articles which we
consume so largely of and do not produce, thus equalizing our exports with our [and] imports. [In case of foreign war] It will give
us command of all the islands refered to, in case of foreign war,
instead of them becoming [and thus prevent an enemy from ever
again possessing himself of] rendezvous upon our very coast, for
our enemy, upon our very coast. [At present] Now our coast trade
between the Atl States bordering on the Atlantic and those bordering on the Gulf of Mexico, is cut in two by the Bahamas and Cuba
[the Antilles]. Twice we must, as it were, pass through foreign
countries to get, by sea, from Georgia to the West Coast of Florida
coastwise.

St. Domingo being free, with a stable government, and de-

~~veloping her resources, has resources as they will~~, [under which her immense resources can be developed] ~~would~~ill give remunerative wages to tens of thousand of laborers not now upon the island. ~~It would~~ This labor will come in canoes, ~~on raf~~ and in every conceivable way from [take advantage of every available means of transportation to abandon] the adjacent islands both for [and seek] the advantages [blessings] of freedom, and its sequence; each inhabitant receiving the reward of his own labor. ~~Slavery in~~ Porto Rico and Cuba ~~would~~ will have to ~~be~~ abolished [slavery] as a measure ~~to~~ of self preservation; to retain its [their] laborers.

St. Domingo will become a large consumer of the products of Northern farms and Manufacturies. The cheap rate at which her citizens will [can] be furnished with food, tools and machinery, will make it necessary that the other islands contiguous [islands] should have the same advantages [in order] to compete in the production of Sugar, Coffee, tobacco, tropical fruits &c. thus opening [This will open] to us a still wider market for our products.

The production of our own supply of these articles will cut off more than One Hundred Millions of our [annual] imports; beside ~~it will~~ largely increasing our exports. With such a picture it is easy to see how our large debt abroad is ultimately to be extinguished. With a balance of trade against us ~~of equal~~ (including interest on bonds held by foreigners, and money spent by our citizens traveling in foreign ~~countries~~ lands) is greater than [equal to] the entire yeald of the precious metals in this country, it is not so easy to see how this result is to be [otherwise] acomplished.

The acquisition of St. Doming is an adherence to the "~~m~~Monroe ~~d~~Doctrine"; it is a measure of national protection: it is assuming [asserting] our just claim to a controlling influence over the great Commercial traffic soon to flow from West to East by way of the Isthmus of Darien; it is to build up our Merchant Marine; it is to build up [furnish] new markets for the products of our farms, shops and manufacturies; it is to make slavery insupportable in Cuba and Porto Rico, at once, and ultimately so in Brazil; it is to settle the unhappy condition of Cuba, and end an exterminating conflict; it is to provide honest means of paying our honest debts, without a long period of privation and want [without overtaxing the people]; ~~it~~It is to provide [furnish] our citizens with [the] necessaries of every day life at cheaper rates than ever before; and it is in fine a rapid stride towards that greatness ~~among nations~~ which the intelligence, industry and enterprise of the Citizens of the United States ~~are~~ entitled ~~to~~ this country to assume among nations.

[Ex. Mansion
May 31. 1870.]

ADf (bracketed material not in USG's hand), DLC-USG, III; DS, DNA, RG 46, Presidential Messages, Foreign Relations, Dominican Republic; copy (of first paragraph, dated May 16, 1870), *ibid.*, RG 59, General Records. On May 28 and June 3, Secretary of State Hamilton Fish recorded in his diary. "President— Reads to me his draft of an intended 'Executive' Message to the Senate, on the San Domingo treaty—I leave with him translation of the form of return of the Election held in San Domingo—:" "The President's San Domingo ~~treat~~ message, sent to Execu Session last Tuesday appeared in yesterdays (Thursday's) N Y Herald—Chandler of Michigan was at my office before I went to Cabinet: he said the publications was 'all right' that it was furnished from the White House—he claimed to know 'all about it'—In Cabinet the publication was spoken of. Prsdt said he had been very much disturbed about it, last evening—that Genl Hillyer had been at the White House & told him of its appearance—That late in the Evening, Keim of the Herald, comes to assure him the copy had been obtained from a Senator—" DLC-Hamilton Fish.

1. On May 15, Fish had written to USG. "Before leaving Washington last evening, I requested Mr. Davis to submit to your consideration a further amendment to the San Domingo treaty, viz.: instead of making the future admission as a State imperative, depending only as to time on the discretion of Congress, to reserve to Congress the right *either* to admit the State, *or* to remit it to a condition of either separate or of confederate independence; the latter in connection with other of the islands of the Gulf. This proposition, it may be expected, would find friends among those who desire the influence of our institutions and our protection to be extended to San Domingo, and to the other islands, but who hesitate upon the question of the absorption of tropical possessions. It is perhaps the most practical mode of establishing a protectorate consistent with constitutional limitations. It would present to the other communities in the West Indies the idea of separation from European dependence, of confederation, and of alliance with this government as their natural protector and friend, in a form the least likely to excite their susceptibilities or their natural pride. Prosperity resulting to San Domingo would stimulate and excite the desire of other colonies to establish similar relations. The right to remit the country to a condition of independence or confederate nationality may either be absolute in Congress, or with the consent of the people and Territorial Legislature of San Domingo. The absolute right in Congress is better, and would secure more strength to the treaty, as it would leave to this government the shaping and the control of the future confederation of the islands, should such confederation be deemed expedient. General Schurz showed me yesterday a can-

vass of the Senate, agreeing, as he said, with one made by Senator Stewart, giving thirty-one Senators opposed to the Treaty. If an amendment such as I suggest would cause the adoption of the treaty it should originate from the Administration. San Domingo, I think, would not hesitate to accede to the treaty with the amendment. It would give them present relief, and the assurance of new growth, strength, and stability. If you approve, I would suggest a few days' delay in calling up the treaty while the idea is being presented, and the opponents of the treaty are being consulted." Allan Nevins, *Hamilton Fish: The Inner History of the Grant Administration* (New York, 1936), pp. 326–27.

On May 16, J. C. Bancroft Davis, asst. secretary of state, wrote to Fish. "The President called a special Cabinet meeting this morning to consider the application of Mr Thornton. First he laid before it your letter of yesterday, which I left at the White House early this morning. He has been busy during the morning preparing a message to accompany the additional article to the San Domingo treaty—but when he read the article, and found that it did not embrace the three points you spoke to me about the other day he Concluded to defer sending it in until your return. In bringing your letter before the Cabinet he seemed to take more kindly to the idea of a protectorate than he did yesterday. Robeson spoke strongly and decidedly for accepting the proposed modification. So did Cox in his milder way. The Presdt appealed to the Atty Genl to know if it might not be recognizing the principle of secession. The Atty Genl answered that the amendment does not contemplate that the people of San Domingo may go away of their own volition, but gave to the United States the power to get rid of them. The Presdt said he was not afraid that that power would ever be exercised. Belknap and Creswell were rather averse to yielding anything to the Senate, but said nothing. Boutwell was not there. After some discussion the question was postponed to enable the President to talk with some of the friends of the Treaty. I am only afraid that Morton will, for purposes of his own give him bad advice. We then brought up Mr Thornton's matters. The Presdt said he regarded the refusal to let the vessel go throgh as unfriendly to England— And added 'I guess we all feel so too'—which occasioned a general roar. It seemed to be felt all round that they might retaliate by shutting up the Wellan[d] canal. After considerable discussion it ended by agreeing that if Thornton would put in writing what he had said to you & me, we would answer that the vessel might go through with stores of provision, & that we should say to him that it will be agreeable to this govt if the home govt will issue a proclamation of amnesty before the jurisdiction is transferred. I have so told Thornton, & he is to write his letter this afternoon. I also told him that the Atty Genl and Belknap had sent the desired telegrams. I have also seen Cushing. He will have his material in shape this week and as the President is bent upon a message, I shall try to get together enough material for you to shape one that will do him credit. If he goes on in the track he was in this morning he will—well he will not do the subject justice." ALS, DLC-Hamilton Fish.

On May 21 and 24, Fish wrote in his diary. "*President* comes to State Dept—Talks of the San Domingo treaty—objects to the proposed amendment which I had requested Davis to suggest—He thinks it was Schurz suggestion. Davis had so told him—& he regards it as the suggestion of an opponent—I tell him that it was wholly my own idea, & had not been mentioned to any one except to Davis for the purpose of being communicated to him (I had written to him on Sunday last from NY. on the subject)   I express the conviction that the

Treaty will be rejected unless some of its opponents are gained over by some new feature, or principle & that this had occured to me as possibly capable of gaing some—He authorises me to see Sumner & some others if I think proper, on the subject—" "Left with the President the Article extending the time for Exchange of Ratification of the San Domingo treaty & a message to the Senate transmitting the Same—Also suggested Amendments to the Treaty—prepared by   —He requests me to send him the proposed Amendment which I submitted to Senator Howard.—also that which I suggested to him in my letter of 15th inst from NY—" *Ibid.*

2. On June 2, USG wrote to the Senate. "In reply to your Resolution of the 1st instant requesting 'in confidence'—any information in the possession of the President 'touching any proposition, offer, or design of any foreign power to purchase or obtain any part of the territory of St. Domingo, or any right to the Bay of Samana'—I transmit herewith a copy of a letter dated 27th of April 1870, addressed to 'Colonel J. W. Fabens, Dominican Minister, Washington,' by 'E. Herzberg Hartmont, Dominican Consul General in London.'" DS, DNA, RG 46, Presidential Messages, Foreign Relations, Dominican Republic. The enclosure is *ibid.*

To Edwards Pierrepont

Washington D. C. June 1st *1870*

DEAR JUDGE:

I owe you an apology for not answering your kind invitation for Mrs. Grant & myself to pay you a visit this Summer earlyer. So soon as as Congress adjourns we will go to our house at Long Branch where we expect to remain pretty closely for the Summer, visiting West Point occasionally however for a few days at a time, during some one of which visits we will avail ourselves of Mrs. Pierrepont's, and your kind invitation.

We will have plenty of room at our Cottage to entertain our friends and will expect to see your self and family there some time during the Summer.

Truly yours
U. S. GRANT

JUDGE E. PIERREPONT,
NEW YORK CITY,

ALS, ICarbS.

To Ulysses S. Grant, Jr.

Washington D. C. June 3d *1870*

DEAR BUCK,

Enclosed I send you $70 00/100. Acknowledge receipt. Your Ma and I will probably be in Boston to meet you when you go there for examination. All are well and send love.

Yours Truly
U. S. GRANT

ALS, The Book Sail, Orange, Calif.

To William S. Rosecrans

Washington D. C. June 5th *1870*

DEAR GENERAL:

Your favor of the 30th ult. enclosing a printed letter addressed to "The People of the U. S."[1] is just received. I will take great pleasure in reading it and in giving such consideration as I may deem practicable and timely.

Whilst the nation is adjusting itself to the changes of the last ten years, and to the payment of our vast debt without oppressive taxation, the people are jealous of new policies which look to an outlay of money. I do not know that your proposition looks to this for I have not yet read it, but will to-day.

Yours Truly
U. S. GRANT

GN. W. S. ROSECRANS,
NEW YORK CITY

ALS, CLU. On June 4, 1870, Horace Porter had written to U.S. Representative James A. Garfield of Ohio. "I got the President to write Gen. Rosecrans a letter in reply to one he sent enclosing his Mexican project, I thought it would help to soften his feelings. He dated his letter simply 'New York'. Will you be kind enough to address the enclosed more definitely if you know whom he is staying with in N. Y.—and oblige . . ." ALS, DLC-James A. Garfield.

On April 11, 1869, William S. Rosecrans had written to USG. "*Confidential,*

& *Personal*. . . . I have officially communicated to the Dept. of State the moribund condition of Mexico, indicated the reasons why humanity and wisdom not to say nessesty demand that you should take some action in the matter. You occupy a position of independence and I congratulate you upon it and upon your inaugural in carrying out which I wish you complete success. But as the condition of this country demands action that might *seem* to interfere with your programme of economy, I wish to suggest that it is only a seeming interference not a real one. Because in the first place if we neglect our opportunities now, it will probably cost us dearly hereafter. 'A stitch in time saves nine'. In the next place what ought now to be done can be effected mostly by private capital and a peaceful, humane and beneficial conquest achieved for the benefit of both nations, which will smoothe the way to a union as close as may be necessary to secure the interests of both countries any probable contingency. The plans I propose will also enable you to enlist in support of the administration great commercial moneyed and banking interests, in measures which will give it glory and prestige at home and abroad. The first is to en[s]ure the construction of two rail road lines from the Gulf to the interior on great commercial lines—One from Vera Cruz or Anton Lizardo to this valley—the other from the best point in the region of Tampico or Tuxpan to Mexico—by American capital and enterprize. Concessions for both these routes have been asked, and if granted and the guarranty of peace and stability obtained would make enterprizes worth millions while they would open up the most beautiful, fertile, and productive regions to our enterprize and immigration. If these two roads were undertaken by the proper men with ample means and energy they could with ordinary prudence control the country. Protection is ~~A~~all that would be necessary to ensure [—] and success. To prepare for this, changes must be made in this Govt. either by a change in the cabinet or its overthrow which last is very likely to happen ere long. To provide the means for the Government we want and at the same time get rid of the debt which hangs over Mexico or rather to reduce it to an amt which it can pay interest and finally extinguish: I propose that an association of American capitalists be formed ~~under~~ on the suggestion of the Administration who will buy the Mexican Bonded debt both domestic and foreign and advance what money She may require to carry out the programme to be arranged these purchasers agreeing to take a percentage of the nominal value of the debt which will give them a very large profit and giving a margin for our Government and Mex. to save a great deal of what Mexico would otherwise have pay for them, while it would at once reestablish her credit. . . . I think, with the chances of national and individual advantage offered and with the aid of your friend A. T. Stewart and other eminent and influential men the interest could be so distributed as to result in an entire and speedy success. The bearer of this Dr C W Brink our Vice Consul here has knowledge of many details in reference to the debt which he can give when required. Apologising for the length of this letter . . ."
ALS, USG 3.

1. William S. Rosecrans, *"Manifest Destiny," "The Monroe Doctrine," and Our Relations With Mexico* (n. p., 1870).

To Hamilton Fish

Washington, D. C. June 8th 18670.

SIR:

Please send a letter to Mr. R. H. Perry,[1] U. S. Commercial Agent to St. Domingo, directing him to answer in writing whether or not he showed his official correspondence with the Dominican Government to newspaper correspondents or other persons, and forward his answer to me at your earliest convenience.

Yours truly

U. S. GRANT

HON. HAMILTON FISH
SECT'Y OF STATE.

LS, DNA, RG 59, Miscellaneous Letters. On June 4, 1870, Secretary of State Hamilton Fish had recorded in his diary. "I told the President of the charges Perry makes against Babcock—& that I had required him to put them in writing which he promised to do—Prsdt had heard of them—says Perry 'has been runing about town, repeating them'—He evidently is inclined not to believe them—says of the officers whom he sent down, he thinks all honest—but ha[d] told Babcock that if any thing dishonorable or dishonest was proved against either, he should answer it with his Commission—(the officers are Babcock, Ingalls, and Sackett)" DLC-Hamilton Fish. See *SRC*, 41-2-234; letter to Hamilton Fish, June 18, 1870.

1. On Oct. 7, 1869, Lt. Gen. Philip H. Sheridan, Chicago, wrote to USG. "The bearer Major Raymond H Perry late of the volunteer army of the U. S., desires the appointment of U. S. Marshal for the western district of Texas. In case of an existing vacancy in said position I cordially recommend him for the place. Major Perry served with credit during the War, and during the years 1865, 6 and 7 was with me in the South. For some time he was Chief of Police at Galveston Texas having been appointed by the late Genl. Charles Griffin. He is an active energetic and fearless man and can be relied upon to do his duty." Copies, DNA, RG 59, Letters of Application and Recommendation; *ibid.*, RG 60, Records Relating to Appointments. On Oct. 18, USG endorsed this letter. "Respectfully refered to the Atty Gen. for such recommendation as he deems proper. If there is a change to be made in the Marshalship I think we can do no better than to take Major Perry" Copies, *ibid.* On Oct. 20, Raymond H. Perry, Washington, D. C., wrote to USG. "I am ready to go at an hours notice to any part of the World alone or in company as you wish, and in any position to serve you, I want to earn your confidance and a reputation, I return to night to my farm in Bristol Rhodes Island where I can be found if wanted, I have taken and can take as desperate chances as any man that lives if necessary, Enclosed are copies of letters from Lt Gen P. H. Sheridan also from Gov A. E. Burnside and Senator H. B. Anthony of R. I. who know me" ALS, *ibid.*, RG 59, Letters of Application and Recommendation. The enclosures are *ibid.* On the same day,

Orville E. Babcock wrote to Fish. "The President directs me to send you the enclosed papers and to say that he thinks Maj. Perry is a proper person to send to Sto Domingo in the place of Mr. Smith, provided you have not already selected one." LS, *ibid.* See *SED*, 41-3-17; *PUSG*, 18, 505–6.

To Zachariah Chandler

Washington, D. C. June 8th 18670

DEAR SENATOR:

Your letter of yesterday enquiring whither I had any consultation with the Ch. of the Com. on Foreign Relations relative to the Sant-Domingo treaty, prior to sending that treaty to the Senate for action, is just rec.d. I did call at Senators Sumner's residence during the first week of Jan.y last for the express purpose of consulting with him relative to the treaty which had been negoetiated. He seemed to be much interested in the matter and requested me to send Gen. Babcock to see him to inform him more fully of the terms of the treaty, the resources of the island &c. I will not pretend to quote the exact language of the Senator but he did reply to the direct question from Col. Forney,[1] who was present during the interview, "whether he would support the treaty," in such language as to leave no doubt upon my mind that he would support it. Col. Forney will sustain this statement, and may remember more exactly than I do the language used by Mr. Sumner.

Truly yours
U. S. GRANT

HON. Z. CHANDLER, U. S. S.

ALS, DLC-Zachariah Chandler. See Charles Callan Tansill, *The United States and Santo Domingo, 1798–1873* (Baltimore, 1938), pp. 383–88; David Donald, *Charles Sumner and the Rights of Man* (New York, 1970), pp. 434–38. On June 18, 1870, Orville E. Babcock wrote to Adam Badeau. "I suppose you are in England though no one has so reported to me. I trust you are and that before this you are in full possession of your office—and all goes well. Your humble servt has been *investigated*, since you left, but I think not hurt much. They were after the President and hoped to hitch something onto me—and thus hurt the old man, . . . We are in the midst of a terrible *struggle* in the Senate, Sumner Shurz, &c. 'versus the President', One vacancy has occurred in the Cabinet—

and if the war is carried on, and the treaty defeated by them, you will see some fighting—equalled only at Vicksburg, Wildrnss Richm, &c &c. He has a large majority with him in the Senate, and you will see his friend's friends will be provided for at the expense of his enemies (friends). He will strike high and low. The fight has opened, and he is as much in earnest, as he was in the Wilderness. Were it not that Sumner, and his followers, have the support of the democrats the treaty would have been confirmed *months* ago. Mr Sumner has opposed—or spoken unkindly of every foreign appointment made by the President, except two, Motley & Jay, and he spares no pains to denounce them. He has lied to the President about supporting the Treaty, and he learns this will be shown up. He made a most cowardly attack upon me in the Senate, but my name was handsomely defended, and Mr Sumners. committee snubbed twice on account of it, As he is a coward. I simply intend to denounce him as a liar and coward—and let the poor *sexless* fool go.—. . ." ALS, MH.

1. John W. Forney, born in 1817, edited newspapers in Lancaster, Pa., and Philadelphia, became influential in state and national Democratic politics, and served as clerk of the U.S. House of Representatives (1851–56, 1860–61). He allied with the Republicans at the onset of the Civil War, founded the *Washington Chronicle*, and served as secretary of the Senate (1861–68). See Forney, *Anecdotes of Public Men* (New York, 1873–81).

On June 6, 1870, Babcock wrote to Forney. "During the last interview between us at your room, when the Dominican Treaty was the subject of our conversation, I think you told me that you were present at the interview between President Grant and Senator Sumner (at the Senator's house), in Dec. last, when the President explained the treaty to the Senator, and the course he had pursued, and expressed a hope that the Senator would support the measure, &c. and that Mr. Sumner replied, 'Mr President I could not think of doing otherwise than supporting the treaty', or words to that effect. Will you please send me an answer by the bearer and inform me whether I am correct in my remembrance of what you told me, . . ." Copy, DLC-Zachariah Chandler. On the same day, Forney wrote to Babcock. "I was present at Mr. Sumner's residence when President Grant called and explained the Dominican treaty to the Senator; and, although I cannot recall the exact words of the latter, I understood him to say that he would cheerfully support the treaty. At the President's request I remained to hear his explanations, and I am free to add that such is my deep regard for Mr. Sumner that his indorsement of the treaty went very far to stimulate me in giving it my own support. I had already said this much to Mr. S., who, however, replies that other information since obtained has shaped his present action." *Washington National Republican*, Dec. 23, 1870.

To Charles W. Ford

Washington D. C. June 8th *1870*

DEAR FORD:

Enclosed I send you power of atty. from G. W, Dent, to me authorizing ~~to~~me to act for him in all matters pertaining to any property he has in the State of Mo. I presume the paper should be recorded in St. Louis Co. and I send it to you for that purpose.

I hope Burns[1] will still stand up to his contract. It is certain I should have had to have done so had the decission been the other way. Has an appeal been taken?

Yours Truly

U. S. GRANT

ALS, DLC-USG. On June 17, 1870, USG telegraphed to Charles W. Ford. "Close with Burns the whole amount to be paid by July fifteenth. if necessary, one third can be paid now" Telegram received (at 11:20 P.M.), *ibid.* Noted on the telegram received is the amount $16,516.50, divided by three ($5,505.50), and payments scheduled for June 18, July 1 and 15.

1. Calvin F. Burnes. See letter to William S. Hillyer, [Jan. 1873].

To Oliver P. Morton

Washington, D. C. June 8th 1870.

DEAR SIR:

My attention has been called to an article from the pen of the Washington correspondent of the New York Evening Post of June the 6th in which this passage occurs: "About the end of Nov. Mr P. reported that Senator Morton had drawn up a proclamation recognizing the Cubans as belligerents which he had taken to the President to sign. The President had, however, declined to sign it as it was antagonistic to the policy which the President expected to follow."

This is entire news to me. You never showed me a proclamation, or any other paper touching our relations with Cuba prepared by you or which you wished me to sign. The statement of the Post correspondent so far as it relates to you in any matter about which I know anything is entirely without foundation.

Yours truly
U. S. GRANT.

HON. O. P. MORTON
U S SENATE.

Copy, DLC-USG, II, 1.

To Hamilton Fish

Washington D. C. June 9th *1870*

DEAR GOVERNOR:

Please furnish my office with copies of all correspondence and information in relation to the arrest, confinement and release of the man Hatch[1] whose statements senator Ferry[2] has received as conclusive evidence against whomsoever he chooses to make charges. I want them to furnish to the committee of investigation ordered yesterday. I shall be absent tomorrow and next day[3] but if the papers are left with Gen. Babcock he will furnish them to the Committee:

Truly yours
U. S. GRANT

HON. H. FISH,
SEC. OF STATE.

ALS, DLC-Hamilton Fish.

1. Davis Hatch, an American citizen, had been imprisoned in Santo Domingo to prevent him from opposing annexation. On Feb. 24, 1870, USG had written to the Senate. "In answer to the Resolution of the Senate of the 21st instant, directing the Secretary of State to furnish the Senate with copies of all correspondence relating to the imprisonment of Mr. Davis Hatch by the Dominican Government, I transmit a report of the Secretary of State, upon the subject." DS, DNA, RG 46, Presidential Messages. The enclosures are *ibid*. See *SED*, 41-2-54; *SRC*, 41-2-234. On Feb. 28, J. C. Bancroft Davis, asst. secretary of state, wrote to Orville E. Babcock. ". . . I fear there is no hope that the treaty will make its way through the Senate. If there ever was a ghost of a

chance the Davis Hatch case will kill it." ALS, Babcock Papers, ICN. On May 6, USG transmitted to the Senate additional information concerning the Hatch case. DS, DNA, RG 46, Presidential Messages. The enclosures are *ibid.* See *SED*, 41-2-54, part 2.

2. U.S. Senator Orris S. Ferry of Conn.

3. On June 6, Babcock wrote to Thomas L. Kane, Kane, Pa. "The President directs me to acknowledge the receipt of your letter of the 3d instant, and to say in reply that, the arrangement of the time &c is in the hands of Senator Cameron, and that he understands the Senator will keep you posted by telegraph. It is possible that the party may not go this week, as there are some measures pending that may require the presence of the President all of the week. If he goes the President says he shall not take Jesse with him. He wishes me to communicate his thanks for your kindness." Copy, DLC-USG, II, 1. On June 9, USG, U.S. Senator Simon Cameron of Pa., *et al.* left Washington, D. C., for a Pa. trout-fishing trip and returned on June 13. See *Washington Chronicle*, June 10, 1870.

To Congress

[*June 13, 1870*]

~~Since~~ ~~When~~ soon after [the opening of the present session of] Congress ~~came together, all (and from time to time since,)~~ all that was officially know by the government of the condition of affairs in Cuba,[1] was ~~reported to~~ communicated, and [from time to time since] all the correspondence that has taken place between Spain and the United States, relative to Cuban affairs, ha~~ve~~s been given [furnished for the information of that body]. ~~With the Up~~ [Previous] to the meeting of Congress I ~~observed~~ [adhered to] the precedents of my predecessors in office in maintaining a strict neutrality in the affairs of Spain, with which government we were at peace. ~~Since Congress came together~~ [During the Session] I would not feel [I have not felt] myself justified in taking a step which might be attended with serious results without the advice of that body [the legislative branch of the Government].

Three times since the begining of the conflict in Cuba American vessels, protected by the United States flag, have been seized [captured] upon the high seas and carried into ~~a~~ Spanish ports. In but one instance has there been any reparation made, [and] then tardily ~~and~~ [up] to ~~this~~ [the present] time, ~~though~~ [though repeatedly demmanded and] often promised, no copies [even] have been furnished this government of the evidence upon which the other two vessels were condemned. [have been furnished to this Government][2] ~~fair and in accordance with our own laws and the laws of Nations no matter how much we as a people may sympathize with the revolutionists. In Now however in~~ [In] view of these facts ~~however~~ and the further fact that Spain, with all her Armies and Armament [the combined power of her army and navy], has not been able to suppress the rebellion ~~in~~ which has [now] continued ~~now~~ almost two years and in view of the ~~cruel manner of conducting the war by Spain,~~ [her failure to protect American citizens] failure of Spain to protect American citizens, or to give them time to prove their innocence of complicity in conspiracy against Spanish authority, as two American prisoners who were executed declared their ability to do and the proximity to our own shores of the seat of war, it becomes a question, how long [we] can ~~we~~ permit this contest without further noticing it? and what ~~is~~ our duty [is] to the unhappy belligerents, ~~and~~ to humanity and to ourselvs. ~~This nation reserves to itself the right to judge when to acknowledge the independence of a people struggling to free themselves from foreign rule. It also reserves the right to judge of the policy of recognizing belligerency, and when such recognition can be extended legally.~~

I believe the time has come when a decided protest should be entered, by the United States, against a further continuence of the strife in Cuba, and against the ~~inhuman and~~ summary manner of ~~killing~~ taking the lives of prisoners, almost as soon as ~~caught, upon after trials which are but little better than mockeries~~ [captured].

~~The statement accompanying this has been prepared by my direction, and so far as it details the policy has my approval. To Congress the question is committed of our future action in this matter is committed.~~ [This grave question is submitted to Congress for its action]

ADf (bracketed material not in USG's hand), DLC-USG, III. On June 13, 1870, Secretary of State Hamilton Fish wrote in his diary. "President read some

passages ~~of~~ which he had written to add to a *part* of the proposed paper submitted by me some time since—he referred therein (as in the paper he read to
me on 2d Inst. (see page 71) to the cruelties practiced in Cuba, specifying the
'Capture' of three American Vessels on the High seas. . . . He then requested
me to read the draft Message I had ~~written~~ read to him this morning—I had
had two copies made—& read it—Gov Cox was unusually silent—Hoar & Robeson urged the necessity of declaring the attitude of the Administration—the
importance of consolidating the opinions of the Party—&c—&c—President evidently wishes to add something which may show condemnation of Spain, &
more of sympathy with Cuba, than wd be drawn from my draft—I contend that
my draft presents a just & impartial summary of the case—condemns each
party—that by adding what the Prsdt has written, its logical effect will be
destroyed   That the conclusion of a Message containing the allegations against
Spain which he made, ought to be a recommendation of a declaration of war—
that the charges which he made were not in all respects accurate, & that if
specific acts of wrong by Spain were alluded to, his summary was not complete—that no specific case should be alluded to unless a carefully prepared
presentation of the whole complaint, were made—& I was not prepared to say
that such presentation might not justify a recommendation of a declaration of
War, 'if it is thought advisable to do so'   It was generally admitted that if War
is to be resorted to it should be by *direct* declaration, & not by embarassing Spain,
by a declaration of belligerency—Agreed unanimously that no condition of facts
exists to justify belligerency—*Cresswell* admits that 'he thinks so—has so
thought for some months—although at one time he favored it.' Finally, the Prsdt
amends his sentences, by refering in general terms to seizures on the high seas,
embargoes of property, & personal outrages—& Robeson adds the concluding
sentence, claiming that, the question of belligerency is distinct from these questions of wrongs, which are being pressed for indemnification &c—& that if not
satisfied they will be made the subject of a future Message—And thus it is
agreed that the Message shall be sent in—It was sent to Congress after 4 PM—
Vide tomorrows Newspapers for the Message & its reception (I think the conclusion reached, both right—& politic)" DLC-Hamilton Fish. Fish had drafted
a message to Congress explaining administration policy of neutrality in Cuban
affairs. ADf, *ibid*. The final version, signed by USG, is in DNA, RG 46, Presidential Messages. See *SED*, 41-2-99; *SMD*, 49-1-162, part 1, pp. 384–89. On
July 10, Fish recorded some remarks by USG: "without refering to other instances, on two important occasions, at least, your steadiness, & wisdom have
kept me from mistakes into which I should have fallen—On one of these occasions you led me against my judgment at the time,—you almost forced me—in
the matter of signing the late Cuban message—and I now see how right it was—
and I desire most sincerely to thank you—The measure was right & the whole
country acquiesces in it—" DLC-Hamilton Fish. See Allan Nevins, *Hamilton
Fish: The Inner History of the Grant Administration* (New York, 1936), pp.
353–63.

1. On Feb. 11, USG had written to the House of Representatives. "In compliance with the resolution of the House of Representatives requesting me to
furnish any information which may have been received by the government in
relation to the recent assault upon and reported murder of one or more American
citizens in Cuba, I communicate a report from the Secretary of State with the

papers accompanying it." Copies, DNA, RG 59, General Records; *ibid.*, RG 130, Messages to Congress. The enclosures are *ibid.*, RG 59, General Records. See *HED*, 41-2-140. On Feb. 18, USG wrote to the House transmitting additional papers. Copies, DNA, RG 59, General Records; *ibid.*, RG 130, Messages to Congress. The enclosures are *ibid.*, RG 59, General Records. See *HED*, 41-2-140, part 2. On July 9, USG wrote to the Senate. "In answer to the resolutions of the Senate of the 26th of May and of the 14th of June last, I transmit a report from the Secretary of State thereupon, and the papers by which it was accompanied." DS, DNA, RG 46, Presidential Messages. On the same day, Fish had written to USG submitting information concerning the seizure of American ships and the imprisonment of American citizens in Cuba. LS, *ibid.* The enclosures are *ibid.* See *SED*, 41-2-108.

2. New page begins; material missing.

To Ebenezer R. Hoar

Washington, D. C. June 15th 18~~6~~70

MY DEAR JUDGE

In accepting your ~~d~~resignation as Atty Genl when the appointment and qualification of your successor, I take this occasion to express to you my high appreciation of the able patriotic and devoted manner in which you have performed the functions of that office   In no less a degree do I do I appreciate the pleasant personal relations which have existed from the beginning of our association officially in public place. Hoping that you will Cary with you, none but pleasant recollections of your connections with the present administration, and with assurances of my personal esteem and friendship I remain,

With Great respect
Yr friend & obt svt
U S GRANT

To HON E R HOAR
ATTY GEN.

Df, OFH; copy, DLC-USG, II, 1. On June 15, 1870, Attorney Gen. Ebenezer R. Hoar had written to USG. "I resign the office of Attorney General of the United States; the resignation to take effect upon the appointment and qualification of my successor." ALS, OFH. On June 17, Secretary of State Hamilton Fish recorded in his diary. "While at dinner Judge Hoar called—He goes home this Evening to return & remain in office until the end of July   The public announcement of his resignation he tells me wa[s] 'owing to one of the leaks at the White House—that the President had given his reply to one of the "*confidential*" clerks to be copied, & thus it had gotten out' hearing it had been telegraphed to the public prints in N. Y. & thus given to the World, he had advised the immediate nomination of his successor to relieve the Prest fro[m] the importunity which wd otherwise follow—. . . In the Evening the President came to see me—Soon I remarked that Judge Hoar's resignation had been a surprise—He said that its announcement was the result of an accident, but being made he determined immediatey to nominate his successor—He did not explain *how* the 'accident' occurred—He refered to the remark he had made at the Cabinet meeting on Tuesday with regard to his wish that all the Members of the Cabinet should sustain his San Domingo treaty—He did not specialy connect Hoar's resignation with this—but I thought the allusion significant, & said that his remark on that occasion, & what he had said to me the day before, about Hoar, & Cox & Boutwell, not sustaining his views on that question had ocurred to me, in connection with this unexpected announcement of the Judge's resignation—His reply was peculiar~~ly~~ & guarded—after a momentary pause, he said 'If it was, no one knows it' Another pause—& he proceeded—'I have a great regard & affection for Judge Hoar—he is a man of great abilities, & learning—& a very charming companion, & true man, & friend—he has not the faculty of making himself popular with politicians. I have said to Senators & others that I mean to recognize my friends—& those who sustain my policy—The Judge told me when Mr Boutwell was appointed that he was willing to withdraw—I have always felt the embarassment of having two Members of the Cabinet from the same State—& you do not know how strongly that has been pressed upon me'— He referred to his desire to appoint the Judge to a seat on the bench of the Supreme Court,—that wd have relieved him of the pressure on the ground of 'two Cabinet officers from one State'—he would have made an excellent Judge— he (the Prest) was greatly grieved by the refusal to confirm him.—He concluded with a warm tribute to the Judges character—" DLC-Hamilton Fish.

On July 29, Secretary of the Interior Jacob D. Cox wrote to Aaron F. Perry. ". . . The Judge has always said that if the presence of two members of the cabinet from [o]n[e] State became embarrassing, he would choo[se to] be the one to step aside; but no allusion [to] the subject had been made for sometime & he was reckoning upon going on as usual when during the hight of the excitement about the San Domingo business, he received a note from the Prest intimating that the time had come when a concession to the Southern States seemed necessary & that for that purpose the Judge would have to make way for a Southern man. Of all this I only know the substance & my statement may not be quite accurate. The Judge immediately took to the President his resignation & learned that Mr Akerman was thought of for the place, Mr A. having been somewhat prominent ~~fo~~ as a candidate for the Circuit Judgeship given to Judge Woods. Judge Hoar recommended that the matter be kept entirely secret till Mr A should accept, so that there might be no scramble for the place, & took special precautions to keep his own part of the correspondence to himself. In some way the matter leaked out from the White House the same day, the President having had his own letter accepting the resignation copied, & as is supposed some one about his office having proved leaky, the press got hold of it, & next morning a correspondent of a paper which had *not* got the news came to Judge Hoar with a despatch from New York asking the meaning of the statement in the 'Times' telegraphic column of that morning that the Atty Gen'l had resigned the day before & his resignation accepted. The Judge refused to give any information but went at once to the President, informed him that some one had abused his confidence, & then advised that the nomination be sent in without delay, which was done. That evening at 7 o'clock I got the 'Times' & started at once to find Judge Hoar to learn what it all meant. Passing down by the Capitol Grounds I met Senator Wilson who stopped me & began to express his regrets at Judge H's resignation & asked me what I knew of the nominee for his place, whom, however, he did not name. Ashamed to confess my ignorance of the whole affair or to ask who the nominee was, I evaded an answer & got into a street car as soon as I could & made for the Judge's lodgings. Thus you will see that all this had sprung up between the Tuesday & Friday cabinet meetings, and as I had not been out of my Department except to go to my house, I had heard nothing of it. What I naturally regarded as the strangest thing about the matter was that on Friday no allusion to it was made at Cabinet meeting, & as the President did not speak of the subject, the rest of us did not feel at liberty to interrogate him about it. I suppose he assumed that we had learned of it from the Judge & his usual reticence seemed to make it hard for him to open the discussion of it at all   That day's silence made it harder to say anything afterward, and so it has never been alluded to. Early the following week I left for the East, was gone a week, & returned with Judge H. I said no allusion was made to the Judge's going—The only correction this needs is to say that on the last cabinet day he was with us, Mr Akerman was also present and on the breaking up of the meeting the Judge said, 'Well Mr. President, I suppose this is the last time I shall meet you here & I shall therefore bid you good bye'— 'Good bye Judge—I hope we shall meet frequently elsewhere, however, & that you will come to see me at Long Branch.' In all this, I am bound to say that I verily believe the President's sincere liking & admiration for Judge Hoar continued, & that I have every reason to be sure that there was not the slightest rub or chafing between them personally. I think it must all be summed up in this— The President had set his heart on an object for which Congressional assistance was indispensable—He had heard frequent iterations of the statement that the Atty Genl was unpopular with a class of Senators and Representatives, & was led to believe that not only the one object might be attained, but power for other purposes also secured by conciliating the dissatisfied in this respect. At the same time Mr Fish was unhappy in regard to his own department & I feared he would insist upon leaving; and as similar Congressional influences might determine his successor in a way not pleasant to my notions, I was seriously contemplating an early return to Cincinnati. The President refused to think of Mr Fish's going for the present at least, & we have settled back into the old quiet, awaiting what may come of the various influences which we know will be actively exerted at Long Branch during the summer. To sum up, the influences in Congress which I regard as the least respectable have achieved a triumph in driving from the Cabinet a man of the most inflexible honesty & bluntness, whose influence was for purity and principle in governmental action, & against the theory of governing by the corrupt use of patronage, under the dictation of Congressmen. I do not see that the President has gained anything in return for this. His force to oppose similar pressure in the future has been weakened, & every member of the cabinet must feel a liability to a similar summary severance of his connection with the Government, which will go far to destroy all personal interest in everything but the work of his own department. . . ." ALS, Cox Papers, Oberlin College, Oberlin, Ohio. See Jacob Dolson Cox, "How Judge Hoar Ceased to be Attorney General," *Atlantic Monthly*, LXXVI, CCCCLIV (Aug., 1895), 162–73.

On July 7, Hoar wrote to USG. "In terminating our official relation, I cannot forbear to express to you the feelings of personal regard and affection to which it has given birth. Since I have been a member of your Cabinet, I have never heard at any meeting a suggestion in regard to any public measure except a desire to promote the public welfare. Meeting as comparative strangers, we have been in our intercourse and relations almost a band of brothers. That your chief motive of action was the desire to deserve well of your countrymen by faithful public service, I believed when you first invited me to act as one of your advisers, and the belief has been strengthened and confirmed by all that I have since seen and known. For the honor which you gave in the selection to a place in the government, I desire to thank you. I have endeavored to repay it by faithful and honest counsel, and am sure that in parting, I leave no one behind me who has a more sincere wish for your success, honor and happiness . . ." Moorfield Storey and Edward W. Emerson, *Ebenezer Rockwood Hoar: A Memoir* (Boston and New York, 1911), p. 213.

To Julia Dent Grant

Washington, D, C,
June 15th 1870

ᴀDEAR JULIA:

All is peace and quiet at the White House. Jesse & your father are well and contented. We hope you and Nellie are having a good time of it, and that Fred[1] has got through his examination creditably.—When you have made up your mind what train you want to leave Jersey City, or Elizabeth, on, telegraph me and I will make arrangements for a car for you.

Love to you, Fred & Nelly.

ULYS.

ALS, USG 3. On June 14, 1870, USG had telegraphed to Julia Dent Grant, West Point, N. Y. "It will be impossible for me to leave Washington this week. All well." ALS (telegram sent at 10:30 P.M.), Richard E. Longacre, Wayne, Pa.

1. On June 26, USG telegraphed to Frederick Dent Grant, Metropolitan Hotel, New York City. "Certainly." ALS (telegram sent at 9:05 P.M.), NN.

To Senate

To the Senate of the United States:

I hereby nominate Amos T. Akerman[1] of Georgia to be Attorney General of the United States vice E. R. Hoar resigned.

U. S. GRANT

EXECUTIVE MANSION.
JUNE 16TH 1870.

DS, DNA, RG 46, Executive Nominations. On June 20, 1870, Henry G. Cole, Marietta, Ga., wrote to USG. "I have been falicitating you and the country on your wise appointment of A. T. Ackerman to be Atorney General of the U. S.— To-day I am pained to see that an effort is [made] to have you withdraw Mr Ackerman's name for that *apt*, I hope Sir, these efforts will not prevale, if they do not, my word for it, that time will show that your appointment of Mr Ackerman is the most wise and judicious that could have bee[n ma]de, And his superior has not filled that place since the dayes of *Wm* Wirt," ALS, *ibid.*, RG 60, Applications and Recommendations. On June 23, the Senate confirmed Amos T. Akerman as U.S. attorney gen.

On March 19, 1869, Lucius J. Gartrell *et al.*, Atlanta, had petitioned USG to retain Henry S. Fitch as U.S. attorney, Ga. DS (11 signatures), *ibid.*, Records Relating to Appointments. In [*March*], Charles H. Prince and Joseph W. Clift wrote to [USG] recommending John Milledge for an appointment. DS, *ibid.* On March 20, Joshua Hill wrote to USG. "I think, it proper to suggest—that unless a better opportunity to provide for my friend Mr. Akerman offers—that at the proper time—he be appointed District Attorney for Georgia—Mr. Akerman, and Mr. T. P. Saffold, whose name has been presented for the office of U. S. Marshal for Ga. are devoted friends. They are equally deserving and modest—and both gentlemen of the highest character. You will remember that Mr. Akermans late letter was addressed to Mr. Saffold—" ALS, *ibid.* A related petition is *ibid.* On April 2, USG nominated Akerman as U.S. attorney, Ga., in place of Fitch; on April 16, the Senate postponed this nomination indefinitely. On April 17, USG nominated Milledge for the position. On Dec. 17, USG nominated Akerman after Milledge resigned.

On Feb. 21, 1870, Akerman, Atlanta, wrote to Milledge. "In reply to your request that I should write something in furtherance of your intended application for an appointment under the present national administration, I can say only what is known to all Georgians at all acquainted with the public men of their State; namely, that you are well qualified for an honorable public station by your personal worth, by your academic and social culture, by your experience in public business, by your devotion to the Union when such devotion was rare in Georgia, by your connection with the Republican party, by the social ban to which political opponents have tried to subject you on account of your vote for President Grant, and by your zealous patriotism. If my attestation of these merits can be of any service to you, you have it in this note, which you can show to whom you may wish." ALS, *ibid.*, RG 59, Letters of Application and Recommendation. On March 14, Milledge wrote to Secretary of State Hamilton Fish. ". . . I held the office of U. S. Dist Atty until Col Akermans disabilities were removed by Congress as soon as they were I resigned the same and if I mistake not sent you a copy of the correspondence I had with him at the time of my appointment—Since my resignation I have been out of employment. Col Akerman was kind enough to give me a general letter to be used when and with whom I saw fit, & which my personal friend Rev Mr Huntington will show you. I desire to present my name as an applicant for a foreign appointment—You know what positions are *vacant*, and the pay attached to each.—I am in need and shall hope to receive under the circumstances, your kind assistance. You can fix me up in some way—My health is suffering for the want of some regular employment. Please interest yourself in my behalf with the President and if you think I had better come on to Washington I will do so as soon as I hear from you. Please make my respects to Mrs Fish . . ." ALS, *ibid.* On July 14, Fitch, Savannah, wrote to William S. Hillyer. "Did you get my last? Do see Grant and Ackerman in person and if I cannot get the appointment of Assistant Atty Genl— leave no stone unturned to secure me a foreign (Germany or French Germany prefered) Consulate—I must see my wife and children or I shall go mad and she is too ill to travel, and may die any time. She writes such beseaching letters to come over and see her and I *cannot* for want of means. I have no fear from what Senator Pratt writes me of my confermation if Grant will only appoint. *Do Do* write at once" ALS, William S. Hillyer Papers, ViU. On July 16, Fitch wrote to Hillyer on the same subject. ALS, *ibid.* No appointments followed.

1. Born in 1821 at Portsmouth, N. H., Akerman graduated from Dartmouth College in 1842, moved to Ga., practiced law, and, after serving in the C.S. Army, became a prominent Republican.

To Gen. William T. Sherman

———

Washington D C
June 17th 1870

GEN.

The Senators from N. C. and some other gentlemen from that State, will call on you (the Sec. of War being absent), to obtain uniforms for State Militia which is about being organized to restore order in their state. Not ~~knowing~~ having the money to pay for the uniforms until the Legislature makes the necessary appropriation, I do not know exactly how they are to get them. I want them to have the uniforms however, and am willing to sign any legal order necessary to accomplish that purpose. It may be well to consult the Judge Advocate Gen on the subject.

Respectfully &c

Your obt. svt.

U. S. GRANT

GEN: W. T. SHERMAN

COMD'G. U. S. ARMY

Copy, DNA, RG 94, Letters Received, 462A 1870. Gen. William T. Sherman endorsed this letter. "I have not a particle of doubt this can easily be accomplished—by ordering the issue of clothing, camp Equipage &c for a full Reg't, to be sent to Raleigh—to be sold to the Governor at prices of their last public auction—his Bond for payment to be accepted on the order of the President" Copy (undated), *ibid.* Related papers are *ibid.*

To Hamilton Fish

Washington D. C. June 18th *1870*

DEAR GOVERNOR:

If Perry should resign his position as Com. Agt. please do not accept it until you see me. I do not think he should be permitted to quit the service until the "Committee of Investigation," before which he has been testifying, has made its report.

Truly Yours

U. S. GRANT

HON. H. FISH.

SEC. OF STATE.

ALS, DLC-Hamilton Fish. The testimony of Raymond H. Perry is printed in *SRC*, 41-2-234. On June 14, 1870, Secretary of State Hamilton Fish had noted in his diary that USG "speaks of the San Domingo treaty—his desir[e] for its ratification—that he wishes all the Members of his Cabinet, & all his friends to use all proper efforts to aid him—that he will not consider those who oppose his policy as entitled to influence in obtaining positions under him—that he will not let those who oppose him 'name Ministers to London' &c a[nd] refers warmly & affectionately to Babcock, whose innocence of the Charges against him he confidently believes—Speaks very strongly against Perry, agains[t] whom he says grave charges were made while in the Army—swindling a Bank in New Orleans: Rape upon a small girl—&c—" DLC-Hamilton Fish.

To John A. Dix

Washington, D. C. June 20th 18670

GN. J. A. DIX,

DEAR SIR:

Yours of the 18th inst. stating that the report had been circulated in Iowa that I had stated that I would not enforce the laws for the collection of taxes, to pay rail-road bonds, if resisted by the citizens, is received. It is hardly necessary for me to deny such a statement. I would hardly invite a community to resist laws which I am sworn to execute. I do however emphatically deny the report, and state further that if it becomes my duty to use force to execute the laws in Iowa, or any other state, I shall do so without hesitation.

Very respectfully
your obt. svt.
U. S. GRANT

ALS, Columbia University, New York, N. Y. On June [18], 1870, John A. Dix, New York City, had written to USG. "Certain persons in Lee county, Iowa, who are resisting the officers of the United States in their efforts to enforce the judgments of the Supreme Court of the United States, have circulated the report that you had said you would not aid those officers in the performance of their duty, if forcibly resisted. I know, of course, that the report is wholly without foundation, but many persons have been deceived by it and encouraged in their resistance of the Federal authority. If you will be so kind as to say that the report is entirely unfounded, I am confident unlawful resistance will cease, and that any further application to you will be unnecessary." Printed as dated June 11 in *Washington Chronicle*, Aug. 13, 1870.

To Charles W. Ford

Washington D. C. June 27th 1870

DEAR FORD:

I am just in receipt of a letter from Geno. W. Dent, San Francisco, in which he says as follows; "A few days ago I called on Jesse Holliday[1] in relation to the Carondelet lands. He informed me that his interest was not ~~with~~ included in Burns 146 arpents. He owns

⅙ of Burns interest but thinks that B has excluded the 5th int. in sale to you. He says he will write to St. Louis and procure all the facts in the premises and advise me. Would it not be well to advise Ford in the mean time to look into Holliday's title? H is disposed to comply with hi[s] former promises."[2] Holliday proposed some time since to compromise on the same terms the others have. I know nothing about what interest he may have, but I want to compromise with all I can. About the last of July I shall go to St. Louis when I want to arrange for having all the lands compromised surveyed into lots of convenient size, and held for sale. Don't you want to act as Real Estate agt.?

Yours Truly

U. S. GRANT

ALS, DLC-USG. On July 2, 1870, Charles W. Ford, St. Louis, wrote to USG. "Your letter & enclosure of the 27th was duly received—Burns deed covers ⅘th leaving ⅕th to Holleday—This is correct. Mr Shepley told me there would be no trouble about Holledays tittle, It could be traced out very readily, I enclose herewith. the power of Atty from Dent to you. duly recorded. I shall be glad to see you out here. I think you ought to come, You will find the 'Butcher Boy', in good trim for you. better than ever before. Will Mrs Grant come out with you? You must let me know in time so that I can find *a place for you to stay*—On the 30th̶1st may—'Decoration day', B Gratz Brown delivered an address at Jefferson City. He thinks it is *pretty good*, I guess—and so do I, and he is so anxious you should read it—that he sent it to me by Houser, of the Democrat, with the request that I should send it to you—So. I enclose it. The weather has been intensly hot for the last three weeks. until. last night we cooled off. Mr & Mrs Casey have been here. He has gone back to N. O. & Mrs Casey to Oakorchard or some other orchard—in Kentucky—I will talk up the land agency business when you come out—I forgot to say—that the McKensie tract or farm near you has been sold. Benton bought the homestead and 140 acres—& paid $27.000 for it—I think he bought for *speculation*," ALS, USG 3.

1. See letter to Charles W. Ford, Nov. 3, 1870.
2. See letter to Charles W. Ford, May 9, 1870.

To James W. Nye

Washington D. C. June 27, 1870

SIR:

In reply to your letter of today, I am pleased to inform you that Gen. Babcock did not exceed my wishes or my verbal instructions to him in connection with the *Confidential Basis*. Gen. Babcock was sent to Sto Domingo to ascertain so far as he could the wishes of the Dominican people and Government with respect to annexation to the United States. If he found them favorable he was directed to ascertain the terms on which they desired annexation. He brought the confidential Basis, which was not binding, or intended to be binding upon either government, unless each saw fit to continue the negotiations. It contains a clause, making it null and void unless accepted and carried into effect.

I also directed the Secretary of the Navy to send, by Gen. Babcock, such instructions to the commanding officer of the U. S. Steamer "Seminola" as would direct him to seize the "Telegrafo", if found on the high seas, and send her to Baltimore for adjudication, she having interfered with our merchant shipping. In transferring these instructions to the commanding officer of the U. S. S. "Tuscarora," Gen. Babcock did no more than was his duty. Gen. Babcock's conduct throughout meets my entire approval.

Yours truly
U. S. GRANT

HON. JAMES W. NYE.
U. S. SENATE.

Copy, DLC-USG, II, 1. James W. Nye, born in 1814 in Madison County, N. Y., practiced law in N. Y., ran unsuccessfully for Congress as a Free Soiler (1848), and became a New York City police commissioner (1857). Nye went to Nevada Territory as governor (1861); following statehood, he was elected U.S. senator (1864). On June 27, 1870, Nye had written to USG. "There is a rumor that General Babcock used your name without authority in reference to the 'Confidential basis' for the annexation of San Domingo, and that Gen. B. exceeded the verbal instruction given him in regard to the 'Telegrapho', and the sending of the 'Tuscarora' after that piratical craft. The Select Committee would be glad to receive from you any explanations or statements you may see fit to make on these subjects—should you think it worth while to notice such imputations."

ALS, OFH. On the same day, Governor Rutherford B. Hayes of Ohio visited USG at the White House. "San Domingo was his pet topic. He did not expect it to be ratified (the treaty). Thought the committee on Foreign Relations badly constituted. *Sumner* as chairman, a man of very little practical sense, puffed-up, and unsound. *Carl Schurz*, an infidel and atheist; had been a rebel in his own country—as much a rebel against his government as Jeff Davis. *Casserly*, a bigoted Catholic who hated England; a learned man and a good man, but his prejudices made him unsafe. I told him I did not know upon what grounds the Administration wanted San Domingo. He in a rapid, brief, but comprehensive way set forth its advantages, described the island, its productions, people, etc., etc., in a most capital way. He said he felt 'much embittered' against Sumner for unjust attacks on Major Babcock. Major Babcock could not defend himself; gave him a fine character. 'I can defend myself, but he is merely a major of engineers with no opportunity to meet a Senator.' " Charles Richard Williams, ed., *Diary and Letters of Rutherford Birchard Hayes* (Columbus, 1924), III, 111–12.

USG received an anonymous undated letter. "we have not had time, to read the testimony, but, we have read this Enclosed item, and we are proud, to know that Gen Babcock's course has been marked with honor. truth and Fidelity, and the Evidence leaves him without a stain. Again, we are glad to know, that this attempt, to injure you or your administration, has failed, and that like the malicious Gold slanders, will rebound upon the authors themselves. Before your nomination, when your claims, and qualifications were being thouroughly Canvassed, it was repeatedly told us that you were not equal, to the high duties and responsibilities of the position, and that your administration would prove a failure, and unequal to the task. We denounced, this spirit of Calumny, which Webster so sternly rebukes, in one of his orations, that would build itself up, upon the ruins of another, and by slander and misrepresentation, and predicted that it would be as successful as any in our history. Despite the abuse of a partisan press, thus far it has been a splendid success. The Republican party has been sustained and strengthened, and the Chicago platform, has been adhered to in the course of the administration. God bless the leader of our armies, 'Without a stain' thats the motto. On your Superior merit, worth and ability, you won your high offices spite of their lies, and without a stain. May it continue to win, by high, conscientious and noble deeds, and your administration. be as successful in the future, as the past. We had rather see this glorious result, than to see our beloved President an Astor or a Stewart. Excuse this hasty line from A. true Friend. . . . The Country will be rejoiced to learn these facts in relation to Gen Babcock. May all who surround our beloved President, have as proud a record. God bless our President, and the members of his administration, and grant them continued success." AL, ICN. The enclosure, a newspaper clipping describing the Senate investigation of Santo Domingo, is *ibid.*

To Hamilton Fish

———

Washington D. C. June [3]0th *1870*

Dear Sir:

Please send message to withdraw the name of Robeson[1] as Consul to Tangiers so as to replace Mathews.[2] Robeson might be informed at the same time that he will be appointed Consul to Leith, and will probably find his commission there on his arrival.

Respectfully
your obt. svt.
U. S. Grant

Hon. H. Fish,
Sec. of State

ALS, DLC-Hamilton Fish. On June 30, 1870, Secretary of State Hamilton Fish wrote to USG. "I send with the nomination of Mr Matthews, & the withdrawal of Robeson, as directed—also a message nominating Robeson to Leith—A despatch recd from Mr Motley says that Fiske has intimated a desire to resign—The term of the Court at which he may be tried is fixed for the 11th July, but the trial may possibly not come off then—& it occurs to me that possibly you would think proper to make the nomination before the Senate adjourns. It would certainly place Robeson more comfortably, & I think would not affect Fiske's trial, or position" ALS, *ibid.* On June 11, John Lothrop Motley, U.S. minister, London, had written to Fish. "*Confidential.* . . . It is my painful duty to call your attention to copies of telegrams received by me and extracts from London papers of recent date, which accompany this Despatch, by which you will learn that the Consul of the United States at Leith, John Safford Fiske, has been arrested at that place and brought to London on a criminal charge. . . . I have also to state to you that Mr. Fiske called at the Legation on the 4th instant, in order to communicate the fact that his name was implicated in the disgraceful affair of the men in women's clothes, now in prison awaiting their trial for felony, and to request some introduction in writing from the Legation to the counsel charged with the prosecution. He thought he could make explanations to that personage which might relieve him from the suspicions resting upon him. He admitted that he had made the acquaintance of the prisoner Boulton at Edinburgh, that he had introduced himself to him, that he had requested him to put on his female attire, that he had received him familiarly at his own house, not in women's clothes however, by invitation eight times, and that he had written letters to him, three of which were in the hands of the prosecution. . . ." LS, DNA, RG 59, Diplomatic Despatches, Great Britain. The enclosures are *ibid.* On June 24, Fish read Motley's letter to USG and to the cabinet. Fish diary, DLC-Hamilton Fish. In an undated cable, Motley wrote to Fish. "Fiske released yesterday on bail. His letter of resignation to you sent on twenty fifth. Vice Consul to-day takes charge of Consulate temporarily" Telegram received (in cipher—on July 1, 11:40 A.M.), DNA, RG 59, Diplomatic Despatches, Great Britain.

1. John T. Robeson, former consul, St. Thomas, Danish West Indies. On June 23, 1869, J. Watson Webb, Washington, D. C., wrote to USG. "Do not suppose I am about to trouble you in regard to my own affairs. I accept your decision as final in regard to myself; but indulge the that you may find it convenient to give my son the appt to West Point. If not, I shall be equally reconciled to such decision. My object in troubling you, is to call attention to the case of Col. *Robeson*, late Consul at St Thomas. He was appointed without his solicitation or knowledge because he was one of the few Union men in West Tennessee; and he with thirteen associates, having escaped from his Rebel neighbors, presented himself to Genl Grant at Cairo. To the question—'What do you want'? His reply was—muskets! He was three times taken Prisoner; & rose to the rank of Colonel, frequently wounded. I first met him at St Thomas in December last. Again February; and he came home with me on the steamer Merrimac. He does not complain of his removal; but he says he cannot lifve in *safety* at home. He seeks therefore, a reappointment at *any distant* Consulate. Whether in India, China, South America or the Pacific, he cares not. He is well qualified for the Post; and I believe, an honest man. His case is a hard one; and I hope you may find it compatable with the public interests, to gratify him." ALS, *ibid.*, Letters of Application and Recommendation. Related papers are *ibid.* On Dec. 6, USG nominated Robeson as consul, Tangier, withdrew the nomination on July 1, 1870, and, on July 9, appointed him as consul, Leith, Scotland.

2. On April 16, 1869, USG appointed Felix A. Mathews as consul, Tangier, but suspended the appointment on Nov. 12. On March 9, 1870, U.S. Representative Aaron A. Sargent of Calif., using White House stationery, wrote to USG. "You remember the interest I take in Felix A Matthews, the Consul at Tangiers, and that I think the evidence is conclusive that he is the victim of a dastardly forgery & slander. I learn this morning that there is a vacancy by death in the Consulship at Tripoli—a place of equal grade. This furnishes an opportunity for you to do justice in a matter that has attracted universal attention and interest in my State. The Republican papers there say you will do justice if investigation shows that Matthews has been foully dealt with. The Copperhead press say the matter will never again be heard from. I believe you will not let an innocent man suffer from the exposed schemes of a scoundrel. I called to suggest that the Consulship at Tripoli be not filled until after an investigation in Matthews case, & that if he is vindicated, & the first letter of the Emperor be shown to be a forgery, that his successor be appointed at Tripoli & he be reinstated." ALS, *ibid.* On July 9, USG reappointed Mathews as consul, Tangier.

To Hamilton Fish

———

Washington D. C. July 1st *1870*

Dear Governor;

As I go away to-day to be absent until the 6th inst.¹ I would like to send to the Senate the name of a successor to Mr. Motley² before starting. The name of Hon. T. F. Freelinghuysen,³ of N. Jersey, strikes me with great favor and if you will have the appointment for him made out I think I will send it to the Senate.

Truly yours
U. S. Grant

Hon. H. Fish
Sec. of State

ALS, DLC-Hamilton Fish. On June 25, 1870, Secretary of State Hamilton Fish wrote in his diary. "Rcd note requesting me to call at the Executive Mansion— Prsdt began by asking if I had seen an article in the NY Tribune of yesterday, (PS—article pasted in margin) refering to my resignation of the State Dept—& appointm't as Minister to England—on being answered in the affirmative, he remarked pleasantly, 'well—you know how little truth there is in it—but I want to explain to you precisely what may have passed so far as I know to have given ~~foundation for it~~—rise to it—' He then said that some three or four weeks ago, some Senators, (naming Morton, Chandler, & Carpenter) were in conversation with him, & remarked that the Senators who were opposing him, especially on the San Domingo treaty, had received more patronage from his Administration, than others who sustained him—That he replied he was aware that such was the case with some, & that he had determined, & had so said to some of his Cabinet, that he would remedy this—that he instanced Sumner & his opposition while he had got Motley appointed to England—but that he intended to recall him, & would do so as soon as he could find the right man to send in his place, but that he must have a first rate man—if they would suggest a suitable person he would appoint him regardless of where he came from—That they expressed themselves much pleased, & separated with the suggestion that they would present a name for the Mission—A short time after Chandler called, & said they had not yet found a name—that it was difficult to find one—that he told him (or perhaps had told the others previously) that he had never thought Motley the right man for London—had thought he should be sent to ~~Londo~~ Vienna.—he told Chandler his original intention with A. T. Stewart in the Treasury, was as he had often told me (he so wrote to me in March last year) to have offered me the Mission to England. Chandler remarked that would be capital—Prsdt did not think I would take it, & he did not know whom to take for Sect. of State, should I leave—& asked how Judge Pierrepont would do for Minister to London—Chandler thought it doubtful if he could be confirmed as such—but if I were nominated to England I would be confirmed, & then Pierrepont might be as Sect of State, as the Senate allows ~~to~~ the Prsdt to select his

Cabinet, more freely than to make other appointments—The President remarked here, 'but I would not have Judge Pierrepont as Sect of State'—wh he meant that he made this remark to Chandler, & now makes it to me, I was not sure, & did not care to ask any question about it—for I know that he feel[s] grateful to Pierrepont, but has not entire confidence in him—He said he told Chandler that Pierrepont[s] nomination for the Cabinet would not do, because although now quite identified with the Republican Party, he was very recently from Tammay Hall, '& there might be other objections' (I supposed this to allude to the $20.000 subscription—paraded &c) Now, said the President, I suppose the Tribune Article may have come from this conversation. so far as I know there is no other authority from me, or from any thing I have said, & I wished to explain this to you, lest you may be disturbed by the article—I replied that I had become somewhat indifferent to such publications, that I had had a large amount of unmerited abuse, & been the object of so much malicious falsehood, that a statement like that he referred to, although calculated, & possibly intended to produce an impression that he desired to get rid me, fell so far short of the malice of other publications that I was comparatively indifferent—He said the publication had worried him, & he had feared it might annoy me—(I imagine it ha[d] been inspired, & suggested by some who have more of his confidence, & who exercise more influence, & hence will prove for his good or that of the Republican party I know that I have been an obstacle in the way of some of these people, who could not use me, & whose plans it has been my lot to defeat—) I then reminded him of my frequently expressed wish to withdraw from the Cabinet—that I should desire to do so as soon as possible—that I wished to avoid the heat of this climate, & could not consent to remain, through the summer—He expressed reluctance, to part with me—Did not know whom he could get to take my place—said Congress would soon adjourn, & then the members of the Cabinet could take vacation—& I could get relaxation &c—I remarked that last summer we had the same prospect, but during the time I was absent, I was worked about as hard, as when here—I enquired whether he intended to hold Cabinet meetings during the Summer as he did last year, & would expect us to attend—for if he did, I must withdraw as I would not be willing to be coming on, as I did last year—He said no—he did not think it would be necessary to hold Cabinet meetings—that he wd come on occasionally from Long Branch, more for appearance, & to satisfy the expectation of querulous persons, than for any necessity. Said that Genl Jackson, used to be absent for several months at a time, & then there was no telegraph—that now the business could be largely transacted by telegraph & if his presence, or that of any officer of the Govt was necessary, they could be summoned immediately—That after the adjournment of Congress I could leave here, & until the middle of October, might not be obliged to be here more than once or twice—perhaps not at all—I said that with that understanding, I would retain the office until October, unless he was prepared to fill it sooner. He ~~asked~~, said 'until the next Session of Congress, won't you?' I replied, possibly I might. I would prefer leaving sooner, & not be obliged to make any arrangements in the Autumn—He said that it would oblige him very much, if I would remain until Congress meets in Decr—Allusion was then made (by him) to the Mission to England—& he asked if I would like it.— I replied 'no—that I would not. I would not be willing to accept it—' I assigned some reasons why it would not be a position to my taste.—He repeated, as he had told me frequently before, that he had intended to remove Motley, who he said represented Mr Sumner more than he did the Administration, & spoke with much warmth of feeling, about Sumner—I said that I thought he was mistaken as to the extent of Sumner's present exercise of influence over Motley—I did not think there was at present any frequency of correspondence—there had been a tendency to follow Sumner when he first went out—but I had not seen it lately— I hope to induce the Prsdt to withhold action as to the removal of Motley—at least for the present—" *Ibid.* Clippings from the *New York Tribune*, June 24, 25, 1870, are *ibid.*

On June 28 and July 1, Fish wrote: "I suggested the nomination of Sumner as Minister to Engl[and]   Prsdt said the proposition had been presented to him, & hi[s] reply had been, that he would nominate him 'on condition that he first resign his seat in the Senate, & with the understanding that he would remove him as soon as the nomination was confirmed'—I presented the names suggested last Eveng by Cameron & Butler—Creswell says that he cannot be confirmed by the Senate—. . . I said jokingly to the Prsdt 'then you don't think well of sending Sumner to England?' His reply was in a different tone from the former remark on the same subject—he said 'I don't like to do it'—but as Boutwell was then leaving the Room, & near the door, he called to him, & asked 'what he thought of it?' Boutwell replied 'that he would not do it, without knowing how it would be rcd by Sumner—that he thought the Prsdt should not put himself in S's power by making the offer to be refused, & thrown up at him'   The matter will be further considered, for it has at least acquired a lodgment as a question of expediency—" "Prsdt asked if I had rcd a note from him, replying 'yes' I said 'but I wish to talk with you before you send in or sign that nomination'   taking me aside I told him that I thought the removal of Motley wd have a very bad effect, it would be attributed to temper—& wd be said that he was punishing Motley for Sumners offenses—that Motley had done nothing since immediately after his arrival in England, that was subject of disapproval the Country wd not consider the removal necessary—and that at least, if determined to remove him, he should give him the opportunity to resign—I urged that he let him remain until next winter—He replied, with much determination, 'that, I will not do—I will not allow Mr Sumner to ride over me'—'but (said I) it is not Mr Sumner, but Mr Motley whom you are striking'   G—'it is the same thing'—F 'the Country will not so understand it'—(G—) 'they will when the removal is made'   I continued to plead, & to urge but to no other avail, than to obtain permission to write to Motley & say that his resignation will be accepted . . . Left Washington for NewYork, in the Evenig—Accompanied the President & Mrs Grant—Genl Butler—Messrs Strong, Kellogg & Starkweather of Connt also in the Cars   During the Evenig the President asked me if I had 'telegraphed' to Motley—I answered 'no—I wrote by mail'—'then (he replied) we will not get his answer in time to send the nomination of a Successor to the Senate before its adjournment—& I must do that'   I said that about the time of the arrival of the letter I had written Motley could be informed by telegraph, that he (the President) desired an answer by telegraph—he said that would answer— He seems very determined in this matter . . ." *Ibid.*

On July 1, Fish cabled to John Lothrop Motley, London. "Private. . . . I am instructed by the President to say that he finds it desirable to make a change in the mission to England, and that he wishes to allow you the opportunity of resigning, in case you feel inclined to do so"   Copy, DNA, RG 46, Presidential Messages. On July 12, Fish cabled to Motley requesting an immediate response.

Copy, *ibid.* On July 14, Motley wrote to Fish. *"Private* . . . In compliance with
the request contained in your telegram of 12th instant I have replied this day
to the above mentioned letters by a telegram in these words; 'I respectfully
request you to inform the President that I feel compelled to decline the offer
which he makes in giving me an opportunity of resigning my post for considerations which are set forth in full in my letter of today.' I have now to observe
in farther explanation of my course that as no reasons are given me why I
should resign the post to which I was appointed by the President fifteen months
ago, with, I believe, the unanimous consent of the Senate, as I myself know of
none & as I am not conscious of having ever omitted to carry out to the best of
my ability the policy & instructions of the President during the period of my
mission, I fail to perceive why I should offer my resignation. . . ." ALS, *ibid.*,
RG 59, Diplomatic Despatches, Great Britain. On Nov. 10, USG wrote to
Queen Victoria informing her of Motley's recall. Copy, *ibid.*, RG 84, Great
Britain, Instructions. On Jan. 9, 1871, USG wrote to the Senate transmitting
correspondence concerning this matter. DS, *ibid.*, RG 46, Presidential Messages.
The enclosures are *ibid.* See *SED*, 41-3-11.

1. On June 17, 1870, USG wrote to Governor James E. English of Conn.
"I have received your letter of the 14th inst, extending to me the hospitalities
of your State. I anticipate great pleasure during my visit and in meeting your
citizens and I shall be happy to conform to any arrangements that may be made
in the matter of reception." Copy, DLC-USG, II, 1. On June 14, English had
forwarded a resolution from the Gen. Assembly of Conn. authorizing the governor "to meet the President upon his entrance into the State, to extend to him
the offer of our hospitalities and to invite him to visit the two houses of this
General Assembly, if they should then be in session." D, OFH. On June 20,
USG wrote to Mayor Jarratt Morford of Bridgeport. "I have the honor to acknowledge the receipt of your letter of the 17th. inst., inviting me to visit
Bridgeport. during my contemplated trip to Connecticut. I have placed myself
in the hands of Senator Buckingham, and cannot deviate from the arrangements he has made for the journey. Should circumstances permit however, it
will give me great pleasure to visit your place and make the acquaintance of
your citizens." Copy, DLC-USG, II, 1. On June 27, Marshall Jewell, Hartford,
wrote to Henry C. Bowen. ". . . Genl Grant writes me that Mrs. Grant will not
come as she cant stand so much work. But Mrs. Jewell has now taken the matter
in hand & I guess will get her here after all. Cant tell, tho, yet. But she evidently
would not come at all had we not got our invitations for her reception all out.
By all this I think it very doubtful if she will try to go to Woodstock any how.
Had we known this in time we could have started earlier from Hfd. on Monday."
ALS, Connecticut State Library, Hartford, Conn.

On July 2, USG, Stamford, responded to a speech by English welcoming
him to Conn. "I cannot find words to express my feelings at this cordial reception to your State; but you will accept for yourself, and through you to the
citizens of your State, my thanks for the welcome extended." *New York Herald,*
July 3, 1870; variant text in *New York Times*, July 3, 1870. Also on July 2,
USG, New Haven, spoke to the Conn. Assembly and Senate. "In attempting to
say anything I feel very much like young gentlemen entering college—they know
a great deal more than they can say. All I have to say is that I am very glad

to meet the gentlemen of the Assembly." "It affords me very great pleasure to be able to address you, briefly as I must, on this occasion. At some future day I will have great pleasure in spending a day, at least, with you in seeing the many objects of interest I will find here. Besides, it will afford me great pleasure to see a people who by their industry contribute so largely to keep down the balance of trade against us." *New York Herald*, July 3, 1870; variant texts in *New York Times*, July 3, 1870, and *New York Tribune*, July 4, 1870. On July 4, USG, enroute by train to Woodstock, Conn., spoke at Plainfield. "I thank you for this reception accorded me this morning. I feel under great obligations to the people of Connecticut and Windham County for the kind reception they have given me. I have met a warm welcome throughout my entire journey through your State, and Windham County is no exception. I thank you for this reception, and am glad to be here." *New York Tribune*, July 5, 1870; variant text in *New York Herald*, July 5, 1870. USG returned to Washington on July 7.

2. On July 5, U.S. Senator Henry Wilson of Mass. wrote to USG. "After much reflection I have decided that duty demands that I should write to you my views touching the proposed removal of Mr Motley. I fear you will make a sad mistake, if you remove him, and I beg you to consider the case carefully before acting. His removal is believed to be aimed at Mr Sumner. Right or wrong this will be the construction put upon it. Can you, My Dear Sir, afford to have such an imputation rest upon your administration? Mr Motley is one of the best known and most renouned of our countrymen. In Let[t]ers he is recognized as one of the foremost living authors of our country or of the world. Office can add Little to his reputation. Removal from offic[e] while it will wound his feelings will not affect his standing among the most cultivated men of the age. I assure you, My Dear Sir, that the men of Massachusetts that gave you more than seventy five thousand majority are proud to number Mr Motley among their most loved and honored sons. They remember that during the war his pen, voice and social influence and position were on the side of his struggling country. They were grateful to you for his appointment as Minister to England. I need not say that they are surprised at the rumor that he is to be removed. They are pained to hear it said that his removal is on account of Mr Sumner's opposition to the St Domingo treaty. His removal will be regarded by the Republicans of Massachusetts as a blow not only to him, but to Mr Sumner. There has been much feeling about the treaty. Imprudent words have been uttered, as they always are when men's feelings are excited. Perhaps Mr Sumner may have said things that may be distasteful to you, but the people of Massachusetts are with him as ten to one. Holding on general principles that the prominent interests of the country would be advanced by a foothold in the Gulf, and wishing to sustain your administration whenever I could do so, I voted for the treaty, though I knew that nine tenths of the people of my state were against it. I had nothing to gain and something to lose by such a vote. I am ready to take the consequences of that vote, but I am not insensible to the fact that the dismissal of Mr Motley under present circumstances will not only be a loss to your administration, but a blow to me. Personally I ask nothing, but I do entreat you, before acting to look well to the matter. Your administration is menaced by great opposition, and it needs peace and unity among the people and in Congress. The head of a great party—the President of the United States has much to forget and forgive but he can afford to be magnanimous and forgiving. I want

to see the President and Congress in harmony and the Republican party united and victorious. To accomplish this we must all be just, charitable and forgiving." ALS, USG 3.

On July 19, Francis G. Young, London, wrote to USG. "I desire to express to your Excellency the warm approbation which in common with all Americans abroad I feel at your action in removing Mr Motley from his place as Minister to Great Britain. During a period of seventeen years passed in great part in Europe, I recall no act of the Executive which has met with such unanimous assent. Mr Motley has the misfortune to disappoint and displease most persons who wait upon him and all are impressed with his unfitness for the post—I have the honor to refer Your Excellency to the U. S. Senators Messrs Conkling and Fenton." ALS, DNA, RG 59, Miscellaneous Letters.

3. Frederick T. Frelinghuysen, born in 1817 into a prominent N. J. family, graduated from Rutgers College (1836), practiced law and held local offices in Newark, and served as state attorney gen. (1861–66) and U.S. senator (1866–69). See letter to Hamilton Fish, July 14, 1870.

To Buenaventura Báez

Washington D. C. July 7th *1870*

Dear Sir:

It is with extreme regret that I inform you of the failure of the treaty for the annexation of San Domingo to the United States. I had hoped a different result.[1] I believe now that if the subject was submitted to a popular vote of the people it would carry by an overwhelming majority. Believing this, has induced me to negociate with your Plenipotentiary for an extension of the treaty for the occupancy of the Bay of Samana. I shall hope that the return of Congress in December next will find that body in a condition to recommend a renewal of the rejected treaty.

With extreme regret for the failure of negociations which I believe of such mutual advantage to the two countries, and with the highest considerations for you personally, I subscribe myself, with great respect;

your obt. svt.
U. S. Grant

President Baez
San Domingo

ALS, General Grant National Memorial, New York, N. Y. On July 8, 1870, USG wrote to the Senate. "I transmit for consideration with a view to its ratification, an additional article to the Convention between the United States and the Dominican Republic of the 29th of November, 1869, for a lease of the Bay and Peninsula of Samana." Copy, DNA, RG 59, General Records. There is no indication that the Senate received or considered this article. See William Javier Nelson, *Almost a Territory: America's Attempt to Annex the Dominican Republic* (Newark, Del., 1990), pp. 127–28.

1. On July 17, U.S. Senator Carl Schurz of Mo. wrote to USG. "*Personal.* . . . Before leaving this city to take part in the political campaign I should be happy to have a conversation with you about matters of importance to the Administration and the party to which we both belong. Recent events which cannot fail to excite a deep and strong feeling among the German population of this country, have devolved an influence and duties and responsibilities upon me more comprehensive than any that had formerly fallen to my lot. I have spoken about them to the Secretary of State, but I should be glad to communicate my views to you in person, for, if ever, it is desirable at this moment that there should be a fair understanding between the administration and myself. I am painfully sensible of the change which our personal relations have suffered in consequence of our differences on the San Domingo Treaty. I have reasons to believe that there has been much mischievous tale-bearing connected with this matter. You have been informed as I understand, that I attacked you personally in the secret deliberations of the Senate. Whoever may have carried that story to you, I pronounce it unqualifiedly untrue. I desire now to remove this erroneous impression, not as a man who has favors to seek—for that is not my condition—but as one who has great interests to serve. When we had our first conversation about the San Domingo Treaty, I told you frankly that I was, opposed to it on conscientious grounds and would endeavor to defeat it. When the Senate had closed the first debate on the Treaty, I beseeched you to drop the matter there, that advice sprang from patriotic motives, and subsequent events have demonstrated its judiciousness so clearly that I should not hesitate to repeat it. In fighting the treaty, I have used all the legitimate means of parliamentary warfare, and, looking back upon my conduct, I have nothing to conceal and nothing for which I should reproach myself. I fervently hope the question is disposed of not to arise again, for it is my sincere and earnest desire to support your Administration with what ability and influence I may possess. This is the motive which impels me to write you this note and to ask you whether and when you will be kind enough to grant me a private interview. May I hope for an answer at your earliest convenience? I intend to leave Washington on Tuesday, to address, on Wednesday Evening, a large German mass-meeting at New York." ALS, USG 3. On July 18, USG wrote to Schurz. "I am in receipt of your letter of the 17th; requesting a private interview. I shall be pleased to see you at any time to day before three o'clock, or tomorrow before the same hour, as may suit your convenience." LS, DLC-Carl Schurz.

To Elihu B. Washburne

———

Washington D. C. July 10th *1870.*

DEAR WASHBURNE:

I have received your recent letters, two in regard to Gen. Anderson. I do not know how anything can be done for the Gen. at present, but I do know, or at least feel, that the aAmerican people will never permit his family to suffer. Should the worst happen the Gen. his family will be taken care of. I would start the matter and what is, or has been, done for Rawlins and Stantons families would probably be done for Gen. Andersons.

Congress is soon to adjourn. The reflection is almost a compensation for the suffering endured during their (its) session. If it was not for the feeling of loyalty of the people, and the almost certainty that a democratic sucsess would be repudiation and surrender to old Southern leaders, there is but little doubt but that the republican party would loose control of the country at the next election. Lack of attention to material interests, rangling among themselves, dividing and allowing the few democrats to be the balance to fix Amendments to every important measure, ~~which th~~ (and voting against the whole bill when brought to a vote) attacking each other, and the Administration, when any individuals views were not conformed to, has put the party in a very bad light. I think every thing will be right two years hens, and that members see the errors they have committed. I shall hope so at least. If we had had a short session of Congress, and harmonious, the party would never have been on as strong a footing as now. All that was necessary to do was to pass the appropriation bills, idmit the outstanding states, pass a funding bill and promise the people a reduction of Eighty Million of taxes at their next session. We could well spare that amount if the public debt bore but 5 prnt

Please present Mrs. Grant's and my kindest regards to Mrs. Washburne and the children. My family are all well. Fred graduates at West Point next June Buck has passed his examination for admittance to Harvard, and Nellie goes off to school at Farming-

[ton] Conn. in the Fall. I regret my negligen[ce] in writing to you but I am just as glad to hear from you as though I wrote by every Mail.

yours Truly
U. S. Grant

ALS, IHi. On May 19, 1870, Elihu B. Washburne had written to USG. "You may know or not know, that my family have gone to spend the Summer at Tours, some four hours and a half out of Paris, by rail. We find living there Genl. Robert Anderson and family and I must confess that my feelings have been greatly interested in regard to them. It seems that the General has only his half pay to live on, togethe[r] with a small pittance that Mrs. A. has. He has for his family a wife, three daughters and one son, a lad of some twelve years. Two of the daughters and the boy are to be educated.—We can well imagine how difficult it must be for a man [of] the rank and position in society of Genl. Anderson, to support such a family on the half pay of a Brigadier General. They say that they foun[d] it utterly impossible for them to live on their means in the United States and they thought that by coming abroad and living in obscurity they might make the two ends meet so long as the General should get his half pay. In locating at Tours last year they took a miserable house and in an unhealthy location because they could get it a low rent. They have been living in the most complete isolation, as they had not the means to go into society. Mrs. Anderson is an invalid and for two months last winter was unable to leave her room. The General, as you are aware has been very feeble for years and utterly unable to attend to any-thing. And now what is most sad, he is very [sick and fears] he will never be much better. Indeed, Mrs. Washburne writes me that she fears he will not live long. . . ." ALS (press), DLC-Elihu B. Washburne. On June 15, Washburne wrote to USG on the same subject. ALS, DNA, RG 94, ACP, 5135 1871.

To Hamilton Fish

Washington D. C. July 14th *1870*

Dear Sir:

I would like to send in the nomination of Mr. Freelinghuysen as Min. to England to-day. If Mr. Motley has not forwarded his resignation the nomination can read vice "Motley" without saying "removed"

Truly yours,
U. S. Grant

Hon. H. Fish
Sec. of State.

ALS, DLC-Hamilton Fish. On July 14, 1870, Secretary of State Hamilton Fish recorded in his diary. "rcd note from President requesting me t[o] send nomination of Frelinghuysen as Minister to London—vice Motley—I take the nomination to him & at the time tell him I think it a mistake—that the Country will not approve it—refer to Frelinghuysen a[s] unexceptionable—but his location in New Jersey is unfortunate—a Small & a Democratic State, receiving in a short time, a Cabinet Officer—a Judge of the Supreme Court, & the first of the Foreign Missions—He says there is a good deal of feeling Among his friends about Motley's retention—He signed the Message making the nomination . . ." *Ibid.* On July 27, Frederick T. Frelinghuysen, Newark, wrote to USG. "Permit me to express my appreciation of the distinguished honor done me in my appointment as Minister to England—an honor the more valuable because originating with one whose confidence I so highly prize—I received the official notification of my appointment on Friday the 22d inst., since then, and before, I have deeply and disinterestedly reflected on the question whether it was my duty to accept the office—And having come to the conclusion that it is not, I regret that the telegrams indicating the result to which I have come, sent—the one on the morning of the 14th inst. as soon as the rumors of my possible nomination took shape in the press—and the other on the morning of the 15th as soon as I heard of my nomination—did not reach their destination in time to lead to the selection of another than myself for the position—Although my mind was fixed on this subject when I telegraphed, yet the most grateful vote of the Senate on my confirmation, which I am aware was to a good degree the result of a natural kind feeling toward a recent associate and also an expression of views as to the national policy, has led me carefully to review the subject—In view of my domestic relations and duties which I was gratified to find in our recent interview you appreciated; my own distaste for diplomatic position; and my conviction that there are others better suited to the office, I am brought to my first conclusions—and shall forward to the Secretary of State a letter declining the office—While I regret that my efforts to avoid the public association of my name with this office were not successful, you will please permit me again to express my high appreciation of the honor conferred—" LS, USG 3.

To Senate

To the Senate of the United States:

I herewith return, without my approval, Senate Bill, No 476.— "An Act to fix the status of certain federal soldiers enlisting in the Union army from the States of Alabama and Florida", for the reasons embodied in the following facts which have been obtained from the office of the Second Comptroller.

The 1st Regt. of Florida Cavalry, composed of six companies, was organized from December 1862 to August 1864 to serve three years. It was mustered out of service November 17th 1865. by reason of General Order from the War Dept. discharging all cavalry organizations east of the Mississippi.

The men of this regiment enlisting prior to July 18. 1864 received twenty-five dollars advance bounty at muster in, and the discharged soldiers, and heirs of those deceased have been paid the same bounty under Act of July 22. 1861.; Joint Resolution Jan'y. 13. 1864 and Act of July 28. 1866. as men enlisted at the same time in other volunteer organizations.

The 2nd Regiment of Florida Cavalry, composed of Seven companies, was organized from December 1863 to June 1864 to serve three years. It was mustered out November 29. 1865, by reason of the order discharging cavalry organizations east of the Mississippi. Most of the men received the twenty-five dollars advance bounty at muster in, and the discharged men, and heirs of deceased men have received bounty under the several acts of Congress cited above, subject to the same conditions which apply to men who enlisted at the same time in other volunteer organizations.

The 1st Alabama Cavalry was originally organized as a one year regiment from December 1862 to September 1863., and two companies of three year men (Companies "I." and "K.") were added to complete its organization. These companies were formerly companies "D." and "E" of the 1st Middle Tenn. Cavalry. Prior to the expiration of the term of the one year men, the Adjutant General of the Army,—of date May 15. 1863., authorized Gen. Dodge to fill up this command, and in accordance therewith the places of the companies discharged by reason of expiration of term, were filled by companies of men enlisted for three years. The original companies A. B. C. D. E. F. G. H and L were organized from December 1862 to September 25. 1863., and were discharged by companies from December 22. 1863 to September 28. 1864 in order as the term (one year) of each company expired. Companies I. and K., mustered in August 1862 to serve three years, were discharged in July 1865 by reason of expiration of term of service. As reorganized under the order above mentioned the regiment consisted of companies A. B. C. D. E and G., organized from Feby.

5. 1864 to Oct 1864., to serve three years; companies F. L. and M., organized from Dec. 29. 1863 to Oct. 31. 1864 to serve one and three years; company H. organized in March and April 1865, to serve three years and companies I and K of the old organization described above. The men of the 1st Alabama cavalry who enlisted for three years have been paid bounty under the several acts of Congress, upon the same principles which apply to other three year volunteers.

The one year men enlisted prior to July 18. 1864., received no bounty, but One hundred dollars bounty has been paid the proper heirs of the one year men of this organization who died in the service in accordance with the Act of July 22d. 1861., under which the regiment was originally organized.

Some of the men of these organizations were erroneously paid by the Pay Department at the time of their muster out of service, they having been paid but one hundred dollars when they should have been allowed three hundred dollars under the Joint Resolution of Jany. 13. 1864. The balance of bounty due these men is being paid by the proper accounting officers. It will be seen by comparing the above statement with the Act. under consideration, that the effect of the Act will be to give the one year men of the 1st Alabama Cavalry, nearly all of whom enlisted in 1862 and 1863 a bounty of One hundred dollars each or a proportionate part according to the time served. It would give each man of companies I and K of the 1st Alabama cavalry one hundred dollars more bounty. The bounty of the other three year men of the 1st Alabama cavalry, 1st Florida cavalry and 2nd Florida cavalry, who enlisted prior to December 25. 1863 and from April 1. 1864 to July 17. 1864 inclusive, and who were discharged by reason of orders from the War Department, will not be affected.

The men enlisting in these organizations under Joint Resolution of Jan. 13. 1864 receive under existing laws one hundred dollars more bounty than they would be entitled to receive if the Act under consideration becomes a law.

In case of deceased men the working of the Act is still more perplexing as the prescribed order of inheritance under Act of

July 4. 1864 is entirely different from that under all other acts.

A large proportion of the claims in case of the deceased men have been settled and bounties have been paid fathers, mothers, brothers and sisters—the proper heirs under existing laws—which under this act would go only to the widow, children and widowed mother. Bounty has also been paid to parents under Act of July 28. 1866 which this Act would require to be paid to the widow although she may have remarried.

Under Act of July 28. 1866. children of age are not entitled, but this act makes them joint heirs with the minor children.

In case of the deceased one year men, and the three year men enlisted under Joint Resolution of Jany. 13. 1864 the effect of this act would only be to change the prescribed order of inheritance.

In case of the three year men enlisted under Act of July 22. 1861. the order of inheritance is changed by this act and the heirs entitled (widow, children and widowed mother) will receive one hundred dollars more bounty than they are now entitled to receive.

It may be well to state that Nov. 14. 1864., the War Department gave authority to enlist men who had deserted from the rebel army as recruits for the 1st Alabama Cavalry, with the distinct understanding that they were to receive no bounty. Such recruits have not been paid bounty and it may be a question whether the act under consideration would entitle them to any.

U. S. GRANT

EXECUTIVE MANSION
JULY 14TH. 1870.

DS, DNA, RG 46, Presidential Messages. See *CG*, 41–2, 5571.

To Congress

[*July 15, 1870*]

TO THE SENATE AND HOUSE OF REPRESNTIVES

Your attention is respectfully called to the necessity of passing the an Indian appropriation bill[1] before leaving adjournment. [the members of Congress separate.] Without such appropriation Indian hostilities are sure to insue, and with them suffering, loss of life and expenditures vast as compared with the amount asked

[The latest intelligence from Europe indicates the imminence of a War between France & North Germany—In view of this, ~~it~~ a sound policy indicates the importance of some legislation tending to ~~increase~~ enlarge the commercial Marine[2] of this Country—The vessels of this Country at the present time are insufficient to meet the demand which the existence of a War in Europ will impose upon the Commerce of the U. S. & I submit to the consideration of Congress th the interests of the Country will be advanced by the opportunity afforded to our Citizens to purchas vessels of foreig construction for the Foreign trade of the Country—An act to this effect, may be limited in its duration, to meet the immediate exigincy]

I suggest to Congress the propriety of ~~extending~~ [further postponing] the time for adjournment with the view of considering the questions herein communicated

[U S GRANT]

ADf (bracketed material not in USG's hand), DLC-George B. Cortelyou. The message transmitted included three additional paragraphs. "The foreign mail service of the United States is in a large degree dependent upon the Bremen and Hamburg lines of Steamers. The Post Office Department has entered into contracts in writing with the two companies above named and with the Williams and Guion lines respectively for a regular and continuous service of two years. The only arrangement that could be made with the Inman and Cunard lines is temporary, and may be broken off at any time. The North German lines are first class in point of speed and equipment, their steamers usually making the trip across the Atlantic in from twenty-four to thirty-six hours in advance of the Williams and Guion line. Should the North German steamers be blockaded, or impeded by France, our postal intercourse with foreign nations, will be greatly embarrassed unless Congress shall interpose for its relief" LS (dated July 15, 1870), DNA, RG 46, Annual Messages. *SED*, 41-2-115. On July 15, 1870, Secretary of State Hamilton Fish recorded in his diary. "President & Cabinet at the Capitol all day until 5 P M when Congress adjourned—President sent a Message to Congress on the subject of the Indian Appropriation bill, & an amendment of the law prohibiting the issuing of American Registry to Foreign built vessels—He wrote the first sentence respecting the Indian bill—I—the second—& Cresswell the part relating to Mail Contracts—. . ." DLC-Hamilton Fish.

1. The bill passed on July 15.
2. On June 25, USG wrote to the Senate. "In answer to the resolution of

the 22d instant requesting to be furnished with 'proposals received from any company or citizens of the United States for constructing and placing iron steam ships in transatlantic service', I transmit herewith the only proposal, of that nature, received by me." DS, DNA, RG 46, Annual Messages. The enclosures are *ibid.* On May 16 and 18, Ambrose W. Thompson, president, International Steamship Co., had written to USG on this subject. Copies, DLC-Ambrose W. Thompson. Printed version, *Letter and Proposals of the International Steamship Company to His Excellency President Grant, Relative to Iron Ship-building Yards,* transmitted in DNA, RG 46, Annual Messages. A printed prospectus describing the company's intention to carry emigrants from Europe is *ibid.* See SED, 41-2-102.

On July 2, Thompson, Philadelphia, wrote to Lewis Dent. "It was my intention to have seen you on the subject of the International Steamship Company so soon as the President should send the papers relating thereto into Congress. To have interested you as Counsel before that was done, might have been misconstrued by political adversaries to the disadvantage of the President, a possibility, I was not willing should be incurred against him—hence the delay in my seeing you after your interview with Genl Beale. I was called from Washington by the death of my daughter; but expect soon to return there, and as early as I can, will have the pleasure of an interview in the expectation of arranging an interest for you contingent upon the success of the measure with you for such counsel and aid as you may be able to give in advancing it from the present position, as also for an Annual Salary for attending to our business ~~with the Post Office Department and Collecting the monthly pay for the mail Service of the Steamers~~ in Washington." Copy, DLC-Ambrose W. Thompson.

On Nov. 12, Nov. 17, Thursday, and Nov. 20, Thompson, New York City, wrote to USG. "*Private* . . . About a week since I learned there was to be a convention of the Governors of the Western States to be held at Indianapolis on the 23d inst. relative to Immigration. On Thursday I was confidentially informed that the movement was intended to act adversely to your renomination, and to be made servicable to secure the nomination of one closely associated with you, by being subsequently made to appear as his, in a popular cause. It occurred to me that it would be a politic move to checkmate this latter object, if the information was correct, by placing before the members of the convention the facts as they now exist, evidencing that through you the only proper steps had already been taken to give practicable protection to the immigration to this Country in advance of present ideas, by American Steamers. I therefore sent to each Governor named, a letter, copy of which is enclosed, and with it the printed documents to show what was, done, and expected to be secured through Congressional action; seeking also to identify them with with the measure. If they act in accordance, of which I have no doubt, an organization of Local Boards will be perfected throughout the Country which may be made entirely reliable as the most efficient basis—that of intelligence, common interest and wealth—upon and from which to act energetically and Successfully in your Cause, which is that of the Nation. The most popular thought of the present time is that of restoring the Commerce of the Country—the only way that that can effectually be accomplished is the one contained in your message referred to in the letters in Exec Doc 102 embracing the proposal of the International Steamship Co. An organization of the Local Boards in furtherance of this object and uniting the Working people with it will give a force in your favor that must overcome any arrayed against you. I intend to go to the Convention for this object, but will work to see you before leaving, to give you the information I have received & to learn your wishes as to movements which may be made" "I leave here tonight for the purpose of seeing you for a few minutes only, on the subject of my letter of the 12th inst I will call at the Executive Mansion at about 10 o'clk Friday morning—if no accident occurs to delay my arrival—and hope you will be able to see me as I desire to return immediately so as to reach Indianapolis early Tuesday morning." "Private . . . I have just found that the copyist made a mistake in writing out the proposal, putting the provision for absolute control of the Yards, in the wrong place, and as new copies cannot be made before I leave for Indianapolis, I send one of the printed forms of the original, with the new provision interlined; and on my return will immediately send or bring fairly written copies. If you could give some such suggestion in you Message, as would convey the idea, 'that the Naval Arm of the United States would be strengthened by having a building yard of the description named to rely upon, that the provisions in the proposal for its construction gives the government its entire control in time of War, and preference at all times for its naval work without the outlay of Vast Sums, thus securing economy and efficiency, while it affords the amplest facilities to restore Commerce by placing, on Our Ocean routes iron steamships built under the most careful government inspection, the better to guarantee safety to life and property, and to secure ~~safety~~ health and protection to Emigrants, that for these reasons you recommended the proposals to the Consideration and approval of Congress.'—such suggestion, would show to the whole country that you were in advance of all movements for securing work to Mechanics and laborers, protection to Emigrants. and—the adoption of the surest means to create to ~~create~~ reliable transportation at low rates for our cereals and other products to foreign markets—and the surest bases for the restoration and permanent support of Our Ocean Commerce. I have found letters from some of the Western Governors in reply to mine (copy of which was sent you) approving and saying they will heartily cooperate. One writes, that the object of the Convention is to get the Control of all Emigrant depots into *government hands*. This is part of the plan which was confidentially given me and of which I spoke—It is believed to be unconstitutional, but all that government in use of its constitutional functions can safely do, was thought to be embodied in the laws relating to the carrying passengers in ships or Vessels." ALS (press), *ibid.*

On Nov. 20, Thompson wrote to Orville E. Babcock. ". . . If a Suggestion such as is made in my private letter to the President can go into the message, it will place him ahead of all parties in this matter—this is the object I wish. and the credit that can be made to enure to him will tell powerfully upon the masses— I hope then you will try to get Something Similar, but better, in the message.— I have rode all night & my head feels to heavy to express myself clearly. If you can suggest in any way that the Secretary of the Navy takes ground in favor of this measure for its economy to the Navy, it will do as much good in getting it *referred* to the *Naval Committees* instead of those on *Commerce*. The latter are not very well composed, and have become bewildred on this subject, connecting it with tariffs and all sorts of things. I have placed the name you gave me, in the list of directors, and will write to Mr Campbell from Indianapolis, or on my return here. If I had time I would go to Chicago to see him. If you should be writing to him please name the matter, and say that we expect you to take the position of Chief Civil Enginer of the Company as soon as we get under way." ALS (press), *ibid*. On Nov. 21, Thompson wrote to USG. "I have the honor to renew the proposal of the International Steamship Company as made in May last to establish Iron Ship building Yards and docks with the addition as suggested, that the same shall in case of War be under the absolute Control of the United States Government, to the exclusion of all other than its own work for Naval and Military purposes. This provision as you justly say, is one the Government Should have inserted and meets the full Concurrence of the Company. As the letter which accompanied the proposals when first made, gives details and Explanations I enclose a copy thereof as applicable to the present renewal of the same." ALS (press), *ibid*. On Nov. 23, Babcock wrote to Thompson. "Your letter enclosing one to the President was received, and the letter delivered as you requested." ALS, *ibid*.

On Nov. 26, Thompson wrote to USG. "*Private* . . . I have just returned from Indianapolis. The Immigration Convention failed in its objects. These objects were,—land, and railroad schemes, underlaid by the plan I mentioned to you. Mr. Young of the Treasy. Department was there. nominally to give statistics of Emigration In *conversing* with the delegates, he urged that a bureau of Emigration should be established under control of the Treasury Department with officers of every description stretching along the railway and steamboat lines for the protection of the Emigrants. *nominally*; the real object was soon made known, and like the railway & land schemes became exposed & failed. The main agent in getting up this plan was a very notorious lobbyist who was denounced by Genl Farnsworth some three or four years ago on the floor of the House, as an 'unclean thing' &c. and who it seems had some reason to believe he would be made Cheif of this 'Bureau of Emigration' when it should be formed. He decieved the Governors of the Northwest States, 'packed' a large portion of the Convention with land agents & railroad Employes, amongst which latter, was a Mr Gwinner, *ticket agent of the Pennsylvania Railroad Co*, and the plan of Roland & others of his clique was, to make this Gwinner, President of the Convention. In this they were frustrated. as in all other movements. The prominent members of the Convention, I mean those whose social and political position placed them above such parties as composed the Clique, gave no countenance to their plans. They all now fully comprehend that you are favorable to any good constitutional course which can be adopted for the safe-guard of those who seek to become citizens. It was a prominent fact developed in this Convention, that every foreigner in it, (and there were very many Germans) depricated, and some denounced, all interference of the kind proposed, as being injurious to Emigrants. Very strong in this position was an old German gentleman named Reemelin from Cincinnati who said he had come over as an Immigrant, and all that Immigrants wanted was to be allowed to take care of themselves, just as Americans did; that this assumption of care for them after their arrival here by government authority was not calculated to make them independent men, but on the contrary—to encourage the lazy to become paupers. and dependents upon the government. I give only these brief points, that you may at once mentally grasp the whole spirit & object of the convention. I now enclose the written copies of my former letter and of the amended proposal, of which my time did not permit to be sent before leaving for Indianapolis last week, when I sent a corrected or interlined printed copy. On my way from Washington I stopped to see Mr Borie and proposed his coming into this mat-

ter. He seems disposed to do so & wanted to look over the papers; these I sent
him. He said he intended soon to make you a visit & would determine shortly
upon the matter. I presume from this he wished to speak with you on it. I told
him I thought you would be gratified to see his name connected with such an
enterprise. I have put his name on the prospectus as one of the Board, so that,
if you think well of it, it may be continued there, or a pen drawn through it,
as you deem best. I so plan it because he may be with you now, or before I can
possibly see him. I saw some prominent politicians of the West, they believe and
emphatically declare that no other than yourself can be elected by the Republican party, and one of the most influential of the state of Indiana, gave me some
of the causes which could defeat in that state, which I will state when I have
the pleasure of again seeing you. Indiana may be in his opinion fully recovered
by the Republican party by the next election, He told me that very many of the
most influential politicians had held back this Autumn for the 'Causes' I have
alluded to." ALS (press), *ibid.* See *Indianapolis Journal*, Nov. 23–24, 26, 1870;
New York Times, Nov. 24–26, 28, 1870; *PUSG*, 18, 406–7.

Speech

[*July 16, 1870*]

MR. MINISTER: It gives me great pleasure to receive, as the
representative of his Majesty; the Emperor of the French, a gentleman so well known and distinguished as yourself.

I can assure you that I shall give a cordial support to every effort which you may make to increase the commercial and industrial
ties between the people of the United States and of France, and to
strengthen and perpetuate the amicable and historical relations
between the two Governments.

Washington Chronicle, July 17, 1870. USG spoke in response to remarks by
Lucien A. Prévost-Paradol, minister from France. "MR. PRESIDENT: I have the
honor to place in your hands the letters whereby his Majesty, the Emperor of
the French, has been pleased to accredit me, in the quality of Envoy Extraordinary and Minister Plenipotentiary to the Republic of the United States. I particularly congratulate myself on having been selected for this high mission at a
time when the traditional friendship of France and the United States is darkened
by no cloud. This happy state of good feeling, which is, so to speak, the natural
and necessary situation of these two great nations, and which has always seemed
to be in accord as much with their true interests as with the traditions of their
history, renders my task near you an easy and at the same time a pleasant one.
To cherish, and thereby to enlarge, between France and the United States, those
industrial and commercial relations which sustain and strengthen political sympathy, such must now be the main object of my efforts, and if I shall be able

to contribute thereto, I shall have faithfully fulfilled the intentions of my journey." *Ibid.* Prévost-Paradol, a prominent writer and journalist born in 1829, committed suicide on July 20, 1870. *Ibid.*, July 21, 1870.

On July 20, Secretary of State Hamilton Fish wrote to USG. "Permit me to suggest the propriety of sending a military guard to the house of Mr Prevost Paradol as a testimonial of respect. None of the Legation are here except Mr Dejardin, the Chancelier and the body lies almost literally without any one to care for it." LS, DNA, RG 45, Letters Received from the President. On July 22, J. C. Bancroft Davis, asst. secretary of state, telegraphed to Horace Porter, Long Branch. "French government declines to Exempt German steamers from Capture Except those now at sea ignorant of war which may enter French port. Same government thanks the President and Officers of this government for respect shown remains of Mr Paradol. Funeral this morning large and imposing. Baron Gerolt present as dean of diplomatic Corps and all members of Cabinet in town, and General Sherman and Admiral Porter in Uniform. No other news—cipher not necessary for this. . . . Secretary leaves tonight for Garrisons" Telegram sent (at 3:35 P.M.), DLC-Hamilton Fish; copy, DNA, RG 59, Domestic Letters. See Pierre Guiral, *Prévost-Paradol (1829–1870): Pensée et Action d'un Liberal Sous le Second Empire* (Paris, 1955), pp. 706–10.

On Aug. 2, Louis L. Molon, "Catholic priest," Elyria, Ohio, wrote to James A. McMaster, editor, *New York Freeman's Journal.* "the following is a letter which I today sent to that degraded being called president grant. TO HIS EXCELLENCY PRESIDENT GRANT. Sir. I just read, in a paper which I call reliable, that you have lately assured, in an official Capacity, the prussian Legation, of your warmest sympathies, in regard to the war to be waged between France and prussia. All right, Sir. I, a French man and a Catholic priest, understand now why paradol the late French minister killed himself. he thought, the poor man, he would find yet the America of Washinghton and Lafayette which he loved and he found the America of the Hessians with grant at their head! ! ! For god's sake, Sir: go to your Senate's Hall with one of your Hessians and with some of that French blood shed at york town for the independance of your Country, put out, yes, put out, I say it again, ungrateful representative of an ungrateful nation put out that noble face of Lafayette, standing on one side of your Vice president's Chair. Let that noble picture not be disgraced any longer; I ask it in the name of france which despises you, put in the place some thing more worthy of you, *Arnold* or *Bismark.* Thanking god that I am *not* an American . . . publish if you deem proper" ALS, InNd.

Endorsement

Approved and the recommendations of the Sec. of the Int. will be carried into execution.

U. S. GRANT

JULY 20TH 1870.

AES, DNA, RG 48, Lands and Railroads Div., Package 129. Written on a letter of July 12, 1870, from Secretary of the Interior Jacob D. Cox to USG. "On the 21st of May last, I laid before you a communication with regard to railroads in the Indian Territory, in which I reported that I found under the legislation of 1866, and the treaties with the Cherokee, Creek, Choctaw and Chickasaw, and Seminole Indians, of the same year; that three railroads in the state of Kansas were authorized to build their lines to a common point on the northern boundary of the Cherokee lands in the Indian Territory, near where the Neosho river crosses said boundary, and that the road which should succeed in first reaching said common point, should be authorized to build a trunk road through the Indian Territory to a point at or near Preston in the state of Texas; and that but one such trunk, from North to South, was authorized to be built. I recommended that, if you should agree with me in the conclusions I reached, the Superintendents for the Central and Southern Indian Superintendencies be appointed a commission to determine which of the said railroad companies should first fully comply with the conditions of the statutes as the same were defined, and to report to this Department when such complete fulfilment should have taken place. The views and findings which I laid before you, were approved by you on the 23d of May, and you directed that my recommendations, including those above referred to, should be carried into execution I have now the honor to state that I have received a report from said Commissioners, dated the 13th day of June, 1870, showing: — 1st — 'That the Union Pacific Railway, Southern Branch, reached the northern boundary of the Indian Territory, in the valley of the Neosho River, on the west side and about one mile therefrom, at 12 M., the 6th day of June, 1870, and that, at that time, there was no other railroad, nearer than sixteen miles of that point.' 2d — 'That on the 9th day of June, 1870, Governor James M. Harvey, of the state of Kansas, the officer specified by Act of Congress to pronounce upon the completion of this railroad, certified over his official seal and signature, that the same was a first class completed railroad to the northern boundary of the Indian Territory.' Under a misapprehension as to the condition of the controversy, between the several roads, before yourself and this Department, the said commissioners proceeded further to make some statements with regard to the Kansas and Neosho Valley Railroad, which reached the northern boundary of the Indian Territory on the 30th day of April, 1870, but at a point about fifteen miles east of the Neosho River, and upon the borders of the Quapaw reservation, through which no right for any railroad company to enter has been granted by the Indians, as I have formerly reported to you in my communication of the 21st of May, above mentioned. I transmit, herewith, a complete copy of said commissioners report, for your information, . . . Upon the receipt of these documents I caused the several parties in interest to be notified that at such time as might be convenient to them, I would sit to hear causes shown, if any there were, why said report should not be received as conclusive of the fact that the Union Pacific Railroad Company, Southern Branch, now called the Missouri Kansas and Texas Railway Company, had first complied with the conditions prescribed for securing the right to construct the trunk road through the Indian Territory. On the 9th inst., the said parties appeared before me, and arguments were heard thereon, which have been this day concluded. The point made by the Kansas and Neosho Valley Railroad Company is, that no satisfactory evidence is before the Department, that the character of said Southern Branch Pacific Railway is that of a good completed road. No testimony was submitted as to the character of the road, but several informal statements, not sworn to, were read or orally made, and a similar class of statements, by way of rebuttal, was made upon the other side. A paper, forwarded with the report of the Commissioners, was also referred to, as showing that the Southern Branch road was not equal in the character of its construction to the Kansas and Neosho Valley road. The circumstances, under which the examination of the Commissioners was made, were such as to satisfy me that said paper was not based upon any actual measurements or specific investigations of the Commissioners themselves, but was probably received with an argument and other papers, irregularly submitted to them by Mr. Joy. I have, therefore, confined my consideration, for the present, to the question whether, under the several statutes authorizing the construction of those roads, the certificate of the Governor of Kansas is the conclusive evidence of the character and completion of the road, required by law. It was admitted, in the argument before me, that such certificate was conclusive and final, for the purpose of entitling the company to its land grants, but not for the purpose of determining its compliance with the 11th section of the Act of July 25. 1866, and determining its right to build the trunk road. If such certificate be the conclusive evidence required by law, inquiry as to facts, *ab extra*—must be unnecessary. If it is not conclusive, but the Department or yourself must determine the fact of the sufficiency of the road upon other testimony, then I should not be satisfied with anything less than a complete examination by a scientific commission, or a full investigation, upon the sworn evidence of experts, who had made a scientific examination. On the question what the law requires, as the evidence of the completion of these roads, I find that, substantially, the same provision is contained in both statutes authorizing the construction, respectively, of the Kansas and Neosho Valley Railroad, and the Southern Branch Pacific Railroad. . . . I am forced, therefore, to the conclusion, that the completion, referred to, must be understood to be a completion in accordance with the terms of the act authorizing the construction of each road, and that, when the road is so completed, it would be accepted, and its patents issued, under the terms of such statute. We have no further inquiry to make with regard to it. I am, therefore, of opinion that such completion, and the quality of the road is not a question of fact to be determined upon any other evidence than that which the statute prescribes, and that the certificate of the Governor of Kansas, that the Southern Branch Pacific Road has reached the northern boundary of the Indian Territory as a completed first class railroad, is conclusive evidence of that fact; and further, that the certificate of Commissioners Hazen and Hoag, that no other road was within fifteen miles of the common point at which said roads were to enter the Indian Territory, is unquestioned by either party, and is, therefore, satisfactory evidence that said Southern Branch Pacific Railroad has first complied with the terms of your order of the 23d of May. If you shall agree with me in this conclusion, I recommend that you give the said Union Pacific Railroad Company, Southern Branch, in accordance with the terms of the 11th section of the statute of the 25th of July, aforesaid, your written approval to construct and operate its line of railroad from said point on the northern boundary of the Indian Territory, to a point, at or near Preston, in the state of Texas, . . . I would further recommend, that, besides the agreement of such company to comply with these terms, they shall further be required, before entering said Indian Territory, to give bond in a reasonable amount, payable to the United States, or to either of the Indian nations, through whose territory they may pass, conditioned that they shall, in every particular, respect the rights of said Indian tribes, and the individuals thereof, as guaranteed by the treaties, and the intercourse and other statutes of the United States; that they shall commit no waste upon said Indian lands, nor take materials therefrom, except under contract with said Indian tribes, or individuals thereof, who may make sales of individual property; such contracts, whether with the nations or individuals to be valid only, when approved by the proper officers of the Indian Department. The counsel for the Cherokee Nation, in a written argument filed with me, have urged that no sufficient legislation yet exists to authorize either of the companies, who might win the race to the southern boundary of Kansas, to enter the Cherokee territory, and that further legislation is necessary, to protect the rights of the Indians, and define the manner in which the privilege of entering, and building a road, should be exercised. After careful examination of this argument, and with the fullest desire to do whatever may be necessary to protect the rights of the Indians in the premises; I am of opinion, that the statutory right to enter the Territory is complete, upon the fulfilment of the conditions precedent, which have been fixed, and that the necessity for your approval of the acts of the railroad company, and their mode of construction, together with your undoubted power to suspend their operations in building, whenever they shall cease to conform to the intercourse laws and other statutes, and to the regulations which you may prescribe, are sufficient to secure proper respect to, and observance of, all the rights of the Indians in the premises." LS, *ibid.*

On May 21, Cox had written to USG. "On the 13th instant, upon a complaint filed in this Department by the duly authorized delegates of the Cherokee Nation, averring that parties alleging themselves to be working parties of the Southern Branch, Union Pacific Railway Company had entered the Cherokee country, and were employed in grading a line for a railway; the officers of said railway company were notified by this Department, that the Cherokee Indians did not recognize their right to intrude upon their territory, and that no work of the kind referred to could be permitted therein, until the Executive should be satisfied, by evidence submitted through this Department, that such entry and occupation was in accordance with law. A similar notice had been given, on the 27th ultimo, to the officers of the Kansas & Neosho Valley Railway Company, who were reported to have entered the Quapaw reservation near the town of Baxter in southeastern Kansas. On Wednesday the 18th instant, the said Southern Branch Union Pacific Railway Company appeared by their counsel and moved for the revocation of said notification and order with respect to them, and the Cherokees, the Creeks, the Kansas and Neosho Valley Railway Company, the Leavenworth, Lawrence and Fort Gibson Railroad Company, and the Atlantic and Pacific Railroad Company, appeared by counsel, to represent their several interests in the questions involved The point submitted for the consideration of the Department, and for your determination, is, what rights have been given to railroad companies to construct railroads through the Indian Territory, and what railroads, if any, are entitled to such privileges and right of way. . . . There is, incidentally connected with the discussion of these questions, the farther one as to the propriety of giving approval to the construction of other railroads through the Indian country than those which may be built in strict accordance with the scheme fixed by the treaties and by legislation. The policy of preserving the Indian Territory as free as possible from intrusion by white settlers, under any form, has been hitherto regarded as firmly established in this country. It has been based upon the well known fact that the Indian tribes, which are brought into closest contact with the whites, have been, uniformly, injured by drunkenness and other vices, which they have seemed peculiarly unable to resist, and the only hope of their complete civilization seems, by common consent, to rest upon our ability to keep them by themselves under stringent laws with regard to the introduction of intoxicating liquors, and in circumstances where immoral intercourse with the whites shall be prevented as thoroughly as possible. The intelligent men among the civilized Indians fully appreciate the necessity of this policy, and their delegations have been extremely earnest in deprecating any course which may throw them into closer contact or more direct competition with our own people, than is absolutely necessary. Negotiations for the removal of Indians from the small reservations in Kansas and Nebraska to the Indian Territory, have been based upon this policy, and, in order to carry it out with any degree of success, it is necessary to adhere to it as firmly as possible. We cannot honestly advise the scattered and small tribes, now within our organized states, to migrate to the Indian country, except upon the honest assurance that there, with the advantages of teachers and mission establishments, and protected from the temptations which have, heretofore, been so ruinous to them, they may work out the problem of their possible civilization and final incorporation into the nation. I, therefore, most earnestly advise, inasmuch, as in the wisdom of Congress, the scheme involving the building of but one trunk railroad through the Territory from north to south, with a branch from Fort Gibson to Fort Smith, and a double line from east to west, meeting in the valley of the Canadian, has been deemed sufficient for the necessities of our own commercial intercourse between different sections of the country; that this scheme be rigidly adhered to, and, that no approval be given to any deviation therefrom." LS, *ibid.*, RG 75, Letters Received, Southern Superintendency. On May 23, USG endorsed this letter. "The views & findings of the Secretary of the Interior herein are approved & his recommendations will be carried into execution—" ES, *ibid.*

On June 6, William P. Ross, Fort Gibson, Indian Territory, wrote to USG. "I have the honor, as presiding Officer of an International Indian Council, held at Okmulgee, in the Muscogee Nation, to forward to your Excellency the enclosed declaration and Appeal, adopted and signed by the Delegations of the Several Nations therein represented on the 4th Instant, and to ask for its statements a favorable consideration." LS, *ibid.* Ross enclosed a document addressed "To the President—Congress—and People of the United States." "The Undersigned representing the Several Nations inhabiting the Indian Territory whose names are hereto appended in view of the perils which surround their people deem it a solemn duty to make this declaration of their views and wishes in regard to their situation. In the beginning we take occassion to publicly affirm our earnest determination to preserve the relations of Amity towards the Government of the United States, now existing. Our interests all centre in peace, peace, with the government and the People of the United States—peace, with our Neighboring brethren and peace, Among the Members of each individual Tribe and Nation. And as the best means of maintaining that relation unimpaired, we deem a just and fair observance of existing Treaty Stipulations with the Government of the United States as indispensable.—We therefore hereby publicly renew our adherence to said Treaties, or to such as may be hereafter duly negotiated. and our purpose to comply Faithfully with all their stipulations, whether originally favorable or otherwise. And we confidently express our conviction that a like spirit of justice and fidelity will mark the conduct of the Governmt towards the owners and inhabitants of the Indian Territory. The people of that Territory were uprooted from their ancient homes, and placed where they now are through the policy, and by the power of the Govt for the benefit and convenience of the whites, with assurances and guaranties of ownership in the Soil, and protection from interference with their privilieges of self Government, and from intrusion upon them, as strong and solemn as language could make them.—If the lapse of time, the increase of the White population, and the march of events have removed us from the wilderness in which we were then plunged unwillingly, and placed us in the way of our Neighbors, the fault is not ours, nor do they invalidate any existing obligations.—We ask nothing from the people and Authorities of the United States, aside from their respect and good fellowship, but what they have promised, *An observance of their Treaties*. Despite all the vicissitudes of our history and the terrible ordeal of war by which we ~~have~~ have been scourged with fire and sword—through no fault of ours, but weakness and inability to sustain ourselves, we feel that we are, even now progressing in knowledge, and improvement in the Arts and Customs of civilization. We desire no change, for the purpose of experiment in the policy of the Government in its dealings towards our people and Territory.— We have no fault to find with their policy as provided for, by our Treaties, all that we crave is a simple and honest administration of that policy by competent and honest means.—We have been charged with opposition to progress, and improvement: but, in refutation of that charge, however humble they may seem, we confidently appeal to our houses—Our farms—Our stocks of horses and cattle, Our Schools, Our churches, and our regularly organized Governments. We are not opposed to progress. We are not opposed to improvement, we are not opposed to civilization, we are not opposed to the christian religion. On the contrary, we acknowledge the conviction that rests upon our minds, that our highest interests, and selfpreservation itself, depend upon progress and improvement, We feel that we cannot safely step backwards, but must press forward, inspired by the spirit of the Age in which we live, in the Arts, pursuits and Achievements of the surrounding civilization. We desire only not to be overwhelmed by the influences brought to bear upon us through the Ambition of Aspiring men, the cupidity of souless corporations, and combinations of whatever name, or the mistaken philanthropy of the uninformed. Our forms of Government are those of our own choice, modeled after your own, and such as are adapted to our condition. Under them—we have prospered when allowed quiet and rest.—The tenures by which we hold our lands is such as we prefer, and such as we beleive to be for the best, for the majority of our people. Observation and reflection lead us to believe that no change can be made in this respects, that will not be fraught with mischief and ruin! We wish no change in regard to either, and confidently appeal to you to arrest all attempts to enforce them upon us, except to the extent and in the manner authorized by our Treaties now in force, or that may be hereafter concluded, by them we are bound, upon them we rely, and we appeal to you as the stronger and more enlightened party to these compacts, to honestly and firmly observe their Stipulations. We do not wish any material changes in our relations to the Government, but we do wish quiet and Security. The constant agitation of questions which vitaly affect our welfare, are full of evil influences upon our progress, We want a consciousness of protection and security; It is in your power to give both, You have promised them. Grant these and we shall fear no evil, we shall apprehend for our race, neither extinction nor degredation. But Progress and Civilization will follow and a brighter page in Indian Affairs will be found in the history of the United States than has yet been recorded. Adopted and signed in International Council at Okmulgee in the Muscogee Nation on Saturday the 4th day of June A D 1870" DS (21 signatures—7 by mark), *ibid.* On June 14, Lewis Downing, "Principal Cheif of the Cherokee Nation," and five others, Washington, D. C., wrote to USG. "we herewith transmit the address of Grand Council held on the first of the presen[t] month at Okemulgee in the Musc[o]gee Nation—for which we ask your care full consideration, as a true expression of the views and sentiments, the hopes and the fears of thos[e] people in relation to the policy of the government toward them—" LS, *ibid.*

On June 14, William A. Phillips, Washington, D. C., wrote to USG. "A short time ago there was an examination, before the Secretary of the Interior as to the powers, or rights of certain railroads to pass through the Cherokee Nation, under certain provisions of law and Treaty. At that time the representatives of the Cherokee nation understood that but two things were decided, namely: *First.* That but one railroad from north to south, and one from east to west should proceed through the Cherokee Nation. *Second* That no road should be permitted to enter it, until the rights of the parties were determined. On the question of the admission of any one road we have not had a hearing. It is a matter of great moment to the Cherokees that no road, with hostile purpose, and making any claim to our lands be permitted to enter We also, insist that, it is impossible for any company to enter safely, until the exact modifications of the intercourse laws are defined and we hold that this is the 'duly authorised by law,' required by the Treaty. We respectfully ask of you, or before the Attorney General, a full hearing of the points involved before any such permission is given. If a hearing is granted to any of the roads, we desire to be notified and to be present to represent the interests of the Cherokee Nation We learn that an attempt has been made to permit the Union Pacific Southern Branch to enter our Country. We have since heard that the order to enter has been countermanded, until a hearing shall be had, which we hope is correct. We are prepared to show FIRST, That the said Union Pacific Southern Branch does not propose to build a branch to Sherman, but, under the law and its plat filed, proposes to go to Ft. Smith To give it the right to build the through line north and south would either defeat the construction of the north and south line, or subject us to new embarrassments, and new clamors for another line. SECOND, That this company, by its specific authority from Congress, is forbidden to enter the Cherokee Nation without our consent which it has not got. These and several other reasons equally forcible we are prepared to show, which would forbid the proposed entry. We held before the Secretary, and still hold that further legislation from Congress is required, and that entering the Indian Territory without it will lead to great confusion" ALS, *ibid.*, Cherokee Agency. On July 12, Charles Nelson, Humboldt, Kan., wrote to USG. "As your Honnor is the only reliable Source that i know of to find out the truth as concern the land question in this part of our State I will now state our case we are poor hardworking men we came here last Febuary and settled on our land or at least we call it ours for when we settled on our land it was called Government land liable to preemption at $1.25 per acre to be paid for the 10th of april A. D. 1871   In the full belief that this was true we set to work to make our newly made homes a comfortable Possible   But now comes the news that we must appear at the Railroad land office of the Mosouri Kansas & Texas Rail way within 30. days for the purchase of our land   well what do we do   we go to some lawyer and ask his advice   he says never mind what they say they are only trying to swindle you   But now comes the tug of war   who shal we believe the lawyer or the land agent   this is the reason i have ventured to write to your Honor and ask your Honors advice   P S we are living on Osage ceded lands   Please answer this my prayer and do us a great favor"   ALS, *ibid.*, Neosho Agency. See *Washington National Republican*, July 14, 1870.

On July 21, Attorney Gen. Amos T. Akerman wrote to USG. "The question which you have submitted to me is this: Which of the two railroad companies, the Missouri, Kansas and Texas Railroad Company, formerly known as the Union Pacific Railroad Company, Southern Branch, or the Missouri River, Fort Scott and Gulf Railroad Company, formerly known as the Kansas and Neosho Valley Railroad Company, has the right, under the acts of Congress and the treaties with the Indians, to construct a railroad through the Indian territory southward from the southern boundary of Kansas? . . . As the result of my investigation, I am of the opinion that the right to build the road through the Indian territory to Texas, belongs to the Southern Branch road, now known as the Missouri, Kansas and Texas road." Copy, DNA, RG 60, Opinions. On July 27, Isaac N. Morris, Washington, D. C., wrote to USG. "The Principal Chief and the Cherokee Delegation, intending to leave for home in a few days, or as soon as the health of Col Adair will permit, request me to say they will be greatly obliged if you will forward a request for the Attorney General to furnish them with a copy of his opinion recently rendered ~~in~~ in the matter of the Missouri, Kansas and Texas Railroad Company, commonly called Parson's company, touching the right of said Company to run their road through the Indian Territory. The Republican newspaper, of this morning, refers to it and to the action of the Executive Department on the question, and the Delegation are, of course, anxious to know exactly what has been determined and this they can only learn from a copy of the official papers. They are bound to submit a full and correct report to their people on all points entrusted to their care, and they direct me to say so. If you will forward the request to me I will see that the Chief gets it" ALS, *ibid.*, Letters from the President. See H. Craig Miner, *The Corporation and the Indian: Tribal Sovereignty and Industrial Civilization in Indian Territory, 1865–1907* (Columbia, Mo., 1976), pp. 31–33.

To Charles F. Hall

Washington, D. C. July 20 18670.

Capt. C. F. Hall.

Dear Sir:

You are hereby appointed to command the Expedition toward the North Pole to be organized and sent out pursuant to an Act of Congress approved July 12th, 1870, and will report to the Secretary of the Navy and the Secretary of the Interior for detailed instructions.

U. S. Grant

DS, DNA, RG 45, Cruises and Voyages (Special). Charles F. Hall wrote to USG to thank him for this appointment. William Evarts Benjamin, Catalogue No. 42, March, 1892, p. 11. Hall, born in 1821, an engraver and newspaper publisher, twice traveled to the Arctic (1860–62, 1864–69) and published accounts of his experiences. See Chauncey C. Loomis, *Weird and Tragic Shores: The Story of Charles Francis Hall, Explorer* (New York, 1971), pp. 232–50.

On July 11, 1870, U.S. Senator Oliver P. Morton of Ind. had written to USG. "I have taken a deep interest in the proposed Expedition to the Arctic Regions, recently brought to the attention of Congress by Captain Charles Francis Hall, through whose energy and efforts an appropriation of $50.000 has just been made. His experience, (and the success that attended his explorations heretofore in the far North), warrants me in earnestly recommending him to your very favorable consideration. . . ." ALS, DNA, RG 48, Appointments Div., Letters Received. Petitions recommending Hall are *ibid.* On July 14, U.S. Representative Washington Townsend of Pa. wrote to USG. "I desire to state that I have in charge a recommendation very extensively signed by Senators and Representatives in Congress asking the appointment of Dr Isaac I. Hayes to the command of the proposed Arctic Expedition and respectfully to request that you delay any appointment for a few days until the credentials of Dr Hayes can be submitted to your consideration." ALS, *ibid.* Also in July, Dr. Isaac I. Hayes wrote to USG requesting command of the expedition. William Evarts Benjamin, Catalogue No. 27, Nov., 1889, p. 7.

On Feb. 13, 1871, Secretary of the Navy George M. Robeson wrote to USG. "I have the honor to enclose herewith for your approval, a letter addressed to the Secretary of the Treasury, requesting him to place to the credit of this Department, the appropriation of $50.000, for organizing an expedition to the North Pole." Copy, DNA, RG 45, Letters Sent to the President.

To William W. Holden

Long Branch. N. J.[1]
July. 22nd. 1870.

Hon. W. W. Holden, Gov. of N. C.
Dear Sir:

Your favor of the 20th. *inst.* detailing the unsettled and threatning condition of North Carolina, is just received, and I will telegraph to the Sec. of War immediately, to send more troops to the State without delay. They will be used to suppress violence and to maintain the law if other means should fail.

With great respect
Your ob'dt Serv'nt
U. S. Grant.

Copy, North Carolina Division of Archives and History, Raleigh, N. C. William W. Holden, born in 1818 in Orange County, N. C., switched allegiance from Whig to Democrat and assumed control of the *North Carolina Standard*, making it the most influential newspaper in the state and an advocate of secession. After losing contests for governor and U.S. senator (1858), his support for Democrats and secession became inconsistent, and he helped to establish a conservative party. He was appointed provisional governor of N. C. by President Andrew Johnson (1865) and elected as Republican governor (1868). On July 20, 1870, Holden had written to USG. "I have declared the Counties of Alamance and Caswell, in this State, in a state of insurrection. I have the power to do this under the Constitution of the State, and in pursuance of laws passed by the General Assembly. I have embodied a considerable number of the militia, have occupied the Counties above named, and have made a number of important arrests. Four of the persons arrested have sued out a *habeas corpus*, and the matter has been argued for several days before Chief Justice Pearson, of the Supreme Court. It is expected that the Chief Justice will deliver his opinion on Friday, the 22d. I have no means of knowing with certainty what his decision will be, but I incline to the opinion that he will substantially sustain me. There are threats of resistance, whatever his decision may be. My purpose is to organize a military court at Yanceyville, Caswell County, at an early day, to try the assassins and murderers now in custody. Col. Kirk, who commands at Yanceyville, apprehends resistance and an attempt to rescue the prisoners. He has 350 available men, native white loyalists, many of them ex-Federal soldiers. But the Ku Klux largely outnumber them in the Counties referred to, and if they should take the field and be joined by others from other Counties the State troops would certainly be in peril. I have in Raleigh one hundred colored troops, sixty white troops, and at Hillsborough fifty white troops, and in Gaston County one company of sixty. My whole available force is not more than six hundred. I think it very important that a regiment of federal troops be at once sent to the State, and that the federal troops here be ordered to come to my aid promptly. The defeat of the State and federal forces in any conflict in this crisis, would be exceedingly disastrous. It may be that the crisis may pass, and that I may be able to punish these assassins and murderers without encountering resistance; but I have deemed it my duty in this emergency to acquaint you with the condition of things, so that you may Judge of the expediency of ordering that I be further aided and supported by federal troops. I am satisfied that very important disclosures will be made as to the Ku Klux organization during the progress of the investigation before the military court. It is believed, from evidence already in hand, that Ex-President Johnson is at the head of the Order, and that Gen. Forest is the commander for Tennessee and North-Carolina. The organization is widespread and numerous, is based on the most deadly hostility to the reconstruction acts, and is, in all respects, very unfriendly to the governments of the reconstructed States and of the United States." ALS, DNA, RG 94, Letters Received, 442P 1870. On July 22, USG, Long Branch, telegraphed to Secretary of War William W. Belknap. "Send troops, six companies if possible, to Raleigh N. C. will write more particulars by mail." Telegram received, *ibid.*; *ibid.*, RG 107, Telegrams Collected (Bound); copies, *ibid.*, Letters Received from Bureaus; *ibid.*, Orders and Endorsements. Related papers are *ibid.*, RG 94, Letters Received, 442P 1870.

On March 10, Holden had written to USG. "I have felt it to be my duty to declare the County of Alamace, in this State, in a State of insurrection. The copy of my proclamation, herewith enclosed, of date March 7, 1870, contains some of the reasons ~~that have~~ for this step. There exists in this State a secret, oath-bound armed organization, which is hostile to the State government and to the government of the United States. Bands of these armed men ride at night through various neighborhoods, whipping and maltreating peaceable citizens, hanging some, burning churches and breaking up schools which have been established for the colored people. These outrages are almost invariably committed on persons, white and colored, who are most devoted in their feelings and conduct to the government of the United States. I can not rely upon the militia to repress these outrages, for the reason that, in the localities in which these outrages occur, white militia of the proper character can not be obtained, and it would but aggravate the evil to employ colored militia. Besides, the expense of calling out the militia would be greater than our people could well bear in their present impoverished condition. Federal troops inspire terror among evildoers, and they have the confidence and respect of a majority of our people. We, therefore, look to and rely on the federal government to aid us in repressing these outrages and in restoring peace and good order. If Congress would authorize the suspension by the President of the writ of *habeas corpus* in certain localities, and if criminals could be arrested and tried before military tribunals, and shot, we should soon have peace and order throughout all this country. The remedy ~~is~~ would be a sharp and a bloody one, but it is as indispensable as was the suppression of the rebellion. I trust, Sir, that you will issue to the commanding general of this department as stringent orders in this matter as the present laws will allow. The commanding general has been prompt to respond to the extent of the power which he has, but I fear this power will not be adequate to effect the desired result. I have the honor to enclose a copy of the State law under which my proclamation was issued; also, a pamphlet containing the testimony of witnesses in the preliminary examination of the Lenoir County prisoners, which will afford some idea of the organization and objects of the Ku Klux Klan."

ADfS, Duke University, Durham, N. C.; copies, DNA, RG 46, Presidential Messages; North Carolina Archives. See letter to Senate, Jan. 17, 1871.

On Aug. 9, Belknap telegraphed to USG. "The following teelegram was received from Gov. Holden yesterday.—Raleigh N. C. 7. Aug. 1870. To. THE PRESIDENT OF THE UNITED STATES Washington   Sir. The Chief Justice of the supreme court of this state sustained by his [A]ssociate Justices has decided that I have a right to declare counties in a [o]f insurrection, and to arrest & hold all suspected persons in such counties. This I have done. But the district Judge Brooks relying on the fourteenth amendment & the act of Congress of eighteen sixty seven, page eighty five, chapter twenty eight, has issued a writ of habeas corpus commanding the officer Kirk to produce before him the bodies of certain prisoners detained by my order,   I deny his right thus to interfere with our local laws in murder cases. I hold these persons under our state law, and under the decision of our supreme court,   Judges, who have Jurisdiction of the [w]hole matter, & it is not, known to Judge Brooks in what manner or by what tribunal the prisoners will be examined and tried,   The officer will be directed to reply to the writ that he holds the prisoners under my order and that he refuses to obey the writ. If the Marshal shall then call on the posse comitatus there may be a conflict but if he should call first on the federal troops it will be for you to say whether the troops shall be used to take the prisoners out of my hands. It is my purpose to detain the prisoners unless the Army of the United States under your orders shall demand them. An early answer is respectfully requested. signed W W. HOLDEN Govr. I referred the ~~ma~~ telegram to the Attorney General and he replied as follows   Attorney Generals Office Washington August 8. 1870   I do not see how the U. S. District Judge can refuse to issue the writ, if the petition makes out a case for it under the habeas corpus act of 1867 (14 statutes 385). If the return uncontroverted, or the facts appearing on proof to the Judge after a denial by the petitioner show the arrest to have been made under lawful state authority, he will remand the prisoners. In determining whether the laws of the state authorize the arrest, he will respect the decision of the state Judges. I advise that the state authorities yield to the U. S. Judiciary. signed. A. T. AKERMAN Atty Genl. No reply has been sent to Governor Holden and I submit his telegram with the opinion of the Attorney General, in which I concur, to you"   ALS (telegram sent), DNA, RG 107, Telegrams Collected (Bound). Printed copies of Holden's telegram and the opinion of Attorney Gen. Amos T. Akerman are *ibid.*, Letters Received from Bureaus.

On Dec. 15, Holden wrote to USG. "I herewith transmit to you my Annual Message, containing a printed statement of all the material facts connected with the effort to preserve peace in North-Carolina in the summer elections of this year, and in which you did me the honor to lend me the aid of National troops. The evidence elicited by the examinations had before the Chief Justice and two of the Associate Justices, seems to me to disclose the existence of a combination, (said to be 40.000 strong in this State,) which may threaten the future peace, if not the safety of the Nation, as it has already disturbed and continues to threaten the peace and safety of the law-abiding people of North-Carolina. I have, therefore, deemed it my duty to lay this evidence before you. I am satisfied that the witnesses were reluctant, because they stood in dread of violence from the Klans, which they were exposing. But enough was elicited to give an idea of the character, purposes and extent of the organization, and to show its dangerous and hostile intentions. Much more full and certain evidence might now be obtained bearing upon these points, and also upon the nature of the murders and other crimes committed by the various Klans in this State. I regret to say that the United States District Judge prevented a fuller development at the time, by an interference with my authority, which has since been decided by the U. S. Circuit Court Judge to have been wholly unauthorized by the laws of the country; but which interference so emboldened the enemies of the government and depressed its friends, that the examinations, which occurred immediately afterwards, were had at great disadvantage, being shorn to a large extent of their intended moral weight with the masses of the people. For two years past this organization has successfully defied the laws and the Courts of this State, and the authority of the Executive; and it is now believed that its leaders having gathered sufficient power, with impunity from punishment, are preparing to execute the first steps in their dangerous revolutionary schemes against the established order of things in this State. Should North-Carolina fall under the absolute control of such a secret and evil-intentioned power, not only the rights but the lives of the friends and supporters of the national government will be rendered unsafe within her territory: And furthermore, the Conspirators will have secured a firm base, from which more daring operations may be projected, aiming at the life, or the control, of the nation itself. Entertaining these views, and knowing that my authority and influence though freely exerted and as freely sustained by the Executive department of the general government, have proven inadequate to stay the growth of this organization, I now transmit the evidence that has been collected of its existence and character to you, for your serious consideration." Copy, *ibid*. The enclosure is *ibid*.

Holden's response to unrest in Alamance and Caswell counties led to his impeachment by the N. C. legislature on Dec. 19. Found guilty on March 22, 1871, of raising an illegal military force and directing wrongful arrests, Holden was removed as governor. On May 20, Holden, Washington, D. C., wrote to USG. "My counsel, my friends and family advise me that it is not expedient, if safe for me to return to my State. My trial has cost me about eight thousand dollars, besides the loss of my salary, five thousand per year. In addition, I am disqualified from holding office in my State, the result of the Judgment of the Senate. I am separated from my family, who are much distressed on that account, and my small estate is being absorbed in necessary expenses. Under these circumstances I respectfully ask for some employment under the government. I am not accustomed to such things, and therefore do not know what I should ask for. I am sure the members of Congress from my State, the Southern members generally, and not a few of the Northern and Western, would sustain my application. Leaving the matter in your hands, with the assurance that, in any event, I am your unwavering friend." ALS, *ibid*., RG 59, Letters of Application and Recommendation. See William C. Harris, *William Woods Holden: Firebrand of North Carolina Politics* (Baton Rouge and London, 1987), pp. 281–311.

1. On July 22, 1870, USG, Long Branch, wrote to Adolph E. Borie. "My family and myself arrived here yesterday finding our house in order and everything ready for housekeeping and receiving friends. I hope we may have the pleasure of receiving you Mrs. Borie and one of the young ladies next week to spend at least one week with us . . . I promise Mrs. Borie not to take you to visit Phila. friends before lunch. Having experienced your weakness once I should

feel culpable if I should lead you into temptation . . ." *The Collector*, 861, (1978), L-737. On July 23, J. C. Bancroft Davis, asst. secretary of state, wrote to USG. "I enclose for your signature three commissions of Deputy Postmasters, and two letters addressed to the Emperor of Morocco, with the request, by the Secretary's direction, that you will forward the same to him for countersignature in the accompanying envelope bearing his address." Copy, DNA, RG 59, Domestic Letters. A letter of the same day enclosing pardons for USG's signature is *ibid.* On July 25, Horace Porter, Long Branch, wrote to Davis. "I return you the papers signed by the President. Having no envelopes along of the kind called gigantic, I have turned yours, like the old woman did with her shawl, your two despatches were received and deciphered all right. They were read with great interest, and constituted the only news we have heard, so far, from Washington" ALS, DLC-J. C. Bancroft Davis. On July 26, Davis wrote to USG. "I enclose for your signature and for return to this Department the accompanying papers, namely, one commission for Assistant Treasurer at St. Louis, Mo.; one for Deputy PostMaster at Sacramento City Cal., and two exequaturs." Copy, DNA, RG 59, Domestic Letters.

To DeB. Randolph Keim

Long Branch, N. J.
July 23d 1870:

This will introduce De B. R. Keim, Diplomatic and Consular Agt. of the United States to Asia, to the representatives of theis ~~U~~Country abroad. Mr. Keim is commended to such representatives as he may come in contact with as a gentleman entitled ~~entitled~~ to their good offices and esteem, and one who will duly appreciate such attentions as he may receive. Having confered the apt. myself, not upon the recommendations of others, but upon personal acquaintance, I do not hesitate to give this commendation.

U. S. GRANT

ALS (facsimile), PHi; DLC-William H. Taft. Born in Reading, Pa., in 1841, DeB. Randolph Keim earned USG's confidence and favor during the Civil War while serving as a correspondent for the *New York Herald*. In 1865–66, he traveled throughout Asia, and from Nov., 1868, to March, 1869, he observed army operations in Indian Territory. See Keim, *Sheridan's Troopers on the Borders: A Winter Campaign on the Plains* (Philadelphia, 1870). On March 16, 1869, Keim, Washington, D. C., wrote to USG requesting an appointment as consul, Foo Chow. LS, DNA, RG 59, Letters of Application and Recommendation. Related papers are *ibid.* On April 12, USG nominated Keim to that post, withdrew the nomination on April 15 in order to nominate Keim as consul, Kiu Kiang. No appointment followed.

On July 19, 1870, Secretary of the Treasury George S. Boutwell wrote to USG. ". . . I recommend the following appointments, at a compensation at the rate of $5000. per annum and actual necessary expenses. W. J. Armstrong, to continue until December 1st 1870. R. B. Dennis to continue until December 1st 1870, and D. B. R. Keim, to continue for the period of one year from date of appointment." Copy, *ibid.*, RG 56, Letters Sent. On the same day, USG appointed Keim, William J. Armstrong, and R. B. Dennis as agents to examine the accounts of consular officers. USG extended Keim's appointment on July 1, 1871 (copy, *ibid.*, Letters Relating to Miscellaneous Appointments), Jan. 18, 1872 (copies, *ibid.*; *ibid.*, RG 130, Executive Orders and Proclamations), and June 4 (copy, *ibid.*, RG 56, Letters Relating to Miscellaneous Appointments). See "DeB. Randolph Keim, Agent of the United States, &c.: The Official Story of an Appointment," *The Keim and Allied Families in America and Europe*, 22 (Sept., 1900), 692–96. For reports from Keim, see *SED*, 41-3-7; *HED*, 42-2-11; *ibid.*, 42-2-317; *ibid.*, 42-3-145; *ibid.*, 42-3-168.

On Dec. 19, 1870, USG wrote to Congress. "I transmit herewith a report of the Secretary of the Treasury, made in compliance with Section 2 of the Act approved July 11. 1870, 'making appropriations for the consular and Diplomatic expenses of the Government for the year ending June 30 1871, and for other purposes.' " DS, DNA, RG 46, Presidential Messages. On Dec. 9, Boutwell had written to USG submitting reports from Keim, Armstrong, and Dennis. LS, *ibid.* The enclosures are *ibid.* Boutwell wrote to USG enclosing additional reports on Jan. 17, 1871 (LS, DNA, RG 59, Miscellaneous Letters), Jan. 28, and April 10 (copies, *ibid.*, RG 56, Letters Sent to the President). On May 2, William A. Richardson, asst. secretary of the treasury, wrote to USG submitting a report from Keim. Copy, *ibid.* On Dec. 4, USG wrote to the House of Representatives. "In compliance with section two of the 'Act making appropriations for the consular and diplomatic expenses of the government for the year ending June 30th 1871,' approved July 11th, 1870, I herewith transmit the names and reports of, and the amounts paid to Consular Agents of the United States." Copy, *ibid.*, RG 130, Messages to Congress. A copy of a letter dated Nov. 28 from Boutwell to USG submitting this material is *ibid.*, RG 56, Letters Sent to the President. On Dec. 12, 1872, USG wrote a similar letter to the House. Copy, DNA, RG 130, Messages to Congress. On Dec. 11, Boutwell had submitted Keim's reports to USG. Copy, *ibid.*, RG 56, Letters Sent to the President. On May 23, Boutwell wrote to USG submitting a report from Keim. Copy, DNA, RG 56, Letters Sent to the President. On the next day, USG wrote to Congress transmitting this material. DS, *ibid.*, RG 46, Presidential Messages. On Jan. 31, 1873, USG wrote to Congress. "In compliance with Section two (2) of the act approved July 11. 1870 entitled, 'An Act making appropriations for the Consular and Diplomatic expenses of the Government for the year ending June 30th 1871 and for other purposes,' I have the honor to submit herewith a letter of the Secretary of the Treasury relative to the Consular Agent appointed under authority of said act together with the amounts paid such Agent; and to transmit the report of the said Agent upon the Consular Service of the United States." Copy, *ibid.*, RG 130, Messages to Congress.

To Lt. Gen. Philip H. Sheridan

Long Branch, N. J.
July 25th 1870.

Lt. Gen. P. H. Sheridan, of the United States Army, is authorized to visit Europe,[1] to return at his own pleasure, unless otherwise ordered. He is commended to the good offices of all representatives of this government whom he may meet abroad.

To citizens, and representatives of other governments, I introduce Gen. Sheridan as one of the most skilful, brave and deserving soldiers developed by the great struggle through which the United States Govt. has just passed.

Attentions paid him will be duly appreciated by the country he has served so faithfully and efficiently.

U. S. GRANT

ALS, DLC-Philip H. Sheridan. On July 29, 1870, J. C. Bancroft Davis, asst. secretary of state, telegraphed to USG. "I received from Berthemy copy of despatch from Duke de Gramont, of which this is translation. 'Please make known to the President of the United States that the Emperor regrets extremely that he cannot authorize General Sheridan to follow the operations of the French army. His Majesty would have been happy to make an exception in favor of a soldier so illustrious but it has been decided on controlling considerations that no foreign officer shall be admitted to headquarters. Gramont.' The documents sent by General Porter have been received." Copy, DNA, RG 59, Domestic Letters. See *Personal Memoirs of P. H. Sheridan* (New York, 1888), II, 349, 358–61. On Sept. 13, Lt. Gen. Philip H. Sheridan, Reims, wrote to USG. "The capture of the Emperor Napoleon, & McMahons army at Sedan on the 1st of Sept. has thrown France into a chaos which even embarrasses the Prussian authorities. It seems to a quiet observer, as though Prussia had done too much— who to negotiate with—who to hold responsible in the final settlement, are becoming grave questions, & one cannot see what will be the result. I was present at the battles of *Beaumont Gravellote* & *Sedan* & have had my imagination clipped, in seeing these battles, of many of the errors it had run into in its conceptions of what might be expected of the trained troops of Europe. There was about the same percentage of sneaks, or runaways, & the general conditions of the battles were about the same as our own. One thing was especially noticeable the scattered condition of the men in going into battle, & their scattered condition while engaged. At Gravellote, Beaumont, & Sedan the men engaged on both sides were so scattered that it looked like thousands of men engaged in a deadly skirmish without any regard to lines, or formations. These battles were of this style of fighting, Commencing at long range, & might be called progressive fighting, closing at night by the French always giving up their position, or being driven from it in this way by the Prussians. The latter had their own strategy up to the Moselle, and it was good and successful after that river was reached the French made the strategy for the Prussians—and it was more successful than their own—The Prussian Soldiers are very good brave fellows, all young scarcely a man over twenty seven, in the first lines They have gone into each battle with the determination to win. It is especially noticeable also, that the Prussians have attacked the French where ever they have found them, let the numbers be great or small, & so far as I have been able to see, though the grand tactics of bringing on the engagements have been good, yet the battles have been won by the good square fighting of the men and junior officers—It is true the Prussians have been two to one except in one of the battles before Metz, that of the 16th of Aug, still the French have had the advantage of very strong positions. Generally speaking, the French soldiers have not fought well— it may be because the poor fellows have been discouraged by the traps into which their commanders have led them but I must confess to having seen some of the '*tallest*' running at Sedan I have ever witnessed, especially on the left of the French position all attempts to make the men stand seemed to be unavailing; so disgraceful was this that it caused the French Cavalry to make three or four gallant but foolish charges, as it were to show that there was at least some manhood left in a mounted French soldier. I am disgusted; all my boy hood fancies of the soldiers of the great Napoleon have been dissipated, or else the soldiers of the 'little Corporal' have lost their élan in the pampered parade soldiers of the man of DESTINY.' The Prussians will settle, I think by making the line of the *Moselle* the German line taking in *Metz* & *Strausburg* and the expenses of the war. I have been most kindly received by the King & Count Bismark & all the officers at the Headquarters of the Prussian Army—have seen much of great interest, especially have I been able to observe the difference between European battles & those of our own country & have not found the difference very great, but that difference is to the credit of our own country. There is nothing to be learned here professionally, but ~~the~~ it is a satisfaction to learn that such is the case. There is much however which Europeans could learn from us. The use of Rifle pits—the use of cavalry which they do not use well— for instance there is a line of communication from here to Germany exposed to the whole of the south of France with scarcely a soldier on the whole line & it has never been touched—There are a hundred things in which they are behind us—. The staff Depts are poorly organized the Q. M Dept wretched &c &c. . . . P. S. We go tomorrow with the Head quats of the King to a point about ~~thi~~[twe]nty miles from Paris." LS, Second Story Books, Washington, D. C.; copy, MiU-C.

1. On July 19, Ambrose E. Burnside, New York City, wrote to USG. "As I told you the other day, [I] am going over to Europe for a few weeks—It has occurred to me that [I] might be of some service to you—if you desire to give me some work to do, ~~such a~~ it will give me great pleasure to serve you—It may be desirable for you to have such information as I could gather ~~fr~~ in three or four weeks, from consultation with our ministers abroad and with the foreign departments of England, France and Prussia—If so, and you ~~may~~ think proper to give me letters accrediting to those governments and to our ministers in the capacity of a confidential agent I will be glad to do what I can—Please dont understand me as applying for an office—I want no pay, but would be glad to serve you in the way I have mentioned—I sail on the 'Scotia' on Wednesd[ay]

next, and return by the 13th of Sept The reason I ~~mention~~ would lik[e] to be accredited is that it would giv[e] me better opportunities of gaining ~~the~~ information that may prove of some value—You will remember I spok[e] to you of Genl Lewis Richmond my asst Adjt Genl all through the war There is a consulate in china vacan[t] Hong Kong I think—Cannot he have it?—He needs something, and deserv[es] it—Anthony has written to Mr Fish about it—Please dont forget that you are to visit us 17th Sept—and I ho[pe] the madam and your children wi[ll] come with you—" ALS, DNA, RG 59, Miscellaneous Letters. On Aug. 19, Col. William B. Hazen, Long Branch, wrote to Bvt. Maj. Gen. Edward D. Townsend. "I have just seen the President and received his promise of going abroad to see the war. . . ." ALS, *ibid.*, RG 94, Letters Received, 492H 1870. In an undated letter, Horace Porter, Newport, R. I., wrote to Townsend. "The President thinks the Sec. of War and Gen. Sherman are both absent from the city, and directs me to say to you that if Gen. Hazen should apply for a leave to visit Europe, he would like to have permission given him to remain in Europe until recalled, reporting monthly to the War Department his address; in other words to give him an indefinite leave in order to let him see as much of the war as possible." ALS, *ibid.*

To Gen. William T. Sherman

Long Branch, N. J.
July 31th[1] 1870.

DEAR GENERAL:

Your letter of the 27th inst. come duly to hand. As I shall be in Washington on Thursday or Friday next I will not answer it further than to say that the General of the Army should, as a matter of course, be stationed at the National Capitol, and that his controll should be equal over all portions of the line of the Army at least. Whether the General of the Army should have any controll ofver the Staff Corps is a matter of law.

I do not understand that the Sec. of War has required all orders to be issued independent of the General, but that in all matters pertaining to discipline, changes of location, &c. orders will be issued hereafter as hereto-fore.

I am delightfully located here and enjoy it very much.

Yours Truly
U. S. GRANT

GN. W. T. SHERMAN,

ALS, DLC-William T. Sherman. On July 27, 1870, Gen. William T. Sherman, Washington, D. C., had written to USG. "I ask your personal consideration to some things, and your answer as early as convenient as it may, influence my action. You remember that when summoned to Washington to succeed you in the command of the Army, you expressed a desire, and made the order that I should exercise a command over all parts of the Army. Gen Schofield was to remain as Secretary of War long enough to initiate the measures. You soon appointed Gn Rawlins and modified the first order, leaving me in the exercise of undefined power, governed by Army Regulations, that did not Contemplate a General, or even name a Commanding General. Gradually the old state of things has been reestablished, and the recent law strips the General of all semblance of power, and the Secretary of War has it, may be very properly ordered that Orders to the Army shall be issued by the War Departmt, through the Adjutant General instead of the General. I do not complain of this, or of any thing, but I wish to Shape my private life to the end, that I may not occupy a ridiculous position. When the Gentlemen of NewYork generously raised a sum of money to enable me to occupy the position you had held, they tendered me the money, or offerred to buy your house and furniture at a cost of $65,000.—I answered them that I preferred not to touch the money, but if they would present me the House it would be a generous gift that would lay me and my family under lasting obligations, and its purchase of you at that price would be equally beneficial to you. The deed was then presented me, and as you know I have been in possession since. As soon as it was apparent that Congress designed to diminish my pay we began to consider whether we could with our family so curtail Expenses as to continue to occupy the house, and it is found almost impossible for the house is large and entails heavy Expense. I first endeavored to sell at $50,000, but failed—I then estimated for the conversion of the house into two houses, one for my self and one for Rent: and that is my present aim, but if my office be a sinecure, ultimately to be stripped and abolished I had better jump to the Conclusion now, and go away. Before taking any steps I ask your personal opinion and wishes in the premises. My family is now in Ohio and I must at once prepare for them in the coming year. If I could dispose of that house on any thing like fair terms I would ask to return to Saint Louis, but it is an Elephant on my hands, and the next best is to ask if you object to my going there when I can dispose of it, even if I have to surrender it back to the donors." ALS, USG 3.

1. Sunday.

To Charles W. Ford

Long Branch, N. J.
Aug. 2d 1870.

Dear Ford:

Your favor of the 29th is just rec'd. It is rather a singular coincidence that not an hour before I rec'd your letter I was thinking of my trip to St. Louis, and wishing that I might receive an invitation to Benton's[1] house instead of having to go to a hotel. I accept of course, with great pleasure. Tell Benton so and that I expect to reach St. Louis on the 10th inst. Will telegraph on the way what train. My party will consist of Dr. Sharp, U. S. Grant Jr. and myself.

Yours Truly
U. S. GRANT

ALS, USG 3.

1. While visiting St. Louis, Aug. 10–12, 1870, USG stayed at the home of William H. Benton.

To Joseph Thomson

Long Branch, N. J.
Aug. 2d 1870.

JOSEPH THOMSON, ESQ.
SIR:

My son, to whom you wrote in reference to the suit of clothes you are making for him, is absent from Long Branch, and will not probably be able to visit New York again before starting West, on Monday next.

I go to Washington on Thursday, day after to-morrow, and will be much disappointed if I do not get the suit of clothes ordered last week before starting.

If possible please forward them to-morrow.

Yours &c
U. S. GRANT

ALS, Herman Blum, Philadelphia, Pa. On Jan. 25, 1870, Horace Porter had written to Joseph Thomson, New York City. "The President directs me to request you to make him a suit of black cloth clothes, double breasted frock coat, pants & vest." Copy, DLC-USG, II, 1. On Feb. 4, Orville E. Babcock wrote to Thomson. "I am directed by the President to enclose you his check for $104.05, amount of your bill of Jany. 26." Copy, *ibid.*

On Oct. 19, 1866, USG had written to "Messrs Spence & Thomson." "Enclosed please find check for $121 50/100, the amount of bill for clothing just rec'd. I ordered at the time my measurement was taken two white vests which did not come. I will now get them in this City. You need not therefore send them. I return by express Gn. Butterfields clothing. Gen. Butterfield is on duty in New York City." ALS, Gallery of History, Las Vegas, Nev. Partial text of this letter is in *PUSG*, 16, 559.

Endorsement

The writer is an old Babtist preacher; entered the service early in the rebellion as Maj. of the 21st Ill. of which regt. I was Col. served throughout the war; was Eighteen months in rebel prisons, and some weeks of the time was confined under the fire of Gilmore's guns at Charleston. I regard Col. McMacin[1] as a good and reliable man.

U. S. Grant

Aug. 5th /70

AES, DNA, RG 48, Applications for Indian Inspector. Written on a letter of July 25, 1870, from Warren E. McMackin, Salem, Ill., to USG. "Having learned that the Superintendencies of Indian Agencies are now to be filled by the appointment of Civilians—I have concluded to ask an appointment to One of them. If you think I am the man for the place—I would like an appointment. (If it can be mad consistently). You know my Claims—as also my Qualifications— and feeling assured that you will do for me what you think to be Just and Right—I shall feel perfectly satisfied with your action in the premicies—" ALS, *ibid.* During the Civil War, McMackin served as maj., then lt. col., 21st Ill. On March 31 and April 14, 1869, USG nominated him postmaster, Salem, but the Senate did not confirm the appointment. On Jan. 6, 1873, USG nominated McMackin as pension agent, Salem. See *PUSG*, 2, 30, 50–51.

1. On Feb. 6, 1871, McMackin wrote to USG. "I address you to ask of you the faver of putting the name of my Son (John Scott McMackin) on the State for a presidential appointment to a Cadetship in the Millitary Schoo Accadamy at West Point. This (11th Congressional) District being represented by a Democrat—a Republican stands no chance for a Congressional appointmett I therefore ask this favor of you and hope it may receive your favorable consideration." ALS, DNA, RG 94, Unsuccessful Cadet Applications.

To Hamilton Fish

Long Branch, N. J.
Aug. 7th 1870.

DEAR GOVERNOR:

I am just in receipt of your dispatch saying that Trumbull says "No" and asking if you shall ask Morrill or Edmunds. The dispatch is dated the 6th however and as I received, and answered, yesterday a dispatch from you indenticle in terms, saying "Morrill first,"[1] I do not answer again by telegraph. As I start for St. Louis in the morning, and possibly my reply may not have been rec'd I write this. If Morrill and Edmunds should both decline I do not know who to name. Pierrepont would represent the country ably but I know from Senators that his nomination would meet with strong objections as would that of Judge Hoar. I think, failing to get either Morrill or Edmunds, I would offer the place to Blaine.

I shall probably be back from St Louis ~~about~~ by the 16th. Before leaving Washington I directed the Atty. General to make out a proclamation for the pardon of the convicted Fenians,[2] giving him the grounds upon which I wanted the pardons granted, and directed the Asst. Sec. of sState to prepare a proclamation[3] of warning to them for the future. Neither will be issued until I return, and not then unless I think it advisable after hearing the views of the Cabinet. I also told Mr Davis to have prepared, and to submit to you before my return, a "Neutrality proclamation"[4] to be issued on my return.

Please present Mrs Grant's and my kindest regards to Mrs. Fish.

Truly yours
U. S. GRANT

HON. H. FISH
SEC OF STATE

ALS, DLC-Hamilton Fish.

1. This two-word message from USG, dated Aug. 6, 1870 (received on Aug. 7) is *ibid.*

2. On Aug. 12, Mayor Nathan Cole of St. Louis presented to USG a

petition requesting pardons for John O'Neill, John Donnelly, and other Fenian prisoners. *Missouri Democrat*, Aug. 13, 1870. See letters to Hamilton Fish, Aug. 18, Oct. 8, 1870.

    3. See proclamation, Oct. 12, 1870.

    4. See letter to Hamilton Fish, Aug. 18, 1870. On Aug. 1, J. C. Bancroft Davis, asst. secretary of state, had written to Horace Porter. "[T]he CoMarshal at San Francisco reports [po]ssibility of fillibustering expedition against French [se]ttlements in Tahiti. Have seen [Be]rthemy—he will instruct French consul to communi[ca]te with Marshal. Have instru Marshal to [be] instructed to watch without incurring [ex]pense. Berthemy says Roessine North[e]rn Prussian Consul at N. Y is forwarding [r]ecruits—Gerolt Prussian Minister admits that he is [fo]rwarding soldiers Men absent here on leave. Have [c]autioned the minister not to violate [n]eutrality laws—He gets angry vexed at caution says no violation in what has been don[e.] Please communicate this to the President and to Secretary of State on arrival when he arrives" ADf (initialed), DLC-Hamilton Fish. On Aug. 2, USG telegraphed to Secretary of War William W. Belknap. "DIRECT TROOPS IN SAN FRANCISCO HARBOR TO OBEY SUMMONS OF U. S. MARSHAL IF CALLED ON TO PREVENT FITTING OUT OF UNLAWFUL EXPEDITIONS." Telegram received, DNA, RG 94, Letters Received, 463P 1870.

To Jane Franklin

Long Branch, N. J.

Aug. 8th 1870.

MY DEAR MADAM,

    Please accept my acknowledgments of your kindness in send me a copy of the "fFate of Sir John Franklin,"[1] your honored and renowned husband. A man who has contributed so much to the world's knowledge of the world as has Sir John Franklin wins the esteem of more than his own Countryman, and when overcome by such a fate as his ishas been, is moarned for by all civilazed nations.

With great respect

Your obt. svt.

U. S. GRANT

LADY JOHN FRANKLIN.

ALS (photocopy), USGA. In 1828, Jane Griffin married Capt. John Franklin, British naval officer and noted arctic explorer. Knighted in 1829, Franklin died in 1847 while leading an expedition in search of a Northwest Passage. On Aug. 6, 1870, Jane Franklin and George W. Childs visited USG at Long Branch. *New York Herald*, Aug. 8, 1870.

1. Probably Francis L. McClintock, *Fate of Sir John Franklin: The Voyage of the "Fox" in the Arctic Seas in Search of Franklin and his Companions* (3rd ed., London, 1869).

To Julia Dent Grant

St. Louis, Aug. 10th *1867*0

DEAR JULIA:

We arrived here at 12 Midnight last night after a very pleasant trip. Buck and Clifford[1] have just started for the farm to spend the day. I shall see Shepley this morning and ascertain his views of the propriety of taking an appeal for the purpose of effecting a compromise for the balance of the Carondelet tract or not. Also try to make arrangements for a lot in Belfontain Cemetery. You need not send a carriage for me on Tuesday[2] Morning. By arrangement we will go to Long Branch without going by New York city and I can not tell exactly the hour we will arrive there on Tuesday. I can easily take a hack at the stand.

Love and kisses to you and the children.

ULYS.

ALS, USG 3. See *Missouri Democrat*, Aug. 10, 1870.

1. Arthur Clifford, son of former Governor John H. Clifford of Mass.
2. Aug. 16. On that day, USG, Cleveland, telegraphed to Julia Dent Grant. "Will be home tomorrow noon" Telegram received, USG 3.

To Julia Dent Grant

St. Louis Mo. Aug. 11th *1870*.

DEAR JULIA:

I leave here in the morning for Chicago where I will remain until Sunday[1] evening and then go directly to Long Branch. I have, on the advice of Mr. Glover, appealed the suit in the Carondelet case in hope thereby of effecting a compromise.—Judge Krum,[2]

Dr. Sharpe and Fred have gone to Belfontain to locate a lot. I made the arrangement for the purchase.

The farm is in fine condition, much better than I ever saw. Elrod has 75 acres of corn which will average more than 50 busels to the acre. Now, while he is not busy, two of his hands are making $100 00 pr. week with his thrashing machine around the immediate neighborhood.—We all took tea with Fent Long[3] last evening. The big pot was put in the little one and every thing done to make the occasion a pleasant one. Nothing could have been nicer or more appropriate than the arrangements he had made.

Love and kisses to you and the children. I will not write again before going back to Long Branch.

ULYS.

ALS, USG 3. See *Missouri Democrat*, Aug. 11, 1870.

1. Aug. 14.
2. John M. Krum, St. Louis attorney.
3. John F. Long.

To Hamilton Fish

Long Branch, N. J.
Aug. 18th 1870.

DEAR GOVERNOR:

I returned, arriving here, yesterday afternoon. Your letter was handed to me too late to get a reply into the mail for this morning boat.—I do not propose a Cabinet meeting for anything I now foresee. In the matter of postponing the issuing of a pardon to the Fenians I see the force of your suggestion and shall adopt it. The Neutrality proclamation was read in presence of all the Cabinet except yourself and the Sec. of the Treas. There is no other matter that I know of now to bring before the Cabinet. Any papers requiring my signature may be sent to me here. I so telegraphed Mr. Davis yesterday before getting your letter.

I hope Edmunds[1] or Blane will accept the English Mission. If neither do there is Ex. Govr Bullock,² of Mass. ~~that~~ whos name might be considered.

Mrs. Grant joins me in sending our kindest regards to Mrs Fish and yourself.

yours Truly
U. S. GRANT

HON. H. FISH,
SEC. OF STATE

P. S. I only give the name of Govr Bullock for your consideration.

ALS, DLC-Hamilton Fish. On Aug. 16, 1870, Secretary of State Hamilton Fish had written to USG. "I always supposed that you would deem it wise to release the persons convicted of participation in the Fenian raid. Purely political prisoners are the worst kind of birds to keep caged. I would however suggest whether it may not be well to postpone the action for a short time. The pardon will produce some irritation among the Canadians, who may in their excitement annoy some of our fishermen. At present they seem inclined to treat them very leniently. The fishing season is over within a few weeks. . . . and it will do no great harm to O'Neill to spend a few weeks in the cool climate of Vermont." William D'Arcy, *The Fenian Movement in the United States: 1858–1886* (1947; reprinted New York, 1971), p. 364. On Aug. 19, Fish, Garrison, N. Y., wrote to USG. "Your letter of yesterday is this moment received—I send by my Son, the Proclamation of Neutrality for your signature—Mr Berthemy has made complaint of some things done by the Germans, & to a certain extent I think his complaints are just—The Germans it seems are engaging Surgeons for their Army—under the pretext that they are non combattants; but they are officers to be employed in the military service, & the Attorney General, I understand, is of the opinion that they come within the provisions of our neutrality law—The issuing of the Proclamation will probably arrest such infractions of the laws, & of our neutral duties—I have Countersigned the Proclamation, so that it can be forwarded directly to Mr Davis & be made public at once—I have barely time to get this ready for Hamilton to take the train at 12 48" ALS (press), DLC-Hamilton Fish.

On Aug. 18, Fish telegraphed to USG. "Shall I send for signature the paper mentioned in my letter? If so when?" ALS (telegram sent), *ibid.* In an undated telegram, USG wrote to Fish. "Papers requiring my Signature may be sent here" Telegram received, *ibid.* On Aug. 18 and 19, Fish wrote to J. C. Bancroft Davis, asst. secretary of state. ". . . I wrote a day or two ago to the President on the subject of the Fenian Pardons & Proclamation, urging postponement—I hope that he will not be in a hurry: but I fear that some persons are pressing it, on the ground that it will have a beneficial effect on some local elections. The question raised by the Atty Genl of the right of a neutral to purchase vessels from a belligerent, during the War, does not seem to have a *present* application—Our Statute prohibits the transfer to an *American Register*, of the vessels of Either belligerent—Does the question come in any shape, into the proposed *Fenian* proclamation? I have not seriously examined it—. . ." "A letter this moment rcd from the President, induces me to send Hamilton to Long

Branch, with the Proclamation, which I think will be signed & forwarded to you, by tomorrows mail—He cannot get there in time for it to go off tonight—I have countersigned it so that it will require only the *Seal*—I have erased the words 'public or carry despatches'—& now think it might have been well to insert 'military' before 'despatches'—but it is done, & let it go as it is—I hope to see it out on Monday—. . . I wrote a longer letter this morning—" ALS and AL (initialed), *ibid.*

1. George F. Edmunds, born in 1828 in Richmond, Vt., was a lawyer and state legislator before being elected U.S. senator in 1866. On Aug. 17, 1870, Fish telegraphed to USG. "Morrill says no—I have enquired of addressed same enquiry to Edmunds—" ALS (telegram sent), *ibid.*

2. Alexander H. Bullock, born in Royalston, Mass., graduated from Amherst College (1836) and Harvard Law School (1840) and settled in Worcester, where he practiced law, edited Whig party publications, and held a series of local and state offices, including three terms as Republican governor of Mass. (1866–69).

To Gen. William T. Sherman

Long Branch, N. J.
Aug. 18th 1870.

DEAR GENERAL:

Your letter of the 7th inst. did not reach Long Branch until after I had left for St. Louis, and consequently is just before me for the first time.—I do not know what changes recent laws, particularly the last Army bill[1] passed, make in the relations between the Gn. of the Army and the Sec. of War. Not having this law, nor other statutes, here I can not examine the subject now, nor would I want to without consultation with the Sec. of War. On our return to Washington I have no doubt but that the relations between the Sec. and yourself can be made pleasant, and the duties of each be so clearly defined as to leave no doubt where the authority of one leaves off and the other commences.—My own views, when commanding the Army, were, that orders to the Army should go through the Gen. No changes should be made however either of the location of troops or Officers without the authority of the Sec. of War. In place, the Gen. commanded them without reporting to the Sec. further than he [c]hose, the specific orders he gave from time to time, but subject himself to orders from the Sec. the latter deriving his authority to give orders from the President.—As Congress has the right however to make rules and regulations for the Govt. of the Army, rules made by them, whether they are what they should be or not will have to govern. As before stated I have not examined the recent law.

Yours Truly

U. S. GRANT

GEN W. T. SHERMAN

ALS, DLC-William T. Sherman. On Aug. 7, 1870, Gen. William T. Sherman, Washington, D. C., had written to USG. "I intended in person last night to acknowledge your letter from Long Branch but there was no time. Of course if you think I should remain in Washn I must do so, and fear I must spend $10,000 to convert my presnt house into two, for I cannot afford with Six children, to spend in mere housekeeping more than my income, and you know that is impossible with so large a house &c. to curtail expenses much. I think the Law, clearly gives the General the Command of the Staff just as much as the Line. There are Certain administrative duties of the Heads of the Bureaux, that devolve by law on the Secretary of War, but the Law approved July 25, 1866, reviving the Grade of General, provides that he shall 'under the direction of and during the pleasure of the President command the Armies of the U S—and that approved July 28 defines the Army to be 'Five Artillery, ten Cavalry, forty five Regimts of Infantry, the Professors & Corps of Cadets, and *such other forces*' as are provided in the act—visiting in succession all the staff corps & Depts. I send you a Copy of a letter you wrote to Secretary Stanton Jan 29, 1866, and ask you to read it. It contains all I ask, and since that time no law or Regulation on the subject has been made excepting by yourself. I also enclose you a copy of Special Orders No 179, issued without consultation with me. If these officers be of the Army, and are ordered about by the Secretary of War, through the Adjt General, without the knowledge of the General of the Army, Who Commands the Army? And of what use is a General? Does not disbandmt follow as a logical sequence? and as a prudent man ought I not to be getting ready? I do not speak to General Belknap about this, because he did not speak to me of his proposed change, and I think you who have had so much experience in both offices, can so easily define the just limit between them. . . . *If possible*— please answer in general terms before you start for St Louis—as the Contractor waits for my answer to his proposals for building" ALS, USG 3. See *PUSG*, 16, 36–38.

On Sept. 2, Sherman, Omaha, wrote to USG. "I have received your most acceptable letter of Aug 18, and assure you that I am perfectly willing to abide by any decision you may make. We had a most enthusiastic meeting at Des Moines, and General Belknap gave us a fine finished address. I have concluded to go on to San Francisco, to attend the Annual Celebration of the Pioneers to be held on the 9th instant—from there I will make a short turn aiming to get back to St Louis via Denver by the 1st of October and so on to Washington without unnecessary delay. Conscious of the heavy burdens already on you, I should refrain from adding one more to your already load of Care, but it seems to me that now is the time to fix clearly and plainly the field of duty, for the Secretary of War, and the Commanding General of the Army, so that we may escape the unpleasant controversy that gave so much scandal in General Scotts time, and leave to our successors a clear field. No matter what the result I promise to submit to whatever decisions you may make. I also feel certain that General Belknap thinks he is simply executing the law as it now stands, but am convinced that he does not interpret the Law reviving the Grade of General— and that of 'fixing the Peace Establishment,' of 1868, as I construe them. For instance I am supposed to control the discipline of the military academy as a part of the Army. Whereas Genl Belknap, ordered a Court of inquiry in the Case of the Colored Cadet, made the detail, reviewed the proceedings & made his order, without my knowing a word of it except through the newspapers, and more recently when I went to Chicago to attend to some Division business I found the Inspector General Hardie under orders from the Secretary of War to go to Montana on some Claim business—all I ask is that such orders should go to the parties through me. If all the staff officers are subject to receive orders direct from the Secretary of War, it will surely clash with the orders which they may be in the act of executing from me or from their immediate Commanders. I ask that Gnl Belknap draw up some clear well defined Rules for my action, that he show them to me before publication, that I make on them my remarks, and then that you make a final decision. I promise faithfully to abide by it, or give up my Commission. Please show this to Genl Belknap, and I will be back early in October." ALS, USG 3. See *Memoirs of Gen. W. T. Sherman* (4th ed., New York, 1891), II, 441–51.

1. See *U.S. Statutes at Large*, XVI, 315–21.

To Schuyler Colfax

Long Branch, N. J
Aug. 21st 1870.

DEAR SIR:

Your letter of the 18th instant, with its enclosures, was duly received. I have read your remarks on "the coming contest"[1] with interest, as well as Dr. Ray's letter. My trip home was pleasant and I found my family all well. Letters had accumulated but I found among them nothin of importance, except (confidential) that Mr. Morrill had declined the English Mission and that Edmunds had made no response. He has not yet. If he declines I am half inclined to offer it to Horace Greeley.² This is confidential too for the present as I may possibly not make the offer.

Please present my compliments to Mrs. Colfax and to S. C. Jr.

Yours Truly

U. S. GRANT

VICE PRESIDENT COLFAX

SOUTH BEND, IN.

ALS, ICarbS. On Aug. 18, 1870, Vice President Schuyler Colfax, South Bend, Ind., had written to Charles H. Ray. "Your letter reached me this morning, & the points are put in it so forcibly, & it was so timely a supplement to what I had said, I should have sent it to ~~him~~ ~~with~~ the President without your suggestion. But he had asked me to send him my article on 'the Coming Contest,' which he had heard of but not read, & having to write him on another topic, I have enclosed your letter to him with mine, in the most natural way possible." ALS, CSmH. On Oct. 9, Colfax wrote to USG. "Home this Sunday, after my month's daily speaking over this doubtful State, (& two more of my 30 speeches to make tomorrow,) I find your reference of *the twins* at Logansport to me, & would suggest that, when they grow up, we should present them with a box of segars! My voice & throat are worn out, by having to speak out doors nearly every day to large crowds, & I have declined all invitations to speak in other States, after our election, not being willing to kill myself off yet. The apathy in our State has been alarming. Meetings on both sides generally meagre & a good deal of local disaffections. Morton has spoken however 8 or 10 times to large crowds; & Cumback, Baker & Pratt have had good audiences. We have done all we could, & now must await the result. I send you a few notices of my meetings, but must add that I am more determined than ever to retire from public life inflexibly at the end of this term. Every where's our friends are unanimous for your reelection, & you will have to make up your mind to that." ALS, ICarbS.

1. See *New York Times*, Aug. 8, 1870.
2. Born in N. H. in 1811, Horace Greeley apprenticed as a printer in Vt., moved to New York City in 1831, and established the *New York Tribune* in 1841. In 1864, Greeley considered USG a more viable presidential nominee than Abraham Lincoln; in 1868, Greeley endorsed USG without enthusiasm. On Jan. 5, 1869, John Russell Young, managing editor, *New York Tribune*, wrote to U.S. Representative Elihu B. Washburne of Ill. "I have your letter of the 24th Decr, and you see what use I have made of its information—I want to say to you that the best thing Grant has done since he wrote that letter to Johnson about Sheridan, were his two speeches which, I see, have been denied, about the Pacific Railroad subsidies and putting men in office. They effect they made on Mr. Greeley's mind was marked. So long as Gen. Grant and his friends made General professions of honesty, they made no more impression upon the country than general professions of virtue always do. They were looked upon as mere *ad captandum* rhetoric. But when he singled out the Pacific Railroad; a mighty interest in itself; and the Louisiana levee—another interest almost as great *to* the office holders, and of interest engrossing all others—and put himself specifi-

cally on the record against them; he showed the country that his words were embodied deeds. All we want from Gen. Grant now, it seems to me, is, to put into his Cabinet men who will thoroughly execute the policy expressed in these recent manifestations. I sincerely trust and pray that he will not give us a Cabinet of men who have no claim upon the party save the fact that they have long been members of its political conventions. I do not think the Republican party expects him to give appointments to men merely because they have ideas. No Republican whom I respect, has expressed a doubt of Gen. Grant's thorough and sincere devotion to Radical principles. What we want from him, however, is, men who will do the work—Some Hercales in the Interior Department, for instance, who will take the many-headed serpent of robbery and strangle it in its various shapes—Indian Rings, Patent Rings, Stationery Rings and Railroad Rings. This work, will, of course, make a tremendous howl among Congress-people. The publication of our little dispatch the other day brought upon us a storm of denial and vituperation. I was told that our correspondent had been hired by Oakes Ames to publish a libel upon Grant; that he was in a state of intense indignation at the false position in which he was placed, &c., &c. But behind all this clamor of hungry office-holders the great people, who pay taxes and who fought our battles, stand ready and yearning to approve a vigorous policy. Gen. Grant has an opportunity now as great as that which Washington had when he became President, or as that which fell to the First Bonaparte at the battle of Marengo. He can put upon America a policy of retrenchment in office, of dignity among office-holders, of reform in the civil service and of course simplicity of Republican practice. I think that we can save the principle of the Tenure-of-Office Bill by amending it. I should be very sorry to see it repealed, because I do not think that Gen. Grant's best interests will be served by plunging him into the sea of political trouble that would arise from the necessity of considering 60,000 offices. And then, after Grant we may have another Andrew Johnson, and it would not be wise to surrender all that we have won from Johnson when we may never ~~again~~ have the power to win it over again.—This is a long sermon upon Statesmanship. I suppose you are bothered with many of them. But you certainly have no one who troubles you less on this subject than I do." ALS, DLC-Elihu B. Washburne. See following letter; letters to Oliver P. Morton, Oct. 21; John Russell Young, Nov. 15; Horace Greeley, Dec. 10, 1870; Glyndon G. Van Deusen, *Horace Greeley, Nineteenth Century Crusader* (Philadelphia, 1953), pp. 304, 366–68, 373–74, 385–88, 390–92.

On April 5, 1869, Greeley, New York City, wrote to USG. "The bearer, Mr John Dolan, is well known as one of the most influential and effective Republicans in the XXIst Ward. He is an able, strong man, whose appointment would, I think, do good at once and permanently. I commend him to your kind regard, believeing that he will prove equal to any responsibility and worthy of any trust." ALS, DNA, RG 59, Letters of Application and Recommendation. On July 6, 1870, John Dolan wrote to USG. "Allow me to address you and say as the time for the Congress to adjourn is at hand I ask of you, to inquire after my papers which has been placed in the hands of Sect. Fish by Hon. B. F Butler which will inform you of my application some time ago, for an appt as Consul to the Port of Belfast or Cork at Ireland . . ." ALS, *ibid.* Numerous related papers are *ibid.* No appointment followed.

On April 24, 1869, James B. Taylor *et al.*, New York City, telegraphed to

USG. "We rejoice in the appointment of Genl Patrick H Jones as Post master" Telegram received, *ibid.*, RG 107, Telegrams Collected (Bound). On the same day, Greeley telegraphed to USG. "I heartily thank you for the appointment of Gen. Jones. no better selection could be made." Telegram received (at 11:20 A.M.,) *ibid.* On April 28, Taylor telegraphed to USG. "Appointment of Jones heartily approved—Tribune and times cordially endorses" Telegram received (at noon), *ibid.*

To Hamilton Fish

Long Branch, N. J.
Aug. 21st 1870

HON. H. FISH,
SEC. OF STATE,
DEAR SIR:

The amnesty proclamation[1] was signed and mailed to Mr. Davis yesterday. It will probably appear in the papers of to-morrow.

Your son tells me that no reply has yet been received from Senator Edmunds? Should he reply in the negative what do you say to the offer of the Mission to Horace Greeley? If you think well of it you may offer it at once, if declined by Edmunds, otherwise leave the matter rest until I see you.

I shall go to Newport on Tuesday and from there to West Point on Saturday. Mrs Grant says she prefers going to Roe's Hotel so that she may spend Sunday, and as much time as possible, with Fred. This will probably be the last time she will see him until after he graduates.

Yours Truly
U. S. GRANT

ALS, DLC-Hamilton Fish. On Aug. 24, 1870, Secretary of State Hamilton Fish, Garrison, N. Y., wrote to USG. "I was on the eve of writing to you when I received your letter mentioning Mr Greeleys name—I had no answer then from Mr Edmunds & proposed suggesting for your consideration the name of William Cullen Bryant—I do not know that I ought to object personally to Mr Greeley, who certainly has ability, & many excellent friends—but he is very full of notions, & very uncertain—he has been used to dictate & control & would not be likely either to obey instructions which he might not like, or to conciliate those with whom he may have to negotiate—He has written harsh things, & called the English statesmen with whom he would have to deal, by harsh names, is very apt to be personal and abusive in his controversies—I think that he would not be able to affect as much, in the position of Minister to England, as almost any other man, with far less ability, but without his peculiarities of temper, & his abruptness of manner, & of language—Politically, his ~~nomination or~~ appointment by you, would, I believe be misunderstood, & would be taken as indicating your favor of one interest which has always been opposed to you—He has never been friendly to you—& has opposed almost every measure of your administration—and his opposition to the Foreign policy pursued under your administration, has been such that his appointment would be regarded, as a change of policy, if not a censure upon that policy which he continually has denounced. It is of but little importance that to me, individually, he has never been friendly—not that he has openly avowed hostility—on the contrary, we are & have been on *good* terms, but he never has been friendly or inclined to give me any support which could be withheld—I have no idea whether or not Mr Bryant woul[d] accept—but I am sure that his appointment would be well received, both here, & abroad. His literary reputation is superior to that of Mr Motley—more people, in this country & in Europe are familiar with his writings—his manners and address are affable, & conciliatory—& he is more prepared in [national] & international questions, than most men connected with the press—The suggestion of his name is wholly my own—If he would accept the office there is no one whose name at present occurs to me that would in my judgment, at the same time fill the position as well, & give so much confidence & satisfaction to the public, both here, & abroad—I think it would quiet all the clamor that the friends of Mr Motley are disposed to make—[S]everal persons have suggested to me the name of William H. Aspinwall. He would be an excellent man, & would command respect & confidence—Governor Morgan has also been recommended—& so have Governor Morton, & Senator Howe Either would make a fitting representative—While writing I have a telegram from Mr Edmunds (now in Michigan) saying he cannot accept—that he has written by mail, but the letter has not yet come to hand I hasten to meet the mail—but hope you will not decide until I shall have the pleasure of seeing you—" ALS (press), *ibid.*

1. See letter to Hamilton Fish, Oct. 8, 1870.

To Virginia Grant Corbin

Long Branch, N. J.,
Aug. 21st, 1870.

DEAR SISTER:

By arrangement of a year's standing Julia and I go to Newport on Tuesday[1] morning next, to be gone there, and at West Point, one week.

But for that we would visit you and Mother this week. I shall go next week however and if Julia is not too much fatigued, or too lazy, with her travelling will take her along. You know I never give any one credit with being fatigued; I always attribute the feeling to another cause.—I hope you are all well. Give my kindest regards to Mother and Mr. Corbin.[2]

Yours truly,

U. S. GRANT.

J. G. Cramer, p. 111.

    1. Aug. 23, 1870.
    2. Abel R. Corbin, born in 1808 in Exeter, N. Y., studied law, then moved to St. Louis in 1836 where he taught school and published the *Missouri Argus*. He served as clerk, U.S. House Committee on Claims (1842–58). In 1863, he settled in New York City and invested in real estate. In an undated note, USG, as gen., wrote to "Gn." "This will introduce to you Mr. A. R. Corbin, of New York City, the gentleman from whom I got my residence. Mr. Corbin calls on business which he will state. Please see him." ANS (facsimile), James Lowe Autographs Ltd. [March, 1992], no. 51. See *HRC*, 35-1-414; John Y. Simon, ed., *The Personal Memoirs of Julia Dent Grant* (New York, 1975), p. 160. On April 25, 1869, Julia Dent Grant wrote to Katherine Felt. "You will be surprised when I tell you I have just finished a letter of congratulation to Miss Jennie Grant—she is to be married on the 13th of May—to Mr Corbin the gentleman you meet at our hous just before you left & I wanted you to set your cap for. You remember him, dont you. He is an old friend of ours & we are all well pleased we think both are doing well. Jennie is geting a good very good husband & Mr Corbin is geting a splendid wife You know of cours that Mame Stillman is to be married soon also—to Col. Pride—Mr Stillman was down here to enquire about him—You know *I* think him extreemly handsome—besides he is very clever—Col Cambell & Mr Plumb looked very much gratifyed when I told them that I was going to write for you to come this way home & spend a week with me.—You know now Mr Plumb is Consul Genl of Cuba, & Cambell is Gov of a great Terretory—Though I would rather go to Cuba th[an] out amonge the Indians—would not you? Be sure & come by the way of Washington home— & make me a visit—& dont dear Kittee ~~ask~~ expect me to write again—you know how harde it is for me to write atall—I want you to come very very much—& would like you to send me word so I can send to the Depo for you All send love & often speak of you with the greatest affection write soon to your friend" ALS, University of Kentucky, Lexington, Ky. See letter to George S. Boutwell, Sept. 12, 1869. On Aug. 9, 1870, Julia Grant, Long Branch, had written to Virginia Grant Corbin. "Allow me to offer yourself & Mr Corbin my congratulations—& to also present my respects to her little Ladyship Miss Jennie Corbin Hopeing to soon have the pleasure of seeing you I will close with much love, from your friend & sister . . . P. S. Nellee & Jessie join in love to the baby" ALS, Marshall B. Coyne, Washington, D. C.

To Edwin D. Morgan

———

Long Branch, N. J.
Aug. 21st 1870.

DEAR GOVERNOR:

Your favor of the 18th inst. inviting Mrs. Grant and myself to dine with Mrs. Morgan and you on Friday next,[1] is just before me. I must return to New York City on Friday, or Friday night, so as to take the morning boat on Saturday for West Point. If the train starts late enough for that I accept, with pleasure, but otherwise must beg you to excuse me.—Please present Mrs. Grant's and my kindest regards to Mrs. Morgan, and accept assurences of my highest regards for yourself.

Yours Truly
U. S. GRANT

HON. E. D. MORGAN.

ALS, New York State Library, Albany, N. Y. On Aug. 24, 1870, Horace Porter, Newport, R. I., wrote: "The President and Mrs. Grant accept with pleasure Governor and Mrs. Morgan's polite invitation to dinner on Friday next, but regret that they will be obliged to leave early, in order to take the night boat for New York on that evening" AN, *ibid.*

1. Aug. 26.

Proclamation

———

BY THE PRESIDENT OF THE UNITED STATES OF AMERICA.
A PROCLAMATION

Whereas, a state of war unhappily exists between France on the one side and the North German Confederation and its allies on the other side;

And whereas, the United States are on terms of friendship and amity with all the contending Powers, and with the persons inhabiting their several dominions;

And whereas, great numbers of the citizens of the United States reside within the territories or dominions of each of the said belligerents and carry on commerce, trade, or other business, or pursuits, therein protected by the faith of treaties;

And whereas, great numbers of the subjects or citizens of each of the said belligerents reside within the territory or jurisdiction of the United States, and carry on commerce, trade, or other business or pursuits therein;

And whereas, the laws of the United States, without interfering with the free expression of opinion and sympathy, or with the open manufacture or sale of arms or munitions of war, nevertheless impose upon all persons, who may be within their territory and jurisdiction, the duty of an impartial neutrality during the existence of the contest.

Now, therefore, I, Ulysses S. Grant, President of the United States, in order to preserve the neutrality of the United States and of their citizens and of persons within their territory and jurisdiction and to enforce their laws, and in order that all persons being warned of the general tenor of the laws and treaties of the United States in this behalf, and of the law of Nations, may thus be prevented from an unintentional violation of the same, do hereby declare and proclaim, that by the act passed on the 20th day of April, A. D. 1818, commonly known as the "Neutrality law," the following acts are forbidden to be done under severe penalties, within the territory and jurisdiction of the United States, to-wit:

1. Accepting and exercising a commission to serve either of the said belligerents by land or by sea, against the other belligerent.

2. Enlisting or entering into the service of either of the said belligerents as a soldier, or as a marine, or seaman on board of any vessel of war, letter of marque, or privateer.

3. Hiring or retaining another person to enlist or enter himself in the service of either of the said belligerents, as a soldier, or as a marine, or seaman on board of any vessel of war, letter of marque, or privateer.

4. Hiring another person to go beyond the limits or jurisdiction of the United States with intent to be enlisted as aforesaid.

5. Hiring another person to go beyond the limits of the United States with intent to be entered into service as aforesaid.

6. Retaining another person to go beyond the limits of the United States with intent to be enlisted as aforesaid.

7. Retaining another person to go beyond the limits of the United States with intent to be entered into service as aforesaid; (But the said act is not to be construed to extend to a citizen or subject of either belligerent who, being transiently within the United States, shall, on board of any vessel of war which, at the time of its arrival within the United States, was fitted and equipped as such vessel of war, enlist or enter himself or hire or retain another subject or citizen of the same belligerent, who is transiently within the United States, to enlist or enter himself to serve such belligerent on board such vessel of war, if the United States shall then be at peace with such belligerent.)

8. Fitting out and arming, or attempting to fit out and arm, or procuring to be fitted out and armed, or knowingly being concerned in the furnishing, fitting out or arming of any ship or vessel with intent that such ship or vessel shall be employed in the service of either of the said belligerents.

9. Issuing or delivering a commission within the territory or jurisdiction of the United States for any ship or vessel, to the intent that she may be employed as aforesaid.

10. Increasing or augmenting or procuring to be increased or augmented, or knowingly being concerned in increasing or augmenting the force of any ship of war, cruiser, or other armed vessel which, at the time of her arrival within the United States, was a ship of war, cruiser, or armed vessel in the service of either of the said belligerents, or belonging to the subjects or citizens of either, by adding to the number of guns of such vessel, or by changing those on board of her for guns of a larger calibre, or by the addition thereto of any equipment solely applicable to war.

11. Begining or setting on foot, or providing or preparing the means for any military expedition or enterprise to be carried on from the territory or jurisdiction of the United States against the territories or dominions of either of the said belligerents.

And I do further declare and proclaim that by the 19th Article of the Treaty of amity and commerce which was concluded between His Majesty the King of Prussia and the United States of America, on the 11th day of July, A. D. 1799, which Article was revived by the Treaty of May 1. A. D. 1828, between the same parties, and is still in force, it was agreed that, "The vessels of war, public and private, of both parties, shall carry freely, wheresoever they please, the vessels and effects taken from their enemies, without being obliged to pay any duties, charges, or fees to officers of Admiralty, of the Customs, or any others; nor shall such prizes be arrested, searched, or put under legal process, when they come to and enter the ports of the other party, but may freely be carried out again at any time by their captors to the places expressed in their commissions, which the commanding officer of such vessel shall be obliged to show;"

And I do further declare and proclaim that it has been officially communicated to the Government of the United States, by the Envoy Extraordinary and Minister Plenipotentiary of the North German Confederation, at Washington, that private property on the high seas will be exempted from seizure by the ships of His Majesty, the King of Prussia, without regard to reciprocity;

And I do further declare and proclaim that it has been officially communicated to the Government of the United States by the Envoy Extraordinary and Minister Plenipotentiary of His Majesty the Emperor of the French, at Washington, that orders have been given that in the conduct of the war the commanders of the French forces on land and on the seas shall scrupulously observe towards neutral powers the rules of international law, and that they shall strictly adhere to the principles set forth in the Declaration of the Congress of Paris, of the 16th of April, 1856,—that is to say—1st That privateering is and remains abolished; 2nd That the neutral flag covers enemy's goods, with the exception of contraband of war; 3rd That neutral goods, with the exception of contraband of war, are not liable to capture under the enemy's flag; 4th That blockades in order to be binding must be effective, that is to say, maintained by a force sufficient really to prevent access to the coast of the enemy; and that although the United States have not adhered to the Declaration of 1856, the vessels of His Majesty will not seize enemy's property found on board of a vessel of the United States, provided that property is not contraband of war;

And I do further declare and proclaim that the statutes of the United States and the law of nations alike require that no person, within the territory and jurisdiction of the United States, shall take part, directly or indirectly, in the said war, but shall remain at peace with each of the said belligerents and shall maintain a strict and impartial neutrality, and that whatever privileges shall be accorded to one belligerent, within the ports of the United States, shall be in like manner accorded to the other:,

And I do hereby enjoin all the good citizens of the United States, and all persons residing or being within the territory or jurisdiction of the United States to observe the laws thereof, and to commit no act contrary to the provisions of the said statutes, or in violation of the law of nations in that behalf;

And I do hereby warn all citizens of the United States and all persons residing or being within their territory or jurisdiction, that while the free and full expression of sympathies in public and private is not restricted by the laws of the United States, military forces in aid of either belligerent can not lawfully be originated or organized within their jurisdiction, and that while all persons may lawfully, and without restriction by reason of the aforesaid state of war, manufacture and sell within the United States arms and munitions of war, and other articles ordinarily known as "contraband of war", yet they cannot carry such articles upon the high seas for the use or service of either belligerent, nor can they transport soldiers and officers of either, —————— —————, or attempt to break any blockade which may be lawfully established and maintained during the war, without incurring the risk of hostile capture, and the penalties denounced by the law of nations in that behalf;

And I do hereby give notice that all citizens of the United States and others who may claim the protection of this Government, who may misconduct themselves in the premises, will do so at their peril, and that they can in no wise obtain any protection from the Government of the United States against the consequences of their misconduct.

In witness whereof, I have hereunto set my hand, and caused the seal of the United States to be affixed.

Done at the City of Washington, this Twenty-Second day of August, [in the year of our] Lord one thousand eight hundred and seventy and of the Independence of the United States of America the ninety-fifth

U. S. GRANT

DS, DNA, RG 130, Presidential Proclamations. A State Dept. draft of this document, with insertions by Secretary of State Hamilton Fish, is in DLC-Hamilton Fish. See proclamation, Oct. 8, 1870; *HED*, 41-3-1, pp. 45–47; *SMD*, 49-1-162, part 3, pp. 605–8.

To Jacob D. Cox

———

Long Branch N. J.
Aug. 22d 1870.

HON. J. D. COX
SEC. OF THE INT.
DEAR SIR:

I understand that you have appointed one day this week to hear arguments in the McGarrahan case. That is well enough because if Congress should fail to settle that case we may have it to do, and the sooner we know all the points of it the better.

However as the matter has been taken in hand by Congress before the incoming of this administration, and as so much fraud is charged, and believed to exist, on both sides, I am not willing that my name should be signed to a patent for either party until Congress has either decided or declared their inability to do so.

I wish you would say to Mr. White,[1] sec, for signing patents, not to put my name to that one except on special orders from me through you. He must not take orders from Mr. Wilson[2] in the

matter. I have grown suspicious of Mr. W. and will tell you why
when I go to Washington next.

Yours Truly

U. S. GRANT

Copies, USG 3; DLC-USG, II, 1. On Aug. 23, 1870, Secretary of the Interior
Jacob D. Cox wrote to USG. "Yours of yesterday is this morning received and I
have given your directions in regard to signing a patent to the New Idria Company, to Mr White by letter, he being confined to his bed by sickness, as I am
informed. On the subject of the McGarrihan business itself, I think you must
have been misinformed as to its status in Congress. According to the formal
opinion given by the Attorney General last year the case is in no such sense
before Congress as to interrupt or impede the action of the Department under
the laws, but parties have the same right to insist upon a hearing & decision
here that they have in any other case when they claim a decision upon their
rights under the explicit provisions of the statutes. Congress has assumed no
peculiar jurisdiction of the subject. McGarrahan petitioned the last Congress,
as he had the two preceding Congresses, to make him a grant of lands in
California included within the boundaries named in a pretended grant to one
Gomez, which the Supreme Court of the United States declared void in 1865.
He has appealed to Congress in vain. At the late session it was again before the
Judiciary Committee of the House of Representatives, and the parties consented
to suspend the contest in this Department till that Committee should pass upon
the matter of the petition. The Committee *did* pass upon it, & by a vote of seven
to three determined to report *against* granting the prayer of his petition, and
directed Mr Peters' of that Committee to draw up their report. Mr Peters'
statement of these facts is filed with the papers in this Department. The New
Idria mining company now claim that their business should be taken up and
disposed of. McGarrahan claims on the other hand that the fact that the Committee did not find the opportunity to make their report to the House should
hold the other parties to still further delay until the next session of Congress.
To this the other side reply that it was the action of the *Committee* that they
consented to await, & quote the printed statements of McGarrahan's counsel
before the Committee to the effect that if the Committee decided against them
they would make no further contest. The Department, as the Attorney General
decided, was not authorized to delay its performance of duty under the law at
all, except by common consent of the parties in interest, and has only taken the
responsibility of delay in cases where manifest equity required it and where
action by Congress is probable. After careful inquiry and investigation I think
it clear that neither of these conditions exist in the present case. McGarrahan's
original claim has been, now for five years, decided by the Supreme Court to
have been utterly fraudulent and void. He immediately made his effort to obtain
relief from Congress and five years of most industrious and as I believe unscrupulous effort has been futile. Pending these petitions to Congress he attempted to obtain a patent from this Department on the ground that the lands
were only agricultural lands & did not contain gold, silver, or quicksilver mines
and might therefore be bought at $1.25 per acre. This was refused by Mr
Browning my predecessor, on the ground that the lands were mining lands, and
the New Idria Quicksilver Mines was notoriously the bone of contention. Mc-

Garrahan then sought to force the Department to issue him a patent by a writ of mandamus from the Court of this District, and after the unprecedented action of that Court in allowing the writ against me after Mr Browning's retirement, the Supreme Court of the United reversed and annulled the proceedings in the Court below in a judgment which reflected with great severity upon all concerned in procuring such action. McGarrahan stands before the Department therefore as a fraudulent claimant who has twice been foiled and condemned in his fraud by the highest Court of the nation, and ~~his~~ whose efforts to procure favor from Congress have also failed. His claim for still further delay, in order that he may try whether he cannot yet obtain legislative action in his favor which may give him that which the Courts have determined that he has no right to under the law, seems to me worse than baseless, and I should feel as if I were party to a wrong upon Congress were I willingly to do anything to subject them to further annoyance from such a source. Under the opinion of the legal adviser of the Government therefore, and in full accordance with my own sense of right and duty, I have said that the Department will no longer delay in proceeding with its business according to law. At this stage I find myself met by another effort at obstruction. McGarrahan brings suit in the same Court of the District for an injunction against the New Idria mining Co, *to forbid them from applying for a patent for the lands they claim under the statute*, and that too although the Company is in *California* wholly out of the Jurisdiction of the Court, nor is it pretended that lawful service of the writ can be made on them. Their *attorneys* here are made defendants & the Court is asked to forbid them from prosecuting their clients' case before the Department which has jurisdiction of it; and this too when in the mandamus case last winter the Supreme Court decided that the jurisdiction of the Department was exclusive and absolute, with which no court could lawfully interfere! The Department is not a party to this suit, yet I have had today a notice served upon me to appear before this Court on the 30th instant and show cause why an *attachment* should not issue against me for directing the Land office to go forward with its business! If the Federal Executive is to be at the mercy of such proceedings as these we shall justly become the contempt of the nation & of the world. To show you still further the unblushing knavery of McGarrahan's conduct, a gentleman allowed me to read a letter directed to him by one of McGarrahan's attorneys, in which the attorney offered for McG. stock in his California claim to the amount of *Twenty thousand Dollars* for the *use of his influence with me* to procure favorable action to him in this Department. As to appearing before the Court, I am at a loss what to do—The Attorney General has gone to Georgia & leaves no assistant who is an experienced advocate, his Department, as you know, not being fully organized—The District Attorney, who would be the one to whom I should naturally go next, is Judge Fisher who was one of the two judges who signed the writ of mandamus last year, & of course he could not defend the department without condemning himself—and Congress last winter, in the act organizing the Department of Justice took away from the other Departments the right to employ special counsel—My belief is that no question more gravely affecting the dignity of the Executive & its independence will be likely to arise during your administration & I think the situation fully warrants your telegraphing the Attorney General, if not all the Cabinet, to meet you here before the 30th For myself, as I am conscious of having only fought fraud with such vigor as I could, I can make no compromise, & if I fail to secure to the fullest extent your approval of my course, I must beg you to relieve me at once from duties which without your support I shall utterly fail in—Begging to be remembered with great respect to Mrs Grant, . . ." ALS, USG 3. On Nov. 10, William McGarrahan, Washington, D. C., wrote to USG. "The statements relative to myself, and my claim to the Panoche Grande Rancho, contained in Mr. Ex-Secretary Cox's letter to you, published in this morning's papers, compel me to address you, and lay before you the following facts, which will enable you to judge in a measure between truth and the statements of Mr. Cox. . . . The fugitive charge made by Mr. Cox that I attempted to secure his favor by bribery is as false as it is vague. I judge my guilt was more in the neglect than in the performance. The other intemperate and defamatory language which Mr. Cox, taking advantage of his official position, has seen fit to use to your Excellency toward me I deem unworthy of notice. The action of your Excellency in giving no credence to it, or any other of his assertions relative to me and my claim, and the few facts in the case as herein presented, are sufficient vindication . . ." *Washington Chronicle*, Nov. 14, 1870. See letter to Jacob D. Cox, Oct. 5, 1870.

William S. Hillyer wrote an undated document on the stationery of Charles P. Shaw, New York City, attorney for McGarrahan. "Mr President I come to you representing the interests of a simple ~~citizen~~ penniless citizen who has not money enough to pay my expenses and who has ~~for years~~ been ~~fought by one of the~~ fighting for years one of the most powerful and wealthy corporations ~~and combinations~~ in the country. I do not ask you to ~~do any~~ listen to the merits of his cause nor to form or express any opinion on the same—I simply ask that you will refrain from doing anything ~~that~~ to adjudicate or determine the rights of either party until Congress which has already assumed juristiction of the case shall have expressed its will in the premises—The ~~case is b~~ controversy is between McGarraghan and the New Idria Mining Company—The matter is now before the judiciary committee of the lower house of Congress and the attorneys of the respective parties have filed ~~before~~ with that committee a written stipulation that ~~the~~ neither party will seek your interference to determine their rights until this Congress shall have acted upon the report of that committee I exhibited to the President a verbatim copy of that agreement. I told him further that Mr Cox had given my client notice that he would on a certain day hear and determine the case—~~That I had reason to believe that~~ That my client believed that Mr Cox had already prejudged the case—(This belief Mr Cox's letter of the clearly shows was well founded—) whether he had or not that his agreement with the Committee of Congress forbade him to submitt the matter at this time to ~~the~~ Mr Cox's adjudication. I told him that such men as Jas F. Wilson Chairman of the judiciary committee of the House in Congress and Bingham chairman of the same committee in this Congress had after a laborious and thorough examination of the case expressed themselves as clearly of the opinion that McGarraghan claim was a just one—That this was a case in which ~~judic~~ official corruption in high places had been charged and in some instances clearly proved— That it involved a charge against Commissioner Wilson of having mutilated the records and papers in his office, all of which matter, ~~was~~ had been submitted to the consideration of the committees—~~In view.~~ I told him further that the New Idria Mining Company were in possession of the property receiving its immense revenues with which they were fighting my client and no damage could ensue to them by reason of the delay—That the utmost delay which could ensue would be until the fourth of next March—In view of these facts and out of a proper

respect to ~~the Congress of the United States which~~ a coordinate branch of the
~~g~~Government ~~of the~~ as well as a matter of ~~comm~~ proper regard for the rights of
~~an humble~~ a poor and humble citizen that he would not permit ~~one~~ a patent to
issue under his signature until the case was disposed of by Congress—~~The~~ Upon
this statement confirmed by the proofs I exhibited to him of the correctness of
the same he ~~assented~~ assured me that the patent should not issue except by his
express direction ~~and~~ and stated that he would not interfere with the matter
while this Congress had it under consideration   He did not intimate and I have
no reason to beleive that he had formed any opinion as to the merits of the controversy—" ADf, Hillyer Papers, ViU. See *HRC*, 41-3-24.

On May 31, 1871, USG wrote to Secretary of the Interior Columbus Delano. "Enclosed I send you application from the Att'y of McGarrahan to have
restored to his client the record of his claim as it was; and also application for
a patent. Please examine the case at your leisure and give me your judgment as
to the course that should be pursued, or whether as heretofore decided upon,
the whole matter should be left with Congress, where the Administration found
it." Copy, DLC-USG, II, 1. On June 15, McGarrahan wrote to Delano. "By the
kindness of the President I have seen his letter to you, transmitting my application to have the record of my patent restored upon the records of the Land
Office, and to direct a patent to issue to me as of the date of that record. The
brief of the late Attorney-General, Hon. E. R. Hoar, in the case of Secretary
Cox *vs.* McGarrahan, and the opinion of the United States Supreme Court in
this case, will explain the reason why I made the application direct to the
President and not to the Department. . . . Now, what I ask of you, Mr. Secretary,
is, that you will be pleased to advise the President to order the restoration of
the record of my patent upon the records of the Land Office to the same condition in which it was placed by the decisions of President Lincoln and Secretaries Smith and Usher, and to remove the unauthorized and illegal erasures
made on it by direction of Mr. Cox, and that an exemplified copy of this un-
mutilated record be delivered to me. The record was in this condition when
President Grant entered upon his duties as President of the United States, and
all I ask is, that he restore this record to the same condition in which it was
when he entered upon the duties of his office. . . ." *SMD*, 45-2-85, pp. 903–5.
On June 16, USG endorsed this letter. "Respectfully referred to the Secretary
of the Interior. It seems to me that if the records of the Interior Department have
been changed, as herein stated, they should be restored to the condition in which
they were when this Administration came into office. In regard to furnishing
Mr. McGarrahan with copies of the original record, I would be guided by
precedents in like cases." *Ibid.*, p. 905. See *HRC*, 45-2-951; Robert J. Parker,
"William McGarrahan's 'Panoche Grande Claim,'" *Pacific Historical Review*,
V, 3 (Sept., 1936), 212–21.

1. On Aug. 23, 1870, Cox wrote to Joseph S. Wilson, commissioner, General Land Office. "I enclose for transmission a note to Mr. White, the President's
Secretary for signing land patents, directing that no patent be signed granting
lands to the NewIdria Mining Company claimed by them, until specific directions so to do shall come from the President through this Department. This
direction is given to prevent any inadvertent issue of a patent in the event of the
decision by the land office or this Department in favor of said company, and to

ensure the deliberate action & knowledge of the President & the Department."
Copy, USG 3. The enclosure to Charles White is *ibid.*

2. On Nov. 21, Henry C. Levens, Boonville, Mo., wrote to USG. "I have
learned through dispatches from the City of Washington that there is danger of
the removal from office that incorruptible and efficient officer Joseph S. Wilson,
Commissioner of the Gen Land office. If there should be any truch in such reports, I would humbly and earnestly implore you in behalf of my County and the
State of Missouri, to let him remain in the office he so honestly fills. By his late
and just opinions he has saved Missouri thousands of acres of 'Swamp Lands'
donated to the State for the education of *poor children*; besides I have been informed by the Receiver at Boonville, John N Gott, that he has at all times when
not inconsistant with his duties, favored *poor persons* and *actual settles*, and
saved them from being swindled out of their rights by '*Land Sharks.*' It is well
known by many in this state that a wealthy and influential Combination was
formed, and suceeded in entering large quantities of 'Swamp Lands' which
rightfully belongs to the several counties in this state, and would probably have
succeeded had it not been for the *timely interference* of *Joseph S. Wilson*, who
ordered all such entries *canceled*, for which the people of Missouri owe him a
debt of gratitude. You may think it presurption in me who occupies such an
obscure and humble position in life, to address one *so far* above me, but I could
not do less than contribute my mite, however little that may be, to save and
sustain in office that honest and faithful servant of the people." ALS, DNA,
RG 48, Appointment Div., Letters Received. On Dec. 14, Thomas Lytle, Treasure City, Nev., wrote to USG. "Some four and a half years ago as agent and
superintendent of the Radical, the Spotted Tiger and the Bald Eagle claims or
mines of Aurora, Esmeralda County, Nevada—I made application for U. S.
Patents for the three above named mines through the Hon. W. T. Lockhart of
Carson City—He not fully understanding the law put me to something over
one thousand dollars useless expense and finally when all was right and ready
for the supervission of the Surveyor General he was out of the State—and before
he returned to confirm the papers, Survey &C. but long after the ninety days
advertising had passed—A certain Mr. E. O. Taylor intervened in an unofficial
way—But as subsequent events have shown the chief Clerk in the Land office
at Washington is an intimate friend and colleague of Mr. E. O. Taylor. The
applications were all sent back from Washington to Carson for tryal—After no
little expense and trouble in the matter I gained the case in two seperate tryals
and fully established the fact that Mr. E. O. Taylor was an imposture had no
right and never had. For which see affidavit of seven practical miners produced
on the tryal and forwarded to the Land office at Washington among other
papers.—Judge Wells of Carson and Hon. W. M. Stewart attended to the matter
at Carson and after carefully examining all the papers &C. pronounced things
right in the premisis more tha[n] two years ago—At which time the Hon W. T.
Lockhart made his final repoart o[n] the three cases to the Land office at Wa[sh]-
ington—Still the Hon. J. S. Wilson respectfully pays no attention to the mat-
te[r] notwithstanding often urged—and the matter has cost us over four thousand dollar[s] in gold coin. Now why it is that after every thing has been made
right and clear and the law fully complied with in all respects that the Hon.
J. S. Wilson will no[t] issue the Patents is not only a mistery to myself but to
all the three companie[s] all of whom are citizens and good Union men—It has

been hinted to me by high Government Officials that the Hon J. S. Wilson is wating for a good, round illeg[al] fee—Now if I have to resort to fraud in order to obtain the rights of an American Citizen—the Patents will never be issued—After all other efforts have failed—I have been forced to address you. and presuming upon your valuable time in hopes that a wrong may be righted and *corruption* (if any exists) be cast out of the Department" ALS, *ibid.*, Lands and Railroads Div., Miscellaneous, Letters Received. On the same day, Jonathan Mulford, Philadelphia, wrote to USG. "When you shall have been made acquainted with the grievance endured by your humble Servant, I trust no apology for addressing you will be deemed necessary, as the object is based legitimately on business, connected with the Land Department at Washington under Commissioner Wilson. Permit me therefore to submit the following—On a Land Warrant (26040) issued at the close of the Black Hawk War for 160 acres, entry was made, and duly registered in Nebraska (1860) on which we paid Taxes regularly up to July 1868, when I was notified we were paying Tax on 40 acres, belonging to another Person. In correspondence from Washington, I found this Person by priority of entry was entitled,—By instructions from Commissioner Wilson, upon my furnishing Certificate from the Records in the County where location was made—relinquishing Deed for 40 acres—and my depositing $150.00 in Land Office at Washington, patent would be issued for same number of Acres in unentered Lands in Nebraska.—Certificate was furnished—relinquishing Deed also, but was unable, and objected to raiseing the money, especially as I regarded it was not equitable, for I only asked the Government to reinstate us in our rights. Haveing narrated the foregoing as preliminary I now proceed to lay before you what from continuous, vexatious and unreasonable delays I am made to suffer. . . ." ALS, *ibid.* See letter to Zachariah Chandler, Sept. 22, 1870, note 1.

To Hamilton Fish

Long Branch, N. J.
Aug. 22d 1870.

DEAR GOVERNOR:

Mr. Southard, of Me. has called to request the transfer, for trial, of Z. Allen, to the Atlantic Sea board. Mr. Allen was first officer of the ship Matterhorn, and killed a sailor, in self defence as is alleged, and is now on his way from Calau to San Francisco for trial. My reply has been that it might be both expensive and inconvenient to bring the prisoner and witnesses to the Atlantic, but that the proceeding can be reviewed here and if there is the appearance of injustice to the prisoner he can be pardoned or granted a new trial. I submit the matter to you however for any action you choose to take. I understand that the young man is of high character and that Gov. Chamberlain, Senator Morrill and Speaker Blaine are much interested in him.

Yours Truly
U. S. Grant

Hon. H. Fish, Sec. of State

ALS, DLC-Hamilton Fish. On July 21, 1870, David J. Williamson, consul, Callao, Peru, submitted papers to Secretary of State Hamilton Fish relating to the case of Zacheus Allen. LS, DNA, RG 59, Consular Despatches, Callao.

To Adam Badeau

Long Branch, N. J.
Aug. 22d 1870.

Dear General:

Your several letters written since your return to England have been received, and read with great interest. I have been negligent about writing you   I would not be surprised if Napoleon should be off his tThrone (he is practically so now) and peace, through the intervention of other Nations, in a fair way of being negociated. The winding up of Congress was much more harmonious and satisfactory than the begining. I think the Republican party stands well before the people. We will loose members of Congress in the Fall elections no doubt because it always happens that the party in power are less active at the election intervening betwen two Presidential elections than the party out.

I have not yet sent any one to take Mr. M's place in England. As you have no doubt learned from the papers Mr. Freelinghuysen declines   It is to be regretted for Mr. F. and his family, are good representative Americans.

The Summer in the United States has been intollerably warm. At Long Branch however we always have a breese which makes the warmest weather in endurable.—Mrs. Grant and the children

send their kindest regards. I shall always be glad to hear from
you, and to get exactly the sort of letters you have written so far,
though I may not write often myself.

Yours Truly

U. S. GRANT

GN. A. BADEAU CONSUL &C.

ALS, Munson-Williams-Proctor Institute, Utica, N. Y. On Aug. 31, 1870,
Adam Badeau, London, wrote to USG. "I have sent by this steamer an application to the Postmaster General in behalf of my only brother Dr. C. W. Badeau,
for the position of 'Physician to the Post Office Dept N. Y. City.' My brother
was a soldier, and is a staunch republican. He has been educated entirely at my
expense, and is I beleive a faithful and skilful young physician. He has had a
position for a year and a half in the Bellevue Hospital, NewYork city, but by
the rules of the institution, he can not hold it longer. He leaves there with the
best certificates from the first men of his profession in America. The place I
ask for him is worth $1500 a year, and the duties are to visit daily any of the
P. O. employees who may report themselves ill, and ascertain if they are unfit
for duty. My brother is 26, and the recent death of my father leaves him no
friend but me to take any peculiar interest in him. I should esteem it a very great
kindness if you would exert your powerful interest in his behalf. . . . It is reported in the newspapers here that I am to be appointed Minister to England. If
I should be, I will not fail to let you know" ALS, NjP.

To Daniel H. Chamberlain

———

I never used the language attributed to me by General Butler
as stated above. I never opposed the reëlection of Governor Scott,
nor spoke disparagingly of him. On the contrary I look upon the
so-called "Reform" movement in South Carolina only as a device
to give the control of the State to the enemies of the party which
has supported me, and which supported our armies and maintained
the Union.

U. S. GRANT

LONG BRANCH, N. J., August 22, 1870.

Washington Chronicle, Sept. 8, 1870. Born in Mass. in 1835, Daniel H. Chamberlain graduated from Yale (1862), studied law at Harvard, then joined the
5th Mass. Cav. as 1st lt. in 1864. He moved to S. C. in 1866, was a member of
the constitutional convention, and, in 1868, was elected attorney gen. On Aug.
15, 1870, Chamberlain, Columbia, S. C., had written to USG. "In a public

speech delivered by ex-Confederate General M. C. Butler, of this State, candidate of the so-called 'Union Reform' party of this State for Lieutenant Governor, he made use of the following language: 'When, a few days since, I visited the capital for the purpose of having my political disabilities removed, and called on that great soldier hero, General Grant, did he say nay? Not at all. He said, go b[a]ck home and beat Governor Scott, for he is no Repub[li]can.' These words were used in a speech at Spartanburg Court-house, in this State, on Thursday, the 4th instant. A statement so astounding, made so publicly, has induced me to ask you, on behalf of our party in this State, if there is any truth in it. If not, can we deny it by your au[t]hority?" *Ibid.* On Aug. 29, Chamberlain wrote to the editor, *Charleston Republican.* "I ask the publication in your columns of the following correspondence. The language quoted in my letter to the President is a *verbatim* extract from the report of General Butler's speech in the Spa[rt]anburg *Republican* of the 11th inst. General Butler has since informed me that he did not use the language there attributed to him, and I have accordingly written to the President to that effect. I desire, however, that the correspondence, without change, may be laid before the public." *Ibid.*

On Oct. 22, Governor Robert K. Scott of S. C. twice wrote to USG. "We have just passed through an Election which for rancour and virulence on the part of the opposition has never been excelled in any civilized community—The Republican Administration has been charged with every crime in the catalogue, and although these charges have been deliberately made and circulated throughout the entire State by nearly if not all of the outspoken champions of the Reform Party, yet no attempt has been made to substantiate a single one of them or to furnish a single particle of proof—The people of the State have had these charges before them, and by an overwhelming majority even in counties where the white population are largely in the ascendency, have decided that there was no foundation whatever for them: and by their votes have shown that the whole tissue of falsehoods was only devised for political capital—Unusual quietness characterised the day of Election throughout the State, and but little disturbance was experienced in any quarter which may be attributable to the presence of detachments of United States troops at the localities where they were most apprehended—In the upper or more northern counties where the white population predominated, fears were entertained that intruders from North Carolina and Georgia would interfere and cause trouble; but it appears from subsequent events that the programme was changed to an attack upon the ballot boxes and, by destroying them, to vitiate the Election. Reliable information has reached this Department that an organized force has appeared at Laurens Court House, assailed the State Constabulary driving them from their position, and killing and wounding several of them, together with a number of private citizens. These desperados seized upon the arms on deposit belonging to the State and drove many of the peaceful inhabitants from their homes creating a general reign of terror and lawlessness. Colored men and women have been dragged from their homes at the dead hour of night and most cruelly and brutally scourged for the sole reason that they dared to exercise their own opinions upon political subjects—For four years the National Government conducted a war for the perpetuity of the Union and the establishment and preservation of the Liberty of the people and those who were its opponents throughout that desperate struggle are the same class of men who now resist its policy and defy the constituted authorities, in their efforts to conform the State Government to the new order of things. In the struggle for National existence the United States Government made citizens of four millions of human beings, who had previously been kept in ignorance and poverty, and thus assumed the responsibility of their education and protection; & and if the state is powerless to secure these people their natural rights the duty clearly devolves upon the National Government to throw around them its arms of protection and the shield of its authority. The Republican party at the recent Election carried nearly every county in the State; even those where the white population were largely in the majority. The respectable portion of the community desire peace and tranquility, and are willing to abide the results of the late war; but this portion of the community is powerless to prevent the inhuman and brutal outrages that are continually being perpetrated in the name and by the authority of those calling themselves democrats. I have within a few moments witnessed in my own office a spectacle that has chilled my blood with horror. Four peaceable and unoffending citizens of Spartanburg county were at the dead hour of night dragged from their homes and lashed on their bare backs until the flayed flesh hung dripping in shreds, and seams were gaping in their mangled bodies large enough to lay my finger in. After this torture they were subjected to nameless indignities too gross and disgusting to be even remotely alluded to, when these fiends in human shape, exhausted by their own attrocities desisted from further torture. A humane gentleman brought these victims of political hate, to this city and quite a number of persons examined their wounds in my office. United States Senator Robertson. and Col Patterson vice President of the Greenville & Columbia. R. R, were present and will fully corroborate my statement. From the information of these gentlemen. your Excellency will also learn the condition of things in this State. and the necessities of the occasion, and will perceive the absolute necessity of military assistance on the part of the General Government. Our state militia are but imperfectly drilled, and are necessarily employed in their daily avocations as laborers, and it would be impracticable to continue them continuously in service, so as to be constantly prepared to arrest and punish the attempts at violence and crime. while their opponents are largely composed of those. who were engaged in the Confederate Armies, accustomed to the use of fire-arms, thoroughly drilled and armed with the most improved weapons, and would consequently possess many advantages over their antagonists. Humanity therefore as well as every sound principle of policy would dictate that regular troops should be employed in this service." "Since the departure of Senator Robertson for Washington, things have assumed a more threatening aspect. I am convinced that an outbreak will occur here on Friday next being the day appointed by law for the counting of ballots. Large bodies of men are congregating in this city and other points, and from the threats made and other indications there can be no doubt of their intentions. It has been and is being publicly said by the Leaders of the Democratic Party, that they will not submit to any election which does not place them in power—It becomes therefore a question with us, whether to surrender unconditionally, or fight. If the latter, then we have the entire floating element of the Confederate Army to contend against, and a body of a thousand such men. could be collected in a very short time. You will readily perceive the folly of attempting to maintain the supremacy of law in the protection of life and property with the inexperienced militia of the state against men of four years experience of actual war. The Hon. Reuben Tomlinson, Auditor of State, Hon Niles G Parker, Treasurer of State, together with Mr Ripley (who has been visiting in the

State for some time and has had a very good opportunity of learning the feeling and determination of the Ex Rebel Element) have kindly volunteered to visit Washington for the purpose of laying before your Excellency the true facts in the case: With the hope that they may be enabled to satisfy your Excellency of the necessity of at once placing a considerable force of U. S. Troops in this state; for unless the General Government gives protection to the Loyal people, and authorities in the late rebellious states. for some years to come, there can be nothing hoped for except a complete surrender of everything to the old ruling classes, which will be followed by anarchy and destruction of all Civil Liberty." LS, DNA, RG 107, Letters Received from Bureaus. Related papers are *ibid.*

On Nov. 23, Thomas Murphy, collector of customs, New York City, telegraphed to USG. "Steamship James Adger sailed Yesterday for Charleston having as passenger Col Jas E. Kerrigan and a gang of roughs for the purpose as I am credibly informed of controlling the organization of the south Carolina legislature" Telegram received (at 10:32 P.M.), *ibid.*, RG 94, Letters Received, 1400M 1870.

To Roscoe Conkling

Long Branch, N. J.
Aug. 22d 1870.

DEAR SENATOR:

I have just been shown a despatch from you to Mr. Cornell[1] stating that you could not well meet me in New York City tomorrow, and expressing surprise rather that I wanted to see you. Before I started ~~w~~West, two weeks ago, I stated to Mr. Murphy, and one or two others, that I should like to meet you, and would try to do so, on my return. Hence the letter to you from Mr. Cornell. I start in the morning for Newport, to remain there until Friday evening.

On Saturday I shall reach West Point where I will reman until Tuesday, the 29th inst. and then return here. I should like very much to meet you before the meeting of the State Convention, and, in the mean time, express the hope that you will go as a deligate. Should I not meet you I will write you a letter, specially if you should be a deligate, expressive of my views as to the Gubernitorial nomination. It was on this subject I wanted to consult, more than advise, with you. New York, the largest, is certainly the most important state to secure a fare election, in, and to secure to the republican party, if it is right. If it is not right a majority of the legal voters are the ones to so declare. The proper nominations should be made to test the strength of parties.—May I expect to meet you either at West Point on Saturday, Sunday or Monday next?

Yours Truly
U. S. GRANT

HON. ROSCOE CONKLING
UTICA, N. Y.

ALS, DLC-Roscoe Conkling. See Alfred R. Conkling, *The Life and Letters of Roscoe Conkling* (New York, 1889), pp. 328–30.

1. On March 25, 1869, USG had nominated Alonzo B. Cornell as surveyor of customs, New York City. On June 25, 1870, USG nominated Cornell as asst. treasurer and treasurer of the assay office, New York City, but withdrew the nomination on June 27. On Oct. 23, 1872, Cornell wrote to USG. "Having been named by the Republicans of the Eleventh Assembly District of the City of New York, as a candidate for the Legislature, I hereby tender my resignation as Surveyor of the Port of New York. During the three and a half years that I have had the honor to occupy this responsible position, so kindly without my solicitations conferred upon me, I have endeavored, to the best of my ability, to faithfully perform its duties; and in retiring from it, I desire to express my sincere thanks for the confidence which has been reposed on me, by your Administration." ALS, DNA, RG 56, Surveyor of Customs Applications.

To J. C. Bancroft Davis

———

Long Branch, N. J.
Aug. 22d 1870.

DEAR SIR:

Enclosed I send a letter addressed to Gen. Badeau which I will be obliged to you if you will have forwarded by the next Mail leaving the State Dept.—I go to Newport to-morrow, to be gone one week. If convenient I would like to have the Fenian Amnesty, and warning, proclamation ready and sent to me here by the time I return.

Yours Truly
U. S. GRANT

HON. J. C. B. DAVIS
ASST. SEC. OF STATE

P. S. Since writing the above I have added a letter to Washburne and one to Jones which I wish you would mail also.

U. S. GR

ALS, DLC-J. C. Bancroft Davis. On Sept. 1, 1870, J. C. Bancroft Davis, asst. secretary of state, wrote to Horace Porter, Long Branch. "I enclose herewith for the signature of the President, the pardon of William Warren and the Exequatur of Henry C. Dallett, Consul for Nicaragua. The pardons of Coleman Briggs and Lewis Veazie, which were forwarded to the President at Long Branch, for his, signature, on the 22d ultimo, have not yet been returned to this Dept." Copy, DNA, RG 59, Domestic Letters.

To William A. Richardson

Long Branch, N. J.
Aug. 22d 1870.

DEAR SIR:

For the office of Appraiser, the new office created under the Chicago Custom House, you may send for my signature the name of Dr. Ray. I do not recollect the initials to the Drs. name but think you may have them in the department. If not any Illinois man in the dept. can give them as the Dr. has long been a leading editor in the state, and is now editing the Chicago Post.

Respectfully &c.
U. S. GRANT

JUDGE RICHARDSON
ASST. SEC. OF THE TREAS.

ALS, DNA, RG 56, Appraiser of Customs Applications. USG appointed Charles H. Ray as appraiser of merchandise, Chicago; Ray died on Sept. 23, 1870.

On Sept. 24, George W. Wood, Chicago, wrote to USG. "I respectfully make application for the appointment of Appraiser under the new law recently passed making this city a port of Entry made vacant by the decease of Dr Ray I presume to ask this not from the slight personal acquaintance with you which perhaps with your cares & duties has been forgotten, but from what you will concede to be good reasons which I believe you have considered to be of paramount importance in all your appointments viz Honesty & Capability. I also claim to have ever been an active worker in the ranks of the Republican party

& to have done somthing towards its success. Never have asked an office but as this is one to which if appointed I can bring a practical experience, having for five years in the service of a large importing house in Boston had the charge of the Custom house business ~~Eleven years~~ & for Twenty five years been in active mercantile business Eleven years of that at Galesburg in this state & five years in this city Although not so well known in political Circles in this city have been an active worker & Knox County will attest I worked to good purpose there I feel that the appointment if made, would be perfectly satisfactory to the leading men here & in the state both in Politics & business There will be forwarded you letters from some leading men which will I trust satisfy you of some of the herin stated & will I trust lead to the bestowal of the favor upon . . ." ALS, *ibid.* Related papers are *ibid.* On Dec. 6, USG nominated L. D. Ingersoll as appraiser of merchandise, Chicago, but, on March 10, 1871, nominated Charles H. Ham to replace him. On Dec. 6, 1871, USG nominated Wood as collector of Internal Revenue, 1st District, Tex.

To Elihu B. Washburne

———

Long Branch, N. J.
Aug. 22d 1870.

Dear Washburne;

When I wrote to you last, although it was but a few days before the declaration of War by France,[1] I had no idea that such an event was even threatening. I was taken by surprise as Napoleon admits he was in one of William's attacks.

The result, if we read right in our papers, has surprised me. I supposed, from the declaration of war coming from the French, ~~that~~ they would be all ready while the Prussians might not be fully so, and therefore, at the begining, the French would have it all their own way. The Prussian military system is so perfect however that I believed, singlehanded, they would be too much for the French in the end.—The war has developed the fact here that every unreconstructed rebel simpathyses with France, without exception, while the loyal element is almost as universally the other way. Poor Napoleon I suppose will retire to private life.

My family are all well and join me in kindest regards to yourself, Mrs. Washburne and the children.—I am always pleased to hear from you, and here after will try to drop you a line more frequently.

U. S. GRANT

ALS, IHi. On Sept. 6, 1870, Elihu B. Washburne wrote to USG. "I have received your letter this morning. Events have marched at a gigantic pace. I saw all that was going on Sunday and have written Gov. Fish quite a long despatch which goes by the open mail of to-day giving a full account of the performances. I think you may read it with interest. I hope to be able to write you more fully by the next mail. I am glad to see the direction of the sympathies of our people, I mean the loyal people. It were impossible for them to have been otherwise. I have had a tremendous job on my hands in protecting the Germans expelled from France, but I have got along very well. The German Govt. has sent me its thanks. Mrs. W. & family in Brussels and all well." ALS (press), DLC-Elihu B. Washburne. On the same day, USG, Monmouth, N. J., telegraphed to Secretary of State Hamilton Fish, Garrison, N. Y. "Davis dispatch from Washburne received I would instruct W. to recognize new government at once" Telegram received (at 11:55 A.M.), DLC-Hamilton Fish. On the same day, Fish telegraphed to USG. "Instructions have been sent to W. according to your telegram—" Telegram sent, *ibid.*

1. On July 20 and 27, Washburne wrote to USG. "The declaration of war caught me at Carlsbad last Saturday and I left for Paris by the first diligence; reaching here Monday night after a hard trip of fifty-two hours. I was very sorry to give up my cure, but in such a terrible crisis this is my post of duty, and here I shall remain, sick or well. I find so much to do, that I can write you but a short letter to go by the open mail of to-day. I send quite elaborate despatches to Gov. Fish. So suddenly did this terrible war break out that the people of Europe have been utterly appalled. No language can measure the probable consequences and results. The damage *already* done to the material interests of the world cannot be repaired in years. Everything is brought to a stand still and ordinary people stand aghast with amazement. But the great crowd are mad with excitement and things are rushed as in a giddy whirl. The words of Thiers, of Jules Favre, of Gambetta counseling a little moderation are drowned in hisses and they are covered with insults. The house of the Venerable Thiers, a man whose great name has illustrated France for half a century is surrounded by a howling mob. And so we go. it is war. war. war on all sides— 'To Berlin', 'down with Prussia', are the cries. I have no time to write you of the causes, but must refer to you to my despatches. How wise was your message to Congress in regard to the shipping, to meet this crisis, and how fatal to the interests of the country that Congress did not heed your suggestions. I am trying to see what I can do in regard to the German Steamers, but I fear nothing can be accomplished. The Prussian archives came to our Legation to-day and the Saxons have asked us for our protection. Dont this show that times have changed, so far as our country is concerned, in a few years. Ten years ago what great power in Europe would have asked the U. S. to protect their subjects? Your message for Mrs. Pope was duly received and Col. Hoffman has written you about it. The suicide of the Dr. was one the strangest and saddest

things that ever happened. I do not want to say anything against Motley but I *do* want to say that I am delighted with the appointment of Mr. Frelinghuysen & so I am with Orth's. My family are at the sea-shore all well and happy. Kindest regards to Mrs. Grant & Mr. Dent . . ." ALS (press), DLC-Elihu B. Washburne. "I shall send you by the despatch-bag, which leaves here on Friday next, a set of the official military maps, showing the field to be operated on by the armies of the two great nations at war. I procured them from the Minister of War, General le Boeuf, and send them to you thinking that they have some interest at the present time. . . . P. S: I shall send copies of these maps to the Department of State and the War Department, as soon as I can obtain them, having been unable to procure all at this time." LS, USG 3. On Aug. 8, Frederick T. Dent wrote to Washburne. "The President directs me to inform you that your letter of July 27th/70 is recved together with the maps of what it was supposed would be the country over which the war between Prussia and France would extend   the President thanks you for the maps notwithstanding the fact that the tide of war rolled in the other direction from the Rhine. The President sends his most cordial and friendly greeting to yourself and family, and with mine . . ." ALS, IHi.

On July 29, Secretary of the Treasury George S. Boutwell wrote to USG. "Passing events in Europe suggest to me the possibility of arrangements with England by which she may be relieved from the Alabama claims and the transfer of the Canadas to the United States accomplished. Not that England could openly transfer the Canadas in payment of the Alabama claims; but she may be ready to enter upon a policy in reference to her American possessions which would result in separation and then in annexation if she were assured that the Alabama question could be so settled as to place her in a position to take a part in European affairs. She has already suffered severely from the effect of her own example; and it is quite probable that in the next few months she will realize more fully the intensive wickedness of her conduct. As now situated she can not with safety take part in the affairs of the continent; and should France prevail in the contest with Prussia, England will be compelled to go to the relief of Belgium and Holland or in humiliation to witness the ~~humiliation to witness~~ the acquisition of those countries by her rival. Anticipating such a contingency she must desire to relieve herself of every weight. Even if the Alabama claims were not an incumbrance her American colonies would be a hindrance rather than a help. I am aware that there is nothing fresh in these suggestions; and my only reason for presenting them is in the opinion I entertain that ~~nothing~~ act would be more advantageous to the country or beneficial to the administration than the peaceful acquisition of the Canadas. Moreover, should England become involved in the European wars the temptation to our people to take part against her would be removed by the circumstance that she had already withdrawn her flag from this continent." ALS, USG 3.

On July 31 and Sept. 12, Washburne wrote to USG. "I wrote you after my return to Paris after the breaking out of the war.—Since that I have received your letter of the 10th inst. I knew that you would feel a world of relief at the adjournment of Congress. My own opinion is that it is the worst Congress that has ever assembled since the foundation of the Government and your characterization of it is perfectly just. I have no doubt that we shall lose a great many members this fall; perhaps the Copperheads may have a majority of the next House. That wont be any worse for us than the present House has been. We now have to bear the responsibility—then the other side will have it. The country will say that your recommendations have been wise and sagacious, and the fault is with Congress not carrying them out. If the opposition have the House and dont adopt your recommendations, we can hold them responsible. Whatever may be the results this fall I shall have no fears for '72. The people will never hand the Country over to the tender mercies of the rebels repudiator and old Copperhead leaders. If the scamps had passed the funding bill three months ago, as they ought to have done, instead of spending all their time in personal quarrels, jobbing and wrangling, you would this day have had five hundred millions funded at 5 per cent. It will now be years before you can fund at that rate—or at any rate. If there be one single acre of the public land that has not been voted away to corrupt monopolists, I wish you would let me know. I want to buy it for my youngest boy. But the worst infamy of all was the running away of the rascals and refusing to adopt the recommendations of your message about the shipping interest. Did ever man entrusted with such vast interests ever behave so before? What a splendid opportunity has been thrown away, to retrieve our Commerce! I hope you will call an extra session in September and submit the question again. I have written Gov Fish very full despatches in regard to war matters. He can tell you about them. I hope I will be able to get along with the increased responsibility of my position, growing out of my protection to the North Germans. It will be a great labor but I am glad to perform it. It is rather working down my two secretaries, but I dont ask them to work any harder than I do. I wish I could see an end to this terrible war, but no man can foretell that. The Emperor has gone with great panache and par[a]de. He took more baggage than you did from Smith's plantation, when you [set] out on the Vicksburg Campaign. Query? will he be more successful? Jones has got to stay at hand this summer to watch little Belgiums. My people are still at the Sea-shore and all very well. I sent old Uncle Jesse DuBois's letter to Captain Pitt, and I presume the Captain will remit a lot of stamps. He has a good many. We have had an intensely hot season here, but it is now cooler. The suicide of Prevost-Paradol created a profound sensation here. If you have a spare half hour at Long Branch I would be glad to have a line from you. With kindest regards to the family . . ." "I hope you will like my letter to Jules Favre, which I send you herewith. I can truly say that his reply is splendid. I intended to have written you by the bag of Friday but after getting off my budget to Gov. Fish I had no time to write you. But I told the Governor about all there was to be said. I would like to see you to tell you of all I have seen here for the last few weeks. Never was a nation so humbled, prostrated and butchered as France has been. I was so glad that the Governor telegraphed your desire for peace. Our Country has never before stood out so prominently as now. Our prompt recognition of the Republic thrilled the whole country, and 'vive l'Amerique' is on all lips. The people demonstrate by calling on me in Legation and by sending addresses &c. &c. and I am alarmed in suddenly finding myself so popular, when I deserve so little. The Government here think I can do great things in working peace, but in such a delicate matter I of course take no steps without instructions. They now want my good offices here, especially and simply as an individual and I have telegraphed the Governor about that. Now that the Empire is surrendered and the Republic established there ought to be an honorable peace made. I dont believe in departing from our traditional policy of non-intervention in European affairs, but if our good offices could do any good they perhaps might be sort of unofficially extended. If you could be instrumental in making a peace, never could a man have so much gratitude. Jules Favre has changed his mind about going away, and so I should remain here as long as he does. When he really removes the Foreign Office, I shall have to follow. I need not say how glad I am always to have a little line from you." ALS (press), DLC-Elihu B. Washburne. On Oct. 28, Fish, Washington, D. C., wrote to USG. "I enclose for your information, a copy of a telegram received this afternoon from Mr Motley concerning Military events in Europe." Copy, DNA, RG 59, Domestic Letters.

On Oct. 31, Washburne wrote to USG. "I have written the Governor some despatches from time to time since the Siege has commenced, but my health has been so bad for the [— — — —] that I have not written much to anybody.— But while my despatches and letters have probably reached their destination, I have nothing in return. I have only received one despatch bag since the siege commenced, and that was brought by General Burnside one month ago. The last despatch I have from the State Department was dated September 8th. I have written the Secretary fully about this matter and I cannot but believe that he will be a good deal disturbed in finding his communications with me shut off by the Prussian authorities. I do not know how far you will all recognize the right of those authorities to prevent the Government of the United States from communicating with its representative to a friendly power. It is no pleasant thing for me during all these grave events, and with all the responsibilities upon me, to be left for so long a time without any advice or instruction from my Government. Entering on the seventh week of the siege, I find my duties still arduous. Last week, after a great deal of negociation and trouble, I got out of the city a large number of our countrymen, and now there are others still wanting to go. As I was not disposed [to] run away from my post of duty when the trouble commenced, (like the English, Austrian, Russian and Italian Ministers) and leave my countrymen to take care of themselves, a great many nationalities have placed their people in Paris under my protection. I have nearly all the South American Republics, as well as the Kingdom of Portugal. The Germans I have had from the beginning, as you know, and they have a great many matters to attend to. I receive at least half a dozen letters every week from Bismarck and have to write as many. It is impossible for me to attempt to write you much about the siege. Paris is holding out vastly better than anybody ever expected. For the last few weeks the bearing of the people has been good. There is not as yet much suffering and I think they can hold out till the first of January. The military operations have driven me out of my house and [I] am [now stopping] with a friend and I would never wish to live any better. A great many people are eating horse meat, and Louis Blanc told me the other day that he found it very good. The best cuts sell for forty cents a pound. Bread is abundant and cheap and vegetables are quite plenty, though not cheap. The stock of wine is almost inexhaustable, and French people can almost live on [— —]. I cannot tell you much about military matters. The number of men with arms in their hands in Paris, is between 400.000 and 500.000, but not half that number of soldiers. The great trouble now is a *leader*. In my judgment Trochu is a failure— a second edition of McClellan, always organizing, but never ready to strike. But what will happen, nobody knows. The present condition of France is deplorable. Thiers is just back, but I know not what he brings. Peace seems impossible on the terms demanded by Prussia. The fall of Paris is only a question of time, and after that—'the deluge.' I propose to remain for the present unless the Governor instructs me to leave. I have no letters from the United States since the first days of September and no letters from my wife, now in Brussels, since the 17th of that month. No news of the October elections. Kindest regards to Mrs. Grant and the children, . . ." ALS (press), DLC-Elihu B. Washburne.

To Frederick T. Dent

Aug. 24th 1870

DEAR DENT:

I wish you would send word to Adams & Co. Express office that there is a pony at the White House, to be shipped to Mr. ~~Haey~~ Hoey[1] at Long Branch, and find out when they will ~~they~~ be ready to take him. ~~You~~ When they are direct Richard to deliver "Little Reb"[2] with his single harness.

We leave here for West Point on Friday evening.[3] I do not know when I will be in Washington again.

Yours Truly
U. S. GRANT

ALS, James S. Copley Library, La Jolla, Calif. Written on stationery of "Fair Lawn, Newport."

1. John Hoey, born in Ireland, became gen. manager of the Adams Express Co. in 1854 and, by 1862, had acquired property in Long Branch. Hoey married actress Josephine Shaw Russell in 1849. See *New York Times*, Nov. 15, 1892; *Entertaining A Nation: The Career of Long Branch* (Long Branch, 1940), pp. 84–85; letter to J. Russell Jones, April 18, 1872.

2. See Jesse R. Grant, *In the Days of My Father General Grant* (New York and London, 1925), pp. 15–16.

3. Aug. 26, 1870.

To William Elrod

Aug. 24th 1870

MR. WM ELROD:
DEAR SIR:

If you [have] not cut down [—] trees you need no[t do] so. The old orch[ard] the one near you[r] house, I want ke[pt] particularly whet[her] it bears good fruit or not. At the White place I have no objection to your cutting away such as is not worth keeping.

After visiting the farm I visited a Wine sellar in the city. It has changed my theory entirely. I find that the Concord grape has no market now, as a wine grape, and to raise more than you have now set out will probably prove a loss. At your convenience some time find out just what grape will find a ready market and plant none other.—I will send you the money in the Fall to purchase young cattle with

AL (signature clipped), Illinois Historical Survey, University of Illinois, Urbana, Ill. Written on stationery of "Fair Lawn, Newport."

To Charles W. Ford

Washington, D. C. Sept. 3d *18*670

DEAR FORD:

I wish, as soon as possible after the receipt of this, you would telegraph me the names one two good men, either of whom you would be willing to endorse, for the Collectorship of the Port of St. Louis. I shall remove Costé on the ground of his course in the present campaign in Mo. Of course I do not want the names of any men who are not supporting the *regular* ticket in your state. If you can suggest the name of a man for the Apprasiership, the new office created, I would be glad of it. If Drake should happen to be in St. Louis I would like you to consult him; but do not delay a day if he is absent. Drake has recommended Shepard but for reasons which I will explain to Mr. D. I would not like to appoint him until after election.

Yours Truly

U. S. GRANT

ALS, DLC-USG. See letter to George S. Boutwell, Sept. 22, 1870.

To Bvt. Maj. Gen. Edmund Schriver

Sept. 8th /70

Appoint Harrison G. Otis[1] of New Jersey & MacComb,[2] son of Gen. McComb,[3] of the Eng. Corps. Cadets at West Point, to fill vacancies "At Large," and send the Apts. to Gn. Pitcher. These young men have been directed to report at West Point where they would receive their formal notice of apt.

U. S. GRANT

GN. SCHRIVER

ANS, Stephen W. Bumball, Mountainside, N. J. On Sept. 9, 1870, Bvt. Maj. Gen. Edmund Schriver, inspector gen., wrote to USG. "I find on my table this morning your memorandum directing the appointment of Harrison G. Otis and Montgomery Meigs Macomb, cadets 'at large, and I have the honor to inform you that the order has had attention." Copy, DNA, RG 94, Letters Sent, USMA.

1. Harrison Gail Otis of N. J., USMA 1874.
2. Montgomery M. Macomb, born in 1852 at Detroit, USMA 1874, had attended Yale University for one year.
3. John N. Macomb, born in N. Y., USMA 1832, served in the 4th Art. until transferred to the corps of topographical engineers in 1838. After Civil War service in Va. he was promoted to col. as of March 7, 1867.

To Roscoe Conkling

Washington D. C. Sept. 8th *1870*

DEAR SENATOR:

Your invitation to Mrs. Grant and myself to visit you, at Utica, was received just as I was starting to Washington. Events in Europe made it necessary for me to to come here at this time, and as I have been traveling so much this Summer, and propose going again the latter part of this month to place two of my children at school, I think I will not be able to accept.

I have seen the result of your convention. If the result was rightly obtained it ought to prove very satisfactory.—A dispatch to Porter to-day, from Murphy, I judge related to the Buffalo Collectorship?[1] I had no intention of making any change there until I become better satisfied than I am yet as to who should be appointed.

Yours Truly

U. S. GRANT

HON. R. CONKLING

U. S. SENATOR

ALS, DLC-Roscoe Conkling.

    1. On April 7, 1869, USG nominated Samuel J. Holley as collector of customs, Buffalo Creek, N. Y. On April 21, G. H. Ball, Buffalo, wrote to USG. "Many of our citizens were surprised and pained, at the appointment of Mr. Saml. Hawly as *collector of customs* for this port. And since some inquiry into his fitness has been made, since his appointment, I think it my duty to say to you, that as the moral sense of the community was outraged by his appointment, his prompt removal would afford great satisfaction. I know that mr. Bennet recommended him with great reluctance, and by what pressure he was brought to do it, I cannot understand. He is generally known to be a gambler; has two sons who are gamblers by profession, ~~and~~ who are to have places in the office; Mr H. freely declares, that he intends to *run* the office, so as to make money, and the skill of three gamblers will be likely to ensure success. I have not a particle of preference for any man for that office, only that he be honest & competent; and I write this, because, I am sure you have been imposed upon in the case of Mr H. as our citizens were imposed upon, by having ~~having~~ him foisted upon them, as candidate for Congress a few years since, when he was little known. I prefer that my name should not be known in this matter, unless necessary to the success of justice. Senator Conkling will vouch for my fidelity in what I say, and also Gen. Garfield of the House. I am pastor of the Niagira Square Baptist Ch." ALS, DNA, RG 56, Appraiser of Customs Applications. On May 3, D. H. Mueller, First Methodist Church, Buffalo, telegraphed to USG. "The charges against my friend Holley are infamous and worthy of no consideration" Telegram received (at 10:00 A.M.), *ibid.* Related papers are *ibid.*

    On Feb. 23, 1870, USG nominated Rodney W. Daniels to replace Holley. On Aug. 4, Holley wrote to USG. "After my interview with your Excellency yesterday I telegraphed Hon Chas J. Folger from Long Branch requesting him to address you a letter in time to have it reach your Excellency while you were at Washington on 5th inst—after my arrival here yesterday P. M. I wrote a letter to Judge Folger at Geneva with Same request—In the matter of the removal of Rodney W. Daniels I am certain you would act promptly if you realized how important it was for the preservation of the ascendency and success of the Republican Party in the 30th Congressional District—With Daniels in the Custom House it is certain a Democratic Member of Congress will be returned this Fall in place of Mr Bennett, and it is almost equally certain the district could not be carried in 1872 for the Republican Party—. . ." ALS, *ibid.* On Nov. 12, Josephus N. Larned, editor, *Buffalo Express*, wrote to USG. "It has become apparent, I think, to most Republicans in this District, that the placing of the chief Federal office here in antagonism with the Representative of the District has not been of good effect upon the party, but on the contrary has contributed not a little to the demoralization which resulted in our disastrous defeat in the late election. I trust that your Excellency will consider whether it may not be desirable to place the Government offices in this city more in harmony with each other and with our Representative" ALS, *ibid.* On Nov. 16, U.S. Representative David S. Bennett of N. Y., Buffalo, wrote to USG. "A Special Agent from the Department has found the present Collector's funds several thousand Dollars short hence you will have no embarrassment in removing him. I desire to renew the application for the appointment of Nathan. C Simons. His Papers from the Hon E. G. Spaulding are on file with the Department" ALS, *ibid.* On Nov. 18, William Dorsheimer, U.S. attorney, and Isaac F. Quinby, U.S. marshal, Rochester, N. Y., telegraphed to USG. "On account of discovery made by Treasury detective Leopold in the Custom house at Buffalo reported by him to the department We think the Collector should be promptly removed. We unite with Mr Bennett in recommending the appointment of Nathan C. Simons" Telegram received, *ibid.* On Jan. 9, 1871, Lyman K. Bass, Buffalo, wrote to USG. "In case of the designation of some person to succeed Mr. Daniels, as Collector of this port, I join in the recommendation that Mr. John Pierce be appointed to that office. He is an old and well known citizen of this city, an honest man, and known as an honest man in this community, a successful business man well qualified to discharge the important duties of the office. . . ." ALS, *ibid.*, Collector of Customs Applications. Related papers are *ibid.* On Jan. 16, Bennett, Washington, D. C., wrote to USG. "I hear from Buffalo, that the Commercial Advertiser clique, together with Mr. Bass, who is no less than their paid Attorney, is urging the name of John Pierce for Collector of Customs. Mr. Pierce keeps a Livery Stable by the side of Mr. Daniels,—has no position in society whatever and no political influence except as a wWard politician. His appointment would be a direct insult to the men of character and standing in community. Now, Mr President, I respectfully submit, that Mr Conkling has carried this matter quite far enough. He seems determined to act with the Commercial Advertiser and that clique, which is not in line with the Administration—opposing openly many measures of yours and weakening very much the future prospects of the Republican party. I beg of you to take this matter in hand and save the good men of the District, who are *your* true friends, from any further disgrace by the elevation of men of the stripe of Mr Daniels to the honored position of Collector of Customs, I regard Mr. Pierce as no better than Mr. Daniels. Mr. Conkling cannot afford to interpose any further opposition to the appointment of such men as Mr. Simons. He was in the Convention that nominated Mr. Lincoln the first time—went with the delegation to Springfield to notify him of his nomination—is a man of character and influence and entirely familiar with our commercial business. I have had one and only one interview with the Senators in relation to this appointment. Mr. Conkling himself acknowledged Mr. Simons to be a good man. Mr. Fenton said if asked he should favor Mr. Simons on account of my recommending him, disclaiming having had anything to do with the appointment of Mr. Daniels except to give his assent. I think however that Mr. Fenton secretly hopes that Mr Conkling's counsel will prevail knowing that if it does it will very much weaken him (Mr. Conkling) with the good men of the District and strengthen himself correspondingly, While I wish to remain on good terms with both of the Senators I desire to do all in my power to strengthen your Administration and must respectfully ignore any interference on the part of the Senators which will tend to weaken it. Herewith I hand you a slip from the 'Buffalo Morning Express' which is the true organ of the Administration having twice the circulation of the Commercial in my District, and also hand you two slips from the 'Commercial Advertiser.' The friends of the Express are very desirous that Mr. Simons should receive the appointment of Collector." LS, *ibid.*, Appraiser of Customs Applications. On Jan. 17, USG nominated John Pierce to replace Daniels, but withdrew the nomination on Jan. 23. Daniels continued as collector of customs.

To William Elrod

Washington, D, C,
Sept. 8th 1870.

DEAR ELROD:

Enclosed I send you check for One ₡Thousand (1000) dollars to be used in the way mentioned when I last saw you. I will endeavor to send you an Alderny bull this fall.

I wrote to you to set out no more concord vines! I am satisfied they will not pay. An investigation by yourself will demonstrate the kind to plant, if any.

AL (signature clipped), Illinois Historical Survey, University of Illinois, Urbana, Ill.

Speech

[*Sept. 9, 1870*]

Mr. PEREZ, I am pleased to receive you as the Minister Resident here of the United States of Colombia. It is not to be doubted that that high honor has been worthily bestowed. Your remarks upon its character show that you propose to enter upon the discharge of the trust with the full understanding of its responsibilities, and in a spirit of candor and good will. It shall be my purpose to meet you in the same spirit, and to endeavor to cause any questions which may be pending, or which may arise between our respective Governments, to be adjusted upon a basis satisfactory to both. The important negotiation to which you allude, justifies the fullest and calmest deliberation for its conclusion. It is to be hoped that, notwithstanding the protracted character of that negotiation it may result in a measure which will insure a successful accomplishment of its great object.

New York Times, Sept. 10, 1870. Santiago Perez, Colombian minister, born in 1830, was an attorney, playwright, and editor who had served in the Colombian government as a senator and cabinet officer. In 1866, he co-founded *El Mensajero*, an opposition newspaper that helped to force President Tomas Cipriano de Mosquera from power. On Sept. 9, 1870, Perez presented his credentials to USG. ". . . I am also very happy to believe, Sir, that in the discharge of my mission, if I succeed in fulfilling it in accordance with the high views of both the Government which sends me and the one which receives me, I shall find a fresh evidence that the sole, enduring and intimate links between nations as between individuals, are to be found in the practice of candor and justice. Undertaking, as heretofore, the examination of all subjects that may present themselves for consideration between our two countries, under the guidance of those controlling principles any difficulty that may arise will be easily surmounted. Such will be the case in the most important negotiations for interoceanic communication by a ship-canal—an undertaking to whose colossal magnitude must be attributed the deficiencies arising in the compact previous to the starting of the work. While a complete and quick agreement upon all the questions to be settled by that treaty ought not to be expected immediately, still the debate, laborious as it has been, must certainly demonstrate in its satisfactory result that in this, as in everything else, all just demands are compatible, and all legitimate interests may work harmoniously." *Ibid.*

Also on Sept. 9, Joaquin Godoy, Chilean minister, presented his credentials, and USG responded. "Mr. GODOY, I receive with pleasure your credentials as the Envoy Extraordinay and Minister Plenipotentiary of the Republic of Chili. It will be an agreeable duty for me to reciprocate the kind spirit on the part of your Government which you say has led to your mission. The United States take a special and lively interest in the welfare and happiness of the Republics of this hemisphere which were formerly dependencies of Spain. I heartily trust that the relations between Chili and her allies on the one side and the mother country on the other, which for some time past have been hostile in a technical sense only, may, with your participation, be restored to a condition of lasting peace and cordiality. For that desirable end I shall earnestly co-operate." *Ibid.*

On Sept. 3, Secretary of State Hamilton Fish, Garrison, N. Y., had written to USG. "The new Ministers from Colombia & from Chili have arrived & are desirous of being presented—I had informed Mr Cortes (the Colombian chargé) of your intention to be in Washington on Friday next & that you would probably receive Mr Perez on that day—Should there be any change in your plans, or should you prefer not to receive these Ministers on that day, or during your next visit to Washington will you do me the favor to advise me by telegraph, that I may inform the Gentlemen, in time—as neither of them is at present in Washington—I hope that you reached home Comfortably & are enjoying cool sea breezes—" ALS (press), DLC-Hamilton Fish. On Sept. 6, Tuesday, USG, Long Branch, telegraphed to Fish. "I will be in Washington Thursday and will meet Chilian minister then" Telegram received (at 4:00 P.M.), *ibid*. On Sept. 7, Fish telegraphed to USG. "Howe says no—Shall I wait until I see you ~~oin Fri~~ Washington on Friday—" ALS (press), *ibid*. On the same day, USG telegraphed to Fish. "Wait until we meet in Washington I go to Washington this evening" Telegram received (at 4:00 P.M.), *ibid*.

To Hamilton Fish

————

New York City,
Sept. 10th 1870.

DEAR GOVERNOR:

Governor Morton desires his nomination to the English Mission kept from the public until he gets back to Ia. so as to save the Governor of the state from embarassment   He says that if his apt. goes to the public all the politicians of the state will be after his place in the Senate. By letting Governor Baker know before the public do he will be able to apt. a Senator at the time the public become aware of the vacancy.

Yours Truly
U. S. GRANT

HON H. FISH
SEC OF STATE

ALS, DLC-Hamilton Fish. On Sept. 10, 1870, USG, New York City, twice telegraphed to Secretary of State Hamilton Fish. "Morton accepts. Send apt to him at Fifth ave. Hotel." "Govr Morton desires his apt be kept from the public until after he gets back to Ia." Telegrams received (at 11:05 and 11:25 A.M.), *ibid*.

Speech

————

[*Sept. 14, 1870*]

You know, Governor, that I don't make speeches, but I m[u]st say that I have been very much pleased to day. I take an interest in agriculture, and I do not know that there is any better way to develop it than these agricultural fairs. I have spent a very pleasant day, and I thank the committee of the society and the citizens of your county generally for the kindness shown me.

New York Herald, Sept. 15, 1870. Attending the Monmouth County Agricultural Fair, Freehold, N. J., USG responded to a speech by Joel Parker, former Democratic governor of N. J. (1863–66). Parker, born in N. J. in 1816, graduated from Princeton (1839), served as Monmouth County prosecuting attorney (1852–57), and, as governor, supported the war, though often criticizing federal policies. During the presidential election of 1868, N. J. had been among the eight states carried by the Democrats. "GENTLEMEN—We have here to-day a distinguished soldier; a man who occupies the highest position in the gift of the people of this country, perhaps the highest position in the world. We need not say, Mr. President, that we are highly gratified that you have thus visited our town on the occasion of our annual Agricultural Fair. We take this visit as a recognition on the part of the Chief Magistrate of the nation of the great importance of the agricultural interest, that interest which is the foundation of our national prosperity. Our people are also very much gratified, Mr. President, that you have selected this county as your residence, and we hope this visit will serve to make you better acquainted with your neighbors and friends. You will find the people of Monmouth a noble-hearted, generous people, and while they have strong and fixed political views they never permit them to interfere with their social relations. I propose, gentlemen, the health of the President of the United States." *Ibid.*

To Hamilton Fish

Long Branch, N. J.
Sept. 14th 1870

HON. H. FISH,
SEC. OF STATE;

It will not be necessary to address a not to Governor Morton to learn when to make known his apt. to England. As soon as he arrives at Indianapolis he will make the matter known to Governor Baker, who will at once appoint Morton's successor to the Senate, or publish his determination to make no apt. until the State Legislature meets in Jan.y. By Thursday of next week, if it is not before given out from Indianapolis, the notice may go from Washington withou[t] correspondence with Morton.

Yours Truly
U. S. GRANT

ALS, DLC-Hamilton Fish. On Sept. 12, 1870, Secretary of State Hamilton
Fish had written to USG. "I enclose copies of telegrams ~~received~~ viz I from Mr
Bancroft—recd yesterday II—from Mr Washburne recd this mornig—Also copy
of reply sent this mornig to Mr Washburne—Will Governor Morton inform me
when his appointment is to be announced? or shall I apply to him—& if so shall
I address him at Indianapolis? a letter arriving there in his absence might be
opened, and its purport thus be prematurely ~~be~~ made public—Sir Edward
Thornton has returned, and confirms the statement that the Provincial authorities
construe the Treaty of 1818 as ~~giving~~ excluding our Fishing Vessels from their
Ports, for the purpose of unloading their cargoes or for any other purpose than
those specially mentioned in the Treaty—he says that they claim, that our vessels never exercised or claimed the right under the treaty of 1818; That the
habit of resorting to their ports for the disembarkment of their Cargos (in
board) arose under the Reciprocity treaty, & that the abrogation of that treaty
remitted them to their rights under the treaty of 1818—I claimed the right under
that treaty, & have pointed him to some incidents connected with the negotiation of the treaty, which he admits present an argument in our favor. I am not
prepared to say it a conclusive argument, or that our right is perfectly clear—
we are investigating the question & will ascertain whether or not our vessels
did resort to those Ports, for the purpose of transfer of cargo, or of trade, prior
to the Reciprocity treaty—I understand that two more of our vessels have been
seized—but have not the particulars—Thornton mentioned the fact as having
been telegraphed to him—. . . P S—I enclose copy of a telegram just now received from Gen Read" ALS (press—tabular material expanded), *ibid.* On
Sept. 16, Fish wrote to USG. "I enclose a letter from Mr William Everett, son
of the late Eduard Everett which will explain itself. Your letter of 14th is
received—I am anxious for an early decision, & hope the new minister will be
prepared to leave at a very early day—The 'Fisheries' question is becoming involved and it appears to me not desirable to begin the correspondence and
negotiations through the minister now in London, who must leave before any
solution of the question is likely to be reached—Sir Edward Thornton, in an
interview yesterday represented the feeling of the People in Canada as being
much excited against the United States, in consequence of the refusal of a Commercial Treaty with them; and more particularly on account of the late Fenian
Raid, with regard to which, however, he expresses the opinion, and said he had
told them they were unjust in holding this Government (which had done more
to defeat it than the Canadian Government) responsible—He says that they
claim that all that is done to the American Fishing Vessels is strictly justified
by the Treaty—The most significant part of his conversation, in connection with
that subject, was a remark, apparently thrown out for the purpose of inducing
a reply that 'it was of the greatest importance, that the two Governments before another Fishing Season, should readjust and settle the whole question, &
thus take it out of the hands of the Provincial Authorities—' I replied that what
had occurred and was taking place would make necessary a decided remonstrance whould would probably be sent to the minister in London. He intimated,
without expressly saying it, that they would be prepared to receive in a good
spirit, any communication from us" Copy, *ibid.* On Sept. 23, Fish wrote to
USG. "I forward herewith for your signature Governor Morton's Commission
as Minister to London, and a ceremonial letter to the Emperor of Austria."
Copy, DNA, RG 59, Domestic Letters.

To Thomas Murphy

———

[*Sept. 20, 1870*]

This letter is respectfully refered to the Collector of Customs, New York City. The letter has been mislaid among many papers and letters that had received attention, and has only just come to my notice. I no doubt saw it when first rec'd but in reading up a whole mail before [re]p[lying] to any part, this has escaped.— Where men risked their lives in defense of their country they should have the preference in all cases of Govt. employment, all other things being equal, over those who did not so serve.

U. S. GRANT

ALS, InFtwL.

To George S. Boutwell

———

Long Branch, N. J.
Sept. 22d 1870.

HON. GEO. H. BOUTWELL:
SEC. OF THE TREAS.
DEAR SIR:

The bolters movement in Mo. differs but little from the successful tactics used in Va and Tenn. to give those states to the democracy. When I was in St. Louis I knew as well what was to be done in convention, by the "bolters" as I know now since the conventi[on] has met. I do not want to favor their movement by fostering in office men who go actively into that movement. Such is our Collector of the Port of St. Louis, Felix Costé.[1] I wish you would have him removed at once and appoint in his stead Gen. Isaac F. Shepard,[2] Ch. Rep. State Central Com. of Mo. His residence is St. Louis. I know him well. He is a writer of some not, a staunch republican, and one of the first officers with me willing to take command of a Colored regiment when orders were rec'd. to organize such troops.

Truly yours

U. S. GRANT

ALS (photocopy), USGA.

1. On May 1, 1869, Orville E. Babcock had written to Samuel M. Breckinridge. "The President directs me to write to you & to state that in accordance with ~~you~~ circumstances that you understand and your statement to him to resign at any time he might designate, he will be pleased to accept your resignation to date from the 30th of June next." Copies, DLC-USG, II, 1, 4. On Dec. 7, USG nominated Felix Costé as surveyor of customs, St. Louis, to replace Breckinridge. On Dec. 6, 1870, USG nominated Elias W. Fox as surveyor of customs. Fox also served as act. collector of customs, St. Louis.

2. On Aug. 12, Henry C. Vinton, St. Louis, wrote to USG. "I take the liberty of saying to you that I am desirous of receiving the appointment of Appraiser for the Port. of St Louis Mo—The Merchants of this city who are doing a very large proportion of the business through the Custom House here, have been kind enough to express themselves in favor of my appointment—Herewith I hand you their *Petition* In the hope my request may meet with favorable consideration . . ." ALS, DNA, RG 56, Appraiser of Customs Applications. The enclosed petition is *ibid.* Letters recommending E. Anson Moore and Charles L. Tucker are *ibid.* On Oct. 27, Isaac F. Shepard, St. Louis, wrote to USG. "I have the honor to acknowledge the receipt of notification of my appointment as Appraiser of Merchandize at this port, for which generous attention at your hands please accept my thanks. I shall strive to make my administration of the duties of the office at once an honor to myself, and a credit to the appointing power. In the matter of Mr. Leaming of Sedalia which I promised you to investigate, I find that a gross injustice would have been done by his removal from office on the belief that he was at all complicated in the bolters' movement. Mr. L. has been continually a firm and earnest friend, not only to your administration, but also to the regular Republican party of the State, who support Governer McClurg for re-election. He was in the Convention at Jefferson City, and labored earnestly to prevent division, and after the bolt stood steadfast by the regular platform and ticket. He has never wavered for a moment, and is now one of our most active workers for success. He has a brother who is understood to be working for the Brown party, and he may have been confounded with him. But of his own fidelity to us and our cause there is no question. I am painfully satisfied, from cumulative evidence that cannot be doubted, that Hon. Chester H. Krum, U. S. District Attorney, is fully against us in State matters, and does not hesitate to avow himself a Brown man, and in favor of the new party. Personally I have no wish for his removal, but you will allow me to say that his retention in office, while Mr. Coste has been removed, will give occasion, as is already the case, for the Germans of St. Louis to charge that only they are to be dealt with. I am informed that Coste has used such imputations against your administration, in speeches at German meetings. You will judge how far this suggestion should have weight. Should you think it wise to make a change, I still think, as I named to you, that Mr. D. T. Jewett of St. Louis is the most desirable appointment.

He is a sharp, sterling, experienced lawyer, and has done distinguished service as a Republican." ALS, *ibid.*, RG 60, Records Relating to Appointments.

Endorsement

Referred to the Secretary of the Interior.

I think Mr. Brockway[1] might with great propriety be assigned to the Indian agency in his own State, to which he has once been appointed and confirmed.

He is a minister, and therefore the new rule adopted will not be violated by his appointment.

I want, besides, to accommodate Senator Howard, whom I regard as an able supporter of the Republican party and of the Administration.

U. S. GRANT.

SEPT. 22, 1870.

Zachariah Chandler: An Outline Sketch of His Life and Public Services (Detroit, 1880), p. 307. Written on a letter of Sept. 21, 1870, from U.S. Senator Zachariah Chandler of Mich. to USG. "Secretary Cox has done my colleague an unintentional but a serious injury. In 1869 the whole Michigan delegation united in recommending the Rev. W. H. Brockway, one of the most popular Methodist clergymen in the State, for Indian Agent. He was nominated and confirmed, but acquiesced in the transfer of Indian affairs to the military. Since the adjournment of Congress, my colleague made a personal request to the Secretary of the Interior, that the Rev. Mr. Brockway be commissioned as Indian Agent for Michigan. Instead of sending the commission, he has sent a man from New Jersey to attend to our Indian affairs. This has given offense to the most numerous and powerful religious denomination in the State and seriously injured my colleague. I ask for my colleague that the New Jersey commission may be immediately revoked, and Mr. Brockway may be at once commissioned. . . . It is really important that this be done at once." *Ibid.* See letter to Zachariah Chandler, Sept. 22, 1870.

On Dec. 8, USG nominated William H. Brockway as Indian agent, Mich., but Brockway declined the position. On March 14, 1871, USG nominated George Bradley for this post. On Oct. 31, 1870, Bradley, Mt. Pleasant, Mich., had written to USG. "please allow an humble Individual to address you in behalf of the Indians residing in Isabella County Michigan   The condition of the Indians is my apologey for troubling you. but hope you can find time and will listen to. and look into the matter. and if possible give them the desired relief   These Indians are known as The *Chippewa Indians* of *Sagenaw*, and portions of the Bands of *Chippewa* Indians of *Swan Creek and Black River* . . ."

ALS, DNA, RG 75, Letters Received, Mackinac Agency. In an undated letter, Bishop Matthew Simpson wrote to USG. "Rev Mr Bradley desires to make some statements in reference to Indian affairs in Michigan. He was for many years a missionary among the Indians at Isabella, and is intimately acquainted with the condition of the tribe, and the matters connected with their reservation. He is a minister in regular standing in the Michigan Conference and enjoys the confidence of those who know him." ALS, *ibid.* On April 18, 1871, after Bradley's death, USG nominated Richard M. Smith as Indian agent.

In an undated petition, John Chatfield *et al.* wrote to USG. "We the Chiefs of the Chippewa Indians of Sagenaw Swan Creek and Black River Bands now living on the Reservation in Isabella County State of Michigan, wish to Speak a few words to our Great Father the President of the United States in behalf of ourselves and our Children   *Whereas* we made Treaties with your Commissioners, one in 1855 and one in Oct. 18th 1864, by which we supposed we were getting a *home* for ourselves and our children, we felt thankful that you was willing to deal so generously by us, and under the Second Article of the Treaty of Augt 2 1855 provision was made for building a Grist-Mill and Saw Mill on our Reservation, which was promptly done—Also provision was made in both of the Treaties as we supposed, by which we were to have patents for our land within at least ten years years from the date of the same. And *Whereas*, About fifteen years have passed away and we have no *patents* yet, although promised them times without number by your Agents. The effect of this delay has nearly ruined us.   we are *discouraged*, and our young men, are not willing to clear any land for other people, and, Whereas, Certain White men Mr *Rust* and *company* made a strong effort to get away from us some fourteen or fifteen thousand acres of the best and most valuable timberedland—, but we feel very thankful that some of our white friends became interested in our behalf, and succeed[ed] in getting us back the land,—but as yet we get no Patents. And now last of all The Agent James W Long, has got our Mill Property, without our knowledge or Consent. The following Deed Shows it which is now recorded in the Records of the county—The mill was built on land selected by J. W. Nicholson for which he recieved a certificate, and possible the Govt has given him a patent. See Article Seventh of the Treaty of Oct 18th 1864 touching this matter   *Now,* Our Great Father We ask you to help us, in our Troubles, and send us a good agent,—one who will sympathize with us in our trouble and poverty and do for us as the 'Treaties' call for and give us what is right and not *Rob* us. We ask again for our *Patents* so we can feel that we own our lands, and we do not see why we cannot have them   We will do the best we can when we feel sure that our *homes* are our own personal property; we do not wish to have any more promises—but our *Patents*" D (signed by mark—docketed as received on Jan. 6, 1871), *ibid.* See *HED*, 42-2-1, part 5, pp. 924–27.

1. Born in Vt. in 1813, Brockway moved to Mich. in 1831, worked as a blacksmith and teacher, and was licensed as Methodist minister in 1833. For twenty-five years, he rode the circuit, served as chaplain at Fort Brady, Mich., and was assigned to Indian missions. He then became active in railroad construction and Republican politics.

To Hamilton Fish

Long Branch, N. J.
Sept. 22d 1870.

HON. H. FISH:
SEC. OF STATE:
DEAR SIR:

I believe the Consulship at Santa Iago de Cuba is vacant? If so, and there is no one to whom the place has been offered, you may appoint A. N. Young,[1] of Ky. He is an excellent and very competant man who served during the entire rebellion, in the Army, his early service being with me. I do not know Mr. Youngs address, but if his apt. is sent to the care of my father, Covington Ky. he will get it.

Faithfully yours
U. S. GRANT

ALS, DLC-Hamilton Fish. On Oct. 4, 1870, Secretary of State Hamilton Fish wrote in his diary. "President suggests to withhold Commission of A N Young, lately appointed Consul at Santiago de Cuba & that with a view to the possible sending him to Turks Island, & one of the two Candidates recommended by Mr Borie for Santiago de Cuba, to that place." DLC-Hamilton Fish. On Dec. 6, USG nominated Alfred N. Young as consul, Santiago de Cuba. See letter to Zachariah Chandler, Sept. 22, 1870.

1. In an undated petition, O. F. Shaw, Ripley, Ohio, Jesse Root Grant, Covington, Ky., et al. wrote to USG recommending Young. DS (16 signatures—docketed as received in Oct., 1870), DNA, RG 59, Letters of Application and Recommendation. Related papers are ibid. Grant endorsed these papers. "I would give it as my deliberate & candid opinion that you cant better fill that place than to appoint Mr Young. And his Army services, & the shabby treatment by his Copper head Company officers; and the fact that you have never appointed a Native of Brown County to any office, all plead in his favor—" AES, ibid.

To Zachariah Chandler

Long Branch, N. J.
Sept. 22d 1870.

DEAR SENATOR:

Your letters, one speaking of the services rendered the re-publican party by Judge Edmunds,[1] and also recommending the re-instatement of Mr. Brockway[2] for the Indian Agency to which he was once appointed, were received to-day. I at once wrote to the Sec. of the Int, to put Mr. B. in, and would have sent the letter to you to read before delivery only that I did not know but you might leave the city before the letter reached there.—You have seen before this that Govr. Morton has been appointed to the English ~~comm~~Mission; I think the time has come when we want something more there than a "Figure head."

No one thinks more of Judge Williams[3] than I do. For the office you speak of howeve I do not think he will suit as well as for something higher, if the occasion arises before the expiration of his Senatorial term.

I shall leave here on Monday next to put my children at school, and then return to Washington prepared to commence a vigorous campaign against Congress.—I hope Senator Howard will understand that if I had thought of it, and had been familiar with the circumstances, I would not have approved the apt. of another than his friend to the Indian Agency in Mich.

Yours Truly
U. S. GRANT

HON. Z. CHANDLER, U. S. S.

ALS, DLC-Zachariah Chandler. On Sept. 24 and 25, 1870, Secretary of State Hamilton Fish wrote to USG. "Personal & *Unofficial*—. . . Senator Chandler called this mornig to urge the withholding of Govr Morton's Commission for the present, on the ground that Indiana is a very close State, & the chance of securing a Senator for the remainder of Morton's term, would stimulate the Democrats to extraordinary exertions, in order to send Mr Hendricks to the Senate: of whom Chandler says he is the ablest man, and the most adroit manager in the Democratic ranks, in the United States—The withholding the Commission will scarce have the effect he desires—The acceptance of the appointment, by Govr Morton, of Minister to England indicates an approaching vacancy in the

Senatorship, & will probably stimulate all the effort which the Democracy can make. I told Senator Chandler that I would write you, presenting his suggestion, & as the mail will possibly bring the Commission from Long Branch, within a day or two, & there is no immediate object in forwarding it for a few days, I will await to hear from you—The Commission for Mr Young as Consul at Santiago de Cuba, which you directed, is forwarded to day for your signature— there have been several applicants for this Consulate, to each of whom I have given the advice to *take their Coffin with them*, in case of appointment—Accompanying it is a Commission for Mr Mattoon as Consul at Honolulu—his recommendations are much stronger than those of any other applicant, & he is very well endorsed politically. There is also a Commission for a Marshal of Consular Court at Chinkiang—a gentleman, long resident there & recommended by the Consul—Also for a Consul at Santos, Brazil—a 'feed-consulate' worth about $200 per annum—the person named is an American (Marylander) long resident there in business, & recommended by the Houses in NewYork, Philadelphia &c. doing business with that place—It is again, very warm here, & excessively dusty—" "Senator Chandler has called to represent certain matters, involving, very seriously, the chances of Republican Success in the pending Elections—We have had a conference with Genl Babcock, who goes tonight to NewYork, to meet you. He is fully ꜰ informed as to the difficulties encountered & is possessed of the views of Senator Chandler (in which I concur) as to the importance & the possibility of overcoming them, & of obtaining, as we hope, a triumph this Autumn, which, very probably, will settle the next Presidential Election—or at least, make success then, if not certain, more easy, & more probable—Genl Babcock will present these views; for which I beg your consideration—trusting that they may Commend themselves to your Approval—" ALS (press), DLC-Hamilton Fish.

On Aug. 4, Calvin S. Mattoon, Washington, D. C., wrote to USG. "I have the honor, very respectfully, to solicit an appointment to the place of Consul at Honolulu, Sandwich Islands. I beg leave to state that about the middle of March 1865, my application for the position named was presented to the lamented late President Lincoln, by the Hon Senator Sherman, the Hon Mr Shellabarger (then my member), the Hon Mr Schenck and others, with the recommendation of the Republican delegation in Congress from Ohio, and other prominent men of my state. I had also the strong verbal endorsement to President Lincoln of Gov. Dennison, then Post Master General. . . . On the strength of the recommendations presented, both President Lincoln and Secretary Seward promised me the appointment as successor of the then incumbent, whose place, it was stated, would be vacant in the fall following. Very soon thereafter the appalling assassinations scences occurred, overwhelming the land with grief. As soon after the accession of Mr *Johnson* to the Presidency as it could properly be done, his attention was called to the circumstances of my pending application, and he signified his readiness to carry out the understanding had in reference to my case. Thus the matter rested, but before the time referred to, when the office would be vacant, had arrived, the differences between Congress and the President had become so serious that I suspended further effort for the time, not being sure but to accept an office under President Johnson at that time even if one could get it, would cast suspicion upon the soundness of his Republican principles I have never compromised my political principles, and have been unswerving in my devotion to the progressive policy of the Republican party.

My standing, character and qualifications, as well as my past political course and present position are, I think, sufficiently attested by the papers to which your attention has been invited. I most respectfully ask a favorable consideration of this renewed application." ALS, DNA, RG 59, Letters of Application and Recommendation. Related papers are *ibid.* On Dec. 6, USG nominated Mattoon as consul, Honolulu.

On July 1, Eli T. Sheppard, consul, Chin Kiang, wrote to Fish. "I beg to inform you that Mr. Geo. W. Lewton has this day tendered to me his resignation as U. S. Marshal at the Consular Court at Chinkiang, and that I have this day appointed Mr. Alferd C. Colquet to act as Marshal at said Consular Court, subject to your approval. Mr. Colquet was the acting Marshal at Chinkiang for nearly two years pevious to Mr. Lewtons appointment and I take pleasure in saying that he is in every respect, well-qualified to discharge the duties of the office. He is a Native of the State of New York and resides, at present in Chinkiang." ALS, *ibid.*, Consular Despatches, Chin Kiang. On Dec. 6, USG nominated Alfred C. Colquit as marshal, Chin Kiang. Also on Dec. 6, USG nominated William T. Wright as consul, Santos, Brazil.

1. James M. Edmunds, born in 1810, former state legislator in Mich., assisted U.S. Senator Zachariah Chandler of Mich. in promoting candidates through the Republican Congressional Committee. In 1870, Chandler told USG that "Judge Edmunds is the Bismark of this campaign." *Zachariah Chandler: An Outline Sketch of His Life and Public Services* (Detroit, 1880), p. 314.

On March 26, 1869, U.S. Senator Henry W. Corbett of Ore. wrote to USG. "Allow me to express the hope that there will be *no* change in the Comr of the Genl Land Office. I do not know as it is contemplated to make a change, I simply wish to testify to the ability of the Hon Jos S. Wilson, his faithful and long public service, his thorough acquaintance with the whole system, seems to make it necessary that he should be continued—My deliberate opinion is, that such services cannot be furnished by any other man in the United States, and my only regret is that he is so inadequately compensated." ALS, DNA, RG 48, Appointment Div., Letters Received. In [*March*], Chandler *et al.* wrote to USG. "Our personal knowledge of the Hon J. M. Edmunds, Our Confidence in his integrity and ability as manifested in every public position in which he has been placed, and especially as seen in his discharge of the duties of Commissioner of the General Land office under the administration of President Lincoln justify and induce our earnest Solicitation for his reappointment to that Bureau. Mr Edmunds was the first prominent victim of Mr Johnsons policy, and Surrendered that place that he might, unembarrassed continue the work of extending Republican organization into the South with the Sole view of the restoration of the States upon a just basis—It is not too much to Say that to his Sagacity and efficiency in this direction the Country is largely indebted for the triumph of the Congressional policy and the Consequent Success of the Republican party. In view of these Services the personal Sacrifices of Mr Edmunds for the Cause, his experience of nearly Six years in the position named and the success which he there obtained, we especially desire and repeat our request that he be appointed to the office Specified   By this appointment the Government will at once Secure the Experience and Capacity essential to So important a trust, and gracefully reward a fidelity to principle which is above place and which none, better than yourself can appreciate" DS (4 signatures), *ibid.*

On April 15, U.S. Representative George W. Julian of Ind. wrote to USG. "I have been a member of the House Committee on public Lands for nearly nine years, & chairman of the Committee nearly seven years, during all which time I have had ample means of knowing both Mr. Wilson & Judge Edmonds, personally & officially. I can speak of them therefore from my own knowledge, & if my word is to be credited I cannot doubt that Mr. Wilson will be relieved & Judge Edmonds appointed in his place. It should be done for the following reasons: 1 Edmonds is most unmistakably a republican, & is known every where throughout the whole country as a representative man in our party, & one of its most effective supporters; while Wilson is a fossil democrat, & has, certainly, no real sympathy or affiliation with our party or its principles. 2 Edmonds is a sagacious & practical man of business, of strong native sense, & of inflexible honesty; while Wilson is a man of rhetoric, of surface accomplishments, & is wholly wanting in the grasp of mind & power of concentration which the position demands. 3 Edmonds believes, with all his might, in saving the public lands for actual settlement & tillage, & in his administration of the Department did every thing in his power to inaugurate his policy; while Wilson has no sympathy with it, & has, to my own knowledge, been the servant of monopolists during his term of service. The only real reforms in the Land Department within the past eight years are fairly to be credited to Judge Edmonds. 4 One of the causes which led to the removal of Edmonds was his decision of upon a controversy between thieving monopolists in California on the one side, & honest settlers on the other, which decision has since been sanctioned by the Federal courts; Mr. Wilson lending himself as the tool of the monopolists, & thereby serving the political influence which gave him the position. 5 Judge Edmonds lost his position, mainly, because he would not become in any degree subservient to Andrew Johnson; while Mr. Wilson, then his chief clerk, took advantage of the fact, & by political sapping & mining, & by his ready service of the monopolists refered to, was able to receive the place he now holds; falsely pretending, of late, to be the friend of Grant & the Republican cause." ALS, *ibid.*

On April 17, John M. Langston *et al.* wrote to USG. "in behalf of the Colored Men of U. S. of America, whom we represent, we respectfully Solicit, the appointment of Hon, J M Edmunds to some prominent, and honorable, position. We do this because of our entire confidence in the man, and from a sense of obligation, we feel, for the great good, he has done our people and the Republican party. permit us to instance, His invaluable Services to the Country, in organiseing our people in the South, thereby enabling them to combine their efforts, (under the reconstruction Laws,) in restoreing that Section upon a basis of Justice, and Equality. He also originated the Southern Homestead Law, by which Thousands, of White, and Colored, poor, and landless, have been made prosperous and happy, by its provisions. His efforts have very largely contributed, to Educate them, in the first dutys, of citysenship and the importance of Sobriety and Obedience to Law. remembering these noble efforts, for the general Welfare of our Country; we ask that they be recognised, and rewarded." DS (5 signatures), *ibid.* On Dec. 6, USG nominated Edmunds as postmaster, Washington, D. C.; on Jan. 11, 1871, Willis Drummond as commissioner, General Land Office.

2. William H. Brockway. See endorsement, Sept. 22, 1870.

3. U.S. Senator George H. Williams of Ore. See letter to Oliver P. Morton, Oct. 21, 1870.

To Charles W. Ford

———

Long Branch, N. J,
Sept. 22d 1870,

DEAR FORD:

You may compromise with Mr. Hulse[1] at $75 00 pr. Arpent.
He says there is but about ten Arpents, that I claim, in his tract,
and he proposes to give $750 00. Let him pay the $75 00 pr. Arpent
for what he has, no more and no less.

I wish some time when you are out riding you would go down
to Carondelet and see the man who lives on the piece of land that I
compromised with Mr. Carlin for, and terminate any lease, or pretended lease he may claim to have, and make a new arrangement
either with the man on the land, or any one else, to rent it for next
year. I may also have taxes to pay on that, and my proportion of
the land got from Burnes.

Your brother has been down here spending a day with me. He
went back last evening.

Yours Truly
U. S. GRANT

ALS, MoSHi. See letter to Charles W. Ford, Oct. 8, 1870.

1. George T. Hulse.

To Marshall Jewell

———

[Sept. 24, 1870]

Your favor of yesterday is received. Mrs. Grant and myself
leave here, for Boston, on Monday[1] next to put our son in college.
We will return about Wednesday to Hartford and remain only
long enough to take Nellie out to Farmington.[2] We will be pleased
to accept your proffered hospitalities for the short time we do remain in your city. Please present Mrs. Grant's and my kindest
regards to Mrs. Jewell and the children.

Kenneth W. Rendell, Inc., Catalogue 174, no. 44. Marshall Jewell, born in N. H. in 1825, became a partner in his father's leather business in 1850, invested successfully in a variety of retail and manufacturing enterprises, and served as governor of Conn. from May, 1869, until May, 1870.

1. Sept. 26, 1870.

2. On Oct. 4, USG wrote to Jewell. "Please take Nellie to your house to remain until we send for her. Did you get my despatches of 2d & 3d" Copy, DLC-USG, II, 5. Ellen Grant returned to Washington soon after enrolling in Miss Porter's School in Farmington, Conn. On Oct. 10, Sarah Porter wrote to her brother. ". . . Miss N. Grant went away last week—Gov Jewell coming for her here & taking her to his house. I should not be utterly surprised if she comes back—Gen Porter & Mr. Belknap tried earnestly to persuade the mother to say she must stay—but in vain—It is a pity—she is a nice child—but no child could be unhurt by such attentions as she receives & she is greatly behind many girls in study—I was some what disgusted by Gov Jewell's subserviency. . . ." ALS, Miss Porter's School. On Oct. 13, Horace Porter wrote to Lt. Col. James H. Wilson that "I was in N. York Monday on my way home, bringing Nellie Grant from boarding school, where she got homesick, and was unfortunately allowed to return." AL (initialed), DLC-James H. Wilson. On Dec. 17, Orville E. Babcock wrote to Henry C. Bowen, New York City. "The President requests me to answer your letter of the 18th of November, and say that by accident the letter had been mislaid. He wishes me to communicate his thanks for your kind interest in his family and to inform you that at present his daughter Nellie will remain at home under private instruction." Copy, DLC-USG, II, 1. See letter to Ulysses S. Grant, Jr., Dec. 8, 1870; *New York Herald*, Sept. 30, 1870; *Cincinnati Enquirer*, Aug. 17, 1879; Mary Clemmer Ames, *Ten Years in Washington: Life and Scenes in the National Capital*, . . . (Hartford, Conn., 1875), pp. 254–55; Jesse R. Grant, *In the Days of My Father General Grant* (New York and London, 1925), p. 100; Ishbel Ross, *The General's Wife: The Life of Mrs. Ulysses S. Grant* (New York, 1959), pp. 218–19.

To Hamilton Fish

Boston Mass.
Sept 28th 1870.

DEAR GOVERNOR:

Dr. Draper,[1] of New York, who you no doubt know personally, goes to Europe, or starts for there, in about ten days. I am asked to give him letters to some of our representatives abroad and promised to do so on my return to Washington. You know the Drs. literary and scientific tastes, and his standing with the people of the U. States, and I wish you would have written in the State Dept.

for my signature, letters to Messrs Marsh,[2] Bancroft,[3] Washburne,
McVeigh[4] and such other ministers as you may think proper, by
the time I return, Sunday next.

Yours Truly

U. S. GRANT

HON. H. FISH
SEC. OF STATE

ALS, DLC-Hamilton Fish. On Oct. 3, 1870, USG wrote to George Bancroft,
U.S. minister, Berlin. "Doctor John W. Draper, President of the University
Medical College of New York visits Europe on a short tour without any public
or political object   You are probably aware of Doctor Drapers professional
eminence and of his great personal worth and social position. I desire to present
him to your acquaintance, and to commend him to such good offices as you may
be able to extend to him in his pursuit of health or of amusement." LS, DLC-
John W. Draper. On the same day, USG addressed identical letters to John
Jay, U.S. minister, Vienna, Wayne MacVeagh, U.S. minister, Constantinople,
and Elihu B. Washburne. *Ibid.*

1. Born in 1811 near Liverpool, John W. Draper studied at London University before emigrating to the U.S. to complete studies in science and medicine
and to begin a career that included important research on light, photography,
telegraphy, and physiology as well as publication in 1863 of the influential
History of the Intellectual Development of Europe.

2. On Feb. 21, 1869, Amasa Stone, Jr., Naples, wrote to USG. "You no
doubt have many advisers, and many of them no doubt have at least one eye to
their own welfare, but I am not aware that I have any other motive in the intrusion of this letter upon you, than to assist in making your administration (for
the success of which I contributed largely) a successful one—I have spent some
time in Italy and have come to the conclusion that Hon. Geo. P. Marsh is the
most influential and popular Embassador at the court of Florence, and that it is
a great credit to our country to have such a representative—You will have no
cause to complain of his acts while he remains there—I learned not through him
that your predecessor lately sent him a Mr Hay as secratary who is not of the
slightest assistance to him as he cannot read or write the Italian language successfully and besides that he is a man of no standing at home, that he tried to
get a living by preaching and failed from the want of piety and personal character—I think a new man in his place would be approved by every one, besides
relieving Mr Marsh from paying for the services of an extra secretary to perform the duties that belong to him . . ." ALS, DNA, RG 59, Letters of Application and Recommendation. On March 10, U.S. Senator George F. Edmunds
of Vt. *et al.* wrote to USG. "The undersigned respectfully, but earnestly urge as
the wish of the people and delegation of Vermont, that Hon George P Marsh be
retained as minister at Florence. Considering the political character and position
of our State, and that this is the only place of chief importance filled by one of
her citizens, as well as the lustre which the reputation and attainments of Mr
Marsh shed upon our nation, we think we do not, in asking this, ask too much."
LS (5 signatures), *ibid.*; LS (press), Marsh Papers, University of Vermont,

Burlington, Vt. On Nov. 5, 1870, Henry P. Hay, Philadelphia, wrote to USG. "Will pardon me for intruding myself on your attention; but I do it without solicitation, and on the behoof of a distinguished diplomat and scholar who is in entire accord with your administration, and an honor to our country. I refer to the Hon. George P. Marsh, the Minister of the United States to the Kingdom of Italy. As you are aware, he was appointed to that position by President Lincoln; which he has ever since most worthily filled; having also for eight years, at a previous time, represented our government in Turkey. Mr. Marsh besides being a highly accomplished literary gentleman, is thoroughly acquainted with the mysteries of European diplomacy, and is frequently consulted by the diplomats of other nations. I speak advisedly, having at one time, been connected with him, as the Secretary of our Legation in Italy. On account of his experience, would he not probably be able to fill satisfactorily the position of our Minister to England?" ALS, DNA, RG 59, Letters of Application and Recommendation. George P. Marsh continued as minister to Italy. See Young, II, 264, 266; David Lowenthal, _George Perkins Marsh, Versatile Vermonter_ (New York, 1958), pp. 281–82, 300.

3. On March 5, 1869, Bancroft wrote to USG. "Pray find time to accept my congratulations on your attaining the unsought for honor of the Presidency. Still more do I wish my country joy of the event. You have exactly that power which is required for the success of an administration, comprehensiveness of view joined with sureness of judgment & force of will to direct. Washington's administration was a glorious one, because he was in truth its chief. Van Buren, in his first three years, left his secretaries to act much on their own responsibility; & in those three years his course was full of reverses; in the fourth year he made himself in truth the head & centre, & his last year was an admirable one. Buchanan let things drift; and under a bright sky the treasury was all but bankrupt. The success of Polk's administration was due to his own vigilance over all. I have not learned, whether the treaty with England on the Oregon or rather Washington Boundary has been accepted by the Senate. We have been unjustly dealt with in former references of boundary questions: that of New-Hampshire was followed by a manifestly wrong award; & on the North Eastern Boundary, the king of Holland found the missing Highlands in the centre of the bed of a river. Of those who made or accepted the treaty now still unfulfilled, & followed the negotiation in all its forms, I alone or almost alone am left alive. Buchanan, Polk, Sir Robert Peel, Lord Aberdeen, as well as Marcy are dead. Our case has _not_ yet _been stated in all its force._ If it must be referred, I should think this court as safe a one as could be found: of the character of the umpire in Switzerland I know nothing. The terms of the treaty are made to suit the English pretensions. Pardon me for alluding to this subject; but of those Americans who watched the course of the negotiation most closely, & who were most trusted, I alone remain; & feel the warmest interest in the result. See what your office is; one of thought & labor; I cannot even wish you joy, without introducing business. I beg my best regards to Mrs Grant, . . . Count Bismarck, who had not dined once during the winter with one of the diplomatic corps, gladly accepted my invitation for yesterday out of his desire to prove to you his regard. I assure you we had a very pleasant time; I never saw Bismarck so much at his ease, & so full of mirth & frolic. ~~as well as gravity~~" ALS, USG 3. On March 4, Count Otto von Bismarck had cabled congratulations to USG. Telegram received (at 12:10 P.M.), DNA, RG 107, Telegrams Collected (Bound). On

March 13, Bancroft wrote to USG. "Congratulations & poems & letters on your induction to office continue to flow in upon me. One of the best, being in print, I send by mail. The Gothe Almanac sent to me for prints or photographs of you, intending to insert an engraving of you in their next volume. But a surer proof of confidence, & one which may encourage Mr Boutwell, is, that yesterday three millions of dollars of our bonds were bought at the Berlin Exchange, at prices varying from 87 to 88. One million was bought by a noted German one who a few years was a bitter friend of the secessionists; a proof that in the breasts of our bitterest enemies skepticism about our future is at an end." ALS, USG 3. USG retained Bancroft as minister to Germany. See *PUSG*, 17, 189–90; M. A. DeWolfe Howe, *The Life and Letters of George Bancroft* (New York, 1908), II, 221–26, 234–35; Russell B. Nye, *George Bancroft, Brahmin Rebel* (New York, 1945), pp. 258, 261–63; Lilian Handlin, *George Bancroft: The Intellectual as Democrat* (New York, 1984), p. 299.

4. On March 8, 1869, Jessup and Moore, Philadelphia, wrote to USG. "Mr Edward Joy Morris our Minister at Constantinople is a personal friend of ours. Mr Johnson was about recalling him when the Senate refused to ratify other nominations. Mr Morris is the only Minister of any Country who has ever caused a Moslem to be executed for the murder of a christian. He has defended the honor of the nation & the liberty of American citizens. He speaks almost every European language fluently, and also Arabic, Turkish & Persian. He is very kind & hospitable to Americans who visit Constantinople, and was loyal, thoroughly so during the War, at the same time neither abused the President, nor talked about Congress. He attended to the duties of his position, and was belied by the same Anonymous scribbler who defamed Motley & others. Hoping that you will bear the above in mind, . . ." ALS, DNA, RG 59, Letters of Application and Recommendation. Related papers are *ibid*. On June 1, 1870, Secretary of State Hamilton Fish recorded in his diary. "President sent me a note (recd in the vestibule) directing the appt of Mr McVey Wayne MacVeagh of Penn—as Minister to Turkey—I ask if he will not give Morris the opportunity to resign— he assents that I ask him by Telegraph to do so—" DLC-Hamilton Fish. On June 4, USG appointed MacVeagh, son-in-law of U.S. Senator Simon Cameron of Pa., as minister to Turkey, replacing Edward Joy Morris. On Dec. 13, Mac-Veagh, Constantinople, wrote to USG. "*Confidential* . . . I believe I have had about enough of the East, and I therefore forward by this mail my application for leave to return home. I write to ask you to do me the kindness to let Gen: Porter inquire at the Department and assure himself that the leave will be sent without unnecessary delay. My domestic reasons for coming home are imperative,—as indeed considerations of my private affairs are also,—but if these causes did not exist I would still be unwilling to stay away while ill-designing men are endeavoring to estrange from you the moral element in American politics in order to carry it to the support of such pure patriots and such Christian statesmen as Twead and Fisk and their man Hoffman—Some things have been done which, with the imperfect knowledge I have, appear to me to be of questionable political wisdom; but nobody has ever pretended that you were infallible. What your friends have asserted, and thank God can truly assert, is that your motives are as upright as your character, and that your only desire is to discharge the duties of your high office with fidelity to the best and highest interests of the people—I loathe and detest the unmoral practices of our politics as much as any man living, and am in favor of many of the changes of which

these disorganizers prate so much; but it makes ones blood boil to hear men talk of reform of corruptions and abuses while they are doing all in their power to hand the country over in 1872 to the tender mercies of the thieves and the harlots of the Tammany ring—Of course I will be quite ready to resign my commission when I reach home, but I am anxious that you should not consider the subject of my successor until after I have told you the true state of things here. My only desire is to give you light in deciding upon the *the kind* of man; and not at all to attempt to interfere in the choice of the individual. Remember both Mrs Mac Veagh and me to Mrs Grant, and in the hope of seeing you at an early day, . . ." ALS, USG 3.

To Abel R. Corbin

***

New York, Sept. 30th *1870*

DEAR SIR:

Your letter of yesterday is just rec'd, and answered by telegraph. I should like very much to go over and spend Sunday with you.

It does not seem that either Julia or myself can go now. I must be here for the funeral[1] to-day, and before leaving Long Branch myself and a portion of the Cabinet[2] agreed to dine at the Union League this evening. Mr Dent and Jesse are alone at the White House and Julia is anxious to get back to them as soon as possible. We thought therefore of going up to West Point in the morning to stay a few hours with Fred, who we will probably not be able to see again before June next, and go to Washington by the night train. If the storm makes any change of programme so that we can get to Elizabeth I will telegraph you.

Kind regards of myself and Mrs. Grant to Jennie and yourself.

Yours Truly,
U. S. GRANT.

MR. A. R. CORBIN,
ELIZABETH, N. J.

ALS, Northwestern University, Evanston, Ill.

1. On Sept. 30, 1870, USG attended the funeral of Admiral David G. Farragut. *New York Times*, Oct. 1, 1870.
2. Secretary of War William W. Belknap, Secretary of the Navy George M. Robeson, and Postmaster Gen. John A. J. Creswell. *Ibid.*

To Charles W. Ford

[*Sept. 1870*]

DEAR FORD your draft on me was "protested" without me, or any member of my family, knowing that it had ever been presented. It seems some one called at my house and enquired whether I was in. Finding I was not, without making known their business, the draft was protested. I enclose you therefore a check to pay the draft, Twenty dollars to pay the lawyer employed by Mr. McGuire, and Five dollars for the expense of protest.

I regard the movement headed by Carl Schurz, Brown & Co. as similar to the Tennessee and Va movements, intended to carry a portion of the Republican party over to the Democracy, and thus give them controll. I wish you would talk to Smith,[1] Newcomb[2] & Easton[3] about this. I hope you will all see your way clear to give the "regular ticket" your support.

U. S. GRANT

ALS, DLC-USG. On Sept. 20, 1870, U.S. Senator Carl Schurz of Mo., St. Louis, wrote to USG. "To day the St. Louis Tribune published the following article: . . . The statement, that 'the movement headed by Carl Schurz, Brown etc. is *intended* to carry a portion of the Republican party over to the Democracy and give them control,' has, I need hardly say, created great surprize among the many old and earnest Republicans, who, as true Republicans, support that movement. It occurs to me that in the article of the Tribune sentences may have been omitted which materially qualify that statement. I shall be greatly obliged to you if you will give me some information about that subject. I enclose also a copy of our address to the people of Missouri containing a plain and straightforward account of the causes of the rupture." ALS, USG 3. The newspaper clipping quoting USG's letter is *ibid*. See Thomas S. Barclay, "The Liberal Republican Movement in Missouri," *Missouri Historical Review*, XXI, 1 (Oct., 1926), 89–91; William E. Parrish, *Missouri Under Radical Rule, 1865–1870* (Columbia, Mo., 1965), pp. 308, 311.

On Dec. 3, M. A. Rosenblatt, Mo. Republican Committee, St. Louis, wrote to USG. "I take great pleasure in recommending to your Excellency's favorable consideration the Hon. Weston Flint of St Louis. He is the founder & Sole proprietor of the Saint Louis Tribune, the only paper, true to the regular Republican organization in this city. For five years, he has been, one of the most active & influential Republicans in the State. Besides his commendable services, he has sunk twenty thousand dollars in the attempt to establish the Tribune. No Republican in Missouri has done more for the Party with less reward than Mr Flint. I have therefore no hesitation, in saying, that before most others he is entitled to honorable recognition at the hands of the present National Administration." ALS, DNA, RG 59, Letters of Application and Recommendation. Related papers are *ibid.* On Dec. 6, 1871, USG nominated Weston Flint as consul, Chin Kiang.

1. On Feb. 15, 1870, USG had nominated Barnabas Smith as assessor of Internal Revenue, 2nd District, Mo.

2. On March 11, 1869, USG nominated Carman A. Newcomb as marshal, Eastern District, Mo. Letters recommending Newcomb are *ibid.*, RG 60, Records Relating to Appointments.

3. On April 5, USG nominated Alton R. Easton as assessor of Internal Revenue, 1st District, Mo. See *PUSG*, 1, 353; *ibid.*, 10, 90.

To Edward M. McCook

Washington D. C. Oct. 3d *1870*

DEAR GENERAL:

This will introduce to you Dr. Sam.l Bard,[1] Editor of the "True Georgian," published in Atlanta, Ga. and which has supported the present Administration from its commencement.

The Dr. wishes to make enquiries of you as to the probable support which a good, well conducted, reliable rebpublican paper might expect to receive in Colorado if he should decide to establish such there.[2] I hope you will give the desired information, and I am satisfied that Dr. Bard will give you a good paper, if he desides to settle among you, or none.

You will probably recollect Dr. Bard as having been appointed Govenor of Idaho by me,[3] an office which he resigned however, after confirmation by the Senate, to keep up his paper in Georgia.

Yours Truly

U. S. GRANT

GENL. ED MCCOOK
GOVR OF COL. TERR.

ALS, DLC-McCook Family. On Oct. 20, 1870, Governor Edward M. McCook of Colorado Territory wrote to USG. "Personal . . . I have forwarded you to-day two petitions from those German Colonists who Came here under the leadership of Carl Wulsten; their misfortunes have been such only, as always follow improvident reliance on future good fortune, and want of judgment in selecting some location for the Colony, where Nature would reward honest labor more bountifully than it has done. I am sure these are the first serious Cases of destitution occurring in the history of this Territory; and for it the sufferers themselves, and not the Territory are responsible. I have already Contributed myself, and Circulated a subscription for their relief; the amount secured will possibly be two thousand dollars. I have also procured work for about forty of them, so you see I have done all in my power for the relief of these impoverished and helpless Germans. I did not wish these petitions to form part of the many annoyances you are subjected to, but it is my duty to forward them, and I do so hoping that they may not lead you to change your opinion of this Country. You know, *Newspaper Eyes* are so sharp now days, that for the next month I shall live in perpetual fear of seeing double leaded headings announcing 'A famine in Colorado.' Mr Chaffee who was nominated as my Especial friend and Choice, has been Elected by the largest majority ever given any Candidate in this Territory; his actual majority is 1720. (Mr Bradfords, the present incumbent was 17) *seventeen,* (17) The official majority is however only 1392; 328 Voters having been disfranchised by Democratic County Commissioners refusing to Establish new precincts in localities where republican Colonists have recently settled. I hope Congress will pass a bill securing the right of suffrage to every Citizen. When I Come to Washington I will explain to you fully this system of disfranchisement. I received your letter in relation to Dr S Bard of the 'True Georgian,' and have written to him fully. Most of the papers here are edited with a pair of scissors and a paste pot; and a man of true genius, originality, and industry, would I think make a mark both for himself and the Country. I hope to welcome Dr Bard as a citizen of Colorado. This Territory has given Your Administration the best endorsement it has yet received, viz: Nearly *one thousand* per cent increase in the Republican majority; and I wish to see the number of your friends editorial and other, increase and multiply." ALS, DNA, RG 107, Letters Received from Bureaus. McCook enclosed a petition of Oct. 5 from Peter Rousselot *et al.* to USG. "In the name of Two Hundred and Fifty men Women and Children of the German Colonization Company of Colfax Fremont County Colorado—who are in a state of destitution, and in the name of humanity, we the undersigned residents of Wet Mountain Valley Colorado would appeal to your excellency that the Government take steps for their immediate relief by furnishing them provisions. They are hard working honest people—and have undertaken to develope a new & wild country & will succeed if they can subsist through the Comming winter. They are without money—all they possessed being invested in machinery which is being put up in a thourough & permanent manner—but all Covered by Mortgage to secure parties who have furnished them with food to date but who refuse to aid them further—rendering them unable to raise money on their property. Their crops have all failed from the early frost—We can assure your excellency that if the Government will furnish them provisions for the winter they will succeed—otherwise there *will be* much *suffering*—as they are far from friends unable to obtain Labor, & to remove their families where they can. This appeal is founded upon our knowledge of of the aforegoing facts, & we trust your excellency will inform them by return mail if they can hope for any immediate assistance from the Government" DS (15 signatures), *ibid.*

On Jan. 16, Carl Wulsten, president, German Colonization Co., Washington, D. C., had written to USG. "The German-Colonization Company of Colfax, Fremont County, and Colorado Territory, consisting of mechanics, laborers and farmers in very moderate circumstances, humbly asks Your Excellency to grant to them the following: 1. To cause such transportation as the members of this Company need for to reach their intended place of settlement in Wet-Mountain-Valley, Fremont County and Colorado Territory, to be furnished by the military authorities of the Western Military Department, at the terminus of the Kansas-Pacific Rail Road, where the said Company will disembark from the Rail Road's Cars about the middle of February, 1870, the departure of said Company from Chicago to be made to the resp. authorities. 2. To furnish one hundred tents to said Company to be used by the same for the protection of their families crossing the plains and at their new settlement intil the families can be sheltered in log-houses or abodes of their own at the terminus of the Kansas and Pacific Rail Road. The tents to be returned to the nearest military post Dezember the first 1870 in good order and condition or the Company to pay for them. 3. To ask the Governor of Colorado Territory to kindly furnish said German-Colony, being organized into the militia organization known as the Colfax Guards according to the statute of Colorado; arms of improved make, if possible the Winchester Rifle.) and sufficient amunition thereto at the terminus of said Kansas and Pacific Rail Road, and to muster said militia organization into the service of the Territory Colorado at said terminus of the Kansas-Pacific Rail-Road.—The Company will consist of about one hundred families and it will be necessary to furnish about one hundred and twenty Rifles and corresponding amunition. With such the Company can protect itself against eventual indian attacks—and need no military escort of any kind. The Company will build fortifications at their Settlement, if such will be allowed by the Government and will then keep up their military organization for the next five years." ALS, *ibid.*, RG 94, Letters Received, 106M 1870.

On Jan. 24, Gen. William T. Sherman telegraphed to Maj. Gen. John M. Schofield. "An German Emigrant Company of a hundred families wish to go from the End of the Kansas Railroad toabout the middle of February—to Wet Mountain Valley—Fremont County, Colorado and the President wants to transport them in Army wagons. If an order is made can you spare the wagons & teams and how many—" ALS (telegram sent), *ibid.*; copies, *ibid.*; *ibid.*, Letters Sent. On Jan. 29, Sherman wrote to Schofield. "You By special direction of the President you may supply the German Emigrant Company, under the leadership of Carl Wulsten with a tent per family not to exceed one hundred in the aggregate all, taking the receipt of the head of the Colony, and transportation from the End of the Railroad to Wet Valley Colorado not to exceed thirty five wagons, with one wagon master & the necessary teamsters to bring back the train." ADfS, *ibid.*, Letters Received, 106M 1870; copy, *ibid.*, Letters Sent.

On Jan. 20, Wulsten wrote to USG. "In my last application I ommitted to ask you for to sanction, that the German Colonization Company of Colfax, Fremont County, Colorado Territory be furnished also with two small howitzers upon carriages with catridge wagons and amunition thereto. The fact of such weapons being in the neighbourhood only, would tend to keeping the indians quiet and as the Colony intends to build up fortifications with permission of the government, two such 4 lbs carronades would greatly tend towards making the Colony secure. The Colony would be willing to pay for the same at the expiration of 5 years and would keep the canons in perfect order and condition. Hoping that the government will also grant this request, and the granting of which will save the government perhaps the keeping of troops in that region . . ." ALS, *ibid.*, RG 107, Letters Received from Bureaus. On Jan. 26, Sherman endorsed this letter. "Respectfully returned to the Secretary of War—If you wish to give away two howitzers &c this is a good chance, but the German Colony would soon find out that they were useless for their purposes, and abandon them by the road side." AES, *ibid.* On Feb. 23, Wulsten, Pond Creek, Kan., telegraphed to USG. "Can I expect any more wagons for the German Colony or not, Pray let me know as soon possible, no, or yes," Telegram received (on Feb. 24), *ibid.*; (press) *ibid.*, Telegrams Collected (Bound). On March 11, Sherman telegraphed to Schofield. "Mr. Carl Wilstan telegraphs from Cheyenne Wells, that he needs twenty more wagons to move his Colony—and that there are plenty at Fort Wallace. The President wants you to order them by or before the 20th." ALS (telegram sent), *ibid.*, RG 94, Letters Received, 106M 1870; copy, *ibid.*, Letters Sent.

On June 23, Wulsten, Washington, D. C., wrote to USG. "There is an other number of people ready to go to Colorado under my leadership. I would pray Your Excellency to again extend the assistance of this government to these people in reference to transportation from the terminus of the Kansas-Pacific Rail Road to their place of destination 'Wet-Mountain-Valley' in Fremont County and 'San-Luis-Valley' in Costilla County in the territory Colorado. The train of government wagons, which transported the German Colony to 'Wet-Mountain-Valley' was in charge of a wagonmaster alike rude and wantonly impertinent, who with some of his teamsters acted in many ways outrageously arbitrary and insulting. I would respectfully ask, that I either be entrusted with the command of any train of wagons for the purpose of transporting emigrants to Colorado or that an army officer be put in command thereof, ensuring the emigrants a courteous and decent treatment. If your Excellency can grant my humble request, I beg to be informed thereof through General Dent before leaving this city next week, when I will give due and timely notice to the War-Department of the exact starting time of our party from Chicago and Springfield Ill. I would also pray Your Excellency to provide our Colony, which is organized as territorial militia with two pieces of canon and necessary amunition to be used in case of emergency and actual attacks by Indians. The colony is living in perfect friendship with the Ute tribe of indians, but may any day be attacked by Apaches and the so called 'Dog soldiers,' who are said to have threathened to exterminate the 'heap Chicago men' now upon their former hunting grounds. So far, the indians generally look upon our settlement, in which I am causing the erection of a strong stockade for defensive purposes, with seeming respect, and as a military post. I uphold guard-duty and drill our men in the use of arms weekly. My plans are to establish one colony upon the other along the mountain valleys of Colorado and New Mexico and by so doing, settle the agrevating indian question in our vicinity peaceably and with lasting effect. Railroads will follow the track of these settlements in a short space of time and the red man will either settle down along its lines or recede into the farther off wilderness, intil he vanishes alltogether, thus allowing civilization to take its more rapid and steady course. By these settlements colonies or towns being made, the general government will save the upholding of expensive military posts, thus reducing actual expences and increasing taxeability, where none is now, opening wide tracts of vertile soil to the people, lessening the burdens of large cities and preventing the establishment of a 'proletariate' so dangerous to a republican form of government and detrimental to the moral status of society. The only and most perplexing difficulty I actually encounter in this enterprise is 'how shall I feed

these people I am bringing out, intil the first harvests can be obtained', and I
again pray Your Excellency to assist my honest endeavors to benefit mankind,
by allowing me to draw government provisions for those allready out and those
coming, intil I am enabled, by the harvested crops, to feed the hundreds without
further aid. I wish Your Excellency to understand, that I am not taking exclusively Germans out. All nationalities are represented in our midst and many
american born citizens have allready joined us. In my estimation it would even
pay this government to carry out the surplus population of large cities and feed
them out west upon homestead lands, intil the first crops are gathered. To enable
me to work better and more effectively I intend asking His Excellency Governor
Edward M. McCook to appoint me a commissioner of immigration to Colorado
Territory. Then, I could more readily bring this colonization business into a
successfull system. Delegate Allen A. Bradford and J. F. Chaves and other
territorial delegates to Congress I think will endorse my plans and endeavors.
In the hopes of meeting Your Excellency's views upon this matter, and praying
for due consideration of the same . . ." ALS, *ibid.*, RG 107, Letters Received,
W194 1870.

On Oct. 19, McCook wrote to USG. "I have the honor to herewith forward
petitions from the Officers and Members German Colonization Society of Colfax,
Fremont County, Colorado, asking the assistance of the Government to relieve
them from a state of destitution. I have, since the reception of their letter, subscribed as liberally as my means will allow, and induced other citizens to contribute towards buying and sending provisions to these suffering people; but the
amount raised will not be sufficient to furnish provisions during the whole
winter; Consequently I forward their petitions with the recommendation that,
if practicable the commanding officer of the nearest post, (Fort Reynolds) be
instructed to issue such rations as they may absolutely require." LS, *ibid.*, Letters
Received from Bureaus. See James F. Willard and Colin B. Goodykoontz, eds.,
Experiments in Colorado Colonization (Boulder, 1926), pp. xvii–xxiv, 29–133.

1. Born in 1825 in New York City, Samuel Bard moved south in 1845,
became a newspaper editor and Democratic politician, served in the C.S. Army,
and resumed his editorial activities as a Republican. See *New York Times*, Sept.
20, 1878.

2. On Oct. 4, 1870, Bard, Washington, D. C., wrote to McCook. "I have
the honor to hand you a letter from his Exellecy the President, asking your
Exellecy to post me, as to the propiety of establishing a *first class* Republican
paper—in your 'Terrytory—' Will you be good enough to do so at once, to
Atlanta Ga—" ALS, DLC-McCook Family.

3. On Nov. 17, 1868, Maj. Gen. George G. Meade, Atlanta, wrote to USG.
"*Personal* . . . Dr Saml Bard Editor of the New Era published in this city, is
about visiting Washington and proposes calling on you to confer in reference
to affairs in this state & to lay before you certain personal matters in which he
is specially interested. It is not necessary for me to say that Dr Bard in his
journal, has been a firm consistent, and energetic advocate of your election, &
if the State of Georgia failed to give you her vote, it was not from the want of
the the most strenuous efforts on his part to produce another result—This much
is fairly due Dr Bard—Nor will it be necessary for me to say to you as Dr B—
will confirm that I have in my administration acted independently of any consideration of the Press, or the influence it might bring to bear for or against

me—I can say the, and do with pleasure, that the course of Dr Bard in his journal by its moderation & conservatism and the light in which it has viewed the great questions of the day, has met with my approval & I have no doubt would with yours if you had had the time to carefully read & study it—I will leave Dr Bard to speak for himself & make known to you his views—the only object of this letter, is to call your especial attention to his case, and to say that his services so far as I can judge of them—not only entitle him to a hearing from you, but also to such favorable consideration, as the multitude of claims on you will justify.—" ALS, DNA, RG 59, Letters of Application and Recommendation. On Feb. 3, 1869, Meade endorsed a petition from "officers of the Army doing duty in the State of Georgia" requesting a federal appointment for Bard. "From personal knowledge of Dr Bard and the course of his paper since my being placed in command—I not only cheerfully concur in the within recommendation, but most strongly urge its being favorably receivd & acted on—" AES, *ibid.*

On March 1, Bvt. Maj. Gen. John Pope, Detroit, wrote to USG. "It gives me pleasure to be given an opportunity to say that Dr Samuel Bard of Georgia Editor of the Atlanta New Era, has been a consistent advocate of Reconstruction in Georgia ever since I first met him there in March 1867—He is a gentleman of education & character and his was the first paper in the South to advocate your nomination to the Presidency He gave my administration of the 3rd Mil District a cordial & efficient support of great value in the reconstruction of Georgia—I do not know what he wants (if any thing) from your Administration but I cannot in justice to him withhold this testimony of his consistent & valuable service to the Republican party during the last two years, nor to his gentleman-like & manly course in the process of restoring his State to its proper relations in the Union" ALS, *ibid.* USG endorsed a card attached to this letter. "To be placed with Dr. Bard's application for Governorship of New Mexico or Arazona." AN (initialed), *ibid.*

On April 2, Bard, Atlanta, telegraphed to USG. "*Private* . . . The appointment of James L. Dunning as Postmaster at Atlanta would be an injury to the Era. Pardon this liberty." Telegram received (at 2:20 P.M.), *ibid.*, RG 107, Telegrams Collected (Bound). On April 13, USG nominated James L. Dunning as postmaster, Atlanta. On April 17, U.S. Senator Richard Yates of Ill. wrote to USG. "Hon. Saml Bard, Editor of the Atlanta New Era, I have known for twenty two years. He is a man of high character and great ability, and has been a true loyal man. His paper, I have read, and it has contributed very largely to our successes in the South—He is in every respect competent and worthy of any position he would accept. I sincerely hope that he may be favored at your hands. Should it turn out that Col. Crow cannot take the appointment of Governor of New Mexico, I think Mr Bard would be admirably adapted to that position. . . . P. S. Should Mr Crow be able to take the oath, then I recommend Hon Mr Bard for Govr of Alaska—and really & sincerely hope he may be favored in this regard, or some other position equal to his merits." ALS, *ibid.*, RG 59, Letters of Application and Recommendation. On July 14, Joshua Hill, Rutledge, Ga., telegraphed to USG. "I recommend Samuel Bard of Atlanta for Marshal of Georgia" Telegram received (on July 15, 8:45 A.M.), *ibid.*, RG 107, Telegrams Collected (Bound).

On Jan. 18, 1870, Amos T. Akerman, U.S. attorney, Ga., Elberton, wrote to USG. "Dr. Samuel Bard has retired from the New Era of Atlanta. His conduct of that paper has been discreet, concilatory and firm. He has endeavored to show the Southern people that the government of the United States, as at present administered, is their friend, and will exercise no rigor except what is made necessary by their own perversity. Because he has sought to cure, rather than to aggravate, this perversity, he has been sometimes accused of a lukewarm attachment to the Republican party. This is a great mistake. He is convinced that the welfare of the country, and particularly of the South, is bound up with the success of that party; but it has appeared to him the part of wisdom to undermine rather than to assault the prejudices which prevail here against that party. As a man of prudence, capacity and integrity and of devotion to the Republican party, he is worthy of an honorable appointment under your administration, and I warmly recommend him for any place requiring those qualities." ALS, *ibid.*, RG 59, Letters of Application and Recommendation. On Jan. 20, Thomas P. Robb, collector of customs, Savannah, wrote to USG. "I respectfully beg leave to address you in behalf of my personal friend, Dr Samuel Bard. In the spring of 1866, I became pecuniarily interested with him in the purchase of 'Atlanta New Era', and have known him since well and intimately. Against him, in all his business transactions, both of a public and private nature, I have never heard the faintest whisper of suspicion, and speaking for myself, I can say, that in all my own individual business relations with him, I have ever found him the soul of honor and integrity. In the conduct of the 'New Era', as its Editor, I am convinced Mr President, that he has ever acted conscientiously, regardless of personal consequences, with a view only to what he deemed the good of the Republican party, and the well-being and success of the Administration. I know of no man in Georgia, who, in my opinion deserves more, and has received so little at the hands of the party with which he is identified. Could he be consistently appointed by you to some Federal Office of honor and Emolument, I am satisfied that it would be not only acceptable to the great majority of Republicans in this State, but that it would also be an appointment that would reflect much credit upon the government and the administration." LS, *ibid.* Related papers and *ibid.*; *ibid.*, RG 60, Appointment Records. On Feb. 4, USG nominated Bard as governor, Idaho Territory. On May 20, Bard resigned the governorship prior to confirmation. LS, *ibid.*, RG 59, Letters of Resignation.

On Dec. 12, 1872, USG nominated Bard as postmaster, Chattanooga. On Jan. 7, 1873, USG wrote to the Senate. "I have the honor to return herewith, in answer to the resolution of the Senate, of the 20th. of December last, requesting it, the Senate resolution of the 12th. of December advising and consenting to the appointment of Samuel Bard to be Deputy Postmaster at Chattanooga, Hamilton County, Tennessee, and accompanying papers." LS, *ibid.*, RG 46, Executive Nominations. USG enclosed letters, petitions, and newspaper clippings protesting the nomination. *Ibid.*, Papers Relating to Nominations. On Jan. 9, the nomination was withdrawn at Bard's request. On Dec. 15, USG nominated Bard as postmaster, Atlanta.

To Jacob D. Cox

Washington, D. C. October 5th 18670

HON. J. D. COX;
SEC. OF THE INT.
DEAR SIR:

Your letter of the Third inst. tendering your resignation as Sec. of the Interior, is just received. As suggested by you it will be accepted to take effect upon the completion of the Annual report of the departpment now being prepared to accompany my message to Congress.

In parting company permit me to say that I highly appreciate the zeal and ability which you have ever shewn in the discharge of all of your official duties. I hope your relations in the new sphere you have pointed out for yourself will prove as pleasant as our relations have been in the past, to me, and that you may fully realize your brightest expectations.

> With highest regards
> Your obt. svt.
> U. S. GRANT

ALS, Jacob D. Cox Papers, Oberlin College, Oberlin, Ohio. On Oct. 3, 1870, Secretary of the Interior Jacob D. Cox, Staten Island, N. Y., had written to USG. "When Congress adjourned in the Summer, I was credibly informed that a somewhat systematic effort would be made before their reassembling in the winter, to force a change in the policy we have pursued in the Interior Department. The removal of the Indian service from the sphere of ordinary political patronage has been peculiarly distasteful to many influential gentlemen in both houses, and in order to enable you to carry your purposes out successfully, I am satisfied that you ought not to be embarrassed by any other causes of irritation in the same Department. My views of the necessity of reform in the civil service have brought me more or less into collision with the plans of some of our active political managers, and my sense of duty has obliged me to oppose some of their methods of action through the Department. I have no doubt whatever that public sentiment will sooner or later sustain these efforts at what I regard needed reforms; but I ought not to overlook the fact that for the present they involve opposition which it may not be for the interest of your Administration to provoke, and as my personal tendency is to be rather more than less persistent in the course to which I am committed, I deem it my duty to place in your hands my resignation of the office of Secretary of the Interior, to take effect as soon as you can conveniently determine upon my successor. The annual report of the Department will be made at an early day, and for this and other reasons I believe the interval prior to the adjourned session of Congress the fittest for such a change. I trust you will permit me to add that as the original acceptance of the position was an interference with plans of life formed as I think with prudence, a return to my private business, so far from being an inconvenience or a disappointment, will only be carrying out what I have most desired to do as soon as it could be done without embarrassment to you or sacrifice of public duty. Indications that you might be already troubled by suggestions on the subject, have induced me to write at once, without waiting my return to Washington. With sincere assurances of my strong desire for the complete success of your administration, . . ." ALS, USG 3.

On Oct. 4, Secretary of State Hamilton Fish recorded in his diary. "Boutwell was saying something about the suggestion that the law establishing the Interior Dept had been repealed by the law passed at the last Session, relating to the Patent Office—and mentiong an opinion published in the papers by Judge Paschal said that the 'McGarrahan' claim was at the bottom of that opinion as he heard that the Secy of the Interior had issued a Patent to the New Idria Co— The President, with much animation & more feeling than I almost ever saw him exhibit, enquired if that were so—Boutwell replied that 'he believed so—had heard so'—President instantly answered 'if it be so, I shall have a new Secretary of the Interior within an hour after knowing that fact' He then mentioned having expressed his wish many months, & having told Gov Cox, at a Cabinet meeting, that he did not wish any Patent issued to either party—that Congress had taken the subject in their hands & he intended to let them decide it—That after hearing that Argument had been heard before the Secy of the Interior, he wrote him, desiring that no patent should be issued, & had received while at Long Branch, a letter from Gov Cox, which had not pleased him—that after speaking very severely of the Counsel in the case, he concluded, by saying 'that he had labored to administer his Department honestly & to keep it free from fraud, corruption, & that if his efforts in that direction were not sustained by the President he would desire to be relieved from his Office' President said he was fond of Cox, & appreciated his thorough integrity, & that his Dept had been better administered by him, than ever before—but this remark had 'cut him severely'—He had shewn the letter to Robeson at Long Branch—While speaking of it, he took a bundle of letters from his drawer, & selected this letter of Cox—& read the passage, which I have given above from memory—He evidently has been much disturbed" DLC-Hamilton Fish. See letter to Jacob D. Cox, Aug. 22, 1870.

On Oct. 13, Horace Porter wrote to U.S. Senator Zachariah Chandler of Mich. "Your letter of the 8th was received. The affair is not to take place till the Secretary finishes his annual report. He is hard at work on it now, or at least is getting in his subordinate reports, but I do not expect it to be done for nearly three weeks. The President is anxious to keep the matter perfectly quiet till it culminates. I am as impatient as you are about it. Good for Penn & Ohio!" ALS, DLC-Zachariah Chandler. On Oct. 18, Manning F. Force, Cincinnati, wrote to USG. "Dont let Governor Cox withdraw from the cabinet. The announcement has produced great anxiety. The great body of men of character throughout the country, are not active politicians. They constitute the political landwehr, and determine the battle in emergencies. The war made them rally to the republican party. They constitute its reserve strength They recognize Gov. Cox' high character and the purity of his administration of affairs. Every

where they regard his resignation as an ill omen. Dont let the republican reserves lose confidence." ALS, OFH. On Oct. 21, Orville E. Babcock wrote to
Chandler, Detroit. "*Personal* . . . Your letter came in due time. The Cox question
is out, and makes some noise. Delano goes in. Boutwell is evidently trying to put
his man in Delanos place, and has gone so far as to suggest Richardson. Now
there must be a true man put th[er]e, one who will remain true to the President,
and not run that department for any one, but the President. I think Delano should
name his successor, and I think Belknap & Creswell, will support him. It might
be well for you to write to Creswell and tell him how important it is to have
a true man there, and that he must unite with Del and secure a man, that will
not belong to Boutwell. We want some one who will carry out Delanos system,
and will be true to the party. Of course you will not allow Creswell to know
that I suggest your writing. Morton has diclined the English Mission, and the
President has accepted the declension. Morton wrote a beautiful letter, it is
sound. Old man in good spirits, has no one in his mind for England. I have been
to see Edmonds (Judge) and had a long talk with him. The President likes the
idea of a permanent organization—for the press. Remember me to the good
people at home." ALS, DLC-Zachariah Chandler.

On Oct. 19, Cox, Washington, D. C., wrote to Porter. "Either you have
misapprehended the purport of Judge Metcalfe's note, or I have not rightly
understood the direction given by the President to Judge Otto in my absence—
I understood that the President directed that leaves of absence in usual form be
granted to clerks going home to vote, *so as to be in uniformity with the other
Departments.* As the matter was performed under that direction, I desire to
know whether the request for an extra grant of time is understood to be made
in the other Departments, so that ours may be made in the same way—You will
see that the request is for an *extension* of leaves already granted under the
President's direction—Probably Judge M. failed to convey this idea, and my only
purpose is to follow the rule of uniformity above suggested—I should not trouble
you again, but Judge M's note was written when I was busily engaged in other
matters & I did not see it." Copy, Cox Papers, Oberlin College. On the same day,
Porter had written to George T. Metcalfe, chief clerk, Dept. of the Interior. "I
have to acknowledge the receipt of your Communication of this date, enclosing
an application requesting that the clerks in the Interior Department, who reside
in the cities of New York and Brooklyn, may be granted a leave of absence for
ten days—the time required to register and vote at the November election. The
President directs me to say that the heads of departments are authorized to grant
all such leaves of absence and that an Executive order in the case will not be
necessary" Copy, DLC-USG, II, 1. On Oct. 20, Porter wrote to Cox. "I have
just received your note of yesterday in regard to the leaves of absence requested
by the clerks. The President & I both misunderstood Gen. Metcalf's letter in
regard to the application being for an extension of leaves already granted. The
President has not given any particular instructions to the heads of departments,
but I find that in the Treasury, and, I believe, some of the other departments,
the clerks from New York, state have been granted leaves to include the 1st and
8th of November, and for the sake of uniformity the President requests that
you will grant the full time applied for. He will give similar instructions to the
other departments." Copy, *ibid.*

On Oct. 18 and 22, Cox wrote to Ebenezer R. Hoar, Concord, Mass. ". . . I
promised you a somewhat fuller story of my resignation, yet I hardly know what

there is to say. Your leaving us as you did, utterly broke down my faith in the President's ability to stand up against the combined efforts of intriguing politicians, and from that moment I was resolved to anticipate them, whenever it should become probable that he would be likely to yield in a way to compromise my plans with regard to the administration of my own department. I told you of the issue I was obliged to make with him on the McGarrahan business. To my letter on that subject he never replied, and has never even alluded to it until since my resignation, when I for the first time learn that he felt hurt at the emphatic way in which I declared that he must either stand by me or relieve me. He has since given explicit directions that no action shall be taken by my Department on that case till after the next session of Congress, although I have told him that the rascality of the whole proceeding & their abuse of the department itself had been such that I should regard myself as stopped from doing my plain duty by the mere bullying of the McGarrahan set. I had no sooner gone on my vacation a month ago, than the attack opened in form. The so-called Pennsylvania association was only the cat's paw, used by Chandler, Cameron, & that ilk to make a noise under cover of which they intended to make their attack on the President's purposes. The first sign of giving way was in Indian matters. Under the President's express authority I had divided the Indian Country among the several mission associations, & among these had given to the Am. Mission Assocn, the Lake Superior region, including Mackinaw & upper Michigan. The Commission for the Mackinaw agency was made out. The person selected had abandoned other employment & was about starting for his post when Chandler wrote to the Prest in his own name & Howard's protesting & insisting upon the reinstatement of the old agent who had made way for an Army officer. The President sent Chandler's letter to the Dept with an endorsement which Judge Otto regarded as a direction to appoint Chandler's man, putting it however, upon the ground that the person had been a methodist minister formerly & therefore was within our rule—ignoring the essential fact that systematic coöperation with the *Societies* was our plan which was thus broken. As I expected, I immediately received a warmly expostulatory letter from the disappointed assocn., asking 'what does this mean?' and protesting against being treated so, as well in their own behalf as in that of the person they had induced to accept the agency. Explanation was impossible. About this time the papers announced Chandler & Cameron as calling on the Prest & insisting upon a change of my rule in regard to sending clerks home to vote. Last year we allowed them to go as an additional vacation but I then notified the Department that *this* year they would be expected to bring such absence within their usual thirty days vacation or else forfeit pay for the extra time. The President gave Judge Otto explicit orders not to observe this rule, made with such ample warning. Chandler went into my Dept & both to Judge Otto & to Gen. Walker of the Census Bureau stormed about my action, saying significantly that six members of the Cabinet & the President were together on these subjects, and they would soon have *seven*. The papers were regularly supplied with Washington Despatches intended to prepare the way for a change, & I think I should have been very blind not to recognize the fact that the time had come when I must bring matters to a focus. My mode of doing it & the result you will see in my letter of resignation & the President's reply, of which I enclose copies, asking you to burn them when read so as to provide agt accidental publicity which I have reason to think the President would dislike. My letter was written at Staten

Island on Monday & mailed in New York Tuesday, reaching Washington of Course on Wednesday, the 5th, the same day on which as you will notice, the acceptance is dated. When you have read both & considered this fact of dates, I think you will see that but one conclusion could be drawn—I had not acted too soon. In my letter I intended to 'call a spade a spade', but did not wish to go out on it, if the President was disposed to give me good backing. Had he said, 'You are mistaken about my being embarrassed by your action, & I will guaranty you freedom in carrying out your ideas,' I should willingly have remained. Whatever embarrassment there is in his most unexpected *form* of meeting the issue I presented was not of my intending. I certainly thought he would at least have expressed some general approval of the Civil Service reform, even if he ac~~ac~~cepted the resignation on the ground that I had personal controversies on my hands. I think he sees this now, & shall be surprized if he does not try to correct the error in his message in some way. But outside of all this, I have been glad to get away because of the general drift of affairs. I understand that the English mission was offered successively to Frelinghuysen Trumbull, Morrill of Maine, Edmunds, & Howe, with the intention of then offering it to Blaine. All declined, but instead of offering it to Blaine, the President suddenly gave it to Morton. You know my opinion of Morton & that I had very pointedly expressed it to the President. True, none of us were consulted except Mr Fish, (who certainly did not like it), but the nomination itself, in view of such known opinions is very like an intimation of want of confidence. If Morton thinks he can gain importance by stirring up a war with England, look out for squalls. Again, the proscription of the followers of Gratz Brown & Schurz I look upon as very unwise. Their bolt looks to me unwarranted, but the administration cant *afford* to proscribe them, and had no need of doing it. Would it have been done but for Schurz's action ~~of~~ on St Domingo? I think we both know how much the President is influenced by considerations which he does not fully acknowledge or define to himself, and the conviction is fastened on me that untoward influences have the upper hand, & I should only be compromised by staying, without doing any real good. So I go. The President is personally cordial & has expressed himself more kindly than I could have asked, but he gives 'no sign' upon the questions of administration on which my issue was made. He says he will stick to the Indian policy & I most earnestly hope he may. . . ." "Your last, acknowledging mine of 18th, is just received. Since writing that letter, I have learned the particulars of the cabinet meeting of Tuesday the 4th Oct. (the day before the President received and accepted my resignation) which throw some further light upon his action. Please recall the situation as it stood up to that time. The President had, on an *ex parte* statement from some one in McGarrahan's pay, written me from Long Branch, directing that no patent should issue on the New Idria Company's application (the only one then pending before me) till he should give explicit directions to that effect, & intimating that no such directions would be given till after the next session of Congress. I had responded to this most earnestly and half indignantly, protesting against such a mode of interfering with the Department. He seems to have brooded over this but said nothing & gave me no reply. Then came the efforts of the intriguers to overrule me in the matter of my general departmental administration. He had made a break in the system of Indian appointments, and had ordered Judge Otto to revoke my rule as to leaves of absence. At this point came the cabinet meeting to which I have referred. In the course of that meeting Boutwell remarked that I had issued the patent to the New Idria Company. The President started & flushed; and said What! Boutwell repeated the remark. Grant then said angrily, If the Sec to sign patents has put my name to that patent I will have him out *instanter*. He then declared that he had given me explicit directions not to have that patent issued without his own order. On this Boutwell said his information must have been incorrect then—for he had no idea that I would issue the patent under such circumstances. Some allusion was then made to the possibility of Wilson (the Land Commr) having done it, the President being evidently under strong irritation. He then fumbled in his drawer, & took out my letter which was written to him at Long Branch in regard to the business, and went on to remark that he had recd a letter from me on that subject which cut him to the quick. He read a detached clause from it, in which I said that as I had only been conscious of fighting fraud with vigor, I must beg him, if I failed to meet his full approval, to relieve me of duties in which without his support I was sure to fail utterly. He then remarked that if he had answered that letter the day he received it, his answer would certainly have been a request for my immediate resignation. To this however, he added some exceedingly complimentary remarks as to my departmental administration—said he really believed the department had never been more honestly or better managed, & that he had the highest esteem for my own character & purposes &c. He interpreted my letter as an insinuation that *he* desired to protect fraud,—a most mistaken interpretation as you shall see from a copy of the letter before long. He added that he had since been glad that he had not answered me, as he should have been sorry to make a break in the cabinet on such grounds. This new statement that the Department had disregarded his direction had induced him to speak of it before the cabinet. You will mark the characteristic fact that he had never intimated displeasure or dissatisfaction to me, or even alluded to the subject, although we had several times met in the interval. Neither has he explained himself on the point to me since he has accepted my resignation, except, in response to direct questions which I put to him after learning the facts. But to return. The cabinet meeting took place on Tuesday, & Judge Otto's accidental absence had prevented a contradiction of the false report on the spot. I doubt whether the President had the evidence of its falsity yet before him, when next morning my letter of resignation came, & he did what he had been glad he did *not* do at Long Branch—he answered on the spot. Of course, he was then ashamed to recall it & explain his action, & his strong natural tendency to drift with fate helped to keep him from frankly telling me he had made a mistake when we met personally—whilst the very character of his acceptance effectually closed my mouth. The thing which troubled me most in the whole business is the fact that the President whilst withholding the correspondence, allows it to be given out as from 'the best authority' &c, that purely personal & family reasons were assigned by me for my act, & that there was no divergence or even question on the matter of the civil service Reform. Crounse, of the N. Y. Times (who is reputed a truthful man) says the President told him this with his own lips. It is even said, on strong evidence, that a letter from the White House to the Editor of a New York paper, (whose name I am not permitted to repeat) assigns exactly the same causes of my action. The unexpected response in public sentiment has invested the transaction with so much more than common importance that I despair of any permanent concealment of the facts, and may be forced to allow the letters to be published in self protection; for after all the stir

in the public mind I should be justly blamed if I had permitted the storm to
gather when there was no truth in the almost universal assumption that the
facts were somewhere near what we know them to be. It would be an attempt to
gather reputation on false pretences for which a man ought to be execrated, &
I should expect to be, if I had done so. A word as to the expression of public
sentiment as it has appeared in the press. Friends have sent me from all parts of
the country, extracts from the papers which show a universality of support ready
to be given a true reform, that is perfectly marvellous. The exceptions are so
few & so insignificant that they prove the rule with a vengeance. One could
weep for grief that Grant had not divined this, and trusting his better impulses
& sympathies given you & me such open & hearty backing as to have made his
administration the Era of a memorable & healthy change in our administrative
history. . . ." Copies, Cox Papers, Oberlin College. On Nov. 2 and 4, Henry V.
Boynton, Washington, D. C., wrote to Cox. ". . . I had a talk with Morton this
afternoon. He was very guarded, but the little he said rather confirmed the assurance I had had elsewhere during the day, that the President has decided to
send the McGarrahan correspondence out. If it goes tonight, I am promised a
sight of it, & whatever comment may be with it. It may be of a character that
we can send a swift antidote along with it. Morton said he heard the President
explain that he read your letter of resignation through hastily, & without considering it further than to see that it was a resignation, wrote his letter of
acceptance & sent it off without even keeping a copy. Morton seemed *very*
anxious to know if I had seen the McGarrahan correspondence. . . ." ". . . I
hear, *in a direct* way, that the President construes your letter to him at Long
Branch on the McGarrahan case as evidence that you were strongly on the side
of New Idria, & that your letter was plainly an *argument* for them to him. He
seems to be as blind to its real character, & to the effect its publication will have
as he was in regard to the letters attending the resignation. . . ." ALS, *ibid.*

On Oct. 28 and Nov. 9, Babcock wrote to Chandler. "*Personal* . . . Yours at
hand. I have not been able to see Clendining yet—shall try to do so soon. They
should *pony* up—in N. Y. & Phil. Murphy has his hands about full just now,
with all of their quarrels there—but he should *come down with the money.* No
news. Cox goes in a day or two. No successor to Delano. Belknap, Creswell,
Robeson & Delano, and *P & I*, have united on Pleasanton, but Boutwell has
defeated us so far. There are a thousand good reasons why Pleasanton should
be made. He is the Dept. Has broken up fraud in N. Y. Has had the nerve to
go for the illicit distilleries in N. Y. is a purely Grant man. Has no scheme of
his own, and has the entire Confidence of Delano who should name his successor—besides many other reasons. I think it would be a good thing for you to
write to the old man. You can post the enclosed slip from the newspaper in
your letter—as an introduction to the subject. Boutwell should not be allowed
to control that office—. The old man should appoint Pleasanton. All well here.
No news. No new *Minister* to England. We are safe for 7th, I think but a bad
man in Delanos place, one that would unite with B—to make capital against
the old man would do much harm. . . . P. S. You must write promptly, or it will
be too late." ". . . No Comr of Int Revenue yet. We are much afraid that Geo B—
will slip a man in there, and if there is a place that wants watching it is the
Treasury. Will you be in W. before the early part of Dec? Trumbull was in to
see the Prest. yesterday—he does not uphold Coxe's Course. John Sherman was
in to day and he does not. The *ejection* did not come too soon, and the old gentle-

man thinks so to. It would have been better to have followed the advice of some friends and applied the foot as he went out.—. . ." ALS, DLC-Zachariah Chandler. USG nominated Alfred Pleasonton as Commissioner of Internal Revenue. On Oct. 31, Porter wrote to Lt. Col. James H. Wilson. ". . . Cox has just cleared out, and if any government ever had a more negative figure-head in its councils I should like to see him. He has published ~~his letter~~ the correspondence upon his resignation which merely proves him a suspicious creature, conscious that he was giving satisfaction no where. The Presidents mistake was in not squelching Cox's insinuations in his letter accepting the resignation. I wanted this done, but good nature again prevailed. Delano is the choice of every one who knows him. . . ." ALS, DLC-James H. Wilson.

On Dec. 15, Cox, Cincinnati, wrote to Hoar. "The various troubles incident to moving and getting settled left me less leisure last month than I expected, and having promised Henry Adams to write an article on Civil Service Reform for the North American, I was obliged to neglect answering your letter till now. With you, I regarded it as incomprehensible that the President should have published the McGarrahan correspondence, with any idea that it tended to explain the true reason for my resignation. That, it certainly could not do, and in as far as it might be held to indicate any reasons for his acceptance of the resignation, I dont see how he could honestly expect to profit by it. I can understand how men of the Chandler sort could have thought that the mere pretence of something connected with that business might be enough to raise suspicion of my character & motives, and have reckoned upon the unscrupulous party organs taking it up and making charges of corruption out of what could not be dire[ct]ly traced to the President's own assertion; but I have been very unwilling to believe that Grant would become party to an attack of that kind. Yet it is hard to avoid the effect of the evidence which goes to show a willingness to use disingenuous means of getting out of his embarrassment. In my last letter I referred to the unquestionable fact that he had repeatedly given to newspaper correspondents & others, what he declared to be the *substance* of my letter of resignation. In one instance he went so far as to enumerate five different reasons of a personal & pecuniary nature which he said were given in the letter; the whole five being fabricated then & there, & no one of them being in the letter. Again he declared to another man that up to that time there had been no correspondence in regard to my resigning, although this was at least a fortnight after his acceptance of the resignation. Finally came the Associated Press dispatch of one of the last days of October. Knowing Gobright's caution in such matters, I sent for him the day before I left Washington, and asked him how he got the information He said it was from the President himself. I then showed him the resignation correspondence in order that he might know how incorrect his statements had been. He expressed regret but said that he of course had to assume that information from such a source was indisputable. I then asked him to go to the President & say from me, that I regarded it a duty to myself to let the correspondence itself be published, as otherwise I must be in a false position which would be intolerable to me. Gobright said he could hardly venture to go to the President, but he could say that in the very conversation they had had, he had intimated that I might give the correspondence out, & the President had said that if I did so he should have no objection, but that *he* himself could not properly do it. The unpleasant feature of all this is the constant and painful effort to carry the idea that it was only out of delicacy to me that there was any hesitation in allowing the letters to be published. There is an insincerity about it, to use the mildest phraze, which has not tended to reassure me in regard to the purpose and the motives in the publication of the McGarrahan letters. It was asserted in some of the papers that the Forney-Thayer clique had declared that I must be entirely broken down in character, in order to save the President from the effects of my resignation; and after the use of a reasonable degree of charity I am of opinion that they deliberately seized upon this mode of doing it, and that the President assented to it with more or less explicitness. It is notorious in Washington that Forney is a stockholder in McGarrahan's claim, and this would make his political and his pecuniary interests work well together. The attempt failed, and after a series of most damaging inconsistencies in statement, and a ludicrous array of officially authorized explanations which ate each other up, the final position of the President as stated in Spinner's letter, was that he agreed with me that the McGarrahan claim was a swindle, but he wanted Congress to pass some special law for the sale of the land for public benefit, and didn't think the New Idria people had any rights. The 'saving the land for the people' seems to have been Ben. Butler's dodge, & is simply contemptible. No intimation of that sort had ever come from him to me, or had been put forward in Congress or out of it that I can learn. The land had been 'saved for the people' when the Supreme Court rejected McGarrahan's claim & the land reverted to the public domain; and we were treating it just as we treat the public lands containing minerals of value, under the general laws. So far as this controversy has gone, I dont think the President can take much satisfaction in it, and he must be aware that he has lost the respect of those of us who knew how untrue have been the assertions on which it has been sought to give the public the idea that a just dissatisfaction with my conduct in this matter had been the real ground of separation. A statement was published in the 'World,' & simultaneously in the Presidential organ here, which declared that when the Cabinet was organized, Grant told us all together that he didnt want this case touched. You & I both know that nothing could be more untrue than this, yet the statement was manifestly prepared at the White House, and after the introductory words by the correspondent, the rest of it was printed within quotation marks, showing that it was given in written form; and I happened to get evidence here that it came from Washington in that way. We know also that the case was frequently up in Cabinet meetings, down to the time of your argument before the Supreme Court, and the reversal of the *mandamus*. I cannot recall a word or expression from the President during all that time that intimated any disagreement with my often avowed purpose of going forward with the New Idria claim whenever the Supreme Court had disposed of that obstacle. I had notified the Judiciary Comee of the House & the parties that such was my attitude, and I shd have been ready to take it up the day after the Supreme Court gave their judgment, had not the parties stipulated before the Comee to wait till the Comee's investigation was concluded. If you remember anything which modifies or contradicts this, I shall be glad to credit the President with it; but my own memory was so void of any dissent on his part or on that of any member of the cabinet, that his Long Branch letter quite astounded me, when it came to interrupt what I then regarded & still regard as the only proper course of proceedure. There were circumstances about the interference that made it peculiarly galling. I was anxious to carry out his ideas to the letter, and the old man who was the Sec. to sign patents being sick, I sent him the

President's instructions in a note. That same night the note was stolen from the old man's room, and the substance of it telegraphed to the newspapers all over the Country with the assertion that it was a Presidential interference to stop my improper action in the case. Mr White, the Sec, insisted that no one had been in his room but our detestable friend I. N. Morris, whom he suspected of taking the paper. Meanwhile also the McGarrahan set, headed by Pascal, had written such abusive & insulting communications to the Department that I felt bound to refuse to allow them to go on file. P. repeated it, and I directed that he should be suspended from practice before the Dept. Then they published their abuse in full, in the Chronicle; deliberately trying to scare me from my duty by the fear of some of their dirt sticking. You can imagine my disgust, when, in the midst of all this, I found that some one of them, by running to Long Branch had got a letter from the President giving them the delay to continue their operations before Congress which they had failed of getting either by their new attempt to use the District Court, or by bullying me. Under the circumstances, my only wonder is that my letter to the President was so moderate—and I would not take back a word from the vigor of my implied protest against such unwarrantable interference with the legal duty of the Department. He ought to have responded, and in lapsing into a moody silence, he did me a wrong & did himself no credit. My suggestion of a cabinet meeting was the best way out for him—yet he did not notice it. I forgave him all this at the time, because I did not know what his published statements have since proven, that the *natural* interpretation of his conduct was the true one, and that it was not his habitual reticence that kept him silent. *My* indignation has arisen since I have learned from his own statements, that he was brooding over the matter, carrying it in his mind to be used as a concealed reason for some subsequent act. This process of disillusion as to his character has not been a pleasant one, for I am not naturally fond of breaking my idols. But take it as it stands—he now is in the attitude of telling the country that he took no notice of my letter in August, giving me no answer, and avoiding all subsequent reference to the subject, *yet* it was the 'true reason' why he accepted my resignation! Further still, that when I wrote a resignation giving *my* reasons, his answer which made no reference to the reasons alleged by me, was equally silent as to those which he now says influenced him! Can it be possible that he thinks this a creditable course of conduct for a President toward a Cabinet officer? I believe the judgment of intelligent people throughout the country has answered that in a way that *I*, at least, have no cause to complain of. The final act of the farce seems to me to be worthy of Sancho Panza's government. I mean his jumping astride of the Civil Service Reform in his message, and looking around to see whether the world does not believe he was there all the while! It was no doubt intended to be part of the proof of my charlatanism, and to clinch the argument that I had been trying like a very demagogue to go out of office on false pretences of reform, while in fact I was dismissed for corruption in the McGarrahan case. The trick was worthy the astute advisers Grant has been listening to instead of heeding & advising with his cabinet; but he must bear the responsibility of having assented to it & done his best to carry it out, even to the final act. That the public have seen through the maneuvre, makes my feeling contemptuous, whereas had they succeeded I should have been wrathfully bearing the burden of an undeserved public disgrace & real loss of reputation. What can we say of the moral perceptions of a man who would make such an attempt to destroy one of whom he has professed the opinion he has of

me, not simply before our August correspondence, but down to the very day I
left, and the day that this plot was invented? I have not referred to the implication of yourself in these attempted aspersions of me, because I really think
that Grant's intellect is so slow that he was not aware of their being any implied
censure of your opinion in the McGarrahan case. If he had been, however, it
could only be of a piece with the rest. He always spoke of you with the greatest
appearance of sincere respect & regard, and I hold it to be one of the prerogatives
of conscious rectitude which you & I may both use, to say that he couldn't feel
any thing but respect if he had wished to. The last use I heard him make of
your name was when in a rambling talk about the English mission, some one
referred to your ~~name~~, & he said he would gladly tender you the place if
Massachusetts was not so strongly represented abroad, and that no one could
fill it better, or be more pleasant personally to him. 'By that token' he could not
have meant mischief to you, & yet by same reasoning, prior to my leaving
Washington I thought it impossible he should willingly do me a wrong. The
fact is, Judge, that the President of the United States ought to be a statesman,
but unfortunately he is not. And 'that reminds me' that I have yet to tell you of
some scenes in which Lewis Dent figured as an appellant, & the President as a
Court of appeals in some matters belonging to my Department, just before I
left. . . ." Copy, Cox Papers, Oberlin College.

On Dec. 27, Fish wrote to Cox. "I am realizing how true it is that if a
thing is not done at the proper time it is apt not to be done at all. When your
letter of 29th November reached me I was very much occupied, & for several
days was quite unable to acknowledge it. The postponement brought me from
day to day to face new & continually recurring difficulties. It cannot be necessary for me to assure you how much & how sincerely I have lamented your
leaving the Cabinet; & while regret of of the fact has been deep, it has been as
keen, if not more so, for what has ensued. I cannot believe that there has been
any necessity for estrangement between you & the President. . . . The sensation
writers, (professional & others) from this City cannot be repressed, & their
arrogance of assumption in claiming authority for their assertions, should not,
I submit, My Dear Governor, be allowed to disturb a friendship such as that
which existed between you & the President, each of whom, knew, respected, &
loved the other. I can see no reason to believe that the President intended, nor
is it by any means a necessary implication, that he designed in any way to impugn
your motives or to question the integrity of your administration of your office. . . ." ALS, *ibid.*

Proclamation

———

BY THE PRESIDENT OF THE UNITED STATES OF AMERICA:

A PROCLAMATION.

Whereas, on the 22nd day of August, 1870 my proclamation
was issued, enjoining neutrality in the present war between France

and the North German Confederation and its allies, and declaring so far as then seemed to be necessary the respective rights and obligations of the belligerent parties and of the citizens of the United States.

And whereas subsequent information gives reason to apprehend that armed cruisers of the belligerents may be tempted to abuse the hospitality accorded to them in the ports, harbors, roadsteads and other waters of the United States, by making such waters subservient to the purposes of war.

Now therefore, I, Ulysses S. Grant, President of the United States of America, do hereby proclaim and declare that, any frequenting and use of the waters within the territorial jurisdiction of the United States by the armed vessels of either belligerent, whether public ships or privateers, for the purpose of preparing for hostile operations, or as posts of observation upon the ships of war, or privateers or merchant vessels of the other belligerent lying within, or being about to enter the jurisdiction of the United States, must be regarded as unfriendly and offensive; and in violation of that neutrality which it is the determination of this Government to observe; And to the end that the hazard and inconvenience of such apprehended practices may be avoided, I further proclaim and declare that from and after the 12th day of October instant, and during the continuance of the present hostilities between France and the North German Confederation and its allies, no ship of war or privateer of either belligerent shall be permitted to make use of any port, harbor, roadstead or other waters within the jurisdiction of the United States as a station or place of resort for any warlike purpose or for the purpose of obtaining any facilities of warlike equipment; and no ship of war or privateer of either belligerent shall be permitted to sail out of or leave any port harbor roadstead or waters subject to the jurisdiction of the United States, from which a vessel of the other belligerent (whether the same shall be a ship of war, a privateer or a merchant ship) shall have previously departed, until after the expiration of at least twenty four hours from the departure of such last mentioned vessel beyond the jurisdiction of the United States. If any ship of war or privateer of either belligerent shall, after the time this notification takes effect enter any port, harbor, roadstead or waters of the United States, such vessel shall be required to depart and to put to sea within twenty four hours after her entrance into such port, harbor, roadstead or waters, except in case of stress of weather or of her requiring provisions or things necessary for the subsistence of her crew, or for repairs; in either of which cases the authorities of the port or of the nearest port (as the case may be) shall require her to put to sea as soon as possible after the expiration of such period of twenty four hours without permitting her to take in supplies, beyond what may be necessary for her immediate use; and no such vessel which may have been permitted to remain within the waters of the United States for the purpose of repair shall continue within such port, harbor, roadstead or waters for a longer period than twenty four hours after her necessary repairs shall have been completed, unless within such twenty four hours, a vessel, whether ship of war, privateer or merchant ship of the other belligerent shall have departed therefrom, in which case the time limited for the departure of such ship of war or privateer shall be extended so far as may be necessary to secure an interval of not less than twenty four hours between such departure and that of any ship of war, privateer or merchant ship of the other belligerent which may have previously quit the same port, harbor, roadstead or waters. No ship of war or privateer of either belligerent shall be detained in any port, harbor, roadstead or waters of the United States more than twenty four hours by reason of the successive departures from such port, harbor. roadstead or waters of more than one vessel of the other belligerent. But if there be several vessels of each or either of the two belligerents in the same port, harbor. roadstead or waters, the order of their depature therefrom shall be so arranged as to afford the opportunity of leaving alternately to the vessels of the respective belligerents, and to cause the least detention consistent with the objects of this Proclamation. No ship of war or privateer of either belligerent shall be permitted, while in any port, harbor, roadstead or waters within the jurisdiction of the United States to take in any supplies except provisions and such other things as may be requisite for the subsistence of her crew, and except so much coal only as may be sufficient to carry such vessel, if without sail power, to the nearest European port of her own country, or in case the vessel is rigged to go under sail and may also be propelled by steam power, then with half the quantity of coal which she would be entitled to receive, if dependent upon steam alone; and no coal shall be again supplied to any such ship of war or privateer in the same or any other port, harbor, road-stead or waters of the United States without special permission, until after the expiration of three months from the time when such coal may have been last supplied to her within the waters of the United States, unless such ship of war or privateer shall, since last thus supplied have entered a European port of the government to which she belongs.

In testimony whereof, I have hereunto set my hand and cause the seal of the United States to be affixed.

Done at the City of Washington this eighth day of October in the year of our Lord one thousand eight hundred and seventy and of the Independence of the United States of America, the ninety fifth.

U. S. GRANT

DS, DNA, RG 130, Presidential Proclamations. See Allan Nevins, *Hamilton Fish: The Inner History of the Grant Administration* (New York, 1936), p. 401.

To Hamilton Fish

———

Washington D. C. Oct. 8th *1870*

DEAR GOVERNOR:

Will you be kind enough to have returned to the Atty. General the proclamation which he prepared for the pardon of Fenian prisoners?[1] It is wanted by the pardon clerk to enable him to give the grounds of pardon in the papers which he is now preparing.

Yours Truly
U. S. GRANT

HON. H. FISH,
SEC. OF STATE

ALS, DLC-Hamilton Fish. On Sept. 9 and Oct. 7, 1870, Secretary of State
Hamilton Fish had written in his diary. "The President asked me about the
(Fenian) Amnesty Proclamation, which he had requested the Atty Genl to prepared—I reply that I have it in my possession the Proclamation prepared by
the Atty. Genl granting pardon, but that I have not prepared the proclamation
of warning which he had contemplated—I had understood him to have concurred
in the views which I presented in a letter to him (in my letter book) advising
the postponement of any steps in this matter until toward the close of the
Fishing Season—He said that such had been his intention—but he thought it
would be well to let the Prisoners out pretty soon—The subject however was
dropped—" "Submitted the draft of a proclamation of warning against violation of international duties, by such means as the assumed Governmental organizations which claim to exercise Legislative Military Powers within the U S (for
example the Fenian Congress & the Cuban Junta) to be issued simultaneously
with the granting of the Pardons (which the President has decided to issue to
the Fenians convicted in connection with the late raid upon Canada)—The draft
was read—at first before it had been read the President hesitated—Boutwell enquired whether it might affect the approaching elections—when the Prsdt read
it, (by himself) he approved, & it was then it was read to the Cabinet. And the
President directed that it be engrossed, & ready for Publication at the same
time that the pardons 'which he has directed the Atty Genl to prepare' shall be
issued—" *Ibid.* A draft of the pardon is *ibid.* See proclamation, Oct. 12, 1870.
On Oct. 10, Fish wrote. "Called upon the President to suggest the necessity
of instructions from the War, Navy & Treasury, for the purpose of carrying out
the provisions of the Proclamation—He directs copies to be sent to each & Also
to the Attorney Genl with instructions in his name, that they issue such instructions as may seem necessary, from each Department In regard to the
Proclamation to be issued on the granting of the Fenian Pardon he says that
the copies of the Indictments in Vermont have not yet been received—he wishes
all the pardons to be issued together & to bear the same date, & the Proclamation also to bear same date, & be promulgated when the Pardons are issued—He
directs the retention of the Pardons already signed by him, & of the Proclamation, until the name of those convicted in Vermont, be received—" DLC-
Hamilton Fish. On Oct. 12, USG pardoned nine men imprisoned for Fenian
activities. *Washington Chronicle*, Oct. 14, 1870.

1. On Sept. 27, William J. McClure, New York City, wrote to USG. "I
respectfully ask your attention to my brother's printed letter, attached to this.
He is now confined at Chatham Prison, England, for complicity with Fenianism
in 1867. The body he addresses has proved itself unworthy of the confidence of
intelligent men, and at its sitting nearly all the political prisoners at Chatham
refused to make statements as to their treatment—feeling that no good would
come to them from anything they might testify in regard to the outrages all of
them have been subject to at the hands of the prison officials, and indirectly of
the British Government. My brother informs me that he applied to see Mr
Motley, during the sitting of the Commission, and succeeded in having Mr
Moran Secretary of Legation, call on him instead. What transpired at the
interview was, on the whole, unsatisfactory to my brother, who entertains an
unfavorable opinion of Mr Moran's Americanism. In view of the appointment of
Hon. O. P. Morton, as successor to Mr Motley, it may be proper to reiterate

that my brother is a native-born American, and fought on the side of the Union during the late civil war. The records of the State Department will doubtless give full information respecting his case. Pardon me for the suggestion, but might it not avail somewhat if the U. S. Govt were to remind the British Govt, in the form of a vigorous letter of protest that American citizens should not be treated, for political reasons, as common convicts. My brother, John McClure, has been in prison over three years, and there is apparently no sufficient excuse, even of safety, in denying liberty to him and his comrades an hour longer. Matters are now as quiet in Ireland as they ever will be there under English rule. I earnestly hope that you will consider this affair worthy your attention and action, at the present time, when republicanism is advancing in Europe, with the promise of free government to the peoples." ALS, DNA, RG 59, Miscellaneous Letters. The enclosure is *ibid*. On Dec. 24, Benjamin Moran, secretary of legation, London, wrote to Fish announcing the release of John McClure and other Fenians from British prisons. ALS, *ibid*., Diplomatic Despatches, Great Britain. See William D'Arcy, *The Fenian Movement in the United States: 1858–1886* (1947; reprinted, New York, 1971), pp. 368, 370–72.

To Charles W. Ford

Washington D. C. Oct. 8th *1870*

DEAR FORD:

I would like to have the ground which I have compromised for near Carondelet surveyed and platted. At the same time the surveyor might note about the amount Mr. Hulse has of land claimed by me and if it does not vary materially from ten Aprpents it may be compromised.

Yours Truly
U. S. GRANT

ALS, DLC-USG. See letter to Charles W. Ford, Nov. 6, 1870.

Proclamation

BY THE PRESIDENT OF THE UNITED STATES OF AMERICA
A PROCLAMATION

Whereas divers evil disposed persons have, at sundry times within the territory or jurisdiction of the United States, begun or set on foot, or provided, or prepared the means for military expeditions or enterprises to be carried on thence against the Territories or Dominions of Powers with whom the United States are at peace, by organizing bodies pretending to have powers of government over portions of the Territories or Dominions of Powers with whom the United States are at peace, or by being, or assuming to be members of such bodies—by levying or collecting money for the purpose, or for the alleged purpose of using the same in carrying on military enterprises against such Territories or Dominions, by enlisting and organizing armed forces to be used against such Powers, and by fitting out, equipping and arming vessels to transport such organized armed forces to be employed in hostilities against such powers:

And, whereas it is alleged, and there is reason to apprehend that such evil disposed persons have, also, at sundry times, within the territory and jurisdiction of the United States, violated the laws thereof by accepting and exercising commissions to serve by land or by sea against Powers with whom the United States are at peace, by enlisting themselves or other persons to carry on war against such Powers, by fitting out and arming vessels with intent that the same shall be employed to cruise or commit hostilities against such powers, or by delivering commissions within the territory or jurisdiction of the United States for such vessels to the intent that they might be employed as aforesaid.

And whereas such acts are in violation of the laws of the United States in such case made and provided, and are done in disregard of the duties and obligations which all persons residing or being within the Territory or Jurisdiction of the United States owe thereto, and are condemned by all right minded and law-abiding citizens—

Now, therefore I. Ulysses S. Grant, President of the United States of America, do hereby declare and proclaim that all persons hereafter found within the territory or jurisdiction of the United States committing any of the afore recited violations of law, or any similar violations of the sovereignty of the United States for which punishment is provided by law, will be rigorously prosecuted therefor, and, upon conviction and sentence to punishment, will not be entitled to expect or reccive the clemency of the Executive to save them from the consequences of their guilt; and I enjoin upon every officer of this government, civil or military or naval, to use all efforts in his power to arrest for trial and punishment every such offender against the laws providing for the performance of our sacred obligations to friendly powers.

In testimony whereof, I have hereunto set my hand and caused the seal of the United States to be affixed.

Done at the City of Washington, this twelfth day of October in the year of our Lord, one thousand eight hundred and seventy, and of the Independence of the United States of America, the ninety fifth

U. S. GRANT

DS, DNA, RG 130, Presidential Proclamations.

Endorsement

Respectfully refered to the Atty. Gen. The U. S. Marshal[1] who signs for Judge Hughes I know personally to be a man who would not give a recommendation that he did not think given for an entirely worthy person. The others signers I do not know personally but have no reason to doubt their entire reliability. If any reason exists for the removal of the present Dist. Atty, I see no objection to the apt. of Judge Hughes.

U. S. GRANT

OCT. 17TH /70

AES, DNA, RG 60, Records Relating to Appointments. Written on a letter of Oct. 11, 1870, from Horace H. Harrison, Thomas J. Harrison, U.S. marshal, and John Ruhm, Nashville, to USG. "We have the honor to recommend Hon A. M. Hughes of Columbia Tennessee for the position of U. S. District Attorney for the Middle District of Tennessee. Judge Hughes was for many years District Attorney General of his District, and served for several years as One of the Circuit Judges of the State, in which positions he acquitted himself with much Credit. He is a man of nerve, firmness and unflinching integrity, a lawyer of ability, and withal a stanch Republican. He will if appointed do his duty and his whole duty in aiding the President in the execution of the laws of the United States in this District" LS, *ibid.*

On April 2, 1869, USG had nominated Robert McPhail Smith as U.S. attorney, Middle District, Tenn. On Dec. 6, 1871, USG nominated Horace H. Harrison to replace Smith, withdrew the nomination on Dec. 11, and renominated Harrison on Jan. 9, 1872. Letters recommending Harrison are *ibid.* On Dec. 29, 1871, Smith, Nashville, wrote to USG. "You have recently been so kind as to reinstate me in the office of U. S. Attorney here. Before leaving Washington, I placed my resignation in Col. Bristow's hands, to be tendered at the instance of Horace H. Harrison, Esq, who had been selected by you as my successor. This was the arrangement made, as Col. Bristow will remember. On my return here, I conferred with Judge Harrison, who wrote to Col. Bristow, expressing the greatest willingness that the resignation should be deferred so as to accomplish substantially the object desired by me. To day I was surprised at the reception of the following letter from the Attorney General: 'Department of Justice, Washington Dec. 26. 1871. R. McPhail Smith, Esq. U. S. Attorney Nashville, Tenn. Sir. I think it proper that the nomination of your successor should be sent in to the Senate at the termination of the recess on the 8th of January; and your resignation will then be considered as tendered to take effect upon the confirmation of your successor. Very respectfully, A. T. Akerman, Attorney General,' This would destroy the effect of the favor kindly extended to me by you; and besides would convert your action into a very unsubstantial formality—The Attorney General was absent from the City when you graciously accorded to me ~~the~~your consent to the arrangement suggested by me in regard to my resignation, & the time when it should be tendered, & he may not have rightly have apprehended the matter—We have no Court here until next March, and there will be but very little, if indeed anything at all, to do in the office here for the next month—So that there can be no object in hastening my resignation, so far as the government is concerned—What business may arise I pledge my self to despatch with the utmost fidelity. And Judge Harrison will *urge* that our original arrangement be permitted to stand. So that I *earnestly* entreat that my resignation may be kept back until the time agreed upon between Judge Harrison & my self shall have arrived, & he shall write in reference to the matter, according to the understanding with Col. Bristow, sanctioned by yourself." ALS, *ibid.*, Letters Received.

On Feb. 10, 1873, Archelaus M. Hughes, Washington, D. C., wrote to USG. "Some two years ago I was an applicant for the office of District Attorney for the middle district of Tennessee That application was made under the belief that the then incumbent would be removed for cause Your Excellency was pleased at that time to recommend my appointment if there was any sufficient reason for the removal of McFail Smith The attorney General thought there was no sufficient cause then existing for his removal Sometime thereafter, new charges were prefered against Smith and he was removed and the present incumbent H H Harrison was appointed I did not then renew my application The election of Judge Harrison to Congress will necessarily as I suppose create a vacancy in the office on the 4th of March next I again most respectfully solicit the appointment For my qualifications and claims I beg leave to refer your Excellency to the recommendation and endorsement then filed by me and now on file in the Attorney Genls office Also to recommendations recently filed and to the inclosed endorsement of some of my friends and neighbors" ALS, *ibid.*,

Records Relating to Appointments. Related papers are *ibid.* On March 6, USG nominated Hughes as U.S. attorney, Middle District, Tenn.

On Feb. 18, 1875, William Spence, U.S. marshal, Nashville, wrote to USG. "I have heard it rumored that H. H. Harrison Member of Congress from this District is wishing to have Hon A. M. Hughes removed from the Office of District Attorney and get himself appointed. I would respectfully Suggest that this Should not be done for the various reasons First Judge A. M. Hughes is much the best lawyer and has done more to make the U. States laws respected and process is much more easily served than under any of his predecessors, and for another reason that Judge Hughes stands much higher in the estimation of the community Socially and politically than Mr Harrison and can and will do the District and state much more good in the comeing political struggle than Mr Harrison possibly can do. there are many other reasons that will be given if Mr Harrison presses his appointment shewing his unfitness for the office. And as Judge Hughes has given satisfaction to the lawyers, the court and the community I am satisfied that Harrisons appointment in his place would be regarded as a calamity by the Republican party not only of this district but the whole state. therefore I hope no change will be made" ALS, *ibid.* Hughes remained in office.

1. Thomas J. Harrison, born in Ky. in 1824, served in the Civil War as capt., 6th Ind., col., 8th Ind. Cav., and bvt. brig. gen. On May 4, 1870, USG nominated Harrison as marshal, Middle District, Tenn.

To Buenaventura Báez

Washington D. C—Oct 17 /70

HIS EXCELLENCY. PRESIDENT BAEZ.:
SAN DOMINGO—
DEAR SIR.

Your favor of the 26th of August, was duly received and should have had an earlier response, only that, at the time of receiving it, I was where I could not get a translation—This goes by the first steamer for San Domingo, since such a translation has been attainable

My interest in extending the authority of the United States over the Territory, and people of San Domingo is unabated—My thorough conviction of the mutual benefits to both peoples, by the Union of the two nations, is unchanged. On the assembling of Congress, I shall make such recommendations as may then seem best for the accomplishment of this object.

I am glad to hear from you, so favorable an account of the condition of your Government, and of the enthusiasm of the people for annexation.

With assurances of my best wishes for your prosperity, and that of the people over whom, you have been chosen to rule.

I subscribe myself, with great respect—

Your Obed' Servt

U. S. GRANT

Copies, DLC-Hamilton Fish; DLC-USG, II, 1. On Oct. 18, 1870, Secretary of State Hamilton Fish wrote in his diary. "The President speaks to me about a letter addressed to him by Prsdt Baez of San Domingo, which he had sent to the Department together with his reply which latter he requested should be forwarded by Steamer to leave tomorrow—(I have ~~taken~~ given directions to have the missive forwarded) He asks if I had read the correspondence, & thinks Baez letter had better be destroyed. I think not, but that as it is a private letter to him, it should not go on the files of the Department, & I will return it to him—~~He asks if the~~ in reply to his question if I had read it, I tell him I read his answer (I have not read Baez letter) & in reply to his question whether 'it was not right', I tell him that I regret that he promised any communication to Congress—that it would be better to be free from any engagements—" DLC-Hamilton Fish.

To Oliver P. Morton

―――――

Washington, D. C. Oct. 20th 1870.

MY DEAR GOVERNOR:

I am in receipt of your letter of the 17th. inst. declining the English Mission, and giving reasons therefor. I heartily concur with you in your action in regard to the Mission, though I sincerely regret the occasion for it. It is easy to get someone to go to England, but very difficult to get one who has my confidence, to the extent you have, without encountering the very embarrassment met with in your case. I will however make another selection and hope to give Satisfaction in the end.

What you say about the confidence of the people in the Administration is very flattering, and I hope the result in 1872 may sustain your judgement, *substituting the republican candidate at that time* for my name in your letter. I do believe that it is of the utmost importance that the republican party should control so long as national issues remain as they now are. Without such control I believe we would lose, largely, the results of our victories in the field. The revenues of the country would be squandered without paying a dollar of interest upon our public debt, or a dollar of pension to the disabled soldiers, soldiers' widows or orphans. The 13th 14th & 15th amendments to the constitution would be dead letters.

I am pleased to learn the improved condition of Mrs. Morton's health, and hope she may speedily be restored to perfect health.

Thanking you for the course you have pursued in regard to the English Mission, your constituents, the Administration, and for the kindly expressions contained in your letter, I subscribe myself—

> Faithfully yours
> U. S. GRANT.

HON. O. P. MORTON, U. S. S.

Copy, USG 3. USG presumably intended this letter as private and wrote a second letter for publication. See letter to Oliver P. Morton, Oct. 21, 1870.

To Charles W. Ford

Washington D. C. Oct. 20th *1870*

DEAR FORD:

John Dent tells me that he has heard that, at one time, White[1] allowed the 80 acres of my farm which he occupied to be sold for taxes, and that some one now holds a tax title ~~for~~ to it. Will you be kind enough to have some one examine the matter, and settle it, for me.

I understand that Chester Crum[2] is bitterly with the bolters in Missouri: I am sorry if this is so. He is a young man who has impressed me most favorably and I regret to see him go, politically, to the very men he stood so gallantly against in their treason.—

Brown I see has thrown off all disguise! This is manly at least:

All should do the same thing, (the leaders I mean) for they intend nothing more nor less than the overthrow of the party which saved the country from disruption, and the transfer of controll to the men who strove for disruption. The conduct of Schurz has been the most inconsistent as well as the most ungrateful to a confiding people.—I regret the course of the Mo. ~~Republican~~; Democrat. The managers of that paper however have chosen to play second fiddle to their old enemy, the Republican, and will be compelled to hold that position or retreat. They will see that the Mo. bolt leads just where the Tenn. and Va bolts did. They will find modern democracy a hard taskmaster, requiring of them daily apologies for their former loyalty.

Yours Truly
U. S. GRANT

ALS, DLC-USG.

1. See *PUSG*, 2, 28; *ibid.*, 17, 27; *ibid.*, 18, 206–7.
2. On Dec. 14, 1869, John W. Noble, U.S. attorney, St. Louis, wrote to USG. "I have the honor hereby to transmit to you my resignation of the office of attorney of the United States in & for the Eastern District of Missouri. For the confidence and support of yourself and your administration in my office I shall ever retain the most grateful recollection." ALS, DNA, RG 60, Letters Received from the President. On Dec. [18], USG endorsed this letter. "W~~i~~ould it not be well to ask Dist. Atty. Noble if he will not reconcider?" AE (initialed), *ibid.* On Dec. 21 and 22, Charles W. Ford, St. Louis, wrote to USG. "I wrote you a few days since, on the subject of Genl Nobles resignation. From what I learn here, I dont think there is much prospect of retaining him. In the expectation of such being the result. Marr, Easton and myself. have been looking about for the right sort of a man to recommend. It resulted in a joint call on Mr Geo A. Madill, whom we solicited to become a candidate for the office of District Atty, and today all the Revenue offices will sign a joint application to you for the appointment—Mr Madill has the approval (to me) of Judge Treat— George W Cline & other prominent lawyers of our bar. including Genl Noble. He is a young man. (say 35)—fine legal abilities and a man of the purest character—and has all the qualities we desire to make a good & efficient officer—I feel considerable interest in the selection of a good man for Dist Atty—as without one. who is honest straightforward & energetic, the Revenue offices are powerless to punish fraud & enforce the laws—I hope he will meet your approbation as I am sure he will that of the public," "I find I am obliged to take the back track in regard to Mr Madill. whom I have recomemed for Dist Atty, in the place of Gnl Noble, on the score of his politics He was represented a good republican—whereas—it turns out—that he was a Seymour & Blair. man, tho' he took no active part, While I am not mistaken as to his qualifications for the position—I commended for, yet, I confess I was misled—not by Madill, but some

of our own friends, as to his politics—and so *I back out*. I must say one word for Mr Madill. This appointm't was not of his seeking. but, he became an applicant, at the joint request of all the Revenue Officers here, I dont know who to recomend now. but, whoever he may be, he will be a union man & in favor of your administration" ALS, *ibid.*, Records Relating to Appointments. On Dec. 23, Noble wrote to USG recommending Chester H. Krum as his successor, a letter followed by other strong letters from St. Louis recommending Krum. ALS, *ibid.* On Jan. 18, 1870, USG nominated Krum. On Oct. 17, Robert J. Hill and William K. Patrick, St. Louis, wrote to USG. "At a meeting of the County Republican Committee of Saint Louis County held this day, the following resolutions were unanimously adopted. Whereas, Chester H. Krum, United States District Attorney for the Eastern District of Missouri, has betrayed the trust reposed in him as a Republican, abandoning the party and giving aid and comfort to the faction that is making war upon the National Administration and conspiring to over throw Republicanism in Missouri; Therefore be it Resolved: That His Excellency, the President of the United States, be respectfully solicited to remove the said Chester H. Krum from office and appoint to his place a sound Republican and qualified Lawyer. . . ." DS, *ibid.* On Nov. 7, 1872, Krum wrote to USG. "Having been elected a Judge of the Circuit Court of Saint Louis County, I have the honor to tender my resignation as Attorney of the United States for the Eastern District of Missouri. In this connection, I beg leave to thank you most sincerely for your uniform friendship and confidence during my term of office. And most heartily and warmly, I ask to congratulate you upon the recent and triumphant vindication, which you have received at the hands of the American People. In the whole experience of our Nation, there have been few events, which, as well as your re-election, have served to assure the perpetuity of our Republican government." ALS, *ibid.*, Letters Received.

To Jacob D. Cox

——————

Washington, Oct. 21st, 1870.

I am still annoyed with Col. Pychlyn's application to have surveying of Chickasaw lands stopped, but I have refused to hear further argument on the subject except through the proper department. Yesterday however I told him that I would have either you or Gen. Parker, or both of you, here at 11 A. M. today and hear what he has to [say]. If you can I wish you would come at that hour and bring Parker with you.

Typescript (brackets included), Cox Papers, Oberlin College, Oberlin, Ohio. On Oct. 17, 1870, USG had written to Secretary of the Interior Jacob D. Cox. "After conversation with Col, Pichland (   ) I am satisfied that the survey of the Chickasaw lands should be stopped if it is not now too late. I hope you will see the Col. and comply with his request if possible." Typescript, *ibid.* Peter P. Pitchlynn, born in 1806, an influential member of the Choctaw nation, was its principal spokesman in Washington, D. C. See *Letter of P. P. Pitchlynn to the People of the Choctaw & Chickasaw Nations Upon the Question of Sectionizing & Dividing Their Lands in Severalty* (Washington, D. C., 1870); Angie Debo, *The Rise and Fall of the Choctaw Republic* (1934; reprinted, Norman, 1961), pp. 211–13; W. David Baird, *Peter Pitchlynn: Chief of the Choctaws* (Norman, 1972), pp. 182–84.

To Oliver P. Morton

————

Washington. D. C. Oct. 21. 1870

Dear Sir:

Your letter of the 19th inst. declining the English mission, with reasons therefor, is received. I fully concur with you in all the reasons which you give for the course which you find it your duty to pursue in the matter, but regret that the country is not to have your valuable services at the English Court, at this important juncture. Your course, however, I deem wise, and it will be highly appreciated by your constituents in Indiana and throughout the country.

With assurances of my highest regards,

I remain very truly
Your obt. svt.
U. S. Grant

Hon. O. P. Morton, U. S. S.

Copy, DLC-USG, II, 1. On Oct. 21, 1870, Secretary of State Hamilton Fish wrote in his diary. "President reads a letter of Gov Morton declining the English Mission, in consequence of the result of the Indiana election having given the Democrats a majority in the Legislature—After the adjournment of the Cabinet, he suggests the name of Senator Williams, of Oregon, saying at the same time, 'he is hardly big enough for the place', to which I assent, & add that the public expects a large man for the place, there are large interests, & a man who will command confidence from his name & reputation should be selected—' He objects decidedly to Wm C. Bryant—does not know a Southern man, who was loyal, & is competent   Says 'my neighbor' (Pierrepont) troubles him with his importunity for an appointment—wishes to come into the Cabinet, but that that cannot be—thinks he might be competent for the mission to England—I tell him, he could not rely on his obeying instructions: that while Dist. Attorney, in the matter of the Cuban Expeditions, he continually disregarded his instructions, when he thought their enforcement might be unpopular, or was against his own sympathies—Gov Cox was named. He says he would not accept it—is desirous of returning to his Profession—& can not afford it—I remark that under existing circumstances the tender of the position would probably be grateful to him, that the only objection to this, is that it is not desirable to have the office declined, & apparently go a begging—He says that Cox would not accept, has told him his plans—speaks of his age, & the size of his family &c   I mention Andrew White—& remind him of his former consideration of the name of Speaker Blaine—I mention the purport of Genl Butler's letter recommending Wendel Philips—Very evidently he will not consider him within the range of possibilities of appointment" DLC-Hamilton Fish.

On Oct. 22, Edward R. Wiswell, New York City, wrote to USG. "On July 13. 1870 I had the honor to write you a letter asking that Hon. W. H. Seward be appointed Minister to England in place of Mr Motley. But as Mr Seward has gone to China, and Mr Motley has ceased to have any influence in England, would it not be better to have a good practical man appointed at once to conduct the negotiations for a prompt settlement of the 'Alabama Claims' and other questions with England. We have waited too long, and have talked too much with England about these Claims. No nation can afford to neglec[t] too long the vindication of Justice. If the[r]e is any strength in the American claim on this 'Alabama' question let us present it promptly and peremptorily for settlement. I am satisfied that there is no better time than the present, nor one in which Englishmen feel that they had better dispose of the matter. All that is wanted is the right man in London to represent the American Government in making a new demand for settlement. Mr Motley is a very nice literary man, but evidently a poor statesman. His milk and water conversations are better at some other Capital in Europe, if he must represent America abroad. Permit me to suggest the name of Caleb Cushing of Massachusetts, who I think would bring about an honorable settlement. For knowledge of international law, and the other qualifications necessary for a minister to England Mr Cushing has certainly a great reputation. Your late appointment at the West—Mr Morton, perhaps indicates an intention on your part to select some Western man for the position. If so who can do better than my old friend Hon Ben. Wade of Ohio. I trust that you will so[on] send some strong man to London." ALS, DNA, RG 59, Letters of Application and Recommendation. On Oct. 29, Vice President Schuyler Colfax, South Bend, Ind., wrote to USG. "The vacancy still existing in the English Mission leads me again to suggest the name of Mr Greeley for it, if he is willing to accept. Travelling extensively this year over this State, & seeing besides a great many leading men from other States, I found a strong feeling in his favor for that place. He is thoroughly familiar with all the points at issue, can argue them in a straightforward way, could not be influenced by dinner parties & has no special reverence for Dukes or Earls. You intimated at Chicago, & wrote me afterwards confidentially that you had him in your mind; & as his health now would rather tempt him to relaxation from daily Edl labors, I think he might accept." ALS, *ibid.* Letters recommending Wendell Phillips, Bishop Matthew Simpson, Alexander Rives, and Benjamin Moran for the post are *ibid.*

To Adam Badeau

WASHINGTON, D. C., Oct. 23d, 1870

DEAR BADEAU,—I am in receipt of your letter in which you speak of the article[1] you propose writing for the British press, and of getting something from Sheridan to aid you in preparing it. I have rec'd but one letter from Sheridan[2] since he has been with the Prussians. It is probably too late for that letter to be of service to you; but I send it. It will at least interest you.—I also send you a review of the reviewer Adams,[3] by Senator Howe.[4] The Adams' do not possess one noble trait of character that I ever heard of, from old John Adams down to the last of all of them, H. B.—In writing your second volume I would advise to steer clear of criticisms of persons on account of your personal acquaintance. For instance you know personally much more of Butler,[5] Meade and others, against whom prejudice may exist, than any one could learn from any authentic record. I would give them all the credit the record entitles them to and particularly avoid personalities. This is voluntary advice however and you can use it as you please.

My family are all very well and wish to be remembered to you. You will learn before this reaches that Morton declines the English Mission. It is because a bitter copperhead[6] would take his place in the Senate should he go. I have not made up my mind now who to send but I will not leave Mr. Motley.

Yours,

U. S. GRANT.

Adam Badeau, *Grant in Peace* (Hartford, Conn., 1887), p. 472. On Sept. 21, 1870, Horace Porter, Long Branch, had written to Secretary of State Hamilton Fish. "The President directs me to forward you the enclosed letter from Badeau, and to request you to read it, particularly that portion which relates to the contemplated publication of an article on the war in Europe. If you approve of it, the President would like you to Send Badeau a cable dispatch authorizing its publication." ALS, DLC-Hamilton Fish. On Sept. 28, Adam Badeau, London, wrote to USG. "I received Gov. Fish's telegram, since the last Steamer sailed, and ~~merely~~ write at once to thank you for your double and prompt compliance with my request. I say *double*, for I was particularly gratified by your sending your answer thro' the Gov; and thus shewing that you reegarded my wish to treat him with all proper respect. I will be very careful to carry out the injunction to make the *political* portion of the article 'historical,' only. I think it will appear in Frazer's Magazine, which is edited now by Froude, the famous historian, with whom I am now in treaty. It will be ready for the next (or November) number. Frazer's is eminently liberal in tone and of high literary character. I hope this time I shall be better paid. The announcement of Mr Morton's appointment took me by surprise I think it means 'business.' As Mr Morton's health will prevent his going much into society, he can only come to accomplish other purposes; and I do not think he would be willing to give up his great position and career in the Senate, unless he expected to add to his reputation here. Besides which, I know your estimate of his ability, and how much he has been in your confidence. I tell every body that he is one of the ablest statesmen in America, one of the leaders of the Senate, and that he has been the Spokesman and peculiar representative of the administration in that body for at least a year. I do hope, dear General, that you will let him know the history of Mr. Motley's career here fully, so that he may understand the evils of insubordination, as they fall back on the insubordinate. I do hope there will be no repetition of what has occasioned you so much trouble. Of course, I cannot tell you any thing about the war, which the telegram and your ministers will not have rendered stale long before this can reach you. It seems now as if the French were bent on their own destruction. They *will* resist, just as the South *would*, long after resistance is wicked because hopeless. I cant blame the Prussians for wanting to make it impossible, that the French should in a few years repeat their aggressions. I suppose you saw a copy of the London Times containing in a letter from a correspondent in America, an account of a strong movement in Canada towards annexation. It looked to me a more feasable plan than any that has been proposed. The one to which I refer was a suggestion that commissioners should be appointed by you, by the Queen and by Canada to consider and report on the whole subject of the relations present and future of the three countries, taking into view, the independence or the annexation of Canada, the Alabama claims, the fisheries, Reciprocity, the Fenian raids and all. This article said that several hundred thousand Canadians favored the scheme, and that its abettors were at work in the United States and here, earnestly. Perhaps however you know all about it. Mr Motley has told me nothing of his official business since my return, and under the circumstances, I could ask him nothing. I hope that my relations with Mr Morton will be such that I can serve both you and him occasionally. I should be very glad if you would let him know that you would not be averse to having him call upon me for such assistance as you or he might think me able, or suitable to render. I am confident that in some emergencies I could be made very useful. I beg you will make my kindest and most respectful regards to Mrs Grant, and remember me affectionately to the children. I hope Fred passed creditably in his June examinations. . . . P. S. I saw a nasty squib in the 'Sun' stating that I was a great deal away from my office. I dont suppose abuse in the 'Sun' will hurt me in your eyes; but I wish to say that since I entered upon my functions, I have not been absent one day, except on account of illness. My health seems now quite restored. The doctors said the illness originated in my exposures in the field." ALS, ICarbS.

On Jan. 17 and 26, 1871, Badeau wrote to USG. "I have received from Mr. Cunningham the Clerk in the War Office who last summer copied some of the records for me, copies of all the letters and telegrams relative to operations of the Armies of the U. S. received at your headquarters between May 1, 1864 and May 1, 1865—'except those contained in packages *G, M, P, V* and *W* of 1864,' which are the packages that can not be found in the War Office—and about which there is a dispute between the War Office and myself; I maintaining that I returned them, and the Dept having no record of the fact. Now, among the telegrams received at the War Office there are copies of all telegrams received by you, as you remember Mr. Stanton ordered all despatches to or from you to be taken off the wires, and brought to him. If you will order that a competent clerk (I should prefer Mr. Cunningham if he is still in the Dept) should go over the books of telegrams received either by Mr Stanton, Gen Halleck or the Adjt General, from May 1, 1864 to May 1, 1865 and make copies of all relating to operations of the armies, or addressed to you, I can still have this very important and really indispensable ~~matter~~ material. I know it is all in the books I describe, for I saw it there last winter when I was studying up the Rosecranz matter for a Cincinnati correspondent. It is extremely important to me to have these telegrams, and I hope you will give the order. I ought also to have copies of all despatches (letters or telegrams), received by Meade, or Butler, or Ord after he took command of the Army of the James, *from their corps commanders, or from division Commanders when these had independent Commands.* You can see the necessity of this at a glance. It will be a long and tedious job to prepare them, but I dont see to what better use either the records of the War Office, or the services of its employées could be put, than to assist in furnishing to history and the future a correct statement of the deeds of those for whom the War Office was created. Will you please, dear General give very explicit and stringent orders in the matter; and direct as much expedition as is consistent with the interests of the public service. I am working hard on my second volume, and these data will be of incalculable value to me. If I get them, I dont think I can want anything more,   I have constant inquiries here in England for my second volume. I want very much to see Early's reply to my letter in the London Standard. Would it be impossible for you to procure me a copy so that I can answer it (without seeming to do so) in Vol 2. I hope you liked my article in Frazer. I have been a little mortified that you took no notice of it; neither of my inquiry as to whether you wanted me to write on politics. I didn't care about writing, but to get no answer at all made it seem to Mr Froude, as if I had been overstating to him my relations with you . . . *P. S. Important*   I want copies of the telegrams relating to military operations in Packages *G, M, P, V,* and *W* that is from Meade, Sherman, Butler, Halleck Stanton Sigel and Banks for ONLY *the months of April and May 1864. The* others are complete. The Initials indicate the name of the command, not of the commanders. I beg you will pardon my troubling you with this, but it is so important that I thought it best to address you on the subject direct" "I enclose copies of two articles, one in the London Times and one in the London News, on the Motley correspondence. I think Gov. Fish's letter perfectly unanswerable; it leaves Mr. Motley not an inch of ground to stand on. It shows also what the position of the administration, and your own views and wishes have been all along. It comes in the nick of time for Gen Schenck. The Governor was very lenient in not publishing the two letters that Mr. Motley wrote *after* he had been rebuked, which were insubordinate in the last degree, defending his position, after he had been informed it was disapproved by you, and saying it would be seen whether the country and the Republican party would endorse him or not. I believe the letters were marked private or confidential but they are *on record*; I think, as *despatches, numbered*; and I copied them for the book here. I suppose the Governor keeps them back to utterly demolish Mr. M. if he comes to time again. There can be no shadow of doubt as to the right to use them, if they become necessary, I am very anxious to have a dozen or more copies of the entire correspondence, as several important people have asked me for them. *They have not been republished here.* Motley has a great many friends among the literary and newspaper people. I send you also a copy of MacMillan for January containing an article on England & America by Lord Hobart, a very prominent man, It is written in the best possible *spirit.* I received word from my brother of his appointment as medical officer in the N. Y. Post Office, and beg to make my most grateful thanks for this new proof of your regard. The youngster is very happy about it, and I think wont disgrace the office. As soon as the English see that Mr Motley has been the obstacle to a settlement of the difficulties between the two nations, I think his popularity even in the circles which he invited to his dinners will wane wonderfully. Americans were very indignant that he never invited *them* to meet his great acquaintances; so the other day I gave a reception and invited every American that I knew in London, and all the English who have shown me any civilities. I told the English in advance that it was an attempt to bring together English and Americans. It stormed frightfully but I had about a hundred people; among them some of the cabinet, the Lord Chancellor, Mr. Hughes, Froude the historian, several members of parliament Kinglake the historian of the Crimean war, Miss Thackeray the daughter of the great novelist, and quite a number of Lords & Ladies to fill up. The prominent Americans were Gov Evans of Colorado, Commodore Rodgers, Paul Forbes, Mrs Hawthorne the widow of our novelist, and so on. They all affiliated. I deviated from the English custom, and introduced people right and left. They say tis the first time in many years so many Americans had been in English society at once. I hope it will do good. Most of the very great English people were out of town, but a great many have written to me to say what a good idea it was. My entertainment was very simple and unostentatious; but I got a receipt for an American punch from Forbes, and John Bull seemed to like it very much. The bowl had to be replenished very often. You decided as I supposed likely about the article for Froude. I told him of it, and he acquiesced. I think it better myself, for me to abstain from discussing the subject in print. Every one looks eagerly for Schenck. I think I shall go to Liverpool to meet him." ALS, USG 3.

1. Comparing the American Civil War with the Franco-Prussian War, including strategies employed by USG and Helmuth K. B. von Moltke, Badeau wrote "Two Great Wars, an Historical Parallel," *Fraser's Magazine*, II (New Series), XII (Dec., 1870), 793–805.

2. On Sept. 13, Lt. Gen. Philip H. Sheridan, Reims, had written to USG the letter probably forwarded to Badeau. See letter to Lt. Gen. Philip H. Sheridan, July 25, 1870.

3. Henry Brooks Adams, born in 1838, the son of former U.S. Minister Charles Francis Adams, served as his father's secretary in London (1861–68), then began writing on political and financial affairs. From the outset of USG's administration, he questioned appointments, particularly that of George S. Boutwell as secretary of the treasury, and distrusted USG's ability to govern. In 1870, Adams wrote that the administration lacked both purpose and "distinctive character," and he described Congress as inefficient and incompetent. "The Session," *North American Review*, CXI, CCXXVIII (July, 1870), 29–62; re-

printed as *A Radical Indictment! The Administration—Its Corruptions & Short-comings* . . . (Washington, 1870). On Sept. 29, Adams stated that "My last article had not only been reprinted entire by several newspapers, but the party press had thought it necessary to answer it, and I cut out some of their notices to send over to you, but forgot to bring them with me. What is more, I am told that the democratic national committee reprinted it in pamphlet form and mean to circulate two hundred and fifty thousand copies of it." J. C. Levenson, *et al.*, eds., *The Letters of Henry Adams* (Cambridge, Mass., 1982), II, 81.

4. In response to Adams, U.S. Senator Timothy O. Howe of Wis. wrote a lengthy article. ". . . The author is proclaimed to be not only a Statesman himself, but to belong to a family in which Statesmanship seems to be preserved by propogation—something as color is in the leaf of the Begonia, perpetuating resemblance through perpetual change. He may fairly be said to have been sired by at least two Presidents and a half. He belongs to a family in which the statutes of descent have preserved, fame, fortune, fondness for affairs, ambition for public employment, and everything but fidelity to opinions. . . . It seems 'the more conservative class of of citizens' have misunderstood the character of the President. Precisely what the mistake is, does not appear—indeed the critic himself does not profess to know. He has made inquiry it seems. But, 'as a rule, the reply to every inquiry comes in, in the form of confessed ignorance—*we do not know why the President is successful, we only know he is successful.*' One would suppose that was enough for a Statesman of the Adams school to know. But it does not satisfy the investigator of the *Review*. Accordingly 'without attempting to explain what is evidently so complicated an enigma,' he ventures to form a partial idea of the mystery. He enters upon a critical analysis of President Grant's mental and moral organization, his education, past experiences, &c., and comes to the conclusion that such influences 'would be likely to produce a course of action in the main practical, sensible and in intention thoroughly honest. But when used by Jay Gould and Abel Rathbone Corbin, with the skill of New York stock brokers, for illigitmate objects, the result is all the more disastrous in proportion to the energy for which the President is so remarkable.' Here is a discovery in physiological science doubtless of much importance to the welfare of mankind. It should not be forgotten that where a man, practical, sensible thoroughly, honest and remarkably energetic, as President Grant is, falls into the hands of Jay Gould & Co., mischief is likely to ensue. But as the critic does not assert that the President has fallen into such hands, and as all know that a man practical, sensible and thoroughly honest, is not likely to fall into such hands, we fail to see how such characteristics should deter the Constitution from restoring itself. . . . It is true, there were two other causes on the calendar involving the same question decided in the Hepburn case. But they were not brought there by 'the President and Congress.' It is not true, that the President undertook to pack the court in order to procure a reversal of that judgment. A more wanton calumny than that was never generated by party spite. Had Congress provided for an additional number of judges after that judgment was pronounced, and had the President selected the number with special reference to their opinions upon that one question, there would be some apology for making such a charge. But neither of these things was done. When that judgment was rendered there were two vacancies on the bench. One was occasioned by the death of Justice Wayne, who died a natural death and was not killed by 'the President and Congress,' although he was a Democrat. And the other was oc-

casioned by the resignation of Justice Grier, who resigned his office, not withstanding he was a Democrat. It was the duty of the President and the Senate to fill those vacancies. The President made both the selections before judgment was rendered in the Hepburn case. Both names were sent to the Senate on the very day that judgment was entered. And their opinions upon the legal tender question had no more influence upon their selection than had their opinions upon the question of papal infallibility. . . . The only other count in this 'scathing arraignment' of the late session is framed upon the transactions connected with the St. Domingo treaty. The President, in the exercise of his undoubted prerogative, negotiated a purchase of that part of St. Domingo under the Dominican Republic. The Senate in the exercise of its undoubted prerogative refused to ratify the treaty. The President is a Republican and so is the Senate. One would think here was an opportunity even for the critic of the *North American* to hit somebody. Clearly the treaty was wise or unwise. If the reviewer would defend the treaty he might make a strong case against a Republican Senate which rejected it. If he would oppose the treaty he might make a strong case against a Republican President who negotiated it. But a hunter stands no more chance of hitting a moose than a mouse unless he can pursuade himself [t]o stand still and take aim. The critic cannot stand still. He will not say the treaty was right and the Senate wrong, or that the treaty was wrong, and therefore the President was wrong." *Wisconsin State Journal*, Oct. 7, 1870; reprinted as *Political History, the Republican Party Defended. A Reviewer Reviewed.* See Levenson, *Letters of Henry Adams*, II, 95.

5. Badeau considered USG's remarks concerning Benjamin F. Butler especially significant because "Butler was the only one of Grant's personal enemies whom he seemed to me entirely to forgive,—until his final illness. I never discussed the subject with him, but the cordiality appeared complete; all rancor was past; although he believed that Butler had said as offensive things of him as any of his adversaries." When reading the manuscript for Badeau's history of the Civil War, USG suggested changes that tempered criticism of Butler's military career. Badeau, *Grant in Peace*, pp. 471–72.

6. On Oct. 13, 1870, Porter, Washington, D. C., wrote to USG, Frederick, Md. "Morton telegraphs from Indiana, Democratic State ticket elected by about two thousand. Legislature still in doubt." Copy, DLC-USG, II, 5.

To William Elrod

Washington D. C. Oct. 23d *1870*

DEAR ELROD:

Mr. Ford has advised me of the arrival of two head of cattle at St. Louis. I presume them to be an Alderney bull and heiffer from New Jersey. If so, and the bull is too young to serve now get another for this year, but keep all the Alderney heiffers until they can go to a bull of their own kind.

I shall send you one of my fast mares with her youngest colt, a two year old filley and the stallion colt, two years old, this week or next.[1] A man will go with them and I will then send more particular directions. There is not one of these anaimals that I want ever to do a days farm, or heavy, work. The mare I gave $1300 00/100 for and would not take ~~twi~~ twice that for her. The filly is Eathan Allen stock, fast trotters, though she is a natural pacer. She will always be small and I do not want a collar ever put on her.

I have the pedigree of the dam of the colt I send you. On the sire side he is Hambletonian.

If you have it I wish you would send some apple butter by Express.

AL (signature clipped), Illinois Historical Survey, University of Illinois, Urbana, Ill.

1. See *Washington Star*, Oct. 31, 1870.

To Charles W. Ford

Washington D. C. Oct. 23d *1870*

DEAR FORD:

I see by my Bank account that the protested drafts for $210 00/100, which you drew upon me has been paid. The check for $235 00/100 which I sent to take up this draft, and to pay $20 00/100 for other purposes, please get the money on and credit me with it.

The cattle which you advised me of the arrival of I presume to be a bull and heiffr, Alderneys, from Hoey's place, Long Branch, N. J. I shall send to Elrod this week, or early next, a fast troting mare, and her filley colt, a two year old filly and my two year old stallion. They are all very fine and I hope will reach the farm in safety.

Yours Truly
U. S. GRANT

ALS, DLC-USG.

To Ulysses S. Grant, Jr.

Washington D. C. Oct. 23d *1870*

DEAR BUCK,

Without anything special to say, but supposing that you are always glad to hear from home, I write you. By this time you must be over all your hardships, and well settled down to your studies. I hope you are doing well, and, above all, are contented. I should like to hear what mark you get in your studies, and how it compares with the class generally. Fred has been doing quite well this year. He has, I think, gone up a section in all his studies, except in Engineering, and two sections in that with the prospect of going up still another. He is up to his limit in demerit however—Your Ma is now very uneasy. Yesterday Jesse, Willie Cole[1] and Dent Casey[2] went off, we suppose to Capt. Ammens, and have not yet returned. You know your Ma is always alarmed if her children are out of sight for any length of time.

Let us hear from you often. Make it a point to write to Jesse and Nellie alternate weeks, and to your Ma each week.

Yours Affectionately
U. S. GRANT

ALS, Evelyn Wooster Burgess, San Diego, Calif.

1. Willoughby Cole, son of U.S. Senator Cornelius Cole of Calif. See Jesse R. Grant, *In the Days of My Father General Grant* (New York and London, 1925), pp. 58–59; John Y. Simon, ed., *The Personal Memoirs of Julia Dent Grant* (New York, 1975), p. 178.

2. Frederick Dent Casey, USG's nephew. See *PUSG*, 3, 271.

To Jacob D. Cox

Washington D. C. Oct. 26th 1870

HON. J. D. COX;
SEC. OF THE INT.
DEAR SIR:

I enclose you a recommendation for an Indian Agency. Generally I send all such recommendations to the head of the department interested, without comment, not intending thereby any special action.

As a policy has been laid down however for the management of indian affairs, and to prevent partially importunities for agencies, I wish you would let Parker prepare a statement of the policy to give to the "Associated Press" for publication. It might be well also to give the agencies ~~that are~~ as they are to be distributed among the different religious denominations.

Yours Truly
U. S. GRANT

ALS, DLC-USG, 1B. See *New York Times*, Oct. 29, 1870.

To William Elrod

Washington D. C. Oct 26th 1870.

DEAR ELROD:

My horses star[t] for St. Louis to-morrow in care of a man who has lived with me for over four years. He will stay a day or two on the farm . . . a fine, fast troting, mare that I want you to breed from. I want you to meet the stock in St. Louis. I will direct Richard (the man who goes with the stock to stay with Ford [— —] you call.—The stock that went out recently is the best thorough bred Alderney. Keep the Alderney stock pure and make butter from their milk. They give but little milk but that is very rich and makes butter which will usuall[y] bring 25 pr. ct. more than common butter. I should think my horses should reach St Louis about Tuesday next. Do not stay away from the election however to go after it

AL (incomplete), Illinois Historical Survey, University of Illinois, Urbana, Ill.

To Charles W. Ford

Washington D. C. Oct. 26th *1870*

DEAR FORD:

The bearer has my horses in charge and is on his way to my farm. Will you be kind enough to direct him where to send them for safe keeping until Elrod comes to the city.

Yours Truly

U. S. GRANT

P. S. Your head clerk and I have introduced him to Mr. Delano who promises to put your matter through without delay.—You have rec'd my letter which speaks of Chester Krum? I was very much pleased with him and should dislike to make any change in his office. If you will talk to Gn. Shepard he will tell you what I said in that matter.

ALS, DLC-USG. On Oct. 28, 1870, Julia Dent Grant wrote to Charles W. Ford. "You have allways been so kind in attending to different matters of buisness for the Genl that I am going to take the liberty of asking you do some thing for me Mrs Casey has purchased several peices of our furneture at Wish ton Wish—& I want that you should send out two furneture cases for it—& give careful directions as to the packing & that they be sure & get *all the pieces* of the bedsteads rollers &c. I would like you to have them shiped to J F Casey Collector at New-Orleans La) I will give you a list of the articels she wants A Rosewood set consisting of A Rosewood bedstead A Rosewood wash stand A Rosewood beaureau with mirror & Mahogany set of A Mahogany bedstead A Mahogany beaureau & mirror A Mahogany Washstand A Mahogany Wardrobe A Mahogany book case & stand (The one in the dineing room I think it is all fastened together) Send also (to Mrs Casey) the matrass belonging to the rosewood bedstead Mama' & Papas pictures & the small oil painting that hang in the parlour Please have these carefully packed.—Mrs L Dent has some little things there a set of bronze & some three or four statuetts & a box of shells if they will bear transportation would you please send them here & any expenses occuring please send me the bills—Your brother made us all most as short a visit as you did—I do not think

I shall forgive you soon—unless you make it up by comeing here this winter which I hope you will   The weather is gloryeous here now—& we are all enjoying it   The Genl & all join me in reguards" ALS, *ibid.*

To E. Shriver

Washington D. C. Oct. 28th *1870*

MY DEAR SIR:

I am in receipt of your very kind letter of the 21st. I am under many obligations for your exertions to secure me an Alderny bull. Since I saw you I have learned that an Alderny bull and heifer have been sent to my place, from New Jersey, by a man whom I authorized to send last Summer. As I had not heard from him I supposed he had not been able to secure them.

You are very considerate in again offering me your beautiful bull calf. The other bull having been sent,—as have all the stock I intend to ship there this Fall,—I shall ask you to accept my thanks for the repetition of the offer.

Again thanking you for your personal exertion in this matter and your many expressions of kindness.

I am very truly Yours
U. S. GRANT

TO MR. E. SHRIVER
FREDERICK. MD.

LS, Vassar College, Poughkeepsie, N. Y.

To Frederick Dent Grant

[*Oct.–Nov.*, 1870]

I am glad to hear, through Prof. Mahan,[1] that you are doing very well, and that by an effort you may go to the 2d section. I hope you will manage to get through the half year[2] without more than your 100 demerit. On the last of August you had that number. In your next write how Otis[3] is doing. I suppose that he is at least up to the 2d section by this time? All are well and send love to you.

U. S. G.

AN (initialed), USG 3. Frederick Dent Grant graduated USMA on June 12, 1871, standing 37 in a class of 41. See *PUSG*, 16, 84–85.

1. Dennis H. Mahan, born in 1802 in New York City, USMA 1824, remained at USMA as instructor and in 1832 was appointed professor of civil and military engineering.
2. Six-month periods at USMA ending May 31 and Nov. 30.
3. See letter to Bvt. Maj. Gen. Edmund Schriver, Sept. 8, 1870.

Calendar

1869, Nov. 1.   James S. Negley, Pittsburgh, to USG. "I have the honor to join with other well known friends of your administration in presenting the name of David Reed to the attention of Your Excellency and in recommending his appointment as one of the judges to be commissioned by you. Mr Reed is a sound consistant Republican—a man of positive and honest convictions—Fair in his dealings—earnest and thorough in his professional methods. He has attained an enviable reputation as a lawyer with a mature and varied experience. Mr Reed is in the prime and vigor of life—of pleasing manners—candid—courteous and affable. We sincerely hope that his claims may not be overlooked through the exactions upon your time or the wishes of many citizens in Western Pennsylvania pass unheeded."—ALS, NNP. On March 19, 1874, USG nominated David Reed as U.S. attorney, Western District, Pa. On June 29, 1876, Joseph Woodwell *et al.*, Pittsburgh, telegraphed to USG. "We—republicans of the city of Pittsburg Protest against the removal of the Hon. David Reed . . ."—Telegram received (at 12:07 P.M.), DNA, RG 60, Letters from the President. Additional telegrams protesting Reed's removal are *ibid.*

1869, Nov. 2.   Grenville M. Dodge, Council Bluffs, Iowa, to Gen. William T. Sherman. "*Strictly Private* . . . I am in receipt of yours ofand am very glad to here that the President feels so kindly towards me. When in New York I had a talk with 'Rawlins' and he was to tell the President my views about U. P. R. R. I am an officer of it but I do not see matters as others do—I know that Genl Grant looks to me to see that the Govt is protected or at least that I should not consent to anythig wherein he might be mislead— Will you say to him in *confidence* for me—not to be under any *circumstances used as coming from me* that I think he should hold from both companys a portion of the bonds either Govt or 1st Mortagee *until* the *road* is *completed as required* by *law*   I believe this to be best for the *stockholders* and *the Government*   I have no doubt both companies will act fully up to the law but if anythig should *happen* and all the bonds be given out, then the President would be blamed—Understand my idea is that the President should act so as to be *all the time safe*—I do not know what the commissi[on] will bring in but think they will be liberral—I dont want the President to do anythig to cripple us but I want him to be *safer*—Now General this is in strict confidence   Rawlins understood it but I fear had no opportunity to talk to the President before he died—and I know I can write you and it will go no further—I dont want General Grant to even tell his cabinet my views as it would be *misunderstood*"—ALS, DLC-William T. Sherman. On Nov. 6, Sherman wrote to Dodge. "Yours of the 2nd was received yesterday, and I went over to the Presidents and read it to him. It seems the matter has been under discussion in the Cabinet and whilst all are very friendly to the Road, the President thinks they hold back enough security for the Completion. The Commissioners have made a favorable Report, and I heard with pleasure the business holds up to a profitable Standard. A Mr Pomeroy & Ex Attny General Evarts were here yesterday to sound me as to my opinion of the Claims to Land & Subsidy of the Atcheson Branch that they told me you would build in case they succeeded—I told them that I thought they had a clear equitable right to connect with the Main Stem at any point East of the 100 Parallel on the same general terms as were given the other branches. I prefer they should not go over to the Republican at all, but to follow substantively the Little Blue, and Cross the Platte, at Old Fort Kearny If they will [accept some] slight modifications, I will do all that I can properly to help them."—ALS, Dodge Papers, IaHA.

1869, Nov. 4.   To Albert De Groot, New York City. "I am in receipt of your letter of the 25th ult., inviting me to participate in the ceremony of unveiling the 'Vanderbilt Bronze' in the city of New York on the 10th inst. It would afford me great pleasure to be present upon this occasion, and to witness the unveiling of a statue commemorative of the distinguished services of one whose life has been spent in developing useful public enterprises; but I find that my public duties will not permit me to be absent from the capital at that time, and I shall therefore not be able to accept your very cordial invitation."—*New York Herald*, Nov. 10, 1869.

1869, Nov. 4.   To John M. Harlan, chairman, Committee of Invitations, Society of the Army of the Tennessee. "Your favor of the 25th of October ult, inviting me to be present at the meeting of the Society of the Army of the Tenn. and the Cavalry Corps of the Mil. Div of the Miss. is received. It is with regret that I have to reply non accepting. The Army of the Tenn. and the Society composed of members of that Grand Army, are mostly men with whom I commenced my services in the suppression of the late rebellion; and I had, too, the honor of being their first commander, under that name—an honer which I feel, and shall always appreciate. It would afford me the greatest pleasure to be present at the union of the 17th & 18th inst. but public duty will prevent. All that I can do, therefore, is to wish you a happy meeting, and express the hope that there may be many more such reunions when I may have the pleasure of being present."—Copies, DLC-USG, II, 1, 4.

1869, Nov. 4.   Ulysses S. Grant, Jr., Exeter, N. H., to USG. "There is no need of my returning home, I have written the reasons"—Telegram received (at 9:00 A.M.), DNA, RG 107, Telegrams Collected (Bound).

1869, Nov. 10.   John A. Griswold, Troy, N. Y., to USG. "Major General John E Wool died at his residence in this city today"—Telegram received (at 10:00 A.M.), DNA, RG 107, Telegrams Collected (Bound).

1869, Nov. 11.   U.S. Representative William D. Kelley of Pa., Philadelphia, to USG. "The family of Cadet Price leave for West Point tomorrow morning under my assurance that he can be permitted to see *them* at the Hotel Fearing that more important matters may have crowded your promise to direct the Superintendent to allow him this privilege I take the liberty of reminding you of it"—ALS, DNA, RG 94, Correspondence, USMA.

1869, Nov. 15. USG endorsement. "Note this case for appointment next June."—AES, DNA, RG 94, Correspondence, USMA. Written on a letter of Nov. 11 from Maria L. Daly, New York City, to USG. "The lady managers of the Union Home and School for the Soldiers children are encouraged to believe that you will favorably consider their petition sent you in June last, to give to Thomas Davis, the best scholar in their Home, and now a lad in his *seventeenth* year, a cadet ship at *West Point* He is very gentlemanly, and of unexceptionable character and whilst pursuing for the last two years higher studies that any of his companions to fit himself for West Point he has acted as drill master for the Institution When you did us the honor to visit the school you were kind enough to praise the order and precision with which the boys went through their exercise and to notice their young captain Davis. As he has now just completed his sixteenth year, we feel a certain responsibility in retaining him any longer with us unless we can give him the certainty of going next Spring to West Point. He is a young fellow of very great promise and is it time that he should fit himself for some profession or trade, otherwise instead of benefiting we should fear to do him an injustice and waste his time and energies in keeping him longer under our care."—ALS, *ibid.* On Aug. 3, Daly had written a similar letter to USG.— ALS, *ibid.* Thomas F. Davis graduated from USMA in 1875. See Harold Earl Hammond, ed., *Diary of a Union Lady, 1861–1865* (New York, 1962).

1869, Nov. 15. USG endorsement. "The Sec. of War will please review this case and make orders either re-instating Lt. Johnson, to put him back to duty, or to enable him to resign as may seem most proper."—AES, DNA, RG 94, ACP, J42 CB 1869. Written on papers concerning the court-martial of Lt. William S. Johnson.—*Ibid.* On Dec. 8, Johnson, Washington, D. C., wrote to USG. "I have the honor to submit the following for your consideration. I was tried before a General Court Martial, and found guilty of the charge preferred against me; the record was submitted to the Judge Advocate General, who reccommended that the judgement of the court be reversed, and *'that I be returned to duty without a stain on my character;'* the proceedings were again referred to the Court—who made a rejoinder to the review of the Judge Advocate General and re-affirmed their finding; without any further action by the Judge Advocate General the findings and sentence were approved, and I accordingly ceased to be an officer of the Army I am an innocent man; I do not ask mercy—I demand justice. . . ." —LS, *ibid.* On Dec. 21, USG nominated Johnson for reinstatement.

On Jan. 11, 1871, Sylvester Larned, Detroit, wrote to USG. "The bearer Lieut Wm S. Johnson, lately discharged by order of the War Dept, deems such discharge a case of great hardship as the Retiring board found him totally unfit for active service—This was the case in which you so kindly renominated him & where Messrs Chandler & Howard, interested themselves in his behalf. As the only way to repair the wrong he seeks an appt as 2d Lieut. I can confidently recommend him as a gentleman of unblemished honor, & one who deserves to be rewarded for his services & sufferings"— ALS, *ibid.*, R443 CB 1870. On Feb. 6, Johnson, Washington, D. C., wrote to U.S. Senator Alexander McDonald of Ark. "I have respectfully to ask your assistance in procuring for me an appointment as Lieutenant in the U. S. army and submit the following for your information. I enlisted in the Volunteer service April 10th 1861, Was wounded while in command of my Company, at the battle of Fayetteville Ark April 18th 1863, twice breveted for gallant and meritorious conduct during the War. Appointed 1st Lieutenant U. S. army. June 12th 1867, and made Regimental Quarter Master 43d Inft. left out of the consolidation on account of total disibility, tried by General Court Martial in the Summer of 1869, found guilty and dismissed the Service, reinstated by the President January 24th 1870. ordered before the Retiring Board of which Brig Gen Irwin McDowel was President: pronounced totally disabled by the Examining Surgeons in attendance, honorably discharged January 1st 1871. Before recieving my final discharge I made application to the Adjutant General asking that I be assigned to duty as 2d Lieutenant, under the provisions of Sect 12 of the act of July 15th 1870. 'provided I was to be mustered out. This request failed to recive favorable consideration. I have further asked to be furnished with any report or findings the Retiring Board may have made in my case, which has also been refused me, I am therefore at a loss to know why I have not been Retired instead of being discharged unless the Sect of War deems my trial and dismissal sufficent reasons for so doing The Presidents prompt action in reinstateing me sets aside the findings of the Court thereby exonerating me from all blame, . . ."—ALS, *ibid.* On March 1, USG endorsed papers concerning Johnson. "I think this nomination should be made. At the same time others of equal merit should go to the Senate."—AES, Mrs. Walter Love, Flint, Mich. On March 22, USG nominated Johnson as 2nd lt., 24th Inf. On May 20, Johnson was retired as capt. On Sept. 10, 1872, Johnson, Springfield, Mo., wrote to USG seeking additional back pay.—LS, DNA, RG 94, ACP, R443 CB 1870. Voluminous related papers are *ibid.*

1869, Nov. 16. Judson Kilpatrick, U.S. minister, Santiago, to USG. "I send you photograps of the Chilian Indians they may be interesting to you as compared with our Indians at home—The two on seperate cards are the War Chiefs of the well-known & brave Arocanians who have ever been independent living in the south of Chili upon extensive pasture lands— These chiefs have lately visited Santiago in great state—"—ALS, OFH.

1869, Nov. 18. Mrs. M. Meads, Washingon, D. C., to USG. "My husband Wm W Meads has been dismised from the Navy Yard at Washington from Charges prefered unknown to himself. I humbly beg your influence with the Hon. G. M. Robeson Sec of the Navy to give my husbands case an investigation for he is sure he can prove his inocence. Mr Meads is an sober and industrious and inofensive man as Every Officer in the Navy yard will testify. he lost his right arm Eighteen years ago and has been employed fourteen years in the Navy yard and filled the position of Quarterman in the Civil Engnrs Dept up to the time of his discharge to the satisfaction of all those under whom he has been Employed. . . ."—ALS, DNA, RG 45, Subject File, Div. PL.

1869, Nov. 20.   Louisa Porteous, Beaufort, S. C., to USG. "You will receive in this Bag a present of *cured orange Preserves grown* on this *Island* —from the Lady who once before had the pleasure of addressing you on the subject of her Property on this Island—. . ."—ALS, DLC-Hamilton Fish.

1869, Nov. 22.   "Neem[a]yer," New York City, to USG. "I will conduct my property myself"—Telegram received (at 3:40 P.M.), DNA, RG 107, Telegrams Collected (Bound).

1869, Nov. 25.   Ellen O'Connell, Jamestown, N. Y., to USG through Secretary of State Hamilton Fish. "This appeal is made by Ellen OConnell of Jamestown chautauqua county and State of new york as she is Informed your Excellency has adopted the same Rules and Regulations that the Duke of Wellington and Lord Hill did with Regard to the claims of the Relatives of deceased soldiers and the widows of deceased soldiers claiming some compensation for Back pay Bounty and prize money and Pension   The said Ellen OConnell Beg leave to approach his Excellency that a son of hers Deceased of the name of Maurice OConnell served with distinction for nearly [t]hree years in the United States army during the Rebellous war and she is glad to say highly distinguished himself . . ."—ALS, DNA, RG 59, Miscellaneous Letters.

1869, Nov. 30.   William R. Smith, Washington, D. C., to USG. "The St Andrews Society of the City of Washington would be delighted to have the honor of your company this evening at 'Amans' 507 ninth Street. to celebrate the anniversary of their Patron St, Andrew,"—ALS, DLC-USG, I, B.

1869, Nov.   H. F. Heisterman *et al.* to USG. "Your Memoralists beg leave most respectfully to represent, that we are residents of the Colony of British Columbia—many of us british subjects and all deeply interested in the welfare and progress of our adopted Country. . . . we respectfully request, that Your Excellency will cause this Memorial to be laid before the Government of the United States, and that in any negociations which may be pending or *undertaken* between Your Government and that of Her Most Gracious Majesty, for the settlement of territorial or other questions, that you will endeavor to induce Her Majesty to *consent* to the *transfer* of *this Colony* to the *United States.* We believe that Her Majesty earnestly desires the welfare and happiness of all Her People, in view of the circumstance that for years she has consented to the annual exodus of tens of thousands of her subjects to the United States and that she will not let political traditions and sentiments influence her against a Measure, which is so earnestly desired by the People of this poor isolated Colony."—DS (43 signatures—docketed as received on Dec. 28), DNA, RG 59, Miscellaneous Letters. Sec *Washington Chronicle*, Jan. 1, 1870. On Jan. 4, Secretary of State Hamilton Fish recorded in his diary. "The Memorial from residents of British Columbia addressed to the President, asking Annexation to the US was brought up by me—agreed that I send a copy to Mr Motley, & shows this, or state its purport, to Mr Thornton—I suggest that our proper course is to abstain from action 'to keep our eyes fixedly on the movement, & to keep our hands off'—the President says 'that is precisely our course of duty' "—DLC-Hamilton Fish.

On July 18, Timothy G. Phelps, collector of customs, San Francisco, wrote to USG. "I desire, most respectfully, to call your attention to a matter which I believe to be of the first importance to the future interests of the United States. I refer to the annexation to the United States of all that portion of the Brittish Possessions lying west [o]f Lake Superior, including Brittish Columbia I beleive from Evidence [t]o me very conclusive that the English [G]overnment is disposed to part with this vast Territory on terms the most advantagious to the United States, and I have every reason to think from conversations had with and declarations made by the prinsipal residents that the great majority of the people of the Territory are openly desirous [o]f annexation . . . But Should you think it unwise to attempt the aquisition on the basis of the Alabama claims, I hope and trust that you, in your wisdom, will adopt some mode by which it may be acquired. It is alledged that Sir Frederick Bruce was favorable to the transfer of British Columbia to us, and it is thought by many that some negotiations were pending between him and Mr Seward at the time of Sir Frederick death Whether this is true or not I am unadvised Should you conclude to Enter upon this negotiation and Should I be able to render the Slightest assistance I trust you will command me"—ALS, DNA, RG 59, Miscellaneous Letters. On Sept. 1, Phelps wrote to USG on the same subject.—ALS, *ibid.*

1869, DEC. 1.   Horace L. Pike, Raleigh, N. C., to USG. "I am an officer of the Army. Am retired on account of the loss of my leg. Have been appointed by Gov Holden one of his aids. A civil officer. Is there any military objection to my accepting such a position—one which is purely honorary? Or if, I was called upon to operate against the Ku Klux with the state militia would it be inconsistent with my being an United States officer?"—ALS, DNA, RG 94, Letters Received, 818P 1869. Gen. William T. Sherman endorsed this letter. "No objection whatever if he is on the Retired List, on the contrary think it very proper"—AES, *ibid.*

1869, DEC. 2.   David Davis, U.S. Supreme Court, to USG. "In the event of a vacancy in the office of District Judge for the Northern District of Illinois, I would beg leave to recommend for the place, Henry. W. Blodgett Esqr ~~for~~ of Chicago—The bar of the district, as I am advised, have united in requesting his appointment. . . ."—ALS, DNA, RG 60, Records Relating to Appointments. Related papers are *ibid.* On Jan. 10, 1870, USG nominated Henry W. Blodgett as judge, Northern District, Ill.

1869, DEC. 2.   "One of Signers," Cincinnati, to USG. "Please remember D B George's petition for supervisorship signed by best firms of Cincinnati also remember Judge Ashburn's recommendation   Clarke is notoriously unpopular in southern Ohio especially in sixth (6th) District"—Telegram received (on Dec. 3, 9:10 A.M.), DNA, RG 107, Telegrams Collected (Bound).

1869, DEC. 3.   USG endorsement. "I hereby approve the aforegoing convention, and in testimony thereof I have caused the seal of the United States to be affixed."—*HED,* 41-3-1, part 3, p. 98. Written on a postal convention between the U.S. and Great Britain.—*Ibid.* USG endorsements on additional postal conventions, *ibid.,* pp. 99–139, will not be printed. On July 2, USG had endorsed a postal convention with Switzerland.—*HED,* 41-2-1, part 1, p. 91. On Aug. 15, Christopher C. Andrews, U.S. minister, Stockholm, wrote to USG. "(unofficial) . . . As a holder of office under you I am naturally interested in having your Administration as famous as possible. *One* of the means to this end is the increase of the country in population and material prosperity. This I think can be promoted by cheapening the means of correspondence between the United States and Europe; thereby affording to newly naturalized citizens facilities for writing back to their country men of advantages (especially on the public lands) in the U. States. *Postage* on a letter of ½ an ounce between Sweden and the U. States is 20 cts in gold! I will not trouble you with an argument on the subject but only say that I think it would be a very useful and important step if the Post master General would procure a radical reduction in European-American postage." —ALS (press), Andrews Papers, Minnesota Historical Society, St. Paul, Minn.

1869, DEC. 3.   W. B. Figures, editor, *The Advocate,* Huntsville, Ala., to USG. "Brevet Maj. Gen. S. W. Crawford, of the 2nd U. S. Infty., is in command in Alabama, subject to Gen Terry's orders at Atlanta, Geo. Gen Crawford has been in this State about 12 months, in which time he has fully mastered 'the situation' in all its phases. He enjoys the unlimited confidence of the Republicans of the State, as well as their entire good wishes, besides having the respect of the opponents of reconstruction. He knows the people, the public men, the trials and difficulties of the past, the struggles of the present, and the dangers of the future. Next year a bitter political contest will take place for the supremacy in Alabama—the Secessionists will make a last, desperate, and malignant effort to regain control, that they may enjoy *power* as before and, practically, render nugatory what has been done. The Republicans, if then successful, will rule the State for many years. To succeed, it is *essential*, almost vital, as all Republicans think, that Gen Crawford should be retained in chief command in Alabama, and vested with the fullest powers possible under the law, as was Gen Ames in Mississippi—reporting direct to Washington, and able to act of his own volition—with a sufficiency of troops to repress disorder, curb the vicious and encourage the timid. This done, all will be well at the next election."—ALS, DNA, RG 94, Letters Received, 361F 1869. On Dec. 26, Gen. William T. Sherman endorsed this letter. "Gnl Crawford commands one of the Regmts that compose the Command of Maj Gn Terry. I have no information that leads me to suppose Gen Terry intends to change his Station, and I think it would be unwise to anticipate Events"—AES, *ibid.*

On Dec. 11, Governor William H. Smith of Ala. telegraphed to USG. "I understand orders have been issued for removing troops from this city. Please have orders suspended until you receive letter"—Telegram received (at 4:00 P.M.), *ibid.*, RG 107, Telegrams Collected (Bound). On the same day, Smith wrote to USG. "I understand that orders have been issued which involve the removal of three companies of the 2nd U. S. Infantry, from this city. The removal of these troops would leave the capital of the State without any troops whatever. I have the honor to request that, unless these orders be based upon some military necessity, they be so modified as to allow those three companies to remain at Montgomery. I consider their presence here very desirable as a precaution against possible turbulence. The officers in command of them are high toned gentlemen; and being known and recognized as such, they are in condition to exercise a useful influence in the line of their official duty, and with the community at large. I hope, also, to be excused for suggesting that the senior officer of the State, Brevet Maj. General S. W. Crawford, be stationed at Montgomery. His headquarters are now at Huntsville; and I have frequently ~~frequently~~ experienced inconvenience on account of his remoteness from the State capital. I think that his presence here would be mutually advantageous to the United States service, and the State of Alabama. Gen. Crawford has been here a sufficient length of time to become familiar with the wants of the State, and the proper relation of the military service to it."—ALS, *ibid.*, RG 94, Letters Received, 788S 1869. On Dec. 12, John G. Stokes, editor, *Daily Journal*, Montgomery, telegraphed to USG. "For Heavens sake dont remove the Troops from Our State or City   We need them & want a special Order from the Secty of War retaining them"—Telegram received (at 4:14 P.M.), *ibid.* Related papers are *ibid.*

1869, DEC. 4.   John H. Freeman, Richmond, to USG. "An opportunity is now offered to provide for me in the vacancy of Colle[c]torship second (2d) Va Dist to be filled today."—Telegram received (at 1:25 P.M.), DNA, RG

107, Telegrams Collected (Bound). USG nominated Freeman as postmaster, Lexington, Va.

1869, DEC. 6. To Senate. "I submit to the Senate for its consideration with a view to ratification an Additional Article to the Convention of the 24th of October, 1867, between the United States of America and His Majesty the King of Denmark."—DS, DNA, RG 46, Presidential Messages, Foreign Relations, Denmark. Related papers are *ibid.*

1869, DEC. 6. To Senate. "The following named Officers of the Indian Department were suspended during the recess of the Senate, pursuant to the provisions of the 2d section of 'an act to amend "an act regulating the Tenure of certain civil Officers" ' Approved April 5. 1869. . . ."—DS, DNA, RG 46, Papers Pertaining to Certain Nominations.

1869, DEC. 6. U.S. Senator Willard Warner of Ala. to USG. "The enclosed telegram has just been received by me. Judge Felder and Hon. Alexander White are two of the ablest and best native Republicans of Alabama and Mr Stow has been for thirty years a resident of Montgomery, is a man of great worth and wealth who remained South during the war and stood unflinchingly by our flag all the time. No better representatives of the native Union men and Republicans of the South can be found than these three men."—ALS, PHi. See W. Brewer, *Alabama: Her History, Resources, War Record, and Public Men* (Montgomery, 1872), pp. 226–27, 461.

1869, DEC. 7. To Senate. "I transmit for the consideration of the Senate the accompanying copy of a correspondence between the Secretary of State and the Minister of the United States at Berlin, in relation to the exchange of the Ratifications of the Naturalization Convention, dated July 27th 1868, between the United States and the Government of Württemberg, which was not effected within the time named in the Convention."—DS, DNA, RG 46, Presidential Messages, Foreign Relations, Germany. The enclosures are *ibid.*

1869, DEC. 7. To Senate. "I transmit for the consideration of the Senate, the accompanying copy of a correspondence between the Secretary of State and the Legation of the United States at Brussels, in relation to the exchange of the ratifications of the Consular Convention with Belgium, signed on the 5th of December, 1868, which was not effected within the time named in the Convention."—DS, DNA, RG 46, Presidential Messages, Foreign Relations, Belgium. The enclosures are *ibid.*

1869, DEC. 8. James R. Allaben, Brooklyn, to USG. "I will be in Washington tomorrow, I beg that I may be heard before further action is taken in regard to the office I now hold,"—Telegram received (at 10:00 A.M.),

DNA, RG 107, Telegrams Collected (Bound). On Dec. 6, USG had nominated Allaben as assessor of Internal Revenue, 2nd District, N. Y., then withdrew his name on Dec. 7. On Dec. 15, USG renewed the nomination; on March 14, 1870, he nominated Albert G. Allen.

1869, DEC. 9. To Senate. "I desire the consent of the Senate to the correction of a clerical error which occurred in nom[in]ating for his confirmation during their last session, the officer herein named. The name of 'Frederick W. Elbreg,' confirmed April 9. 1869, to be Assistant Surgeon, United States Army, should read, 'Frederick W. Elbrey.' "—DS, DNA, RG 46, Papers Pertaining to Certain Nominations.

1869, DEC. 9. U.S. Senator Simon Cameron to Frederick T. Dent. "The bearer, Col Thomas, is the gentleman to whom I desired Gen Grant yesterday to grant a few moments. The President yesterday promised me to see Col Thomas, and I beg you to procure him an audience"—LS, Harry S. Truman Library, Independence, Mo.

1869, DEC. 10. Horace Porter to Edward Y. Goldsborough, U.S. marshal, Baltimore. "The President's attention has been called to the insertion of the advertisements of your office in the enclosed paper. As its course has been uniformly antagonistic to the Gov't the President suggests that it would be well to withhold from it the public patronage, and confine the patronage to the loyal papers."—Copy, DLC-USG, II, 1.

1869, DEC. 11. U.S. Delegate José Francisco Cháves of New Mexico Territory, Washington, D. C., to USG. "Juan Andres Abeita and Juan Rey Lucero, Pueblo Indians, Principal men of the Pueblo of Ysleta in New Mexico, and authorized Delegates of all the Indian Pueblo towns of New Mexico, came under my care and protection to Washington recently, and are now here, awaiting an opportunity to pay their respects to their 'Tata Grande' (Great Father). These Indians have come as the representatives of all the Pueblo towns in the Territory of New Mexico, to lay their grievances before you and to solicit your parental care and kindness towards them. This class of Indians have, since the Treaty of Guadalupe Hidalgo, always been held and treated as wards of the Government, and have stood related to it as children to a parent. Although living chiefly in the settlements and within the precincts of civilization, as distinguished from the wild, nomadic portion of their race, they have never been treated as citizens, but rather as children; and in a political point of view, have been totally dependent. They are a harmless, orderly and loyal people, always obedient to the law, and in every conflict between the savage and civilized man, they promptly espouse the cause of the latter, as illustrated in the alacrity, efficiency and valor with which they coalesced with the military authority of the United States, on numerous occasions, in the pursuit and castigation of predatory Indian tribes. These poor, simple-minded people afford examples of morality and thrift worthy of emulation, within the very limited sphere of their opportunities, which are of the most circumscribed and primitive character. While the wild and savage tribes who infest and devastate the country are looked after with solicitude and care by the Government, these friendly and upright people are almost entirely neglected. The former have an amplitude of Agents to visit them, to advise them, and learn their wants; they have schools of letters, of agriculture and mechanism; they are annually made the recipients of presents, and in various ways are made the subjects of humane attention and friendly solicitude on the part of the Government. To the latter none of these marks of consideration and kindness are extended, except that they have *one* Agent to look after the interests of nineteen Pueblo communities, extending over a vast region of country (a distance of 300 miles intervening between the two Pueblos most remote from each other), but they have no schools, no instruction in agriculture and the mechanic arts, and receive no tokens whatever of the solicitude of their Great Father for their advancement in the path of moral, social and material progress. I would respectfully submit, whether it would not be wise on the part of the Government, as a matter of policy, and to its honor as a measure of humanity, to institute a system for the education of these Indians, and for their instruction in agriculture, and to some extent in the mechanic arts. They are an apt and industrious people, and if supplied with the principal agricultural and mechanical implements and favored with instruction in the science of husbandry, and the arts of mechanism, they would soon become excellent farmers and skilfull artizans The foundation of moral and material progress is laid deep and broad amongst them, and a little of the fostering care herein suggested would be promptly repaid by their rapid advancement and the developement of results advantageous to the Government, and beneficial to the general interests of society. I beg leave, in their name, to lay before you a grievance which they sorely feel, and of which they humbly but most seriously complain. It is the imposition upon them of an Internal Revenue Tax, which has been carried so far that some of them have been indicted in the U. S. District Court for selling their little products without license and are thus held amenable for the violation of a law of which they were totally ignorant, and which, considering their filial and dependent relation to the Government, cannot equitably if legally be put into operation against them. I appeal to your sense of justice and humanity to take such steps for their relief in this matter as may be concordant with your official obligations and views of public duty. The two Pueblo Indians herein mentioned have come to Washington not on an errand of pleasure or idle curiosity, but with the legitimate purpose, as the representatives of all the Pueblo towns in the Territory of New Mexico, of entreating their '*Tata Grande*' or Great Father, in which light they regard the President of the United States, to alleviate the grievances and disadvantages under which they labor, as herein faintly and imperfectly delineated. As they are poor and their outlay of coming here, though small, is to them heavy, I respectfully ask that their necessary expenses in making this visit, be reimbursed to them. Such a mark of kindness will be gratefully appreciated and I am sure that it will not be a fruitless investment on the part of Government. I beg leave, in conclusion, to state that the fact of your having wisely selected one of their own race to preside over the Indian Bureau at Washington has had no small degree of influence over the minds of the Pueblo Indians in sending this delegation here to intercede in their behalf. That fact, together with your own ever well known views of policy towards the Red man, inspires the hope that their mission will meet the wish and favor of their Great Father."—Copy, DNA, RG 75, Letters Received, Pueblo Agency.

1869, DEC. 11. John S. Loomis, National Land Co., New York City, to USG. "I take sincere pleasure in introducing Mr Alexander McDonald President of the Miners National Association of great Britain He is exerting important influence to move large emigration to Pacific Railway lands and mining districts of america. He will call today at eleven (11) with Col Geo O Evans"—Telegram received (at 9:25 A.M.), DNA, RG 107, Telegrams Collected (Bound).

1869, DEC. 13. Edward J. Gay, "Plantation," La., to Julia Dent Grant. "Presuming upon old family acquaintance, I take the liberty of introducing my son John H. Gay, who is going to school in Maryland and avails of the holiday season to make a visit to Washington. It would be gratifying to my son to meet the Chief Magistrate of our nation, and as no introduction could prove so agreeable as one by yourself, if it should be convenient, I will thank you to confer upon him that honor. Although in the distant south we feel none the less interest in current events affecting the public welfare and especially in all that appertains to the President and his family. We look forward with pleasure to the future when as neighbours in St Louis County, we hope to meet Genl Grant free from the cares which now surround him and in the enjoyment of the measure of his fame amply filled."—ALS, Louisiana State University, Baton Rouge, La. On Sept. 16, 1874, Gay, New Orleans, telegraphed to USG. "Just arrived from Saint Louis, find quiet and order which will speedily prevail throughout the State—if left alone, As an old neighbor, family friend and well wisher I appeal to you, not to re-instate Kellogg I will forfeit my head if under the new State government the rights of the colored men are not fully respected, their welfare is my welfare, I am no politician I speak for the good of my country, allow the people of Louisiana to hail you as their Father, their best friend,"—Telegram received, DNA, RG 60, Letters from the President. Similar telegrams are *ibid.*

1869, DEC. 14. James L. Crane, Springfield, Ill., to USG. "A few months ago there appeared in the public prints a statement charging Col. John Logan U. S. Marshall for the Southern District of Illinois with some financial improprieties in his official operations. I desire to say to you that I have known Mr. Logan for a number of years to be a high minded, honorable, Christian gentleman. It would take very strong & clear proof to make his old neighbors & friends believe that he would knowingly do any thing dishonorable. It is feared that the complaints against Logan are the result of some rivalry or spite. Of this, however, I would not decide. But it would seem that a good character which a man has for years been trying to build up, & that the peace & happiness of a quiet & well-cultivated family should not be allowed to be disturbed or overthrown, without at least a fair hearing. Mr Logan desires the fullest investigation, & that *he do not be required to retire from his present official position without it.*"—ALS, DNA, RG 60, Letters from the President. See *PUSG,* 15, 562. USG appointed John L. Routt to replace John Logan.

1869, DEC. 14. Joseph M. Humphreys, collector of customs, Richmond, to USG. "On the 16th day of July 1866. a little over 3 years ago, I was appointed Collector of Customs for the Port of Richmond Va. and Confirmed by the Senate—this before the defection of President Johnson. I was appointed On account of services I had rendered my government during the war of rebellion at the earnest solicitation of the late Hon John M Botts. . . . Having faithfully performed the duties of my office to the entire satisfaction of the Department with the testimony On file from all the Merchants having business in the office I respectfully ask to be renominated."—ALS, DNA, RG 56, Collector of Customs Applications. On May 20, 1870, Charles S. Mills, Richmond, wrote to USG. "Learning that the term of appointment of Mr J. M. Humphreys as Collector of the Customs for the port of Richmond will soon expire, I take pleasure in testifying to the gentlemanly manner in which he has transacted the duties of his office, and to the aid and support which he has ever extended to loyalty wherever existing. . . ."—ALS, *ibid.* On June 28, Cornelius Harris, John Taney, and A. R. Brooks, Richmond, wrote to USG. "I learn with deep regret that a movement is on foot, to remove Col J. M. Humphreys, under the flimsy pretext that, the Political Necessity requires it. I will assure you Mr President that you can afflict us in no greater way than disregard Our Known, tried and trusty friends, and appoint *Such men* as B. W. *Gillis*—or. *Washburn* Whose only thought is money, and I feel called upon to say to you that the appointment of Gillis will be productive of untold Evils, he does not command The respect of fifty Colored men in Richmond, and Can never again be considered by them for any place of emolument or Honor, I hope Sir if you have *determined* on the removal, that you will give us Some One more acceptable to the Collored Man."—LS, *ibid.* On July 13, USG nominated Joseph M. Humphreys for reappointment as collector of customs, Richmond.

On Jan. 27, 1871, Bosanquet W. Gillis, editor, *Richmond State Journal,* wrote to USG. "You were kind enough to say to me in my recent interview with you, that you had at one time favorably considered my application for the position of Collector of Customs at this port. I desire to say now that, if a change is still contemplated in that office, I may not in any sense be considered an applicant, and to further add that, in my opinion the appointment of Dr G. K Gilmer, whose name you mentioned in connection with this position, would not only be highly creditable to your administration, but would tend greatly to harmonize and strengthen the party here. As I stated to you, my sole desire is to keep my paper in a condition where it may be of the greatest use to the party, and to contribute to our success in the coming Presidential contest. Any thing that your administration may feel disposed to do in furtherance of this our common object will be gratefully appreciated by me."—ALS, *ibid.* On Jan. 28, U.S. Representative Charles H. Porter of Va. wrote to USG. "I received a communication from Richmond this morning, from a member of the Legislature—a gentleman of the utmost reliability—who informs me that on yesterday Dr. Geo. K. Gilmer solicited him, but unsuccessfully, to sign a recommendation for his appointment as Collector of Customs, at Richmond, in place of Colonel J. M. Humphreys, and stated to him that he had a letter from Senator Lewis of a recent date, to the effect that Col. Humphreys was to be removed, and a telegram from J. Ambler Smith (Son of Assessor Smith) now in Washington, which declared that a change had been determined on in the Collectorship'. My correspondent adds, 'I only saw the telegram, which said in substance, "get all the signatures you can, and come to Washington to-night— a change has been determined on" &c. After our Conversation of yesterday morning, I know full well that young Smith could not base his telegram on any assurances received from yourself, but he must have received encouragement in some quarter, especially ~~as~~ as Dr. Gilmer left Richmond last night, in compliance with the request contained in Smith's telegram, and is in Washington to-day. As already ~~stated~~ intimated, I have no idea that you will cause the removal of Col. Humphreys, and will only say that if at any time in the future, it should be contemplated, I have only this very reasonable request to make, that I may be notified, and if my unqualified wish, as the Representative of the district, that he should be retained, cannot be gratified, I pledge myself to show by proof which will abundantly satisfy you, that the Republican *party* of Richmond, and the district, most earnestly desire his retention in that position, And if this should not be deemed sufficient, will demonstrate that such is the wish of the party throughout the *State.* As regards his personal, and official integrity, and the ability, and faithfulness with which he discharges every duty of his office, none, I believe, have ever had the temerity to question."—ALS, *ibid.*

On Feb. 1, Andrew Washburn, pension agent, Richmond, wrote to USG. "I beg leave to ask your favorable attention to the claims of Dr. G. K. Gilmer for appointment to some federal office. . . ."—ALS, *ibid.* On Feb. 2, Mills *et al.* wrote to USG. "The undersigned, desiring the success and continuance of your administration for a second term, respectfully represent to you that the majority of white voters in the state over the colored is about thirty thousand, that this disparety is constantly increasing, that the downward tendency of the Republican Party, its odium and repulsiveness to the whites, can only be checked and made acceptable and attractive to them by being represented by a better and different class of men. We think every Federal office in the state should be held as far as possible by natives and northern men whose character would give respectability to the party, and to the office, and we think the appointment of Dr G K Gilmer to the Collectorship of this Port will tend to do all this   Unfortunately the prejudice against northern men who have recently settled among us is so great, and in many instances justly so, that many of them cannot command the respect, the confidence, or the votes of many republicans."—DS (5 signatures), *ibid.* Related papers are *ibid.* In [*Feb.*], Samuel C. Fischer, Yahn Deuringer, and Charles Pflugfelder wrote to USG. "We present ourselves before you as a committee duly appointed by the organization of Republicans in the City of Richmond, known as the Central Committee of the 'German Republican Club', . . . we do not hesitate to say that the office of Collector of Customs in this City, as at present managed and controlled is a mere political machine, and that its presiding genius, Mr Jos M Humphrey's is the greatest enemy to the party and your administration that can be found in our city. In view of these facts we have thought it proper to present to you this paper; as presiding officers with our signatures attached, in the hope that your Excellency will take some speedy action in the premises,   We have no name to offer you as a suitable candidate for this position, but would merely say that there are scores of men in the City who are sound Republicans, who would fill the office with credit to the party and your administration."—DS, *ibid.* On Feb. 14, Deuringer and Pflugfelder wrote to USG recommending George K. Gilmer for collector of customs, Richmond.—LS, *ibid.*

On Oct. 3, 1872, William A. Richardson, act. secretary of the treasury, wrote to USG transmitting documents suspending Humphreys and designating Mills as collector of customs, Richmond.—Copy, *ibid.*, Letters Sent. On Dec. 5, 1870, Elizabeth Van Lew, postmaster, Richmond, had written to USG. "Permit me to introduce to you the bearer Dr. Chas. Mills, one of our best and most worthy citizens   You will find Dr. M—a scholar—speaking with fluency the French language—and what is better—an honorable and courteous gentleman. I know no one I could so highly commend for the position he ~~seeks~~desires   Dr. Mills was the Republican choice for one of the best city offices at our late sham election—"—ALS, *ibid.*, RG 59, Letters of Application and Recommendation. Related papers are *ibid.* On Dec. 5, 1872, USG nominated Mills as collector of customs, Richmond.

1869, DEC. 15.   To Henry T. Blow, U.S. minister. "I received your letter of the 25th. of October, and the two sacks of coffee therein mentioned have just reached us. It is very fine and Mrs. Grant and I are greatly obliged to you for your kindness."—LS, DNA, RG 84, Brazil, Miscellaneous Correspondence. On Oct. 25, Blow, Rio de Janeiro, had written to USG. "I have taken the liberty of sending you by this 'Steamer,' two sacks of very fine old coffee, one 'Mocha' the other Java, both grown in Brazil. I think Mrs. Grant will say that they cannot be excelled, anyhow I trust you will accept them with my warmest wishes for the health and happiness of yourself and family. My wife presents her compliments and desires me to say that she hopes to give Mrs. Grant, some account of life in Brazil by the November Steamer. I beg Sir to express to you, how deeply I feel the death of Genl Rawlins; he belonged to that class of true and strong men, that our country can poorly afford to lose, at a time when so much has yet to be accomplished."—ALS, IHi.

1869, DEC. 15. To House of Representatives. "In answer to the resolution of Decr 9th 1869, requesting a copy of the charges, testimony, findings and sentence in the trial by Court Martial of Passed Assistant Surgeon Charles L Green, USnavy I transmit herewith a report, from the Secretary of the Navy to whom the resolution was referred."—Copy, DNA, RG 130, Messages to Congress. On Dec. 14, Secretary of the Navy George M. Robeson had written to USG transmitting the information.—Copy, *ibid.*, RG 45, Letters Sent to the President. See *HED*, 41-2-30.

1869, DEC. 15. To House of Representatives. "In answer to the Resolution of the House of Representatives of the 13th instant requesting a copy of official correspondence on the subject of Cuba, I transmit a Report from the Secretary of State to whom the Resolution was referred."—Copies, DNA, RG 59, General Records; *ibid.*, RG 130, Messages to Congress. Printed as *HED*, 41-2-22. On Dec. 14, Secretary of State Hamilton Fish had written to USG. "The Secretary of State, to whom has been referred the Resolution of the House of Representatives; of yesterday, requesting the President, if not inconsistent with the public interest, to communicate to that House a copy of any correspondence with the Minister of the United States at Madrid referring to Cuba, of the instructions to that minister, and of any correspondence with the Government of Spain relating to that subject, has the honor to report, that it is not deemed advisable at this time to comply with the request contained in the Resolution."—Copy, DNA, RG 59, General Records. On Dec. 20, Fish wrote to USG. "The Secretary of State to whom was referred the Resolution of the Senate of the 8th instant, requesting the President to communicate to that Body 'if in his opinion not incompatible with the public interest, any information he may have in his possession in regard to the progress of the revolution in Cuba, and the political and civil condition of the Island'—has the honor to lay before the President extracts from late correspondence between the Department of State and the Spanish Minister accredited to this Government, Mr Lopez Roberts. . . ."— LS, *ibid.*, RG 46, Presidential Messages. The enclosures are *ibid.* On the same day, USG transmitted these documents to the Senate.—Copies, *ibid.*; *ibid.*, RG 59, General Records; *ibid.*, RG 130, Messages to Congress. Printed as *SED*, 41-2-7.

1869, DEC. 16. To John L. Motley, U.S. minister to Great Britain. "This will introduce to you Hon. J B Chaffee of Colorado. I commend him to your confidence and regard."—Transcript, USGA (ALS, Boston Public Library, Boston, Mass.).

1869, DEC. 17.   Thomas L. Kane, Kane, Pa., to USG. "I break through my resolution not to write to you for appointments to office; assured that it will do you credit to interfere in favor of one of the bravest and most deserving soldiers of the War. *Colonel William Rickards* of Franklin Penna. ought to have the Appraisership in Philadelphia vacated by the resignation of Dr. Wilmer Worthington. . . ."—ALS, DNA, RG 56, Appraiser of Customs Applications. No appointment followed. On June 18, 1870, Kane wrote to USG. "*Nicholas P. Trist* asks for the Postmastership at Alexandria Va, should a vacancy occur. I infer from the letter on my table that Mr Trist is in narrow circumstances, & would be grateful for this modest post in reward for the services which he has rendered to his country. I am old enough to remember when Mr Trist was even more intimately in the confidence of General Jackson than the public believe any gentleman of your military family to have been in yours. And when, no longer a boy I visited the White House which you now inhabit, I remember how strong a man he was there, before he left the State Department to go to Mexico, where he so unexpectedly thwarted the designs of Mr Polk's unscrupulous administration. Had he, after turning upon his own party, courted their opponents, he might have risen very high. But he prefered to keep his pride and his consistency, remaining in the shade to which his anti-slavery principles doomed him under succeeding Democratic Administrations. Are there good men around you who may be forgotten by a future generation 'Knowing not Joseph'? Those of your supporters who may survive to see the Administration of 1890 will be grateful to it if it compliments us in keeping from want the old age of faithful friends of yours. To day there still remain not a few disciples of your predecessor Thomas Jefferson, who will thank you for befriending Mr Trist."—Copy, DLC-Nicholas P. Trist. See *PUSG*, 18, 412–16.

1869, DEC. 18.   USG endorsement. "Unless the records in the War Dept. show more than is seen from papers yet placed before me Capt Gay may be nominated to the Senate for restoration."—AES, DNA, RG 94, ACP, G87 CB 1869. Written on papers concerning Maj. Ebenezer Gay, 17th Inf., who had been cashiered on June 3, 1869, for drunkenness on duty.—*Ibid.*

1869, DEC. 18.   "Chambers & Cattell," Philadelphia, to USG. "Limit Government gold or it will ruin importers and manufacturers, Will have to discharge workmen now, Oblige old friends"—Telegram received (at 4:00 P.M.), DNA, RG 107, Telegrams Collected (Bound).

1869, DEC. 21.   U.S. Senator John Sherman of Ohio to USG. "I most heartily join in the request made for the appointment of Louis T. Peale as a Cadet in the Naval Academy for the reason stated by Profr Henry. I personally know young Peale as a bright active and deserving lad who without doubt will ~~obtain~~ maintain a high rank in the school. His Grandfather certainly deserves this much ~~from~~ of Executive favour"—Copy, American Philosophical Society, Philadelphia, Pa. In an undated letter, Joseph Henry wrote to USG. "Contrary to my usual custom, I take the liberty to commend the application for an appointment to the Naval Academy of the grandson of Mr. T. R. Peale, of this city. Mr. Peale has been, for many years, a faithful and efficient servant of his country with but small remuneration. He is a son of the celebrated painter of Revolutionary times, the only survivor, with one exception, of the Rocky Mountain Exploring Expedition under Major Long, was the naturalist of the United States Exploring Expedition and is, now, one of the principal Examiners in the Patent Office. His grandson, Lewis T. Peale, his only surviving offspring, and the candidate for the appointment, is a lad well qualified by talents, education and gentlemanly habits to do honor to the Navy."—LS (press), Smithsonian Institution Archives. Louis T. Peale attended the U.S. Naval Academy, but did not graduate.

1869, DEC. [22].   To New England Society, New York City. "I have received your kind invitation, and should be more than pleased to attend your anniversary dinner; but so many matters of public importance claim my attention that I am reluctantly forced to say that I cannot be with you."— *New York Tribune*, Dec. 23, 1869.

1869, DEC. 22.   To Senate. "In answer to the Resolution of the Senate of the 20th instant in relation to correspondence between the United States and Great Britain concerning questions pending between the two countries since the rejection of the claims Convention by the Senate, I transmit a Report from the Secretary of State upon the subject and the papers by which it was accompanied."—DS, DNA, RG 46, Presidential Messages. The enclosures are *ibid.* See *SED*, 41-2-10.

1869, DEC. 22.   James F. Casey, collector of customs, New Orleans, to USG. "I have telegraphed Secretary Boutwell for permission to visit Washington on business connected with a reduction of force of employes   Please request him to allow special Agent Kinsella to accompany me   I desire to leave tomorrow evening"—Telegram received (on Dec. 23, 9:20 A.M.), DNA, RG 56, Letters Received; *ibid.*, RG 107, Telegrams Collected (Bound).

1869, DEC. 29.   Governor Alvan Flanders of Washington Territory, Washington, D. C., to USG. "Since my arrival in this City I have seen by the papers that General Solomon has been [a]ppointed Governor of Washington Territory. If [t]his be true, it is of course also true, that I have [b]een removed. What charges there may be against me I have no means of knowing, escept so far [a]s I gather them from the news papers, which appear to be as follows. First, that I have vetoed many of the acts of the Legislative Assembly, and have thus [o]bstructed the necessary legislation of the Territory. Second—that I opposed the election of Mr Garfield, present Delegate from Washington Territory. There may have been other charges made against me, but if so I do not know what they are. . . .”—LS, DNA, RG 59, Washington Territorial Papers. The enclosures are *ibid.* On Jan. 10, 1870, USG nominated Edward S. Salomon as governor, Washington Territory. Recommendations are *ibid.*, Letters of Application and Recommendation. Related papers are *ibid.*, RG 46, Senate 41B-A5, Papers Pertaining to Executive Nominations. On Jan. 19, Secretary of State Hamilton Fish wrote to U.S. Senator James W. Nye of Nev. “I have the honor to acknowledge the receipt of your note of the 17th instant and to inform you, in reply, that Governor Flanders is still in office. The intent of the nomination of his successor Sent to the Senate was to effect his removal, with the advice and consent of the Senate.”—Copy, *ibid.*, RG 59, General Records. On March 6, 1871, Salomon wrote to USG. “I received leave of absence for Sixty days dated January 7th 1871. This leave expires tomorrow. I did not leave the Territory until January 28th, and as nearly 4 weeks of my time is taking up in traveling from and [to] my territory I respectfully ask for an [ex]-tension of my leave for 30 days.”—ALS, *ibid.*, Washington Territorial Papers. On Sept. 18, Joseph S. Vansant, Olympia, wrote to USG. “As a citizen of Washington Territory and a life long republican, having served in the army from June 62 to the close of the war—desiring that the republican party shall prosper and be represented on the Pacific slope by men of whom we need not blush to recognize I desire to call your personal attention to the conduct of Edwin Solomon the present Governor of this Territory, as his continuance in office leads me to infer that his doings are not known by you else he would be summarily dismissed and not be allowed to bring disgrace on the party and serve as capital to the democrats: First he was appointed Governor and arrived in Olympia in May 1870—during the month of June he left here and was gone in the East until August—after a sojourn of about four months he again took his departure about the 23d Dec and was absent until about the 21st April—thus, out of 2ten months he was absent ~~five~~ seven—during most of which time we were entirely without a visible head to our Territorial Govt—there having been no Secretary. But the great and most serious charge—the one which bears heavy on the party —causing honest men to hang their heads—is his complicity in the late affair —the defalcation of the Receiver of Public money—in which he is charged as being, if possible, more guilty and culpable than the Receiver himself; which is briefly this. On the 23 July Special Rev. Detective R H. I. Leopold arrived on the evening stage from Portland and immediately proceeded to the office of F. M Lamper Receiver & Depository of Public money—demanded the keys and an examination of the funds and papers pertaining to that office. The result was the discovery of a deficit of about $34.000— while in the safe was found a memoranda note or notes signed by Gov.

Solomon for the major part of said deficit—a note of L Hirsch, a store-keeper and brother in law of Solomon for quite a large sum—note of B B Tuttle Stumpage Collector et al. all of whom are intimately connected with the Governor and are here known as the Governor's ring . . ."—ALS, *ibid.*, Letters of Application and Recommendation. On Oct. 27, Salomon submitted his resignation.—ALS, *ibid.*, Letters of Resignation.

1869, DEC. 31. Governor Harrison Reed of Fla. to USG. "I have the honor to request that you will restore to the office of U. S. Marshall for the Northern Dist. of Florida, Major Alexander McGruder, a true & faithful republican, a gallant officer of the Union Army who was mutilated & crippled in battling for his country; Major M. was removed upon misrepresentation & without cause. A more honest & faithful officer never existed & it was *because* he was honest & faithful that the plan was laid for his removal. I understand the appointee is about to resign—if not, he is a member of our state Legislature & should be removed. He uses his office against the republican administration here & in the interest of corrupt men. You will but do justice to a most capable & honest man & a patriotic soldier if you restore h̶i̶m̶ Major Mcgruder to the position from which he was removed without cause. You will also aid republican govt in Florida by so doing."—ALS, DNA, RG 60, Records Relating to Appointments. USG had appointed George E. Wentworth to replace Alexander Magruder as marshal.

1869, [DEC.]. Peter Doxtator, Bennett's Corners, N. Y., to USG. "The object of this communication is to obtain, my right in a peice of land, known as the Canestoge Indian land situate in the County of Lancaster, State of Pennsylvania, I am of the Oneida tribe of Indians and a desendent as many others of this trine are of from relatives of those Indians Who were Massacred by the Whites in 1763. . . ."—ALS (docketed as received on Dec. 29), DNA, RG 75, Letters Received, New York Agency.

[*1869*]. Jesse Root Grant to USG. "P. S. This was sent over here by Mr Gallager to examine & endorse—I dont see that any thing further is necessary—I think Col Hodges deserves as much of the Government as any man in Kentucky"—AES, CSmH. Written on a letter from William D. Gallagher to USG.—LS (fragment), *ibid.* The letter probably concerned Ky. Republican Albert G. Hodges, editor and publisher, *Frankfort Commonwealth.* See Lincoln, *Works,* VII, 497.

[1869]. Clark Mills to USG. "It is doubtless known to you that I am now engaged on the 'Great National Historical Lincoln Monument' and congress having already donated sufficient number of captured cannon for all the Statuary thereby lessening the expense of them nearly one half. The money has been, and is being raised by the friends of those persons who are to be placed on the monument of which several are modeled and ready for casting in bronze There is still a small sum to be raised for the bas-relieves and allegorical figures. This monument is not only a monument to the heroes and martyrs of the late civil war, but also a monument to the Artist who designed it. In view of this fact therefore I propose to undertake the casting of the bronze doors for the House of Representitives (the models of which are now ready) and to expend the entire profits of the same, on the bas-relieves and allegorical figures of the monument. I will give any security that the government may please to require, that the work shall be done as well, if not better than the Senate doors (done by the Ames company) and for the same price. Would it be presumptuous in me in requesting the influence of the President with the Secretary of the Interior, (who has the power to give the contract) in behalf of the greatest monument in the World."—LS, DNA, RG 48, Miscellaneous Div., Letters Received. Mills designed the National Lincoln Monument to stand seventy feet high and include thirty-six statues, but the project was never completed. See *New York Times*, March 12, 1869; *Washington Star*, Dec. 24, 1870; *American Art Review*, 2 (1881), 131.

1870, JAN. 1.　"Not Signed," Brooklyn, to USG. "The cuban citizens here resident bid you happy new year and they hope that you will cause their beloved country to enjoy also a free and happy new year"—Telegram received (at 9:20 A.M.), DNA, RG 107, Telegrams Collected (Bound). In a petition dated Jan., H. W. Rogers, Jr., *et al.*, Chicago, asked USG to recognize the "CUBAN INSURGENTS as A BELLIGERENT POWER." —DS (146 signatures), *ibid.*, RG 59, Miscellaneous Letters. In an undated letter, submitted as part of a resolution, R. S. Cantine, John Dickson, and N. D. Bradley wrote to USG. "The members of Eureka Lodge No 69 A. F. & A. M. in Camden Mills, Ill., would respectfully but earnestly call your attention to the recent assassinations of Members of the Masonic Fraternity in Cuba, under the instructions of the Spanish Government influenced under and by the dictation of a Catholic Priest. The offence of these poor Men was that they met in a Masonic Lodge. It appears that a number of those unfortunate men who were assassinated were American Citizans— Therefore we as American Citizens, as well as members of the Masonic Fraternity memorialize your Excellancy to hold the Spanish Government responsible for the blood of our Brethren, and to demand from the Government of Spain Strict and full Satisfaction for this grave offence against our Countrymen and to meet out to the Government of Spain Speedy Judgement as the blood of our Brethren calls to us from the ground to avenge th[e]ir death—This we respectfully submit to your Excellency praying that this our memorial may meet with your favorable consideration."—Copy (docketed as received on April 7), *ibid.*

1870, JAN. 3.　Mary Crawford, Enon Valley, Pa., to USG. "I seat myself to write to you for information,　I am the widow of Robbert M Crawford who was a soldier of Co H 46 regt Pa vol　he was killed by guerillas Dec 20 in 63 in Lincoln Co near Fayettesville Tenn,　previous to his death

General Slocum who was in command at that time had issued an order &
carried into effect that for every man that was killed by guerillas there was
a tax of $3000 laid on the citizens of said Co $1000 was to go to the
government & the other $2000 to the widow or nearest friend of the de-
ceased   I never received any of the money or any word from it only
that it was coming to me if justice was done   Alexander Selfridge was
Capt of the Co at the time. the tax was collected & the government was
charged with it. I supposed you would know of it and could do something
for me as I stand in need,   please to send me Gen Slocum address . . . Please
to answer as I would like to hear from you about it"—ALS, DNA, RG 107,
Letters Received from Bureaus.

1870, JAN. 3.   Samuel M. Jones, Versailles, Ind., to USG. "I hope you
will excuse me for Trespassing upon your time with this communication,
It has been my intention to visit the *Capitol* during the Winter, but owing
to my legal engagements it will be out of my power to do so before the
middle of March next. And at the suggestion of Senator Pratt I address
you this communication calling your attention to my application for a
Judicial position in one of the Territories. You will recollect that in April
last Senator Pratt with the Republican Delegation of Congressman from
Indiana, presented my papers to you in person, (and at your suggestion
left them in your care) requesting my appointment as Chief Justice of
Wyoming or some one of the contiguous Territories. My friends at that time
and since, (owing to the reputation that I had acquired from my own
energies, and the endorsements of the first men of our State, and *our* earley
associations) felt sanguine of my success. I was compelled by my business
engagements to leave Washington the next morning after I called on you at
the White House, though against the advice of my friends there at the time,
but I did not desire to be foun*d booring* my friends for three months about
the Capitol in order to procure an appointment. . . ."—ALS, DNA, RG 60,
Records Relating to Appointments. Related papers are *ibid.*

1870, JAN. 4.   Governor John W. Geary of Pa. to USG. "Permit me to
call your attention to the meritorious services of Capt. Jas. Forney, of the
U. S. M. C. On the 11th of July, 1864, a detachment of eight howitzers
and one hundred and fifty marines were detached by Commander C. K.
Stribling, to proceed to Havre de Grace, Md., under the command of Lieut.
Com'r Harris, Capt. Forney being in command of the marines. The day following their arrival at Havre de Gra[c]e Com'r Harris was recalled to Phil-
adelp[hia, —] Capt. Forney in command of the detachment. On the arrival
of the detachment at Havre de Grace they found there several companies of
one hundred days' men, and two companies of volunteer troops who had
been in service, in all about one-thousand men. By order of Gen'l Wallace,
commanding the department, Capt. Forney assumed command of these also.
The object of the expedition was to repel a rebel raid under the command
of Major Gen'l Gilmor, which threatened the ferries at Havre de Grace

and the borders of Pennsylvania. It was of vital importance that the rebel force should be defeated. Capt. Forney's arrangements were so well made, and his forces so disposed, that in a skirmish at Gunpowder Bridge, the detachment had a skirmish with the enemy's cavalry which resulted in their entire defeat. Upon the arrival, [a f]ew days subsequently, of Major-Gen'l French, at Havre de Grace, that officer commended Capt. Forney for the manner in which he had conducted this successful affair. The presence of his force, as disposed by him, intimidated the enemy, prevented the accomplishment of their designs, and forced their retreat. Capt. Forney, for these and other gallant services, ask's the brevet of Lieut.-Colonel, to which I earnestly commend him, and to which I regard him as eminently entitled. By conferring this brevet, you will reward a deserving man and confer a favor upon, . . ."—ALS (torn), OFH. Capt. James Forney, U.S. Marine Corps, was confirmed as bvt. lt. col. on March 25. On April 8 and 13, 1869, USG had nominated Forney as bvt. maj. for "gallantry in action against the savages of Formosa, to date from the 13th of June 1867."—LS, DNA, RG 46, Executive Nominations. Forney was the son of John W. Forney.

1870, JAN. 4.   Mrs. E. L. Moore, Beverly, N. J., to USG. "My husband George H. Moore of San Francisco Cal. has a large claim against Mexico— In consequence of recent heavy losses in business, I turn my attention, with some little hope, upon this claim—and I *entreat your momentary attention* —will you oblige me by informing me what is the prospect of a settlement of these claims—If any—when will it take place—and in what do you suppose will consist the indemnity—will it be in money or lands—I hope you will pardon my trespass upon your momentary attention and ascribe it to its true cause—namely that of enᵃabling my two sons to complete their studies —one is engaged in the study [of] science—is a graduate of Yale College [sci]entific department—has been in Germany nearly two years in the prosecution of his scientific studies, and in a few months hopes to obtain his degree of Dr of Phylosophy—My other son is a *deaf mute*—was educated at the Hartford Institution—he has been a student of art for some years— has been a pupil at the 'Ecole des beaux arts' *Paris*—for three years, and is at present in Spain—prosecuting his studies in art—he has fine talents and is full of artistic enthusiasm—has made fine progress—I am exceedingly anxious to sustain my sons until they complete their courses of study— this is the cause of my extreme anxiety—Any information you can give me on this subject, will place me under many obligations to you—"—ALS (torn), DNA, RG 76, Mexican Claims, Letters Received, 1869–76.

1870, JAN. 5.   USG endorsement. "I think this apt. probably will be the best to make in the Middle district of Tenn."—AES, DNA, RG 60, Records Relating to Appointments. Written on a letter of Jan. from U.S. Representative William B. Stokes of Tenn. to USG. "I have the honor to ask of you the appointment of. Col. Joseph. H. Blackburn. of Tennessee. as U. S.

Martial for the middle division of Said State in place of. Mr. Glasscock.
the present incumbent. at the expiration of his term, about the 20th of this
inst. . . ."—ALS, *ibid.* On Jan. 24, USG wrote to Attorney Gen. Ebenezer
R. Hoar. "On farther enquiry I think it will be better to nominate Blackburn, whos name I believe is before you, for Marshall of Middle Tenn."—
ALS, *ibid.* Related papers are *ibid.* Joseph H. Blackburn was confirmed on
Feb. 18. On May 24, 1875, USG issued a pardon for Blackburn, convicted
of forgery.—Copy, *ibid.*, RG 59, General Records.

1870, JAN. 5.   Judge Advocate Gen. Joseph Holt to USG through the
AG. "Capt. C. H. Pierce, 2d Artillery is tried at Fort Tongass, Alaska Territory, under the following charges:—1. Tyrannical conduct, to the prejudice of good order and military discipline. 2. Conduct unbecoming an
officer and a gentleman. 3. Drunkenness on duty. . . . The prosecution of
this officer is thought, from its character, to have been prompted by ill will,
although several of the charges of misconduct against him have been to
some extent made out in proof. The Court has found that the acts of the
accused which led Mr. Murphy to prefer the charges, were not unwarranted; the evidence is beleived to show them to have been firmly, but at
the same time calmly and courteously done. In the presence of a state of
facts like this, and bearing in mind his unblemised record of military
service, it would appear unjust to permit his accuser to accomplish his ruin
by adducing exaggerated proofs of an act of excess occurring six months
previously, another on Christmas day twelve months before, and yet
another on a 4th of July, of eighteen months standing. It is believed that
the interests of the service do not call for the dismissal, or the severe punishment, of this officer."—Copy, DNA, RG 153, Letters Sent. Capt. Charles H.
Peirce was mustered out as of Dec. 31.

1870, JAN. 5.   H. E. Baker, editor, *Advertiser & Tribune*, Detroit, to
USG. "Although personally a stranger to you, I make bold to write you
briefly because of the interest I feel in the right disposition to be made of
a very important office in this State, & which I have every confidence you
desire to fill properly if you can ascertain who the fittest man for the position
is I allude to the U. S. District Judgeship for this the *Eastern* District of
Michigan in place of Judge Wilkins retired on account of age As I understand, there are or have been three prominent candidates for the place, viz:
Hon Hovey K Clarke, John S Newberry Esq & Hon John W Longyear.
I further understand that Mr Longyear has secured the united recommendation of our Congressional delegation & relies upon that almost entirely to
secure your nomination I think I speak the almost unanimous sentiment
of the bar & of intelligent men in the District when I say that his appointment to this very important place would be a public misfortune. The reasons
for his recommendation are purely political & have no reference to his fitness or qualifications whatever—. . ."—ALS, DNA, RG 60, Records Relating to Appointments. The petition of the Mich. congressional delegation

and papers recommending Hovey K. Clarke, John S. Newberry, and Henry T. Backus are *ibid.* On Jan. 20, Charles A. Trowbridge, New York City, wrote to USG. *"Private* . . . I understand there are two or three aspirants for the vacancy occasioned by the resignation of Judge Wilkins (in Michigan) of the United States Court—Will you permit me to name, as a suitable person for that position, Luther S. Trowbridge of Detroit—His age is 35—He was educated at Yale College—and graduated at the Cambridge law school in 1855. He was admitted to practice in the Courts of Michigan and the United State Courts, in 1857 where he is now practicing—Is a sound lawyer and a perfectly uncorruptable man and has every qualification for the Bench—He Commanded the 10th Michigan Cavalry during the War—I write this note entirely without his knowledge—"—ALS, *ibid.* On Feb. 7, USG nominated John W. Longyear as judge, Eastern District, Mich.

1870, JAN. 7. Secretary of the Navy George M. Robeson to USG. "I have the honor to return the letter of Thomas M. Brown to you, making charges against Wm. H. Lyons, Master Machinist at the Navy Yard, Norfolk, Va. I respectfully call your attention to the enclosed copy of a communication from the Commandant of the Navy Yard, Norfolk, to whom the whole subject was referred."—Copy, DNA, RG 45, Letters Sent to the President.

1870, JAN. 8. Orvil L. Grant, Chicago, to Frederick T. Dent. "Will you please read the enclosed letter as see if you can consistently get a situation for her. I beleive she is a worthy lady I never saw her but she is a relative of Mr Smith of Albany who is one of the best friends I have and to whom I am under many obligations. It is exceedingly unpleasent to me to make applications and I know it must be equally annoying to you to be bored with them. I intend to make some developments against Bloomfield that will astonish the Rev Department and cause his removal or convince all honest men that the present Administration wink at frauds and corruptions. The present Administration must pin its hopes of success upon an honest collection of the Revenue and a reduction of the public debt, and I beleive it my duty to my Govt and my brother to expose or report frauds when I know they exist"—ALS, ICarbS.

On June 18, Orvil Grant wrote to USG. "The matter that I referred to in my note, and which I expected Dr. Lampber to explain to you, was in reference to a proposition made by Gen. Bloomfield to the distillers who had been evading the law, and whose distilleries were seized. Mr. Crosby, who is Gen. Bloomfield's confidential assistant, was authorized to make overtures to distillers, and for a certain sum of money ($20,000) paid into the hands of any man whom they might select, he (Bloomfield) would place with the man all the papers and evidence he had against the distillers, with the positive assurance that the cases would not be prosecuted. Mr. Crosby was afraid to approach the distillers, as it might have a bad effect, and proposed to me that if I would act as a third party and get the distillers to raise the money, I was to retain part as my fee. I feel, of course, suspicious about the honesty of his intentions, and thought it might be a ruse to see whether I would loan myself for such work or not, and I gave him to understand that unless I had positive assurances that Bloomfield would carry out in good faith all that was proposed, that nothing could be done. He gave me such assurances, and said that he was authorized by Bloomfield to make such overtures, that I knew that he and Bloomfield had discussed the question, and that he (Bloomfield) had instructed Crosby to make such propositions. I have had nothing to do with it, but know and can prove by men under oath that such propositions were made to them. These are all facts that I most positively know, and can swear to them, and can prove every word of it by men under oath; and I also know there are men here as gaugers and storekeepers who have assisted the distillers in stealing whisky, and received their pay for doing it, and that Bloomfield knew it, and still retains them in office. If Bloomfield were to take his solemn oath that such is not the case, such strong evidence can be brought to bear that you would be convinced that he had perjured himself by such evidence. A few months ago a Supervisor from Pennsylvania was here, and seized Kerckhoffer & Co.'s distillery, but Jussia's brother-in-law was storekeeper or ganger, I have forgotten which, and after the Supervisor left the case was not prosecuted. I know no reason for it unless it would commit Jussin's brother-in-law. There is not one man in the Revenue Department here who has a particle of political influence, and the success of the party here demands some change. The party is trying for it. Ayres has worked hard for the party, and his appointment as Supervisor would give general satisfaction. If I could see you, I would tell you much more than I like to commit to paper, even worse than I have written, and equally true, yet I might not as easily prove it. I have written you enough that you may know that you have a dishonest man in office. Now that you are apprised of the fact, you are individually responsible for his dishonesty in the future. I have gained my knowledge of the whole affair in the strictest confidence, and, to tell it, I am betraying that confidence, and the only apology I can make for doing a man so great an act of injustice is that my duty to you is stronger than my word or confidence to one who is instrumental in defrauding the Government and ruining your reputation, for all the frauds of your appointees fall upon you and the party. I prefer that you do not use this letter publicly, but remove Bloomfield, and, if necessary to prove all I have written, I can and will do it, and a great deal more. I think I know where parties are stealing under the protection of the Revenue officers, which an investigation would prove, and when you get a proper man in charge of the revenue here I will put him at work, but to make the report now will only injure me and not cause stealing to be stopped. It would injure me because the officers would cover it up, which would show me up as making a false report. I do hope you can see the necessity of a change, and that you will try to preserve the integrity of your party and your position by removing such men. If you wish to retain thieves and scoundrels in office, you alone must

be responsible for it. I would like to see you personally and tell you a little that I know about Cuban bond corruption. You would then know why one or two prominent Republicans worked so hard for recognition, and why they make such strong attacks on you. I got my information from Mr. Taylor, who tried a bribe for my influence. I know he was preparing to make proposals, for he had letters which he showed me authorizing him to do so."
—*New York Tribune,* Jan. 5, 1871.

Orvil Grant later told a reporter: "Yes; I wrote a letter of that kind quite a long time ago. But, now that it has got into print, I couldn't swear that I wrote all it says—a very strong letter, I am sorry to say. *Reporter—* Are the charges against Gen. Bloomfield and Col. Jussen made there correct? . . . *Mr. Grant*—I believe not, as I have since been informed. When that letter was written, I was misinformed and prejudiced against both gentlemen. I have since found that I did not rightly understand the matter at all, and I wrote not long since a letter to the President expressing my regret for having unintentionally prejudiced him against honorable men and good officers. I also, in that last letter, recommended that Bloomfield and Jussen be retained in office. . . . *Reporter*—Then I understand you to say that you think the offices of Supervisor and Collector are worthily filled by Bloomfield and Jussen? . . . *Mr. Grant*—Yes. Please be good enough to say for me in the REPUBLICAN that I apologize to both gentlemen for the unfortunate manner in which they have been misrepresented. I am glad, however, that I have let my brother know the true state of things in a letter which I wrote to him not long since. I hate being mixed up in anything of the kind, and can never too much regret the circumstance. . . . *Reporter—* The last letter you wrote to the President was private also, wasn't it? *Mr. Grant*—Yes, and (excitedly) how under heavens ever the document got publicity beats me. There must be some foul play—I can't understand it. . . . *Reporter*—The President will be very much annoyed, I guess? *Mr. Grant* (reflectively)—Yes, of course he will. That annoys me more than my own personal feelings in the matter. My near relation to the President has always, up to this time, kept me out of ever meddling with political matters. As I said before, I'm a plain business man, and KNOW NOTHING ABOUT POLITICS. The President has enough to worry him without having me dragged into public notice. I'm very sorry for the whole thing. 'Tis most torturing and mortifying to me. . . ."—*Chicago Republican,* Jan. 6, 1871.

On Jan. 8, following a meeting with U.S. Senator Roscoe Conkling of N. Y., Secretary of State Hamilton Fish wrote in his diary. "He refers to a recent publication of a letter of Orville Grant, to the President, in terms of regret—that the Prsdt is being damaged by such things, & expresses the hope that something may be done to arrest such interferences—that the popular mind is arrested by & holds such trifling incidents, to the disadvantage of the President—that he is being injured by the Dents &c—&c— whether I cannot say something to him—It is a very delicate matter. I appreciate what he says & wish it could be prevented—am aware of the feeling on the subject, & on the retention of so much of 'Military' about the 'personelle' of the White House—but do not see how it can be remedied—" —DLC-Hamilton Fish.

1870, Jan. 9. Nathan Ranney, St. Louis, to USG. "I inclose you the old soldiers cry in the hope to touch your heart Jno E Wool Just left was my commander at Plattsburg—The dry pines we burned on the banks of the Saranac shielded the British Sharp Shooters and Indians who were picking off our men at our guns in Fort Brown also preventing us from accurately seeing their big guns on their batteries—After this forlorne hope was finished we Silenced their guns on two batteries in two hours. This was the 2d day of the 5 days Battle Let me know through your private Secretary if you are willing to help the men now tottering on the verge of the Grave"— ALS, OFH. On Jan. 14, Orville E. Babcock wrote to Ranney. "The President directs me to acknowledge the receipt of your letter of Jany. 9th containing a report of the Convention of the Veterans of 1812, and to say that the men who fought for the preservation of our nation have always his entire sympathy. The President directed me also to say that he will with pleasure approve any measure Congress may pass in the behalf of the Veterans of 1812."—Copy, DLC-USG, II, 1.

1870, Jan. 10. To Senate. "In response to the resolution of the Senate of December 9, 1869, 'requesting the information in possession of the President or any of the Departments, relating to the action which has been had in the district of Virginia, under the act "authorizing the submission of the constitutions of Virginia, Mississippi and Texas to a vote of the people, and authorizing, the election of State Officers provided by the said constitutions, and members of Congress," Approved April 10. 1869', I have the honor to transmit herewith the reports of the Secretary of State, the Secretary of War and the Attorney General, to whom, severally, the resolution was referred."—DS, DNA, RG 46, Annual Messages. Numerous enclosures are *ibid.* Printed as *SED*, 41-2-13.

1870, Jan. 10. Jacob C. Patrick, Walcott, Iowa, to USG. "In behalf of myself and thousand of others I would Respectfully ask a favor of you one that I am constrained to beleive you will grant having a large family to Support and having no other dependence But my limited Pension which I Dearly Earnt in defence of our dearly Beloved Country In wiche I lost my right arm ask you if you canot appoint me to an office or to Speak more Plainly there are a good many Post offices in Small country towns that Pay Small Percntage but with the aid of my Pension would help me to maintain my family above the beggry Elements of this world (again not to vindicate or to undermind any man wich is beneath my Principles) for Instance the Post office at Walcott Scott Co Iowa Is conducted By a Rich man while I myself and family cannot Scarcly have the necessites of life its a hard Story to relate but nevertheless true I think according to ability that govt offices to a great Extent ought to be Given to those who Risked ther lives & lost there limbs left thire familys in short left every thing for the country they thought So much of   In conclusion I would Humbly ask of you this one favor   as Refferances are Preffrable I am a Member of the Methodist E. Church   ~~Pleas~~ Please Refer to my worthy Paster ~~Rev S~~ Rev Cyrus Morey Durant Muscatine Co Iowa   P S I tried time and again to get something to do to releive my fast retiring wants but almost Inbaaribley without avail   I hope Genl you will ~~give~~ consider this appeal worthy of notice as my reccord is good at the war dept of this country   I am Striving to make it good in that department that knows no ~~Sorr~~ Sorrows nor wants and again ask of you this favor   may the Lord Crown all your Efforts with Sucsess is my Prayer"—ALS (docketed as 1871), DLC-Benjamin F. Butler.

1870, JAN. 10.   Spotted Tail, Capt. De Witt C. Poole, 25th Inf., *et al.*, Whetstone Agency, Dakota Territory, to USG. "The undersigned, people, Chiefs and Head-men of Brulé and Ogallala Sioux, Half-breeds, Whites, and Officers of the United States Army, resident and located at and near Whetstone Agency, Dakota Territory, have to respectfully represent; that John Richard Jr. (commonly known as 'John Reshaw') formerly residing near Fort Laramie, in an unfortunate affair at said Fort, killed a soldier in the service of the United States, in August 1869, and made his escape, and is now among Indians located in or near Powder river country;—that said Richard being a half-breed has great influence among said Indians, and on account of his supposed banishment from among the whites—his former associates—we have been led to fear that he would use his influence, to create among them an increased animosity to the whites, and endeavor to bring on a war in the Spring—but having been informed by his father and friends that if pardoned by the Government—he would return to his people —use his influence among Indians for peace—and in every way conduct himself as a good citizen of the United States, we therefore your petitioners pray that he may be pardoned and allowed to return—believing as we do, that it will result in much good toward preserving peace—not only among Indians now away from reservations—but also among those upon reservations, for which your petitioners as in duty bound will ever pray."—DS, DNA, RG 94, Letters Received, 5I 1870. Related papers are *ibid.* On June 8, Attorney Gen. Ebenezer R. Hoar wrote to U.S. Attorney Joseph M. Carey, Cheyenne, Wyoming Territory. "Such extenuating circumstances are shown to the President to exist in relation to the case of John Richard, jr. otherwise called John Richards. jr. who is indicted in the Territory of Wyoming for murder, as satisfy him that, if tried and convicted, it would be a proper case for the exercise of Executive clemency—and as public considerations of grave importance render it more suitable that if such clemency is to be extended action should be had at once, you are directed to enter a *nolle prosequi* upon that indictment, and not to have any process issued for the arrest or detention of said Richard upon that charge"—Copy, *ibid.*, 774S 1870. Related papers are *ibid.*

1870, JAN. 11. USG veto. "I return herewith, without my approval, Senate Bill No. 273, entitled, 'An Act for the relief of Rollin White' for the reasons set forth in the accompanying communication, dated December 11th 1869, from the Chief of Ordnance."—DS, DNA, RG 46, President's Messages. See *SED*, 41-2-23.

1870, JAN. 11. USG endorsement. "The recommendation of the Secretary of War is approved."—Copy, DNA, RG 107, Orders and Endorsements. On the same day, Secretary of War William W. Belknap had favorably endorsed a letter of Jan. 10 from Col. Wager Swayne "concerning claim of Mrs. E. M. Perkins, for restitution of $500.00 in gold, seized while on deposit in the Citizen's Bank, New Orleans, and appropriated to the use of the United States, by Gen. B. F. Butler,—and recommends that this claim be submitted to the President with a recommendation that the Q. M. General, for the benefit of whose department the money was appropriated, be directed to return it to the claimant."—*Ibid.*

1870, JAN. 11. To Queen Victoria. "I have received the letter which Your Majesty was pleased to address to me on the 14th of December 1869 informing me that Her Royal Highness, the Princess of Wales, Daughter of His Majesty the King of Denmark, Consort of your dearly beloved son, His Royal Highness Albert Edward, Prince of Wales, Duke of Saxony, Prince of Saxe Cobourg and Gotha, &c: &c: was safely delivered of a Princess on the 26th of November last. I pray Your Majesty to accept my cordial congratulations upon this event and to be assured that I take a lively interest in all that concerns the happiness and prosperity of your Royal House, and so I recommend Your Majesty and Your Royal House to the protection of the Almighty."—Copy, DNA, RG 84, Great Britain, Instructions. On May 6, 1869, and June 24, 1870, USG sent similar letters to Queen Victoria regarding the births of a son and daughter to Princess Helena Augusta Victoria.—Copies, *ibid.*

1870, JAN. 11. John E. Bryant, Atlanta, to USG. "I send my resignation as post master at Aug[us]ta tonight I give particulars by letter."—Telegram received (on Jan. 12, 10:00 A.M.), DNA, RG 107, Telegrams Collected (Bound). Bryant had been nominated as postmaster, Augusta, on Dec. 6, 1869, to replace Foster Blodgett, suspended from office by USG on May 18. On May 20, Governor Rufus B. Bullock of Ga. wrote to Horace Porter. "The Press despatches this afternoon announce the removal of Blodgett and appointment of Bryant as Postmaster at Augusta, We can hardly believe that it is true, Mr Blodgett has been one of the most efficient supporters of reconstruction, is the chairman of our party organization, and is every way worthy & competent to fill his position as Postmaster, He was recommended to the pPostmaster General for retention by the President of state senate, speaker of House, other leading Republicans and myself, If any charges are made against him, I ask the President as a favor to myself that Mr Bl[o]dgett be not removed or suspended until he can be heard [from]   There is no charge that can be made good against him that will justify his removal, and his suspension will be hailed by the rebels as a victory"—Telegram received (at 8:15 P.M.), *ibid.* On the same day, Attorney Gen. Henry P. Farrow of Ga. telegraphed to Porter. "Bryant wages open warfare upon the republican party in Georgia and his appointment as Postmaster at Augusta over Blodgett the Chairman of Republican state central committee will tend to overthrow our organization and will render our lives less secure by destroying party prestige   do help us"— Telegram received (on May 21, 9:00 A.M.), *ibid.* On May 21, noon, Porter telegraphed to Bullock. "I showed your despatch to the President and P. M. G. The final decision is in favor of Bryant"—Copy, DLC-USG, II, 5. On May 22, Farrow and J. R. Johnson telegraphed to USG supporting Blodgett.—Telegram received (on May 23, 11:00 P.M.), DNA, RG 107, Telegrams Collected (Bound). Between Jan. 22 and 24, 1870, Bryant telegraphed to Porter. "Please ask the President to delay appointing my successor until he receives letter from me which I send today. I hear that a man named Jacob R Davis is an applicant. Davis betrayed us and acted with the democrats in the election for state officers and ratification of the state constitution   I saw him vote the democratic ticket. We are laying the foundation for a strong republican party. I give particulars by letter. I ask for nothing for myself. Please say so to the President. I wish to show him that one man in Georgia does not work for office. We will break the Blodgett bullock ring of bad men and rally the best men of Georgia to the support of General Grant's administration"—Telegram received (undated —marked as received at 2:45 P.M.), *ibid.* On Feb. 14, USG nominated Charles H. Prince as postmaster, Augusta. See *SED*, 41-2-37; *ibid.*, 41-2- 43; Ruth Currie-McDaniel, *Carpetbagger of Conscience: A Biography of John Emory Bryant* (Athens, Ga., 1987), pp. 88–111.

1870, JAN. 11.   Anson Burlingame, Berlin, to USG. "Permit me to enclose the application of my son for an appointment 'at large' to the U. S. Military academy at West Point. For particulars in relation to him I most respectfully refer you to our mutual friend General Badeau."—ALS, DNA, RG 94, Correspondence, USMA. The enclosure is *ibid.* No appointment followed.

1870, JAN. 11.   Governor William Claflin of Mass. to USG. "Genl Cowen of Ohio will honor the administration if appointed   You have no better or truer friend or one who did more efficient service in 1868"—Telegram received (at 12:13 P.M.), DNA, RG 107, Telegrams Collected (Bound). On Aug. 30, 1869, Claflin had written to USG recommending Benjamin R. Cowen's appointment as collector of Internal Revenue, Cincinnati.—LS, *ibid.*, RG 60, Records Relating to Appointments. Additional papers recommending Cowen for appointment as U.S. marshal, southern district of Ohio, are *ibid.* On Nov. 26, 1870, Governor Rutherford B. Hayes of Ohio wrote to USG recommending Cowen as commissioner of Internal Revenue. —LS, *ibid.*, RG 56, Appointment Div., Treasury Office, Letters Received. Related papers are *ibid.* No appointment followed.

1870, JAN. 11.   Mrs. E. A. Keough, Fort Monroe, Va., to USG. "As there is a vacancy in the Quarter Master's Dept. M. S. K. Capt John E Blaine having sent in his resignation I Respectfully claim the Promis You made me, while Sec War, that You would appoint my husband Mr John, W, Keough. a M. S. K. he has been in this Dept. since the close of the War, and has a thourough Knowledge of the buisness. His application, and letters of Recomendation, have all been before You, they are on file in the Post Office Dept in Washington; His whole life has been spent in the service of his Country, and now it lays with the President whether he will reward him. for his long and faithfull services or not. sincerley praying that the President will gladen our hearts, the begining of this New Year, . . ."—ALS, DNA, RG 94, ACP, 4732 1874.

1870, JAN. [12].   USG endorsement. "My present judgement is against accepting the resignation of present Marshall."—AE (initialed), DNA, RG 60, Records Relating to Appointments. Written on a letter of Jan. 10 from William R. Thrall, Columbus, to U.S. Representative John A. Bingham of Ohio. "In view of the resignation of General Hickenlooper, Marshal of the Southern District of Ohio, I beg to call your attention and that of the President to my application for appointment to that vacancy. It was made in March last, and embraces recommendations from the republican party of Ohio . . . It has urged my appointment with astonishing unanimity, and so intense has been its feeling, together with the desire that the Office should be in hands to make its importance available to the republican party in the future, that the effect may have the appearance of persecution towards the incumbent, but nothing is more foreign to the truth—. . ."—ALS, *ibid.*

On Dec. 4, 1868, Judge Humphrey H. Leavitt, U.S. District Court, Cincinnati, had written to USG. "I hope you will pardon me for bringing to your notice, at this early day, the case of Gen. A. Hickenlooper, the present efficient Marshal of the United States, for the Southern District of Ohio. His term of office under his present appointment will not expire for eighteen months or more; but he is apprehensive, that upon the incoming of the new administration, efforts will be made for his removal, and the appointment of some one in his place. . . ."—ALS, *ibid.* Additional recommendations are *ibid.*; copies in Cincinnati Historical Society, Cincinnati, Ohio. Andrew Hickenlooper had been appointed U.S. marshal, Southern District, Ohio, in 1866. See *PUSG*, 16, 523.

On Feb. 27, 1869, Benjamin R. Cowen, National Republican Executive Committee, Cincinnati, wrote to USG. "I have the honor to call your attention to the fact that Gen. A. Hickenloper, is present U. S. Marshal for this District—that his term is unexpired, but that the most active measures are being taken by certain parties to have him removed. You know Gen. H.

personally, & So well that he needs no word of commendation from me, but I would merely State that his discharge of the duties of his present position has been as prompt, faithful and Satisfactory as you know his army Service to have been. I would therefore most earnestly urge that he be retained in his place not only as a reward for past services, but because he is *honest, capable & faithful.*"—ALS, DNA, RG 60, Records Relating to Appointments. On May 26, Henry T. Cole, Cincinnati, telegraphed to USG. "While Hickenlooper is many miles away attending bedside of his dying mother, charges against him are being presented before Attorney General, In common justice he should be informed of their exact nature, and allowed an opportunity to meet and repel them,"—Telegram received (at 7:00 P.M.), *ibid.*; (press) *ibid.*, RG 107, Telegrams Collected (Bound). On the same day, Secretary of War John A. Rawlins wrote to Hickenlooper. "Dont allow the information you have received to trouble you one particle. I am sure you will not be disturbed in your place by the President, and certainly not without allowing you an opportunity to be heard. I will speak to the Prest. but believe me it is all right. My health is improving. With kindest regards to you and yours."—LS, Cincinnati Historical Society. On June 14, Walter Q. Gresham, West Point, N. Y., wrote to Hickenlooper. "In the course of quite a long conversation with the President last night I brought up your case, and asked him what had been done & he told me that he had had not *and would not remove* you—You can now dismiss the matter for no opposition can harm you—I told the President that his frinds were your frinds and that he could do nothing that would please them more than standing by you—"— ALS, *ibid.*

On June 19, Bingham wrote to USG. "I beg leave to call your attention to the enclosed letter of the Republican Committee of Vinton County, Ohio, addressed to the State republican Committee at Columbus, Ohio, by which it is shown that Genl Hickenlooper, Marshal of the Southern district of Ohio, has appointed J. G. Swetland deputy marshal and who in the words of the Committee is 'a most bitter enemy of your administration and a zealous worker against the interests of the republican party' By the papers on file in the Attorney General's Office, it appears that similar appointments have been made in many other counties of the district. I am advised that Genl. Hickenlooper replies to the Attorney General that he had to select these men in democratic counties in order to get competent men, and was willing to remove them upon a proper shewing and request of republicans To the first part of this statement, I reply that there is not a county in Ohio in which earnest and good republicans, equally competent and equally trustworthy could not have been found To the second part, I have to reply in the words of the Committee, found in the enclosed letter that they called the attention of Genl. Hickenlooper, some weeks previous to the 7th instant, to the facts above stated concerning his deputy in Vinton County and at the same time 'recommended a reliable Union man to the place,' but that the marshal has not 'even condescended to acknowledge receipt of their communication.' I beg leave to add further, for I must be brief, that from the evidence on file it is clearly shewn that Genl Hickenlooper was active in the *Johnson* movement, in 1866, to divide and destroy the republican party in Ohio, and that in the struggle of 1868, he did nothing to aid the party in the great contest, decided by the October elections, until after the battle was fought and won and his party was on the retreat, *when* he offered his contribution. Is it not clear that if the October elections upon which the fate of the country was suspended had resulted adversely to the Union party that Genl Hickenlooper would have been as swift to offer his contribution to the victorious party. There is another fact I desire to state—that by the statement of H. Carey esqr, of Xenia, Ohio, special Counsel for the government, which statement is on file, these democratic deputies of the Marshal, obstructed the execution of the revenue laws; and it appears, by the public papers in Cincinnati, also, that some twenty indictments for violation of the revenue laws in that district, found in April last, were moved to be set aside for the reason *that the Marshal substituted men on the grand jury at their own special request*, thereby disqualifying the jury and invalidating the indictments. This ought to be enough. No man, Mr President, can be more highly recommended to you for the place than is Mr Wm R. Thrall—late a soldier of the Union Army, and whose application is one file in the Attorney General's Office   Mr President: I but present the request of the great body of the Union party in Ohio, when I ask that the Incumbent be superseded by Dr Thrall—and that without delay, to the end that the marshal's Office may no longer be used for the benefit of our political enemies in a state in which we can not at present spare a single Office, a single man nor a single vote. The success of the party may depend this fall on your action on this subject."—LS, OHi. Letters to USG recommending Thrall are in DNA, RG 60, Records Relating to Appointments. On June 29, Hickenlooper, Cincinnati, wrote to Horace Porter. "I have the honor to herewith transmit my refutation of charges contained in a letter of 19th inst addressed to the President . . ."—ALS, *ibid.* The enclosures are *ibid.*

On Dec. 22, Porter wrote to Hickenlooper. "The President and the Attorney General have decided from motives of public policy to appoint a successor to fill the office of Marshal in your district, and the President suggested that I should write you in this unofficial manner to inform you of the fact and to say that if you prefer to tender your resignation no action will be taken until you have forwarded it to this office."—Copy, DLC-USG, II, 1. On Jan. 1, 1870, Hickenlooper resigned.—ALS, USG 3.

On Oct. 26, Hickenlooper wrote to Secretary of War William W. Belknap. ". . . I am really sorry for the Presidents sake that he made this position—I would however like exceedingly to see a gentleman selected as my successor who is not alone entirely competent for the position, but one who would also add increased strength to the administration; such a person is Genl. Cowan   I understand Dr Thrall and his friends have relinquished their claim, and given up all hope, which I can assure you without prejudice, and in all sincerity, is a fortunate thing for the administration. He was not a fit man in any respect and a more unpopular one (outside of a very small clique, who were doing the 'you tickle me &c' business) could not have been selected. . . ."—ALS, NjP. On Dec. 7, USG nominated Thrall to replace Hickenlooper.

1870, JAN. 12.   To Edwin D. Morgan. "May Mrs. Grant and myself expect the pleasure of a weeks visit from you, Mrs. Morgan & Miss McCorkle commencing say on Monday the 24th instant? We will be much gratified to have you come at that time, if convenient to you, and if not on any subsequent week that may be more convenient. Please present my kind regards to Mrs. Morgan and your son & daughter, and accept the same to yourself."—ALS, New York State Library, Albany, N. Y.

1870, JAN. 12.   Judge Advocate Gen. Joseph Holt to USG through the AG. "Brevet Lieut. Col. Walter B. Pease, Captain, 17th Infy., is tried at Richmond, Va., under the following charges:—1. Conduct unbecoming an officer and a gentleman   1. In appearing in a drunken condition at the Post Trader's store at Camp Grant, and exposing himself thus to enlisted men and citizens; he being at the time officer of the day. This Sep. 25. 1869. 2. At the same place and time, drawing his sword and following one Kitchener, employee of the Post Trader, and conducting himself in an abusive and threatening manner towards him, in the presence of soldiers and citizens, and this after an altercation with said Kitchener, and calling him a liar. *Acquitted* under both specifications. 3. In that, on or about Sept. 10. 1869, he did, while in a drunken condition, attempt to ride on horseback into a house of ill-fame in Richmond, thereby creating a disturbance in the public street and attracting a large crowd. He being so dressed at the time as to indicate that he was an officer. Finding—Guilty. 4. On the same day and about the same time, going to the 1st Police Station in Richmond and enquiring for the chief of Police; and on being informed he was out, replying (in a boisterous manner)—'I am Col. Pease, and want my orders obeyed;' continuing in this conduct in and about said station until arrested, and when brought before Capt. Parker of the police, saying to him: 'I am in command here, (by God) and I want you to know it.' Finding, Guilty, as amended. 2. Drunkenness on Duty. As officer of the day, at Camp Grant, Va, Sept. 25, 1869. Acquitted. The accused is found guilty under the 1st charge, and sentenced: To be dismissed. . . . It is not improbable that some punishment of less severity than dishonorable dismissal, may effectively redeem this officer from the habits under which he is shown to have recently, on one or two occasions lost his self control."—Copy, DNA, RG 153, Letters Sent. On Feb. 8, Capt. Walter B. Pease, 17th Inf., Camp Grant, Richmond, wrote to Holt. "I have the honor to request from you a decision on the following point, viz: Am I, during my suspension from rank and pay for six months, (my sentence as mitigated by the President upon your recommendation) entitled to quarters and fuel at this Post, where my company is serving, and the Hd Quars of my Regiment, and if so what should, or would be my relative rank in selecting quarters? . . ."—ALS, *ibid.*, RG 94, Letters Received, 204M 1870.

1870, JAN. 13. To George Croledge. "The beautiful copies of your Almanac for 1870 for Mrs. Grant and myself were duly received. Please accept my Thanks for your kind consideration."—Daniel F. Kelleher Co., Inc., Sale 566, Oct. 3, 1984, no. 2186.

1870, [JAN. 15]. James Richardson to USG. "This cane was made by the donor with a common penknife from a young cedar tree cut in front of Vicksburg, Miss., about the time of General Pemberton's surrender. The first star from the ferrule was made from a piece of the floating battery used by the Confederates in the attack on Fort Sumter in 1861; the centre star from a piece of eldar cut from a stump near to the spot where General Grant stood at the surrender of General Lee, at Appamattox Court-house, Va.: the top star from the ball extracted from the 'dead line' at the Andersonville prison, Ga. By pulling the tassel a gold pencil will be seen."—*Washington National Republican*, Jan. 17, 1870.

1870, JAN. 17. Maj. Horace R. Wirtz, Washington, D. C., to USG. "I have the honor to respectfully submit this application, asking to be reinstated in the Medical Staff of the U. S. Army, or rather to have *my resignation annuled* or *canceled*, which is to take effect, the *1st March 1870*. The circumstances of my case are simply these. I have two children. I was sent out to New Mexico, in the early days—1847—& the standard of morality was not very high there. Most of the older officers had illegitimate children (officers now high in command) & the younger ones, of whom I was one, copied more or less after their seniors. This was *twenty years ago*; I had the misfortune to be encumbered with two children, a boy, half Mexican, & a white child. Unlike many others, I educated my children, & brought them up respectably; & while I was stationed at Ft. Hamilton (the last 2 or 3 years) I had the boy & girl under my own roof. I lived in a little cottage near the Fort, & the children passed as my *nephew* & *niece*. Nobody made impertinent inquiries, & the ladies of the garrison frequently called on my daughter, & treated her with the greatest kindness. When I went to Oregon last Summer, I sent my *boy* to New Mexico, but the *girl* had no home but mine. She had completed her education, was now about 17 years old, & I thought to establish her permanently as a teacher on the Pacific coast. So I took her with me, imagining that the people would treat her as they had done in the East. But I found the case different. They were jealous, apparently, of her accomplishments, for though only a child, she was intelligent beyond her years. The result was, they abused her, they said she was not my niece, & was probably my mistress. I was shocked at this, & came out openly, & acknowledged she was my *daughter*. But they had a nice piece of scandal, & it was too sweet a morsel to be dropped thus. They persecuted her & myself in all manner of ways; & finally a lady universally respected in Portland, who pitied my child & who knew all the circumstances of the case, took her to her home with her own daughters. One of the young married officers now spoke of putting charges against me for introducing a female under false pretences. . . . The companions who started in life with me, & who studied Medicine, are now in high positions in civil life. I gave up every thing for the army; & now for a simple error of judgment & because I could not control the scandal of a country village, —at 45 years of age, grown gray in service, habituated to army customs, unacquainted with civil life, I am thrown out on the world to begin again. It is a hard lot for a gentleman of refined associations: for one who from the earliest years has known nothing but the army. I ask the attention of the Executive to my situation: I have yet many years of activity before me, & all I seek is to be allowed to *remain in a service*, where I have spent the very *flower* of *my days*, & where I have left a record I am not ashamed of." —ALS, DNA, RG 94, ACP, 521 1874. On the same day, Col. Rufus Ingalls, Willard's Hotel, Washington, D. C., wrote to USG. "I have known for years' past that Dr. Wirtz of the Army had some natural children who were usually styled his Nephew & Niece. The reputed Niece accompanied the Doctor to Oregon, where it would seem, he fell into embarrasment, which resulted in his tender of his resignation, as I really believe, from bad judgment on his part. He wished to escape publicity. I think he practiced no evil in any way. He is an old Army officer of great merit & standing as a Medical man, & has rendered good service to the country. In common with his many friends, I hope you will be pleased to excuse & restore him"— Copy, *ibid.* On Oct. 29, 1869, Wirtz, San Francisco, had written to USG at length concerning his case.—ALS, *ibid.* Related papers are *ibid.* On Jan. 24, 1870, Bvt. Maj. Gen. Edmund Schriver, inspector gen., wrote an endorsement. "The order accepting Dr. Wirtz' resignation is to be rescinded by order of the President of the U. S. Communicated by order of the Secy of War."—Copy, *ibid.*, RG 107, Orders and Endorsements.

1870, JAN. 17.   Governor Robert K. Scott of S. C. to USG. "I have the honor herewith to transmit a concurrent resolution of the General Assembly of South Carolina—'petitioning the President of the United States relative to the construction of warehouses at the Quarantine Station in Charleston.'" —LS, DNA, RG 56, Letters Received. The enclosure is *ibid.*, along with related documents.

1870, JAN. 18.   To Alfred L. Pearson, Pittsburgh. "I regret that public duties prevent my accepting the polite invitation to be present at the Reception given by the G. A. of R. on Wednesday, Jany. 26th."—Copy, DLC-USG, II, 1.

1870, JAN. 18.   To E. S. Stanley, Newport, R. I. "The copy of your beautiful poems in your own hand writing came to me to day. I shall read them

with pleasure. Please accept my thanks for your kind consideration."—
Copy, DLC-USG, II, 1.

1870, JAN. 18.   Horace Porter to John Arthur, Paris. "I am directed by
the President to acknowledge the receipt of your letter of the 23d of November, and the safe arrival of the wine which you were kind enough to
send him. He desires me to convey to you his thanks and say that he finds the
wine very fine. You will please ship to him twelve (12) cases of it, and
draw upon him at sight for the amount. Ship in care of Moses H. Grinnell,
Collector of the Port at New York City."—Copy, DLC-USG, II, 1.

1870, JAN. 18.   Horace Porter to Alfred N. Duffié, consul, Cadiz. "I am
directed by the President to request you to be so kind as to order him two
(2) quarter pipes of good sherry, drawing upon him at sight for the amount.
Send in care of Moses H Grinnell Collr. of the Port at New York City."—
Copy, DLC-USG, II, 1. On Feb. 1, 1869, Bvt. Maj. Gen. Rufus Ingalls,
New York City, had written to USG. "General A. N. Duffié is an applicant
for a position abroad under the General Government and it gives me great
pleasure to bear testimony to his gallant and valuable services in the Army,
both as a Field and General Officer, during the late Rebellion, and to his
moral worth and excellence as a man. The zeal and fidelity with which he
performed his duties when in the military service, if brought to bear in a
civil capacity, would certainly render him a valuable and efficient officer,
and I shall be much pleased to hear that the Government has availed itself
of his services."—LS, DNA, RG 59, Letters of Application and Recommendation. On March 20, Frederick T. Dent wrote to Secretary of State
Hamilton Fish. "This is the case I spoke to you about in the Cabinet yesterday—if Gen Duffie cannot have the place he asks for, do give him a
Consulate elsewhere—for he deserves it and will prove a usefull officer—he
is a good linguist,   I hope he may get Brussels"—ALS, *ibid.* Related papers
are *ibid.* Duffié was confirmed on April 21.
     On Nov. 17, 1870, Amasa Stone, Jr., Cleveland, wrote to USG. "Dur-
ing the winter of 1868–9 I visited Cadiz Spain with my family and a large
party of American friends, and while in the city the insurrection occurred,
and several hundred persons were killed and wounded—We found Col
Farrell acting as our American Consul—At the time the excitement in the
city was very great, and it required much vigilence, energy and discretion
on his part, and it gratifies me to be able to state that the impressions of
our party were that Col Farrell was equal to the occasion, and that he performed his duties to our government faithfully and well, and should he
receive a similar appointment, or any other from the government, I have
no doubt he would perform his duties satisfactorily"—ALS, *ibid.* Related
papers are *ibid.* No appointment followed. On Feb. 7, 1871, Raymond F.
Farrell, Washington, D. C., wrote to USG. "When I presented Gen'l W. S.
Hillyer's letter to you, a few weeks ago, you informed me that the Secretary
of state had stated that there were charges preferred against me whilst

discharging the duties of consul at Cadiz, Spain. I have the honor to inform you that Mr Fish has told me that he has been misunderstood, because no charges have been preferred against me since 1868, and then I was doing my duty as instructed by the Secretary of state and the secretary of the Treasury, and both of these officers have approved and commended my conduct. My offenses consisted in declining to allow dishonest wineshippers to defraud our revenue, and for so doing they have had the Spanish Government to request my removal The U. S. Government, when it found, after three trials at Boston, that it could not convict these dishonest wineshippers, athough the testimony clearly proved their guilt, compromised the matter and realised one hundred and seventeen thousand ($117,000) dollars in the same, to wit, the seizure at my request. My services were rewarded by removal at the request of the Spanish government, although I was the only consular officer in Spain who earned his small office by services in the Army of the Tennessee, and as an editor of a loyal journal at Cincinnati when no longer able to serve in the field I know your sense of equity too well—I know you are not the man either as private citizen, general, or chief magistrate—to believe that you would not tolerate the removal of an officer who has rigidly obeyed the laws and honestly thwarted the proceedings of dishonest foreigners; but I am not seeking for restoration but simply to prove to you that there are no charges against me but what I consider creditable to my administration of the office of U. S. consul at Cadiz and in proof of my statement I beg you to call upon the Secretary of state for a copy of *all* the charges and my reply to the same, and upon your decision I shall confidently rely being assured, of my knowledge of your sense of justice and equity, that it will be fair and impartial."—ALS, *ibid.*

1870, JAN. 19. Bvt. Maj. Gen. Oliver O. Howard to USG. "A worthy gentleman of New York bringing letters from gentlemen of the best character, Mr C. E. Larrabee desires a *private* interview with you on some very important business both personal & public—"—ALS (press), Howard Papers, MeB.

1870, JAN. 19. Mrs. Elizabeth J. Bragg, Gaines, N. Y., to USG. "I wrote you sometime ago, for, aid to get the remains of my husband from Cypress Hills Cemetery, N. Y. but received no answer, and thought I would write again. I do not beg for money, only an order or something of that sort, so that I can get him home cheaper. he died on his way home on a furlough, and wished to be brought home, but I am poor and with poor health, and after trying five years, to acumulate enough to get his body home: I have written to A J Case, U S Undertaker and they charge so high for removal that I fear I shall have to give it up, unless you will kindly help me in some way. His name, Wm J Bragg Company C 8th N. Y. Heavy Artilery, Col Peter A Porter. He was wounded at Battle of Coal Harbour. He died 13th of August 1864. He had served two years. the number of his grave is 1648.

I should be very glad of any aid for it is my dearest wish to get his remains home as he wished with his dying breath. my post office adress is Gaines Orlean Co Arad Thomas gets my pension for me of Albion Orlean Co"— ALS, DNA, RG 107, Letters Received from Bureaus.

1870, [JAN. 19]. Thomas H. Leabourn speech. "MR. PRESIDENT: A convention of letter-carriers, composed of delegates from a large number of States, has been in session in this city. Our object is to induce Congress to increase our pay. Having finished our business, we could not think of leaving this city without first paying our respects to you. I may say we have a twofold object in this: First, because you are the Chief Magistrate of this country; and, second, because in this small number around you a large majority were comrades with you and followed you on many a hard fought battle-field. Permit me to say, Mr. President, that we and the 1,300 letter-carriers we represent approve of your policy of retrenchment; yet we rejoice that in that retrenchment you do not strike at the workingmen of the country."—*Washington Chronicle,* Jan. 20, 1870. "The President said it afforded him pleasure to meet the letter-carriers from the many large cities. He thought that, on account of the high rates of house rent and the heavy cost of the necessaries of life in large cities, they should be paid such salaries as would afford them a fair living, and said that his sympathies were with them in their endeavors to secure increased compensation."—*Ibid.*

1870, JAN. 19. Emma A. Wood, Washington, D. C., to USG. "I would most respectfully submit the following statement of facts—My husband, Bvt. Major Geo. W. F. Wood, U. S. Army, having been ordered to Indianola, Texas, died in that place of yellow fever. He had served throughout the war with Mexico, and, returning, was scarcely able to reach home from the dreadful effects of the Mexican diarrhoea, with which disease he was constantly afflicted until his death. . . . I applied to the Pension Office; but here I was met by the announcement that yellow fever was not considered in 'the line of an officer's duty,' and I must obtain a Special Act of Congress—I applied to Congress and, from one cause and another, year after year passed, until six had nearly gone before I received a pension. Then when the bill had been again brought forward, a member, who could scarcely have thought of the injustice he was doing, objected to it unless payment were made to begin at the date of the approval of the bill instead of the time of my husband's death, . . . My husband died Nov. 8th 1854, my pension commenced June 19th 1860. I would now most respectfully ask you to consider the case and award me the pension for the intervening years—It is but three hundred dollars ($300 00) a year—and even for the six years would make but a small difference to the Government—though of so very great importance to me—I respectfully submit my case to your consideration—"—ALS, DNA, RG 48, Miscellaneous Div., Letters Received. See *SRC,* 34-3-393.

1870, [*Jan. 20*]. Speech. "You are welcome, and in reference to continuing your 'good father,' as you say, I must answer that I have long thought that the two nations which you represent, and all those civilized nations in the Indian country, *should be their own wards and good fathers. I am of the opinion that they should become citizens*, and be entitled to all the rights of citizens,—cease to be nations and become States."—*New York Times*, Jan. 26, 1870. USG spoke in response to remarks made by a delegation of chiefs from the Cherokee and Creek nations. "Mr. President, we call here to-day to offer our fealty to you as our recognized guardian and ward, and to pray you, Sir, to continue our good friend and father."—*Ibid.* On Jan. 20, Commissioner of Indian Affairs Ely S. Parker had escorted the delegation to the White House.—*Washington Chronicle*, Jan. 21, 1870.

1870, JAN. 21. USG endorsement. "I am cognizant of the efficient and valuable services rendered by Gen. A. Gibbs in the suppression of rebellion."—AES, DNA, RG 233, 41A–D1. Written on a petition of Jan. 13 from Peggy F. Gibbs, New York City, to Congress, requesting an increased pension.—DS, *ibid.* Related papers are *ibid.*

1870, JAN. 21. Frederick F. Low, San Francisco, to USG. "The appointment of Hon T. G. Phelps as Collector of the Port gives great satisfaction here. It is an appointment fit to be made."—Telegram received (on Jan. 22), DNA, RG 107, Telegrams Collected (Bound). On Jan. 13, USG had nominated Timothy G. Phelps as collector of customs, San Francisco; on Jan. 24, he was confirmed.

1870, JAN. 22. Orville E. Babcock to B. B. Blair, Georgetown, Ohio. "The President directs me to acknowledge the receipt of your letter and to say in reply that, the place you desire is given by the Commissioner of Internal Revenue and not by the President. He advises you to apply through the collector of Int. Revenue for your district to the Commissioner. The President sends his kind regards to you and other friends in Georgetown." —Copy, DLC-USG, II, 1.

1870, JAN. 24. Col. Robert Allen, San Francisco, to USG. "Confidential. If the changes in contemplation involve the appointment of any acting Quarter Master General who will habitually act as chief, may I ask that my claims to the place considered. Have written you."—Telegram received (on Jan. 25, 1:00 P.M.), DNA, RG 107, Telegrams Collected (Bound).

1870, JAN. 24. John Tyler, Jr., Washington, D. C., to USG. "*Confidential. . . .* You cannot, Mr President, have failed to analyse the recent movement in the Congress upon the Virginia question. The object of the Ultra-Radical Leaders cannot be otherwise than apparent to you. The meaning is too plain to admit of doubt. Not only is Virginia and the Southern States

and People to be crushed in beneath the Political banner of Sumner & Butler, in view of the Presidential contest in 1872, but you yourself are to be
subordinated to the purposes of the Ambition of the one, and the malicious
Vengeance of the other, who is also not without his aspirations. . . . Be an
Automaton to Sumner and to Butler and your Public Career will close upon
you in 1872–3 with only a contemptuous Sneer and a derisive smile from
them. But your position just now has been rendered by their action truely
enviable. In my judgement the game is in your hands and they really stand
at your mercy. One quick, rapid & impetuous movement will prove decisive.
*Veto the Virginia Bill, and call for a General Convention of the American
People to frame a new Constitution of Government, with Powers more
clearly defined, and better adapted to the progress of the age & the wants
of the Republican Empire.* . . . I know it would be attended with additional
Suffering on the part of the People of Virginia, but this they would cheerfully bear under the new hope with which they, in common with the whole
Country, would become inspired. I believe that, under the continuation for
the time being of a provisional Military Government, they would hail your
officers as their best friends, fraternize with them and rush to your Standard.
And as with Virginia so with the entire South & West, especially if the
Capital was removed to the Mississippi Valley. *By the Step you would
inaugurate a new Popular Power in control of the Nation and strike down
the Malign influences of New-England.* In the preparation of such a Message I know of but one man that I implicitly believe fully adequate to the
task. . . . This Person to whom I refer is Jeremiah S Black of Pensylvania.
He was at Willards Hotel on Saturday last, but may have proceeded to his
Residence in Pensylvania. He was at one time, it is true, a friend of your
Predecessor, but you may remember broke with him entirely about the
period of your own difficulties in that direction. But be this as it may, *I
know of no one so ponderously fitted for the task. . . .*"—ALS, Tyler Papers,
College of William and Mary, Williamsburg, Va.

1870, JAN. 25. To Dr. Evanson, Torquay, England. "I take pleasure in
acknowledging the receipt of your letter of Jany. 4th. and of the volumes
you were so kind as to send to me. I fully concur with all you say of the
goodness of the late Geo. Peabody. Please accept my sincere thanks for
your kind consideration."—Copy, DLC-USG, II, 1. On Sept. 26, 1869,
John W. Garrett, president, Baltimore and Ohio Railroad, Baltimore, had
written to USG. "Confidential. . . . After a very interesting visit, from the
18th to the 23rd inst., Mr. Peabody left us for Philadelphia, and on yesterday proceeded to New York. His health is very infirm, and he suffered from
great debility. I fear that we may never again have the gratification of seeing
him. You may not be aware, as he has not permitted it to be ~~publishedly~~
known, that Mr. Peabody will leave for England on Wednesday ~~next~~ next,
by the Scotia. In conversing on the subject, he expressed to me much regret
that he had not had the pleasure of meeting you again.—I give you this
information, as in view of his vast additional benefactions in our country,

you might desire, if aware of his intended departure to address him a farewell note.—"—Copy, DLC-Garrett Family.

1870, JAN. 25.   To Governor Joseph W. McClurg of Mo. "The copy of your message with your compliments came to me to day. Feeling great interest in the State of Missouri, I shall read it with more than ordinary interest. Please accept my sincere thanks for your kindness."—Copy, DLC-USG, II, 1.

1870, JAN. 25.   Orville E. Babcock to Laura Keene, Wall's Opera House, Washington, D. C. "The President requests me to acknowledge your polite note extending to him a box at the Opera house, to thank you for your kindness and to say that he will accept for next Friday evening."—Copy, DLC-USG, II, 1.

1870, JAN. 28.   Attorney Gen. Ebenezer R. Hoar endorsement. "Respectfully transmitted to the President—I see no just and legal objection to the findings and sentence of this military commission."—AES, OFH. Written on a letter of Jan. 25 from Secretary of War William W. Belknap to Hoar. "I have the honor to transmit, herewith, for the action of the President, as provided by law, the accompanying record of the trial by military commission of James L. Stephenson, a civilian, resident within the Fifth Military District, for the murder of two freedmen."—LS, *ibid.*

1870, JAN. 28.   "Republican Committee," Visalia, Calif., to USG. "It is general wish of this community to retain present receiver of land office." —Telegram received (at 4:00 P.M.), DNA, RG 107, Telegrams Collected (Bound).

1870, JAN. 29.   To Congress. "I herewith transmit to Congress a report, dated 29th instant, with the accompanying papers, received from the Secretary of State, in compliance with the requirements of the 18th section of the Act entitled 'An Act to regulate the diplomatic and consular systems of the United States', approved August 18. 1856."—DS, DNA, RG 46, President's Messages; *ibid.*, RG 233, 41A–D1. See *SED*, 41-2-29.

1870, JAN. 29.   U.S. Senator James Harlan of Iowa to USG. "I have known Gen. Heath, Secretary of New Mexico, twelve or fifteen years. He was a firm outspoken Democrat, until the beginning of the recent war, when he united with the *Republican Party*,—since which he has adhered unswervingly to its principles and organization. I know by correspondence, and through other channels, that he has been an active supporter of this administration, and the reconstruction policy of Congress.—That he is well qualified for the office he now holds, there is no question. I therefore recommend his retention."—ALS, University of Iowa, Iowa City, Iowa. On April 3, 1869, USG had nominated Edward L. Perkins as secretary, New

Mexico Territory, to replace Herman H. Heath. On Oct. 4, Anna Rosa Heath, Washington, D. C., had written to USG. "On the arrival of my husband Gen. Heath in NewMexico he became the editor of the republican press at Santa Fé, which, under the influence of his enthusiastic appreciation of your character, was the first journal west of the Mississippi river, and per in the United States, to unfurl your name for the high position you now occupy. And General, I take the liberty of inclosing a copy of that paper, containing an article which shows, that his devotion to you in the past, remains at this time, unfaltering and true. Trusting that his fidelity may meet the just reward of your favor, . . ."—ALS, DNA, RG 59, Letters of Application and Recommendation. Related papers are *ibid.* On Oct. 29, Perkins, Philadelphia, wrote to USG. "The matter respecting which I craved an interview with you (while at Hon. A. E. Borie's), & which I, during my interview with you in Washington on Monday last neglected to mention, is briefly this—As you are aware, there is not money in the Treasury this year sufficient to pay the debts & defray the expenses of the Secretarys office—. . ."—ALS, *ibid.*, New Mexico Territorial Papers. On Dec. 29, Governor William A. Pile of New Mexico Territory telegraphed to USG. "Need Secretary immediately   Heath embarrassing greatly   Perkins I fear corrupt   Collusion with him   an honest Capable man satisfactory"—Telegram received (at 2:25 P.M.), *ibid.*, RG 107, Telegrams Collected (Bound).

On Jan. 10, 1870, USG nominated Henry Wetter as secretary, New Mexico Territory; on Feb. 4, he nominated Heath as marshal, New Mexico Territory. On Feb. 13, U.S. Delegate José Francisco Cháves of New Mexico Territory wrote to USG. "A few days ago you nominated Mr. H. H. Heath for U. S. Marshal for the Territory of New Mexico. I withdrew a protest which I had failed against the appointment of Mr. Heath chiefly with a view of relieving you from all embarassment in the matter, and have ever since felt, and now feel an earnest desire to see your purpose in regard thereto consummated by the favorable action of the Senate. Feeling thus, you may well imagine that I am pained to learn that General Pile has telegraphed to the Hon. Lyman Trumbul, chairman of the Committee on the Judiciary, to reject the nomination. I feel it my duty to make this fact known to you and hope that the interest which I feel in the subject matter, as well as my desire for the success of your administration in regard to its appointments, may relieve me of the necessity of making an apology for so doing. It seems to me that General Pile might find enough to do within the legitimate sphere of the duties of the position which you have entrusted to him, without stepping beyond that sphere to oppose and embarrass you in your plans and purposes in regard to other appointments."—ALS, *ibid.*, RG 60, Records Relating to Appointments. Related papers are *ibid.* Heath's nomination was withdrawn on April 27.

On May 7, Pile wrote to USG. "I received this morning a telegram from Senator Schurz saying you was dissatisfied with my telegraphing behind your back to the judiciary Committee to reject Heath after having recommended his nomination. There is a Serious misunderstanding in reference to my action in this matter. How it has occurred I cannot even guess. I most respectfully request your careful consideration of the following Statement of facts When I first came here in August last I was favorably impressed with Genl Heath; and when in Washington last October I spoke favorably of him to you. Your very decidedly expressed unfavorable opinion and especially what you said about his dismissal from the Army (of which I had not heard until then) for corruption in the matter of condemnation and sale of Horses when a battallion of his regiment was mustered out of Service: produced the impression that I was mistaken as to his character and merits. When I reached Saint Louis on my return I found he (Heath) had been writing letters to Saint Louis abusing me personally. Mrs Heath reached St Louis two days afterwards on her way to Washington and called on me requesting my return to aid in secureing his (Heath's) reappointment. I had that day received a letter from Mr Perkins Stating that he would Start for New Mexico about October 15th I showed this letter to Mrs Heath, saying it was useless to press his reappointment and that you was not favorably [*dispo*]sed to Genl Heath. She replied that Perkins was deceiving me—that he wanted money and further conversation which led me to a strong belief that there was a a corrupt bargain between Heath and Perkins—I then *distinctly* declined to help him in anyway in reference to that or any other office—to be mixed up with office trading—I maintained this attitude steadily after my return here refusing several times to recommend him. After the Legislature met and Heath was embarrassing the public business and opposing the measures I deemed essential for the good of the Territory I sent you the sent you the enclosed telegram (marked "B") which [e]xpresses my convictions of Heath at that time I have not recommended him for any office Since. If any such recommendation is on file in Washington my name has been used without my knowledge or consent. You will see by telegram enclosed and marked "C" that I did not ask Heath's *rejection* but delay of his confirmation. This telegram was brought me by S B Elkins U S Dist Atty. and I was urged to sign it to secure delay until the persons whose business was connected with the office of Marshal could be heard from This was before I knew that Heath had been nominated by you to repair a wrong you then thought had been done him—So soon as I learned this fact from Col Chaves I at onced declined to make any further opposition and have nither written nor telegraphed a word to any one since against him Now Mr President this is as near as I can remember a frank and full Statement of all the facts in this Heath matter. I assure you on my honor that no double dealing nor two sided course has been pursued by me. I may have done Heath and Perkins injustice in my telegram to you of *Dec* 29th (see copy) and in believeing a corrupt bargain existed between them. but I assure you it was not intentional and that I had good and reasonabl~~ye~~ ground for my belief and action. I shall hasten to repair any wrong to either of them so soon as convinced of it If there is any matter yet unexplained I will cheerfully make further explanations called for. I need not State ~~to~~how much I regret that any unpleasant or unfavorable impressions should be produced in your mind and especially that you should think me capable of 'double' dealing'. I renew all I said in my letter of 30th *Ult* as to the personal harship of a removal *it would be ruinous to me.* Relying on your accurate sense of justice, and renewing my thanks for previous kind consideration . . ."—ALS, *ibid.*, RG 59, New Mexico Territorial Papers. The enclosures are *ibid.* See *PUSG*, 16, 428–30.

On July 25, Joseph G. Palen, chief justice, New Mexico Territory, wrote to USG. "It is rumored here (and we trust correctly) that Mr. Wetter Secretary of this Territory is to be removed; I trust before any definite action is taken in regard to his removal and the appointment of a successor, that you will [awai]t the arrival of Judge B. J. Water[s] who has just gone east, to close up his business t[here] preparatory to moving out here, and who will fully advise you of the condition of Affaires here   The Judge has closed the Spring terms of his Courts, and has obtained leave of absence from the Attorney General to go east for the purposes above mentioned, and expects to visite Washington about the twentieth of August, when he will be able to give you a fair and unbiassed statement of Affaires here, And what in the opinion of the Republicans of the Territory should be done   That the interests of the Republican party, the People and the Territory demand the removal of Mr Wetter there can be no doubt"—ALS, DNA, RG 59, New Mexico Territorial Papers. On Feb. 11, 1871, William Breeden, clerk, Supreme Court, New Mexico Territory, *et al.*, Santa Fé, wrote to USG. "The undersigned republicans in the Territory of New Mexico, respectfully request in case of a vacancy in the office of Secretary that Hon. B. J. Waters, now Associate Justice of the Sup. Court of said Territory be appointed to fill the same. . . ."—DS (16 signatures), *ibid.* An undated petition from Breeden *et al.* requesting Wetter's removal is *ibid.* On May 6, Palen *et al.* wrote to USG. "We the undersigned, Citizens of the Territory of New Mexico, and members of the Republican party, respectfully recommend the appointment of Dr. J. S. Martin of Kansas, to the Office of Secretary of said Territory, in place of Henry Wetter the present incumbent."—DS (5 signatures), *ibid.*, Letters of Application and Recommendation. Related papers are *ibid.* On May 23, 1872, U.S. Senator John Scott of Pa. wrote to USG. "The enclosed tender of resignation is forwarded me, in the hope that the nomination of Mr Arny [w]ill be withdrawn, and that the incumbent, Maj. [W]etter, may be permitted to resign, instead of being [d]isplaced by the appointment."—LS, *ibid.*, New Mexico Territorial Papers. The enclosure is *ibid.* USG nominated William F. M. Arny to replace Wetter and requested that Arny's appointment be delayed until June 30.

1870, JAN. 31.   To Hugh Mulholland, Elizabethtown, Ky. "The order designating you to perform the duties of Assessor of Internal Revenue 4th District of Kentucky, vice Wm M. Spencer suspended is hereby revoked, and upon the receipt of this communication you will turn over the office to

Wm M. Spencer whose suspension therefrom has been revoked."—Copy, DNA, RG 130, Executive Orders and Proclamations. On the same day, USG wrote to William M. Spencer. "The order suspending you from the office of Assessor of Internal Revenue 4th District of Kentucky, is hereby revoked, and you will upon the receipt of this communication resume the duties of said office."—Copy, *ibid.* On Oct. 9, 1869, James M. Fidler, Lebanon, Ky., had telegraphed to USG. "The appointment of Mullholland as assessor 4th Dist. Kentucky is an outrage, Will show the same at once Will be in Washington October 14th Hold up commission"—Telegram received (on Oct. 11, 9:00 A.M.), *ibid.*, RG 107, Telegrams Collected (Bound). Nominated on Dec. 6, Mulholland, Louisville, had telegraphed to USG on Dec. 22 and 28. "Please grant me time to refute any complaints that may be made against me" "Will forward you evidence that any charge against me as a gentleman soldier officer & republican is utterly false,"—Telegrams received (at 2:30 P.M.), *ibid.* On Jan. 31, 1870, Secretary of the Treasury George S. Boutwell wrote to USG. "In accordance with instructions received from the Executive Mansion, dated Jan'y. 25th 70 I transmit herewith for your signature an order revoking the suspension of W. M. Spencer from the Office of Assessor of Internal Revenue 4th District of Kentucky, and also an order revoking the designation of Hugh Mulholland to perform the duties of such Office, vice W. M. Spencer suspended." —Copy, *ibid.*, RG 56, Letters Sent.

On March 24, 1871, Solicitor Gen. Benjamin H. Bristow wrote to USG. "Dr Hugh Mulholland of Kentucky was a surgeon of Volunteers in the late war against the rebellion and has been a consistent republican and friend to your Administration. He is a gentleman of intelligence and excellent character. I hope you will see proper to give him the Consular appointment for which he now applies."—ALS, *ibid.*, RG 59, Letters of Application and Recommendation. Related papers are *ibid.* No action followed.

1870, JAN. 31. To Senate. "I transmit to the Senate in answer to their resolution of the 28th instant the Report of the Secretary of State with accompaniments."—Copy, DNA, RG 59, General Records.

1870, JAN. 31. Senate resolution. "RESOLVED, That the President of the United States be requested, if in his judgment not incompatible with the public interests, to furnish the Senate with a copy of the correspondence of J. Ross Browne with the State Department during his late residence as Minister in China."—DS (by George C. Gorham, secretary), DNA, RG 59, Miscellaneous Letters. In March, a response was drafted for Secretary of State Hamilton Fish. ". . . The correspondence referred to is contained upon over twelve hundred closely written ~~manuscript~~ folio pages of manuscript, and further includes some printed pamphlets. . . ."—ADf, *ibid.* A notation on the resolution reads: "This Resolution was never answered."— AN, *ibid.*

1870, [JAN.]. USG endorsement. "Refered to th[e] Sec. of War who will please reappoint. This Officer intends resigning when restored."—AE (initialed), DNA, RG 94, ACP, C94 CB 1870. Written on an undated letter from Thomas Cummings, former capt. and bvt. maj., 19th Inf., to USG. "I have the honor to petition you for reinstatement in the U. S. Army. By virtue of General Order No 7 dated Headquarters of the Army Dec. 31st 1869, I have been cashiered the service, and for the furtherance of my petition I respectfully call your attention to the following services rendered, during and since the late rebellion. . . ."—ALS, *ibid.* A petition of Jan. 17 accompanied this letter. "The undersigned, Officers of the 19th Infantry, respectfully represent, that *Thomas Cummings,* . . . in their judgment and opinion, based on personal observation of his habits and conduct, has been of unsound mind for a considerable time, to such extent as to render him more or less irresponsible."—DS, *ibid.* Nominated on Feb. 21, Cummings was confirmed on March 28 and resigned as of July 15.

[1870, JAN.]. George W. Daniel *et al.*, Booneville, Ky., to USG. "Your attention is most respectfully called to the fact that there are numerous bands of Ku Klux roaming through this part of Kentucky to the terror of our best citizens. It is perfectly astounding and heart rending to witness their many depredations committed upon the people in this part of the State. Their hanging, murdering or whipping of Radical or Union men is of almost nightly occurrence It is alarming to think that the Rebel party has an overwhelming majority of nearly One hundred thousand in the State and to know that this party has resolved itself into a Ku Klux party for the purpose of hunting down and killing Union men all over the State. This is the 8th Congressional District of Kentucky and the only District of Kentucky that is true and loyal to the Government of the United States and it is very hard that our loyal people in Kentucky should be at the mercy of these murderous men We have no loyal member in the Congress of the United States except Col S M Barnes from this District, and he is trying for his seat in Congress now, to appeal to. Consequently under the circumstances, which is life or death, to us, we gladly call on you as the Chief Executive of the nation to extend to us the protection of the Government of the United States, of which we are a part We ask in the name of humanity and in the name of all that is sacred and dear to a people situated as we are to send a Regiment of Colored Soldiers to the town of Richmond Madison County Kentucky, and let them subsist off of those rich Rebel Ku Klux and hunt down and punish those midnight assassins who are a perfect terror to the Country Union men all over the State are afraid to speak aloud against these bands. We refer you to *Col* S M Barnes now in Washington from this District if you doubt what we say. In Gods name send the Soldiers at once . . . Please Don't give our names to no one except to *Col* S M Barnes. If it was known ~~that we had wri~~ to the Ku Klux that we had written this letter to you Our lives would pay the forfeit"—LS, DNA, RG 94, Letters Received, S1155 1869. On Jan. 14, Gen. William T. Sherman wrote to

Secretary of War William W. Belknap. ". . . The letter reports specifically a state of facts existing in Owen [*Owsley*] County Kentucky, that cannot be amended by the limited military force now subject to my control: and even had we the necessary force it would be of doubtful legality, how far it could be employed. The Commanding officer of the Departmt in which Owen County Kentucky lies has only one Regimt of Infantry for the States of West Virginia, Kentucky and Tennessee. Of course he cannot station a Whole Regimt in Owen County for the protection of the Union people there, for there are more than a hundred Counties in his jurisdiction similarly situated. Then a Military force stationed in Kentucky, is not vested with authority that enables it to punish Murderers or Robbers. It could hardly protect a man fleeing to it for safety, for a writ of habeas Corpus, would take such a man out of its custody and remand him to a Jury of the very men from whom he has fled. Even in Mississipi, a state still out of the Union, we have been unable to protect our own officers, as in case of Colonel Crane: Much less in Kentucky, where the Civil Law prevails. Until some Law is passed by Congress defining clearly how the military force can act lawfully and effectually in cases of this kind, I would suggest that the Military Authorities do not undertake to interfere. I respectfully suggest the whole matter be submitted to Congress."—ALS, *ibid.*

1870, FEB. 1. USG endorsement. "Approved—"—Copy, DNA, RG 104, Letters Sent to the Mint. Written on a letter of Jan. 31 from Secretary of the Treasury George S. Boutwell to USG. "I have the honor to suggest for your approval, the appointment of the following gentlemen as Special Commissioners for the annual Assay at the Mint of the United States at Philadelphia, . . ."—Copy, *ibid.*

1870, FEB. 2. To Senate. "In answer to the Resolution of the Senate of the 8th ultimo, I transmit a report from the Secretary of State and the papers which accompanied it."—DS, DNA, RG 46, Presidential Messages. On the same day, Secretary of State Hamilton Fish had written to USG. "The Secretary of State to whom was referred the Resolution of the Senate of the 8th ultimo requesting the President, if in his judgement consistent with the public interests, to communicate to the Senate such information as may be in the possession of the Government relating to the presence of the Honorable William McDougall at Pembina, in Dakota Territory, and the opposition by the inhabitants of Selkirk Settlement to his assumption of the Office of Governor of the North West Territory, lately said to have been transferred by the Hudson's Bay Company to the Dominion of Canada, has the honor to lay before the President the papers mentioned in the subjoined list which contain the information called for by the Resolution."—LS (incomplete), *ibid.*; copy, *ibid.*, RG 59, General Records. The enclosures are *ibid.*, RG 46, Presidential Messages. See *SED*, 41-2-33. In [Jan., 1871], James Wickes Taylor wrote to USG. "About a year ~~since~~ Since, I called the attention of the Senate to the fact, that the people of the Red River Settlement, north of Minnesota, had successfully resisted an attempt by [the] Dominion of Canada to impose an arbitrary Government upon them. By the intervention of Great Britain, the Hudson Bay Company had ~~been in-deed induced to~~ become a party to the transfer of their territorial claims to Canada and, in anticipation of that transfer, ~~the~~ Canada passed an act providing a Government for the vast districts between Lake Superior and the Rocky Mountains and extending from the northern frontier of the United States to the Arctic Ocean. It is surprising that a measure, which no one now defends, should have passed with so little consideration. . . ."— ADf, Taylor Papers, Minnesota Historical Society, St. Paul, Minn.

1870, FEB. 2.   Samuel L. Gouverneur, Frederick, Md., to USG. "In an interview lately with Mr Fish, Secretary of State, he said, that any applica-tion by me to be sent abroad by the Administration, would be fruitless and of no avail. I am not, and do not propose to become an office seeker, but I am unaware of any reason why the Hon Secretary of State should so pe-remptorily refuse to listen to such claims as I may conceive I have upon the Goverment, in so emphatic a manner. I was removed as Consul at Foo Choo during the last hours of the Administration of James Buchannan at the request of John. E. Ward of Georgia then Minister to China, whose ani-mosity I had incurred for having denounced him as a traitor to his country, and for prostituting his office to his personal profit. At this time Jeremiah Black, and Trescott of South Carolina his personal friends were Secretary and asst. Secretary of State. I can prove to your satisfaction the manner in which I was sacrificed to my patriotism. Independent of this however, I consider myself as the representative of a former Administration entitled to consideration above the dictum of Mr Fish. In a few years your children will hold the position I do, when I trust their claims will meet with more favour than has been extended to me. I have tried to condense in these few lines, but would like to speak to you of these things should you feel disposed to give me your attention, and should feel honored by an acknowledgment of the reciept of this."—ALS, DLC-Hamilton Fish. On April 17, 1869, Gouverneur had written to Secretary of State Hamilton Fish requesting a consular appointment at Shanghai.—ALS, DNA, RG 59, Letters of Ap-plication and Recommendation.

1870, FEB. 3.   USG note. "The Sec. of War will please revoke so much of orders No   as retires Dr. McDougall and Dr. Satterl~~y~~ee."—ANS, Gal-lery of History, Las Vegas, Nev. On Feb. 14, 1871, USG wrote to the Sen-ate. "I nominate the Officers herein named for promotion in the Army of the United States. *Medical Department.* Lieutenant Colonel *Charles Mc-Dougall*, Assistant Medical Purveyor, to be Chief Medical Purveyor, with the rank of Lieutenant Colonel, February 22. 1869. vice Satterlee. retired. [since retired.] Lieutenant Colonel *Robert Murray*, Assistant Medical Pur-veyor to be Chief Medical Purveyor with the rank of Lieutenant Colonel,

February 22. 1869. vice McDougall, retired. Surgeon *Robert C. Wood*, to be Assistant Medical Purveyor with the rank of Lieutenant Colonel, February 22. 1869. vice McDougall, promoted. [since retired.] . . . [NOTE] Under the laws and regulations these Officers became entitled to promotion to the grades for which they are above nominated, and their names were submitted to the Senate prior to the Act of March 3. 1869. prohibiting further appointments and promotions in the Staff Corps. I deem it an Act of Justice to the Officers, that these promotions should be made from the dates they became entitled thereto."—DS (brackets in original), DNA, RG 46, Papers Pertaining to Nominations. On March 6, USG sent the same letter to the Senate.—DS, *ibid.*; copy (dated March 10), *ibid.*

On Feb. 1, 1870, Maj. Gen. John M. Schofield, St. Louis, wrote to USG. "Dr McDougall informs me that he is about to apply to you for an appointment to the Naval Academy for his grandson Charles McD. Adams. From your personal knowledge of the Doctors long, faithful and meretorious service and of his present circumstances, I am sure it will cause you as much pleasure to grant him this favor as it will me and all who know him. I will therefore only express the earnest hope that you may find it practicable to grant the Doctors request. I am glad to be able to add that the young man himself is highly worthy of a naval appointment."—Copy, DLC-John M. Schofield.

1870, FEB. 3. To Senate. "I herewith lay before the Senate, for the consideration and action of that body, in connection with a Treaty of December 4th 1868 with the Seneca Nation of Indians now pending, amendments to said Treaty proposed at a Council of said Indians held at their Council House on the Cattaraugus Reservation, in New York, on the 26th ultimo. A letter of the Secretary of the Interior of the 3rd instant, accompanies the papers."—DS, DNA, RG 46, Presidential Messages, Indian Relations. On Feb. 3, Secretary of the Interior Jacob D. Cox had written to USG transmitting the documents.—LS, *ibid.* Related papers are *ibid.* See *SRC*, 41-2-145.

1870, FEB. 5. Proclamation. "Whereas certain additional articles to the Treaty now in force between the United States of America and the Ta-Tsing Empire, signed at Tientsin, the 18th day of June, 1858, were concluded and signed by their Plenipotentiaries at Washington, on the 28th day of July, 1868, which additional articles are, word for word, as follows: . . . Now, therefore, be it known that I, Ulysses S. Grant, President of the United State of America, have caused the said additional articles to be made public, to the end that the same, and every clause and article thereof, may be observed and fulfilled with good faith by the United States and the citizens thereof. . . ."—*Washington Chronicle*, Feb. 7, 1870. See Charles I. Bevans, comp., *Treaties and Other International Agreements of the United States of America, 1776–1949* (Washington, D. C., 1968–76), 6, 680–84.

1870, FEB. 5. USG endorsement. "Respectfully refered to the Sec. of the Treas, I am inclined to think, from the verbal statements made in this case, that the request should be granted."—AES, DNA, RG 56, Collector of Customs Applications. Written on a letter of Feb. 3 from U.S. Senator John F. Lewis of Va. *et al.* to USG. "The undersigned, members of Congress from Virginia, would respectfully ask that Lewis W. Webb, the present Collector of customs at Norfolk be retained in Office."—LS, *ibid.*

1870, [FEB. 5]. Letter of introduction. "Colonel Louis Zimmer, of North Carolina, goes to Europe in the interest of the Southern Union Land Company, to induce emigration to the Southern States of America. The South holds out great inducements to an industrious population, both in the productiveness of the soil and in the cheap rate at which it can be acquired. Labor, also, can be employed to a much larger extent and at fairer wages than is now supplied."—*Washington Chronicle*, Feb. 8, 1870.

1870, FEB. 5. Orville E. Babcock endorsement. "*Respectfully referred to the Honorable Secretary of War.* & especial attention called to this case when appointments are made."—ES, DNA, RG 94, Correspondence, USMA. Written on a letter of Feb. 3 from William Maynadier, Washington, D. C., to USG. "I have the honor to request an appointment to the United States Military Academy at West Point, and in support thereof I submit the following. My father, Major Henry E. Maynadier, 12th U. S. Infantry, graduated at West Point in 1851, in the Artillery; was transferred to the 10th Infantry; served through the late War in Mississippi Flotilla, in the Volunteer and Regular Army and was breveted a Major General of Volunteers for gallant and meritorious conduct and died at Savannah Ga., while in command of his Post on Dec. 3d 1868 leaving my mother with five young sons to educate and support and only a pension of $25 00/100 per month to depend upon. My father's father, Bvt. Brig. Gen. Wm Maynadier, Colonel of Ordnance, is still an officer of the Army having done and is still doing good service to his country. My mother's father Capt. Thomas Barker, 1st U. S. Infantry, served in early youth as a volunteer officer in the war of 1812 and was afterwards appointed in the 1st U. S. Infantry. He served with that Regiment for many years and died in Florida from disease contracted in the swamps while on duty, and her only brother, Bvt. Major Thomas Barker, Lieut. 23d U. S. Infantry served through the entire Rebellion in the 2d California Cavalry and was appointed, at the close of the war, in the 23d Reg't. U. S. Infantry; he also died in the service just one month after my father's death. Hoping that this application may meet your aprobation and that I, too, may devote my life to the service of my country, . . . P. S. I was born at Baton Rouge Barracks, Louisiana, on the 5th day of May A. D. 1853, my present age is, consequently, between 16 and 17 years."—ALS, *ibid.* Maynadier failed to graduate from USMA.

1870, Feb. 5.   Henry Apps, Fort Wayne, to USG. "Please excuse the liberty I take in writing You,   On Aug 20th/62 Under Genl Burnside 83d Regiment Pensylvania Volunteers, Company I Capt. John Sell, was wounded same Year in Oct in Battle on the Potomac near old canal which was thrown up for an Embankment at that time,   I was promoted to carry of the dead & wounded at that Battle was wounded by An Officers Horse striking me in the Back by his foot, Was taken to Alexandria Maryland remained there untill last of Dec same Year, then removed to Ft Shuyler U S Hospital was dischargd for disabibility Applied to C G Bruce War claims agt Cleaveland Ohio in ~~Feby~~ Feby/64 for a Pension gave him a certificate from P Falkner Examining Surgeon Erie Pensylvania   C G Bruce sent the certificate to the War Department but no answer has ever been recd   I would not trouble Your Excelency but I have been burnt out   My own health very poor in consequence of my wound in Battle my Wife's health also extrememely poor & any favour the Goverment is pleased to extend to me, will be very thankfuly recd   Please Excuse ~~the~~ my writing direct to You Mr Presdent as I do not know what other course to take"—ALS, DNA, RG 107, Letters Received from Bureaus.

1870, Feb. 7.   Orville E. Babcock to G. Forrest Walter, San Francisco. "The President directs me to say in answer to your letter of Jany. 25. that he has never had a private secretary by the name of E. A. Protois, and that he is not aware that there has ever been any person by that name employed as a clerk or otherwise."—Copy, DLC-USG, II, 1.

1870, Feb. 7.   Horace Porter to U.S. Delegate Selucius Garfielde of Washington Territory. "I am directed by the President to acknowledge the receipt of your note of the 4th. with a pamphlet on 'Economy and retrenchment,' and communicate his thanks for your kindness. He desires me to say that the subject has been referred to the Secretary of War."—Copy, DLC-USG, II, 1. *Economy and Retrenchment. Vancouver. W. T., vs. Portland. Oregon* (Portland, 1869), includes a memorial of Jan. 7, 1868, from the Washington Territorial legislature to USG, secretary of war *ad interim*, protesting plans to transfer military hd. qrs. and supply depot at Fort Vancouver to Portland.—DNA, RG 94, Letters Received, 1616S 1869. On Feb. 4, 1870, Col. Rufus Ingalls, New York City, wrote to U.S. Senator Henry W. Corbett of Ore. ". . . You remember that Genl. Grant once told us that he would give the *order* in favor of Portland—. . ."—ALS, *ibid.* Related papers are *ibid.*

1870, Feb. 8.   To House of Representatives. "In answer to the resolution of the House of Representatives of the 3d instant, calling for the number of Copies of 'The Tributes of the Nations to Abraham Lincoln,' now in possession of the Department of State, I transmit a report from the secretary of

State and the paper which accompanied it."—Copies, DNA, RG 59, General Records; *ibid.*, RG 130, Messages to Congress. See *HED*, 41-2-128.

1870, Feb. 8. S. B. Moody, San Jose, Calif., to USG. "Please withold appointment of Post Master here for two 2 weeks"—Telegram received, DNA, RG 107, Telegrams Collected (Bound). On March 2, Charles G. Thomas was confirmed as postmaster, San Jose.

1870, Feb. 8. Robert A. Parrish, Jr., Philadelphia, to USG. "I have a just Claim on the Govt of France, for nearly Five Millions of Dollars, the evidence of which is on file in the Departt of State. An adverse decision as to its validity, was made some years ago by the under-clerks of that Departt, based upon *absolute mistatements of the Law, and misrepresentations of the facts* as I have since demonstrated. My appeals for a further examination of the subject are nevertheless refused:—which I cannot but deem a cruel injustice. . . ."—ALS, DLC-Hamilton Fish.

1870, Feb. 9. To J. Langdon Ward, secretary, Union League Club, New York City. "The very cordial invitation from the U. L. Club to be present at the annual reception on the evening of the 16th inst., reached me to day. It would afford me much pleasure to accept the invitation if my public duties would admit. Please communicate to the Club my thanks for the honor conferred by selecting the anniversary of the battle of Donalson for the pleasant occasion."—Copy, DLC-USG, II, 1.

1870, Feb. 9. Secretary of the Interior Jacob D. Cox to USG. "I have the honor to return, herewith, the copy of an act, entitled 'an act for the relief of Alinzor Clark, and to state that I am aware of no special reasons which should induce you to withhold your approval thereto."—LS, OFH.

1870, Feb. 10. USG proclamation concerning reciprocity of consular jurisdiction with "France, Prussia and the other States of the North German Union, and Italy. . . ."—DS, DNA, RG 130, Executive Orders and Proclamations.

1870, Feb. 10. Judge Advocate Gen. Joseph Holt to USG. "The within named applicant, J. H. Leavenworth, was by Special Order of the War Department, of Sept. 26, 1863, dishonorably discharged from his connection with the military service of the United States, as Colonel 2d Colorado Vols., with loss of all pay & allowances. His case having been subsequently referred to this Bureau for examination, a report upon the merits of the same, (of which the within is the copy furnished by the applicant,) was made on Feby. 18, 1864, to the President, in which it was recommended that the said order be recalled, and an order of honorable discharge substituted. This report the President approved by an endorsement over his signature, on March 5, 1864, of which endorsement a copy is also within.

In that endorsement the President stated that he had come to the conclusion that Col. Leavenworth had done 'nothing to censure and all to commend,' and he ordered that the 'recommendation' of this Bureau 'be carried into effect,' at the same time expressing the desire that Col. Leavenworth 'might be replaced in the military service as soon as it could conveniently be done.' (He did not, however, it may here be noted, subsequently reënter the military service, but was appointed an Indian Agent.) On March 26, '64, the direction of the President was complied with, in and by an order of the Secretary of War of that date revoking the original order of Sept. 26th '63, and directing that Col. Leavenworth be honorably discharged as of the date of said original order, with pay to that date. He was thereupon so discharged and paid. Col. Leavenworth now applies for the issuing of a new order in his case as a modification of the order of March 26, 1864. . . ."—Copy, DNA, RG 153, Letters Sent.

1870, FEB. 10.   E. C. Banfield, solicitor of the treasury, to USG. "I have been requested to call your attention to the matter of the U. S. v. The Representatives of John S. Fillmore, late Paymaster &ce, now pending in the District Court of Colorado Territory. Said Fillmore was an Additional Paymaster U. S. A. and died in December 1864, in default to the Government in about $80.000. leaving a large real and personal estate, more than enough to pay said debt to the United States . . ."—LS, DNA, RG 206, Letters Sent (Press).

1870, FEB. 11.   Governor Rutherford B. Hayes of Ohio to USG. "I am very anxious that my friend Gen Schneider should obtain the appointment he wishes. His claims and merits are fully shown by his papers on file, and I now write merely to solicit special attention [to] them."—LS (press), OFH. On March 25, 1867, USG had favorably endorsed papers recommending Edward F. Schneider, former lt. col., 8th Kan., for appointment as bvt. brig. gen.—ES, DNA, RG 94, ACP, 243S CB 1867. On Dec. 9, 1869, William Dennison, Columbus, Ohio, wrote to USG recommending Schneider for a consular appointment in Europe.—ALS, *ibid.*, RG 59, Letters of Application and Recommendation. On Jan. 20, 1870, Hayes wrote to USG supporting an appointment.—LS, *ibid.* Numerous letters addressed to USG urged that Schneider go to Europe to recover his health, damaged by wartime service.—*Ibid.* No appointment followed; Schneider died in July, 1871.

1870, FEB. 12.   Horace Porter to Secretary of State Hamilton Fish. "I am directed by the President to transmit to your department for such further disposition as the laws of the United States require; Senate Bill No 47., entitled 'An Act for the relief of S and H. Sayles'. This bill was received by the President on the first instant, and no action having been taken on it, becomes a law by constitutional limitation."—Copy, DLC-USG, II, 1. For the claim of S. and H. Sayles, see *SRC*, 41-1-2.

1870, FEB. 14.   Horace Porter to Moses H. Grinnell, collector of customs, New York City. "I am directed by the President to say that he would be pleased to have Harry Burton of Staten Island appointed to some position in the Custom House, if you can find a vacancy. Young Burton is the son of the late Gen. Burton and the President desires to appoint him to either the Military or Naval Academy next year, and would be glad if he can have some position under you where he can support himself in the mean time."— Copy, DLC-USG, II, 1.

1870, FEB. 15.   To Senate. "In reply to a resolution of the Senate of the 9th instant, in relation to the Central Branch, Union Pacific Rail-Road Company, I transmit a copy of a letter addressed to me on the 27th ultimo by the Secretary of the Interior. It contains all the information in my possession touching the action of any of the Departments on the claim of that company to continue and extend its road and to receive in aid of the construction thereof lands and bonds from the United States."—DS, DNA, RG 46, Annual Messages. See *SED*, 41-2-45.

1870, FEB. 15.   Secretary of the Interior Jacob D. Cox to USG. "I have the honor to lay before you a letter from the Commissioner of Ind'n Affairs, to this Department, bearing date the 12th inst., relative to the complaint of Edward Dwight, a Choctaw Indian, and a resident of the Choctaw Country, who requests that steps be taken by the Office of Indian Affairs, to restore his property seized by the United States Marshal for an alleged violation of the Internal Revenue laws of the U. S. and to indemnify him for damages thereby sustained. The Commissioner incorporates in his letter the order issued by the Office of Internal Revenue, bearing date the 25th ulto, in relation to the Country west of Missouri and Arkansas, Known as the 'Indian Territory, and appointing officers to execute, within its limits, Sundry provisions of an Act entitled 'An Act imposing taxes on distilled Spirits and tobacco, and for other purposes,' approved July 20th 1868. The delegations of the several tribes or nations, residing within said Territory, have presented a protest against said order and request that your attention be invited to the subject. The letter, of the Commissioner of Indian Affairs, and the accompanying papers present the case with such fullness as renders unnecessary a more specific statement of it in this communication. In order that the action of the Executive branch of the Government may be authoritatively settled, I have the honor to submit to you the propriety of referring them to the Attorney General, and of instructing him to advise you whether the said Act applies to, and is in force within the said Indian Territory and if yea, to what extent."—LS, DNA, RG 75, Letters Received, Choctaw Agency. On Feb. 16, Cox wrote to USG. "I have the honor to return, herewith, a resolution of the Senate of the 14th instant, which was received, by reference from the Executive, on the 15th instant, asking for information whether 'any officer of the government has extended the Revenue laws over the Cherokee Country or has attempted to enforce the payment of taxes by

Cherokees on products manufactured by them in the Cherokee Nation, and sold within the Indian Territory.' A communication from this Department, containing all the information in its possession in relation to the enquiry contained in the resolution, was laid before the President on yesterday. As the Treasury Department has jurisdiction of the subject upon which the Senate calls for information, a reference of the resolution to the Secretary of the Treasury is respectfully suggested."—Copy, *ibid.*, RG 48, Indian Div., Letters Sent. See *SJ*, 41–2, p. 242. On Dec. 28, 1871, Attorney Gen. Amos T. Akerman wrote to USG. "On the 7th of March 1870, you referred to Mr. Hoar, then Attorney General, for an opinion upon the legal questions involved, a communication to yourself from Mr. Cox, then Secretary of the Interior, on the subject of the complaint of Edward Dwight, a Choctaw Indian, who requested that steps should be taken by the Office of Indian Affairs to restore his property, seized by the United States Marshal for an alleged violation of the internal revenue laws, and to indemnify him for damages sustained by such seizure. I have no doubt that the reason why the required opinion was not immediately given by Judge Hoar was, that the question was then before the Supreme Court of the United States, in the cause known as *The Cherokee Tobacco*. That cause has since been argued, and the decision of the Supreme Court is in 11 Wallace Reports 616. The Court decides in that case that the 107th section of the Internal Revenue Act of July 20. 1868 (15 U S. Stats., 167), extends the internal revenue laws, imposing taxes on distilled spirits, fermented liquors, tobacco, snuff, and cigars, over the Indian Territory; and the principle of this decision covers the case of Mr. Dwight, and shows that he is not entitled to the relief which he asks from the Office of Indian Affairs."—LS, DNA, RG 75, Letters Received, Choctaw Agency.

1870, FEB. 15.   James Speed, Washington, D. C., to USG. "Alfred Allen, Esq., is applying for a foreign Mission—Permit me to say that I have known Mr Allen from my boyhood & can confidently say that he is a most worthy gentleman—He is well qualified to represent our government abroad—His position during the rebellion was most decided & worked hard for & accomplished as much [in] his sphere as any man in Ky—He desves well & I hope will be rewarded by the government—"—ALS, Free Library of Philadelphia, Philadelphia, Pa.

1870, FEB. 16.   To House of Representatives. "In answer to the Resolution of the House of Representatives of the 10th instant, I transmit a report from the Secretary of State, with accompanying documents."—Copies, DNA, RG 59, General Records; *ibid.*, RG 130, Messages to Congress. On Feb. 15, Secretary of State Hamilton Fish had written to USG. ". . . The Secretary of State has the honor to report to the President that according to the correspondence on record and on file in this Department, the Spanish Government failed through derangement in its finances for many years after the execution of the Treaty, punctually to pay the interest due to the United

States under the Convention of 1834. The allegation of inability to make those payments appears to have been acquiesced in by the Administrations for the time being. Finally, however, in the year 1847 an arrangement was entered into, which has always been regarded as confidential, by which payment of the interest was to be made by drafts drawn in Havana on New York. It is understood that this arrangement was approved by the claimants or a majority of them. Payments under this arrangement have been made with reasonable punctuality. After the passage of the legal-tender Act of 1862 payment appears to have been offered and accepted in drafts payable in currency. . . ."—Copy, *ibid.*, RG 59, General Records. See *HED*, 41-2-139.

1870, FEB. 16. To Senate. "In response to the resolution of the Senate, of the 8th. inst., asking 'how much of the appropriations heretofore made, amounting to One hundred thousand dollars, to provide for the defence of certain suits now pending in the Court of Claims, known as the Cotton Cases, have been expended, and to whom the same has been paid, for what services rendered and the amount paid to each of said persons, and also the number of clerks in the Treasury department and other persons, with their names, engaged or occupied in the defence of said suits;' I herewith transmit the report of the Secretary of the Treasury to whom the resolution was referred"—DS, DNA, RG 46, Presidential Messages. See *SED*, 41-2-47.

1870, FEB. 16. Orville E. Babcock to Isaac Cook, St. Louis. "The President requests me to acknowledge the receipt of your letter of Feb. 8th. relating to the case of your Imperial Champagne of the vintage of 1868. and to say in reply that the case came in good order and is a fine article. The President directs me to communicate his sincere thanks for your kind consideration"—Copy, DLC-USG, II, 1. On Oct. 6, Horace Porter wrote to Cook. "Enclosed please find the Presidents' check for two hundred and forty dollars, the amt. of your bill of Oct. 1. for 12 cases of wine. Please acknowledge the receipt."—Copy, *ibid.* On Jan. 21, 1873, William H. Benton and John M. Krum, St. Louis, wrote to USG. "We observe that the Senate has made material changes in the Vienna Exposition Bill—The amendment contemplates the appointment of 'Artizans' &c If this is so Mr Isaac Cook will prefer to go as *Artizan* & he is Eminently fit as he represents a leading & very important interest in the Mississippi Valley—the manufacture of native wines We make this change in our recommendation with the consent of Mr Cook & as he expects to be an Exhibitor at Vienna we hope he may be sent in the capacity designated—believing from the great interest he taken in the matter that he will do credit to the position & truly represent the interests of the country."—LS, DNA, RG 59, Letters of Application and Recommendation. On March 17, Levi P. Luckey wrote to Cook. "The President directs me to inform you that you are a Commissioner with Gen. Van Buren to the Vienna Fair, and hence there was no necessity for appointing you as one of the Artisans. Your position gives you the same pay as would be received as an Artisan."—Copy, DLC-USG, II, 2.

1870, FEB. 16.   Orville E. Babcock to C. Hendrickson, New York City. "Your letter informing the President of the case of wine you brought from Spain and left in the hands of the authorities in N. Y., came in due time. The President directs me to inform you that the case arrived in good condition, and to communicate his thanks for your kindness."—Copy, DLC-USG, II, 1.

1870, FEB. 16.   Secretary of the Navy George M. Robeson to USG. "I have the honor to submit herewith for your approval or disapproval, the record of the proceedings of a General Court Martial in the case of Surgeon Wm. Johnson, Jr. sentenced 'To be dismissed from the service of the United States.' "—Copy, DNA, RG 45, Letters Sent to the President. Surgeon William Johnson, Jr., was dismissed from the U.S. Navy on Feb. 19.

1870, FEB. 16.   Maj. George P. Ihrie, "The Accredited Agent of Alaska to the Congress of the U. S.," Ebbitt House, Washington, D. C., to USG. "In the event of Alaska being created into a Judicial and Land District, (which I suggested to the Committees on Territories) I beg to recommend Judge Samuel Storer, son of the late Admiral Storer, U. S. Navy, and residing in Sitka, Alaska, for Judge of the Judicial District of Alaska, and Mr. J. Henry Kinkead, also residing in Sitka, for U. S. Marshal of said District. Judge Storer is a Lawyer by profession, a 'Republican' in politics, and admirably suited for the position. Mr. Kinkead is also eminently qualified for the office of U. S. Marshal."—ALS, DNA, RG 60, Letters from the President.

1870, FEB. 17.   To Senate. "I transmit to the Senate in answer to their Resolution of the 24th ultimo the report from the Secretary of State with accompaniments."—LS, DNA, RG 46, Presidential Messages. On the same day, Secretary of State Hamilton Fish had written to USG transmitting a list of persons holding commissions issued by the U.S. Dept. of State.—DS, *ibid.* See *SED*, 41-2-46.

1870, FEB. 17.   John Eaton, Jr., Washington, D. C., to USG. "The important cases for removal I have delayed transmitting, a little, to give the facts more exactly. W. B. Gaw is Civil Engineer in charge of the Tennessee River improvements at Chattanooga salary, $3000—; T. B. Kirby is his clerk or Secy, salary $1500—. Both have been well known to me as opponents of Congressional reconstruction, and especially Mr. Kirby as a writer for the vilest rebel papers of the state—But recently since affairs have gone so badly in Tennessee, they have been joined in a way to do special harm & become specially obnoxious to men true to the government—Although both were officers in the Union army and of colored Regiments, they are the special intimates of Mr. James a member of the present Legislature who seeks notoriety as an assailant of our Government and its officers, & has been among those men proposing to remove Genl Thomas's portrait from the state Library—in which Mr. Gaw has been his open defender, while Mr. Kirby edits the 'Times' a dirty rebel paper in which he apparently sets no limits to his lying—Mr. Gaw aids him in the support of the paper, and is, I am assured, the endorser of his notes given for its purchase. In a word the Government supports two men, when its friends can scarcely live, and out of that government support they assail & viturperate the government & its friends—These men are on General Weitzel's rolls, but he can not I am sure be aware of these facts—Besides Mr. Gaw I am sure from my personal knowledge of him is far from a proficient Engineer—Indeed his capacity to speak & write English although a native of the country is below par, and he could hardly get along passably in this respect were it not for Mr. Kirby—Lest any one should say it is easy to remove & difficult to fill, I recommend for Mr. Gaw's place Prof. Henry Pomeroy, a native of N. York, graduate of Union [College], and Assist. Engineer on the N-York Canal; also Engineer in Charge of the section of a R. R. running out of Toledo Ohio; also tutor of Mathematics for sometime in Union college & in an Institution at Troy N. Y. & Prof. in Appleton University Wis, whence he became a Major in a Wis. Reg. then Lt. Col, and has for sometime been Principal of an Academy in Tenn—where he went for his health; & now resides at Chattanooga—He has recently been tendered the professor ship of Mathematics in a college at St. Louis, also an appointment in the Naval Observatory here—Of his superior fitness for the place there can be no question—There are a plenty good men for clerks about there & he could select intelligently—"—ALS (brackets in original), DNA, RG 77, Explorations and Surveys, Letters Received. On March 14, Brig. Gen. Andrew A. Humphreys, chief of engineers, wrote to Secretary of War William W. Belknap reporting that Thomas B. Kirby had left government employment in Dec. 1869, and that William B. Gaw had been dismissed on March 8, 1870.—LS, *ibid.* Related papers are *ibid.*

1870, FEB. 18. To James Mitchel. "The very cordial invitation of the Knights of St. Patrick to dinner on St. Patrick's day, is before me. I regret that my public duties prevent my enjoying the pleasure an acceptance would afford. Please communicate my thanks to your society for the kind consideration shown me."—Copy, DLC-USG, II, 1. See *New York Times*, March 18, 1870. On March 7, USG wrote to Bernard Finney, St. Louis. "I have the honor to acknowledge the receipt of the very kind invitation of the Knights of St. Patrick to attend the annual re-union on the 17th inst. I regret that my public duties will not permit me to accept. Please accept my thanks for the kind sentiments expressed in your letter."—Copy, DLC-USG, II, 1. See *Missouri Democrat*, March 18, 1870. On March 7, USG wrote to C. J. Sander, Philadelphia. "I am in receipt of a diploma of membership and your letter informing me that I have been elected an honorary member of the Saengerbund vocal musical Society. It affords me great pleasure to accept this evidence of your consideration. I regret that my public duties will not permit me to accept your polite invitation to attend the annual ball on the 15th. inst."—Copy, DLC-USG, II, 1. On the same day, USG wrote to Louis Newberger, Indianapolis. "I have received your letter of the 1st inst., informing me that I had been elected an honorary member of the Mathesian Society of your University. It affords me much pleasure to accept this compliment, and I have to request you to communicate to your society my thanks for their kind consideration."—Copy, *ibid.* On March 10, USG wrote to Robert Patterson, Philadelphia. "I am in receipt of your pleasant letter containing an invitation of the Hibernian Society to dine with them on the 17th: It would afford me much pleasure to join you at the dinner, but my public duties prevent. I wish you a very happy time— Please present my compliments to the Society and express my regret. Please to present my compliments to Mrs Patterson, and accept my sincere thanks for the invitation to your home."—Copy, *ibid.*

1870, FEB. 18. Secretary of the Treasury George S. Boutwell to USG. "I have the honor to state that I am in receipt of a communication from the Commissioner of Customs of even date herewith, wherein he reports that the Collector of Customs at the port of New Orleans has not unfrequently, in his possession amounts of the public moneys larger than the penalty of his official bond. The Commissioner suggests in view of the fact above given, that an increase be made to the amount of the bond of said officer, from $60,000. to $100,000. In this behalf I would respectfully call attention to the *Act of May 15, 1820.* whereby the President is authorized to increase the bonds of Collectors, and other officers, whenever, in his judgment, such action shall be demanded by the interests of the public service. This matter is respectfully referred to the President with the recommendation that it be favorably considered."—Copy, DNA, RG 56, Letters Sent to the President.

1870, FEB. 18. Robert R. Lunsford, Bonsack, Va., to USG. "This is to call your attention to the fact that a large proportion of the Registrars appointed by Brevet Major General Canby in june last to revise the Registration lists in Virginia, have not been paid for their services. and in reply to many inquiries made to the Pay. Master. General. at Richmond Va and also to Gen Canby. they say that all the money appropriated by Congress for that purpose has been exhausted. and that no further payments can be made until further appropriations are made by Congress. Your Excellency will therefore please Memoralize Congress (in behalf of those Registrars who are unpaid, many of whom are very poor men) to make the needed appropriation."—ALS, DNA, RG 107, Letters Received from Bureaus.

1870, FEB. 19. USG endorsement. "Let special attention be called to this case when apts. come to be made"—Copy, DNA, RG 94, Correspondence, USMA. Written on the docket of letters addressed to USG recommending Almer H. Wells, Kalamazoo, for appointment to USMA.—*Ibid.* No appointment followed.

1870, FEB. 19, Saturday. Governor Oden Bowie of Md. to USG. "Captain Commerell of the english ship dines with me on Monday evening. Can you and one 1 or two 2 of your Cabinet join us at dinner spend the night with me go to the Naval ball that evening and pass the day as you prefer. If you will come on Monday evening I can fix the dinner hour for seven 7 oclock. An hour after the arrival of the train. If you will come I will also invite the British Minister. An early answer desired."—Telegram received (at 3:45 P.M.), DNA, RG 107, Telegrams Collected (Bound). On Feb. 24, Secretary of the Navy George M. Robeson wrote to USG. "I have the honor to inform you that in compliance with your request the Commandant of the Marine Corps has been directed to order the Marine Band to be in attendance at the Executive Mansion at 7 o'clock this evening."—Copy, *ibid.*, RG 45, Letters Sent to the President. On Feb. 24, Capt. John E. Commerell of the *Monarch* met USG at the White House during the evening and, on Feb. 25, members of the cabinet were entertained on board the *Monarch* at Annapolis. See *New York Times*, Feb. 25, 26, 1870.

1870, FEB. 21. To House of Representatives. "I transmit to the House of Representatives in answer to their Resolution of the 7th instant a report from the Secretary of State with accompanying documents."—Copies, DNA, RG 59, General Records; *ibid.*, RG 130, Messages to Congress. On the same day, Secretary of State Hamilton Fish had written to USG transmitting documents concerning diplomatic correspondence between the U.S. and Spain concerning the rebellion in Cuba.—Copy, *ibid.*, RG 59, General Records. See *HED*, 41-2-160.

1870, FEB. 23. To Senate. "I transmit to the Senate, in answer to their Resolution of the 14th instant, a Report from the Secretary of State with accompanying documents."—DS, DNA, RG 46, Presidential Messages. On the same day, Secretary of State Hamilton Fish wrote to USG transmitting correspondence concerning protection of American interests in Japan.—LS, *ibid.* See *SED*, 41-2-52. On March 10, USG wrote to the Senate. "I transmit to the Senate in answer to their Resolution of the 28th ultimo, a report from the Secretary of State, with accompanying documents."—DS, DNA, RG 46, President's Messages. On the same day, Fish wrote to USG concerning the administration of extraterritoriality and the protection of American interests in China and Japan.—LS, *ibid.* Related papers are *ibid.* See *SED*, 41-2-58.

1870, FEB. 24. USG endorsement. "Let the lands herein referred to be sold agreeably to the recommendation of the Secretary of the Interior."—Copy, DNA, RG 48, Indian Div., Letters Sent. Written on a letter of Feb. 23 from Secretary of the Interior Jacob D. Cox to USG. "I have the honor to submit, herewith, reports of the Commissioner of Indian Affairs dated the 3rd July 1869, and the 17th inst., respectively, in relation to the lands set apart for the use of the Friends Shawnee labor School and the School of the American Baptist Missionary Union—under the provisions of the Shawnee treaty of May 10. 1854. (Stat. at Large Vol. 10. p. 1053.) Approving the recommendation of the Commissioner of Indian Affairs, I respectfully request that the President order the sale of the lands as indicated in the report of that Officer of the 3rd July 1869."—Copy, *ibid.*

1870, FEB. 25. USG endorsement. "Let special attention be called to this application."—AES, DNA, RG 94, Correspondence, USMA. Written on a letter of Nov. 14, 1869, from Capt. C. R. Perry Rodgers, "U. S. S 'Franklin.'—Marseilles," to Capt. Daniel Ammen. "I have determined to ask the President for one of those appointments at large through which the country has provided that the [s]ons of its faithful servants may enter West Point. I may not hope for a congressional appointment, for during the last 36 years, I have served in the Navy afloat too steadily to have formed any of those local ties through which I might obtain local [i]nfluence. I beg therefore that, as one of my nearest and dearest friends, you will bring to the notice of the President my earnest application that my son Alexander may receive a Cadet's appointment at West Point. He is seventeen years old, manly, intelligent, and has never given me anxiety or trouble. You know the lad, and can speak for him personally. He is now at the Imperial College at Versailles, the President of which will bear witness to his capacity, diligence, and excellent character. His father, his grandfather, and both his great grandfathers, have served the country faithfully in arms. He bears the name of my brother, who was killed at Chapultepec, while leading the storming party of the 4th Infantry. The President was then a Lieutenant in that Regiment, and will, I am sure, remember his old comrade, and may not be unwilling to perpetuate in the army the name of one whose virtues and honorable death endeared his memory to his companions in arms. . . ."—LS, *ibid.* Alexander Rodgers graduated from USMA in 1875.

1870, FEB. 25. Orville E. Babcock to Governor Lucius Fairchild of Wis. "The President directs me to inform you that he is still holding an appointment to the Naval Academy for the orphan you wished appointed from the Asylum, and requests, that if you do not wish to send the name you will please inform him that he may appoint some boy and give him the time to prepare. The President fears the note sent to you some two weeks since may not have reached you or have been delayed."—Copy, DLC-USG, II, 1. On March 3, Fairchild telegraphed to USG. "I have orphan boy to present for Naval Cadetship this year,"—Telegram received (at 1:10 P.M.), DNA, RG 107, Telegrams Collected (Bound). Possibly on the same day, Fairchild wrote to USG. "Thanking the President for his offer to appoint a cadet in the Navy from the Soldier's Orphans' Home at Madison."—(Undated) Walter Evarts Benjamin, Catalogue No. 27, Nov., 1889, p. 6. On March 7, Babcock wrote to Fairchild. "I am directed by the President to acknowledge the receipt of your letter of the 3d inst., and to inform you that you are authorized to send to him, any time before the 10th day of next February the name of the orphan you may select from the Asylum, and that he will give him an appointment when the appointments are made for next year. The President wishes me to communicate his thanks for the kind sentiments expressed in your letter."—Copy, DLC-USG, II, 1.

1870, FEB. 25.   Judge Henry W. Blodgett, U.S. District Court, Chicago, to USG. "Understanding that the friends of Hon. M. E. Hollister of Ottawa in this state intend to ask for him an appointment to one of the Territorial Judgeships, I take occasion to say that I have known Judge Hollister intimately for over twelve years; and cheerfully bear my testimony to his sterling worth as a Citizen and Jurist—His long experience at the Bar at an early day in this state when our legal and social institutions were forming gives him an experience particularly valueable for a new country while his experience on the Bench in later years has made for him whenever know a rare reputation for uprightness and Judicial ability—If you shall deem it consistent with your views of duty to appoint him I have no doubt but his official Conduct will reflect Credit upon your choice—"—ALS, ICHi. Judge Thomas Drummond, U.S. Circuit Court, favorably endorsed this letter.—AES, *ibid.* On March 16, 1871, USG nominated Madison E. Hollister as associate justice, Idaho Territory. In April, 1869, U.S. Representative Burton C. Cook of Ill. had written to USG requesting Hollister's retention as consul, Buenos Aires.—ALS, DNA, RG 59, Letters of Application and Recommendation.

1870, FEB. 26.   To Secretary of State Hamilton Fish. "Messrs Stokes and Maynard of Tenn. join in recommendation of Fielding P. Meigs, of their State, for one of the consulships now vacnt. I think it will be well to make this appointment, the one recommended by Senator Warner, of Ala. and also the one from Cal."—ALS, DLC-Hamilton Fish. On May 11, 1869, U.S. Representatives William B. Stokes and Horace Maynard of Tenn. *et al.* had written to Fish recommending Fielding P. Meigs for a consular appointment.—LS, DNA, RG 59, Letters of Application and Recommendation. On March 4, 1870, USG nominated Meigs as consul, Montevideo.

1870, FEB. 26.   N. R. Draper to USG. "According to your advice, I have seen Mr. Davis about my uncle's business and he says that Mr. Fish must have misunderstood him, if he told you that the Dept. could not interfere in the matter. Mr. Davis also told me that the matter was in *your* hands and that you could make Mayaguez an independent consulate: whereupon Mr. Smith—whom Mr. Davis had called in to consult—said that the old Spanish government would allow but one consulate on the island; but that if the new government would allow it, both Mayaguez and Ponce were large shipping-ports and of sufficient size to have each a consul. Mr. Davis said that the laws of the old government would probably not affect the new one at all and seemed to think it was very probable that consuls could be appointed both at Ponce an[d] Mayaguez. I do not propose to trouble you any further about the matter, but simply thought I had better tell you the results of my inter-view with Mr. Davis."—ALS, DNA, RG 59, Miscellaneous Letters.

1870, FEB. 28. USG endorsement. "This appointment I want to give when appointment come to be made in June."—AES, DNA, RG 94, Corre-spondence, USMA. Written on a letter of Feb. 25 from Mrs. Anson L. Brewer, Washington, D. C., to USG. "In compliance with your remarks to Senator Sherman and myself this morning, I beg leave to make my applica-tion for the appointment of my son Edwin P. Brewer to be a cadet at large to West Point, His Father Maj: A. L. Brewer was killed while Paymaster of the U. S. A. Feby 1866 by the blowing up and burning of the steamer J. R. Carter in the Mississippi river near Vicksburg, . . ."—ALS, *ibid.* Ed-win P. Brewer briefly attended USMA in 1871 and was appointed 2nd lt., 7th Cav., as of Aug. 31, 1876.

1870, [*Feb.*]. Thomas G. Bell, U.S. Navy boatswain, *et al.* petition to USG. "The petition of the undersigned, a committee of the warrant officers of the United States Navy, respectfully represents: That in the year eighteen hundred and sixty-four your committee presented a petition to Congress asking for the enactment of a law giving assimilated rank to the warrant officers of the United States Navy. These officers are composed of boatswains and gunners of the line, and carpenters and sailmakers of the staff, all of whom receive their warrants from the President of the United States. Their duties, and the reasons submitted to Congress in support of their claim for assimilated rank, are as follows: . . ."—*HMD*, 41-2-58, pp. 3–5.

1870, MARCH 1. USG endorsement. "Call special attention to this case when appointments come to be made."—AES, DNA, RG 94, Correspon-dence, USMA. Written on a letter of Feb. 26 from Simon Wolf, Washing-ton, D. C., to USG. "Hamlin Spiegel son of Col M. M. Spiegel, late of the 120th Ohio volunteers, desires to be appointed to West Point, he is a bright, intelligent lad, 16 years of age, speaks and writes English and German fluently, his honored father was killed in the Red River Expedi-tion under Banks, although he was dangerously wounded in front of Vicks-burgh, he refused to stay at home, but Continued in the service, and lost his life in the discharge of duty, You would Confer a favor on a gallant boy, do honor to the memory of a brave soldier, and Convince many admirers that you aim to do Justice, to all men irrespective of Color or religion."—

ALS, *ibid.* Edward Salomon endorsed this letter. "I heartily concur in the foregoing recommendation. Col. Spiegel was a brave and gallant officer. His widow resides in chicago, where her untiring and noble efforts to educate her children have caused the admiration of all who know her."—AES, *ibid.* A note on the docket indicated that Hamlin Spiegel was too young to receive the appointment.—AN, *ibid.* On June 2, Secretary of War William W. Belknap noted: "The President directs that appointment as Cadet be given to Hamlin Spiegel in 1871 unless he can be appointed prior thereto in place of some appointee failing—"—ANS, *ibid.* Hamlin Spiegel never attended USMA. See Frank L. Byrne and Jean Powers Soman, eds., *Your True Marcus: The Civil War Letters of a Jewish Colonel* (Kent, Ohio, 1985), p. 339.

1870, MARCH 1. To Robert L. Brown. "Official notification of your rejection by the Senate on the 18th of February 1870. having been this day received, you will turn over the office of Collector of Internal Revenue for the 23d District of Pennsylvania to J. M. Sullivan whose suspension therefrom has been this day revoked."—Copy, DNA, RG 130, Executive Orders and Proclamations. On the same day, USG wrote to John M. Sullivan. "The order suspending you from the office of Collector of Internal Revenue for the 23d District of Pennsylvania is hereby revoked, and you will upon the receipt of this communication resume the duties of said office."—Copy, *ibid.* On June 28, 1869, Thomas Williams, Allegheny County, Pa., had telegraphed to USG. "The telegraph reports the removal of Mr Sullivan Collector of this District an officer of great popularity, nominated at my own instance, admitted on all hands to be above exception endorsed with unexampled unanimity by the party, by both the Senators in Congress from this state, and by all who have represented these counties in the other House for the last twenty two years and vouched for by your superviser as the very best of thirteen in his District and equal to any other in the Country, in favor of a new man of doubtful abilities and more than doubtful orthodoxy as a republican . . ."—Telegram received (at 11:30 A.M.), *ibid.*, RG 107, Telegrams Collected (Bound). Nominated on March 7, 1870, Sullivan was confirmed on March 8.

1870, MARCH 1. To Congress. "I transmit to Congress a communication from the Secretary of State with the accompanying documents, relative to the claims of citizens of the United States on the Government of Venezuela which were adjusted by the Commission provided for by the Convention with that Republic of April 25, 1866."—DS, DNA, RG 46, Presidential Messages. On the same day, Secretary of State Hamilton Fish had written to USG. "The Secretary of State has the honor to submit to the President the accompanying correspondence between the Department of State and the Minister of the United States to the Republic of Venezuela relating to the failure by that Republic to comply with its agreements to make payments of principal and interest awarded to citizens of the United States by the

mixed Commission formed under the Convention of April 25 1866. . . ."
—Copy, *ibid.*, RG 59, General Records. See *HED*, 41-2-176; *HRC*, 41-2-79; *SMD*, 41-2-162. On March 31, Fish wrote to USG. "The Secretary of State has the honor to submit to the President further dispatches from the Minister of the United States to the Republic of Venezuela relating to the failure by that Republic to comply with its agreements under the Convention of April 25, 1866: and also sundry documents transmitted to the Secretary of State by the Confidential Agent of Venezuela on behalf of that Government, for the purpose of establishing that there were irregularities in the execution of the mixed commission under the Convention which they claim may invalidate a portion of the award. The Secretary of State respectfully suggests that all the papers be transmitted to Congress to be considered in connection with the correspondence contained in House Executive Document No. 176 of the present session."—Copy, DNA, RG 59, General Records. On the same day, USG wrote to the Senate and House of Representatives. "I transmit to Congress a further communication from the Secretary of State, with the accompanying documents, relative to the claims of Citizens of the United States on the government of Venezuela which were adjusted by the Commission provided for by the Convention with that Republic of April 25 1866."—Copies, *ibid.*; *ibid.*, RG 130, Messages to Congress. The lengthy enclosure is *ibid.*, RG 46, Presidential Messages.

1870, MARCH 1. Frederick Killam, Washington, D. C., to USG. "I have the honor to present to your Excellency a brief statement for your kind consideration. I have sustained the Republican principles of this great Government as a Citizen and a Soldier. I served my country faithfully during the late war for three years and three months, and was thereby disabled which unfits me from performing manuel labor, and in order to obtain an honest living for myself and family, I must have employment of a light nature. Mr President, I have filed an application endorsed by the Conn' delagation and presented to the Hon' W. W. Belknap Secretary of War, by two of the members, Messrs Kellogg and Strong, for an appointment as Temporary Clerk, and have sought this interview thinking that you might give me a line to the Hon' Secretary influencing him to give employment to one who is in actual need. I should gladly accept of a place as Messenger or Watchman in his department."—ALS, DNA, RG 107, Appointment Papers.

1870, MARCH 2. Maj. Gen. John M. Schofield, St. Louis, to USG. "I take pleasure in reccomending Mr Thos P. Hill of Virginia, whose political desabilities I am informed have been removed by congress, as in All respects worthy of the appointment of U. S. Attorney."—Copy, DLC-John M. Schofield. No appointment followed.

1870, MARCH 3. To House of Representatives. "I transmit herewith, in response to the Resolution of the House asking for information in relation to the repairs of Spanish war vessels at the docks of the United States, the report of the Secretary of the Navy to whom the resolution was referred."—Copy, DNA, RG 130, Messages to Congress. On March 2, Secretary of the Navy George M. Robeson had written to USG. ". . . In reply to the resolution, I have the honor to state, that informal application was made to this Department, on behalf of the Spanish Government, for permission to deposit the armament and part of the equipment of the ships referred to, in the Navy Yard at NewYork, preparatory to going into private dock for repairs. It was replied that such an application should be made only through the State Department. No further application has since been made. There is no law or treaty stipulation on this subject known to the Department, but it has always been our uniform practice towards all nations with whom we are at peace, (and that of Spain and other nations towards ourselves) to afford, in our navy yards, to the officers of war ships needing repairs, such of the required facilities as did not interfere with our own work. By this reciprocal custom, the officers of the ships referred to, would be entitled, should they require it, to the use of our government docks when disengaged. This is not likely to be the situation of the docks, however, and they will not be cleared for the purpose."—Copy, *ibid.*, RG 45, Letters Sent to the President. See *HED*, 41-2-177.

1870, MARCH 7. James F. Casey, collector of customs, New Orleans, to USG. "Your letter received and answered."—Telegram received, DNA, RG 107, Telegrams Collected (Bound). On March 11, Casey telegraphed to USG. "Letter from Gov Warmouth mailed you today, explaining matters here & strongly reccommending Herwig for retention as special deputy collector"—Telegram received (on March 12, 6:00 A.M.), *ibid.* Philip F. Herwig retained the position. On March 31, Casey wrote to USG. "I cordially recommend the application of Mr Wm M. Aikman for the appointment of Assistant Appraiser, now vacant, at this port, to your favorable consideration. I have known him for a number of years and can endorse him not only as a good republican but also as a competent business man. Senator Morton by whom he is strongly endorsed will call upon you in relation to his application for appointment"—LS, *ibid.*, RG 56, Appraiser of Customs Applications. No appointment followed.

1870, MARCH 7. Columbus Delano, commissioner of Internal Revenue, to USG. "Doubts having been expressed as to the power of the President to restore a suspended civil officer to duty, after making a nomination to the Senate of a person to fill his place, and after that nomination has been rejected by the Senate, I have had the following correspondence with Hon. Charles P. James Counsellor at Law, in relation to the matter. I enclose that correspondence to you with the respectful request that the opinion of the Attorney General upon the question may be obtained"—LS, DNA, RG 60, Letters from the President. The enclosure is *ibid.* On April 2, Attorney Gen. Ebenezer R. Hoar wrote to USG. ". . . The President, in the case upon which my opinion is asked, has, in effect, asked the concurrence of the Senate in the removal of the officer suspended by the appointment of another, and the Senate have refused to concur. Their whole action upon that proceeding is thus terminated, and I am of the opinion that the President has the same legal right and authority to revoke the suspension and to restore the officer before making another nomination, as he would have had if he had made no nomination whatever; and this construction of the law is most consistent with the spirit and purpose of the statute and with the due exercise of the constitutional powers of the President."—Copy, *ibid.,* Opinions.

1870, MARCH 9. Governor Onslow Stearns of N. H. to USG. "New Hampshire first 1st to formally nominate you now endorses the first 1st year of your administration."—Telegram received, DNA, RG 107, Telegrams Collected (Bound).

1870, MARCH 10. To Senate. "In answer to the resolution of the Senate of the fourth instant, in relation to the 'Trans Continental, Memphis, El Paso, and Pacific Railroad Company', I transmit reports from the Secretary of State and the Secretary of the Interior, with accompanying papers,"—DS, DNA, RG 46, Presidential Messages. The enclosures are *ibid.* See *SED,* 41-2-59.

1870, MARCH 10. William Boyle, Washington, D. C., to USG. "An application has been filed by the following persons, with the Hon: Secretary of State recommending me as a suitable person to be appointed to a consulship in England. The object and purpose chiefly of the parties recommending me is, to have some one in England who can give information in regard to the Silver mining interests of Nevada. A large amount of English Capital is already invested in mining in Nevada, and a much larger amount could be obtained, if proper representations and information from a reliable source could be furnished. . . ."—ALS, DNA, RG 59, Letters of Application and Recommendation. Related papers are *ibid.* No appointment followed.

1870, MARCH 11. Bvt. Maj. Gen. Oliver O. Howard to USG. "I wish to recommend Mr *A. P. Clark* to you for employment in clerical or other duty requiring competency & intelligence—He is a member of the board of Aldermen of Washington but as there is no little compensation there—He needs some other work—I [thought] perhaps Genl Porter, Babcock *or* Michler might set him to some work. He was & is a strong friend of the administration"—ALS (press), Howard Papers, MeB.

1870, MARCH 11. Elihu B. Washburne to USG. "Michael Chevalier, a Senator of the Empire, is one of the prominent men of France, distinguished for his high character, intelligence and liberality. He has visited the United States and has always been one of our best friends. He has addressed me a communication on the subject of the Nicaraguan Canal, which, he has requested me to forward to you. I have the honor, therefore, of transmitting it by the despatch bag which leaves to-day. You will probably send it to the State Department, where it will have all the consideration to which it is entitled"—ALS (press), DLC-Elihu B. Washburne.

1870, MARCH 12.   Secretary of the Navy George M. Robeson to USG. "I have the honor to acknowledge the receipt, through the Department of State, of a copy of a Resolution passed by the Senate on the 7th instant, requesting the President of the United States to communicate certain information regarding the African Slave Trade; and to make the following report upon so much of the Resolution as pertains to the Navy Department. Previous to the late rebellion, a regular squadron of vessels of the United States Navy was maintained on the coast of Africa. During the rebellion the squadron was withdrawn, and since the reestablishment of our foreign squadrons, such assistance as has been rendered by the Navy, in suppressing the African slave trade, has been extended by the European Fleet and South Atlantic Fleet. The vessels of these fleets or most of them are furnished with a special warrant to exercise the rights and privileges under the treaty of April 7, 1862, between the United States and Great Britain, for the suppression of the African Slave Trade. A copy of this warrant is herewith enclosed. The vessels of the North Atlantic Fleet have also been supplied with these warrants. The accompanying lists show the number of vessels in the three fleets authorized in 1869 and 1870 to search for slavers. So far as this Department is advised, the traffic in human beings between the Coast of Africa and the Continent is carried on to a very limited extent. The Swatara, of the European Fleet, returned from an extended cruise on the African coast in April, 1868. Commander Jeffers reported that the Slave Trade was entirely suspended. The Canandaigua, of the same fleet, arrived at New York from a similar cruise in February 1869. Captain Strong reported that from all the information he could gather 'Slaves are no longer exported from Africa, but it is from the reason that it does not pay, now that all the old markets are closed against them.' The 'Quinnebang,' of the South Atlantic Fleet, made an extended cruise on the South West Coast of Africa in the year 1868. Commander Barrett furnished the Department with a copy of a communication addressed to him by Judge Pringle from which the following is an extract: 'From all I have been able to learn on the subject, my opinion is that the African Slave Trade on the West coast has nearly ceased. Occasionally a slaver escapes, but the vigilant watch maintained renders the business so precarious that few men are bold enough to engage in it. I understand that one slaver, and only one, succeeded in getting away from the West coast and over to Cuba during the last year. On the south-east coast, however, the Trade continues. It is estimated that no less than 40,000 slaves are carried off annually—the greater portion of them to Arabia.' The Portsmouth, of the South Atlantic Fleet, sailed from Rio de Janeiro on the 24th of January last, for a cruise on the South West Coast of Africa."—Copy, DNA, RG 45, Letters Sent to the President. See *CG,*

41–2, 1624, 1728. On June 3, USG wrote to the Senate. "I transmit to the Senate for consideration, with a view to its ratification, an Additional Convention to the Treaty of the 7th of April, 1862, for the Suppression of the African Slave Trade, which Additional Convention was signed on this day in the city of Washington, by the Plenipotentiaries of the High Contracting Parties."—DS, DNA, RG 46, Presidential Messages, Foreign Relations, Great Britain. The additional convention abolished the mixed courts which had been established in 1862. The papers are *ibid.* On Sept. 16, USG instructed Secretary of State Hamilton Fish to issue "My Proclamation of an additional Convention with Great Britain relating to the Suppression of the Slave Trade."—DS, NN. A copy of the printed proclamation is *ibid.* See W. E. Burghardt Du Bois, *The Suppression of the African Slave-Trade to the United States of America, 1638–1870* (New York, 1896).

1870, MARCH 14. To Senate. "In reply to your resolution of the 14th. of February, requesting to be informed whether I desire that any of the Indian Treaties now pending before you be considered confidentially, I have to inform you that there are none of them which I object to having discussed in open session."—DS, DNA, RG 46, Presidential Messages, Indian Relations. On March 28, Commissioner of Indian Affairs Ely S. Parker wrote to Secretary of the Interior Jacob D. Cox. "I have the honor to enclose herewith a petition from the Council of the Swan Creek and Black River Chippewas and Munsee & Christian Indians, to the President and Senate of the U. S. asking that they be permitted to withdraw their assent to the treaty with them now pending in the Senate, and that a new treaty may be made with them."—Copy, *ibid.* The enclosure and related papers are *ibid.* On Jan. 24, 1871, USG favorably endorsed these papers. —AES, *ibid.*

1870, MARCH 14. U.S. Senator John Sherman of Ohio to USG. "In pursuance of our conversation about the Cleveland Post Master, I beg leave to state my reasons for advising the appointment of John W. Allen. He is a gentleman of the highest character—long a member of Congress, and for many years identified with all measures to promote the growth and striking prosperity of that city. He is recommended by a great number of leading citizens in all branches of business. From a careful examination of the papers on file and from my correspondence, I believe he is supported by a majority of all the voters. He is not offensively identified with the unfortunate divisions now existing among our party friends in Cleveland. He is the second choice of nearly all parties, and his papers have since been signed by a number of the most prominent of those who had recommended Mr. Wade. He is recommended by both the Republican papers of Cleveland, which, considering their rivalry with each other, is a strong evidence of the popular approval of Mr. Allen. He is supported by Mr. Upson, the Member from the District, who may properly be consulted as to a local appointment. My private correspondence assures me that this nomination of an old and worthy citizen, who will devote his entire time and personal attention to the office, is most in harmony with the policy of the Adminstration to appoint a man who will do the duties of Postmaster, rather than one who is fully employed in other pursuits. As to Mr. Wade, he is certainly not a popular man, and has no special claim from past services—party position, ability, or fitness for this office. It will be construed as a mere personal compliment for Senator Wade, who does not live in Cleveland or in that District. I would gladly render any kindness to Senator Wade himself— but I do not think a local contest for Postmaster of Cleveland ought to be influenced by his choice, but only by the good of the service, and the good of the party, and the wishes of the Republicans of that City alone."—Copy, DLC-John Sherman. On March 29, USG nominated John W. Allen as postmaster, Cleveland.

1870, MARCH 15.   Bvt. Maj. Gen. Oliver O. Howard to USG. "I wish to recommend t[o] your most favorable consideration Dr H N. Howard—who was a surgeon of volunteers during our late war & won an excellent reputation in his department—After the war he labored a long time with great fidelity & success in my bureau in the care of infirm & aged freedmen—If there is any office of public trust, especially connected with his profession, in your gift that he can have, he will not disappoint you—"—ALS (press), Howard Papers, MeB.

1870, MARCH 16.   USG endorsement. "Let special attention be called to this application when appointments come to be made."—AES, DNA, RG 94, Correspondence, USMA. Written on a letter of March 14 from Lt. Col. John Newton, Washington, D. C., to USG. "I have respectfully to solicit a Cadets appointment to the military academy for my son Virginius. M. Newton—who was 17 years old, on the 8th day of December 1869. His name has been enrolled in the War Department for more than a year."— ALS, *ibid.* Related papers are *ibid.* Virginius M. Newton entered USMA in 1871 but did not graduate.

1870, MARCH 16.   USG endorsement. "After the Apt. already ordered for Arazona T. please consider this application favorably for the next ╪Territorial Judgeship"—AES, DNA, RG 60, Records Relating to Appointments. Written on a letter of March 5 from L. H. Chandler, Richmond, to USG. "L. M. Shumaker—is, as I understand, an applicant for a judicial position in one of the Territories. For several years I have been upon the most intimate terms with him. When his native state, Virginia, seceded, he cast his fortunes with her, although opposed to the doctrine of secession— In this he but followed the example of thousands of men who, however mistaken, were good men, but were led away by state pride. The moment the war came to a close he accepted the condition of things, became outspoken in his advocacy of the Union—attached himself to the republican party, and with pen and tongue rendered yeoman's service—He is a man

of fine ability, occupied a prominent position at the bar, and, for some time
past, has been filling the office of a circuit Judge with credit to himself, and
to the satisfaction even of his political opponents. Ostracized for his opinions, he would like, for a time, to seek a fresh field for labor. I sincerely
hope he may be successful in his desire of obtaining a situation at your
hands, for I feel confident you cannot make a better appointment—"—ALS,
ibid. Additional letters to USG on this subject are *ibid.* No appointment
followed.

1870, MARCH 17.   Bvt. Maj. Gen. Oliver O. Howard to USG. "Sojourner
Truth quite an aged & distinguished colored woman earnestly working for
years for her people—desires to see the *President*—She will pray for him
surely but more heartily if she sees him—"—ALS (press), Howard Papers,
MeB. On March 31, USG met Sojourner Truth and gave her his autograph.
See *Narrative of Sojourner Truth* (1878; reprinted, New York, 1968), pp.
233, 273–75.

1870, MARCH 17.   Elihu B. Washburne, Paris, to USG. "The result in
New Hampshire is not bad to take. It is the financial and economical policy
of the administration that did the business. How splendidly Boutwell has
sustained you in your policy and wishes. 'I told you so.' His success is my
vindication and my excuse for so constantly thrusting him before you. I
thank you, for making John Eaton Jr Commissioner of Education in place
of old Barnard, who was simply a scamp and ought to have been turned out
long ago: I was always opposed to that Bureau, but the appointment of so
good a man as Eaton goes a little way in reconciling me to it. I am appalled
at the schemes of robbery before Congress in the way of subsidies of land
& money for rail-road corporations. I pray you will give that matter your
serious attention and I hope to God you will veto the first bill that comes
before you that either grants an acre of land or a dollar of money. The profli-
gate and stupendous grants already made will be regarded in amazement
and horror in future time. The people are tired of that thing, and if the
question of more subsidies, either in land or money, were submitted to
them, not one vote in a hundred would be for subsidies. That is the true test.
I wish you would think over what I write you. Ask Joe Wilson of the Land
Office to give you the figures of the Empires already voted away to these
private corporations. A well considered and elaborate veto would electrify
the country and would endear you more than ever to the masses of the people.
Generations yet to come who want cheap land will rise up and call you
blessed. I ache to see your Proclamation announcing the adoption of the
15th Amendment. It will be next in importance to Lincolns Imancipation
Proclamation. I shall be sorry if the Senate dont let in Josh Hill from
Georgia & confirm Bradley. The rejection of Hoar was simply infamous.
Fremont is after a rail-road grab. Ask Gov. Fish about his stupendous
swindle here in the sale of five millions of dollars of his worthless bonds.
Anything that Fremont has anything to do with ought to be vetoed on

general principles. Every one of our children has been sick—two of them very sick—within the last two weeks, and I have been having attacks of the ague again and confined to my house. Fortunately Mrs. W. has kept up. She unites with me in kindest regards to yourself and family."—ALS (press), DLC-Elihu B. Washburne.

1870, MARCH 18. Bvt. Maj. Gen. Oliver O. Howard to USG. "Permit me to introduce to you Capt. Fred Tiedemann now of Philadelphia but formerly an Aide on the staff of Genl. Schurz, in my command—Capt. Tiedemann was a gallant and able officer, and desires to talk with you about a soldiers widow who is in extreme poverty."—ALS (press), Howard Papers, MeB.

1870, MARCH 21. USG endorsement. "These papers are from the Ex Officer of the Army who I recommended to see the Sec. of State relative to one of the vacancies likely to be created in the State Dept. by Act of Congress."—AES, DNA, RG 59, Letters of Application and Recommendation. Written on a letter of March 17 from Adalbert Fell, Georgetown, D. C., to Secretary of State Hamilton Fish requesting a clerkship in the State Dept.—ALS (in French), *ibid.* Related papers are *ibid.* On Dec. 17, 1869, Judge Advocate Gen. Joseph Holt had written to USG through the AG concerning Fell's court-martial.—Copy, DNA, RG 153, Letters Sent. On Dec. 20, Mathilde Fell, Baltimore, wrote to USG. "I have the honor to address herewith most respectfully your Excellency in behalf of my husband Lieut. Adalbert Fell 2d U. S. Artillery, who was tried by a General Court Martial & is now awaiting his sentence for an offence, the circumstancus of which you will kindly allow me to state in a few words. My husband, having received information that real estate worth $3000. gold was left to him in Germany & having been unable to negociate a loan committed himself so far as to sell his Payaccounts to two different parties, being under the impression at the time that he would be able to redeem the same before the would be due. My husband, knowing, that he was guilty put in his place to that effect, at the same time stating the circumstances, connected with this unfortunate and sad affair. I would now most respectfully ask your Excellency, that in receiving my husband's case you will kindly take in consideration, that he has served his Country faitfully ever since April 1861 as a Soldier and officer, that he was wounded in two battles and that he was never charged with any offense before. Hoping you will kindly excuse the liberty taken in addressing your Excellency . . ."—ALS, *ibid.*, RG 107, Letters Received from Bureaus. On Jan. 3, 1870, Holt endorsed this letter. "Respectfully returned to His Excellency the President, whose attention is invited to a full report in this case, addressed from this Bureau to the President, through the Adjutant General, on the 17th ult. In that report this Bureau expressed itself as disposed to concur in a recommendation of the court, that that portion of the sentence which imposed imprisonment be remitted by the pardoning power. But the case was so aggravated an one, of repeated fraudulent transfers of his pay rolls, by this officer, that no *further* clemency could, in any event, be advised."—ES, *ibid.* On Feb. 10, Fell wrote to USG requesting reappointment to the army so that he could resign.—ALS, *ibid.*, RG 94, ACP, F23 CB 1870. No action followed.

1870, MARCH 21. USG endorsement. "Please leave this vacancy until after the 1st of June."—AES, DNA, RG 60, Records Relating to Appointments. Written on a letter of the same day from U.S. Delegate Selucius Garfielde of Washington Territory, Washington, D. C., to USG. "The confirmation of Orange Jacobs as Chief Justice of Washington Territory, by the senate, leaves his position of Associate Justice vacant. Wm Lair Hill, recommended by senator Williams for that position, has declined, as will be seen by the enclosed telegram. I enclose recommendations in favor of Henry G. Struve for that position, and beg to add my endorsement to the list. I have known Mr Struve for several years in the territory, and know him to be a lawyer of much ability, and a republican of good record. His appointment to the bench would give very general satisfaction and I respectfully request that it be made."—ALS, *ibid.* Related papers are *ibid.* On June 18, USG nominated Roger S. Greene to be associate justice, Washington Territory. On Dec. 3, 1872, USG nominated Henry G. Struve as secretary, Washington Territory.

1870, MARCH 21. U.S. Representative John F. Farnsworth of Ill. to USG. "I earnestly but respectfully recommend the appointment of Mr Wm H. Donoho, to some place—a clerkship, or some other position where he can by diligence, and his undoubted capacity, earn a livelihood for himself & family—"—ALS, OFH.

1870, MARCH 23. Bvt. Maj. Gen. Oliver O. Howard to USG. "The bearer E. J. Maddox Esq: was under my direction for four years—is now a resident of Powhatan Co—. Va—In all his work he gave great satisfaction—He is a man of carefulness & integrity—I commend him to your favorable consideration"—ALS (press), Howard Papers, MeB. On March 24, Howard wrote to USG recommending E. J. Maddox for appointment as assessor of Internal Revenue.—Copy, DNA, RG 105, Letters Sent. No appointment followed.

1870, MARCH [24]. USG endorsement. "If a letter, or Vice Consulate, can be given to Mr. Phelan which will give him the security he asks I would like to have it extended to him."—AES, DNA, RG 59, Miscellaneous Letters. Written on a letter of March 15 from John C. Hamilton, Washington, D. C., to Frederick T. Dent. "Before I left this City—Mr Michael Phelan—a Maker of Billiard tables—being one of my tenants—asked me to request a favor in his behalf of the President, whom he stated that he was acquainted with. I promised to do it—but in the short interview I had last week, it escaped my recollection. He said, he proposed revisiting Ireland—his native country—that he was *engaged in the trouble* of *1848* &, if not protected, that he might be arrested. His request is the favor of some paper from the President for that purpose. It occurred to me, that were he appointed a Vice Consul—merely for that purpose only—he not intending to remove—that this might do—But of the propriety of this—the Secy of State is a better judge that I am,—& if proper to be done at all—some better expedient might be adopted. As I have no right to addres the President directly on this subject, I take leave to write to you. Phelan is really a very recspectable manner & known to be so—If you can reply—please do it."—ALS, *ibid.* No appointment followed.

1870, MARCH 25.   To Senate. "In answer to the Resolution of the Senate of the 15th ultimo, I transmit a report, with accompanying papers, from the Secretary of the Navy, to whom the resolution was referred."—DS, DNA, RG 46, Presidential Messages. The report listing ironclad ships of the U.S. Navy is *ibid.* See *SED*, 41-2-72.

1870, MARCH 25.   Dorothea A. Cooke (Mrs. Jay Cooke), Germantown, Pa., to USG. "We have made special arrangements for Ulysses tonight Can he possibly stay   please answer"—Telegram received, DNA, RG 107, Telegrams Collected (Bound).

1870, MARCH 28.   USG endorsement. "Referred to the Atty. Gen."— Robert F. Batchelder, Catalog 75, 1990, no. 42. Written on a letter from U.S. Delegate Allen A. Bradford of Colorado Territory to USG concerning the reappointment of a judge, probably Moses Hallett, chief justice, Colorado Territory. On April 4, USG nominated Hallett for reappointment. On Feb. 23, 1874, Henry M. Teller and Alfred Sayre, Denver, wrote to USG. "As the term of Office of Moses Hallett Cheif Justice of the Supreme Court of the Territory of Colorado, will soon expire, we most respectfully request his reappointment, . . ."—LS, DNA, RG 60, Records Relating to Appointments. On March 26, USG renominated Hallett.

1870, MARCH 28.   USG endorsement. "Unless there are charges against Judge Noggle, proven sufficient to demonstrate his unfitness for this position, I think it advisable to withdraw the nomination of his successor"— Robert A. Siegel, New York City, Catalogue 289 [1965], no. 12A. On March 9, USG had nominated Benjamin J. Waters as chief justice, Idaho Territory, to replace David Noggle, but withdrew the nomination on April 22 and nominated Waters as associate justice, New Mexico Territory. On April 8, 1871, Waters resigned.—ALS, DNA, RG 60, Records Relating to Appointments. On Feb. 14, 1877, Jessie F. Noggle, New Brighton, Pa., wrote to USG. "Will you be so kind as to inform me whether there was one named Noggle, appointed some years ago, by you, as Chief Justice of

Idaho. Pleas inform me also if you can what his full name was; and where he resided at the time the appointment was made, and what his P. O. address is at the present time. Hoping you will condescend to give me the desired information . . ."—ALS, *ibid.*, Letters Received from the President.

1870, MARCH 28. To Robert B. Potter. "Your letter of the 21st reached me in due time. The very kind invitation would have been accepted at once had I not already been offered and accepted rooms at the Continental Hotel. Mrs. Grant joins me in sending kind regards to yourself and Mrs. Potter for the very polite invitation and the kind sentiments contained in your letter."—Copy, DLC-USG, II, 1. On April 9, USG addressed a meeting of the Society of the Army of the Potomac in Philadelphia. "I am happy to meet so many of my old comrades of the Army of the Potomac. I should be glad if I could fully express my feelings on this occasion. I regret that I cannot do so, and I can only warmly thank you for this kind reception."—Copy, DLC-Society of the Army of the Potomac. On the same day, USG attended the society's banquet at the Continental Hotel. See *New York Times*, April 10, 11, 1870.

1870, MARCH 28. Orville E. Babcock to U.S. Representative Benjamin F. Butler of Mass. "I am directed by the President to inform you that, as President of the National Asylum for disabled Soldiers, you are authorized to forward to him the names of two of the orphan boys under charge of your asylum, for appointment, one to the Military Academy at West Point, the other to the Naval Academy at Annapolis. The candidate for appointment to the Naval Academy may be presented between now and February next, and will be appointed to enter in June 1871—The name of the candidate to the Military Academy may be presented at any time before June 1871. and will be appointed to enter in June 1872,—one year after as the law requires."—LS, DLC-Benjamin F. Butler.

1870, MARCH 28. Secretary of the Interior Jacob D. Cox to USG. "I have the honor, herewith, to lay before you, for such action in the premises as you may deem appropriate, a copy of a letter dated the 25th instant, from the Commissioner of Indian Affairs, and accompanying communication, of the 18th inst., from W. F. M. Arny, Esqr, in relation to the violation, by miners and others, of the treaty of March 2d 1868, with various bands of Utah Indians of Colorado and NewMexico."—Copy, DNA, RG 48, Indian Div., Letters Sent. On Jan. 19, 1871, Horace Porter wrote to George C. Gorham, secretary, Senate. "The nomination of W. F. Arney to be Indian Agent (Pueblo Agency) New Mexico, sent to the Senate yesterday—should read 'W. F. M. Arny'. The President requests that you cause the correction to be made and this letter will be your warrant for so doing."—Copy, DLC-USG, II, 1.

1870, MARCH 28.   M. Blain, Marseilles, to USG requesting assistance in obtaining the death certificate of François Michel Pignatel.—ALS (in French), DNA, RG 59, Miscellaneous Letters.

1870, MARCH 29.   To House of Representatives. "In reply to your resolution of December 20th 1869, asking whether any citizens of the United States are imprisoned or detained in military custody by officers of the Army of the United States, and if any, to furnish their names, date of arrest, the offences charged together with a statement of what measures have been taken for the trial and punishment of the offenders, I transmit herewith the report of the Secretary of War, to whom the resolution was referred."—Copy, DNA, RG 130, Messages to Congress. See *HED*, 41-2-225.

1870, MARCH 31.   To House of Representatives. "In answer to the resolution of the House of Representatives of the 7th instant relating to fisheries in British waters, I transmit a report from the Secretary of State and the papers which accompanied it, and have to state that the commanding officer of the naval steamer ordered to the fishing grounds, will be instructed to give his attention, should circumstances require it, to cases which may arise under any change which may be made in the British laws affecting fisheries within British jurisdiction with a view to preventing, so far as it may be in his power, infractions by citizens of the U. S. of the 1st Article of the treaty between the U. S and Great Britain, of 1818, the laws in force relating to fisheries within British jurisdiction or any illegal interference with the pursuits of the fishermen of the United States."—Copies, DNA, RG 59, General Records; *ibid.*, RG 130, Messages to Congress. See *HED*, 41-2-239.

1870, MARCH 31.   USG endorsement. "This is refered to the Sec. of State with the view of having all the places refered to in the enclosed letter looked into to see if all the incumbents might not be removed and their places given, one to Mr. Lucas and the remainder to other States not now having their share of patronage."—AES, DNA, RG 59, Letters of Application and Recommendation. Written on a letter of March 28 from Josiah M. Lucas, Washington, D. C., to U.S. Representative John A. Logan requesting a consulship at Dundee or Leith, Scotland, or Kingston, Canada.—ALS, *ibid.* Related papers are *ibid.* On May 10, 1871, USG nominated Lucas as consul, St. John's, Canada, but withdrew the nomination on May 18. Also on May 18, USG nominated Lucas for the consulship at Singapore but withdrew the nomination on May 19. On May 29, Lucas wrote to USG. "I owe it to my character and friends to inform you of the exceeding unpleasant and humiliating position in which I find myself placed. In my appointment to the Consulate at St. Johns, Canada, I was well pleased and received I am told, a unanimous confirmation (not excepting the vote of Senator Ed-

munds)   I have said that I had been placed in a very humiliating position
and I confess that I have never had my feelings more deeply humiliated. I
felt happy and no little elated in the contemplation of filling a post so
acceptable to my wife and self. I had been informed by Sec'y Fish two
weeks in advance of the meeting of the Senate that I should have the place.
He told me that I would have time to return to Illinois and make my arrangements. This I had done and secured my bondsmen—having been furnished
with blank forms. I had made some pecuniary sacrifice to avoid delay—my
My wife had made her arrangements to the same end. I was congratulated
by relatives and friends in Ohio, Illinois and Missouri. The *Press,* of which
I had been an editor for congratulated me and thanked you for the consideration you gave to a stedfast and undeviating friend. But, alas, our fondest
hopes were doomed to be blighted. The great commonwealth of Vermont
through One of her Senators was concealed in ambush, the instrument of
my discomfiture. Had he asked for a reconsideration and then put it to
vote, he would have most signally failed—this he knew—hence his questionable strategy. I mean no disrespect to the Senator, but am forced to
admire the fatherly care he takes of the people of his State. But do object to
the means to which he resorted, after leaving the impression upon the minds
of my Senators as well as other friends in the Senate that he would not
interfere with the confirmation   Senators have spoken freely to me on the
subject. As to *Singapore,* it would be nothing less than Suicidal, at my time
of life, and with a delicate wife to go to so unhealthy and inhospitable a
region. I have thought it would have suited a Vermonter quite as well as an
Illinoian. I trust, Sir, you will appreciate my feelings, for realy, I feel
ashamed to return home and undergo the freequent explanations to friends,
as well as to undergo the the sneers and taunts of Democrats. Mr. President
there is a very Simple *panacea* at hand, that would be *just* and doing *no
wrong*   There are three places to which I would call your attention—*Hamilton,* Canada, is filled by a Mr. Blake, who for convenience hails from
Kansas,—he has filled first Ham Fort Erie, then Hamilton for the past seven
or eight years. The *last 'Register'* shows his appointment at Hamilton—
previous ones show his occupancy of Fort Erie, now filled by a Mr
Phillips of Maine—the State where Mr. Blake really belongs. Besides Mr.
Blake before his appointment to Fort Erie was a clerk in one of the Departments here, appointed from Maine. He agrees fully with any Administration!
Dundee, is held first by the son then the father, since April 1861. He is a
Scotchman and his return to this country is doubtful. *Tunstall,* England,
is held by a Mr Runnells, is held of Iowa from *whence* an appointment has
just been made to Singapore! *I make the charge* that Mr. Runnells has for-
feited his position *beyond* a *doubt.* He has not only violated his oath, but
the law of Congress, and the rulings of the Departments to which he is
responsible. I am prepared to prove my assertion. *He has made no report*
to either Department since his incumbency, now over two two years. *I respectfully ask* for *one of these places.*"—ALS, *ibid.* On the same day, USG

endorsed this letter. "If it is practicable to give Mr. Lucas one of the places he asks for I wish it done."—AES, *ibid.* USG appointed Lucas as consul, Tunstall.

1870, MARCH 31.   To Macmillan and Co. "I am in receipt of a beautiful copy of the Life of Lord Fairfax, for which I am indebted to you. The subject is one of great interest: The volume is one that I shall read with much pleasure. Please accept my sincere thanks for your kindness."—Copy, DLC-USG, II, 1.

1870, MARCH 31.   William R. Vaughan, Richmond, to USG. "Civil law defied near Hampton   citizens dispossessed   state requires Government aid action necessary"—Telegram received, DNA, RG 107, Telegrams Collected (Bound).

1870, APRIL 1.   USG endorsement. "Call special attention to the application when apt. come to be made in June next."—AES, DNA, RG 94, Correspondence, USMA. Written on a letter of March 29 from Patsy Jackson, Madison, Ind., to Gen. William T. Sherman. ". . . My son James Jackson (I am the widow of Gen James S Jackson who fell at the battle of Perryville Ky) would like to enter the academy at West Point if he could procure an appointment, . . . I do wish him thoroughly educated,—and have not the means to defray the expense, for almost our entire property was in negros, My husbands widowed mother and Aunt, both childless, live with me   save a few hundred dollars they lost all. Besides the disagreeableness of living under rebel rule, I found it impossible to live in Ky and educate my children, so moved to this place Madison, Indiana, where I found property cheap and public schools good, . . ."—ALS, *ibid.* On April 1, Sherman endorsed this letter. "I knew Gen Jackson well. He was the first Kentuckian that offered his Services to Genl Anderson at Cincinati. Brave enthusiastic, almost rash he fought till killed at Perryville. I heartily approve this application"—AES, *ibid.* James B. Jackson graduated from USMA in 1877.

1870, APRIL 1.   USG endorsement. "If the status of David R. Smith is such that his nomination can be withdrawn I think a message to that effect had better be prepared to send to the Senate to-day. It will be easier to renominate Mr. Smith hereafter, if injustice is done him, than to get him out of office after confirmation."—AES, DNA, RG 46, Papers Pertaining to Nominations. Written on an undated document from Mayor Sayles J. Bowen of Washington, D. C., to USG. "At the regular meeting of the Board of Metropolitan Police held on the 31st ult. after full discussion the following preamble and resolutions were unanimously adopted.—*Whereas,* It has been announced in the papers that David R. Smith has been nominated by the President of the United States, to the Senate for confirmation as a Justice of the Peace for the county of Washington, District of Columbia, and whereas this Board deems said Smith totally unfit both as respects moral character and qualifications for the position, he being addicted to profane, vulgar and indecent language and to the excessive use of intoxicating drink, and having advised violaters of the laws to continue such violations and being now before the Supreme Court of the District of Columbia, for malfeasance in office, besides having been guilty of other acts unbecoming a Magistrate and a conservator of the peace of the community, therefore—*Resolved*, by this Board, that the President be requested to withdraw the nomination of said Smith, from the Senate, and that in the event of his name not being withdrawn, that the Senate be requested to reject his nomination. *Resolved*, That a copy of this resolution signed by the President and Secretary of this Board, be furnished the President of the United States, and the Hon. Hannibal Hamlin, Chairman of the Senate Committee, on the District of Columbia."—DS, *ibid.* Related papers are *ibid.*, RG 60, Records Relating to Appointments.

1870, APRIL 1. Sigismund Kaufmann, New York City, to USG. "Genl Pleasanton and myself representing the soldiers and German republicans most earnestly desire the appointment of Morris Friedsam as assessor of the fifth (5th) district."—Telegram received, DNA, RG 107, Telegrams Collected (Bound). On April 4, James B. Taylor, New York City, telegraphed to USG. "I have seen Mr Willmann since he wrote you. he will accept the Assessorship I have consulted with many German & American republicans All agree his appointment will give universal satisfaction and I have no doubt of it myself."—Telegram received (at 1:35 P.M.), *ibid.* On April 1, USG nominated Andreas Willmann as assessor of Internal Revenue, 5th District, N. Y., but Willmann declined the position. Morris Friedsam received the appointment. On Dec. 12, 1871, USG nominated Willmann as collector of Internal Revenue, 9th District, N. Y.

1870, APRIL 5. USG endorsement. "Refered to the Sec. of War. If practicable let the retirement take place."—AES, DNA, RG 94, Letters Received, R191 1870. Written on a letter of March 21 from Ransom Balcom, N. Y. Supreme Court, Binghamton, to USG. "I take the liberty of recommending that Colonel Isaac S. Catlin be placed on the retired list of Army Officers. Colonel Catlin raised the first Company of Volunteers in this part of the State for the Union Army in 1861. He left a good legal practice and Served the United States during the War. He was brave & gallant. He lost a leg on the battlefield, and deserves to be honored and well paid for his devotion to the flag of his country.—It is so extremely difficult for him to wear a cork-leg that he was compelled to leave the office of Dist. Atty. in the County of Tioga after the close of the War, to which office he had been elected by the people.—He went back into the Army after retiring from the office of Dist. Atty. But I learn the difficulty he experiences in wearing a cork-leg makes it almost impossible for him to continue in the Military Service of the country. I heartily recommend that he be placed on the retired list. In doing this I think I Speak the Sentiments of all his friends & acquaintances who are very numerous in this Section of the country."—ALS, *ibid.* Related papers are *ibid.*

1870, APRIL 6. To House of Representatives. "In answer to your resolution of the 7th ultimo. requesting to be furnished with a copy of orders, correspondence, reports of councils with Indians by Military and Civil officers of the Government in possession of the Interior and War Departments relating to difficulties with the Cheyenne, Comanche, Arapahoe, Apache and Kiowa tribes of Indians, during the year 1867, &c, &c., I herewith transmit the reports received from those departments."—Copy, DNA, RG 130, Messages to Congress. Related papers are *ibid.*, RG 94, Letters Received, 102R 1870; *HED*, 41-2-240.

1870, APRIL 6. To Senate. "In accordance with the provisions of the 1st Section of the Act of Congress, approved 24 January 1865, I nominate Paymaster John H. Stevenson, to be advanced fifteen numbers in his grade for 'extraordinary heroism', during the war of the rebellion, as particularly set forth in the accompanying report from Captain M. B. Woolsey, U. S. Navy, so as to take rank from the 4th May 1866 and next after Paymaster F. H. Hinman."—DS, DNA, RG 46, Nominations. Related papers are *ibid.*, Papers Pertaining to Nominations.

1870, APRIL 13. To James O. P. Burnside. "Your letter of the 9th inst. containing an invitation to attend the lecture of Mr. James E. Murdoch on Thursday Evening the 14th is recd. I regret my inability, on account of a previous Engagement for that Evening, to be present and listen to the 'impressions and recollections of Abraham Lincoln' by so distinguished an Orator."—LS, DLC-USG, 1B. James O. P. Burnside, former capt., Veteran Reserve Corps, nominated as 2nd auditor, Treasury Dept., by President Andrew Johnson, but rejected by the Senate, unsuccessfully sought a consular appointment from USG. James E. Murdoch, born in Philadelphia in 1811, an actor and lecturer, gave patriotic readings at camps and hospitals during the Civil War.

1870, APRIL 14. To Congress. "I transmit to Congress a Report from the Secretary of State, relative to results of the proceedings of the Joint Commission at Lima under the Convention between the United States and Peru of 4th. December 1868, and recommend that an appropriation be made to discharge the obligation of the United States in the case of the claim of Esteban G. Montano, to which the report refers."—DS, DNA, RG 46, Presidential Messages. The enclosure is *ibid.* See *SED*, 41-2-81.

1870, APRIL 14. To John B. Ketchum, New York City. "I have received your letter of the 10th inst., informing me that I have been elected one of the Vice-Presidents of the Military Post Library Association. It affords me much pleasure to accept this compliment, and I have to request you to communicate to the members of the Association my sincere thanks for their kind

consideration, and the sentiments expressed in their communication."—
Annual Report of the U. S. Military Post Library Association, 1870–71
(New York, 1871).

1870, APRIL 14.   To Edwin D. Morgan. "Will you please ask Mr. Russell to accompany you this afternoon, at 5, to take a family dinner with Mrs.
Grant and myself?"—ALS, New York State Library, Albany, N. Y.

1870, APRIL 14.   Governor Rutherford B. Hayes of Ohio to USG. "I am
personally & intimately acquainted with Gen Wm H. Enochs now a member of the House of Representatives of Ohio from Lawren[c]e County. He
served in the Command to which I belonged during the last three years of
the War. He is a lawyer of ability and promise. As an officer he was conspicuous for all soldierly qualities—for courage, fidelity, efficiency capacity
and patriotism. His fidelity to duty, his upright and honorable character and
his general ability fit him to fill satisfactorily any official position he is
likely to seek. I accordingly commend his claims to full investigation."—
ALS (press), OFH. No appointment followed.

1870, APRIL 20.   To House of Representatives. "In answer to your Resolution of the 21st ultimo, requesting to be informed—'whether any portion of the military forces of the United States have been sent into the
counties of Bourbon, Crawford and Cherokee, in the State of Kansas, and
if so; when, what number, for what purpose and on whose procurement;
and also whether they have been required to erect there any winter quarters, forts, fortifications or earthworks, and if so; what, for what purpose
and at whose expense; and at what probable expense to the Government
have all said acts been done'—I transmit herewith a Report, dated 18th
instant, from the Secretary of War, to whom the Resolution was referred."
—Copy, DNA, RG 130, Messages to Congress. See *HED*, 41-2-270. On
May 24, 1869, Governor James M. Harvey of Kan. had written to USG.
"I have made application to Gen. Schofield for a sufficient force of regular
troops to preserve the peace in the several counties of this State comprised
within the so-called Cherokee Neutral Land. The reasons which have urged
me to this step are fully set forth in the application, which, I am informed,
has been forwarded to your Excellency, through the Lieutenant General.
The reasons why regular troops are preferable to militia for this service
were also clearly stated, and it seems to me should be controlling. Since
said application was made I have received such additional information from
the authorities of Crawford county, and other responsible persons, as convinces me of the necessity of employing the services of a military force at
once. I therefore respectfully request that you authorize Maj. Gen. Schofield
to send to such points in the disturbed region as may be proper a sufficient
number of mounted troops, under command of a discreet officer, to preserve
the peace, and to prevent violence towards the railroad or other interests of
that locality."—LS, DNA, RG 107, Letters Received from Bureaus. Re-

lated papers are *ibid.* On Aug. 12, Isaac N. Morris, Washington, D. C., wrote to USG. "I received your kind reply last evening. This morning I called to see Genl: Rawlins who informed me that the Gov: of Kansas had already made requisition for troops, and I believe they were ordered upon the Neutral Lands, in compliance with his request. But they have rendered no service, in consequence of being Infantry; and being stationed at such a distance from parties engaged at work upon the Rail Road that they have not known of the outrages until after they were perpetrated. What is wanted, and what is indespensible to the peace of the district of country, and to the safety of Railroad parties is a Cavalry force. Without it all wook upon the road must remain suspended, and ruin to the Company and the prospects of the road must be the result. As it is now, *mob violence* reigns supreme. Will your Excellency therefore be pleased to direct the Sec: of War on the receipt of this, to order such cavalry to the Neutral Lands, as in his judgement may be required, by the evidence before him. Let me assure you that I am not using idle words, when I say that prompt action should be had. The necesity of notifying the intruders on the Neutral Lands, who were not embraced in the Treaty, that they will be required to surrender the possession to the purchasers, is a separate and distinct question from the one now occupying the attention of the Interior Secretary touching the right of those embraced in the treaty to take the lands at the valuation. But I will not discuss that question now. Knowing that you will appreciate the importance of the suggestions I have made and expecting an immediate reply . . ."— Copy, *ibid.*, Letters Received, M332 1869. On Aug. 17, Morris wrote to Secretary of War John A. Rawlins. "As I shall Sstart for Illinois before your return I leave for you another letter which I received a day or so ago from Mr Joy, with accompanying documents. I think you and the Cabinet will find them of importance, not only as establish what has been heretofore said in regard to the riotous conduct on the Neutral Lands, but as showing the bad conduct of Hon Sidney Clarke, who stated to Genl Parker Commissioner of Indian Affairs, a few days ago, that Mr Joy had withdrawn his proposition to let the settlers have their lands for from $5. to $2. per acre. This statement you will find contradicted in the present letter of that Gentlement to me herewith sent. The argumentative letter which I address to the President is not only intended for his consideration but the Cabinets. I hope you will hand it to his Excellency after carefully reading it; and do me the favor to drop me a line at Quincy what has been concluded on as soon as the next Cabinet meeting is over. . . . P S I have explained to Mr Joy that the Government could not, in respect to its dignity, *threaten* to issue an order—that it could only issue it or refrain from doing it—and that after it was issued would be the time to compromise. The order would stimulate and not retard a settlement of all troubles"—ALS, *ibid.* On the same day, Morris had written to USG. "Your note to me stating that, 'until reports are received from parties now in the West, as to metes and bounds taken up by actual settlers before sale to Joy, I do not see how Government is to interfere—except on requisition of Governor of Kansas,' merits a further response than the brief one I addressed you on the 12th Inst. . . ."—Copy, *ibid.* Related papers are *ibid.* On Sept. 1, Horace Porter wrote to Morris. "I saw the President with reference to the removal by Government of intruders from Neutral lands, spoken of by you in yours of this inst. and am directed by him to inform you that he has postsponed the consideration of the subject in accordance as requested by you."—Copy, DLC-USG, II, 1, 4. On Oct. 8, Gen. William T. Sherman wrote to Maj. Gen. John M. Schofield, St. Louis. "I telegraphed you yesterday about the condition of affairs in the neutral lands below Fort Scott in Kansas. I was of the impression that the trouble between the Railroad and the squatters had long since ceased, but Mr Morris of Illinois is here from Mr Joy and represents the settlers as still engaged in burning ties, obstructing the building of the railroad &c   The President gave an order to General Rawlins just before his death to have a company of Cavalry sent there to protect the road, but General Rawlins never gave me the order   I dont now know what troops if any you have there, but the President says we are bound to maintain Mr. Joy in the possession and enjoyment of the lands he bought of the Indians, under a treaty approved by the Senate. If therefore you have not already sent any Cavalry there, you will please send a company with orders to protect the property of Mr Joy and the Railroad against violence from the resident citizens. . . ."—Copy, DNA, RG 94, Letters Sent. On Oct. 24, 1870, R. P. Hadley, Girard, Kan., wrote to USG. "One year and a half ago, I with others was induced to leave Clermont Co Ohio, to Seek homes on government Lands in the West and I landed in Crawford Co Kan and find there is a dispute about the land. Some Say it belongs to Joy, others Say not. Now Sir please inform me concerning this land.   will we have to purchase of James F Joy, or the Government.   this Land is in the South East of the State and is called the Cherochee Neutral Lands. others Say it is New York Indian land, and there is a Number of Setlers here that does not know what to do.   as I have been with you on Several ocasions from East to South I hope to hear Som advice from you Soon, if you will Humble your Self So much as to oblige . . ."—ALS, *ibid.,* RG 75, Letters Received, Cherokee Agency. See *PUSG,* 18, 594–95; Craig Miner, "Border Frontier: The Missouri River, Fort Scott & Gulf Railroad in the Cherokee Neutral Lands, 1868–1870," *Kansas Historical Quarterly,* XXXV, 2 (Summer, 1969), 105–29.

1870, APRIL 20. Harry H. McConnell, Fort Richardson, Tex., to USG. ". . . I was reduced to the ranks, and my discharge withheld by Brevet Brig Genl. James Oakes, Colonel 6th Cavalry, on the representation to the the C. O. 5th Mil. District that I would be found responsible for certain deficiencies existing in the Subsistence department of this post. The board ordered to investigate this deficiency, found me *innocent,* but I was tried on *other charges, substantiated only* by the word of an officer *self convicted* of appropriating public monies and stores to his own use, and sentenced to one years confinement at the post where my company should be serving. . . ."

—ALS, DNA, RG 107, Letters Received, S222 1870. The enclosure is *ibid*. On May 10, Charles H. T. Collis, Philadelphia, wrote to USG. "I have been asked to write you in reference to the case of ~~Qr Mast~~. Comsy. Sergt. McConnell, now under sentence for embezzlement of Govt. funds &c— While I do not desire to encourage the use of extraneous influence upon such subjects, I desire to say that from information imparted to me by his friends I believe it to be a case which should commend itself to your most merciful consideration—"—ALS, *ibid*. Related papers are *ibid*. See *PUSG*, 18, 448.

1870, April 20.   "Mennil," Paris, to USG concerning a pension possibly due him because of the death of his brother, Louis B. Mennil, Sept. 4, 1864, while serving in the Garibaldi Guards.—ALS (in French), DNA, RG 59, Miscellaneous Letters. On May 6, Orville E. Babcock endorsed this letter to the State Dept. requesting a translation, which is *ibid*.

1870, April 20.   Stephen Miller, former governor of Minn., Hamilton, Nev., to USG. "I hoped never to ask for Office:—but I came here at the solicitation of my brother, engaged in mining, and am financially ruined— Having by this removal lost my identity with my old state I cannot apply through my old Representatives who I know feel friendly toward me. If you can without inconvenience favor me with a paying appointment *any- where*, suited to my capacity, I will be very faithful to my trust, and grate- ful to yourself—With kind regards to Mrs Grant and your children, . . ." —ALS, OFH. On Sept. 3, 1873, U.S. Senator Alexander Ramsey of Minn., St. Paul, wrote to USG recommending that Miller be appointed minister to Sweden.—ALS, DNA, RG 59, Letters of Application and Recommenda- tion. Related papers are *ibid*. No appointment followed.

1870, April 23.   Secretary of State Hamilton Fish to USG. "I enclose a copy of a telegram received yesterday evening from General Sickles an- nouncing that orders have been sent from Madrid to Havana for the release of the Aspinwall."—LS, OFH. The cable of April 8 from Daniel E. Sickles, U.S. minister, Madrid, to Fish is in DNA, RG 59, Diplomatic Despatches, Spain. A related letter is *ibid*. On Jan. 21, Spanish officials seized the U.S. steamship *Colonel Lloyd Aspinwall*, suspected of carrying weapons to Cuban rebels. On April 22, Fish recorded in his diary. "Read recent telegraphic cor- respondence with Sickles & suggested that more decided measures seemed to be imminently necessary—Spain is trifling with u[s] promises fairly, but performs nothing—President suggests writing or telegraphing to Sickles that unless the Aspinwall is released, we will detain the Spanish War Steamer now in NY—I think we should not threaten this but if it be de- termined as the best course, to seize her first, & give notice that she will be released on release of the Aspinwall, & satisfactory explanation   Hoar sug- gests immediate arrest, & Robeson seems to concur—says he can do it—I inquire, has he the force to do so—Hoar replies, 'we have all NY'—I answer 'yes" but will all NewYork prevent her discharging her guns—& what is to answer them'—'that would be War'—Robeson then says she is on a private dock—but subsequently says she *was*—is not sure in what condition she even is—I call attention to the condition of the Spanish Ministry their weakness at home, & probable willingness for a War, in which, to lose Cuba, would involve no National dishonor—I think that possibly they may give the orders for the release of the Aspinwall—if not, we may direct Sickles to ask his passports & return—this wd not necessarily be War— & might not lead to it, though possibly, & perhaps probably it would— Belknap says he would like the detention of the Frigate in NewYork— President directs Telegram to Sickles, not to withdraw his note—Robeson is to report the present Condition of the Frigate—& matters to remain until Tuesday—"—DLC-Hamilton Fish. See *SED*, 41-2-108, pp. 114–43.

1870, APRIL 26. To House of Representatives. "In answer to the Resolution of the House of Representatives of the 9th instant, I transmit a report from the Secretary of State and the papers which accompanied it."—Copies, DNA, RG 59, General Records; *ibid.*, RG 130, Messages to Congress. The enclosure is *ibid.*, RG 59, General Records. The report of Samuel B. Ruggles, delegate to the International Monetary Conference, is in *HED*, 41-2-266. On Jan. 9, 1872, USG wrote to the Senate. "In answer to the Resolution of the Senate of the 19th of December, last, calling for certain correspondence relating to the subject of International Coinage, not heretofore furnished, I transmit herewith, a report from the Secretary of State with the papers which accompanied it."—DS, DNA, RG 46, Presidential Messages. Related papers are *ibid.* See *SED*, 42-2-16.

1870, APRIL 28. USG endorsement. "Accepted."—AES, DNA, RG 60, Records Relating to Appointments. Written on a letter of April 25 from Richard S. Field, Princeton, N. J., to USG. "Being unable by reason of illness to give any attention to my official duties, and seeing no prospect of an early restoration, I beg leave to resign my office as United States District Judge for the District of NewJersey"—ALS, *ibid.* Letters to USG recommending former U.S. Representative John T. Nixon of N. J. as Field's successor are *ibid.* On April 28, USG nominated Nixon.

1870, [APRIL]. USG endorsement. "This applicant was a former resident years of age, and apts. made now being for June /71."—AE, DNA, RG 94, Correspondence, USMA. Written on a letter of April 28 from David S. Corser, Webster, N. H., to USG asking admission to USMA.—ALS, *ibid.* Related papers are *ibid.*

1870, [APRIL]. USG endorsement. "This applicant was a former resident of Santa Cruz. His mother lives there now. He was a soldier under me during the rebellion. If there are not strong reasons for retaining present incumbent I think the apt. had better [be] made."—AES, DNA, RG 59,

Letters of Application and Recommendation. Written on a letter of April 21 from James I. McDonald, Heathsville, Va., to USG. "I have the honor to request the appointment of Consul to Santa Cruz, in the Danish West Indies I deem it proper, to state that I have been a resident of the Island, and now have relatives residing there"—ALS, *ibid.* On July 13, USG nominated John H. Hutchinson as consul, Santa Cruz, Danish West Indies; Hutchinson declined the post.

1870, APRIL. Gideon J. Pillow, Memphis, to USG. "I am sure you will appreciate the motives, which prompt this communication. My personal knowledge of your character, and the generous impulses of your Heart—as shown in the Terms of surrender granted to Genl Lee, and your Report of the Temper and feeling of the southern People, after your tour through the south, all combine to satisfy my mind of your disposition to do *justice* to the southern people. I am encouraged by the knowledge, to address you,— (though I do not do so without hesitation)—on public matters. I have no motive Mr President to mislead you—I am *indentified* with the well being of the Country, & cannot but feel a deep and lively interest, in its prosperity and greatness. I refer to my own *quiet*, & submission to the authority of the Government, since the termination of the war, as proof of the sincerity of what I shall say in this letter. I beg to say to you Mr President upon the Honour of a Soldier and a Christian Gentleman, that if the Government will manifest a *little Respect* for the southern People—by treating them with confidence—as you are said to have contemplated doing—by an act of general amnesty, that you would do more towards re-uniting the Country, and giving it, all the blessings of real peace, than it is possible, for Congress ever to affect by its reconstruction acts. You have a better knowledge of the southern People, than have the Public men of the North—As a Soldier they respect and Admire you. The firmness with which you resisted Mr Johnsons wish to have the Govt prosecute Genl Lee and others—in violation of the Honour of your Terms to his Army, wore greatly on the Heart of the southern People. . . . That there bad men in the south is not denied—that there are acts of violence, is not denied; But these bad men are not of the *Leaders* nor generally of the *rank* & *file* of the late Confederate Army. With rare exceptions—all that class are *orderly* and *submissive* to the Laws— But even these bad men, & these acts of violence, are *magnified* an *Hundred fould*, in the public Prints for political effect. . . ."—ALS, OClWHi.

1870, APRIL. Miss. Representative Hugh M. Street *et al.* to USG. "We, the undersigned citizens of Kemper county and State of Mississippi, your memorialists, humbly and most respectfully beg leave to represent unto your Excellency;—that in the month of June 1869 Wm P. Brack a citizen of said county and State was arrested by the military, charged with the murder of one Proudy Peden (Cold) and conducted to Lauderdale Station— a military post in said State, where he was subsequently tried by a military Commission, convicted and sentenced to hard labor in prison at Ship Island in said State, for what period is to your memorialists unknown. Your memorialists reposing implicit confidence and trust in your Excellency's great sense of justice and humanity, and being fully impressed that your Excellency would not wittingly permit the innocent to suffer for the deeds of the guilty:—and inasmuch as the questionable character of the testimony submitted at the trial of the prisoner was such as to create great doubt as to his guilt, indeed, such as to force on the mind of the unprejudiced, almost positively the conclusion of his innocence, most respectfully beg leave to submit to your Excellency's consideration a concise, but substantial outline of said testimony—to wit—On the night of the 16th of May 1869 the said Proudy Peden was murdered by a party of men masked.—Berry Peden (Cold) son of the deceased testified that he identified the prisoner as one of said party. Two colored women who, with the said Berry Peden had cherished feelings of animosity towards the said prisoner, testified to the same effect. On the other hand Horace Cole Tisdale (Cold) Louis Tisdale (Cold) and the wife of the latter, who were at the residence of the prisoner during the night in question, testified that the prisoner was at his home during the entire night,—this was substantially corroborated by the testimony of the prisoner's wife, thereby conclusively establishing his innocence by an alibi, by three unbiased and disinterested witnesses, corroborated by his wife whose unexceptionable good character affords no reason to doubt the veracity of her testimony,—and this opposed by the questionable proof of identification of the prisoner—masked as represented, and amid the darkness of the night, by witnesses whose testimony was suggested in hate, a desire of revenge and a thirst for the blood of their victim; yet, the prisoner was convicted. . . ."—DS (197 signatures), Smith College, Northampton, Mass. Governor James L. Alcorn of Miss. favorably endorsed this petition.—AES, *ibid.* An undated petition from Nancy Jane Brack *et al.* to USG is in DNA, RG 94, Letters Received, 814B 1870. On Dec. 9, U.S. Senator Adelbert Ames of Miss. endorsed this petition. "Respectfully referred to the President of the U. S. I hope a pardon *will not* be granted. Mr Brack was tried and found guilty of murder by a military tribunal. The proceedings are in the War Dept and can be found if necessary."—AES, *ibid.* Related papers are *ibid.*

1870, MAY 2. Secretary of State Hamilton Fish to USG. "General Acosta, the Minister from Colombia, having applied for the appointment of a time to take leave of you, I have taken the liberty to name a quarter before twelve on tomorrow, the 3d instant for that purpose if this should be agreeable to you. ~~This will enable~~ The General would then be enabled to fulfil his wish to take the train for NewYork at a quarter before one so that he may emba[rk] on the steamer of th[e] 5th for Aspinwall."—ADf (initialed), DLC-Hamilton Fish.

1870, MAY 3. Secretary of the Interior Jacob D. Cox to USG. "I have the honor to submit herewith, for your consideration and, if approved, your

signature, a proclamation of the public sale of certain lands in the Territories of New Mexico and Colorado, in August next."—LS, OFH. On May
13, USG issued the proclamation. See *HED*, 41-3-1, part 4, p. 109.

1870, MAY 4. Secretary of War William W. Belknap to USG. "I have
the honor to return to you the letter recently addressed to the U. S. Minister
at Brussels by Maj. Genl. Bormann, Aide-de Camp to His Majesty the King
of the Belgians, soliciting a testimonial from the U. S. in recognition of the
great value to their military service of his metallic time-fuze for explosive
projectiles, and to report, with reference thereto, that the Bormann Fuze has
been used in the army of the U. S., with various modifications, since the
year 1851, and has been generally regarded as a most excellent device.
During the late war large numbers of this fuze were used, with very satisfactory results. In view of these facts, it is recommended that the thanks
of Congress be tendered to General Bormann for the benefits the U. S. have
derived from his invention, generously placed by him at the service of all
who needed the same. It is also advised, as a preliminary measure, that
the subject be referred to the Navy Dept. for report."—Copy, DNA, RG
107, Letters Sent to the President.

1870, MAY 5. USG endorsement. "I think it will be well to confer this
appointment."—AES, DNA, RG 60, Applications and Recommendations.
Written on a letter of March 2 from Thomas Settle, Raleigh, N. C., to
USG. "I learn that a bill is before Congress which provides that The
President shall appoint _____ commissioners, to revise the laws of the
United States. Should the bill become a law, I beg leave to suggest for your
consideration the name of Victor C. Barringer, Esq, of this State, as a suitable person to be appointed on said commission. Mr Barringer is a sound
lawyer, and has had much experience in revising and codifying laws. He is
at present, one of the Code commissioners of this State. He was one of the
first men of prominence in the State, to go before the people and advocate
the liberality, wisdom, justice and mercy of the reconstruction measures.
He is a zealous friend of your administration, and has contributed much
to the success of the Union cause in this State."—ALS, *ibid.* On May 4,
U.S. Representative Norman B. Judd of Ill. wrote to USG. "The Delegation in Congress from North Carolina propose to recommend Victor Barringer Esq. of that state as one of the commissioners to revise the Statutes
I earnestly concur in that recommendation. Mr Barringer's legal knowledge
literary qualifications and experience eminently qualify him for the position.
It is an opportunity to extend a little patronage in a Southern direction that
ought to be seized"—ALS, *ibid.* On June 23, USG wrote to the Senate.
"I desire that the names submitted to the Senate June 4th 1870 for Commissioners under the 'Act to provide for the revision and consolidation of
the statutes of the United States etc' should stand in the following order:
1st, *Charles P. James*, of Dist. Columbia; 2d, *Benjm Vaughan Abbott*, of

N. Y. 3d, *Victor C. Barringer*, of N. C."—DS, *ibid.*, RG 46, Papers Pertaining to Certain Nominations.

1870, MAY 5.   U.S. Representative William B. Allison of Iowa to USG. "I learn a vacancy is about to arise in the office of Secy of Legation at Constantinople & that Porter. C. Bliss Esq would accept the place. I take pleasure in giving testimony of his eminent capacity for that place & I hope you may find it convenient to give him the appt at an early day."—ALS, DNA, RG 59, Letters of Application and Recommendation. U.S. Representative James J. Winans of Ohio *et al.* favorably endorsed this letter.—AE (23 signatures), *ibid.* A related letter is *ibid.* On July 8, following the resignation of James St. Clair Boal, USG nominated Porter C. Bliss as secretary of legation, Mexico City. On Jan. 26, 1875, Thomas H. Nelson, former U.S. minister, Washington, D. C., wrote to USG. "Mr. James St Clair Boal accompanied me to Mexico as Secretary of Legation in 1869 and faithfully discharged the duties of that position, so long as he chose to retain it. Mr. Boal is a gentleman of superior talents, and attainments and irreproachable integrity. He is a thorough master of the French and Spanish languages, while his abilities, address and prudence, eminently fit him for a diplomatic or consular career. I am sure that he will acquit himself in whatever position that may be assigned to him with credit to himself and honor to his Country."—ALS, *ibid.* Related papers are *ibid.* No appointment followed.

1870, MAY 7.   Secretary of the Navy George M. Robeson to USG. "I have the honor to inform you that the necessary instructions have been issued for the attendance of the Marine Band at the grounds of the Executive Mansion, this evening, and every Saturday evening, until further orders."—Copy, DNA, RG 45, Letters Sent to the President.

1870, MAY 9.   Secretary of the Interior Jacob D. Cox to USG. "I have the honor to submit, herewith, a copy of a report from the Commissioner of Indian affairs, dated the 6th inst., and accompanying papers, in relation to the two children rescued from the Kiowa Indians in 1868, for whose benefit a Joint Resolution was passed by Congress, and is now awaiting the signature of the President. I concur with the Commissioner in the views expressed in relation to the subject, and recommend that said Resolution do not receive the Executive approval."—LS, NNP. On May 17, the joint resolution for the relief of former captives Helen and Heloise Lincoln became law without USG's signature.—*CG,* 41-2, 3540.

1870, MAY 9.   Alfred P. Hall, Front Royal, Va., to USG. "alow me to adress you those few Lines Hopeing to comunicate Some matters of importance   on the 20 ~~day~~ Night of August last too Black men wer taken fron this place who wer in Jail awaiting trial wer taken out and Hung Dead

By the neck   Efforts wer made to ferret out the party but without success   I
Have finel blank proof of the mater this far that I am personly acquainted
with the leader of the party and He may be arrested now at any tim provided a force of too or three good tried men can be Had   I will also Say
that He is a notorrous caracter and any man Who Ever belonged to the
Northern army canot reside in Peace Near Him and I Being one He Has con-
trived to Have me arested or rather was the leader of the party Who arested
me   knoweing that I Had His Secret I Supposed He considered it unsafe
for me to run at large   1 am in Jail in front royal uppon Suspition of
Haveing Stolen a Horse Yet I can bring Evidence Sufficient to prove to
the contrary but I consider it very unsafe for me to remain Has as it is
known I Have the Secret and am liable to meet the Same fate at any time   I
Have Beene in Here too Days   if you wish I will if you will Send three or
four good men arrest this Cut throat and Bring Him with us also I will
remain under arest untill trial with pleasure   Hopeing to Hear from you
Soon . . . General your Honor I Should prefer this kept Secret if you please
Untill I get away or if it please your Honor to Send for me I can Be Found
at Front Royal Jail in the County of warren State Va"—ALS, DNA, RG 60,
Letters from the President. Attorney Gen. Ebenezer R. Hoar endorsed this
letter. "Not requiring action by the President—the matter being wholly of
State jurisdiction—I cannot advise sending to Front Royal jail for Mr. Hall
before his trial for horse stealing—"—AES, *ibid.*

1870, MAY 9.   William G. LeDuc, Washington, D. C., to USG. *"Private
and Confidential* . . . I desire to call your attention to a portion of an article
in the 1st & 2nd pages of Packards Monthly herewith submitted in reference
to the Rebel Archives therein mentioned. A Gentleman of intelligence a
Rebel once rich now poor, who claims to have and I am satisfied has knowledge of the place of concealment of these 'Presidential Archives' and also is
well acquainted with the custodians of these Documts and has personally
seen them, wishes to sell certain of these papers & Books to the United
States. Thinking I might be of some service to the Government in this
and possibly that the whole of these Rebel Archives might be obtained
I have consented to lay the matter before you for your consideration. Should
you desire any further information or action I await your inquiries or orders"
—ALS, DNA, RG 59, Miscellaneous Letters. See Dallas Irvine, "The Fate
of Confederate Archives," *American Historical Review,* XLIV, 4 (July,
1939), 823–41.

1870, MAY 10.   USG endorsement. "Accepted."—AES, DNA, RG 94,
Letters from the President. Written on a letter of the same day from George
P. Fisher, Washington, D. C., to USG. "Having been nominated by Your
Excellency and confirmed by the Senate, as U. S. Attorney, for the District
of Columbia, to take effect on the 14th instant, I hereby tender my resignation, as a Justice of the Supreme Court of the District of Columbia, to take
effect, upon the appointment and qualification of my successor. Permit me,

Mr President, to suggest, that the business of the court is such as to advise the early appointment of my successor."—ALS, *ibid.*

On April 22, USG nominated David C. Humphreys to replace Fisher as associate justice, Supreme Court of D. C. On March 25, 1869, U.S. Senator Willard Warner of Ala. *et al.* had written to USG. "We have the honor to most Earnestly recommend to you Judge D. C. Humphreys of Alabama for the Mission to Spain, or for South American Mission. Judge Humphreys is an old resident of the South, has always been a Union Man, is an able and distinguished lawyer, a man of the purest character and an Earnest Republican. His appointment would gratify all parties and would be a wise and just recognition of Southern Union Men."—LS, *ibid.*, RG 59, Letters of Application and Recommendation. Additional papers are *ibid.* On March 25, 1870, U.S. Senator George E. Spencer of Ala. *et al.* wrote to USG. "We respectfully recommend the Honorable David C. Humphreys of Alabama to be appointed Consul to Honolulu Sandwich Islands. Mr Humphreys is a man of fine ability, a native unionist and a thorough & tried republican."—DS (11 signatures), DLC-Benjamin F. Butler. On Jan. 13, 1873, USG nominated Humphreys as judge, District of Ala.

1870, MAY 10.   To W. B. Spooner, Francis F. Emery, and A. L. Coolidge, Boston. "I am in receipt of your letter of the 7th inst. inviting me to attend a meeting of the New England Shoe & Leather Association. on the 14th inst. I regret that my public duties will not permit me to be absent from the Capital at that time and that I shall therefore not be able to be present. Wishing you every success in the promotion of the object for which your Association has been organized . . ."—Copy, DLC-USG, II, 1.

1870, MAY 10.   Henry A. Heath *et al.*, Whitefield, Maine, to USG. "We the Undersigned, Sympathisers with and supporters of the present Administration; being acquainted with Willard W. Edgcomb of The Town of Whitefield Lincoln County, State of Maine; know him to be a man of Integrity, Sobriety and Abillity, and a republican of good standing. We therefore recomend, and pray that you appoint him, Consul, at Cape-Town, in the British Colony of the Cape of Good Hope South Africa—the present incumbent being an appointee of Ex President Johnson. Mr Edg-comb is a Ship-master and well acquainted with the above named place, having several times been to that Port."—DS (23 signatures), DNA, RG 59, Letters of Application and Recommendation. Related papers are *ibid.* On April 17, 1871, USG nominated Willard W. Edgecomb as consul, Capetown. On April 1, 1873, Heath *et al.* petitioned USG to appoint Edge-comb as consul gen., Shanghai.—DS, *ibid.* No appointment followed.

1870, MAY 11.   USG endorsement. "Let special attention be directed to this application when apts. come to be made."—AES, DNA, RG 94, Correspondence, USMA. Written on a letter of May 7 from David Hunter, Washington, D. C., to USG. "I have the honor most respectfully to apply for the appointment of Cadet at the U. S. Military Academy at West Point, for my adopted son, Hugh Lenox Scott, born in Danville, Kentucky, on the 22d Sep. 1853—son of the Revd Dr Wm M. Scott, and a direct descendant of Dr Ben. Franklin of Revolutionary memory."—ALS, *ibid.* Hugh L. Scott graduated from USMA in 1876.

1870, MAY 14.   Harriet N. Melcher, Boston, to USG. "Allow me to perform the sad but grateful duty of thanking you for the very beautiful gift, with which you acknowledged the services of my late dear husband, (Capt Melcher) in the cause of humanity. Capt Melcher received the watch and was deeply sensible of your thoughtful kindness, and he hoped to express his gratitude in person, . . . I shall keep the watch as a cherished memento of the past and a precious legacy for his child, whom I hope it will teach to emulate his father's virtues and prove an incentive to employ his moments in deeds of charity and love. With sentiments of respect and esteem . . ."— ALS, DNA, RG 59, Miscellaneous Letters.

1870, MAY 15.   William Thomas Hubbard, Springtown, N. J., to USG. "I request of you to do me a favour if you pleas Sir, that is to see if you can find my Mother which was sold out of the state of Maryland about 14 years ago   She belong to a man by the name of Charles Smith and she was the wife of Perrie Hubbard and the last I heard of her she was at Macon Georgia and Her name was Tobitha Hubbard"—ALS, DNA, RG 105, Hd. Qrs., Letters Received.

1870, MAY 19.   Secretary of the Navy George M. Robeson to USG. "I have the honor to submit, herewith, for your signature, commissions for Master J. E. Morse and Chaplain G. A. Crawford prepared agreeably to the confirmation by the Senate on the 10th inst."—Copy, DNA, RG 45, Letters Sent to the President. On April 28 and May 2, USG had nominated George A. Crawford as chaplain and Jerome E. Morse as master, U.S. Navy. On Jan. 8, 1872, USG nominated Morse as lt. On July 13, 1874, Robeson wrote to USG. "I have the honor to submit for your orders the records of the proceedings of a Naval Retiring Board in the case of Lieutenant Jerome E. Morse and Assistant Paymaster E. E. Lewis: and respectfully recommend that you concur in the opinions of the Board in these cases."—Copy, *ibid.*

1870, MAY 19.   Edwards Pierrepont, U.S. attorney, New York City, to USG. "In this election the Democrats will *count* some 55 thousand majority —In this city they *count* at least, 28 thousand more than they poll—Congress *can* pass a law under which we can be protected—the XV amendment gives the *power*; whether Congress has the *courage* I know not; but cowardice never wins—This state voted for Gen. Grant by at least 20 thousand—it was *counted* for Seymour. If this is to be continued the sober citizens will cease to vote—that is certain—There is no trouble about the power of Congress—We had plenty of Republicans during the first years of the war, who doubted the power of Congress to save the nation, and but for the pressure & fanaticisms of certain passionate maen, (which was wisely used by able patriots,) the nation would have perished—Next fall we elect new members of Congress—This *State* is for your administration—If Congress will pass a wise law under the XV amendment & if you will, with stern will, direct that faction cease—that new and complete organization be made—that the national power be used for national success—that the President be the head, & that able men of courage act as his lieutenants & all under military diciplin, we can save this state, and not otherwise"—ALS, OFH.

1870, MAY 21. To Senate. "I transmit to the Senate in answer to their resolution of the 18th instant, calling for information relative to the passage of any English or Canadian Steamer through the canal of Sault St Marie, a report from the Secretary of State with accompanying papers."— DS, DNA, RG 46, Presidential Messages. The enclosure is *ibid.* See *SED,* 41-2-88. On May 3, Governor Henry P. Baldwin of Mich., Detroit, had telegraphed to USG. "Information apparently reliable is furnished me that the Canadian Government are intending to send troops within a day or two from Collingwood to Red River via Sault St Marie Canal. is it your wish that I direct the Superintendan[t] of Canal not to allow its use for that purpose without positiv[e] instructions from Washington"—Telegram received (at 11:55 A.M.), DNA, RG 59, Miscellaneous Letters; copy, *ibid.,* RG 46, Presidential Messages. On May 13 and 20, Baldwin wrote to USG. "I have the honor to acknowledge the receipt of the communication of the Honorable Secretary of State, of May 3d in reply to my telegram to your Excellency, of same date; in which the Secretary—states your desire, that no military expedition of any foreign power, whether of troops or of boats intended for the purpose of taking part in any military or warlike expedition, or of warlike material, be allowed to pass through the Saut Ste Marie Canal, without express instructions from the Goverment at Washington. Immediatly on receipt of the letter of the Secretary of State, instructions were mailed to the Superintendent of the Ste Mari[e] Canal, a copy of which is herewith enclosed requesting that no vessel known to be laden with troops—or war material of a foreign power intended for the purpose of taking part in any military or warlike expedition, should be allowed to pass through the Canal without express permission from the Goverment at Washington, or from myself in behalf of th[e] Federal Goverment; These instructions wer[e] received by the Superintendent on the Nin[th] of May, at which time the Algoma—a Canadian Steamer, believed to have on boar[d] war material for the Red River expedition, had already passed through the Canal. On the tenth of May, the Canadian Steamer Chicora, approached the Canal—laden with Provisions and supplies—believed to be for troops that are to follow on a warlike expedition to the Red River; this belief was strengthened by the fact, that before approaching the Canal, the Steamer had landed on the Canada side of the river, a large number of boats with men to handle them. The Superintendent acting under the instructions contained in my letter of May 5. refused to allow the passage of the Steamer through the Canal. A copy of the Superintendents letter detailing the circumstances of the case is herewith transmitted. I also enclose copy of my letter of this date to the Superintendent. I shall hope to receive from your Excellen[cy] further advices on this subject." "I had the honor to receive on the 17th inst—a telegram from the Acting Secretary of State, bearing date Washington May 16—informing me that the British Minister at Washington, had notified the Department of State, that the diff[i]culties in the Red River country, had been amicably arranged &c.—that your Excellency desired him to say, that under these circumstances, the Federal Government—does not desire to oppose the passage of the Chicora and other vessels of that class through the Canal, so long as they do not carry troops or munitions of war. In conformity with the views expres[sed] in the telegram herein noticed, I maile[d] by first steamer, (on the 18th) to the Superintend[ent] of the Saut Ste Marie Canal, instructions to permit the passage of the *Chicora* an[d] other Canadian Steamers, so long as they do not carry troops or munitions of war."—LS, *ibid.*, RG 59, Miscellaneous Letters. On April 18, George Francis Train, "Your successor as Chief Magistrate of America," had written to USG. "A Canadian Army is invading Red River Country through American Territory (Canal Sault St. Marie). In name of Ten Million Fenians I protest against this National outrage, while American Citizens are being tortured in British Bastiles and Alabama Claims unpaid. Our Flag is already sufficiently dishonored by the inactivity of your Administration, without submitting to this disgrace."—Paul C. Richards, Catalogue 11 [1964], no. 376.

1870, MAY 23 or 25. To House of Representatives. "I transmit to the House of Representatives in answer to their resolution of the 5th instant a report from the Secretary of State and its accompanying papers."—Copies (dated May 25), DNA, RG 59, General Records; (dated May 23) *ibid.*, RG 130, Messages to Congress. Secretary of State Hamilton Fish had written to USG concerning a claim by John R. Brady against the government of Venezuela.—Copy (dated May 25), *ibid.*, RG 59, General Records. Both printed as dated May 23 in *HED*, 41-2-279.

1870, MAY 24. Chief Justice Salmon P. Chase to USG. "You are doubtless aware that the house formerly occupied by Jefferson Davis at Richmond, has been occupied since the overthrow of the rebel Government as Head Quarters by the General Commanding in that District. I understand that the property belongs to the City of Richmond; an intention to give it to Mr. Davis, or in some way appropriate it as an Executive Residence for the President of the Confederate States, having never been carried into effect. The property has never been confiscated, and the title, therefore, remains, as I suppose, unaffected by the rebellion. The great calamity which has recently fallen upon Richmond makes it necessary to provide a place for the sittings of the Court of Appeals & Chancery Courts, formerly held in the Capitol; and this House offers the best location. Nothing, I suppose, is necessary, in order to its restoration to the City, except a simple military order; but of this the War Department is doubtless best informed. I have been requested to ask your favorable consideration of this matter; and as Virginia is within my judicial Circuit, and as a very recent visit to Richmond, immediately after the recent terrible disaster, has given me a very vivid sense of the necessity in which the wish for the restoration of the property, originates, I do so without delay. Your own feelings, I am sure, would prompt you if it were possible, to anticipate the wishes of the Citizens."—ALS, DNA, RG 60, Letters from the President. On April 27, the collapse of the second floor of the Va. capitol, where the court of appeals met, killed 62 people.—*New York Times*, April 30, 1870.

1870, MAY 25.   Edwin D. Morgan, New York City, to USG. "It is now pretty certain that Judge Folger has been chosen one of the two minority Judges of the Court of Appeals. I presumed that many applications have already been made, for Judge Folgers Vacancy in Sub. Treasury. It seemed to me, a year ago, that the Administration would do a wise thing, if it turned away from all these men and parties Connected with money cliques *in this city*, and Selected for that very Confidential and responsible office of Asst Treasurer, some capable and high toned Republican from the country, who would be free from all promises or entanglements of any kind. Such a man, was well chosen in Folger. Now my advice is to do the Same thing again, and fill, the vacancy with another man from the Interior of the State,   Fortunately there is just Such a man in Genl Thomas Hillhouse and I most earnestly advise his appointment. He is a man of Superior qualifications well known, and Universally esteemed."—ALS, DNA, RG 56, Asst. Treasurers and Mint Officials, Letters Received. On July 1, USG nominated Thomas Hillhouse as asst. treasurer, New York City, to replace Charles J. Folger. On March 2, 1874, Secretary of the Treasury William A. Richardson wrote to USG. "I have the honor to return herewith H. R. No. 253— 'An Act for the relief of Thomas Hillhouse, assistant treasurer of the United States in New York city' and to inform you that I know of no objection to its receiving your approval."—Copy, *ibid.*, Letters Sent to the President. USG approved the bill.—*CR*, 43–1, 1995. On June 26, Hillhouse wrote to USG. "As you are aware, the commission as asst treasurer, which I had the honor of receiving from you, will expire on the eleventh day of July next ensuing. However gratifying a reappointment might be to me personally, as an evidence of your approval of my official conduct in the past, I am sensible it affords no reason why I should be continued in office, and I await your decision in the matter, confident it will be such as will best promote the public interests, and prepared, either to resign my trust into other hands, or to discharge its duties for such further term as you may designate"—ALS, DNA, RG 56, Asst. Treasurers and Mint Officials, Letters Received.

1870, MAY 28. To Senate. "In answer to the resolution of the Senate of the 24th. instant, I transmit a report from the Secretary of State, and the document by which it was accompanied."—DS, DNA, RG 46, Presidential Messages. On the same day, Secretary of State Hamilton Fish had written to USG enclosing a report of Dec. 18, 1869, from Henry T. Blow, U.S. minister, Brazil, concerning commercial interests with South America.—LS, *ibid.* See *SED*, 41-2-92.

1870, MAY 28. N. Chalmers, Levuka, Fiji, to USG. "I have perhaps taken an unwarrantable liberty in addressing my letter to you, but the urgency of the case must be my apology—A Mr George Winter, a land-owner in Fiji is or was lately resident in Washington D. C. & I believe intends remaining for some time—His interests are at stake here, and as a personal friend; I have written him the enclosed letter warning him of what is now taking place It is in the hope that Mr Winter is known at the President's levées, or that some of the gentlemen connected with the Government have made his acquaintance, that I have taken the liberty of asking you to endeavour to place this letter in his hands & I feel sure that it is in your power to do so. Trusting that you will excuse the freedom I have taken . . ."—ALS, ICarbS.

1870, MAY 29. To Mrs. Charles Griffin stating that Julia Dent Grant will receive her before noon.—Howard S. Mott, Inc., Catalog 207 [1983], no. 71.

1870, MAY 31. To S. Carl Kapff, Steuben House, New York City. "I am in receipt of your letter of May 24th, inviting me to be present at the laying of the corner stone of the Steuben monument. I regret that my public duties prevent my accepting the invitation and thus contributing in a feeble manner to the ceremony to commemorate the services of one who came to the aid of our country in her early struggle for national existence, one whose name will never be forgotten as long as the principles for which he gave his valuable services are preserved."—Copy, DLC-USG, II, 1. See *New York Tribune*, May 21, June 2, 1870.

1870, MAY 31. Secretary of the Navy George M. Robeson to USG. "I have the honor to submit herewith a nomination of Captain Philip R. Fendall, Marine Corps, for the Brevet rank of Major in said corps, for gallant and meritorious services at Port Royal, Hatteras Inlet and Sewell's Point; also for First Lieutenant George B. Haycock, Marine Corps, for the Brevet rank of Captain in said corps for gallant and meritorious services in aiding the defeat of a rebel raid at Gunpowder bridge, which threatened the ferries at Havre de Grace, and the borders of Pennsylvania."—Copy, DNA, RG 45, Letters Sent to the President.

1870, MAY. Thomas W. Egan, New York City, to USG. "In July last I had the honor to receive from you a note to the Secretary of the Treasury requesting him to confirm my appointment as Weigher in the New York Custom House, which Gov. Boutwell did—It seems that immediately upon my assumption of the position, men were hired to work up if possible a case of fraud on my part against the Government and before I had fairly gotten the office under my control, I was arrested on Such a charge, deprived of my position and have been held under bail for trial ever since, although upon the preliminary examination before a Commissioner of the U. S, all the claim which the prosecution could prove or attempt to prove amounted to (34 80) Thirty four Dollars & Eighty cents, I was not permitted to prove that this amount, if wrongfully charged to Govt was done so, by my foreman with whom I had left vouchers signed in blank to serve during my temporary absence from the city. The whole case is purely one of political persecution—and I appeal confidently to your Excellency to direct that a—nolle prosequi—shall be entered in my case While I was Collector of the 9th Internal Revenue District in this City—Millions of Govt funds passed through my hands, and of all the New York Collectors I beleive I am to this day the only one who has settled his accounts squarely and against whom the Treasury has no claim I appeal to Genl Grant who knows of my services in the field during the late Rebellion, to releive a man who has so often risked his life for his country, from the odium & annoyance of this persecution—My country has given me nothing for Services—I certainly have a right to expect that I Shall not be unjustly punished A synopsis of the evidence in my case—as taken before the U. S. Commissioner can be furnished if required—but I beleive in so petty a case of persecution, Genl Grant will without hesitation direct a nolle prosequi to be entered. I feel confident that a direct reference of my case to the Hon E. Pierrepoint U. S District Attorney for this District will confirm my statements."—ALS, DNA, RG 60, Letters from the President. On June 7, Attorney Gen. Ebenezer R. Hoar endorsed this letter. "Not a case proper for the President's interference. Letter sent to T. W. Egan, informing him that he should apply to the Dist. Atty."—AES, *ibid.* On July 22, 1864, and July 24, 1866, USG had favorably endorsed Egan for promotion.—*SRC*, 49-1-1534, pp. 3–4. See *PUSG*, 12, 359, 436. On Aug. 8, 1874, Egan wrote to USG requesting an appointment to USMA for his son; no appointment followed. —ALS, DNA, RG 94, Unsuccessful Cadet Applications.

1870, JUNE 2. USG endorsement. "The order within referred to is hereby revoked, as recommended by the Secretary of the Interior"—ES, DNA, RG 75, Letters Received, Calif. Superintendency. Written on a letter of the same day from Secretary of the Interior Jacob D. Cox to USG. "At the request of the Commissioner of Indian Affairs, I have the honor to recommend the revocation of the Executive order of June 7. 1869, suspending Billington. C. Whiting, from his office as Superintendent of Indian Affairs for the District of California, . . ."—LS, *ibid.* On Feb. 15, 1871, USG nominated Billington C. Whiting for reappointment as superintendent of Indian affairs, District of Calif.

1870, JUNE 2.   Secretary of the Interior Jacob D. Cox to USG. "I have the honor herewith, to lay before you a copy of a communication, dated today, from the Commissioner of Indian Affairs, enclosing a copy of a telegram from A. E. Farnham, Chief Clerk of the Central Superintendency, reporting the presence of white trespassers upon the Kaw diminished Indian Reserve in Kansas, and respectfully recommend that immediate steps be taken with a view to the removal of the trespassers, as suggested by the Commissioner of Indian Affairs."—LS, DNA, RG 94, Letters Received, 85I 1870. The enclosures are *ibid.*

1870, JUNE 2.   Elizabeth L. Pond, Utica, N. Y., to Julia Dent Grant. "I am sorry to intrude upon you again, when you have so many complicated cares. I have received a satisfactory statement from the Pension Office, regarding my Land Warrant, and am very grateful for your efforts in my behalf. I read with astonishment Mr. Willard's bill, granting pensions to the surviving soldiers and sailors of the war of 1812, but *excluding* widows married after the close of the war. In the room next to mine is an old lady, eighty in August, married in 1816, whose husband enlisted as a mechanic, and received a land warrant, which he sold for sixty dollars. I am seventy eight in March. We were both married after the war, and our husbands were honest yeomen, who served their country according to their capacity. We have gone through life poor, and have reached the Home of the Homeless. A pension would cheer our few remaining days. And how much good it would do other poor soldiers' widows, destitute of home comforts, and daily led to feel that they are in the way of the rising generation. My dear madam, I humbly entreat you, before your Husband signs the bill, to use your influence to have the poor widows included, without any reference to the time of marriage, and you will receive our lasting gratitude."—ALS, DNA, RG 48, Miscellaneous Div., Letters Received. USG approved the bill.—*CG,* 41–3, 1285.

1870, JUNE 3.   To Senate. "I transmit to the Senate, in answer to their resolution of the 18th ultimo a report from the Secretary of State with an accompanying paper."—DS, DNA, RG 46, Presidential Messages. On the same day, Secretary of State Hamilton Fish had written to USG. "The Secretary of State, to whom was referred the resolution of the Senate; of the 18th ultimo, requesting the President, 'if in his opinion not inconsistent with the public interests, to communicate to the Senate any recent correspondence of Mr Bancroft, the Minister of the United States at Berlin, relating to political questions in Germany', has the honor to lay before the President the accompanying paper."—LS, *ibid.* The enclosure is *ibid.* See *SED,* 41-2-94.

1870, JUNE 3.   U.S. Representative Benjamin F. Butler of Mass. *et al.*
to USG. "We earnestly recommend the appointment of Wm L Hanscomb
Esq as naval constructor   His Long experience his energy capacity and
faithfulness to the interests of the Goverment commend his appointment as
beneficial to the public service"—DS (8 signatures), DLC-Benjamin F.
Butler. William L. Hanscom had resigned as naval constructor in 1866.
On Feb. 15, 1871, Secretary of the Navy George M. Robeson wrote to
USG. "I have the honor to return herewith the Resolution (S. R. 108) 'to
authorize the President to permit William L. Hanscom, late a Naval Constructor of the Navy of the United States, to withdraw his resignation of
that office,' and to say that no objections are known to exist to your approving the authority given you to permit Mr. Hanscom to withdraw his resignation; but that, in view of all the circumstances attending the case, action
should not be taken further until a full investigation can be had."—Copy,
DNA, RG 45, Letters Sent to the President. The next day, USG approved
the resolution. See *CG*, 41–3, 1118–24, 1293.

1870, JUNE 4.   G. W. Stidham and Sanford W. Perryman, Creek delegates, Washington, D. C., to USG. "We have been instructed by our people
to lay before you their objections to the organization of a Territorial Government over the Indian Territory, and in doing so, would beg leave to assure you that your Red children the Creek Nation of Indians entertain
the utmost confidence in your just appreciation of their dependence, and
rest their hope that you will not allow any infraction upon their rights secured by *solemn Treaties* with them."—Copy, DNA, RG 75, Letters Received, Creek Agency. The enclosure is *ibid.*

1870, JUNE 6.   To Gen. William T. Sherman inviting him to a reception
for the "delegation of Indian now in Washington. . . . The Cabinet and
their ladies and most of the Diplomatic Corps with their ladies are to be
present also . . . There has been no invitation sent to any one but those
coming expressed a desired to be present."—Sotheby's, Sale No. 4998, Jan.
26, 1983, no. 62. Sherman endorsed this letter. "Absent at time of it's
receipt . . ."—*Ibid.* On June 7, Secretary of State Hamilton Fish recorded
in his diary. "Last Evenig the Prsdt had given a reception to the Indian
Chieftains now in the City—(Sioux Indians) Spotted tail, & his suite—&
Red Cloud & his—The Diplomatic Corps, were present—"—DLC-Hamilton
Fish. On June 2 and 9, USG held meetings with representatives of the
Brulé and Oglala Sioux.—*New York Times*, June 3, 7, 10, 1870; *SED*,
41-3-39, pp. 42–43; D. C. Poole, *Among the Sioux of Dakota: Eighteen
Months' Experience as an Indian Agent, 1869–70* (1881; reprinted, St.
Paul, 1988), pp. 164–69, 181–87.
       On June 18, J. R. Whitehead *et al.* wrote to USG. "Your Memorialists
beg leave to respectfully represent that they are citizens of the United States
and residents of the young Territory of Wyoming; that they have been

attracted thither to settle on the fertile soil, and delve in the rich mines of this embryo state, by confidently expecting that the fostering care, and generous protection for which the Government of the United States has always, heretofore, been noted, would be extended to the pioneers of civilization, who are now pushing forward the car of progress through the valleys and over the mountains of the Rocky Range. But alas! we fear that the recently proclaimed policy of the Interior department in relation to the Indian tribes of our Territory, reverses the former order of things and transfers the 'fostering care' and 'generous protection' of the government from the pioneers to a few bands of murderous savages. . . . The Indians should be restricted to moderate reservations, and instructed to produce their means of subsistence by agriculture, and not be left to subsist by the chase Humanity for the indians (if there is any) would dictate this as the only means of civilizing, and preserving these savages from soon becoming extinct as a race Your memorialists further represent that the development of the resources of Wyoming, would be speedily and materially enhanced, by giving effect to the late act of Congress establishing a mail route through this Indian country from Cheyenne City to Helena Montana, by ordering service thereon. The Country through which the mail would be carried would soon become settled by farmers and stock raisers; and a line of settlements established from the Gallatin valley to the Great National highway. . . ."—DS (113 signatures), DNA, RG 75, Letters Received, Wyoming Superintendency. A similar petition to USG concerning "Indian relations and postal affairs" is *ibid.*

1870, June 8. USG endorsement. "Please present this case to me for review."—AES, DNA, RG 94, ACP, R56 CB 1870. Written on a letter of June 3 from José A. A. Robinson, Washington, D. C., to U.S. Representative Benjamin F. Butler of Mass. "I have the honor to herewith present a statement of the facts in my case together with those that appear on the record of my trial. . . ."—ALS, *ibid.* On June 10, USG nominated Robinson for reinstatement as 2nd lt., 1st Art. On Aug. 7, Butler, Gloucester, Mass., wrote to Secretary of War William W. Belknap. "It appears that young Robinson, of whom I have had conversation with you, who was renominated by the President, was by mistake not reported on and not confirmed by the Senate General Ames, who was upon the Military Committee, says that he supposed him to have been reported upon; therefore I say mistake I know that you were not in favor of his renomination, but the President having determined it, I write you in confidence that the nomination, having failed through inadvertence, will be now followed by an appointment during the recess which may be submitted anew to the Senate."—LS, *ibid.* On Feb. 22 and Oct. 22, 1867, USG as gen. and secretary of war *ad interim* had favorably endorsed Robinson's appointment as 2nd lt.—ES, *ibid.*

1870, June 9. Elihu B. Washburne, Paris, to USG. "Marshal Le Boeuf, the Secretary of War here, is a bluff, off-hand, frank and brave old soldier.

At his official reception last night he was unusually cordial and made haste to tell me that he had in the Corps Legislatif, on that day, read a letter of yours in debate with great effect. The debate sprung up on a question of some soldiers voting at the late election here. The letter he read was one you addressed to Stanton in regard to our soldiers voting during the war. I send you the debate cut from the Official Journal. I told the old marshal I should send it to you, and he seemed immensely gratified and said that I must also send to you his kindest personal regards. I know you will be gratified at the endorsement of your letter by a man so eminent and so distinguished in his profession, as Marshal Le Boeuf."—ALS (press), DLC-Elihu B. Washburne. See *PUSG*, 12, 212–15.

1870, JUNE 11. Bvt. Maj. Gen. Oliver O. Howard, Washington, D. C., to USG. "A few young men in the Depts. (~~eight or ten~~ five or six) have been elected as delegates to the International Convention to be held at Indianapolis the 22nd inst—I wish to ask for them upon their application a special ten days leave to attend this young men's christian association convention. I shall not be able to go owing to my *trial* & other public requirements. My case was closed last night by my own statement except the summing up & the action & report of the Committee"—ALS (press), Howard Papers, MeB.

1870, JUNE 13. Elihu B. Washburne to USG. "I take great pleasure in presenting to you Major Kodolitsch a distinguished officer of the Austrian Army. The Major visits the United States under the direction of his Government to inform himself in regard to matters in his profession. I have assured him of a cordial reception by the officers of our own army, and if you could commend him to Genl. Belknap, he could be put in the way of accomplishing his mission."—ALS (press), DLC-Elihu B. Washburne.

1870, JUNE 15. U.S. Senator Oliver P. Morton of Ind. to USG. "I beg leave to recommend Isaac. P. Gray for the Consulship at St Thomas. He is every way worthy."—ALS, OFH. Numerous letters recommending Isaac P. Gray for appointment as U.S. minister to Venezuela are in DNA, RG 59, Letters of Application and Recommendation. On June 17, USG nominated Gray as consul, St. Thomas, Danish West Indies; on Aug. 22, Gray declined the appointment.

1870, JUNE 18. John Eaton, Jr., commissioner of education, to USG. "Understanding that an act has passed adding another Judge to the Supreme Court of this District to whom as the junior member of the Court the law provides shall be assigned the business of the Orphan Court—abolished by the same act, I would Respectfully but urgently recommend for the place, General John Oliver, a citizen of Little Rock, and member of the Arkansas bar. You know well his special merits as a Union officer in the recent war. My relation to what he has done as a patriotic citizen since the war has given me an opportunity of forming most favorable opinion of his excellent ability, attainments, cultivation, and uncompromising integrity. Too much cannot be said in commendation of his prudent and trustworthy efforts in the reorganization of the State of his adoption in the South. I believe few are more deserving of Government consideration and that he is well qualified for the position, and will fill it ably, and to the satisfaction of yourself and all just men."—LS, DNA, RG 60, Records Relating to Appointments. Related papers are *ibid.* On June 29, USG nominated John M. Oliver as associate justice, Supreme Court of D. C., and withdrew the nomination on July 14.

1870, June 18. Alfred Pleasonton, collector of Internal Revenue, New York City, to USG. "A number of your political as well as personal friends have requested me to state to you the qualifications of Mr Wm R. Page, of Virginia, for the position of Consul at *Port Said*, Suez Canal, for which position Mr Page is an applicante. Mr Page is a gentleman who has resided abroad in Turkey & other countries of Europe for a number of years, he is an excellent linguist in the Oriental languages as well as those of Europe, he is perfectly familiar with the consular & diplomatic service; & in a position such as that of Port Said—where the intercourse it may be said will be with all the different nationalities, I consider the qualifications of Mr Page as peculiarly adapted to the position besides I believe he will do credit to the office from his character & standing as a gentleman. For these reasons I have been induced to intrude this recommendation in favor of Mr Page." —ALS, DNA, RG 59, Letters of Application and Recommendation. Related papers are *ibid.* On Dec. 6, USG nominated William R. Page as consul, Port Said.

1870, June 21. Secretary of the Navy George M. Robeson to USG. "I have the honor to submit, herewith a nomination of Seventy Ensigns to be Masters in the Navy, and one for Seventy-three Midshipmen to be Ensigns in the Navy, all to fill vacancies in the respective grades."—Copy, DNA, RG 45, Letters Sent to the President.

1870, June 23. To Albert Edward, Prince of Wales. "Your dispatch of this evening is received. America and Great Britain have reason to feel gratified at the successful connection of the far East with them by the submarine cable."—*Washington Chronicle*, June 24, 1870. On June 23, the Prince of Wales had cabled to USG. "I feel sure you will rejoice with me on the completion this Evening of submarine telegraphic communication between Great Britain & America with India."—Telegram received (at 7:10 p.m.), DNA, RG 59, Miscellaneous Letters. On the same day, Horace Porter endorsed this cable. "Respectfully refered to Sec of state   The President is not certain whether this is genuine or a hoax. If considered genuine please send a reply in his name."—AES, *ibid.* On June 23, Richard Southwell Bourke, viceroy of India, cabled to USG. "The Viceroy of India for the first time speaks direct by telegraph with the President of the United States. May the completion of this long line of uninterrupted communication be the emblem of lasting union between the Eastern and western world"—Telegram received (at 10:35 A.M.), *ibid.* On the same day, USG cabled to Bourke. "The President of the United States joins in the hope of the Vice Roy of India, that the union this day completed between the Eastern & Western World may be lasting and may tend to closer intercourse and relations—"—Copy, *ibid.*

1870, June 23. To James McCosh, president, Princeton College. "I am in receipt of your letter and have to thank you for your very cordial invitation to attend the approaching commencement of Princeton College. It would afford me great pleasure to be present upon that interesting occasion, and witness the commencement exercises of one of our most honored institutions of learning. I regret however that my public duties will not permit me to leave the capital at that time and that I am therefore compelled to decline." —Copy, DLC-USG, II, 1. McCosh had written to USG inviting him to follow George Washington's example by attending commencement.—William Evarts Benjamin, Catalogue No. 27, Nov., 1889, p. 8.

1870, June 24. James Atkins, collector of customs, Atlanta, to USG. "I have the honor very respectfully to make application to your Excellency for the position of United States District Attorney for the District of Georgia, recently made vacant by the appointment and confirmation of Hon. Amos T. Akerman to the position of Attorney General of the United States. . . ."— ALS, DNA, RG 60, Records Relating to Appointments. On Feb. 21, 1872, USG nominated Atkins as collector of customs, Savannah. On July 26, 1874, Helen King Atkins, Hampton, Ga., wrote to USG. *"Personal.* . . . My husband of whom I speak is at his post of duty assigned by yourself—James Atkins Collector of Customs at port of Savannah   Separated so widely as you are, from every day life at the South; it is scarcely possible for you to realize what it is to be a Republican in Georgia—It implys isolation, contempt, ostracism, & ignominy, & yet such is my beloved husband, a native born Georgian, & in this under the circumstances lies his greatest sin! . . . I write to beg that you will send him to St. Petersburg—in place of Mr. Jewell whom you have recently recalled. . . ."—ALS, *ibid.,* RG 59, Letters of Application and Recommendation. On March 9, 1875, James Atkins, Savannah, wrote to USG requesting an appointment as district judge, Ark. —ALS, *ibid.,* RG 60, Records Relating to Appointments. Related papers are *ibid.* On Feb. 23, 1876, Atkins wrote to USG. *"Personal* . . . I have the honor to enclose herewith my *formal* application for reappointment as Collector of Customs at this port. . . ."—ALS, *ibid.,* RG 56, Collector of Customs Applications. The enclosure is *ibid.*

1870, June 28. Mrs. R. V. Dent, Washington, D. C., to USG. "You will pardo[n] the liberty I again take to trouble you, in regard to my Husbands appointment in the Qm Mst Dept   I called to see Gen Meigs and he requested me to say to you that on receipt of your note he immediately wrote to Hon Sec of War ask[ing] him to appoint Mr Dent to the first vacancy, and that I should go and see the Sec, myself,   I did so and he said the letter was merely referred and could do nothing for him unless ordered by you to appoi[nt] him,   trusting you will grant [this] favor to relieve my Husband from the hard labor at which he is now employed, . . ."—ALS, DNA, RG 107, Appointment Papers.

1870, June 29.   Bvt. Maj. Gen. Oliver O. Howard to USG. "I wish to recommend to you an excellent man for the position of Judge of the Police Court of this District Judge *Henry B. Fernald.* This gentleman is a resident of Washington, an man of high character, good reputation, of learning & experience and I believe from what I have learned of him that he is eminently fitted for this office. It is of considerable importance to the freedmen of this place to have a just & able man at that post."—ALS (press), Howard Papers, MeB. On June 15, Henry B. Fernald had written to USG requesting the appointment.—ALS, DNA, RG 60, Records Relating to Appointments. No appointment followed.

1870, June 29.   L. C. Norvell, Washington, D. C., to USG. "I called to see you this A. M. on my return from N. York but could not get admittance I leave for Home at 2.10 P M via Cincinnati   Mr Casey desired me to see you in his b[e]half and to say that He wanted me appointed Genl appraiser of the south vice Kellogg as He Kellogg was a democrat and He Casey would furnish the proof from his office . . ."—ALS, DNA, RG 56, Appraiser of Customs Applications. Related papers are *ibid.* No appointment followed.

1870, June 30.   USG endorsement. "Please send in nomination to-morrow."—AES, DNA, RG 60, Records Relating to Appointments. Written on a letter of June 30 from U.S. Senator Matthew H. Carpenter of Wis. *et al.* to USG. "We arnestly recommend Captain Franklin W. Oakley of Beloit Wisconsin to be appointed marshal of the United States for the Western Judicial District of Wisconsin   Capt Oakley is a gentleman of high character, lost his right arm in the union army during the late war, is thoroughly qualified for the place, and we are very anxious that he should be appointed"—LS (4 signatures), *ibid.* On April 1, USG had nominated Franklin W. Oakley as postmaster, Beloit, but withdrew the nomination on April 4. On July 1, USG nominated Oakley as marshal, Western Dist., Wis.

[1870], June.   "X Y," Washington, D. C., to USG. "Strictly Confidential . . . I wrote you on the 29th of April, a letter which I hope you have received   Besides much also which I said. I made the following suggestion 'Beware of the men in high stations, & the most of there subordinates, *who were brought here by Chase, when Secretary of the Treasury, & have been*

left in Office by you' I affirmed as a very general rule, they are extremely
hostile to you, and *secretly* but *zelously* working to elect Mr Salmond P
Chase to the Presidency in 1872. . . ."—AL (initialed), USG 3.

1870, JULY 2.   U.S. Representative Cadwallader C. Washburn of Wis.
et al. to USG. "The Subscribers respectfully recommend the Honorable
Charles M Webb of Grand Rapids, Wisconsin for appointment as United
States District Attorney for the Western District of Wisconsin, lately established by Acts of Congress. Mr Webb is a resident of the 6th Congressional District"—LS (7 signatures), DNA, RG 60, Records Relating to
Appointments. On July 9, USG nominated Charles M. Webb as U.S. attorney, Western District, Wis. Papers recommending Webb's reappointment
in 1874 are *ibid.*

1870, JULY 8.   Daniel B. Cox, Philadelphia, and Robert P. Morton, Wilmington, Del., to USG. "Haveing been informed of a will relating to the
heirs of Samuel Miles formely of this city (Philadelphia) haveing died in
Rio Jainaro Brazil about the year 1848, our parents being neglectfull we
being Children of the heirs, (who are now dead.) We, have had influential
men working for us: and we have had one letter from the Consul at Rio
stateing that he had turned our business over to his successor in office, and
since then we have had no satisfaction. Now our object in writeing to you
is we deem it the onley safe course to persue in the matter, haveing gone as
far as our means would allow, our idea being that you would write directly
to the Consul himself and get the nessessary satisfaction for us, as we
thaught a letter from you to our Consul in Rio would have more power
than from us, in doing this you would confer a great favour, and we will
ever be greatful"—LS, DNA, RG 59, Miscellaneous Letters.

1870, JULY 8.   Andrew J. Rodgers, Washington, D. C., to USG. "Believing it to be propper that I should do so, I very respectfully ask leave to
submit the following facts to you. In March last, I was, at the instance of
the Hon. George S. Boutwell, Secretary of the Treasury, employed as Counsel, by the Hon. R. S. Hale, Speccial Counsel for the United States Treasury,
to look up & produce, for the benefit of the U. S. Government, certain existing evidences going to show whereby the Govt had been, & is still being
defrauded out of large sums of money by Claimants who have sued, & are
still suing through the Court of Claims.—. . . The case of one Morris Kohen
vs. the United States, was then needing especcial attention, in as much as
the Claimant had obtained judgement in the Court of Claims, & the Treasury's Counsel had taken it up to the Supreme Court, & was then expecting
the judgement to be returned sustained. To this case Judge Hale urged my
special attention. In order to produce certain important facts necessary to
stay the judgement, & reopen this case, I had either to go, or send to the
State of Georgia. In order to faciltitate my movements, Judge Hale paid me,
on account a retaining fee of Two hundred & fifty dollars, But it so occured

that I could not then go to Georgia. I therefore sent a man, but he was unable to procure the evidences for which he was sent & return as early as I had agreed to produce them in order to meet the exigences of this case. In consequence of this, as I am informed, the judgement has been paid.— . . . I am informed that the Treasury's Speccial Counsel does not desire me to proceed any farther with regard to said Kohn case, or any other cases. It is therefore I come directly to you, the Chief Exective of these United States, & affirm that if I am by you, authorized & empowered, with Commission & Means to proceed, I will, in the capacity of Counsel, as well for the Govt, as my certain clients, produce, or cause to be produced, certain of the Archieves of the late Confederate Govt, among which are many of the so-called Confederate Cotton Loan Records; together with certain other documentary & oral evidences, all of irrefutable character, going to show very nearly the amount of so-called Confederate Cotton, & other property seized, & when seized, & by what officers seized by authority of the United States during the late War. . . ."—ALS, DNA, RG 60, Letters from the President. See Charles C. Nott and Samuel H. Huntington, *Cases Decided in the Court of Claims of the United States, at the December Term for 1868,* . . . (Washington, D. C., 1870), IV, 436–47.

1870, JULY 8. U.S. Representatives Cadwallader C. Washburn and Amasa Cobb of Wis. to USG. "For the purpose of relieving the President from any embarrassment in regard to the appointment of Judge of the Western District of Wisconsin, we beg leave to withdraw the recommendations we have made. In doing so we adhere to the opinions we have heretofore expressed to you."—LS, OFH. On July 1, USG had both nominated and withdrawn the nomination of James C. Hopkins as judge, Western District, Wis., but renominated him on July 9. See *Wisconsin State Journal,* July 2, 8, 9, 1870.

1870, JULY 9. USG endorsement. "Approved"—AES, DNA, RG 60, Records Relating to Appointments. Written on an undated letter from William B. Snell to USG. "I have the honor to request the appointment of Alexander. T. Grey of Washington. D. C. as a Justice of the Peace—for said District." —ALS, *ibid.*

1870, JULY 9. To Senate. "In answer to the resolutions of the Senate of the 26th of May and of the 14th. of June last, I transmit a a report from the Secretary of State and the papers by which it was accompanied."— Copies, DNA, RG 59, General Records; *ibid.,* RG 130, Messages to Congress. On the same day, Secretary of State Hamilton Fish had written to USG. "The Secretary of State, to whom was referred the resolution of the Senate of the 26th of May, last, requesting the President 'to furnish to the Senate copies of papers, correspondence, testimony and other information in the case of the American Brig Mary Lowell, captured by the Spanish gunboat Andalusia in the year 1869, on the Bahama banks;' and also the resolution of the Senate of the 14th of June last requesting the President 'unless in his judgement it is incompatible with the public interests, to transmit to the Senate all information in possession of the Government showing that during the hostilities in Cuba any American citizens have been executed without proper trial, or any American vessels have been seized upon the high seas, or the property of any American citizens has been confiscated, or Embargoed, with full particulars in Each case, and to state, also, what steps, if any, have been taken in reference thereto' has the honor to lay before the President the information called for by the said Resolutions. . . ."—Copy, *ibid.*, RG 59, General Records. See *SED*, 41-2-108.

1870, JULY [11]. USG endorsement. "If the 4th is Fox Dist. please appoint and notify Dr. Newman and Gen. Pleasonton."—AE (initialed), DNA, RG 94, Correspondence, USMA. Written on a letter of July 11 from John P. Newman, Washington, D. C., to USG. "Mrs Newman has just received a telegram from William W. Giddings, her nephew, that he resides in the Fourth Congressional District. N. Y. Will you please inform us. if you appointment."—ALS, *ibid.* William W. Giddings did not attend USMA.

1870, JULY 11. USG endorsement. "Refered to the Sec. of State. I have no objection to the apt. recommended within."—AES, DNA, RG 59, Letters of Application and Recommendation. Written on a letter of July 8 from U.S. Senator Alexander Ramsey of Minn. to USG. "I would respctfully recommend George F. Potter Esq for the appointmt of Consul at Winnepeg British North America   he is a gentleman of respectability character and experience in public affairs"—ALS, *ibid.* On May 3, USG had nominated Samuel T. Day as consul, Winnipeg. On Aug. 5, Governor Harrison Reed of Fla. wrote to USG. "I have the honor to recommend the appointment of Geo. W. Driggs of this place for Consul to Winnipeg in place of Dr. Day declined. Mr. Driggs has been Assistant Secretary of State for the past two years & is an accomplished & competent officer & will do honor the position & administration. He was a gallant soldier in the Union Army during the war & deserves this testimony of respect from the government."—ALS, *ibid.* On Sept. 14, Secretary of State Hamilton Fish wrote to USG. "I enclose a copy of a telegram received this afternoon from Mr Motley, & also one received yesterday—That last received is not hopeful for a speedy termination of the War—I send also a commission appointing Mr Taylor Consul at Winnipeg—this gentleman is Senator Ramsey's friend, and a very competent & excellent appointment, it will be—There is need of filling the place speedily, & I hope that you may think well of Mr Taylor for the position—All is quiet here—and the usual routine runs on—With most respectful regards to Mrs Grant . . ."—ALS (press), DLC-Hamilton Fish. On Dec. 6, USG nominated James W. Taylor as consul, Winnipeg; on Dec. 9, George W. Driggs as consul, Turks Island.

1870, JULY 11.   Secretary of the Navy George M. Robeson to USG. "I have the honor to report in reference to S. R. 96. referred to me that the said resolution was passed upon the recommendation of the Navy Department, and that no reasons are known why it should not receive the approval of the President."—LS, OFH. On July 12, USG signed the resolution appointing Lt. Charles Pendleton and Lt. Richard P. Leary, both retired, as lt. commanders on the active list.—*CG*, 41–2, 5482.

1870, JULY 12.   USG endorsement. "Refered to the Sec. of State. I have no objection to the making of this apt.mt."—AES, DNA, RG 59, Letters of Application and Recommendation. Written on a letter of July 1 from U.S. Representative Charles W. Buckley of Ala. *et al.* to Secretary of State Hamilton Fish recommending the appointment of N. H. De Nyse as consul, Brindisi.—DS (3 signatures), *ibid.* On July 14, Secretary of State Hamilton Fish wrote to USG. "The South Carolina Senators have given the name of Mr Kingman as Consul at Brindisi—Senator Sawyer requests the nomination be sent in as soon as possible saying there will be an Executive Session—& that the nomination will be confirmed today"—ALS (press), DLC-Hamilton Fish. On March 17, 1871, USG nominated Samuel H. Kingman as consul, Brindisi.

1870, JULY 12.   To Senate. "I transmit to the Senate for consideration with a view to its ratification, a convention between the United States and Austria concerning the rights privileges and immunities of consuls in the two countries, signed at Washington on the 11th. inst."—Copies, DNA, RG 59, General Records; *ibid.*, RG 130, Messages to Congress.

1870, JULY 13.   To Thomas A. Scott, J. Gillingham Fell *et al.*, Philadelphia. "I am in receipt of your very polite invitation to be present with my staff at the Reception Ball to be given to the 7th Reg. N. G. S of N. Y. at the Stockton Hotel, Cape May, Friday July 15. It would afford me much pleasure to accept, but my official duties will prevent my leaving the City on Friday. Thanking you for your kind consideration, . . ."—Copy, DLC-USG, II, 1. See *New York Times*, July 15–17, 1870.

1870, JULY 13.   To Senate. "I transmit to the Senate, in answer to their Resolution, of the 8th instant, a Report from the Secretary of State and the papers which accompanied it."—DS, DNA, RG 46, Presidential Messages. On the same day, Secretary of State Hamilton Fish had written to USG enclosing papers relating to emancipation in Cuba.—DS, *ibid.* The enclosures are *ibid.* See *SED*, 41-2-113.

1870, JULY 14.   USG endorsement. "Refered to the Sec. of War. I understand that Capt. Bowen wrote a letter recalling his resignation the day after having forward it. If so he may be permitted to withdraw."—AES, DNA, RG 94, ACP, 5489 1872. Written on a letter of the same day from

U.S. Senator Matthew H. Carpenter of Wis. to USG. "I respectfully, but earnestly, request that the acceptance of the resignation of Capt. E. C. Bowen, U. S. A. be revoked."—LS, *ibid.* On July 8, USG had endorsed papers concerning Capt. Edgar C. Bowen. "Unless under charges the resignation of Capt. Bowen may be withdrawn"—Charles Hamilton Auction No. 119, April 19, 1979, no. 193.

1870, JULY 14.   To Senate. "I transmit to the Senate, in answer to their Resolution of the 7th instant, a report from the Secretary of State, with accompanying documents."—DS, DNA, RG 46, Presidential Messages. On the same day, Secretary of State Hamilton Fish had written to USG concerning the condition of commercial relations between the United States and Latin American countries.—DS, *ibid.* See *SED,* 41-2-112.

1870, JULY 14.   To Senate. "I transmit for consideration with a view to its ratification, a Convention between the United States and the Republic of Salvador for the surrender of fugitive criminals, signed at San Salvador on the 23d day of May last."—DS, DNA, RG 46, Presidential Messages, Foreign Relations, Salvador. The enclosure is *ibid.*

1870, JULY 14.   To Senate. "I transmit for the consideration of the Senate with a view to ratification a Convention between the United States and His Majesty the King of Sweden and Norway, relative to the citizenship of natives of the one country who may emigrate to the other. A Protocol on the subject is also herewith transmitted."—DS, DNA, RG 46, Presidential Messages, Foreign Relations, Sweden and Norway. The enclosure is *ibid.*

1870, JULY 15.   To Senate. "In answer to their resolution of the 9th instant, I transmit a Report from the Secritary of State and the papers which accompanied it."—DS, DNA, RG 46, Presidential Messages. On July 14, Secretary of State Hamilton Fish had written to USG. "The Secretary of State, to whom was referred the resolution of the Senate requesting the President to inform the Senate if Chinese Coolies are being imported into the United States in violation of the Act of February 19th 1862, has the honor to report: That Information has been received from Gen'l Le Gendre, the consul at Amoy that the Chinese Government has limited the Exportation of Chinese laborers to the vessels of the Treaty Powers, and the consul seems to be of the opinion that the effect of this will be to decrease or to prevent this sort of emigration. . . ."—DS, *ibid.* Related papers are *ibid.* See *SED,* 41-2-116.

On July 29, Attorney Gen. Amos T. Akerman wrote to USG. "I enclose to you copies of two letters with their enclosures just received from the United States Marshal of California. The matter upon which he writes is so serious that I have thought it proper to put you in immediate possession of the information which he communicates. It is more than possible he exaggerates the danger; still the eye of the government should be kept upon the subject. I do not see how the Executive can interpose unless called upon by the state authorities under Article IV, section 4, of the constitution. I shall direct the Marshal to be on the alert if any breach in the late act known as the enEnforcement act should be committed, for sections 16 and 17 of that act protect civil rights, and forbid special taxes upon emmigrants from foreign countries; but I do not see that anything further can be done at present. The persons leading the anti Chinese movement do not seem to be of much consideration Yet where popular passions are so inflammable, it may grow to be serious. Possibly it may be well to have some of the military at hand for emergencies."—Copy, DNA, RG 60, Letters Sent.

1870, JULY 15. T. C. Medary, editor, *Lansing Mirror*, Lansing, Iowa, to USG. "At the request of one of our citizens, I take the liberty of addressing you on a matter of justice to a very worthy person. Charles Lloyd of this city was fortunate enough to receive the appointment for a cadetship at West Point. He went there, was examined and *rejected* for deficiency in grammar. The boy was so positive that he *could* pass a satisfactory examination, that, I believe, he went to Washington and laid his case before the Secretary of War. He instructed him to return to West Point and go through another examination. He did so, was examined by the proper authority, and declared all right. After this, refusal was made to accept him on the grounds that, should he be admitted, others who had been rejected would also have to be admitted. His rejection created universal surprise throughout this community, for he is considered a ripe scholar, an honorable, upright and worthy boy in every respect, and his acceptance was not doubted. Hon. Wm B. Allison, Representative from our District, advises the boy to remain at West Point and see if something cannot be done for him. You, Hon Sir, have it in your power to intercede for him and see that justice is done a young man who does not merely wish to get an education at the Government's expense, but who desires to spend his life as a soldier. By giving this matter your personal attention, whether the result should be favorable or not, you will receive the thanks of hundreds of the boys friends, . . ."—ALS, DNA, RG 94, Correspondence, USMA. Charles F. Lloyd graduated from USMA in 1874.

1870, JULY 16. USG endorsement. "Refered to the Sec. of War and his attention called to endorsements."—AES, DNA, RG 107, Appointment Papers. Written on papers supporting the retention of War Dept. clerk William B. Johnson, a disabled veteran.—*Ibid.*

1870, JULY 16. Secretary of the Navy George M. Robeson to USG. "At the request of certain voluntary exiles to Brazil, who were by your direction, afforded a passage in the U. S. Steamer 'Quinnebaug,' from that country to the United States, I have the honor to enclose herewith a copy of a communication received from them, in which they express their gratitude for the kindness which has been extended to them."—Copy, DNA, RG 45, Letters Sent to the President. On July 30, E. Ribet, Natchez, wrote to USG. "Please allow me, as a friend of the Government, to thank you for enabling those poor men, women and children in Brazil to return home. It was and is an act of the greatest humanity. But *your* noble exertions, cannot stop here, when you are assured that at *Para* Empire of Brazil, there are some four or five poor American familys who are suffering and want to get home. Amongst those is the Gaston family, which left Mobile, Ala., in June 1867, to whom the Brazillian Government refuses to give passports. In truth, they are *really prisoners* there. Have those people sent home and God will bless you for the *deed*."—ALS, *ibid.*, RG 59, Miscellaneous Letters. A newspaper clipping describing the return of these exiles is *ibid.*

1870, JULY 18. Horace Porter to U.S. Representative James A. Garfield of Ohio. "I read your letter in regard to the Ohio Fair to the President. He says he did not intend to be understood as definitely accepting, for his engagements are such that he would not like to make a promise when he might find himself unable to accept. If he can, however, he will be present." —Copy, DLC-USG, II, 1.

1870, JULY 18. Secretary of State Hamilton Fish to USG. "I enclose a telegram from Mr Bancroft concerning our Bonds in Berlin. A copy has been sent to the Secretary of the Treasury."—Copy, DNA, RG 59, Domestic Letters. George Bancroft, U.S. minister, Berlin, had cabled to Fish. "War forces sale of millions of American bonds. Treasury can buy here very low and help our credit."—Telegram received (on July 18, 3:30 P.M.), USG 3.

1870, JULY 19. USG authorization. "*I hereby authorize and direct the Secretary of State to affix the Seal of the United States to* my power authorizing John Lothrop Motley to exchange the ratifications of the Adddition Convention to the Convention of April 7. 1862 between Great Britain & the U. S. for the suppression of the African slave Trade . . ."—DS (facsimile), Paul C. Richards, Catalogue 222 [1987], no. 213. A similar document of the same day is in IHi.

1870, JULY 19. Caroline Cates Woodward, Huntsville, Tex., to Julia Dent Grant. "I hope you will pardon the liberty I take in addressing you this letter—The feelings and affections of a mother must be my apology for the boldness I take in writing to you—Not desiring to take much of your time I will proceed to state my object in thus addressing you—Some time in the Spring of the year in 1867 my son James M. Cates was tried and convicted by a military commission at Vicksburgh Miss—upon a charge of horse stealing and sentenced to five years hard labor at the Dry Tortugas, where he is now confined under said sentence—. . ."—ALS, DNA, RG 94,

Letters Received, 431C 1870. An enclosed letter of July 22 from Maj. Nathan A. M. Dudley, penitentiary superintendent, Huntsville, to USG is *ibid.*

1870, JULY 20. USG order. "An additional sum of One dollar and fifty cents is hereby allowed to the pay of enlisted men in the Navy of the United States. This order to take effect from the 1st instant."—Copy, DNA, RG 130, Executive Orders and Proclamations.

1870, JULY 20. USG order. ". . . Willam Sherman, Thomas B. Shannon and Calvin Brown, of California are hereby appointed Commissioners to examine and Report to the President of the United States upon the road and Telegraph Line authorized by said Act, and the Joint Resolution of Congress, approved June 28, 1870, to be constructed by the Southern Pacific Railroad Company of California."—Copy, DNA, RG 130, Executive Orders and Proclamations.

1870, JULY 21. Henry Heynemann, New York City, to USG. "At the time of the surrender of Genl Lee, I carried the flag of Peace from Boston to Washington, when I had the honor to be introduced to You by Mr Andrew Johnson, at that time President of the United States Little I dreamed of at that time that I should ever be selected by a Hundred Thousand Freemasons, all good and faithful Citizens of the United States, to address You in their behalf They pray through me, relying on Your wisdom, Your spirit for Justice and Your love of Freedom to use Your kind offices in behalf of the Ten Freemasons, who yet suffer the most horrible treatment at the hands of the Spaniards in Cuba, . . ."—ALS, DNA, RG 59, Miscellaneous Letters.

1870, JULY 25. E. V. De Graff, De Graff's Military and Collegiate Institute, Rochester, N. Y., to USG. "I would make an application to have my college come under the law passed July 28, 1866, The law reads, Viz: That for the purpose of promoting knowledge of military science among the young men of the United States, the President may, upon application of an established college within the United States with sufficient capacity for 150 male students, detail an officer of The Army to act as President, &c. My College has been established two years and has had 200 pupils in attendance. I have made it thoroughly military as I could, and have gained decided success. Any reference desired can be given by such men as Gen. Quinby, Gen J. H. Martindale and others. Our population is 80000 and the Western part of York State will support it."—ALS, DNA, RG 94, Letters Received, 328D 1870. On Aug. 2, De Graff repeated his request to USG.— ALS, *ibid.* Related papers are *ibid.*

1870, JULY 25. John S. Foster, Sydney, to USG. "being a native of the United States and knowing the Law with regards Dischargeing Seaman from American Ship feeling that I have suffered grate rong by the Law not being properly carryed-out in my case—I have a few facts to lay before you to show how Seaman are treated here by the Consel . . ."—ALS, DNA, RG 59, Miscellaneous Letters.

1870, JULY 28.   John V. Singer, Livingston, Guatemala, to USG complaining that Asa C. Prindle, commercial agent, Belize, "and the Offishels of Balieze took forsably away from me the Schooner Walter Clayton and her Cargo with out enny right what ever."—ALS, DNA, RG 59, Miscellaneous Letters.

1870, JULY 29.   Charles Jonas, "Prussian Silesia," to USG. "Two months ago I left America for the purpose of visiting my *native* country (Bohemia), to see my aged mother. I was born a subject of Austria, but left that country ten years ago, being at that time 19 years old, and have since become naturalized in America. On applying for my passport, I asked Gen'l H E Paine, to lay the facts of my case before the State Department and inquire whether I can rely upon the protection of our Government, if any emergency should arise that would make an appeal to it necessary. Having been assured of the complete protection of the American Government, I started on my journey. At Berlin I have been advised by Mr. Bancroft, to make my intention known to Mr. John Jay at Vienna, before crossing the Austrian frontier and I therefore addressed a letter to him. Great was my astonishment, when I learned from his reply, that he 'would not advise my returning to Bohemia with any idea that he can certainly protect me, if I were owing military service at the time of my departure, ten years ago.' Now, my mother is sick and cannot undertake a journey to meet me beyond the Austria[n] frontier. If I do not see her now, there is very little probability that I shall ever see her in this life again, and I am sure, this awful disappointment will hasten her deat[h.] In this horrible, agonizing situation I appea[l] to you, Sir, imploring you to give orders to the American minister at Vienna, to accord to me the protection, which an American citizen can rightfully claim. The Austrian officials will not dare to touch me, if they know that the Government of our Republic is ready to shield me against injustice and outrage; and whereas I didn't run away from military conscription, they have no right to consider me their slave, as I am now a citizen of the United States. I sincerely trust, Sir, that you will kindly intercede on my behalf and also cause a reply to be sent to me, addressed as follows: Charles Jonas, 29 Langenstrasse, Bremen, Europe."—ALS, DNA, RG 59, Miscellaneous Letters. See Karel D. Bicha, "Karel Jonas of Racine: 'First Czech in America,'" *Wisconsin Magazine of History,* 63, 2 (Winter, 1979–80), 122–40.

1870, AUG. 2.   A. E. Smith, Glenwood, Iowa, to USG. "The Indian question is one which agitates, and is of vital importance not only to the frontier but the whole nation. It has resolved itself into extermination, or means whereby a lasting peace can be obtained. Aside from the extreme frontier the policy of extermination finds very few to uphold it, and in this age cannot be thought of. Then how to make permanent peace. Undeniably the Indians must except in the internal affairs of their tribes be governed by the whites untill advanced in civilization   let it be proved to the leading and most influential Indians and through *them* to their Tribes that their highest intrest lies in friendly relations with us, relations that we will honestly maintain. To this end let one of the most influential men from each of the strongest tribes be sent or induced to go to Dept. Hd. Qrs. to confer with and act as part of the Indian Bureau, let the tribes by *them* know that good faith *is* intended and their intrests guarded   in the meantime induce all possible to go onto their reservations. Admitting the treachery of Indian character still this plan seems feasible. The cheifs could not but feel the importance of being called into the council of the Nation   let them be made to feel it, if no other way through [*one*] of the distinguishing traits of Indian character Vanity."—ALS, DNA, RG 75, Letters Received, Miscellaneous. On the same day, M. D. MacIntyre, "Forks Solomon River," wrote to USG complaining about Indian depredations in Kan.—ALS, *ibid.*

1870, AUG. 9.   Judge Advocate Gen. Joseph Holt to USG. "This application for the pardon of 'Joe Walker,' freedman, confined at Sing Sing for the murder of Scipio Shannon, colored, has been referred to this Bureau from the Department of Justice; Walker having been tried by Military Commission convened in South Carolina in January, 1866. The charge in the case was murder, but the accused was convicted of manslaughter only, and sentenced to be imprisoned for ten years at hard labor. The sentence was finally approved in March, 1866. The crime of the accused was evidently manslaughter, and the findings of the court were clearly correct. The sentence imposed is also deemed a fitting and proper one. The accused and deceased, while somewhat under the influence of liquor, had engaged in a scuffle, to which the first provocation had apparently proceeded from accused in his charging deceased with cheating him at cards. It is not clear who first struck the other, but it is shown that deceased having got the better of accused threw him upon the floor. Accused then rose and stabbed deceased twice with his clasp Knife, inflicting two mortal wounds. There is no evidence whatever that the *deceased* used a Knife or had one, or had or used any weapon whatever, nor was it so pretended in the written defence of accused at the trial, which was devoted solely to an argument that the crime was not murder but manslaughter only. Upon the sworn testimony, therefore, the present application is false in stating that the deceased drew a knife upon accused, as also in stating that deceased declared his determination to take the life of accused, and also in averring that the deceased threw accused down three times; it is also in other respects exaggerated and generally unreliable. . . ."—Copy, DNA, RG 153, Letters Sent. On Sept. 9, Bvt. Maj. Gen. Edmund Schriver, inspector gen., endorsed this letter. "The President has this day declined favorable action on this case."—Copy, *ibid.*, RG 107, Orders and Endorsements.

1870, AUG. 10.   Bvt. Brig. Gen. Cyrus B. Comstock, Duluth, to USG. "I learn that there is a possibility of the removal from his position as Overseer or Superintendnt (under Gen. J. H. Simpson) of the dredging in the Patapsco river below Baltimore of Mr D. C. Ronsaville   Mr. Ronsaville was Overseer of the government work at Fort Carroll under me some years since and was efficient, honest, and thoroughly faithful. Since that time (1857) he has been almost or quite continuously engaged under the U. S. in similar duties at Baltimore and I learn still bears the same high reputation. The officer there desires to retain him and I do not think he could be replaced by another, with advantage to the service"—ALS, DNA, RG 77, Explorations and Surveys, Letters Received.

1870, AUG. 10.   T. W. Clark, Wausau, Wis., to USG.   "having been a soldier of your old Army of the Tennessee and fought with you at Pittsburg Landing and elsewhere. I take the liberty to send you a copy of an account of my newly invented Breech Loading Cannon   I have offered it for sale to the Belligerent Powers of Europe but if Uncle Sam wants it he can have the preference *every time*—I would like to go into a Government Gun Shop and show the workmen how to make these guns   the price I ask for the invention is one Million Dollars in American Gold   terms of payment $1.000 in advance the Balance on completion of the first successful gun— it would be worth a thousand times that Amount in time of war—please to refer this matter to the Sec of War or appoint some experienced Artillery Officer to investigate it and report—I am unable to make a Model but will send Drawings and Specifiations to the Patent office as soon as I can get the Drawings made. Please to let me know you opinion in regard to the value of such an invention and more particularly your opinion about the possibility of keeping a gun cool in such rapid firing—hoping to hear from you . . ."—ALS, DNA, RG 156, Correspondence Concerning Inventions.

1870, AUG. 11.   Gennaro Zagarizo *et al.* to USG soliciting money for a Protestant church in Lecce, Italy.—LS (in Italian—5 signatures), DNA, RG 59, Miscellaneous Letters.

1870, AUG. 16.   George T. Vaughan, Linden, Tex., to USG. "I respectfully call your attention to the subjoined Petition for the Pardon of *George S. Franks* who is now confined in the Penitentiary of Texas at Huntsville under a sentence of a Military Commission assembled pursuant to the laws of the U. S. at Jefferson in the fall of *1869*. Although the offense with which the accused was charged is murder and was cognizable by the civil authorities of the State, yet, since he was tried pursuant to laws of the U. S. by the commission these petitioners have well considered the power to pardon in the case is vested in ꝯYour eExcellency by the Constitution . . . These petitioners make no question about the legality of the trial, conviction and sentence in the case, admitting all the proceedings to be legal, they place the case before your Excellency as one eminently proper for the exercise

of the pardoning power which is granted to the chief Magistrate in the
Constitution and which can not be abridged, modified or withdrawn except by amendments adopted in the manner prescribed therein. Mr. Franks
is a poor man—he has no money to employ counsel to represent him before
your Excellency at Washington, hence, his friends hope to be excused for
addressing an informal communication in his behalf—These petitioners
await your action in the premises with a great deal of anxiety and respectfully requ[e]st that you cause the same to be communicated to me at this
place—"—ALS, DNA, RG 94, Letters Received, 1172M 1870. The petition is *ibid.* On Nov. 9, Vaughan wrote to Attorney Gen. Amos T. Akerman
about this matter.—ALS, *ibid.* On Nov. 25, Judge Advocate Gen. Joseph
Holt endorsed this letter. "Respectfully submitted to the Secretary of War,
with a copy of an unfavorable report made in this case on Sept. 10, 1870,
upon an application of which the within is apparently a copy or a duplicate.
The views expressed in said report are still entertained. A copy of said
report was also, (upon a repetition of the application,) enclosed to the
Secretary of War on Oct. 31st last, with an endorsement to the effect that
no favorable action could be advised. This therefore is the third application
for clemency in the case. As before, no recommendation for remission of
sentence could be made. But inasmuch as this party was convicted by a
Military Commission in Texas under the Reconstruction laws, it would
have been supposed that his case would have come within the order of the
President of Oct. 10th last, extending pardon to all such convicts in that
State, and releasing them from confinement. It would appear from the
within papers that the applicant was still in confinement up to the 9th inst.,
the date of the within letter of his attorney. Why action has not been taken
in this case, under the order of the President, is not known at this Bureau."
—ES, *ibid.*

1870, AUG. 27. U.S. Representative Thomas A. Jenckes of R. I., Providence, to USG. "I respectfully recommend Jonathan Russell Bullock of
Bristol in this State, as a suitable person to be appointed to the office of
Solicitor of the Navy Department, as the same is established by the act
creating the Department of Justice. Mr Bullock has had a long & extensive
practice at the bar; has been a Judge of the Supreme Court of this State &
of the District Court of the United States for the District of Rhode Island,
and is in every way competent & qualified for the performance of the duties
of the Naval Solicitorship."—ALS, DNA, RG 45, Subject File, Div. VA.
A related letter is *ibid.* No appointment followed.

1870, AUG. 28. D. J. Dinsmore, Eureka, Kan., to USG. "I was once *Ned*
the spy. I was once *Nig* the Guide. I was once Black Eagle of the Potomac.
I was D. D. Will The spy and Guide. I entered the army in /.61. I was
wounded eleven times. I received neither Bounty or Pension and am Somewhat disabled from the effects of my wounds. Instead of asking a Pension
from Government I would ask the privilege of entering a Section of land

in town 26. Range 10. East Greenwood County Kansas For a Cattle Ranche, as the decision of Congress only permits actual Settlers to hold 160 acres and the same is not large enough for a Ranche."—ALS, DNA, RG 48, Lands and Railroads Div., Letters Received.

1870, AUG. 29. Mrs. E. Brady, Mitchell, Ind., to USG. "I have been trying to get a Pension from the government But all my Efforts have proved unsuccessful so I have concluded to appeal to you to know if you *can* or *will* do any thing for me, I know I am justly Entitled to one if any Soldiers Widdow Ever was Although my Husband was not in the so called United States service, But sworn into the Home Guard service, By order from the President of the United-States through the Governer of Indiana To impede the proggress of Morgans Raid through the Country & in consequence came to his death, For which his Widdow has never received but Ten dollars as payment for his life & service & I appeal to you to know if this is just & right & to ~~ask~~know if you cannot & *will* have a law passed to the Effect that I may receive a pension at once as well as those who are not justly entitled to what this Government has allowed them without one *Excuse*, All my Case has been properly made out & sent to Pension Office with this Effect, My prayer is that this may find favor in your Eyes, Other acts have been passed more difficult than this & less just, Hopeing this may not be cast aside as useless Trash . . ."—ALS, DNA, RG 48, Miscellaneous Div., Letters Received.

1870, AUG. 29. Martin F. Conway, Washington, D. C., to USG. "Two rival Committees are now engaged in soliciting contributions of money from Clerks and other employees of the Government, for electioneering purposes, in behalf of the Republican Party. I take the liberty to state to your Excellency (as being above all others interested in the success of the Republican Party) that I have in my possession a receipt from Mr. Tullock for the sum of seventy-five dollars, ($75) contributed by me in the Campaign of 1869, (the Presidential) in response to a summons of this kind. I was holding a second class Consulate in France—the one at Marseilles—of which General Starring, the agent sent out by the Government to examine into the condition of our Consulates, reported 'that it was the best organized and the best conducted of any of our sea port Consulates in France,' or words to that effect. This office was the only favor I had ever received from the Republican Party. *Yet it was taken away from me.* My contribution of $75, attested by the signatures of General Schenck, chairman, and Mr. Tullock, Secretary, of Committee, was pleaded in vain, in my behalf. Now, Sir, in the face of facts like this, how can you expect officeholders to contribute to the support of the Republican Party."—ALS, DNA, RG 59, Letters of Application and Recommendation. On April 5, 1869, Conway, Marseilles, had written to U.S. Senator Henry Wilson of Mass. "I have just received a letter from Dr Howe, which informs me that 'the politicians' in Washington are saying that I should be removed from this Consulate because I was a friend of Chase, and would have voted for him if he had been nominated. . . ."—ALS, *ibid.*

1870, AUG. 30.   William C. Mullen, Marengo, Ill., to USG.   "please a[ll]ow me the privelage of addressing your (Exelency)   we the soldiers of this vicinity wish to know the perticulars of the bill allowing Soldiers the rigght of Homesteading *Govn* Land   we are not certain as to its provissions and *now* will you please send me a Specimen of the bill"—ALS, DNA, RG 48, Lands and Railroads Div., Letters Received.

1870, AUG. 30.   Elihu B. Washburne to USG.   "You know the Hon. R. M. McLane of Baltimore, formerly a Member of Congress and our Minister to China, as a most accomplished, intelligent and estimable gentleman. Mr. McL. has resided much in Paris and I have seen much of him, particularly since the breaking out of the war, and he has been exceedingly kind in giving me the benefit of his assistance in many matters coming before me in the terrible whirl I have been in. I have insisted he should call and see you on his return home & tell you how I am getting on, and more than that, to give you an account of the 'situation.' No man is better posted than he is, or can give you a more interesting account of things in Europe than he can. I am sure you will be delighted to see him."—ALS (press), DLC-Elihu B. Washburne.

1870, SEPT. 1.   Secretary of the Interior Jacob D. Cox to Frederick T. Dent.   "The law provides *no payment* for an asst Private Sec. to sign Land Patents, and only provides for such an appointment to take effect when the number of patents is greater than the Priv. Sec. can sign with due industry, or when by sickness or absence he is unable to sign. The custom therefore is to have a clerk already in the Dept act, & I should recommend the President to follow the practice, since the appointment can be of no value to Mr Parrish without payment & would not operate for more than a month in the year at most. My belief is that one of my own clerks (I mean one of the Department proper & not of the Land office) should perform that duty, so as to be directly under my own Eye & control. If you know of any special facts which ought to vary this judgment, I shall be happy to learn them: otherwise I should incline to recommend that the President act as above indicated—Please let me know early tomorrow, if you think of anything further on the subject."—ALS, ICarbS. On Dec. 8, USG nominated Joseph Parrish as secretary to the president to sign land patents.

1870, SEPT. 5.   To William W. Smith from Long Branch.   "Can you and Family visit us here, from seventh till fourteenth, or from nineteenth till twenty fifth of this month—as most convenient"—Telegram received, Washington County Historical Society, Washington, Pa.

1870, SEPT. 5.   G. Dawson Coleman, Lebanon, Pa., to USG. "My brother who has resided in Paris for the last—Eighteen years. Came over to pay us a visit with his family—Since he left the war has broken out—(he came over in the same vessell with Paradol) He has a house in Paris, and his valuables are deposited in the Bank of France—He is anxious to return to see after his affairs—and as there may be some trouble in crossing the lines or getting into Paris—I would consider it a great favor if you could instruct the State Department to make him a bearer of Despatches, or give him some temporay official position to enable him to get in and out of Paris—He expects to sail in the Layfayette September 17th By the time he reaches it is probable the war will be over—but no one can tell. I will abandon my claims on the Collectorship of Faernandina for this office for my brother. . . . My brothers name is Robert—his wife and two sons accompany him."— ALS, DNA, RG 59, Miscellaneous Letters.

1870, SEPT. 8.   USG endorsement. "~~Mr~~Col. Calloway is a most estimable man, trusty in every way. He was an officer of the regiment I started out with in the begining of the rebellion and I regarded him as one of the best men in it."—AES, DNA, RG 60, Records Relating to Appointments. Written on a letter of Aug. 29 from James E. Calloway, Tuscola, Ill., to USG. "Since my interview with you at Chicago, during your recent visit at that place, I have learned that W. N. Jones associate Justice of the Territory of Wyoming, has been nominated by the Republican party for Delegate to Congress and that he will doubtless resign very soon, if he has not already done so—In the event Judge Jones resigns, I present myself as a candidate for the position. I trust that I am qualified to fill the position and think I will have no trouble to get good endorsements from my own State. As I stated to you at Chicago, my desire is to make my future home, in some one of the Territories, and as you named Colorado as the most desirable one of them I would rather prefer a home there but from my knowledge of Wyoming, I will be satisfied to locate there, with a view of becoming a permanent citizen of that country. Your Excellency very kindly Stated that you would bear in mind, my application and I assure you, that I will endeavor to discharge the duties faithfully in the position desired in the event of my appointment. Thanking you for your kind expressions in my behalf, and wishing you health happiness and great success in administering the affairs of our government."—ALS, *ibid.* Related papers are *ibid.* See *PUSG,* 2, 29–30, 77; *ibid.,* 16, 516.

On Dec. 15, U.S. Delegate James M. Cavanaugh of Montana Territory wrote to USG. "I Very respectfully beg leave to recommend Alexander H. Beattie—of Montana—as Secretary for that Territory. Mr Beattie is one of the leading Republicans of the Territory—And is strongly endorsed by Governor Potts—and all the Federal Officials—as well as by the prominet members of his party—I personally know that his appointment would be most acceptable to the people of Montana. Hoping that you may be pleased

to designate Mr Beattie for the position named—. . ."—ALS, DNA, RG 59,
Letters of Application and Recommendation. On Dec. 16, USG nominated
Calloway as secretary, Montana Territory. On April 12, 1871, Governor
Benjamin F. Potts of Montana Territory wrote to USG. "I have the honor
to inform you that your friend Col. James E. Callaway the new Secretary of
Montana has arrived and assumed the duties of his office—Col. C. is all
that you represented him to be—'a valuable acquisition to the Territory'
He appears to be well satisfied with his new position and goes to Work as
though he meant business. I thank you for the appointment of such a man
and believe he will be an ornament to the Service. I have so much confidence
in your judgement that I request you to look about—and if you have a
young friend—who wants to come West—give him the Receivership of the
Public Lands at Helena Montana an office worth $3000 per annum. The
present incumbent is totally *incompetent* for *the position* and I think I can
[—] unworthy of the position because of a want of integrity. The Office
is a very desirable one for a young man and if you can think of a worthy
young man I would be glad you would confer it upon him. We have high
hopes of being able to carry Montana for the Republican party at the
coming Election in August. Peace and good Will exists between the Whites
and Indians in this Territory"—Copy, Montana Historical Society, Helena,
Mont. On Dec. 15, 1869, USG had nominated Richard F. May as receiver,
land office, Helena; on April 23, 1872, he nominated Solomon Starr to
replace May.

1870, SEPT. 10.   Louis Bernard Berkmeyer, Moscow, to USG. "I. Louis.
Bernard. Berkmeyer. Surgeon Dentist. practising in Moscow do petition
That I may receive the sanction of Your Excellency to place the National
Arms of America. upon my signs and advertisements. under the favour of
the permission granted to me by Mr George. T. Allen. United States Consul
in Moscow. and dated June 1st 1870. and which said permission has been
accepted and signed by His Excellency. The Governor General of Moscow.
The Grand Master of the Police. and the Medical Committee. and which
said permission they have accepted. under the good faith and supposition.
that the American Consul. had full power so to grant. by virtue of his Office.
I am now informed by the American Minister that I have no right to place
the National Arms of America. upon such authority. and that the same
must be removed. otherwise proceedings will be taken against me   I am
likewise in danger of being criminated by the Medical Committee for an
attempt to defraud. by illegal honours. and the Signatures to my permission. deem it necessary that I should re[c]eive an apology. or other such
suitable explanation. as will free me. from any liability to criminal proceedings. and at the same time clear my character from any ungentlemanly
aspersion. Having studied the art of dentistry in America. and being the
only user of American Material. (as applied by me in my practise.) in
Russia as Surgeon Dentist (American.) I do therefore pray that I may be
allowed to continue the use of the National. Arms. without let or hindrance.

and under the permission granted to me by the United States Consul. And I do request. that should my application be refused. that I may know for my absolute vindication. by what law the American Consul granted the permission. and under what special authorization can favours be granted (in the absence authorising right.) Should this matter extend further. I shall be under the painfull necessity of calling upon the American Authorities. for an explanation of why I am placed in this awkward and at the same time criminal position Enclosed are copies of my permission. with the Governor. General. Police Master and the Medical Committee papers."—ADS, DNA, RG 59, Miscellaneous Letters. Related papers are *ibid.*

1870, SEPT. 10. Hugh Campbell, St. Louis, to USG. "This will be handed by my valued friend Mr *Alexr Henderson* Consul of U. S. at Londonderry, Ireland, who arrived at N York, a few days ago. He is, like myself a naturalised citizen, having resided at and near Pittsburg, many years; where he not only acquired a comfortable independence, but made many friends. He then left for his native country (Ireland) where he married; and was soon afterwards appointed Consul at Derry. My brother Robert and I, are on his official bond Since then he has been removed about half a dozen times by Prest Johnson and yourself;—and as often reinstated by the sudden resignation of each fresh appointee, who gladly returned the archieves of the office to him, and went back to seek more lucrative positions The office of Consul at Londonderry affords an income from fees, amounting to from $200. to $250. per annum! Your hungry office seekers would starve on on this sum; and each in succession, has retired in dignified disgust, when they ascertained the income & *no pickings* Mr Henderson is an enthusiastic American. During the many years he has held the office, there are many proofs in the Dept' of State of his earnestness & energy Recently he has incured some expenses in protecting & defending American Citizens and of course has some claims to submit to the Dept of State. I have not the honour of a personal acquaintance with Mr Fish. Permit me therefore to request that you will say to the Secretary, that I indorse Mr Henderson, whom I have known for over twenty years, as an honest man; who deserves generous and kind treatment from the Government"—ALS, DNA, RG 59, Letters of Application and Recommendation. On Oct. 4, George H. Stuart, Philadelphia, wrote to USG. "My friend, Alexander, Henderson Esq. U. S. Consul at Londonderry, being about to visit Washington, desires the pleasure of a short interview with you, which if you can find it convenient to give him, I shall feel personally obliged therefor. I have been acquainted with Mr H. for a number of years and any statement he may make, is worthy of the fullest Credit."—ALS, *ibid.* Related papers are *ibid.*

1870, SEPT. 10. Joseph Paw-ne-no-pah-she, governor, Osage nation, *et al.* to USG. "We the undersigned chiefs and Counsellors of the tribe of 'Great and Little Osage Indians' in National Council assembled would respectfully present: That the Bill making provision for the sale of our Lands, and the removal of our people to the Indian Territory—which passed Congress July 15th 1870—has been read and explained to us by the Commissioners you sent to us for that purpose. We feel satisfied that it is your intention to deal fairly with us. We are assured that the Bill is the work of our friends, and not of Speculators. We therefore, are not willing to show a want of gratitude to our friends, by rejecting it—We accept the Bill as binding upon us and our people—at the same praying that we may be allowed to purchase a larger tract of country from the Cherokees, than that provided in th[e] Bill refered to. . . ."—DS (23 signatures), DNA, RG 75, Letters Received, Neosho Agency. On the same day, John D. Lang and Vincent Colyer, Montgomery, Kan., endorsed this document. "The above petition is reccommended to the favorable consideration of the President and Secretary of the Interior"—ES, *ibid.* Related papers are *ibid.*

1870, SEPT. 11.   2nd Lt. Joseph E. Griffith, Keokuk, to USG. "As I informed you when in Washington I have long ago decided to resign my Commission in the Army. I have therefore, just tendered my resignation and asked a year's pay & allowances. I hope that you can find no good reason to refuse me this desire of my heart. I can not support my wife & 2 children on my present rank & pay—I am poorer pecuniarily today than when I shouldered my musket in 1862. and my only inference from staying in the service is that I must live from hand to mouth. My education warrants my asserting that I can make money in civil life honestly, and that I can lay away some for old age. I trust, Mr President, that you accept my very kindest thanks for the many acts of personal friendship you have seen fit to extend to me—and I hope that you will ever regard me as your protegé. My earnest efforts ever will be to lead such a life that you will never regret having assisted me in my darker days. I would like to have you write to me & any advice you may offer will be thankfully received. Give my regards to Mrs G & Miss Nellie."—ALS, DNA, RG 94, ACP, W240 CB 1870. See *PUSG,* 8, 503, 523–24.

1870, SEPT. 12.   John Bailey, Mo. Penitentiary, Jefferson City, to USG. "May it Please your Excellency; The undersigned—formerly a private member Co. A. 10th U. S. Cavalry, Colored Troop; but now a convict in the Missouri Penitentiary, by reason of a verdict rendered against him by a general Court Martial; 'convened at Fort Harker, Kansas, May the 28th 1868, pursuant to ~~general~~Special Orders No. 104, current series . . . and of which, Bvt Lieut Col. F W. Benteen, Capt 7th Cavalry U. S. A.' was President. begs submissively to lay before your Excellency The following Statement of facts, and to petition your Excellency to pardon, restore to liberty, and forever set free, the signer hereof,   I John Bailey am a Colored man, Enlisted in the 10th U. S. Cavalry after having served a term of enlistment, during the 'Slaveholders rebellion,' I deserted my regiment, on or about the 24th day of May 1868. Was apprehended on or about the 30th day May 1868, was tried; as before stated—and sentenced to serve,—

in the Penitentiary, at Jefferson City Missouri, the unexpired term of my
Enlistment. After have served a year and more, of my sentence, I appealed
to the War Department for a reduction of my sentence, which was, granted,
my sentenced being reduced to three (3) years of penal servitude; When
I left my Company, I accompanyed five Others, who induced me to go *with
them* They too were apprehended tried and sentenced, in the same manner and degree as my self—. Since the reduction of my sentence, two (2)
of the five, in whose company I deserted, *have been pardond* And I pray
that as our Offence was identicaly the same so may our punishment be
equal and alike. I have been imprisoned long enough to have discoverd my
folly, and to have become heartily ashamed of it. I have and do most bitterly
repent of my wrongdoing. Justice is satisfied, The law has been upheld,
and amply Vindicated, The Crimnal is a reformed man, and Mercy demands that, he be released. I have a much loved wife,—and To Small sisters, who are dependant upon me for their daily food, and who without my
assistance are reduced to a state of abgect poverty and misery—My wife
mourns for me in my degradation and absence. My child-Sisters are suffering for food, and are growing up in ignorance, for want of means to procure
the most limited education. I have no money, no powerfull friends to inter-
ceede for me, but I hope your Excellency, will *not* under such circumstances
refuse to hear, and answer, my prayer, for liberty. Should I be released, I
solemnly assure your Excellency that, I shall become a good, honest and
industrious Citisen; and that, your Excellency shall never have Occaison to
regret my release."—ALS (ellipses in original), DNA, RG 107, Letters
Received from Bureaus.

1870, SEPT. 13.   Daniel Macauley, mayor, Indianapolis, to USG. "Hon.
John N. Scott, City Judge of Indianapolis during the past two years, and
Major in the Vol. Service during the war is an applicant for the position of
Associate Justice in the United States Court for Wyoming Territory. He
was badly wounded during the war, is a man of excellent reputation and
attainments, a firm and valuable member of the Republican Party, a worthy
and capable Judge and one whom the Republicans here would delight to see
honored by the appointment."—ALS, DNA, RG 60, Records Relating to
Appointments. Related papers are *ibid*. No appointment followed.

1870, SEPT. 14.   George Opdyke, New York City, to USG. "Application
has been made to the Department of State by the friends of Genl. Chs. W.
leGendre, our Consul at Amoy, China, for his promotion to the Diplomatic
corps. Allow me to say a word about Genl. leGendre. He entered the Service in 1861, as Major of the 51st N. Y. V; for his brillant Services at
Roanoke Island, he was made one of the five land and naval officers who
were included in the resolutions of thanks of the people passed at the grand
meeting, at Cooper Institute, this city, on the 22 Feb 1862, of which, I beleive, the Hon. Secretary of State, Mr Fish, was an officer. At Newbern he
was almost fatally wounded in the front. Returning to the field, on his

recovery, he was again Severly wounded, in the Second battle of the Wilderness, whe he lost an eye by a rebel bullet. He was at the Siege of Vicksburgh, and his regiment was the first to enter Jackson, Miss. It was natural that such Services gradually and constantly caused him to be promoted, from a Major to the high rank from which peace in turn releived him. When he was in Hospital at Annapolis with his last wound, the march of Lee rendered it necessary that that city Should be put into a state of defense and that task devolved on him. You will remember that, at that time, the Maryland Convention was Sitting at Annapolis, and that, although they desired to flee to a place of safety, he adroitly prevented them doing so, and on the other hand, employed them in the defence. To his welltimed energy, the safety of Annapolis was to a great extent attributed; and President Lincoln spoke of it in terms of the highest praise. You are officially acquainted with his diplomatic Successes in Southern China; and I need allude to them only for the purpose of saying that they have Secured Substantial benefits to American Commerce, and have been most Satisfactory to other nations as well as our own. Under these circumstances I beg to commend Genl. LeGendre to your favorable consideration for appointment as Minister to Peru or Chilé or promotion to other fields where he can continue to Serve the country."—Copy, DNA, RG 59, Letters of Application and Recommendation. Related papers are *ibid.* On April 9, 1872, USG nominated Charles W. LeGendre as minister to Argentina, but the nomination was not confirmed. In Dec., LeGendre resigned as consul, Amoy, to become an advisor to the Japanese government.—*New York Times,* Jan. 28, 1873. On Jan. 25, 1873, Orville E. Babcock wrote to LeGendre. "I am indebted to you for two very interesting letters and should have written you before this had I not supposed from your first letter that you still expected to return to the U. S. I am glad you have such a nice position I know you can fill it—and I have no doubt [th]at in a little time the Japanese gov't will find [y]our services so valuable that you will be retained so long as you wish active life—I have read your long account with much pleasure, and have explained it to the President and also to Secty Fish. The President told me to send you his Congratulations and to wish you all success. The Secty of State has communicated with Minister Low [a]s you wished—and I trust you will find in him a kind support.—. . ."—ALS, DLC-Charles W. LeGendre. Related papers are *ibid.*; Babcock Papers, ICN.

1870, SEPT. 15.   To U.S. Senator Justin S. Morrill of Vt. from Long Branch declining to attend the Vt. state fair.—Paul C. Richards, Catalogue 4, no. 122.

1870, SEPT. 15.   U.S. Senator Lyman Trumbull of Ill., Chicago, to USG. "I had given Capt. N. Pope a letter to the Sec. of the Interior in regard to the Indian Superintendency of Montana before I knew of the appointment of Mr. Viall to that position and I now write to commend Capt. Pope for the Superintendency of Idaho which I understand to be vacant."—Copy, DLC-Lyman Trumbull. On Dec. 8, USG nominated Jasper A. Viall as superintendent of Indian affairs, Montana Territory, and Nathaniel Pope as superintendent of Indian affairs, New Mexico Territory.

1870, SEPT. 16.   John W. Hall, Goshen, Md., to USG. "I feel that to address you on the occasion, that caused me to grasp my pen this moring, is no more than right. I have contemplated deeply, to find what is the best means of accomplishplishing a good end, for Wisdom teaches:—choose the best means efor accomplishing the best end. Now then Sir, on visiting my reliatves, I find that they, with others of the neighborhood, have strove & are striving to rear a church, they have it wethr-boarded, and covered, and have had for a month, but but on account of cant git any way to have lumber hawled from Washington, here they have not finished it. And Sir, when I arri I arrived here, I found them so anxious and they are yet for learning, that I was so interrogated, ten &and 12 times a day to stay and teach for them, thus I gave them my promise after concidering the matter; and I thought to ask your approval was right. These people have not had any aid whatever eith ei in education, church building or other waise. We all hear that the Bureau do not pay and send out teachers any more, but we do not know it for cirtainly; therefore I interrogate you to know if is is so. And if it is; is it not wise in me to open private school. Rev. Mr. J. W. Alvoid gave me some books to distribute to poor children, on raising a school and I feel it my dudty to teach these my fellow counry men. I Please let me know what can be done, as or can not on the part of the Bureau, and what you think is the best way for me to proceed with raising this school. Sir, I have many contemplations of school hours; but believe to remain from there a while is just as well providing, I can git occupation for, as it is said I believe, that 'Education is not confined to College walls. D Direct Goshen Post-Office Montgomrey Co. Md. Believe me Sir, I am yours truly, with all the Sympathy due you as a worthy Pres."—ALS, DNA, RG 105, Letters Received.

1870, SEPT. 19.   Charles R. Brayton, Providence, R. I., to USG. "I beg to decline the appointment, as U. S. Consul at Cork, Ireland,—the state of my family affairs precluding my acceptance of it—Grateful for the honor done me, in naming me for so honorable a position—. . ."—ALS, DNA, RG 59, Letters of Resignation and Declination. On July 11, USG had nominated Brayton as consul, Cork. On Dec. 8, USG nominated Brayton as pension agent, Providence.

1870, SEPT. 19.   George Russel, Washington, Pa., to USG. "All the United States Officers here will vote against Capt Donly for Congress here this fall. Judge McKennan, Marshall Murdoch, Gared Hall Asst Marshall, James B. Ruple U. S. Assessor and all theer Sons, in all 11 or 12 votes, besides their influence—: If you have any influence with them you had better write to them. they are all your appointments"—ALS, Washington County Historical Society, Washington, Pa.

1870, SEPT. 20.   To Secretary of the Navy George M. Robeson from Long Branch. "Please suspend order relieving Port Admiral, New York Harbor until I return to Washington, and fu until further orders."—ALS, deCoppet Collection, NjP. On Sept. 19, USG had telegraphed to Robeson. "Suspend order relieving Port Admiral New York Harbor until I return Washington and until further orders"—Telegram received, DNA, RG 45, Letters Received from the President. Placed on the retired list in July, 1862, Rear Admiral Silas H. Stringham served as port admiral, New York City, from April, 1869, to June, 1872.

1870, SEPT. 20.   Brig. Gen. Oliver O. Howard to USG.   "*confidential* . . . Having some special work in Kentucky I have given Mr. Burbridge temporary employment at a small monthly allowance—His friends are very anxious for you to give him some employment—and now recommend him strongly for the position of *Surveyor General of Colorado*, in place of an alleged 'Johnson man.' I know you do not act from *personal policy*—but would not some honorable appointment for the General be *wise*—Gen. Runkle endorses him fully—His services from his *war* record & acts, fate him to persecution—You may have considered the case more fully than I have, but from several facts that were brought to me I have thought it best to write you—"—ALS (press), Howard Papers, MeB. Stephen G. Burbridge, former bvt. maj. gen. of vols., received no appointment. See *PUSG*, 7, 358; *ibid.*, 13, 18–21.

1870, SEPT. 20.   John Fitzgerald, National Soldiers Home, Dayton, to USG. "From the above, you will see that I am an inmate of said asylum. I will be seventy years of age, on the 21st of December next, and am no pensioner. I have fo[ur] little girls who depends entirely upon me for support. I had ten sons in the volunteer service, nine of whom were killed;— there wives securing their pensions.—and the tenth one, came home minus left arm. I had four in the 106 Illinois, and four besides myself in the 53 Illinois, and two the old seventh (7) Illinois. Now Genl what I want to know is this, Can you find me something that I can do in or[der] to support my little children, and send them to school. I can refer you to Govenor Palmer of Illinois, Col Cushman of the 53rd, Govenor Hays of Ohio, and numerous others, all of whom are well acquainted with me. Govenor Yates US. Senator from Illinois, now in Washington City, to whom I can also refer you to, has known me for a long time; and Genl I wish you would see him, and for the sake of my children try and do something for me, and your name shall ever be held with greatful rememberance."—ALS, DNA, RG 107, Appointment Papers.

1870, SEPT. 21.   W. H. D. Bowen, New York City, to USG. "I have the honor of submitting the enclosed diagram to your consideration It is the sectional View of an Explosive Cannon-Ball—Between its merits and demerits your excellency will doubtless discriminate, and I should consider myself only too fortunate to receive your opinion"—ALS, DNA, RG 156, Correspondence Concerning Inventions. The enclosure is *ibid.*

1870, SEPT. 23.   John Eaton, Jr., commissioner of education, to USG. "On my return here I learn there is some activity springing up at Memphis in regard to the appointment to me made to the office of appraiser created by late act of Congress, & lesst it should reach you in your absence and occasion some embarrassment I take the liberty to write you that papers with the recommendation of the member of Congress have been filed here in the Treasury in favor of Judge Barbour Lewis who has done so much for Republicanism there, & who will accept the office. I have much that I would like to say but must delay until I see you here. I notice the Democrats are trying to conduct a campaign under the pretext of regard for Farragut, hoping thereby to make some persons not specially favored with discrimination, believe that they are the special friends of dead soldiers & sailors, and that you the chief character of the war are jealous of the honor paid the old sailor."—ALS, DNA, RG 56, Appraiser of Customs Applications. On Feb. 7, 1871, USG nominated Barbour Lewis as appraiser of merchandise, Memphis.

1870, SEPT. 23.   Governor William W. Holden of N. C. to USG. "I learn that Capt. R. T. Frank of the 8th Infantry has applied to be transferred to the Artillery or Cavalry arm of the Service, under the new army bill. He prefers the Artillery. Capt. Frank has seen considerable service in the Southern Department, and has acquitted himself well under trying circumstances. He is, in all respects, so far as I can judge, an excellent Officer. He has conducted himself so well and has performed such important services in this State, that I trust you will pardon the liberty I take in requesting, as I do most respectfully that you will order the transfer which he desires." —LS, DNA, RG 94, ACP, F41 CB 1870; ADfS, Duke University, Durham, N. C. On Dec. 15, Capt. Royal T. Frank, 8th Inf., transferred to the 1st Art. Related papers, including a USG endorsement of Nov. 4, 1865, approving bvt. promotion for Frank, are in DNA, RG 94, ACP, F41 CB 1870.

1870, SEPT. 23.   David X. Junkin, First Presbyterian Church, New Castle, Pa., to USG. "Understanding that THOMAS HENRY Esq, of this city, is an applicant for the appointment of CONSUL, at the port of Canton China, I take the liberty of saying that Mr Henry is, in my judgment, *well qualified* for the position. He is a member of the Lawrence County bar—is a gentleman of good mind and education—of upright character, sober, discreet and attentive to business, and I think will make a good officer. His grand-father represented this District in congress for many years previous to 1844, his father was prominent as the republican candidate for nomination, at the pending election; and the applicant himself is worthy of your confidence. He was a major in the Union army, and behaved gallantly. His appointment would gratify a large body of your friends; whilst the friends of Christian Missions, will be glad to have at that station, a gentleman whose Christian morality will not dishonour our holy Religion."—ALS, DNA, RG 59, Letters of Application and Recommendation. Related papers are *ibid*. No appointment followed.

1870, SEPT. 26.   Charles J. Smith, Rochelle, Va., to USG. "I respectfully transmit to you through the mail, an application for a consulate, and proceed to furnish the reasons which, I hope, will be considered sufficient to support it. I am a naturalized american citizen of English birth, 52 years old, have been a resident of this section of Va since 1836, and a citizen since 1850, having come to this country when 18 ys old. In 1861, though differing in no way way else from the people here, I maintained my allegiance to the federal powers, and consequently became the object of rebel persecution. Judicially & mobbishly, I was hunted with unmitigated fury till I was forced, in the night of the 4th thursday in may, I was compelled to seek safety in flight and became a refugee. . . . If you have the report of the adjutant Genl of Penna. at hand, you will find my name as a medical officer commissioned, and assigned to the 69th Penna. Vet Vols. 3rd Brig 2nd Div. 2nd Corps. My usefulness & capacity in the federal Army may be judged by the Genl Orders, which I have in my possession, detailing me to duty first to the Second Div Field Hosp at Patrick's Station & subsequently to the Genl Depot Field Hospl at city point. In any loyal state or people, I could experience a pride at being present with my Regimt at the surrender of Lee, but, here 'tis a crime and I have been made to feel it. I was mustered out with my Regt near Munson's Hill on the 10th July 1865, & finally disbanded at Camp Cadwallader on the 15th, where I had to bid adieu to as brave a set of fellows as you had in your army, again to experience the horrors of lonely & unprotected loyalty, and to find my home dismantled & my property pillaged & destroyed, the federal troops under Genl Sheridan participating. I sought, through the Bureau of Refugees to reclaim some of my property which I found. The Bureau could not interfere. I applied to the military authorities. They referred me to the courts. This I regarded as nonsense, & designed only to relieve themselves of a little trouble, & to worry me into an acquiescence with the existing chaotic condition of things. I soon saw that I could receive no redress. My time & means were being wasted hunting what I was destined never to find, viz the aid of a government. The rebels derided, defied, and threatened me; telling me 'when the yankees give us back what they stole from us, we will give you back what we took from you.' I abandoned the whole thing in disgust, and concluded, as the rebels would not reciprocate in a business way, to try to make a living

for my family by manal labor upon my house less & ruined farm. For five years I have been lost sight of by the government I defended, & for 5 years I have been subjected to the most abject slavery, the only recognition of my being a citizen being in the collection of taxes from me, and in a summons from the overseer to work with my spade upon the road. Mr President I hope it will be your pleasure to redeem me from this Siberian bondage . . ."
—ALS, DNA, RG 59, Letters of Application and Recommendation. Related papers are *ibid.* No appointment followed.

1870, Sept. 30.   Mary E. Coffee, Burnet, Tex., to USG and Secretary of the Treasury George S. Boutwell. "I respectfully ask leave to state to you the grievance & wrong, my husband 'W. B. Coffee' sufferred from the United States Government. The said W. B, Coffee was a true and loyal citizen of the United States, as has been proven in the Census Office; In the year 1859 he was appointed Deputy Marshal for the western district of Texas; his Census work comprised the Counties of Burnet, San Saba, Mason, Menard, Concho & McCulloch,   for the four last named Counties, neither he or any other person has recieved any payment or satisfaction in any form whatever   The said W. B. Coffee hired a man to go with him through the four Counties of Mason, Menard, Concho and McCulloch, on account of the danger from Indians, and suffered many hardships in doing the work, but the work was done and the returns made out and mailed. The said W. B. Coffee's life at this time was in great danger from the fury of the Rebels, who way-laid & threatned his life, from the commencement of the war, 'till he left the Country and took refuge in New Orleans after it was taken by the Federals & where he remained until the suppression of the Rebellion. After peace was made the said W. B. Coffee returned to Texas, and recieved from A. J. Hamilton Provisional Governor of Texas the appointment of State agent to collect, cotton,—wool, horses, mules &c belonging to the State. With much trouble, after expending, five hundred and fifty dollars of his own money, he got possession of one hundred and five bales of cotton, belonging to the State of Texas, the United States Officers siezed this cotton, and left him without compensation. W. B. Coffee's contract with Gov Hamilton was that he should recieve, one fourth of the proceeds of all State property collected by him,   Cotton at the time of the seizure was worth, from 25 to 28 cts pr lb, the bales weighing from 5 to 6 hundred lbs pr bale. The said W. B. Coffee was in Washington City in the winter of /67 trying to get something on this claim, and finally was offered eleven hundred and sixty dollars, which necessity compelled him to recieve; his property was destroyed after he left Texas during the rebellion and his family treated with much indignity,   from these causes and other troubles and hardships connected with the rebellion he died insane not long after his return from Washington,   his widow and orphan were left destitute,   since the Census work of 1860, they have suffered for food and raiment, and now by the work of my own hands I procure the necessaries of life. I made appliance to Mr M. C. Hamilton U. S. Senator from Texas to revive this matter for me but he refused to have any thing to do with it   I humbly beg you as the Head of the Govt to bring these remembrances, before the next Congress, to whom I appeal for justice and relief. . . . I hope for information if not asking too much"—ALS, DNA, RG 56, Cotton and Captured and Abandoned Property Records.

1870, OCT. 1.   USG endorsement. "Let the within named officers be assigned to duty as within mentioned till further orders from the Secretary of the Navy"—ES, DNA, RG 45, Letters Received from the President. Written on a document of Oct. 4 assigning twelve naval officers on the retired list to duty.—DS, *ibid.*

1870, OCT. 1.   To James T. Ely, Chicago. "In accepting your resignation as Assistant Private Secretary, tendered to take effect at the close of the present month, I am happy to recognize the ability, integrity and efficiency with which you have discharged the duties of the position"—Copy, DLC-USG, II, 1. On Nov. 14, 1868, Governor Richard J. Oglesby of Ill. had written to USG. "James T. Ely, of Chicago will hand you this note   should you have time for a few moments conversation with him he will in full explain his object—and wishes—All I desire to say is that Mr Ely is a gentleman of high personal character—of strict integrity who understands the obligations of a private relation,—iIn his profession he is an expert—I have no hesitation in recommending him to your favorable notice—"—ALS, OFH.

1870, OCT. 2.   A. J. Smith, Harrisonville, Ill., to USG. "I take the Pleasure to write you a few lines to inform you that I am a Soldier of your Command in the W̶west and have voted for you at the Last Electtion to which you was Elected Cheif Exective of our Country and I See in Some of the Papers that we are intiled to Land warrant and iff So I wish you would give Some information about the matter as wee only one Claim agent our Conty and he is a man that was oppesed to Subperesing the Rebilion and I Dont to give him half of the worth of my Dues to me of the Country   if you will Sent me the address to who has the ishuing of Land warrants I Can have my discharge filled out By a gustice of the Peace and Send them myself as would Like to go west this winter and Lay my Land in Kansas Before the valuable Land is takeing up . . . Later   it asking a great deal of you But as I am Cripled I Like to Save the 15 Dollars which have to Pay the Claim agent   So if I have the name of officer that autherised to ishu the warrants I Can Sent him my Dicharges"—ALS, DNA, RG 48, Lands and Railroads Div., Letters Received.

1870, OCT. 3.   Andrew J. Mock, Sun Cliff, Pa., to USG. "I have this Morning taken the opprtunity of Asking you what the law is one the soldiers land wheather they must Stay on the land A certin lengh of time to secure it or not or weather the goverment will give him A title for 160 Achres by going and picking A pice where ever it suits him best   I am A soldier was

drafted in the fall of 64, and was in the Servic 5 month   I got nothing
but my monthly pay   Mr president I never saw you but once that time I
seen you riding fast our hospital at washing   I was wounded was int in the
fight at petersburgh   I belonged to the 45 Pa Regiment   therefore if you
will let me know what the law is and how A Soldier must improve his land
to secure it I would like it very much   Nothing more at present . . . Please
let me know the whole state of affairs"—ALS, DNA, RG 48, Lands and
Railroads Div., Miscellaneous, Letters Received.

1870, OCT. 4.   To Fred Bertsch, Cincinnati. "I am in receipt of your letter
of the 29th ult. informing me of my election as an honorary member of the
Am. Sharpshooter's Society and inviting me to be present at the festival
this month. I accept with pleasure the membership in your Society but regret
that my public duties will not permit me to be absent from the capital at
this time."—Copy, DLC-USG, II, 1.

1870, OCT. 4.   To Theodore Cook. "I am in receipt of your letter of Sept.
10th. inviting me to attend the sittings of the Southern Commercial Convention to be held in Cincinnati during the present month. It would afford
me great pleasure to be able to be present, but my public duties will not
permit me to leave the capital at this time. I earnestly hope the convention
may be successful in the object of its meeting and that the interests of commerce may be greatly benefitted by its deliberations."—Copy, DLC-USG,
II, 1.

1870, OCT. 4.   To Edward McMurdy, president, Industrial Exhibition
Co. "I am in receipt of your letter of the 1st ult. informing me that I have
been elected one of the Regents of your Institution. I accept with pleasure
the position and hope that the undertaking may meet with the success which
it deserves."—Copy, DLC-USG, II, 1. McMurdy sought private and public
funds to build an exhibition hall in New York City, but the project failed
amidst accusations of fraud. See *New York Times*, Nov. 6, 1873; April 10,
1876.

1870, OCT. 4.   F. Montgomery, editor, *Logan (Ohio) Republican*, to USG.
"In the matter of the appointment of Marshal for Southern Ohio, everything
is going on encouragingly for Col. F. F. Rempel. You will remember you
promised at Long Branch to give us all the time we needed. Senator Sherman
has made us the same promise, and requested me to visit you again on the
subject, which I may do. In the meantime, if you will give us the opportunity
we will show you that Col. Rempel is by all m odds the choice of the people
for the office"—ALS, DNA, RG 60, Records Relating to Appointments.
No appointment followed. Papers recommending Ferdinand F. Rempel for
a consulship are *ibid.*, RG 59, Letters of Application and Recommendation.
On Dec. 3, 1872, USG nominated Rempel as postmaster, Logan.

1870, OCT. 5.   Governor Harrison Reed of Fla. to USG. "It becomes my imperative duty to inform you that in several counties of this State the officers of the law are overawed & civil government set at defiance by organized bands of enemies of the government, & that these organizations are incited by political demagogues to prevent the people from a free exercise of their rights of suffrage. It will be impossible without the aid of a Military force to secure a fair vote at the election in November. The employment of State Militia will only exasperate & extend the evil. I am compelled therefore to request that you order to this State immediately at least five companies of Federal Soldiers, under command of energetic & faithful officers to be subject to my disposition for not exceeding four weeks, to be used as a police force to protect the people against violence in the discharge of their duties as freemen at the polls on the 8th November."—ALS, DNA, RG 94, Letters Received, 1240 1870. On Nov. 1, U.S. Senator Thomas W. Osborn of Fla., Tallahassee, telegraphed to USG. "Governor is absent   Adjutant General of Georgia telegraphs he has no orders to send troops to Florida   shall we have them   it is very important"—Telegram received (at 6:10 P.M.), *ibid.* Gen. William T. Sherman endorsed this telegram. "Recent orders have taken every company in Dept of the South so that only one company of Inf. is in ~~Kentucky~~ Tennessee one Company in Mississipi—two in Kentucky 4 in Georgia—& 6 in S Carolina—16 in Alabama   Shall any go from Alabama to Florida?—"—AES, *ibid.* On Nov. 2, Bvt. Maj. Gen. Edward D. Townsend also endorsed this telegram. "This being submitted to the President, he decides that there are no troops available which can be sent to Florida, all being fully employed at places of great importance   So inform Senator Osborne."—AES, *ibid.* On Nov. 4, Osborn, Jacksonville, Fla., telegraphed to Secretary of War William W. Belknap. "If we can have the support we expected we shall carry the state   if not the probabilities are decidedly against us and many assassinations will be committed"—Telegram received (at 8:30 P.M.), *ibid.* On Nov. 5, Sherman telegraphed to Maj. Gen. Henry W. Halleck, Louisville. "The President orders that you send immediately two Companies from the neighborhood of NewOrleans to Tallahassee to report to the U. S. Marshall for Election week & then to return to their post—"—ALS (telegram sent), *ibid.* On Nov. 17, Reed wrote to USG. "Through treachery & intimidation a republican majority of over 10.000 has been overcome & the Democrats or rebels now proclaim their purpose to seize the government by violence, depose the Executive, by assassination if necessary, & drive from the state all leading republicans. Two companies of infantry sent us to secure the execution of the Enforcement law would have saved us. I now most respectfully ask that you order to this state for our protection one full regiment of U. S. troops to remain here until the Legislature adjourns in February. The capitol is liable at any time to be seized by armed hords of outlaws & unless you extend *immediate* assistance we cannot sustain Republican government in Florida . . . P. S. All action must remain secret until the troops are on the ground."—ALS, *ibid.* On Nov.

22, Belknap wrote to Reed. "In reply to your letter of the 17th inst to the President asking military protection for the State Capitol during the session of the Legislature I beg to inform you that orders have this day been given for stationing two companies of troops at Tallahassee, wh. number it is hoped will be sufficient, as a greater number cannot be withdrawn from other stations."—Df, *ibid.* Related papers are *ibid.*

1870, OCT. 5. William T. Spence *et al.*, Savannah, to USG. "We the undersigned delegates to the Republican Convention to Nominate candidates for Congress in the 1st Congl District in Order to secure harmony as well as to Express the wishes of a large Majority of the Republicans in that Vicinity, do respectfully, but Earnestly, recomend the appointment of C. P. Goodyear, Collector of Customs for the District of Brunswick. He is prompt, energetic, Capable and of sound integrity."—DS (14 signatures), DNA, RG 56, Collector of Customs Applications. On Jan. 11, 1871, USG nominated Charles P. Goodyear as collector of customs, Brunswick, Ga., but withdrew the nomination on Jan. 19.

1870, OCT. 7. Horace Porter to Secretary of the Navy George M. Robeson. "I am directed by the President to say that the attendance of the Marine Band at the grounds of the Executive Mansion, will not be required again this season."—LS, DNA, RG 45, Letters Received from the President.

1870, OCT. 8. U.S. Representative Halbert E. Paine of Wis., Milwaukee, to USG. "I am advised that Hon. A. G. Miller, Judge of the U. S. District Court, for the Eastern District of Wisconsin, will probably soon resign, in accordance with the provisions of the recent Act of Congress; and that he may possibly do so on, or before, the reassembling of Congress in December. For more than five years it has been, and still is, my earnest wish to succeed Judge Miller, whenever he shall see fit to resign; and, upon his resignation, I shall make formal application for the appointment. I take occasion to inform you of this *now* because I shall have no previous notice of the time of his resignation, and a new appointment might be decided upon without knowledge of my intended application and before the presentation of my own papers."—ALS, PHi. On Nov. 18, 1873, Paine, Washington, D. C., wrote a similar letter to USG.—ALS, NNP. A letter of Dec. 1, 1870, from U.S. Representative James A. Garfield of Ohio to USG recommending Paine as judge, court of claims, is in DLC-James A. Garfield. No appointment followed.

1870, OCT. 10. USG endorsement. "Refered to the Sec. of War."—AES, DNA, RG 107, Letters Received from Bureaus. Written on a letter of Aug. 30 from Morris Downs, Washington, D. C., to Bvt. Maj. Gen. Joseph K. Barnes, surgeon gen., requesting "to be enlisted in the general service United States Army, for duty as messenger or Watchman, . . ."—ALS, *ibid.*

1870, OCT. 12. USG endorsement. "Refered to the Atty. Gn. to know if U. S. Commissioners are subject to removal."—AES, DNA, RG 60, Letters from the President. Written on a letter of Oct. 7 from Governor Joseph W. McClurg of Mo. to USG. "I herewith enclose a letter from J. R. Winchell one of the Editors of the Hannibal Courier, a most excellent and most reliable gentleman, true republican &c. You will see that it relates to a case about which I telegraphed. The name however is not 'Gern' as I had it, but *Moses P Green.* Mr Winchell's letter explains the case. The acts or words of disloyalty were known to one of the registrars and the Board were *required by the law* to place him Dodge on the rejected list, which was done. For this Green, U. S. Commr caused the arrest &c of the registrars. I presume they will in few days be properly released. *My object* now is to suggest the removal of Green if it can be. I have not been able to see the law as to appointments & removals in such cases—But I forbear making any further suggestions, knowing that, with the facts before you, whatever can be done will be speedily done that the registrars may resume their work and complete it in time for the election. Should *Green* be sustained, we may look for like interference in one half or more of the Counties in the State."—ALS, *ibid.* The enclosure is *ibid.*

1870, OCT. 15. To Governor Rufus B. Bullock of Ga. "Please express my regrets to the Legislature of Georgia at not being able to accept their invitation to attend the State Fair at Atlanta. My duties will not admit of so long an absence from Washington at this time."—Copy, DLC-USG, II, 5. The letter, dated Oct. 17, is printed in *Chicago Times,* Oct. 22, 1870. On Oct. 14, Attorney Gen. Amos T. Akerman had written to USG. "I send you a dispatch just received from Gov. Bullock. On every personal and political account, I should be delighted for you to visit Georgia. I go tonight to New York for Mrs. Akerman, to return Monday. Please answer Gov. B's telegram"—ALS, OFH.

1870, OCT. 15. U.S. Senator Thomas F. Bayard of Del. to USG protesting plans for use of U.S. troops during the election. "I denounce as a slander any allegation that necessity exists or can exist for so offensive an invasion of our State laws."—William Evarts Benjamin, Catalogue No. 42, March, 1892, p. 4.

1870, OCT. 15. U.S. Representative Robert C. Schenck of Ohio, Dayton, to USG. "Judge Leavitt, of the U. S. Dist. Court for the Southern Dist. of Ohio, has confidentially informed a friend of his & mine in Cincinnati, that in January, on account of his advanced age, he means to avail himself of the law which permits him to retire from the Bench; & he is desirous that this friend should succeed him. I take the liberty, in his behalf, of writing to ask whether you have contemplated the probability of such a vacancy, & in that case made up your mind as to the person to be appointed. The gentleman I refer to does not wish to present his name or testimonials, nor to have his friends in Ohio make any movement with a view to asking his appointment unless the question of selection remains entirely open."—ALS, OFH. On Oct. 20, Orville E. Babcock wrote to Schenck. "I am directed by the President to acknowledge the receipt of your letter of the 15th, and to say in reply that there are many recommendations, in anticipation of the retirement of Judge Leavitt but the matter is entirely open."—Copy, DLC-USG, II, 1.

On April 12, 1869, James Loudon, Georgetown, Ohio, had written to USG. "I notice that Congress has passed a Law Reconstructing the Courts. I suspect that some of the old Judges will avail themselves of the provisions of this Law and retire from the Bench & among them I should expect Judge Levit of Ohio to do so, as he is a very old man. If that should occur I should be pleased to see Col D. W. C. Loudon occupy Judge Levits place. . . ."— ALS, DNA, RG 60, Records Relating to Appointments. On Dec. 23, Governor Rutherford B. Hayes of Ohio wrote to USG. "I am personally acquainted with Phillip B Swing of Batavia and know his reputation as a lawyer. He is an upright and honorable gentleman and a learned and able lawyer. He is recognised by his brethren of the bar in Southern Ohio as a man whose personal character and professional ability and knowledge fit him to fill creditably and acceptably an important judicial position."—ALS, *ibid.* Related papers are *ibid.* On March 29, 1871, USG nominated Philip B. Swing as judge, Southern District, Ohio, in place of Humphrey H. Leavitt. See *PUSG*, 15, 555; *ibid.*, 16, 377–78.

On Aug. 13, 1869, Jesse Root Grant, Covington, Ky., had written to USG. "I understand that Judge Carter of Cin, will be an applicant for the district Judge ship in the southern district of Ohio when vacated by Judge Levit After Phillip Swing, for whom I entertain the very highest personal consideration, I know no man that I would prefer for that situation than Judge Carter—The Judge is a native of Cincinnati—has served ten years on the Bench—And as far as I know or have ever heared has given general & universal satisfaction to all concerned"—ALS, DNA, RG 60, Records Relating to Appointments. On Nov. 19, George W. Morgan, Mount Vernon, Ohio, wrote to USG. "I have known the Hon A. G. W. Carter, whose name is presented to Your Excellency for one of the associate Judgeships, and join with his numerous friends in cordially commending him to your consideration. He is not only a good lawyer, but a gentleman of fine culture and would adorn the position to which he aspires."—ALS, NNP. On Dec. 21, A. G. W. Carter, Cincinnati, wrote to USG. "I am informed by the telegrams from Washington that there is, or there is about to be a vacancy in the office of *Chief Justice of Washington Territory*; and I write this respectfully to say, that I would gladly accept the appointment if you would be pleased to tender it to me.—You are aware that my application for appointment as Circuit U. S. Judge has been pending before you, but as I see you have given the place to another, I shall rest quite satisfied if I should be so fortunate to obtain from your hands a judicial office in one of the Territories. Hoping to receive favorable consideration, . . ."—ALS, DNA,

RG 60, Appointments, Washington Territory. On Oct. 13, 1870, Carter
wrote to USG. "As I am an applicant to you for the position of U. S. Judge
of this Southern District of Ohio, in the event of the retiring of Judge
Leavitt I enclose to you two additional letters,—one from Gov. R. B. Hayes
of this state, and the other from your father. Both of these letters were voluntarily offerred and I feel quite happy in being so recommended. I shall
esteem myself fortunate indeed, if I receive this appointment at the hands
of a President whom I so much admire and respect."—ALS, *ibid.*, Records
Relating to Appointments. The enclosures are *ibid.* On March 6, 1871,
Carter wrote to USG. "As you are aware, my name is before you as a candidate for the position of United States Judge of this District soon to be
made vacant by the resignation of Judge Leavitt. He told me a few days
ago that he would retire from his office, during next month, and in our conversation expressed himself formally to me as his successor; though he said,
from motives of delicacy he was unwilling to take any active part. . . ."—
ALS, *ibid.*

On Nov. 30, 1870, Leavitt, Cincinnati, had written to USG. "Some
days since, at the request of my friend, Gen. N. C. McLean, I took the liberty of addressing your Excellency a letter, stating that the General's name,
among many others, might be submitted to you, for the office of Judge for
this District, when it should become vacant. To avoid any misconstruction
of my letter, I beg leave to say, that in endorsing Gen. McLean, as a worthy
and honourable gentleman, and a respectable member of the Bar, I did not
say, or intend to say, he was superior in fitness for the place, to others whose
names will be presented to your Excellency. I could not consistently have
done this. You may perhaps remember, that in the brief interview I had
the honor to have with your Excellency, at Long Branch, in September last,
I expressed my preference for the Hon. R. M. Corwine for the judgeship.
And my views have undergone no change since. . . ."—ALS, *ibid.* On
March 17, 1871, Joseph H. Barrett and Benjamin Eggleston, *Cincinnati
Chronicle*, wrote to USG. "*Personal.* . . . Understanding that a nomination
for District Judge in place of Judge Leavitt, resigned, will soon be sent
to the Senate, we beg leave to ask your earnest consideration of what we
believe to be the nearly unanimous opinion of your true political friends
here—in regard to the generally anticipated appointment of Philip B.
Swing. We assure you, in all kindness, that it will be an unpopular and
distasteful appointment here—to the bar in general, and to the influential
Republicans to whom you must look for support. If you have been assured
otherwise, permit us to say in all frankness, you have not been candidly
dealt with in regard to it. There is already much disaffection—permit us
to say in all freedom and plainness of language—in regard to some appointments already made here, and we greatly fear the effect of adding now that
of Mr. Swing. That we are actively your friends, with no favors to seek for
ourselves personally, we trust you understand so well as to give us credit
for entirely proper motives in what we have thus made bold to say. We had
thought it not improbable that your mind would incline favorably towards

Hon. Richard M. Corwine, as Judge Leavitt's successor; and of course we have at this moment no knowledge but that such has been all the while your preference. He is universally regarded as an able lawyer; as District Attorney formerly he is entirely familiar with the practice of the District Court; he is one of your warmest and most faithful friends; and his appointment—whatever adverse opinion you may have heard from any quarter—will be regarded with favor. We beg you to consider whether it is not the best possible selection to be made, under all the circumstances, and at this particular juncture. Not presuming to trespass upon you further in this matter, and cordially desiring the continued success of your Administration, . . ." —LS, *ibid.*

On Jan. 5, Manning F. Force, Cincinnati, had written to USG. "A gentleman, a member of the bar here, has asked if I would be willing that a representation should be made to you, suggesting me for the District Judge in case Judge Leavitt should resign. He said he understood that such an application would be agreeable to you. His reason for saying so was, that a gentleman in New York lately remarked, you had said you were prepared to appoint me to that office, but desired a recommendation from half a dozen responsible persons in Cincinnati. It is true that a judgeship is the only office I care to hold in time of peace. It is also true that such an office should not be solicited. A judge should freely take his oath of office—to administer justice without fear and without favor. For that reason, whenever members of the bar have asked me if they should take any steps to forward my name, I have discouraged them.—For a double reason. If I should be appointed upon their recommendation after consulting me, a sense of obligation might impair my absolute impartiality. If I should not be appointed, their effort in my behalf might bring upon them the displeasure of the successful applicant. But if this report is correct, the matter stands differently. If you are ready of your own mind to make the appointment but only desire confirmation of your purpose from trustworthy persons here, I would feel that I owed the place to your spontaneous pleasure, not to their efforts; and, besides, in that case, the persons who recommended would run no risk of incurring ill will. I have therefore requested the gentlemen who have spoken to me to do nothing unless there should be some assurance that such action would be agreeable to you. If the Attorney General should write to responsible persons here, or to the judges of the Supreme Court of the State, or the governor, perhaps the most trustworthy information could be obtained. This is speaking to the President pretty frankly, but I am sure it is not disrespectful."—ALS, *ibid.*

On Feb. 4, Aaron F. Perry, Cincinnati, wrote to USG. "I send herewith a number of letters and testimonials of the character and abilities of Hon. R. B. Warden. He is a man of excellent intelligence, fine abilities and pure character, capable of filling any place at the Bar or on the Bench with credit to himself and the community. He has held the office of Judge of Common Pleas in this county: the office of Reporter of the Supreme Court of the State, and of Judge of the Supreme Court of the State and is yet comparitively a young man, with full capacity for labor. He is a good and successful speaker, both at the Bar, and on the stump. He has not, I understand, called your attention to any appointment which he would like. But I speak without mental reserve, when I say that I think he can be of great service in our public affairs, if encouraged to try by some adequate token of appreciation. His private circumstances are not such as to permit of his giving much time to public affairs, unless in a situation to derive some benefit from his services. The District Judgeship of the Central district, should such District be formed, or of this District, would no doubt be pleasant to him. I would not hesitate to recommend him for either place. I am aware, however, that you have in mind for this District, another man, to whose appointment I neither feel nor wish to make opposition: and also aware that I have no claims to meddle in the Central District. I can, however, thus place before you my estimate of the character and influence of Judge Warden and commend the subject to your favorable recollection. . . . P. S. I have concluded for the present not to send the letters referred to." —ALS, *ibid.* On Feb. 16, Robert B. Warden, Cincinnati, wrote to USG. "My friend, Mr. Perry, informs me that he has directed the attention of your Excellency to the supposed fitness of the undersigned to be put into some place of public service. . . . I have thought, from what I have seen in the papers, that it may happen, or that it may already have happened, that it is may soon be the duty of your Excellency to think of selecting a proper person to be Commissioner of Patents. The accidents of my life, some of my habits and tastes, and some of my studies in art and science, not to speak particularly of my legal studies, have led me to believe, that I could be of public service in that office, of which some of the duties are at least quasi-judicial. While I would prefer to have a judgeship, I fear that that can not be; and if I could secure your good opinion for the place I have named, and if an appointment for that place has to be considered, I have, after much reflection, come to the conclusion that to suggest my name as above, might not seem immodest or otherwise improper. But, in spite of the private need I have mentioned, I would not ask an office on that account." —ALS, *ibid.*, RG 48, Letters Received.

1870, OCT. 18. To Ferdinand Dupré, Manchester, England. "I take pleasure in acknowledging the receipt of your work the 'Rationale of Hygiene' which has safely reached me, and have to request you to accept my thanks for your kind consideration."—Copy, DLC-USG, II, 1. Dupré had written *The Rationale of the Application of Hygiene, the Principles of Health, to the Prevention and Elimination of Disease . . .* (Manchester, 1869).

1870, OCT. 18. To A. D. Gale, New Lebanon, N. Y. "I have received the set of harness you were so kind as to send me and have to request you to accept my sincere thanks for it. It is of very fine workmanship and pleases me very much."—Copy, DLC-USG, II, 1.

1870, OCT. 21. To Edward Harris, Woonsocket, R. I. "Through the politeness of Mr Holden, I am in receipt of the beautiful piece of cassimere of your manufacture. I am glad to see that such fine work is done by Americans and I hope the day is not far distant when we shall be able to equal the world in all sorts of clothes and be able not only to supply the home demand but to export. With many thanks for your kindness, . . ."— Copy, DLC-USG, II, 1. Born in 1801, Harris was a prominent textile manufacturer and philanthropist.

1870, OCT. 22. Columbus Delano, commissioner of Internal Revenue, to USG. "I have the honor to transmit a report of J. B. Wass to Supervisor S. B. Dutcher dated October 18th, in reference to an effort made by him with twenty-four assistants Assessors to destroy certain illicit distilleries in Brooklyn, and also a communication to this Office made by Supervisor Dutcher dated October 21st recommending the employment of a military force of not less than five hundred men to assist the civil authorities in suppressing illicit distillation in Brooklyn. N. Y. These reports induce me to recommend that you will comply with the request of Supervisor Dutcher and place under his directions the military force which he suggests for the purposes therein stated. Without this force I am satisfied that illicit distillation in that City will go on as heretofore. My opinion is that feeble and insufficient efforts such as have been heretofore made tend to increase rather than diminish the flagrant violations of law which have defied all efforts hitherto made."—LS, DNA, RG 94, Letters Received, 698A 1869. Related papers are *ibid.*

1870, OCT. 22. George E. Welles, assessor of Internal Revenue, Toledo, to USG. "Understanding that the term of Office. of Gen'l Patrick S Slevin as collector of Customs at this Port will expire during this winter. I write for the purpose of saying that in my opinion he should be reappointed. I have known the General intimately since I was a Boy first as a prominent Lawyer. and subsequently. as a brave and gallant soldier in command of the 100th Regt of Ohio Vol Infantry, with which he served with distinction in the 23rd Army Corps, until in August 64, in front of Atlanta where in leading a charge upon the Enemies works He was severely wounded and permanently disabled but rejoined his command as soon as able, and seved until the close of the war . . ."—ALS, DNA, RG 56, Collector of Customs Applications. Related papers are *ibid.* On March 10, 1871, USG nominated Patrick S. Slevin for reappointment as collector of customs, Miami District, Ohio.

1870, OCT. 24. Walter R. Gregory *et al.*, Becker County, Minn., to USG. "The undersigned citizens of the newly settled county of Becker, in the State of Minnesota, would respectfully but earnestly represent to Your Excellency that during the whole summer and fall we have suffered from the depredations of roving indians from the different bands of the Chippewa nation north of us,   Our prairies have been repeatedly fired by them, and great quantities of hay destroyed, leaving settlers without any provision for their stock, during our long and severe winter. Houses have been robbed and families terrified, till citizens leave their homes only to have their households in a state of continual fear and suspense   These outrages culminated last evening in the robbery and probably murder of Mr Gunner Carlesen, one of our best citizens. . . ."—DS (105 signatures), DNA, RG 75, Letters Received, Chippewa Agency.

1870, OCT. 25.   USG endorsement. "Approved."—ES, DNA, RG 75, Letters Received, Miscellaneous. Written on a letter of Oct. 24 from Ely S. Parker, Indian commissioner, to Secretary of the Interior Jacob D. Cox. "I have the honor to recommend that the President be requested, under the 6th Section of the 'Act making appropriations for the current and contingent expenses of the Indian Department,' &c. approved July 15, 1870. to discontinue the Idaho, Nevada, Wyoming, Dakota, Utah and Colorado Superintendencies; and that the Fort Hall Agency, in Idaho, and the Shoshonee and Bannock Agency, in Wyoming, be attached to the Montana Superintendency; the Nez Percé Agency, in Idaho, to the Oregon Superintendency; the Agencies in Nevada, to the California Superintendency; the Agencies in Colorado with the Uintah Agency in Utah, to the New Mexico Superintendency; and that the several Agents in Dakota, be authorized to report direct to this Office."—LS, *ibid.*

1870, OCT. 26.   Secretary of the Navy George M. Robeson to USG. "I have the honor to submit, herewith, for your signature, warrants for carpenters H. R. Philbrick and John L. Davis and Sailmaker George F. Douglass, of the Navy, all of whom have performed the probationary period required at sea."—Copy, DNA, RG 45, Letters Sent.

1870, OCT. 27.   USG endorsement. "Refered to the Sec. of the Navy with whom Lt McClure's business is."—AES, DNA, RG 45, Miscellaneous Case Files. Written on a letter of Oct. 24 from William McKennan, Washington, Pa., to USG. "This note is to introduce Lieut. George M. McClure, of the Navy, who will hand it to you—My close relations with some of Lieut. McClures connections in Allegheney Co., where his family resides, furnish me with such means of knowledge of him as enable me to say that, by reason both of his professional merit and service and his personal character, he is altogether worthy of your confidence—"—ALS, *ibid.* An Oct. 1868 report of a board of examiners denying promotion to Lt. George M. McClure is *ibid.* McClure was placed on the retired list as of Nov. 9, 1868.

1870, OCT. 29.   Louis Foy to USG. "I have tried in every way as a poor colored man to get justice of the Courts of my [su]it that is wanted justices to try my case but because [I] was a colored man they would not, and I wish to appeal to you as my President [to] let my case be tried under the civil rights bill, I was badly beaten and shot in my [o]wn house by some white Rebels in *Terrell, Co, Geo,* (I own there twenty acres of land, a mule, stock &c and had a good crop) Living next to a Justice of the Peac[e] who was not at home (but if he had been would not have protected me) went over to a Justice of the Peace in Lee, Co, Geo who the second night after I was there being present allowed the *Klu Klux* to come and take me down to a bridge at night Two miles off, and shoot me *through* and *through* and when I fall off into the creek 15 feet below in the dark I drift off a mile they still shooting at me and I crawl to a frinds who cares for me and I am able to slip off to this point, wont you order the Marshall here Maj Wm H. Smythe U. S. Marsha[ll] or Judge John Pope U. S. Dist Atty to arrest my persecutors and try them &c. as I am too poor to go to any expence. I am here on the place of Col J. N. Griffins"—ALS, DNA, RG 60, Letters from the President.

1870, OCT. 31. To Dmitrii G. Glinka, Russian minister to Brazil. "I have the honor to acknowledge the receipt of your valuable work upon the 'Science of human Society.' which you were kind enough to send me. I beg you will accept my sincere thanks for your consideration and for the kind expressions contained in your letter."—Copy, DLC-USG, II, 1. Glinka had written *La Science de la Société Humaine* (4th ed., Rio de Janeiro, 1867).

1870, OCT. 31. Jane Hollis, Elkton, Md., to USG. "Would you be kind enough to inform me how much money there is remaining yet in Washington for me, and if I must come down, to please send me sufficient cash to bear expenses. I am the widow of William Hollis. I would like to know how much money there is yet and whether or not I must come down to get— or if you could send it to me"—ALS, DNA, RG 56, Letters Received.

Index

All letters written by USG of which the text was available for use in this volume are indexed under the names of the recipients. The dates of these letters are included in the index as an indication of the existence of text. Abbreviations used in the index are explained on pp. xiv–xviii. Individual regts. are indexed under the names of the states in which they originated.

Abbott, Benjamin V. (of N.Y.), 422–23

Abeita, Juan Andres (Pueblo), 342

Able, Daniel (of St. Louis), 7n

Acosta, Santos (Colombian minister), 135n, 421

Adair, William P. (Cherokee), 208n

Adams, Charles F. (minister to Great Britain), 321n

Adams, Charles M. (midshipman applicant), 383

Adams, Henry (writer), 299n, 318, 321n–23n

Adams, John (U.S. President), 318, 322n

Adams Express Co., 6, 259 and n

Adamson, Thomas, Jr. (U.S. consul), 87n–88n

Agriculture, 18, 36, 43, 74, 75, 82n, 125, 127n, 134n, 156, 241n, 266–67, 267n

Aikman, William M. (of New Orleans), 400

Akerman, Amos T. (U.S. Attorney General): appointed, 171n, 172n, 174, 174n–75n, 437; disabilities removed, 175n; renders opinions, 208n, 212n, 226n, 389, 444; prepares pardons for Fenians, 222, 305, 306n; involved with McGarrahan claim, 242n; involved with appointments, 290n–91n, 309, 310n, 471; endorsement to, Oct. 17, 1870, 309; administers dept., 378, 450, 468; endorsement to, Oct. 12, 1870, 468; urges USG to visit Ga., 468

Alabama, 16n, 55n, 67n, 68n, 192–95, 339–40, 341, 425, 466

Alabama (C.S. Navy), 29–31, 45n, 48n, 87n, 256n, 317n, 319n, 338, 350, 428

Alamance County, N.C., 210n, 211n, 212n, 213n

Alaska, 35, 40, 76, 99 and n, 290n, 356, 391

Albany, Ga., 104n

Albany, N.Y., 140 and n, 357

Albion, N.Y., 372

Alcorn, James L. (Gov. of Miss.), 421

Aldama, Miguel (of Cuba), 48n

Alexandria, Va., 65n, 349, 385

Algoma (Canadian steamship), 427

Allaben, James R. (assessor), 341–42

Allegheny County, Pa., 474

Allen, Albert G. (assessor), 342

Allen, Alfred (of Ky.), 389

Allen, Elisha H. (Hawaiian minister), 81, 81n–82n

Allen, George T. (U.S. consul), 454, 455

Allen, Henry (of Port-au-Prince), 15n

Allen, John W. (postmaster), 403–4

Allen, Robert (U.S. Army), 373

Allen, Zacheus (prisoner), 246–47, 247n

Allison, Joseph (of Philadelphia), 64n

Allison, William B. (U.S. Representative), 423, 444

Alvord, J. W. (Congregationalist minister), 459

American Missionary Association, 295n

American Philosophical Society, Philadelphia, Pa.: document in, 349–50

Ames, Adelbert (U.S. Senator), 45n–46n, 96n, 340, 421, 434

Ames, Mrs. (of St. Louis), 111n

Ames, Oakes (U.S. Representative), 65n, 150n–51n, 231n

Ames Co. (Chicopee, Mass.), 353

Amherst College, Amherst, Mass., 227n

Ammen, Daniel (U.S. Navy), 325, 395

Ammen, Jacob (of Ohio), 83n

Amnesty, 133n, 158n, 232, 252, 305, 306n, 420, 450

Amoy, China, 443, 457, 458

Andalusia (Spanish gunboat), 441

Anderson, Robert (U.S. Army), 190, 191n, 412

Anderson, Thomas D. (Baptist minister), 141n

Andersonville, Ga., 368

Andrew, John A. (Gov. of Mass.), 86n

Andrews, Christopher C. (minister to Sweden), 339

Angier, Nedom L. (Ga. treasurer), 105n–6n

Annapolis, Md., 394, 458

Anthony, Henry B. (U.S. Senator), 114–15, 115n, 162n, 218n

Anton Lizardo, Mexico, 161n

Apaches, 288n, 414

Appomattox Court House, Va., 368

Apps, Henry (of Fort Wayne), 385

Arapahoes, 414

Arctic Ocean, 137n, 209 and n, 223 and n

Argentina, 144n, 458

Arizona Territory, 290n, 404

Arkansas, 53n, 71n, 83n–84n, 85n, 86n–87n, 95n, 435–36, 437
Armstrong, William J. (consular agent), 215n
Arnold, Abraham K. (writer), 58 and n
Arnold, Benedict, 201n
Arny, William F. M. (Indian agent), 378, 409
Arthur, John (of Paris), 370
Ashburn, Judge, 339
Aspinwall, William H. (of New York City), 233n
Aspinwall, Colombia, 421
Associated Press, 299n, 326
Astor, William B. (of New York City), 180n
Atchison, Kan., 334
Atherton, Joseph B. (of Honolulu), 88n
Atkins, Helen King (wife of James Atkins), 437
Atkins, James (collector), 437
Atlanta, Ga., 103n, 174n, 285, 289n, 290n, 291n, 339, 437, 468, 473
Atlanta New Era (newspaper), 289n, 290n–91n
Atlanta True Georgian (newspaper), 285, 286n
Atlantic and Pacific Railroad Co., 204n
Augusta, Ga., 362–63
Aurora, Nev., 245n
Austin, Tex., 133n
Austria, 258n, 435, 442, 447
Ayres, 358

Babcock, Orville E. (secretary to USG): writes for USG, 4n, 12n, 52n, 93n, 133n, 136n–37n, 167n, 220n, 270n, 360, 373, 375, 385, 390, 391, 395, 396, 409, 469; family of, 94n; as secretary, 95n, 279n, 384, 401, 418; negotiates with Santo Domingo, 122n, 123n, 162n, 163, 163n–64n, 166, 166n–67n, 176n, 179 and n, 180n; refuses to dispense patronage, 142n; asked to intercede with USG, 198n–99n; conveys political information, 275n; influences appointments, 294n, 298n–99n, 458
Backus, Henry T. (of Mich.), 357
Badeau, Adam (U.S. consul-general): asked for appointment, 10n; provides advice, 45n; USG invites to dine, 58n; nominated as consul-general, 142,

143n; informed about Santo Domingo treaty, 163n–64n; receives political news, 247; letter to, Aug. 22, 1870, 247–48; requests appointment for brother, 248n; USG writes to, 252; letter to, Oct. 23, 1870, 318; as historian, 318, 318n–20n, 321n, 323n; friend of Anson Burlingame, 363
Badeau, C. W. (brother of Adam Badeau), 248n, 321n
Báez, Buenaventura (president, Santo Domingo): negotiates with Orville E. Babcock, 123n; letter to, July 7, 1870, 188; pursues annexation, 188, 311–12, 312n; letter to, Oct. 17, 1870, 311–12
Bahamas, 27, 155, 441
Bailey, John (prisoner), 456–57
Bailly, Joseph A. (sculptor), 52n
Baker, Conrad (Gov. of Ind.), 230n, 266, 267
Baker, Eugene M. (U.S. Army), 119n, 120n
Baker, H. E. (of Detroit), 356
Baker, R. Tarvin (of Ky.), 89n
Balcom, Ransom (N.Y. Supreme Court), 413–14
Baldwin, Henry P. (Gov. of Mich.), 68n, 69n, 427–28
Baldwin, Mary McCook, 111n
Ball, G. H. (Baptist minister), 262n
Ballard, Bland (U.S. District Judge), 95n
Baltimore, Md., 179, 342, 374, 406, 449
Baltimore and Ohio Railroad, 374
Bancroft, George (minister to Germany): sends reports, 268n; assists U.S. travelers, 280 and n, 447; letter to, Oct. 3, 1870, 280n; advises USG, 281n–82n; corresponds with Hamilton Fish, 341, 432; reports on U.S. bonds, 445
Banfield, E. C. (solicitor of the Treasury), 387
Banks, Nathaniel P. (U.S. Representative), 60n, 320n, 362, 397
Banks, 161n, 453
Bannocks, 474
Baptists, 141n, 221, 262n, 395
Barbadoes, Frederick G. (of Mass.), 11n
Bard, Samuel (*Atlanta True Georgian*), 285, 286n, 289n–91n
Barker, Thomas (U.S. Army), 384

Barnard, Henry (commissioner of education), 43, 405
Barnes, John S. (writer), 58 and *n*
Barnes, Joseph K. (U.S. Army), 467
Barnes, Lucien J. (of Little Rock), 84*n*–85*n*, 86*n*–87*n*
Barnes, Sidney M. (of Ky.), 380
Barrett, Edward (U.S. Navy), 402
Barrett, Joseph H. (of Cincinnati), 470–71
Barringer, Victor C. (of N.C.), 422, 423
Bass, Lyman K. (of Buffalo), 263*n*
Bassett, Ebenezer D. (minister to Haiti), 9, 10*n*–11*n*, 12*n*
Batavia, Ohio, 469
Bates, Alice L., Los Angeles, Calif.: document owned by, 57*n*
Baton Rouge, La., 384
Baxter Springs, Kan., 204*n*
Bayard, Thomas F. (U.S. Senator), 468
Beale, Edward F., 197*n*
Beattie, Alexander H. (of Montana Territory), 453–54
Beaufort, S.C., 337
Becker County, Minn., 473
Bedford, Pa., 65*n*
Belfast, Ireland, 231*n*
Belgium, 35, 94*n*, 256*n*, 257*n*, 341
Belize, British Honduras, 447
Belknap, William W. (U.S. Secretary of War): administers dept., 39–41, 49, 135*n*, 136*n*, 158*n*, 223*n*, 288*n*, 335, 362, 369, 375, 380, 382, 384, 385, 392, 398, 399, 410, 413, 415, 422, 434, 435, 438, 442, 444, 449, 450, 466, 467; letter to, Dec. 9, 1869, 49; administers Reconstruction, 96*n*, 103, 104*n*, 106*n*, 107*n*, 132*n*, 133*n*, 210, 211*n*, 212*n*, 340, 381; endorsements to, Feb. 1, 1870 (2), 107*n*; administers Indian policy, 119*n*, 120*n*; supports Santo Domingo annexation, 158*n*; absent, 175, 218*n*; telegram to, July 22, 1870, 211*n*; clashes with William T. Sherman, 218, 219*n*, 227–28, 228*n*, 229*n*; telegram to, Aug. 2, 1870, 223*n*; advises about Ellen Grant's education, 279*n*; dines with USG, 283 and *n*; influences appointment, 294*n*, 298*n*; endorsement to, Nov. 15, 1869, 335; endorsement to, [Jan.], 1870, 380; note to, Feb. 3, 1870, 382; endorse-

ment to, March 16, 1870, 404; endorsement to, April 5, 1870, 413; recommends policy concerning Spain, 419; endorsement to, July 14, 1870, 442; endorsement to, July 16, 1870, 444; endorsement to, Oct. 10, 1870, 467; mentioned, 360, 366–67
Bell, Thomas G. (U.S. Navy), 397
Beloit, Wis., 438
Benedict, Charles L. (U.S. District Judge), 17*n*, 63*n*
Bennett, David S. (U.S. Representative), 262*n*, 263*n*–64*n*
Bennett's Corners, N.Y., 352
Bent, Silas (oceanographer), 137*n*
Benteen, Frederick W. (U.S. Army), 456
Benton, Caroline E. (of Philadelphia), 110*n*
Benton, John C., 111*n*
Benton, Mortimer M. (of Covington, Ky.), 111*n*
Benton, William H. (of St. Louis), 7, 178*n*, 220 and *n*, 390
Berkmeyer, Louis Bernard (dentist), 454–55
Berlin, Germany, 255*n*, 280*n*, 282*n*, 341, 363, 432, 445, 447
Berthemy, Jules (French minister), 216*n*, 223*n*, 226*n*, 238
Bertsch, Fred (of Cincinnati): letter to, Oct. 4, 1870, 465
Beverly, N.J., 355
Bigelow, John (minister to France): letter to, Feb. 19, 1870, 112; seeks son's USMA appointment, 112, 112*n*–14*n*; letter to, Feb. 7, 1870, 112*n*
Bigelow, John, Jr. (U.S. Army), 112, 112*n*–14*n*
Bighorn Mountains, 120*n*
Bingham, John A. (U.S. Representative), 117*n*, 243*n*, 364, 365–66
Binghamton, N.Y., 413
Birmingham, England, 144*n*
Bismarck, Otto von (Chancellor of Germany), 201*n*, 217*n*, 258*n*, 276*n*, 281*n*
Black, Jeremiah S., 374, 382
Blackburn, Joseph H. (marshal), 355–56
Black Hawk War, 246*n*
Black River (Mich.), 271*n*, 272*n*
Blacks: in Haiti, 8–9, 9*n*–15*n*; in Philadelphia, 10*n*, 11*n*; as soldiers, 10*n*, 210*n*, 270, 380, 392, 456–57; in Cin-

Blacks (*cont.*)
cinnati, 11*n*–12*n*; celebrate ratification of Fifteenth Amendment, 12*n*,
130–31, 132*n*, 138*n*; in Va., 13*n*; in
Ga., 20, 105*n*, 107*n*; education of, 43,
131; as laborers, 50 and *n*; appointment of, 50*n*; and Santo Domingo,
74–75, 154, 156; in N.C. militia,
210*n*, 211*n*; violence against, 211*n*,
249*n*–50*n*, 375, 420, 423–24, 448,
474–75; at USMA, 229*n*; friend of,
277*n*; in La., 344; in Richmond, 345,
346; trade in, 402–3; visit USG, 405;
try to reunite families, 426; in Washington, D.C., 438
Blain, M. (of Marseilles), 410
Blaine, James G. (U.S. Representative), 79*n*, 144*n*, 222, 225–26, 247,
296*n*, 317*n*
Blaine, John E. (U.S. Army), 364
Blair, B. B. (of Georgetown, Ohio),
373
Blair, Francis P., Jr. (vice presidential
candidate), 86*n*, 87*n*, 314*n*
Blake, Freeman N. (U.S. consul), 411
Blanc, Louis (of France), 258*n*
Blatchford, Samuel (U.S. District
Judge), 48*n*
Bliss, Porter C. (secretary of lega-
tion), 423
Blodgett, Foster (of Augusta, Ga.),
107*n*, 362–63
Blodgett, Henry W. (U.S. District
Judge), 339, 396
Bloomfield, Ira J. (supervisor), 357–
59
Blow, Henry T. (minister to Brazil):
letter to, Dec. 15, 1869, 347; sends
coffee to USG, 347–48; fosters com-
merce, 430
Blum, Herman, Philadelphia, Pa.:
document owned by, 220
Boal, James St. Clair (secretary of le-
gation), 423
Bogotá, Colombia, 135, 136*n*
Bolaye, Sophia, 147*n*
Boles, Thomas (U.S. Representative),
86*n*
Bolles, John A. (U.S. Navy Judge Ad-
vocate), 62*n*–63*n*
Bond, Hugh L. (U.S. Circuit Judge),
66*n*
Bonsack, Va., 393
Book Sail, The, Orange, Calif.: document owned by, 160

Booneville, Ky., 380
Boonville, Mo., 245*n*
Booth, Edwin (actor), 10*n*
Borie, Adolph E. (of Philadelphia):
visited by Ambrose W. Thompson,
199*n*–200*n*; letter to, July 22, 1870,
213*n*–14*n*; invited to Long Branch,
213*n*–14*n*; in politics, 273*n*; USG
visits, 376
Borie, Elizabeth M. (wife of Adolph
E. Borie), 213*n*
Bormann, Charles G. (Belgian army),
422
Boston, Mass., 40, 63*n*, 85*n*, 88*n*,
115*n*, 160, 254*n*, 278, 279–80, 371,
425, 426, 446
Boston Public Library, Boston, Mass.:
document in, 348–49
Botts, John M. (of Va.), 345
Boulton, Ernest, 181*n*
Bourbon County, Kan., 415
Bourke, Richard Southwell (viceroy):
telegram to, June 23, 1870, 437
Boutwell, George S. (U.S. Secretary of
the Treasury): recommends reforms,
24; letter to, Jan. 14, 1870, 80–81;
involved in appointments, 84*n*, 185*n*,
215*n*, 269, 282*n*, 294*n*, 298*n*, 384,
431; described, 90*n*; views on Reconstruction, 133*n*; administers dept.,
141*n*, 209*n*, 350, 379, 381, 389, 390,
393,445,463; misses cabinet meeting,
158*n*, 225; and Santo Domingo, 171*n*;
covets Canada, 256*n*; letter to, Sept.
22, 1870, 269–70; comments on Mc-
Garrahan claim, 293*n*, 296*n*–97*n*; offers political advice, 306*n*; appointed,
321*n*; endorsement to, Feb. 1, 1870,
381; endorsement to, Feb. 5, 1870,
384; praised, 405; investigates fraud,
439; mentioned, 61*n*, 99*n*
Bowdoin College, Brunswick, Maine:
documents in, 371, 401, 404, 405,
406, 407, 435, 438, 460
Bowen, Edgar C. (U.S. Army), 442–
43
Bowen, Henry C. (*New York Independent*): letter to, April 21, 1870, 143;
sends USG commemorative publication, 143 and *n*; receives USG family
news, 186*n*, 279*n*
Bowen, Sayles J. (Mayor of Washington, D.C.), 412–13
Bowen, W. H. D. (inventor), 461
Bowie, Oden (Gov. of Md.), 66*n*, 394

Bowles, Samuel, II (Springfield, Mass. *Republican*), 55n

Boyle, William (of Nev.), 401

Boynton, Henry Van Ness (newspaper correspondent), 298n

Boys in Blue (veterans' society), 138n

Brack, Nancy Jane (wife of William P. Brack), 421

Brack, William P. (prisoner), 420–21

Bradford, Allen A. (U.S. Delegate), 286n, 289n, 408

Bradley, A. Alpeora (Ga. senator), 107n

Bradley, George (Indian agent), 271n–72n

Bradley, Joseph P. (U.S. Supreme Court), 55n–56n, 57n, 323n, 405

Bradley, N. D. (of Camden Mills, Ill.), 353

Brady, James T. (attorney), 118n

Brady, John R., 428

Brady, Mrs. E. (of Mitchell, Ind.), 451

Bragg, Elizabeth J. (of Gaines, N.Y.), 371–72

Bragg, William J. (N.Y. Vols.), 371–72

Brayton, Charles R. (pension agent), 459

Brazil, 3n, 76, 87n, 134n, 144n, 156, 347–48, 430, 444–45, 475

Breckinridge, Samuel M. (surveyor), 270n

Breeden, William (of New Mexico Territory), 378

Bremen, Germany, 196n

Brevil, M. J. E. (French consul), 223n

Brewer, Anson L. (U.S. Army), 397

Brewer, Mrs. Anson L., 397

Brewer, Charles (Boston merchant), 85n

Brewer, Edwin P. (U.S. Army), 397

Bridgeport, Conn., 186n

Briggs, Coleman, 253n

Brightwood, D.C., 51n

Brindisi, Italy, 442

Brink, C. W. (U.S. vice consul), 161n

Bristol, Pa., 87n

Bristol, R.I., 162n, 450

Bristow, Benjamin H. (U.S. Solicitor General), 95n, 310n, 379

British Columbia, 337–38

British Guiana, 75

Brockway, William H. (Indian agent), 271 and n, 272n, 274, 277n, 295n

Brooklyn, N.Y., 139n, 294n, 341, 353, 473

Brooks, A. R. (of Richmond), 345

Brooks, George W. (U.S. District Judge), 212n, 213n

Brown, B. Gratz (of Mo.), 178n, 270n, 284 and n, 296n, 313

Brown, Calvin (of Calif.), 446

Brown, Egbert B. (of St. Louis), 7n

Brown, Robert L. (collector): letter to, March 1, 1870, 398

Brown, Thomas M., 357

Brown County, Ohio, 273n

Browne, A. K. (of Washington, D.C.), 73n

Browne, J. Ross (minister to China), 379

Browning, Orville H. (U.S. Secretary of the Interior), 103n, 241n, 242n

Brownlow, William G. (U.S. Senator), 3n

Brown-Séquard, Charles E. (physician), 92n

Bruce, C. G. (of Cleveland), 385

Bruce, Sir Frederick (British minister), 338

Brulés, 361

Brunswick, Ga., 467

Brussels, Belgium, 93n, 255n, 258n, 370, 422

Bryant, John E. (of Augusta, Ga.), 362–63

Bryant, William Cullen (*New York Evening Post*), 232n, 233n, 316n

Buchanan, James (U.S. President), 281n, 382

Buckingham, William A. (U.S. Senator), 186n

Buckley, Charles W. (U.S. Representative), 442

Buenos Aires, Argentina, 396

Buffalo, N.Y., 261–62, 262n, 263n

Buffalo Commercial Advertiser (newspaper), 263n, 264n

Buffalo Express (newspaper), 262n, 264n

Bullitt, W. A. (of Louisville, Ky.), 4n

Bullock, Alexander H. (of Mass.), 226, 227n

Bullock, Jonathan R. (of Bristol, R.I.), 450

Bullock, Rufus B. (Gov. of Ga.): administers Reconstruction, 61n, 103n, 104n, 105n, 106n, 107n, 362–63; letter to, Oct. 15, 1870, 468

Bumball, Stephen W., Mountainside, N.J.: document owned by, 261

Bunker, Charles (of Hawaii), 85n–86n

Burbridge, Stephen G., 460

Burch, 61n

Burgess, Evelyn Wooster, San Diego, Calif.: document owned by, 325

Burke, Ricard O. (Fenian), 116n

Burlingame, Anson (Chinese envoy), 363

Burnes, Calvin F. (of Mo.), 145n, 146n, 147n, 149n, 165 and n, 177–78, 178n, 278

Burnet, Tex., 463

Burnside, Ambrose E. (of R.I.): letter to, Feb. 24, 1870, 114–15; asked to support reelection of Henry B. Anthony, 114–15; recommends appointments, 162n, 218n; travels in Europe, 217n–18n, 258n; during Civil War, 385

Burnside, James O. P. (of Washington, D.C.): letter to, April 13, 1870, 414

Burson, John W. (Union Pacific Railroad), 5, 5n–6n

Burton, Harry (of Staten Island), 388

Burton, Henry S. (U.S. Army), 388

Butler, Benjamin F. (U.S. Representative): involved in Reconstruction, 61n, 374; letter to, Jan. 24, 1870, 89–90; champions USG, 89–90, 90n; recommends appointments, 185n, 231n, 317n, 433, 434; interested in McGarrahan claim, 300n; during Civil War, 318, 320n, 323n, 362; assists orphans, 409

Butler, David (Gov. of Neb.): letter to, Nov. 23, 1869, 15–16; supports Fifteenth Amendment, 15–16, 16n

Butler, Matthew C. (of S.C.), 248, 249n

Butler, Roderick R. (U.S. Representative), 96n

Butler, Pa., 84n

Butterfield, Daniel (U.S. Army), 98n, 111n, 221n

Cadiz, Spain, 370–71

Cairo, Ill., 182n

Calais, France, 75

Caldwell, Henry C. (U.S. District Judge), 53n

California: courts in, 72n–73n; interested in Hawaii, 82n, 85n, 88n; appointments in, 139n, 140n, 182n, 375, 386, 396; Pioneers Association, 228n; McGarrahan land claim in, 241n, 242n; land controversies in, 277n; vols., 384; Indians in, 432, 474; Chinese in, 443–44; railroads in, 446

California, University of, Los Angeles, Calif.: document in, 160

Callao, Peru, 246, 247n

Calloway, James E. (secretary, Montana Territory), 453, 454

Cambridge, Mass., 86n

Camden, N.J., 132n

Camden Mills, Ill., 353

Cameron, Simon (U.S. Senator), 79n, 84n, 167n, 185n, 282n, 295n, 342

Campbell, Benjamin H. (marshal), 93n–94n, 198n

Campbell, Hugh (of St. Louis), 455

Campbell, John A. (Gov. of Wyoming Territory), 120n, 234n

Campbell, Robert (of St. Louis), 455

Camp Cadwallader, Pa., 462

Camp Grant, Richmond, Va., 367

Canada: U.S. relations with, 32, 33, 44n, 45n, 49n, 268n, 427–28; border with, 117n; Fenians raid, 151, 152n, 226n, 306n; uprising in, 158n; annexation discussed, 256n, 319n, 337–38; reorganized, 381, 382

Canadian River, 205n

Canandaigua (U.S. Navy), 402

Canby, Edward R. S. (U.S. Army), 65n, 393

Cantine, R. S. (of Camden Mills, Ill.), 353

Canton, China, 461

Cape Town, South Africa, 425

Carey, H. (of Xenia, Ohio), 366

Carey, Joseph M. (U.S. District Attorney), 361

Carlesen, Gunner (of Minn.), 474

Carlin, Delphy (of Mo.), 138–39, 139n, 144, 146n, 149, 278

Carlin, Mary (of Mo.), 139n

Carlsbad, Austria, 255n

Carondelet, Mo., 138–39, 139n, 144–45, 145n–46n, 149 and n, 177–78, 178n, 224, 278, 307

Carpenter, Benjamin D. (of Brightwood, D.C.), 51n

Carpenter, Matthew H. (U.S. Senator), 71n, 183n, 438, 443

Carrington, Edward C. (U.S. District Attorney), 64n–65n

Carson City, Nev., 245n
Carter, Alfred G. W. (of Cincinnati), 469–70
Cartter, David K. (D.C. Supreme Court), 53n–54n
Case, A. J., 371
Casey, Emily (Emma) Dent (sister-in-law of USG), 178n, 327n
Casey, Frederick Dent (nephew of USG), 325 and n
Casey, James F. (brother-in-law of USG), 178n, 327n, 350, 393, 400, 438
Casserly, Eugene (U.S. Senator), 180n
Caswell County, N.C., 210n, 212n, 213n
Cates, James M. (prisoner), 445
Catholics, 60n, 111n, 141n, 180n, 201n, 323n, 353
Catlin, Isaac S. (U.S. Army), 413–14
Cattaraugus Reservation (N.Y.), 383
Cattle, 264, 323, 324, 326, 328, 451
Cavanaugh, James M. (U.S. Delegate), 453–54
Cecil County, Md., 15n
Census, 43
Centaur (U.S. Navy), 47n
Cerre, Gabriel, 147n
Cessna, John (U.S. Representative), 65n–66n
Chaffee, Jerome B. (U.S. Delegate), 286n, 348–49
Chalmers, N. (of Levuka, Fiji), 430
Chamberlain, Daniel H. (S.C. attorney general): letter to, Aug. 22, 1870, 248; questions USG's political preferences, 248n–49n
Chamberlain, Joshua L. (Gov. of Maine), 247
Chambers and Cattell (of Philadelphia), 349
Chandler, Lucius H. (of Va.), 404–5
Chandler, Zachariah (U.S. Senator): collects for Edwin M. Stanton fund, 80n; involved in appointments, 93n, 183n–84n, 271n, 274, 274n–75n, 276n, 293n, 294n, 295n, 298n–99n; advocates Santo Domingo annexation, 157n, 163, 183n; letter to, June 8, 1870, 163; letter to, Sept. 22, 1870, 274; assists officer, 336
Chapultepec, Mexico, battle of, 395
Charles XV (King of Sweden and Norway), 443

Charleston, S.C., 221, 249n, 251n, 369
Chase, Salmon P. (U.S. Chief Justice), 428–29, 438–39, 452
Chatfield, John (Chippewa), 272n
Chattanooga, Tenn., 67n, 291n, 391, 392
Chautauqua County, N.Y., 337
Cháves, José Francisco (U.S. Delegate), 289n, 342–44, 376, 377
Cherokee County, Kan., 415
Cherokees, 202n, 204n, 207n, 208n, 373, 388–89, 456
Chevalier, Michel (of France), 401–2
Cheyenne, Wyoming Territory, 120n, 150n, 361, 434
Cheyennes, 414
Cheyenne Wells, Colorado Territory, 288n
Chicago, Ill.: courts in, 70n, 396; Republican convention at, 84n, 180n; Board of Trade, 110n; USG visits, 111n, 224, 317n, 453; meteorological observation at, 137n; customhouse, 253, 253n–54n; emigrants leave, 287n, 288n; whiskey fraud in, 357–59; mentioned, 61n, 94n, 136n, 162n, 198n, 229n, 339, 353, 392, 458, 464
Chicago, University of, Chicago, Ill.: document in, 96n
Chicago Historical Society, Chicago, Ill.: documents in, 93n–94n, 396
Chicago Post (newspaper), 253
Chicago Republican (newspaper), 359
Chicago Tribune (newspaper), 70n
Chickasaws, 202n, 315 and n
Chicora (Canadian steamboat), 427–28
Childs, George W. (friend of USG), 79n, 223n
Chile, 4n, 29, 265n, 266n, 336, 458
China: minister to, 4n, 379, 452; U.S. relations with, 36–37, 458; consuls in, 182n, 214n–15n, 218n, 285n, 382, 425, 457–58, 461; legation in, 275n, 276n; William H. Seward visits, 317n; U.S. Marines in, 355; treaty with, 383; protection of U.S. interests in, 394; illegal immigration from, 443–44
Chippewas, 271n, 272n, 403, 473–74
Choctaws, 202n, 316n, 388, 389
Cincinnati, Ohio: blacks in, 11n–12n; merchants from, 80; petition from, 116n, 117n; newspapers in, 300n,

Cincinnati, Ohio (*cont.*)
320n, 371; appointments in, 339,
468, 469, 470, 471, 472; Internal
Revenue in, 363, 366; during Civil
War, 412; sharpshooter festival at,
465; commercial convention at, 465;
mentioned, 89n, 111n, 172n, 199n,
293n, 299n, 364, 438
Cincinnati Chronicle (newspaper), 470
Cincinnati Historical Society, Cincin-
nati, Ohio: documents in, 364, 365
(2)
City of Paris (steamship), 117n
City Point, Va., 462
Civil Rights Act, 475
Civil Service, 231n, 292n, 296n, 297n,
299n, 301n
Claflin, William (Gov. of Mass.), 363
Clarendon, George W. V. (British for-
eign secretary), 31
Clark, A. P. (of Washington, D.C.),
401
Clark, Alinzor (inventor), 386
Clark, T. W. (of Wausau, Wis.), 449
Clarke, Hovey K. (of Mich.), 356–57
Clarke, Reader W. (3rd Auditor of the
Treasury), 339
Clarke, Sidney (U.S. Representative),
416
Clayton, Powell (Gov. of Ark.), 83n–
84n
Clendining, 298n
Clermont County, Ohio, 417
Cleveland, Orestes, Jr. (of N.J.), 111n
Cleveland, Ohio, 224n, 385, 403–4
Clifford, Arthur, 224 and n
Clifford, John H. (of Mass.), 224n
Clift, Joseph W. (of Ga.), 174n
Cline, George W. (St. Louis attorney),
314n
Coal, 305
Cobb, Amasa (U.S. Representative),
440
Coburn, John (U.S. Representative),
69n
Coën, David, 122n
Coffee, Mary E. (of Burnet, Tex.),
463–64
Coffee, W. B. (of Tex.), 463
Coffee, 134n, 156, 347–48
Cold Harbor, Va., battle of, 371
Cole, Cornelius (U.S. Senator), 325n
Cole, Gordon E. (of Minn.), 72n
Cole, Henry G. (of Marietta, Ga.),
174n

Cole, Henry T. (of Cincinnati), 365
Cole, Nathan (Mayor of St. Louis),
222n–23n
Cole, Willoughby, 325 and n
Coleman, G. Dawson (of Lebanon,
Pa.), 453
Coleman, Robert (of Paris), 453
Colfax, Schuyler (U.S. Vice Presi-
dent): recommends appointments,
79n, 317n; letter to, Aug. 21, 1870,
229–30; advises USG, 229–30, 230n;
mentioned, 55n
Colfax, Colorado Territory, 286n,
287n, 289n
Collingwood, Canada, 427
Collis, Charles H. T. (of Philadel-
phia), 418
Colombia, 28, 44n, 135, 135n–37n,
264–65, 265n, 421
Colonel Lloyd Aspinwall (steamship),
418–19
Colorado Territory, 285, 285n–89n,
321n, 386, 387, 408, 409, 422, 453,
460, 474
Colquit, Alfred C. (marshal), 275n,
276n
Columbia, S.C., 248n, 250n
Columbia, Tenn., 309n
Columbia University, New York, N.Y.:
document in, 177
Columbus, Ohio, 364, 365, 387
Colyer, Vincent (Indian commissioner), 120n, 456
Comanches, 414
Commerce: with Ecuador, 4n; U.S.
merchant marine facilitates, 20, 124–
26, 179, 196 and n, 197n–200n,
255n, 257n; with Santo Domingo, 74,
75, 76, 134n, 155, 156; with Hawaii,
81, 81n–83n, 84n, 88n; whaling, 84n,
88n; in Alaska, 99 and n; U.S. exports, 127n; customs regulations affect, 141n; with Mexico, 161n; with
France, 200 and n; railroads affect,
205n; through fishing rights, 226n,
268n; neutrality protects, 236; with
Brazil, 275n; with Latin America,
430, 443; with China, 458; convention encourages, 465
Commerell, John E. (British navy),
394
Compiègne, France, 60n, 92n
Comstock, Cyrus B. (U.S. Army), 449
Concho County, Tex., 463
Concord, Mass., 54n, 86n, 294n

Congregationalists, 143n
Conkling, Roscoe (U.S. Senator): letter to, April 12, 1870, 140; involved in appointments, 140, 262n, 263n–64n; letter to, Aug. 22, 1870, 251–52; USG consults, 251–52; invites USG to visit Utica, 261; letter to, Sept. 8, 1870, 261–62; discusses Orvil Grant letter, 359; mentioned, 188n
Connecticut, 63n, 185n, 186n–87n, 279n, 399
Connecticut State Library, Hartford, Conn.: document in, 186n
Conscription, 56n
Constantinople, Turkey, 35, 49n, 280n, 282n, 423
Conway, Martin F. (U.S. consul), 451–52
Cook, Burton C. (U.S. Representative), 396
Cook, Isaac (of St. Louis), 390–91
Cook, Theodore: letter to, Oct. 4, 1870, 465
Cooke, Jay (financier), 408
Coolidge, A. L. (of Boston), 425
Copley Library, James S., La Jolla, Calif.: document in, 259
Corbett, Henry W. (U.S. Senator), 276n, 385
Corbin, Abel R. (brother-in-law of USG): identified, 234 and n; letter to, Sept. 30, 1870, 283; invites USG to visit, 283; influences USG, 322n
Corbin, Jennie (niece of USG), 234n
Corbin, Virginia Grant (sister of USG): letter to, Aug. 21, 1870, 233–34; invites USG to visit, 234; marriage, 234n; mentioned, 283
Cork, Ireland, 231n, 459
Cornell, Alonzo B. (surveyor), 251, 252n
Cornell University, Ithaca, N.Y.: document in, 63n; faculty, 86n
Corser, David S. (USMA applicant), 419
Cortes, Enrique (Colombian chargé d'affaires), 265n
Corti, Luigi (Italian minister), 148 and n
Corwine, Richard M. (of Cincinnati), 470, 471
Costa Rica, 29
Coste, Felix (act. collector), 260, 269, 270n
Costello, Augustine E. (Fenian), 117n

Costilla County, Colorado Territory, 288n
Cotton, 127n, 390, 440, 463
Council Bluffs, Iowa, 71n, 333
Courts-Martial: in C.S. Army, 87n; of officers, 335–36, 406–7; of naval surgeons, 348, 391; for drunkenness, 349, 356, 367; of deserter, 456–57
Covington, Ky., 89n, 111n, 273 and n, 469
Cowen, Benjamin R. (of Cincinnati), 363–65, 366
Cox, Daniel B. (of Philadelphia), 439
Cox, Jacob D. (U.S. Secretary of the Interior): letter to, Nov. 7, 1869, 5; regulates railroads, 5, 6n, 201, 202n–5n, 388, 401, 416; administers dept., 42, 43, 209, 353, 386, 421–22, 431–32, 452; on foreign policy, 44n, 169n; considers appointments, 54n–55n, 221; administers Indian policy, 100, 100n–101n, 102n, 103n, 118–19, 120n, 202n, 271 and n, 274, 315 and n, 326, 383, 388–89, 395, 403, 409, 423, 432, 456, 458, 474; on Santo Domingo annexation, 158n, 171n; on resignation of Ebenezer R. Hoar, 171n–73n; considers resigning, 172n; endorsement to, July 20, 1870, 201; endorsement to, May 23, 1870, 205n; endorsement to, Aug. 5, 1870, 221; letter to, Aug. 22, 1870, 240–41; addresses McGarrahan claim, 240–41, 241n–43n, 244n–45n; endorsement to, Sept. 22, 1870, 271; letter to, Oct. 5, 1870, 292; leaves cabinet, 292, 292n–302n; letter to, Oct. 21, 1870, 315; letter to, Oct. 17, 1870, 315n; considered as minister to Great Britain, 317n; letter to, Oct. 26, 1870, 326; endorsement to, Feb. 24, 1870, 395; endorsement to, June 2, 1870, 431; endorsement to, Sept. 8, 1870, 453; endorsement to, Oct. 25, 1870, 474
Coyne, Marshall B., Washington, D.C.: document owned by, 234n
Crane, James L. (of Springfield, Ill.), 344–45
Crane, Joseph G. (U.S. Army), 381
Crawford, George A. (U.S. Navy), 426
Crawford, Mary (of Enon Valley, Pa.), 353–54

Crawford, Robert M. (Pa. Vols.), 353–54
Crawford, Samuel W. (U.S. Army), 339–40
Crawford County, Kan., 415, 417
Creeks, 202*n*, 204*n*, 205*n*–7*n*, 373, 433
Creswell, John A. J. (U.S. Postmaster General): administers dept., 41–42, 339; involved in appointments, 88–89, 140, 248*n*, 294*n*, 298*n*; on Santo Domingo annexation, 158*n*; opinion on Cuba, 169*n*; considered as minister to Great Britain, 185*n*; writes part of message to Congress, 196*n*; dines with USG, 283 and *n*; mentioned, 44*n*, 362
Crockett, Joseph B. (Calif. Supreme Court), 72*n*–73*n*
Croledge, George (writer): letter to, Jan. 13, 1870, 368
Cromwell, Edward (of New York City): letter to, Feb. 16, 1870, 109; promotes home for disabled veterans, 109 and *n*
Crosby, Mr., 357–58
Crounse, Lorenzo L. (*New York Times*), 297*n*
Crowe, Charles C. (Gov. of New Mexico Territory), 290*n*
Cuba: U.S. policy toward, 25, 26, 28, 44*n*–45*n*, 46*n*, 47*n*, 48*n*, 165–66, 167–68, 169*n*–70*n*, 306*n*; filibustering expeditions to, 26–27, 47*n*, 316*n*; slavery in, 76, 156, 402, 442; U.S. commerce with, 134*n*; U.S. vessels seized near, 167–68; U.S. legation in, 234*n*; revolt in, 348, 353, 359, 394, 418, 419; citizens in Brooklyn, 353; U.S. citizens executed in, 441, 446; mentioned, 29, 75, 155
Cumback, William (of Ind.), 230*n*
Cumberland County, Pa., 53*n*
Cummings, Thomas (U.S. Army), 380
Cunard Steamship Co., 196*n*
Cunningham, Ross (War Dept. clerk), 319*n*, 320*n*
Curtin, Andrew G. (minister to Russia), 84*n*, 454
Curtin, Richard, 259, 326, 327
Curtis, William W. (clerk, General Land Office), 245*n*
Cushing, Caleb, 47*n*, 158*n*, 317*n*
Cushman, William H. W. (Ill. Vols.), 460

Dahlgren, Madeleine V. (wife of John A. Dahlgren): letter to, Jan. 24, 1870, 90
Dakota Territory, 361, 381, 474
Dallett, Henry C. (Nicaraguan consul), 253*n*
Daly, Maria L. (of New York City), 335
Danbury, Conn., 98*n*
Daniel, George W. (of Booneville, Ky.), 380–81
Daniels, Rodney W. (collector), 262*n*, 263*n*, 264*n*
Danville, Ky., 426
Dartmouth College, Hanover, N.H., 175*n*
Davenport, Iowa, 72*n*
Davis, David (U.S. Supreme Court), 69*n*, 70*n*, 71*n*, 339
Davis, Edmund J. (Gov. of Tex.), 132*n*
Davis, Edmund S. (surveyor), 245*n*
Davis, J. C. Bancroft (Asst. Secretary of State): conducts Spanish diplomacy, 46*n*–47*n*; on annexation of Santo Domingo, 157*n*, 158*n*, 166*n*–67*n*; reports Prévost-Paradol funeral, 201*n*; dept. duties of, 214*n*, 225, 226*n*–27*n*, 232, 252–53, 253*n*, 255*n*, 396–97, 428; on Franco-Prussian conflict, 216*n*, 222, 223*n*; letter to, Aug. 22, 1870, 252–53
Davis, Jacob R. (of Ga.), 363
Davis, James W. (contractor), 150*n*
Davis, Jefferson (C.S.A. President), 180*n*, 428
Davis, John L. (U.S. Navy), 474
Davis, Noah (U.S. District Attorney), 18*n*
Davis, Thomas F. (U.S. Army), 335
Dawes, Henry L. (U.S. Representative), 89–90, 90*n*
Day, Mr., 88
Day, Samuel T. (U.S. consul), 441
Dayton, Ohio, 460, 468
Dearborn, William N., Nashville, Tenn.: document owned by, 97
De Graff, E. V. (of Rochester, N.Y.), 446
De Groot, Albert (of New York City): letter to, Nov. 4, 1869, 334
DeHaas, F. S. (Methodist minister), 111*n*
Dejardin, Paul (French diplomat), 201*n*

Delano, Columbus (U.S. Secretary of the Interior): administers Internal Revenue, 39, 139*n*, 149, 327, 373, 400, 473; recommends appointment, 67*n*; letter to, May 31, 1871, 244*n*; addresses McGarrahan claim, 244*n*; endorsement to, June 16, 1871, 244*n*; enters cabinet, 294*n*, 298*n*, 299*n*

Delany, Martin R. (of Ohio), 55*n*

Democratic Party: in South, 53*n*, 289*n*; influences U.S. Supreme Court, 54*n*, 322*n*–23*n*; in Md., 66*n*; in Ga., 86*n*, 105*n*, 106*n*, 363; receives Republican defectors, 90*n*, 269, 284 and *n*; opposes Santo Domingo annexation, 164*n*; in Calif., 182*n*; Tammany Hall, 184*n*, 283*n*; may win congressional elections, 190, 256*n*–57*n*; in N.J., 192*n*, 267*n*; in N.C., 210*n*; in Ill., 221*n*, 411; in S.C., 250*n*; in N.Y., 262*n*, 426; in army, 273*n*; in Ind., 274*n*–75*n*, 316*n*, 318, 323*n*; denounced, 277*n*; in Colorado Territory, 286*n*; in Mo., 313–14; publicizes criticism of Republicans, 322*n*; in Washington Territory, 351; in Memphis, 461; in Fla., 466; mentioned, 349, 375, 438

Denmark, 35, 341, 362

Dennis, R. B. (consular agent), 215*n*

Dennison, William (of Ohio), 79*n*, 275*n*, 387

Dent, Anna Baine (wife of Lewis Dent), 327*n*

Dent, Ellen Wrenshall (mother-in-law of USG), 327*n*

Dent, Frederick (father-in-law of USG): discusses politics, 133*n*; lost Carondelet property, 145, 146*n*, 147*n*; in good health, 173; at White House, 283; picture of, 327*n*; mentioned, 92*n*, 256*n*

Dent, Frederick T. (secretary to USG): discusses appointments, 7*n*, 139*n*, 357, 370, 407–8; acquires Carondelet property, 145, 146*n*, 147*n*; as secretary, 151*n*–52*n*, 288*n*, 342, 452; locates cemetery lot, 224; writes for USG, 256*n*; letter to, Aug. 24, 1870, 259; ships horse, 259; mentioned, 359

Dent, George W. (brother-in-law of USG): owns Carondelet property, 138, 144, 145*n*, 146*n*–47*n*, 165, 177,

178*n*; receives appointment, 139*n*–40*n*

Dent, John C. (brother-in-law of USG), 313

Dent, Lewis (brother-in-law of USG), 197*n*, 302*n*

Dent, Mrs. R. V. (of Washington, D.C.), 437–38

Denver, James W., 139*n*

Denver, Colorado Territory, 228*n*, 408

De Nyse, N. H., 442

Deserters, 87*n*, 195

Des Moines, Iowa, 228*n*

Detroit, Mich., 65*n*, 68*n*, 290*n*, 335, 427

Detroit Advertiser & Tribune (newspaper), 356

Deuringer, Yahn (of Richmond), 347

Dickinson College, Carlisle, Pa.: document in, 52; graduate of, 53*n*

Dickson, John (of Camden Mills, Ill.), 353

Dillon, John F. (U.S. Circuit Judge), 71*n*–72*n*

Dinsmore, D. J. (of Eureka, Kan.), 450–51

Dinsmore, William B. (of New York City), 111*n*

Dix, John A.: during Civil War, 63*n*; letter to, June 20, 1870, 177; as railroad official, 177 and *n*

Dodge, Grenville M., 71*n*–72*n*, 193, 333–34

Dodge, Mr. (of Mo.), 468

Dodge, William E. (of New York City), 49, 63*n*

Dolan, John (of New York City), 231*n*

Donley, Joseph B. (U.S. Representative), 459

Donnelly, John (Fenian), 223*n*

Donoho, William H., 407

Dorsheimer, William (U.S. District Attorney), 263*n*

Douglass, Charles R. (son of Frederick Douglass), 138*n*

Douglass, Frederick (black leader), 10*n*, 138*n*

Douglass, George T. (U.S. Navy), 474

Downing, George T. (black leader), 11*n*

Downing, Lewis (Cherokee), 207*n*

Downing, McCarthy (British parliament), 116*n*

Downs, Morris, 467

Doxtator, Peter (Oneida), 352

Drake, Charles D. (U.S. Senator), 55n, 260
Draper, John W. (physician), 279, 280n
Draper, N. R., 396–97
Driggs, George W. (U.S. consul), 441
Drummond, Thomas (U.S. Circuit Judge), 70n–71n, 92n, 396
Drummond, Willis (General Land Office), 277n
Dublin, Ireland, 117n
Dubois, Jesse K. (of Springfield, Ill.), 257n
Dudley, Nathan A. M. (U.S. Army), 446
Duffié, Alfred N. (U.S. consul), 370
Duke University, Durham, N.C.: documents in, 65n, 211n, 461
Duluth, Minn., 449
Dundee, Scotland, 410, 411
Dunn, Fannie E., 110n
Dunn, William M., Sr. (U.S. Army), 110n
Dunning, James L. (postmaster), 290n
Dupré, Ferdinand (writer): letter to, Oct. 18, 1870, 472
Durant, Iowa, 361
Dutcher, Silas B. (supervisor), 473
Dwight, Edward (Choctaw), 388, 389
Dyer, Alexander B. (U.S. Army), 362

Early, Jubal A. (C.S. Army), 320n
Easton, Alton R. (assessor), 72n, 284, 285n, 314n
Eaton, John, Jr. (Commissioner of Education), 95n, 391–92, 405, 435–36, 461
Eaton, Lucien B. (marshal), 94, 94n–96n, 150n
Ecuador, 3n, 4n, 126–27, 127n
Edgecomb, Willard W. (U.S. consul), 425
Edinburgh, Scotland, 181n
Edmunds, George F. (U.S. Senator): considered for minister to Great Britain, 222, 225–26, 227n, 229, 232 and n, 233n, 296n; recommends appointment, 280n; considers appointment, 410–11
Edmunds, James M. (postmaster), 274, 276n–77n, 294n
Education: of blacks, 10n, 12n, 43, 211n, 457, 459; land sales support, 102n; USG emphasizes, 131; for Indians, 205n, 206n, 343, 395; at Harvard, 227n, 248n; in Mo., 245n; at Yale, 248n, 261 and n; of USG's children, 274, 278, 279n, 325, 328–29, 329n; commissioner of, 405; at Princeton, 437; in military science, 446
Egan, Edward E. (USMA applicant), 431
Egan, Thomas W. (weigher), 431
Eggleston, Benjamin (of Cincinnati), 470–71
Egypt, 436
Eichelberger, Grayson (of Md.), 66n
Elberton, Ga., 290n
Elbrey, Frederick W. (U.S. Army), 342
Elizabeth, N.J., 173, 283
Elizabethtown, Ky., 378
Elkins, Stephen B. (U.S. District Attorney), 377
Elkton, Md., 475
Elliott, Jehu T. (Ind. Supreme Court), 69n
Ellis, George E. (of Boston), 85n
Elrod, William (farm manager): letter to, March 27, 1870, 127–28; manages USG's farm, 127–28, 128n, 225, 259–60, 264, 323–24, 326–27; letter to, Aug. 24, 1870, 259–60; letter to, Sept. 8, 1870, 264; letter to, Oct. 23, 1870, 323–24; letter to, Oct. 26, 1870, 326–27
Ely, James T. (asst. secretary to USG): letter to, Oct. 1, 1870, 464
Elyria, Ohio, 201n
Embry, Bowling (postmaster), 5n
Embry, J. O. (customhouse clerk), 5n
Embry, James H. (of Ky.), 3, 5n
Emerson, Ralph Waldo (author), 86n
Emery, Francis F. (of Boston): letter to, May 10, 1870, 425
Emmons, Halmer H. (U.S. Circuit Judge), 69n
English, James E. (Gov. of Conn.): letter to, June 17, 1870, 186n
Enochs, William H. (Ohio representative), 415
Enon Valley, Pa., 353
Erie, Pa., 385
Erskine, John (U.S. District Judge), 110n
Esmeralda County, Nev., 245n
Eunche, Mr. (of Mo.), 149n
Eureka, Kan., 450

Evans, George O., 344

Evans, John (Gov. of Colorado Territory), 321*n*

Evanson, Dr. (of Torquay, England): letter to, Jan. 25, 1870, 374

Evarts, William M. (attorney), 7*n*, 17*n*, 48*n*, 333

Everett, Edward (of Mass.), 268*n*

Everett, William, 268*n*

Exeter, N.H., 334

Exeter, N.Y., 234*n*

Fabens, Joseph W. (Dominican minister), 153, 159*n*, 188

Fairchild, Lucius (Gov. of Wis.), 116*n*, 395–96

Fairfield, Iowa, 71*n*

Farmington, Conn., 190–91, 278, 279*n*

Farnham, N. C. (clerk), 432

Farnsworth, John F. (U.S. Representative), 199*n*, 407

Farragut, David G. (U.S. Navy), 283 and *n*, 461

Farrell, Raymond F. (U.S. consul), 370–71

Farrow, Henry P. (Ga. attorney general), 363

Faulkner, Peter (of Erie, Pa.), 385

Favre, Jules (of France), 255*n*, 257*n*, 258*n*

Fayetteville, Ark., 336

Fayetteville, Tenn., 353

Felder, Adam C. (of Ala.), 341

Fell, Adalbert (U.S. Army), 406–7

Fell, J. Gillingham (of Philadelphia), 442

Fell, Mathilde (of Baltimore), 406

Felt, Katherine (of Galena), 234*n*

Fendall, Philip R., Jr. (U.S. Marine Corps), 430

Fenians: imprisoned in Great Britain, 115, 115*n*–18*n*, 428; raid Canada, 151, 152*n*, 268*n*, 319*n*; pardoned, 222, 223*n*, 225, 226*n*, 305, 306*n*–7*n*; amnesty for, 232, 252

Fenton, Reuben E. (U.S. Senator), 60*n*, 93*n*, 188*n*, 263*n*–64*n*

Fernald, Henry B. (of D.C.), 438

Fernandina, Fla., 453

Ferry, Orris S. (U.S. Senator), 166, 167*n*

Ferry, Thomas W. (U.S. Representative), 68*n*

Fidler, James M. (of Lebanon, Ky.), 379

Field, Richard S. (U.S. District Judge), 419

Fielding, Wrenshall D. (storekeeper), 139*n*

Fifteenth Amendment: ratification celebrated, 12*n*, 137, 138*n*; praised, 13*n*, 14*n*; ratified, 15–16, 16*n*, 91, 130–31, 132*n*–33*n*, 313, 405, 426, 427; protection sought under, 15*n*; considered in Miss., 96

Figures, W. B. (of Huntsville, Ala.), 339–40

Fiji, 430

Filkins, Morgan L. (postmaster), 140*n*

Fillmore, John S. (U.S. Army), 387

Finance: national debt, 20, 22, 23–24, 37, 44*n*, 61*n*, 160, 257*n*, 282*n*, 313; currency, 21–22, 23, 38, 44*n*, 322*n*, 323*n*; tariffs, 23, 32, 35, 44*n*; government appropriations, 89–90, 90*n*, 190, 372, 405; U.S. credit abroad, 92*n*, 445; and U.S. merchant marine, 124–26; related to Santo Domingo, 134*n*, 156–57; Mexican investment, 161*n*

Finney, Bernard (of St. Louis): letter to, March 7, 1870, 392

Fischer, LeRoy H., Stillwater, Okla.: document owned by, 127–28

Fischer, Samuel C. (of Richmond), 347

Fish, Hamilton (U.S. Secretary of State): makes diplomatic appointments, 3, 85*n*, 87*n*, 142, 143*n*, 144 and *n*, 175*n*, 181 and *n*, 218*n*, 231*n*, 273 and *n*, 274*n*–75*n*, 276*n*, 282*n*, 296*n*, 370–71, 382, 396, 401, 406, 410, 411, 412, 441, 442; schedules diplomatic interviews, 12*n*, 127*n*, 265*n*–66*n*, 421; submits reports, 16*n*, 49*n*, 96 and *n*, 115 and *n*, 116*n*–17*n*, 118*n*, 350, 375, 379, 381, 385–86, 389–90, 391, 394, 398–99, 401, 410, 414, 419, 427, 428, 430, 432, 440–41, 442, 443; administers dept., 27, 46*n*, 60*n*, 93*n*, 94*n*–95*n*, 147–48, 201*n*, 223*n*, 246–47, 247*n*, 255*n*, 257*n*, 258*n*, 279–80, 318*n*, 341, 351, 387, 407, 408, 427, 436, 445, 455; reports cabinet meetings, 44*n*–45*n*, 47*n*–48*n*, 55*n*, 90*n*, 196*n*, 293*n*; forwards contribution to Edwin M. Stanton fund, 80*n*; as gov. of N.Y., 97*n*; opposes Santo Domingo annexation, 122*n*–23*n*, 123–24, 124*n*, 134*n*–35*n*,

Fish, Hamilton (*cont.*)

157n–59n, 162 and n, 163n, 166 and n, 176 and n, 312n; reports ratification of Fifteenth Amendment, 132n–33n, 138n; conducts foreign affairs, 135 and n, 136n, 153n, 214n, 240n, 268n, 458; involved in politics, 141n, 170n–71n, 189n, 302n, 359–60; deals with Fenians, 152n, 225–26, 226n–27n, 305, 306n, 307n; policy toward Cuba, 168n–70n, 348, 394, 418–19; may resign, 172n, 184n; seeks successor for John L. Motley, 183, 183n–86n, 191, 192n, 222, 225–26, 227n, 232, 232n–33n, 266 and n, 267, 268n, 316n–17n, 320n–21n; in Canadian affairs, 338; suppresses slave trade, 403; reports reception for Indians, 433; during Civil War, 457; mentioned, 337, 405

—Correspondence from USG: letter to, Nov. 6, 1869, 3; letter to, March 22, 1870, 123–24; letter to, April 19, 1870, 142; letter to, April 25, 1870, 144; endorsement to, [May], 1869, 144n; letter to, May 11, 1870, 147–48; letter to, June 8, 1870, 162; letter to, June 9, 1870, 166; letter to, June 18, 1870, 176; letter to, June 30, 1870, 181; letter to, July 1, 1870, 183; letter to, July 14, 1870, 191; letter to, Aug. 7, 1870, 222; telegram to, Aug. 6, 1870, 222n; letter to, Aug. 18, 1870, 225–26; undated telegram to, 226n; letter to, Aug. 21, 1870, 232; letter to, Aug. 22, 1870, 246–47; telegram to, Sept. 6, 1870, 255n; letter to, Sept. 10, 1870, 266; telegram to, Sept. 6, 1870, 266n; telegram to, Sept. 7, 1870, 266n; telegrams to, Sept. 10, 1870 (2), 266n; letter to, Sept. 14, 1870, 267; letter to, Sept. 22, 1870, 273; letter to, Sept. 28, 1870, 279–80; letter to, Oct. 8, 1870, 305; letter to, Feb. 26, 1870, 396; endorsement to, March 21, 1870, 406; endorsement to, March [24], 1870, 407; endorsement to, March 31, 1870, 410; endorsement to, May 29, 1870, 412; endorsement to, [April], 1870, 419; endorsement to, July 11, 1870, 441; endorsement to, July 12, 1870, 442

Fish, Hamilton, Jr., 226n, 232

Fish, Julia K. (wife of Hamilton Fish), 175n, 222, 226

Fishback, George W. (*Missouri Democrat*), 110n

Fisher, George P. (U.S. District Attorney), 242n, 424–25

Fisher, John (U.S. Representative), 148 and n

Fisk, James, Jr. (speculator), 282n

Fiske, John S. (U.S. consul), 181n

Fitch, Henry S. (U.S. District Attorney), 174n, 175n

Fitch, Thomas (U.S. Representative), 73n

Fitzgerald, John (of Dayton), 460

Flanders, Alvan (Gov. of Washington Territory), 350–51

Flint, Weston (U.S. consul), 284n–85n

Florence, Italy, 111n, 280n

Flores, Antonio (Ecuadorian minister), 126–27, 127n

Florida, 75, 83n, 95n, 192–95, 352, 384, 466–67

Florida (C.S. Navy), 87n

Fogg, Peter (of Boston), 115n

Folger, Charles J. (N.Y. judge), 262n, 429

Foo Chow, China, 214n–15n, 382

Forbes, Paul S., 321n

Force, Manning F. (of Cincinnati), 293n–94n, 471

Ford, Augustus (brother of Charles W. Ford), 278, 327n

Ford, Charles W. (friend of USG): manages USG's business, 6–7, 76–77, 128n, 138–39, 139n, 144–46, 149 and n, 165 and n, 177–78, 219–20, 278, 284, 307, 313, 323, 324, 326, 327 and n; appointed collector of Internal Revenue, 7n; recommends appointments, 72n, 139n, 314n–15n; denounces John McDonald, 149, 149n–50n; active in politics, 260, 284; assists Julia Dent Grant, 327n–28n

—Correspondence from USG: letter to, Nov. 12, 1869, 6–7; letter to, Jan. 3, 1870, 76–77; letter to, April 7, 1870, 138–39; telegrams to, April 25, 1870 (2), 139n; letter to, May 5, 1870, 144–45; letter to, May 9, 1870, 145–46; telegrams to, May 13, 1870 (2), 146n; letter to, May 16, 1870, 149;

letter to, June 8, 1870, 165; telegram to, June 17, 1870, 165n; letter to, June 27, 1870, 177–78; letter to, Aug. 2, 1870, 219–20; letter to, Sept. 3, 1870, 260; letter to, Sept. 22, 1870, 278; letter to, Sept., 1870, 284; letter to, Oct. 8, 1870, 307; letter to, Oct. 20, 1870, 313–14; letter to, Oct. 23, 1870, 324; letter to, Oct. 26, 1870, 327

Fordham, N.Y., 115n

Formosa, 355

Forney, James (U.S. Marine Corps), 354–55

Forney, John W. (*Washington Chronicle*), 163, 164n, 300n, 355

Forrest, Nathan B., 211n

Fort Abercrombie, Dakota Territory, 120n

Fort Brady, Mich., 272n

Fort Brown, N.Y., 360

Fort Carroll, Md., 449

Fort Donelson, Tenn., battle of, 386

Fort Erie, Canada, 411

Fort Gibson, Indian Territory, 205n

Fort Hall, Idaho Territory, 474

Fort Hamilton, N.Y., 368

Fort Harker, Kan., 456

Fort Jefferson, Fla., 445

Fort Kearny, Neb., 334

Fort Laramie, Wyoming Territory, 361

Fort Monroe, Va., 364

Fort Reynolds, Colorado Territory, 289n

Fort Richardson, Tex., 417

Fort Ripley, Minn., 120n

Fort Schuyler, N.Y., 385

Fort Scott, Kan., 417

Fort Smith, Ark., 205n, 207n

Fort Sumter, S.C., 368

Fort Tongass, Alaska, 356

Fort Vancouver, Washington Territory, 385

Fort Wallace, Kan., 288n

Fort Wayne, Ind., 385

Foster, John G. (writer), 58 and n

Foster, John S. (seaman), 446–47

Foster, Lafayette S. (of Conn.), 63n

Fourteenth Amendment, 20, 38, 132n, 212n, 313

Fox, Elias W. (surveyor), 270n

Fox, John (U.S. Representative), 441

Foy, Louis (of Terrell County, Ga.), 474–75

France: U.S. diplomacy with, 33–34, 35, 44n, 302–5; USG's interest in, 91, 91n–92n; revolution in, 92n, 93n; consuls in, 113n, 386, 451; expects war with Germany, 196 and n; minister to U.S., 200, 200n–201n; at war with Germany, 201n, 216n–18n, 235–40, 254, 255n–56n, 257n–58n, 318n, 319n, 321n, 441, 445, 452, 453; colonizes Tahiti, 223n; claim against, 386; U.S. ship at, 395; interested in Nicaraguan canal, 401–2; legislature of, 435; mentioned, 110n, 175n

Frank, Royal T. (U.S. Army), 461

Frankfort Commonwealth (newspaper), 352

Franklin, Benjamin, 426

Franklin, Jane (wife of Sir John Franklin): letter to, Aug. 8, 1870, 223; sends book to USG, 223 and n

Franklin, Sir John (Arctic explorer), 223 and n

Franklin, Pa., 349

Franklin (U.S. Navy), 395

Franks, George S. (prisoner), 449–50

Franz Josef I (Austrian Emperor), 268n

Frederick, Md., 66n, 323n, 328

Frederick William III (King of Prussia), 238

Freehold, N.J., 267n

Freeman, John H. (postmaster), 340–41

Frelinghuysen, Frederick T. (of N.J.): recommends appointment, 56n; considered for minister to Great Britain, 183, 191, 192n, 247, 256n, 296n; identified, 188n; declines nomination, 192n

Frémont, John C., 405

Fremont County, Colorado Territory, 286n, 287n, 288n, 289n

French, E. R. (pardon clerk), 305

French, William H. (U.S. Army), 355

Freyre, Manuel (Peruvian minister), 29, 47n

Friedsam, Morris (assessor), 413

Front Royal, Va., 423, 424

Froude, James A. (*Fraser's Magazine*), 319n, 320n, 321n

Gaines, Myra Clark (of New Orleans), 66n

Gaines, N.Y., 371, 372

Gale, A. D. (of New Lebanon, N.Y.): letter to, Oct. 18, 1870, 472

Galena, Ill., 70n, 93n

Galesburg, Ill., 254n

Gallagher, William D., 352

Gallatin River, 434

Gallery of History, Las Vegas, Nev.: documents in, 220n–21n, 382

Galveston, Tex., 162n

Gambetta, Léon (of France), 255n

Gambling, 262n

Garesché, Alexander J. P. (of St. Louis), 139n

Garfield, James A. (U.S. Representative), 160, 262n, 445, 467

Garfielde, Selucius (U.S. Delegate), 351, 385, 407

Garrett, John W. (Baltimore and Ohio Railroad), 374–75

Garrison, N.Y., 201n, 226n, 232n, 255n, 265n

Gartrell, Lucius J. (of Atlanta), 174n

Gaston (of Mobile), 445

Gaston County, N.C., 210n

Gaw, William B. (of Chattanooga), 391–92

Gay, Ebenezer (U.S. Army), 349

Gay, Edward J. (of La.), 344

Gay, John H. (of La.), 344

Geary, John W. (Gov. of Pa.), 354–55

General Grant National Memorial, New York, N.Y.: document in, 188

Geneva, N.Y., 262n

George, D. B., 339

Georgetown, Ohio, 373, 469

Georgia: Reconstruction in, 19–20, 61, 61n–62n, 92n, 103, 103n–8n, 132n, 285, 289n–91n; Democrats in, 86n; appointments in, 174n, 290n, 362–63; Republicans in, 174n–75n, 437, 467; intruders from, 249n; investigation in, 439–40; garrisoned, 466; state fair, 468; mentioned, 110n, 174

Germantown, Pa., 408

Germany: travelers to, 111n, 447; immigrants from, 141n, 189n, 199n, 285n–89n, 347; at war with France, 196, 201n, 216n–17n, 218n, 235–40, 254, 255n–56n, 257n–58n, 318 and n, 319n, 321n; steamship lines from, 196n; violates U.S. neutrality, 223n, 226n, 303–5; treaties with, 238; U.S.

diplomacy with, 281n, 341, 432; U.S. bonds purchased in, 282n; consular jurisdiction in, 386; mentioned, 175n, 355, 406

Gerolt, Baron F. von (Prussian minister), 34, 201n, 223n, 238

Gibbs, Alfred (U.S. Army), 373

Gibbs, Peggy F. (of New York City), 373

Giddings, William W. (USMA applicant), 441

Gillis, Bosanquet W. (*Richmond State Journal*), 345–46

Gillmore, Quincy A. (U.S. Army), 221

Gilmer, George K. (of Richmond), 346, 347

Gilmor, Harry (C.S. Army), 354

Girard, Kan., 417

Glascock, Edwin R. (marshal), 356

Glenwood, Iowa, 447

Glinka, Dimitrii G. (Russian minister to Brazil): letter to, Oct. 31, 1870, 475

Gloucester, Mass., 434

Glover, Samuel T. (St. Louis attorney), 138–39, 139n, 140n, 145, 146n, 147n, 224

Gobright, Lawrence A. (newspaper correspondent), 299n

Godoy, Joaquin (Chilean minister), 265n, 266n

Gold, 21, 22, 44n, 76, 93n, 127n, 180n, 241n, 245n, 349, 449

Goldsborough, Edward Y. (marshal), 342

Gomez, Vicente P., 241n

Goodyear, Charles P. (of Ga.), 467

Gordon, George Hamilton, Lord Aberdeen, 281n

Gorham, George C. (U.S. Senate secretary), 379, 409

Goshen, Md., 459

Gott, John N. (Receiver of Public Lands), 245n

Gould, Jay (speculator), 322n

Gouverneur, Samuel L. (of Frederick, Md.), 382

Graham, Walter L. (of Butler, Pa.), 84n

Gramont, Antoine, Duc de (French foreign minister), 216n

Grand Army of the Republic, 369

Grand Cayman Island, 75

Grand Rapids, Wis., 439

Grant, Ellen (daughter of USG): travels with Julia Dent Grant, 173; sent to school, 190–91, 274, 278, 279n; welcomes cousin's birth, 234n; mentioned, 325, 456

Grant, Frederick Dent (son of USG): attends USMA, 173, 190, 232, 283, 319n, 325, 328–29, 329n; telegram to, June 26, 1870, 173n; letter to, [Oct.–Nov., 1870], 328–29

Grant, Hannah Simpson (mother of USG), 234

Grant, Jesse Root (father of USG): letter to, Jan. 15, 1870, 88–89; active in patronage, 88–89, 89n, 273 and n, 352, 469, 470; as postmaster, 89n

Grant, Jesse Root, Jr. (son of USG), 167n, 173, 234n, 283, 325

Grant, Julia Dent (wife of USG): discusses patronage, 7n, 139n; plans Christmas gathering, 57; charitable activities of, 73n–74n; praises Edwin M. Stanton, 78n; meets son in Boston, 160; letter to, June 15, 1870, 173; traveling, 173 and n; telegram to, June 14, 1870, 173n; travels with USG, 185n, 232, 233–34, 235 and n, 278, 283; invited to Conn., 186n; letter to, Aug. 10, 1870, 224; letter to, Aug. 11, 1870, 224–25; informed about USG's travels, 224–25, 224n; telegram to, Aug. 16, 1870, 224n; health of, 234; conveys family news, 234n; withdraws Ellen Grant from school, 279n; concerned about children, 325; ships furniture, 327n–28n; introduction to, 344; issues invitations, 367, 415; receives visitors, 430; receives appeals, 432, 445; mentioned, 90n, 111n, 147n, 159, 178n, 190, 222, 226, 243n, 247, 256n, 258n, 261, 281n, 283n, 319n, 347, 348, 368, 409, 418, 441, 456

Grant, Orvil L. (brother of USG), 357–59

Grant, Ulysses S.: early life, 4n, 68n, 80–81, 94n; finances of, 6–7, 58n, 76–77, 138–39, 139n, 144–46, 145n, 146n–47n, 149 and n, 165 and n, 177–78, 178n, 224, 278, 284, 307, 313, 324; receives gifts, 7–8, 8n, 234n, 328, 337, 347–48, 368, 370, 390, 391, 472, 473; administers Reconstruction, 15–16, 61, 61n–62n, 103 and n, 104n, 105n, 107n, 108n,

210, 210n–13n, 466; enforces neutrality in Cuba, 27, 165–66, 167–68, 169n–70n; Indian policy, 38–39, 100, 103n, 118–19, 119n–20n, 195–96, 271, 296n, 315 and n, 326, 383, 403, 433; equestrian statue of, 51, 52n; owns horses, 51, 128, 178n, 259, 324, 326, 327; Supreme Court appointments, 54n, 55n, 77–78, 79n, 171n; visits Pittsburgh, 56n; entertains relatives, 57 and n, 58n; receives books, 58 and n, 223, 368, 369–70, 374, 412, 472, 475; visits Long Branch, 58n, 111n, 146, 159, 172n, 184n, 210–83 passim, 293n, 296n, 297n, 298n, 300n, 301n, 318n, 452, 458, 460, 465, 470; attends Mary Surratt's trial, 64n; donates to charity, 73 and n; Santo Domingo policy, 74–76, 121, 122n–23n, 123–24, 124n, 133–34, 134n–35n, 153–57, 157n–59n, 162 and n, 163, 163n–64n, 166 and n, 176 and n, 179, 180n, 183n, 188, 189n, 311–12, 312n; visits New York City, 78n, 185n, 235 and n, 266 and n, 275n; meets Prince Arthur, 90 and n; trustee of Rawlins fund, 97, 97n–98n; visits Chicago, 111n, 224, 317n, 453; supports Henry B. Anthony, 114–15; sells house to William T. Sherman, 121, 219n; promotes U.S. merchant marine, 124–26; owns St. Louis farm, 127–28, 128n, 224, 225, 259–60, 264, 323–24, 326–27, 328; praises George H. Thomas, 128, 129n; punishes Winfield S. Hancock, 129n–30n; announces ratification of Fifteenth Amendment, 130–31, 137, 138n; encourages interoceanic canal, 135, 135n–36n; sends Adam Badeau to London, 142, 143n; plans visit to St. Louis, 145, 178 and n, 219–20; warned about John McDonald, 149, 149n–50n; ill, 152n; goes trout fishing, 166, 167n; accepts Ebenezer R. Hoar's resignation, 170, 170n–73n; nominates Amos T. Akerman, 174; during Civil War, 182n, 221, 257n, 273, 319n–20n, 435, 453, 456; replaces minister to Great Britain, 183, 183n–86n, 187n–88n, 191, 192n; visits Conn., 186n–87n; belittles Congress, 190; vetoes bills, 192–95, 362; promoted for reelection, 200n; accused of being pro-German, 201n; re-

Grant, Ulysses S. (*cont.*)
　action to Franco-Prussian War, 216*n*–
　17*n*, 235–40, 302–5; administers
　army, 218, 227–28; purchases clothes,
　220, 220*n*–21*n*; visits St. Louis, 222,
　224–25, 224*n*, 227, 228*n*, 269; in
　Cleveland, 224*n*; visits USMA, 232,
　233, 235, 251, 259; visits Newport,
　R.I., 232, 233, 235*n*, 251, 252, 259–
　60, 259*n*, 260*n*; servant of, 259, 326,
　327; encourages veterans' preference,
　269; makes travel plans, 278, 283;
　photographs of, 282*n*; accepts Jacob
　D. Cox's resignation, 292, 292*n*–
　302*n*; prohibits filibustering, 307–9;
　supervises railroad, 333–34; attends
　theater, 375; in Philadelphia, 376,
　409; secretary of war *ad interim*, 385;
　inspects South, 420; offered C.S.A.
　archives, 424; sends gift of watch,
　426; threatened, 438–39; personal
　secretary resigns, 464
Grant, Ulysses S., Jr. (son of USG):
　letter to, June 3, 1870, 160; examined
　at Harvard, 160, 190; clothes for,
　220; travels with USG, 220, 224;
　attends Harvard, 274, 278, 325; let-
　ter to, Oct. 23, 1870, 325; in N.H.,
　334; visits friends, 408
Grant, Ulysses S., 3rd (grandson of
　USG): documents owned by, 57*n*,
　61*n* (2), 97*n*–98*n*, 98*n*, 105*n*–6*n*,
　139*n*, 145–46, 146*n*, 146*n*–47*n*, 149,
　160*n*–61*n*, 173, 178*n*, 187*n*–88*n*,
　189*n*, 192*n*, 219–20, 219*n*, 224,
　224–25, 224*n*, 228*n*, 228*n*–29*n*,
　240–41, 241*n*–43*n*, 244*n*–45*n*, 256*n*
　(2), 281*n*, 282*n*, 282*n*–83*n*, 284*n*,
　292*n*–93*n*, 312–13, 319*n*–20*n*, 320*n*–
　21*n*, 328–29, 366
Grant Association, Ulysses S., Carbon-
　dale, Ill.: documents in, 223, 269–70
Gravellote, France, battle of, 216*n*
Gray, Isaac P. (of Ind.), 435
Great Britain: U.S. diplomacy with,
　27, 29–32, 33, 34–35, 48*n*, 49*n*,
　256*n*, 268*n*, 317*n*, 350; owns Carib-
　bean islands, 75; Prince Arthur visits
　USG, 90 and *n*; imprisons Fenians,
　115, 115*n*–18*n*, 306*n*–7*n*, 428; Anti-
　Slavery Society, 138*n*; governs Can-
　ada, 151, 158*n*, 337–38, 382; natu-
　ralization treaty with, 152–53, 153*n*;
　U.S. diplomats in, 163*n*, 401; min-
　ister to, 183, 183*n*–86*n*, 187*n*–88*n*,

191, 192*n*, 222, 225–26, 229–30,
232, 232*n*–33*n*, 247, 248*n*, 266, 267,
268*n*, 274 and *n*, 281*n*, 294*n*, 296*n*,
298*n*, 302*n*, 312, 313, 316, 316*n*–
17*n*, 318, 319*n*, 320*n*–21*n*, 348–49;
Ambrose E. Burnside visits, 217*n*; ex-
plores Arctic, 223 and *n*; minister to
France, 258*n*; universities in, 280*n*;
boundary treaties with, 281*n*; postal
convention with, 339; Miners National Association, 344; in War of
1812, 360; Queen congratulated, 362;
naval ship, 394; suppresses slave
trade, 402, 403, 445; fisheries, 410;
colonies of, 425; extends interoceanic
cable, 436; mentioned, 180*n*, 374,
427, 462
Greeley, Horace (*New York Tribune*):
　recommends appointments, 17*n*–18*n*;
　proposes Cuban policy, 46*n*; consid-
　ered for minister to Great Britain,
　230, 232, 232*n*–33*n*, 317*n*; identified,
　230*n*; in politics, 230*n*–31*n*, 232*n*
Green, Charles L. (U.S. Navy), 348
Green, Moses P. (of Mo.), 468
Greene, Roger S. (Washington Terri-
　tory Supreme Court), 407
Greenville and Columbia Railroad,
　250*n*
Greenwood County, Kan., 451
Gregory, Robert C. (Ind. Supreme
　Court), 69*n*
Gregory, Walter R. (of Becker County,
　Minn.), 473–74
Gresham, Walter Q. (of Ind.), 5*n*,
　59*n*, 69*n*, 365
Grey, Alexander T. (of D.C.), 440
Grier, Robert C. (U.S. Supreme
　Court): letter to, Dec. 15, 1869, 52;
　resigns, 52, 53*n*, 56*n*, 79*n*
Griffin, Charles (U.S. Army), 162*n*
Griffin, Mrs. Charles, 430
Griffins, J. N. (of Ga.), 475
Griffith, Joseph E. (U.S. Army), 456
Grinnell, Moses H. (collector): asked
　for appointment, 5*n*, 388; subscriber
　to Rawlins fund, 97, 97*n*–98*n*; not in
　Washington, D.C., 140; appointed,
　140*n*–41*n*; replaced, 141*n*; as collec-
　tor of customs, 370
Griswold, John A. (of Troy, N.Y.),
　334
Guatemala, 447
Gunpowder Bridge (Md.), 355, 430

Gurnee, Walter S. (of New York City), 61n

Gwinner, Henry W. (Pennsylvania Railroad), 199n

Habeas Corpus, 17n, 210n, 211n, 212n, 381

Hadley, R. P. (of Girard, Kan.), 417

Haiti, 8–9, 9n–15n, 122n

Hale, R. S. (Treasury counsel), 439

Hall, Alfred P. (of Front Royal, Va.), 423–24

Hall, Charles F. (Arctic explorer): argues over command, 137n; letter to, July 20, 1870, 209; commands expedition, 209 and n

Hall, Gared (asst. marshal), 459

Hall, John W. (of Goshen, Md.), 459

Halleck, Henry W. (U.S. Army), 320n, 466

Hallett, Moses (Colorado Territory Supreme Court), 408

Halpin, William G. (Fenian), 116n–18n

Ham, Charles H. (appraiser), 254n

Hamburg, Germany, 196n

Hamilton, Andrew J. (Gov. of Tex.), 463

Hamilton, John C., 407–8

Hamilton, Morgan C. (U.S. Senator), 463–64

Hamilton, Canada, 411

Hamilton, Nev., 418

Hamilton County, Tenn., 291n

Hamlin, Hannibal (U.S. Senator), 413

Hampton, Ga., 437

Hampton, Va., 412

Hancock, Winfield S. (U.S. Army), 129n–30n

Hannibal, Mo., 468

Hanscom, William L. (U.S. Navy), 433

Hardenbergh, James R. (surveyor general), 88n

Hardie, James A. (U.S. Army), 229n

Hardy (Sister of the Sacred Heart), 111n

Harlan, James (U.S. Senator), 375

Harlan, John M. (of Louisville): letter to, Nov. 4, 1869, 334

Harris, Charles C. (Hawaiian minister of finance), 84n

Harris, Cornelius (of Richmond), 345

Harris, Edward (of Woonsocket, R.I.): letter to, Oct. 21, 1870, 473

Harris, Ira (of N.Y.), 63n–64n

Harris, James H. (N.C. legislator), 50n

Harris, Thomas C. (U.S. Navy), 354

Harrison, Horace H. (U.S. District Attorney), 309n–10n, 311n

Harrison, John C. S. (Union Pacific Railroad), 6n

Harrison, T. W. (of West Va.), 64n

Harrison, Thomas J. (marshal), 309, 309n–10n, 311n

Harrison, William H. (U.S. President), 6n

Harrisonville, Ill., 464

Hartford, Conn., 84n, 186n, 278, 355

Hartmont, Edward H. (Dominican consul-general), 123n, 159n

Harvard University, Cambridge, Mass.: graduates of, 86n, 227n, 248n; Ulysses S. Grant, Jr., attends, 160, 190, 274, 278, 325; document in, 163n–64n

Harvey, James M. (Gov. of Kan.), 202n, 203n, 415, 416

Haskell, William G. (Universalist minister), 97, 98n

Hatch, Davis, 166, 166n–67n

Hatteras Inlet (N.C.), 430

Havana, Cuba, 47n, 390, 418

Havre, France, 86n

Havre de Grace, Md., 354, 430

Hawaii, 81, 81n–88n, 144n, 275n, 276n, 425

Hawkins, Isaac R. (U.S. Representative), 96n

Hawley, Joseph R. (of Conn.), 84n

Hawthorne, Sophia P. (wife of Nathaniel Hawthorne), 321n

Hay, Henry P. (secretary of legation), 280n, 281n

Haycock, George B. (U.S. Marine Corps), 430

Hayes, Isaac I. (Arctic explorer), 137n, 209n

Hayes, Rutherford B. (Gov. of Ohio): recommends appointments, 67n, 73n, 363–64, 387, 415, 460, 469, 470, 471; forwards resolution regarding George H. Thomas, 129n; visits White House, 180n

Hayes Library, Rutherford B., Fremont, Ohio: documents in, 62n–63n, 63n, 64n (2), 65n (3), 66n–67n, 120n, 127n, 129n (2), 140n–41n, 170, 170n, 179n, 186n, 293n–94n,

Hayes Library, Rutherford B. (*cont.*)
336, 354–55, 360, 375, 386, 387,
407, 415, 418 (2), 421–22, 426–27,
435, 440, 442, 464, 468, 468–69
Hazen, William B. (U.S. Army),
202*n*, 203*n*, 218*n*
Head, George E. (writer), 58 and *n*
Heath, Anna Rosa (wife of Herman
H. Heath), 376, 377
Heath, Henry A. (of Whitefield,
Maine), 425
Heath, Herman H. (secretary, New
Mexico Territory), 375–77
Heathsville, Va., 420
Heisterman, H. F. (of British Colum-
bia), 337–38
Helena, Montana Territory, 434, 454
Henderson, Alexander (U.S. consul),
455
Hendricks, Thomas A. (of Ind.), 274*n*
Hendrickson, C. (of New York City),
391
Henry, Joseph (Smithsonian Institu-
tion), 350
Henry, Thomas (of New Castle, Pa.),
461–62
Henry, William (of New Castle, Pa.),
462
Henson, A. W. (of Cincinnati), 11*n*–
12*n*
Hepburn, John Bell (of Port-au-
Prince), 13*n*–14*n*
Hepburn v. *Griswold*, 323
Herwig, Philip F. (deputy collector),
400
Hesing, Anton C. (*Illinois Staats Zei-
tung*): letter to, June 13, 1870, 111*n*
Hewit, Mrs. Henry S., 111*n*
Heynemann, Henry (of New York
City), 446
Hickenlooper, Andrew (marshal),
364–67
Highland Falls, N.Y., 112
Hill, Joshua (of Ga.), 174*n*, 290*n*,
405
Hill, Robert J. (of St. Louis), 315*n*
Hill, Thomas P. (of Va.), 399
Hill, William L. (of Ore.), 407
Hillhouse, Thomas (asst. treasurer),
429
Hillsboro, N.C., 210*n*
Hillyer, Curtis J. (of Calif.), 73*n*
Hillyer, William S. (friend of USG),
157*n*, 175*n*, 243*n*–44*n*, 370

Hillyer, William S., Jr. (of New York
City), 111*n*
Hinman, Frank H. (U.S. Navy), 414
Hirsch, L. (of Washington Territory),
352
Hitch, Henry F. (of New York City),
87*n*
Hoag, Enoch (Indian superintendent),
202*n*, 203*n*
Hoar, Ebenezer R. (U.S. Attorney
General): involved in appointments,
17*n*, 64*n*, 70*n*, 86*n*, 93*n*, 95*n*, 162*n*,
314*n*, 408; advises USG, 45*n*; renders opinions, 48*n*, 106*n*–7*n*, 150,
151*n*, 241*n*, 244*n*, 400–401; nominated for U.S. Supreme Court, 54*n*–
55*n*, 92*n*, 171*n*, 405; undated endorsement to, 70*n*; endorsement to,
Dec. 22, 1869, 95*n*; endorsement to,
May 17, 1870, 150; opposes Santo
Domingo annexation, 158*n*, 171*n*;
endorsement to, Oct. 18, 1869, 162*n*;
in Cuban affairs, 169*n*, 418–19; letter
to, June 15, 1870, 170; resigns, 170,
170*n*–73*n*; replaced, 174; considered
for minister to Great Britain, 222,
302*n*; in McGarrahan claim, 241*n*,
244*n*, 300*n*, 302*n*; Jacob D. Cox consults, 294*n*–98*n*, 299*n*–302*n*; endorsement to, Dec. 18, 1869, 314*n*;
letter to, Jan. 24, 1870, 356; administers dept., 356, 361, 365, 366, 375,
424, 431; asked about Indian taxation, 388; endorsement to, March 28,
1870, 408; mentioned, 7*n*, 360
Hobart, Vere Henry, Lord Hobart,
321*n*
Hodges, Albert G. (*Frankfort Commonwealth*), 352
Hoey, John (friend of USG), 259 and
n, 324
Hoff, Henry K. (U.S. Navy), 28, 46*n*,
47*n*
Hoffman, John T. (Gov. of N.Y.),
282*n*
Hoffman, Wickham (secretary of legation), 255*n*, 257*n*
Holden, Mr., 473
Holden, William W. (Gov. of N.C.):
buys uniforms for militia, 176*n*; letter
to, July 22, 1870, 210; upholds Reconstruction, 210, 210*n*–13*n*, 338;
impeached, 213*n*; assists army officer,
461
Holladay, Ben, 110 and *n*, 145*n*, 147*n*

Holladay, Jesse (of San Francisco), 145*n*, 147*n*, 177–78, 178*n*
Holladay, Notley C. (wife of Ben Holladay), 110 and *n*
Holley, Samuel J. (collector), 262*n*
Hollis, Jane (of Elkton, Md.), 475
Hollister, Gideon H. (minister to Haiti), 10*n*, 12*n*, 13*n*–14*n*
Hollister, Madison E. (Idaho Territory Supreme Court), 396
Holt, Joseph (U.S. Judge Advocate): recommended for U.S. Supreme Court, 53*n*; recommends appointment, 65*n*; asked for opinions, 176, 335; renders opinions, 356, 367–68, 386–87, 406–7, 448, 450
Hong Kong, 218*n*
Honolulu, Hawaii, 82*n*, 83*n*–88*n*, 275*n*, 276*n*, 425
Hooper, Samuel (U.S. Representative), 80*n*
Hopkins, James C. (U.S. District Judge), 440
Horton, E. (of Port-au-Prince), 14*n*–15*n*
Hospitals, 47*n*, 88*n*, 248*n*, 385, 414, 458, 462
Houser, Daniel M. (*Missouri Democrat*), 178*n*
Howard, Horatio N., 404
Howard, Jacob M. (U.S. Senator), 65*n*, 68*n*–69*n*, 159*n*, 271 and *n*, 274, 295*n*, 336
Howard, Oliver O. (U.S. Army): recommends appointments, 371, 401, 404, 406, 407, 438, 460; introduces Sojourner Truth, 405; on trial, 435
Howe, John H. (Wyoming Territory Supreme Court), 150, 150*n*–51*n*
Howe, Samuel Gridley (of Mass.), 451
Howe, Timothy O. (U.S. Senator): considered for minister to Great Britain, 233*n*, 266*n*, 296*n*; criticizes Henry Adams, 318, 322*n*–23*n*
Howe, William W. (of La.), 53*n*
Hoy (Sister of the Sacred Heart), 111*n*
Hubbard, John H. (of Litchfield, Conn.), 63*n*
Hubbard, Tobitha (slave), 426
Hubbard, William T. (of Springtown, N.J.), 426
Hudson's Bay & Puget Sound Agricultural Co., 32
Hudson's Bay Co., 381, 382

Hughes, Archelaus M. (U.S. District Attorney), 309, 309*n*–11*n*
Hughes, Mr., 321*n*
Hulse, George T., 278 and *n*, 307
Humboldt, Kan., 207*n*
Humphreys, Andrew A. (U.S. Army), 392
Humphreys, David C. (U.S. District Judge), 53*n*, 425
Humphreys, Joseph M. (collector), 345, 346, 347
Hunt, Ward (of N.Y.), 54*n*
Hunter, David, 425–26
Huntington, 175*n*
Huntington Library, Henry E., San Marino, Calif.: documents in, 69*n*, 230*n*, 352
Huntsville, Ala., 339, 340
Huntsville, Tex., 445, 446, 449
Hurlbut, Stephen A. (minister to Colombia), 28, 135 and *n*, 136*n*
Hutchinson, John H. (U.S. consul), 85*n*
Hyacinthe, Père (Catholic priest), 60*n*

Idaho Territory, 285, 291*n*, 396, 408–9, 459, 474
Ihrie, George P., 391
Illinois, 69*n*, 70*n*, 86*n*, 92*n*, 93*n*, 111*n*, 253, 339, 344–45, 411, 416, 453
Illinois Historical Survey, University of Illinois, Urbana, Ill.: documents in, 259–60, 264, 323–24, 326–27
Illinois Staats Zeitung (newspaper), 111*n*
Illinois State Historical Library, Springfield, Ill.: documents in, 73*n*–74*n*, 76–77, 91, 110, 110*n*, 111*n* (4), 190–91, 254–55, 256*n*, 347–48, 445
Illinois Volunteers, 221 and *n*, 453, 460
Immigration, 34–35, 44*n*, 117*n*–18*n*, 152–53, 153*n*, 197*n*–200*n*, 339, 344, 384, 443
India, 182*n*, 436, 437
Indiana: Republicans in, 5*n*–6*n*, 93*n*, 200*n*; courts in, 69*n*, 70*n*; elections in, 230*n*; elects senator, 266 and *n*, 267, 274*n*–75*n*, 316 and *n*, 318; vols., 311*n*; Democrats in, 316*n*, 318, 323*n*; during Civil War, 451; mentioned, 317*n*, 354
Indiana Historical Society, Indianapolis, Ind.: document in, 69*n*–70*n*

Indianapolis, Ind., 5n, 6n, 59 and n, 69n, 70n, 197n–98n, 199n, 267, 268n, 393, 435, 457

Indianola, Tex., 372

Indians: policy toward, 38–39, 292n, 295n, 296n, 326, 447–48; treaties with, 100, 100n–103n, 205n–8n, 272n, 383, 403, 409, 417; Peace Commission, 118–19; hostilities with, 119n–20n, 132, 287n, 288n, 361, 414, 434, 448, 463, 473–74; appropriations bill, 195–96, 196n; superintendents, 202n, 203n, 221n, 431–32, 458–59, 474; railroad on lands of, 202n–8n; missionaries among, 205n, 272n; Okmulgee council, 205n–7n; mismanagement of, 231n, 341; agents, 271, 271n–72n, 274, 343, 387, 409; on reservations, 315 and n, 352, 432; in Chile, 336; in New Mexico Territory, 342–44; in War of 1812, 360; pardoned, 361; delegations visit White House, 373, 433; taxed, 388–89; educated, 395; kidnap children, 423; consider territorial government, 433; moved to Indian Territory, 455–56; mentioned, 234n, 454

Indian Territory, 101n, 132n, 202n–8n, 214n, 388–89, 433, 455–56

Ingalls, Rufus (U.S. Army), 162n, 369, 370, 385

Ingersoll, L. D. (appraiser), 254n

Inman Steamship Co., 196n

International Steamship Co., 197n–200n

Iowa, 53n, 71n, 72n, 100, 177 and n, 411

Iowa, University of, Iowa City, Iowa: document in, 375

Iowa State Department of History and Archives, Des Moines, Iowa: document in, 333–34

Ireland, 49n, 115n–18n, 141n, 151, 152n, 259n, 307n, 392, 393, 408, 455, 459

Irwin, William R. (Indian commissioner), 103n

Isabella County, Mich., 271n, 272n

Isleta Pueblo, New Mexico Territory, 342

Italy, 35, 148 and n, 258n, 280n–81n, 386, 449

Ithaca, N.Y., 85n

Jackson, Andrew (U.S. President), 184n, 349

Jackson, James B. (U.S. Army), 412

Jackson, James S. (U.S. Army), 412

Jackson, Patsy (of Madison, Ind.), 412

Jackson, Miss., 45n, 96n, 458

Jacksonville, Fla., 466

Jacobs, Orange (Washington Territory Supreme Court), 407

Jamaica, 75

James, Charles P. (of D.C.), 400, 422

James, Mr. (Tenn. legislator), 392

James Adger (steamship), 251n

Jamestown, N.Y., 337

Jamestown (U.S. Navy), 88n

Japan, 36, 394, 458

Jay, John (minister to Austria), 164n, 280n, 447

Jeffers, William N. (U.S. Navy), 402

Jefferson, Thomas (U.S. President), 349

Jefferson, Tex., 449

Jefferson City, Mo., 178n, 270n, 456, 457

Jeffords, Elza (Miss. judge), 66n–67n

Jenckes, Thomas A. (U.S. Representative), 450

Jenks, Charles W. (*The Bureau*), 136n–37n

Jersey City, N.J., 173

Jessup and Moore (of Philadelphia), 282n

Jewell, Esther D. (wife of Marshall Jewell), 186n, 278

Jewell, Marshall (Gov. of Conn.): recommends appointment, 63n; arranges Julia Dent Grant visit, 186n; letter to, Sept. 24, 1870, 278; provides hospitality, 278, 279n; letter to, Oct. 4, 1870, 279n; as envoy extraordinary to Russia, 437

Jewett, Daniel T. (of St. Louis), 270n–71n

Jews, 397–98

Johnson, Alexander S. (of Utica, N.Y.), 17n

Johnson, Andrew (U.S. President): impeached, 3n; befriended, 5n; condemned, 54n, 211n, 231n, 275n, 276n, 277n; appropriations under, 89; appoints Jesse Root Grant, 89n; appointees of, 210n, 280n, 282n, 414, 425, 455, 460; in politics, 366; friend of, 374; planned to prosecute Robert E. Lee, 420; mentioned, 230*n*, 345, 446

Johnson, J. R. (of Ga.), 363

Johnson, James M. (Lt. Gov. of Ark.), 83*n*

Johnson, John H. (D.C. justice of the peace), 65*n*

Johnson, Reverdy (minister to Great Britain), 29, 31, 117*n*, 152

Johnson, William, Jr. (U.S. Navy), 391

Johnson, William B. (War Dept. clerk), 444

Johnson, William S. (U.S. Army), 335–36

Johnston, John W. (U.S. Senator), 45*n*

Jonas, Charles, 447

Jones, J. Russell (friend of USG): as minister to Belgium, 91, 92*n*, 93*n*, 94*n*, 110*n*, 111*n*, 253, 257*n*, 341, 422; resigns as marshal, 93*n*; letter to, May 18, 1870, 110*n*; letter to, Dec. 12, 1871, 111*n*

Jones, Patrick H. (postmaster), 232*n*

Jones, Samuel M. (of Versailles, Ind.), 354

Jones, Thomas L. (U.S. Representative), 89*n*

Jones, William T. (Wyoming Territory Supreme Court), 453

Joy, James F. (railroad official), 203*n*, 416, 417

Judd, Norman B. (U.S. Representative), 111*n*, 422

Julian, George W. (U.S. Representative), 277*n*

Junkin, David X. (Presbyterian minister), 461–62

Jussen, Edmund A. (collector), 358, 359

Kaeo, Peter Y. (of Hawaii), 85*n*

Kalama, Queen (of Hawaii), 88*n*

Kalamazoo, Mich., 394

Kamehameha V (King of Hawaii), 81*n*, 82*n*, 84*n*, 85*n*, 86*n*

Kanaina, Charles (of Hawaii), 85*n*

Kane, Thomas L. (of Kane, Pa.), 167*n*, 349

Kane, Pa., 167*n*, 349

Kansas: courts in, 72*n*, 456; Indians in, 100*n*, 101*n*, 103*n*, 205*n*, 415–17,

432, 448; railroads in, 101*n*–2*n*, 202*n*–8*n*, 415–17; land policy in, 207*n*–8*n*, 450–51, 464; vols., 387; patronage involving, 411

Kansas and Neosho Valley Railroad, 202*n*–8*n*

Kansas Pacific Railroad, 287*n*, 288*n*

Kapff, S. Carl (of New York City): letter to, May 31, 1870, 430

Kaufmann, Sigismund (of New York City), 413

Kaws, 100 and *n*, 101*n*, 102*n*, 103*n*, 432

Keene, Laura (actress), 375

Keim, DeB. Randolph (newspaper correspondent): explains newspaper leak, 157*n*; letter to, July 23, 1870, 214; as consular agent, 214, 214*n*–15*n*

Kelley, William D. (U.S. Representative), 334–35

Kellogg, Lucius D. (appraiser), 438

Kellogg, Stephen W. (U.S. Representative), 185*n*, 399

Kellogg, William P. (Gov. of La.), 344

Kemper County, Miss., 420

Kentucky, 3*n*, 4*n*, 5*n*, 94, 95*n*, 178*n*, 273, 352, 378–79, 380–81, 389, 412, 460, 466

Kentucky, University of, Lexington, Ky.: document in, 234*n*

Keokuk, Iowa, 456

Keough, John W. (of Fort Monroe, Va.), 364

Keough, Mrs. E. A. (of Fort Monroe, Va.), 364

Kerckhoffer and Co., 358

Kerrigan, James E., 251*n*

Ketchum, John B. (of New York City): letter to, April 14, 1870, 414–15

Killam, Frederick, 399

Kilpatrick, H. Judson (minister to Chile), 336

Kinglake, Alexander W. (British historian), 321*n*

Kingman, Samuel H. (U.S. consul), 442

Kingston, Ontario, Canada, 410

Kinkead, J. Henry (of Sitka), 391

Kinney, Constance (of Washington, D.C.), 111*n*

Kinsella, T. J. (customs agent), 350

Kiowas, 414, 423
Kirby, Thomas B. (of Chattanooga), 391–92
Kirk, George W. (N.C. militia), 210n, 212n
Kitchener, Mr. (post trader employee), 367
Kline, Thomas (of Waynesboro, Va.), 87n
Knox County, Ill., 254n
Kodolitsch, Major (Austrian army), 435
Kohn, Morris (claimant), 439–40
Krum, Chester H. (U.S. District Attorney), 270n, 313, 315n, 327
Krum, John M. (St. Louis attorney), 224, 225n, 390
Ku Klux Klan, 210n, 211n, 212n–13n, 338, 380, 475

Labor, 7–8, 8n, 20, 32, 36, 50 and n, 125, 156, 286n, 344, 372, 443
Lafayette, Marquis de, 201n
Lafayette (steamship), 453
Lampber, Dr., 357
Lamper, F. M. (of Washington Territory), 351
Lamson & Goodnow Manufacturing Co. (Shelburne Falls, Mass.): letter to, Nov. 17, 1869, 7–8; presents cutlery to USG, 7–8, 8n
Lancaster, Pa., 164n
Lancaster County, Pa., 352
Lander, Edward (of Washington, D.C.), 65n
Land Policy: for Indians, 39, 100n–103n, 272n, 455–56; public land sales, 42, 422; to promote black settlement, 50n; for immigrants, 199n; for railroads, 202n–8n; McGarrahan claim, 240–41, 241n–45n, 293n, 295n–302n; speculation, 245n–46n; corrupt, 257n; administration of, 276n–77n; disputed in Kan., 416, 417; Homestead Act, 450–51, 452, 464, 465
Lang, John D. (Indian commissioner), 456
Langston, John M. (of Ohio), 11n, 277n
Lanier, James F. D. (of New York City), 111n
Lansing, Iowa, 444
Larned, Josephus N. (*Buffalo Express*), 262n–63n

Larned, Sylvester (of Detroit), 335–36
Larrabee, C. E., 371
Lauderdale Station, Miss., 420
Laurens, S.C., 249n
Lawrence County, Ohio, 415
Lawrence County, Pa., 461
Laycock, John C. (of Philadelphia), 152n
Leabourn, Thomas H., 372
Leaming, Mack J. (assessor), 270n
Leary, Richard P. (U.S. Navy), 442
Leavenworth, Jesse H. (Indian agent), 386–87
Leavenworth, Kan., 149n
Leavenworth, Lawrence, and Fort Gibson Railroad, 204n
Leavitt, Humphrey H. (U.S. District Judge), 364, 468, 469, 470, 471
Lebanon, Pa., 453
Leboeuf, Edmond (French minister of war), 256n, 434–35
Lecomte, Ferdinand (writer), 58, 58n–59n
LeDuc, William G., 424
Lee, Robert E. (C.S. Army), 368, 420, 446, 458, 462
Lee County, Ga., 475
Lee County, Iowa, 177n
Leffingwell, Hiram W. (of St. Louis), 76, 77n
LeGendre, Charles W. (U.S. consul), 443, 457–58
Leith, Scotland, 181 and n, 182n, 410
Lenoir County, N.C., 211n
Leopold, R. H. I. (Treasury agent), 263n, 351
Leopold II (King of Belgium), 422
Leroy, N.Y., 147
Levens, Henry C. (of Boonville, Mo.), 245n
Lewis, Barbour (appraiser), 461
Lewis, Enos E. (U.S. Navy), 426
Lewis, John F. (U.S. Senator), 346, 384
Lewton, George W. (marshal), 276n
Lexington, Va., 341
L'Hommedieu, Stephen S. (of Cincinnati), 111n
Liberia, 55n
Lima, Peru, 28–29, 414
Lincoln, Abraham (U.S. President): praised, 9n, 13n, 14n, 458; appointees of, 53n, 70n–71n, 84n, 87n, 92n, 275n, 276n, 281n, 282n; USG com-

pared with, 132*n*; reelection doubted, 230*n*; considers McGarrahan claim, 244*n*; receives presidential nomination, 263*n*; monument to honor, 352–53; printed tributes, 385–86; commends Jesse H. Leavenworth, 386–87; issues Emancipation Proclamation, 405; subject of lecture, 414; calls out militia, 451; mentioned, 102*n*

Lincoln, Helen (Indian captive), 423

Lincoln, Heloise (Indian captive), 423

Lincoln County, Maine, 425

Lincoln County, Tenn., 353

Lincoln National Life Foundation, Fort Wayne, Ind.: documents in, 78*n*–79*n*, 79*n*, 269

Linden, Tex., 449

Liquor: imported into Hawaii, 82*n*; regulated in Alaska, 99 and *n*; for Indians, 205*n*; soldiers abuse, 349, 356, 367, 448; whiskey frauds, 357–59; wine sent to USG, 370, 390, 391; taxed, 388, 389; used in excess, 413; illicit distilleries, 473

Lis, General (of Haiti), 14*n*

Litchfield, Conn., 63*n*

Little Blue River (Kan.), 334

Little Rock, Ark., 53*n*, 435

Liverpool, England, 117*n*, 280*n*

Lively, Frederick (of Boston), 115*n*

Livingston County, N.Y., 86*n*

Lizzie Major (schooner), 27, 44*n*

Lloyd, Charles F. (U.S. Army), 444

Loan, Benjamin F. (of Mo.), 71*n*

Lockhart, Warren T. (of Carson City, Nev.), 245*n*

Lockland, Ohio, 83*n*

Logan, John (marshal), 344–45

Logan, John A. (U.S. Representative), 410

Logan, Ohio, 465

Logansport, Ind., 230*n*

London, England: agreements signed at, 29, 152; U.S. legation at, 110*n*, 111*n*, 117*n*, 183*n*, 192*n*, 248*n*, 268*n*, 307*n*, 317*n*, 318*n*, 321*n*; consul-general at, 142, 143*n*; newspapers in, 319*n*, 320*n*; mentioned, 159*n*, 176*n*, 181*n*, 185*n*, 188*n*, 280*n*

Londonderry, Ireland, 455

Long, James W. (Indian agent), 272*n*, 295*n*

Long, John F. (of St. Louis County), 225

Long, Stephen H. (U.S. Army), 350

Longacre, Richard E., Wayne, Pa.: document owned by, 173*n*

Long Branch, N.J.: USG visits, 58*n*, 111*n*, 146, 159, 172*n*, 184*n*, 210–83 passim, 293*n*, 296*n*, 297*n*, 298*n*, 300*n*, 301*n*, 318*n*, 452, 458, 460, 465, 470; exposes USG to bad influences, 172*n*; mentioned, 324

Longyear, John W. (U.S. District Judge), 356, 357

Loomis, George (West Va. judge), 65*n*

Loomis, J. Porter (U.S. Navy), 136*n*

Loomis, John S. (of New York City), 344

Loudon, De Witt C. (of Ohio), 469

Loudon, James (of Georgetown, Ohio), 469

Louisiana, 130*n*, 230*n*–31*n*, 344, 400

Louisiana State University, Baton Rouge, La.: documents in, 79*n*, 79*n*–80*n*, 344

Louisville, Ky., 3*n*, 4*n*, 95*n*, 379, 466

Loury (of Ky.), 48*n*

Love, Mrs. Walter, Flint, Mich.: document owned by, 336

Low, Frederick F. (of San Francisco), 373, 458

Lucas, Josiah M. (U.S. consul), 410–12

Lucero, Juan Rey (Pueblo), 342

Luckey, Levi P. (secretary to USG), 390–91

Lunsford, Robert R. (of Bonsack, Va.), 393

Lyons, William H. (Norfolk Navy Yard), 357

Lytle, Thomas (of Treasure City, Nev.), 245*n*–46*n*

Macauley, Daniel (Mayor of Indianapolis), 457

McClellan, George B. (U.S. Army), 258*n*

McClellan, Robert H. (of Galena), 70*n*

McClure, George M. (U.S. Navy), 474

McClure, John (Fenian), 116*n*, 306*n*–7*n*

McClure, William J. (of New York City), 306*n*–7*n*

McClurg, Joseph W. (Gov. of Mo.): recommends appointment, 71*n*; supported for reelection, 270*n*; letter to, Jan. 25, 1870, 375; as gov., 375; supervises elections, 468

McConnell, Harry H. (U.S. Army), 417–18

McCook, Alexander M. (U.S. Army), 111*n*

McCook, Edward M. (Gov. of Colorado Territory): as minister to Hawaii, 83*n*, 84*n*; letter to, Oct. 3, 1870, 285; promotes territorial development, 285, 285*n*–86*n*, 289*n*

McCorkle, Miss, 367

McCosh, James (Princeton College): letter to, June 23, 1870, 437

McCrary, George W. (U.S. Representative), 66*n*

McCulloch, Hugh (U.S. Secretary of the Treasury), 371

McCulloch County, Tex., 463

McDonald, Alexander (of Great Britain), 344

McDonald, Alexander (U.S. Senator), 83*n*, 84*n*, 336

McDonald, James I. (of Heathsville, Va.), 419–20

McDonald, John (supervisor), 139*n*, 149, 149*n*–50*n*

McDougall, Charles (U.S. Army), 382–83

McDougall, William (of Canada), 381

McDowell, Irvin (U.S. Army), 336

McGarrahan, William (of Calif.), 5, 240–41, 241*n*–45*n*, 293*n*, 295*n*–302*n*

McGregor, Iowa, 119*n*

McGrew, James C. (U.S. Representative), 64*n*

McGrew, John S. (surgeon), 85*n*

MacIntyre, M. D. (of Kan.), 448

McKee, William (*Missouri Democrat*), 149*n*

McKennan, William (U.S. Circuit Judge), 56*n*, 57 and *n*, 64*n*, 459, 474

MacKenzie, 178*n*

Mackinac Island, Mich., 295*n*

McLane, Robert M. (of Md.), 452

McLean, Nathaniel C. (of Cincinnati), 470

McMackin, John S. (USMA applicant), 221*n*

McMackin, Warren E. (of Salem, Ill.), 221 and *n*

MacMahon, Maurice de (Marshal of France), 216*n*

McMaster, James A. (*New York Freeman's Journal*), 201*n*

McMichael, William (of Philadelphia): letter to, April 5, 1870, 129*n*

Macmillan and Co.: letter to, March 31, 1870, 412

McMurdy, Edward (of New York City): letter to, Oct. 4, 1870, 465

Macomb, John N. (U.S. Army), 261 and *n*

Macomb, Montgomery M. (U.S. Army), 261 and *n*

Macon, Ga., 426

MacVeagh, Wayne (minister to Turkey), 280 and *n*, 282*n*–83*n*

Maddox, E. J. (of Va.), 407

Madill, George A. (St. Louis judge), 314*n*–15*n*

Madison, Ind., 412

Madison, Wis., 396

Madison County, Ky., 5*n*, 380

Madrid, Spain, 348, 418

Magruder, Alexander (marshal), 352

Maguire, John (of St. Louis), 139*n*, 146*n*, 284

Mahan, Dennis H. (USMA), 328, 329*n*

Mail, 196*n*, 197*n*, 255*n*, 256*n*, 257*n*, 258*n*, 434

Maine, 135*n*, 143*n*, 144*n*, 246, 296*n*, 411, 425

Manchester, England, 472

Maps, 77, 256*n*

Marcy, William L. (U.S. Secretary of State), 281*n*

Marengo, Ill., 452

Marietta, Ga., 174*n*

Marr, James S. (supervisor), 149*n*, 314*n*

Marseilles, France, 395, 410, 451

Marsh, George P. (minister to Italy), 111*n*, 280 and *n*

Marshall, William R. (Gov. of Minn.), 83*n*

Martin, J. S. (of Kan.), 378

Martin, J. Sella (black leader), 50*n*

Martindale, John H. (of N.Y.), 446

Marvin, William (of Fla.), 53*n*

Maryland, 15*n*, 65*n*, 66*n*, 92*n*, 275*n*, 344, 354–55, 426, 458

Mary Lowell (brig), 27, 44*n*, 440

Mason County, Tex., 463

Masons, 353, 446

Massachusetts, 63*n*, 171*n*, 187*n*–88*n*, 226, 227*n*, 248*n*, 302*n*, 317*n*

Massachusetts Historical Society, Boston, Mass.: document in, 59–60

Mathews, Felix A. (U.S. consul), 181 and *n*, 182*n*

Matterhorn, 246

Mattoon, Calvin S. (U.S. consul), 275*n*–76*n*

Maupin, A. T. (postmaster), 87*n*

Maxwell, Edwin (West Va. judge), 65*n*

May, Richard F. (land office receiver), 454

Mayaguez, Puerto Rico, 397

Maynadier, Henry E. (U.S. Army), 384

Maynadier, William (U.S. Army), 384

Maynadier, William (USMA cadet), 384

Maynard, Horace (U.S. Representative), 396

Maysville, Ky., 3*n*, 4*n*

Meade, George G. (U.S. Army), 289*n*–90*n*, 318, 320*n*

Meads, Mrs. M. (of Washington, D.C.), 336–37

Medary, T. C. (of Lansing, Iowa), 444

Medicine: fevers, 47*n*; disabled veterans, 109; insanity, 115*n*–16*n*, 380; physicians, 248*n*, 279, 280*n*; water cure, 255*n*; surgeons, 368–69, 379, 382, 391, 404, 462; yellow fever, 372; dentist, 454–55

Meigs, Fielding P. (U.S. consul), 396

Meigs, Montgomery C. (U.S. Army), 362, 438

Melbourne, Australia, 88*n*

Melcher, Capt., 426

Melcher, Harriet N. (of Boston), 426

Memorial Day, 178*n*

Memphis, Tenn., 95*n*, 96*n*, 420, 461

Memphis, El Paso & Pacific Railroad, 401

Menard County, Tex., 463

Mennil, Louis B., 418

Merrimac (steamship), 182*n*

Metcalfe, George T. (Interior Dept. clerk), 294*n*

Methodists, 73, 73*n*–74*n*, 111*n*, 262*n*, 271 and *n*, 272*n*, 295*n*, 361

Metz, France, 217*n*

Mexican War, 342, 372, 395

Mexico, 160*n*–61*n*, 349, 355, 423

Michie, Peter S. (U.S. Army), 113*n*–14*n*

Michigan, 68*n*, 69*n*, 86*n*, 233*n*, 271, 271*n*–72*n*, 274, 276*n*, 295*n*, 356–57

Michigan, University of, Ann Arbor, Mich.: document in, 216*n*–17*n*

Michigan Central Iron Co., 58*n*

Michler, Nathaniel (U.S. Army), 401

Miles, Samuel (of Philadelphia), 439

Milledge, John (U.S. District Attorney), 174*n*, 175*n*

Millen, Henry A. (of Ark.), 84*n*–85*n*

Miller, Andrew G. (U.S. District Judge), 467

Miller, Peet, and Opdyke (of New York City), 63*n*

Miller, Samuel F. (U.S. Supreme Court), 53*n*

Miller, Stephen (of Nev.), 418

Mills, Charles S. (of Richmond), 345, 346–47

Mills, Clark (sculptor), 352–53

Mills, D. H. (of Albany, N.Y.), 140*n*

Milwaukee, Wis., 70*n*, 71*n*, 467

Mining, 240–41, 241*n*–46*n*, 293*n*, 295*n*, 296*n*–97*n*, 298*n*, 299*n*, 300*n*–302*n*, 344, 401, 409, 418

Minnesota, 71*n*, 72*n*, 83*n*, 382, 418, 473–74

Minnesota Historical Society, St. Paul, Minn.: documents in, 339, 381–82

Mississippi, 20, 21, 40, 45*n*–46*n*, 66*n*, 95*n*, 96 and *n*, 340, 360, 381, 397, 420–21, 466

Missouri: patronage in, 7*n*, 285*n*; courts in, 71*n*, 72*n*; marshal in, 77*n*; 1st Light Art., 86*n*; Indians in, 100, 102*n*; land policy in, 245*n*; elections in, 260, 327, 468; party strife in, 269, 270*n*, 284 and *n*, 313–14, 314*n*, 315*n*; U.S. attorney for, 314*n*–15*n*; prisoner in, 456; mentioned, 165, 375, 411

Missouri, Kansas, and Texas Railroad, 202*n*–8*n*

Missouri Argus (newspaper), 234*n*

Missouri Democrat (newspaper), 110*n*, 149*n*, 178*n*, 314

Missouri Historical Society, St. Louis, Mo.: documents in, 55*n*, 71*n*, 278

Missouri Republican (newspaper), 314

Missouri River, Fort Scott and Gulf Railroad, 208*n*

Missouris, 100 and *n*, 102*n*

Mitchel, James: letter to, Feb. 18, 1870, 392

Mitchell, George H. (of New York City), 111*n*

Mitchell, Ind., 451
Mobile, Ala., 445
Mock, Andrew J. (of Sun Cliff, Pa.), 464–65
Moffett, Samuel G. (U.S. consul), 88n
Molon, Louis L. (Catholic priest), 201n
Moltke, Helmuth K. B. von (German army), 321n
Monarch (British navy), 394
Monmouth, N.J., 255n
Monmouth County, N.J., 266–67, 267n
Monroe County, Ill., 464
Monroe Doctrine, 45n, 46n, 75, 154, 156
Montana, Historical Society of, Helena, Mont.: document in, 98n
Montana Territory, 229n, 434, 453, 454, 458, 459, 474
Montano, Esteban G. (Peruvian claimant), 414
Montevideo, Uruguay, 396
Montgomery, F. (of Logan, Ohio), 465
Montgomery, Ala., 340, 341
Montgomery, Kan., 456
Montgomery County, Md., 459
Moody, S. B. (of San Jose, Calif.), 386
Moore, E. Anson (of Mo.), 270n
Moore, Frank (asst. secretary of legation), 257n
Moore, George H. (of San Francisco), 355
Moore, Mrs. E. L. (of Beverly, N.J.), 355
Moran, Benjamin (secretary of legation), 117n, 306n, 307n, 317n
Morey, Cyrus (of Durant, Iowa), 361
Morford, Jarratt (Mayor of Bridgeport, Conn.): letter to, June 20, 1870, 186n
Morgan, Edwin D. (of N.Y.): recommends appointments, 54n, 429; approves appointment of Edwin M. Stanton, 79n; considered for minister to Great Britain, 233n; letter to, Aug. 21, 1870, 235; invites USG to dinner, 235 and n; letter to, Jan. 12, 1870, 367; plans visit to USG, 367, 415; letter to, April 14, 1870, 415
Morgan, Eliza W. (wife of Edwin D. Morgan), 235 and n, 367
Morgan, George W. (of Mount Vernon, Ohio), 469
Morgan, John H. (C.S. Army), 451

Morgan Library, Pierpont, New York, N.Y.: documents in, 58n, 63n–64n, 64n, 69n, 72n, 333, 423, 467, 469
Morgantown, West Va., 65n
Mormons, 92n, 120n
Morocco, 181, 182n, 214n
Morrill, Justin S. (U.S. Senator), 458
Morrill, Lot M. (U.S. Senator): opinion on Santo Domingo treaty, 135n; considered for minister to Great Britain, 222, 227n, 229, 296n; assists constituent, 247
Morris, Edward Joy (minister to Turkey), 282n
Morris, Isaac N. (friend of USG), 208n, 301n, 416–17
Morris, William G. (marshal), 223n, 443–44
Morse, Freeman H. (U.S. consul-general), 142, 143n
Morse, Jerome E. (U.S. Navy), 426
Morton, Lucinda B. (wife of Oliver P. Morton), 313
Morton, Oliver P. (U.S. Senator): on McGarrahan claim, 5, 5n–6n, 298n; in Ind. politics, 93n, 230n, 323n; supports Santo Domingo treaty, 158n, 183n; letter to, June 8, 1870, 165–66; favors Cuban rebels, 165–66; recommends commander for Arctic expedition, 209n; prospective minister to Great Britain, 233n, 266 and n, 267, 268n, 274, 274n–75n, 294n, 296n, 306n, 312, 313, 316 and n, 317n, 318, 319n; letter to, Oct. 20, 1870, 312–13; letter to, Oct. 21, 1870, 316; recommends appointments, 400, 435; as gov. of Ind., 451
Morton, Robert P. (of Wilmington, Del.), 439
Moscow, Russia, 454–55
Moselle River, 217n
Moslems, 282n
Mosquera, Tomas Cipriano de (president, Colombia), 265n
Motley, John Lothrop (minister to Great Britain): conducts Alabama claims diplomacy, 30, 31, 153, 338, 445; aids U.S. travelers, 110n, 111n, 348–49; aids Fenians, 116n, 306n; Charles Sumner supports, 164n; reports arrest of U.S. consul, 181n; replaced, 183, 183n–86n, 187n–88n, 191, 192n, 233n, 247, 256n, 317n, 318, 319n, 320n–21n; reports Franco-

Prussian War, 258n, 441; criticized, 268n, 282n; letter to, Dec. 16, 1869, 348–49; mentioned, 176n
Mount Pleasant, Mich., 271n
Mount Vernon, Ohio, 469
Mueller, D. H. (of Buffalo), 262n
Mulford, Jonathan, 246n
Mulholland, Hugh (assessor): letter to, Jan. 31, 1870, 378–79
Mullen, William C. (of Marengo, Ill.), 452
Mullett, Alfred B. (architect), 52n
Muncie, Ind., 5n, 6n
Mungen, William (U.S. Representative), 93n
Munson's Hill, Va., 462
Munson-Williams-Proctor Institute, Utica, N.Y.: document in, 247–48
Murdoch, Alexander (marshal), 459
Murdoch, James E. (actor), 414
Murphy, Eugene P. (U.S. Army), 356
Murphy, Isaac (Gov. of Ark.), 83n
Murphy, Thomas (collector): nominated, 141n; advised about patronage, 142n, 269; active in politics, 251, 261, 298n; provides political information, 251n; letter to, Sept. 20, 1870, 269
Murray, Robert (U.S. Army), 382
Murtagh, William J. (*Washington National Republican*), 51n
Muscatine County, Iowa, 361

Nantucket, Mass., 86n
Naples, Italy, 280n
Napoleon III: controls Atlantic cable, 33; Elihu B. Washburne visits, 60n, 91, 91n–92n, 93n; sends minister to U.S., 200 and n; captured, 216n, 217n; at war with Germans, 238, 247, 254, 257n
Nashville, Tenn., 5n, 309n, 310n, 311n, 392
Natchez, Miss., 445
Nebraska, 15–16, 16n, 71n, 72n, 205n, 246n
Neem[a]yer (of New York City), 337
Negley, James S. (U.S. Representative), 64n, 333
Nelson, Charles (of Kan.), 207n–8n
Nelson, Samuel (U.S. Supreme Court), 54n
Nelson, Thomas H. (minister to Mexico), 423
Neosho River, 202n

Netherlands, 35, 256n, 281n
Nevada, 73n, 179n, 245n–46n, 401, 474
New Albany, Ind., 69n
Newark, N.J., 188n, 192n
Newberger, Louis (of Indianapolis): letter to, March 7, 1870, 393
New Berne, N.C., 457
Newberry, John S. (of Mich.), 356–57
Newberry Library, Chicago, Ill.: documents in, 166n–67n, 180n, 458
New Brighton, Pa., 408
New Castle, Pa., 461–62
Newcomb, Carman A. (marshal), 284, 285n
Newcomb, Horatio C. (of Indianapolis), 69n
Newcomb, Wesley (of Ithaca, N.Y.), 85n–86n
New Hampshire, 281n, 401, 405
New Haven, Conn., 186n
New Idria Mining Co., 241n–42n, 243n, 244n, 293n, 296n–97n, 298n, 300n
New Jersey, 64n, 183, 192n, 261 and n, 267n, 271n, 323, 328, 419
New Jersey Historical Society, Newark, N.J.: document in, 56n
New Lebanon, N.Y., 472
New London, Conn., 84n
Newman, John P. (Methodist minister): letter to, Dec. 24, 1869, 73; dispenses charity, 73 and n, 74n; nephew of, 441
Newman, Mrs. John P., 441
New Mexico Territory, 288n, 290n, 342–44, 368, 375–78, 409, 422, 459, 474
New Orleans, La., 40, 66n, 75, 138, 176n, 178n, 327n, 344, 350, 362, 393, 400, 463, 466
Newport, Ky., 89n
Newport, R.I., 218n, 232, 233, 235n, 251, 252, 259–60, 259n, 260n, 369
Newspapers: in New York City, 47n, 88n, 93n, 183n, 184n, 230n, 232n, 297n, 300n, 319n; in Washington, D.C., 51n, 164n, 301n; in Chicago, 70n, 253; report French news, 92n–93n; in Memphis, 95n, 96n; in St. Louis, 110n, 149n, 150n, 178n, 234n, 284n, 314; *Illinois Staats Zeitung*, 111n; report treatment of Fenians, 116n, 117n, 232; report Indian

Newspapers (*cont.*)
affairs, 119n, 120n; print USG interview, 134n, 138n; print USG's message prematurely, 157n; discuss Santo
Domingo treaty, 162; report Cuban
news, 165–66, 169n; resignation
leaked to, 171n–72n; in Calif., 182n;
in N.C., 210n; Civil War correspondent, 214n; in Great Britain, 248n,
319n, 320n; in Charleston, S.C.,
249n; in Buffalo, 262n, 263n, 264n;
in Colombia, 265n; in Atlanta, 285,
286n, 289n, 290n–91n; in Colorado
Territory, 286n, 289n; Associated
Press, 299n, 326; sensationalize Mc-
Garrahan claim, 300n, 301n; in Ala.,
339; print patronage advertising,
342; in Detroit, 356; in New Mexico Territory, 376; in Tenn., 391,
392; in Cleveland, 403; mentioned,
135n, 142n, 180n, 192n, 208n, 352,
411, 444, 465, 468, 470
Newton, John (U.S. Army), 404
Newton, Virginius M. (USMA cadet),
404
New York: patronage in, 16–17, 17n–
18n, 342, 413; fort in, 40; former
residents of, 61n; courts in, 63n, 413;
state engineer, 97n; veterans in, 109;
legislature praises George H. Thomas, 129n; Fenians in, 152n; Republicans in, 251–52, 261, 262n–63n,
429; Democrats in, 262n; fraud in,
298n; Indians in, 383, 417; election
in, 426–27; National Guard, 442;
Sing Sing prison, 448; mentioned,
136n, 140n, 141n, 158n, 159n, 276n,
280n, 392, 438, 446
New York City, N.Y.: customhouse,
5n, 7n, 140n, 141n, 142n, 251n, 269,
388, 391, 431; Booth's Theatre, 10n;
blacks in, 12n; courts in, 17n, 63n,
64n; Spanish ships visit, 29, 418–19;
Cuban relief meeting in, 46n; Cooper
Institute, 46n, 109n, 457; newspapers
in, 47n, 88n, 93n, 230n; publishers
in, 58 and n; shipping from, 75, 76;
USG visits, 78n, 185n, 235 and n,
251, 266 and n, 275n, 283; veterans'
aid in, 109 and n, 335; Germans in,
141n, 189n; Republicans in, 141n,
219n, 231n, 252n, 413; hotels, 173n,
266n, 430; Tammany Hall, 184n;
tailors in, 220 and n; U.S. Army in,
221n; German army recruits in, 223n;

postmaster at, 232n; attorneys in,
243n; post office in, 248n, 321n; patronage in, 275n, 441; stockbrokers
in, 322n; Vanderbilt Bronze unveiled,
334; New England Society, 350; vols.,
371, 457; Union League Club, 386;
politics in, 426; U.S. treasurer at,
429; during Civil War, 457; exhibition hall, 465; mentioned, 49, 54n,
73n, 79n, 87n, 97 and n, 98n, 111n,
117n, 118n, 146n, 159, 160, 161 and
n, 177n, 179n, 197n, 198n, 217n,
224, 234n, 279 and n, 280n, 289n,
294n, 296n, 306n, 317n, 329n, 337,
344, 357, 370, 373, 374, 385, 390,
402, 414, 421, 436, 446, 455, 460,
461, 468, 471
New York Evening Post (newspaper),
165–66
New York Freeman's Journal (newspaper), 201n
New York Herald (newspaper), 157n,
214n
New-York Historical Society, New
York, N.Y.: documents in, 63n (2)
New York Independent, 143 and n
New York Public Library, New York,
N.Y.: documents in, 58, 173n, 403
New York State Library, Albany, N.Y.:
documents in, 114–15, 235, 235n,
367, 415
New York Sun (newspaper), 319n
New York Times (newspaper), 171n,
232n, 297n
New York Tribune (newspaper), 183n,
184n, 230n, 231n, 232n
New York World (newspaper), 171n,
300n
Nez Percé, 474
Nicaragua, 4n, 29, 253n, 401–2
Nicholson, J. W., 272n
Nickerson, Benjamin R. (of Calif.),
139n
Nipsic (U.S. Navy), 136n
Nixon, John T. (U.S. District Judge),
419
Noble, John W. (U.S. District Attor-
ney), 7n, 314n
Noggle, David (Idaho Territory Su-
preme Court), 408–9
Noggle, Jessie F. (of New Brighton,
Pa.), 408–9
Norfolk, Va., 357, 384
Norment, Samuel (D.C. police commis-
sioner), 111n

North American Review, 299n, 323n

North Carolina, 14n, 65n, 175–76, 176n, 210, 210n–13n, 249n, 338, 384, 422, 461

North Carolina Division of Archives and History, Raleigh, N.C.: documents in, 210, 211n

North Easton, Mass., 65n

Northwestern University, Evanston, Ill.: document in, 283

Norvell, L. C., 438

Norway, 148n, 443

Norwich, Conn., 63n

Notre Dame, University of, Notre Dame, Ind.: document in, 201n

Noyes, Crosby S. (*Washington Star*), 51n

Nunn, David A. (minister to Ecuador), 3 and n, 4n, 96n

Nye, James W. (U.S. Senator): letter to, June 27, 1870, 179; informed about Santo Domingo, 179 and n; identified, 179n; mentioned, 351

Oahu, Hawaii, 82n, 86n

Oakes, James (U.S. Army), 417

Oakley, Franklin W. (marshal), 438

Oak Orchard, Ky., 178n

Oaths, 20, 104n, 105n, 106n, 107n

Oberlin College, Oberlin, Ohio: documents in, 54n–55n, 171n–73n, 292, 294n, 294n–96n, 296n–98n, 299n–302n, 302n, 315, 315n

O'Connell, Charles U. (Fenian), 116n

O'Connell, Ellen (of Jamestown, N.Y.), 337

O'Connell, Maurice, 337

O'Donovan, Dennis (of New York City), 118n

Oglalas, 361

Oglesby, Richard J. (Gov. of Ill.), 464

Ohio: courts in, 67n, 68n, 69n; vols., 67n, 96n, 116n, 397, 473; legislature praises George H. Thomas, 129n; Sherman family in, 219n; Republicans in, 275n, 403–4; appointments in, 363–67, 415, 465, 468–71, 473; fair in, 445; mentioned, 117n, 293n, 317n, 411

Ohio Historical Society, Columbus, Ohio: document in, 365–66

Okmulgee, Indian Territory, 205n, 207n

Oliver, John M. (of Little Rock), 435–36

Olympia, Washington Territory, 351

Omaha, Neb., 16, 71n, 228n

Oneidas, 352

O'Neill, John (Fenian), 223n, 226n

Opdyke, George (of New York City), 457–58

Ord, Edward O. C. (U.S. Army), 320n

Oregon, 281n, 316n, 368–69, 474

Orleans County, N.Y., 372

Orphans, 109, 313, 395–96, 409, 435, 463

Orr, Ann Jane (of Mo.), 127–28, 128n

Orth, Godlove S. (U.S. Representative), 256n

Osages, 100 and n, 101n, 102n, 208n, 455–56

Osborn, Thomas W. (U.S. Senator), 83n, 466

Oswego, N.Y., 63n

Otis, Harrison G. (U.S. Army), 261 and n, 329

Otos, 100 and n, 102n

Ottawa, Ill., 396

Otto, William T. (Asst. Secretary of the Interior), 294n, 295n, 296n, 297n

Owsley County, Ky., 381

Packard's Monthly, 424

Page, William R. (U.S. consul), 436

Paine, Halbert E. (U.S. Representative), 447, 467

Palen, Joseph G. (New Mexico Territory Supreme Court), 378

Palmer, Frank W. (U.S. Representative), 67n

Palmer, John M. (Gov. of Ill.), 460

Panama, 74, 135, 135n–37n, 155, 156

Paraguay, 29, 144 and n

Pardons, 133n, 222, 223n, 225, 226n, 232, 246, 253n, 305, 306n, 448, 449–50, 457

Paris, France: U.S. legation at, 60n, 61n, 91, 91n–93n, 110, 255n, 256n, 257n, 434, 452; education in, 111n, 355; Germans near, 217n; Congress of 1856, 238; besieged, 258n, 453; wine from, 370; mentioned, 115n, 191n, 418

Parker, Capt. (Richmond police), 367

Parker, Ely S. (Commissioner of Indian Affairs): administers Indian policy, 39, 315, 326, 388, 395, 403, 409, 423, 431, 432; escorts Indian

Parker, Ely S. (*cont.*)
delegation, 373; involved in land
sales, 416; recommends policy, 474
Parker, Joel (of N.J.), 266–67, 267n
Parker, John M. (N.Y. judge), 63n
Parker, Niles G. (S.C. treasurer),
250n–51n
Parrish, Joseph (secretary to USG),
452
Parrish, Robert A., Jr. (of Philadel-
phia), 386
Parsons, Levi (railroad official), 208n
Partridge, James R. (minister to Ven-
ezuela), 398–99
Paschal, George W. (of Washington,
D.C.), 293n, 301n
Patapsco River (Md.), 449
Patents, 43, 231n, 293n, 350, 449
Patrick, Jacob C. (of Walcott, Iowa),
360–61
Patrick, William K. (of St. Louis),
315n
Patrick's Station, Va., 462
Patterson, James W. (U.S. Senator),
93n
Patterson, John J. (Greenville and Co-
lumbia Railroad), 250n
Patterson, Robert (of Philadelphia):
letter to, March 10, 1870, 393
Paul, Mrs. James W. (of Philadel-
phia), 110n
Paw-ne-no-pah-she, Joseph (Osage),
455–56
Payne, Daniel A. (African Methodist
Episcopal bishop), 12n
Peabody, George, 374–75
Peale, Charles Willson (artist), 350
Peale, Louis T. (midshipman), 349–
50
Peale, Titian R. (of Philadelphia), 350
Pearre, George A. (of Md.), 65n–66n
Pearson, Alfred L. (of Pittsburgh):
letter to, Jan. 18, 1870, 369
Pearson, Richmond M. (N.C. Supreme
Court), 210n, 212n
Pease, Walter B. (U.S. Army), 367–
68
Pease, William B. (U.S. Army), 120n
Peck, Clement A. (of Tenalleytown,
D.C.), 51n
Peden, Proudy, 420, 421
Peel, Robert (British statesman), 281n
Peirce, Charles H. (U.S. Army), 356
Peirce, Henry A. (minister to Hawaii),
85n

Pemberton, John C. (C.S. Army), 368
Pembina, Dakota Territory, 120n, 381
Pendleton, Charles H. (U.S. Navy),
442
Pennsylvania: Indians in, 38, 352;
courts in, 56n, 64n; Republicans in,
84n, 333, 462; appointments from,
282n, 398; during Civil War, 355,
430; mentioned, 79n, 167n, 293n,
295n, 358, 374
Pennsylvania, Historical Society of,
Philadelphia, Pa.: documents in, 71n,
214, 341, 467
Pennsylvania Railroad, 199n
Pennsylvania Volunteers, 353, 354,
385, 462, 465
Pensions, 42–43, 221n, 313, 337, 360,
372, 373, 384, 385, 406, 418, 432,
451, 460
Perez, Santiago (Colombian minister),
264–65, 265n
Perkins, Edward L. (secretary, New
Mexico Territory), 375, 376, 377
Perkins, Elias (U.S. consul), 84n
Perkins, Mrs. E. M., 362
Pernambuco, Brazil, 87n, 88n
Perry, Aaron F. (of Ohio), 171n, 471–
72
Perry, Raymond H. (commercial
agent), 162, 162n–63n, 176 and n
Perryman, Sanford W. (Creek), 433
Perryville, Ky., battle of, 412
Peru, 4n, 29, 47n, 48n, 414, 458
Peters, John A. (U.S. Representative),
241n
Petersburg, Va., 110n, 465
Pflugfelder, Charles (of Richmond),
347
Phelan, Michael, 407–8
Phelps, Timothy G. (collector), 139n–
40n, 338, 373
Philadelphia, Pa.: blacks in, 10n, 11n;
fort in, 40; attorneys in, 64n; navy
yard, 90n; honors George H. Thomas,
129n; newspaper, 164n; merchants,
275n; appointment in, 349; USG
visits, 376, 409; mint, 381; Saengerbund Society, 393; Hibernian Society,
393; mentioned, 52n, 56n, 57n, 87n,
110n, 152n, 197n, 213n, 246n, 281n,
282n, 298n, 334, 354, 374, 406, 414,
418, 439, 442, 455
Philadelphia, Free Library of, Philadelphia, Pa.: documents in, 57n, 389
Philbrick, Henry R. (U.S. Navy), 474

Phillips, Andrew C. (U.S. consul), 411
Phillips, Wendell, 317n
Phillips, William A., 207n
Piegans, 119n–20n
Pierce, John, 263n, 264n
Pierrepont, Edwards (U.S. District Attorney): letter to, Dec. 3, 1869, 16–17; recommends appointments, 16–17, 17n, 64n–65n; resigns, 17n; advises USG, 47n, 48n; assists Edwin M. Stanton, 78n; minister to Great Britain, 111n; letter to, June 1, 1870, 159; invited to Long Branch, 159; proposed as minister to Great Britain, 183n, 222, 316n–17n; rejected for secretary of state, 183n–84n; comments on politics, 426–27; as district attorney, 431
Pignatel, François Michel, 410
Pike, Horace L. (of Raleigh, N.C.), 338
Pile, William A. (Gov. of New Mexico Territory), 376–78
Pillow, Gideon J. (of Memphis), 420
Pitcher, Thomas G. (U.S. Army), 261
Pitchlynn, Peter P. (Choctaw), 315, 315n–16n
Pitt, Capt., 257n
Pittsburgh, Pa., 56n, 64n, 333, 369, 455
Pittsburg Landing, Tenn., 449
Plainfield, Conn., 187n
Platte River, 334
Plattsburg, N.Y., 360
Pleasonton, Alfred (collector), 141n, 298n, 299n, 413, 436, 441
Plumb, Edward L. (U.S. consul-general), 46n, 47n, 234n
Plymouth, N.C., 14n
Polk, James K. (U.S. President), 53n, 281n, 349
Pomeroy, Henry (of Chattanooga), 392
Pomeroy, Samuel C. (U.S. Senator), 333
Ponce, Puerto Rico, 397
Pond, B. F. (Lamson & Goodnow Manufacturing Co.), 7, 8n
Pond, Elizabeth L. (of Utica, N.Y.), 432
Pond Creek, Kan., 288n
Poole, De Witt C. (U.S. Army), 361
Pope, Caroline O. (wife of Charles A. Pope), 255n

Pope, Charles A. (of St. Louis), 255n–56n
Pope, John (U.S. Army), 290n
Pope, John D. (U.S. District Attorney), 475
Pope, Nathaniel (Indian superintendent), 458–59
Port-au-Prince, Haiti, 10n, 11n, 13n–15n
Porteous, Louisa (of Beaufort, S.C.), 337
Porter, Charles H. (U.S. Representative), 346
Porter, David D. (U.S. Navy), 46n, 108, 122n, 201n
Porter, Horace (secretary to USG): corresponds for USG, 5n, 6n, 46n, 48n, 96n, 107n–8n, 129n, 201n, 220n, 235n, 318n, 342, 362–63, 366, 370, 385, 387, 388, 390, 409, 417, 436, 445, 467; involved in appointments, 84n–85n, 261, 293n, 298n, 299n; secretarial duties of, 122n, 132n, 160, 214n, 216n, 218n, 223n, 253n, 282n, 294n, 401; eschews patronage, 142n; discusses Ellen Grant's education, 279n; reports election results, 323n
Porter, John K. (N.Y. judge), 48n
Porter, Mr., 279n
Porter, Peter A. (N.Y. Vols.), 371
Porter, Sarah (Miss Porter's School), 190–91, 279n
Portland, Maine, 40
Portland, Ore., 351, 369, 385
Port Royal, S.C., 430
Port Said, Egypt, 436
Portsmouth (U.S. Navy), 402
Portugal, 258n
Poston, W. T. (of Memphis), 95n
Potter, George F., 441
Potter, Robert B. (of Philadelphia): introduced, 110n–11n; letter to, March 28, 1870, 409
Potts, Benjamin F. (Gov. of Montana Territory), 453, 454
Powder River, 361
Powhatan County, Va., 407
Pratt, Daniel D. (U.S. Senator), 175n, 230n, 354
Presbyterians, 461, 462
Prescott, Canada, 85n
Preston, Stephen (Haitian minister), 12n
Preston, Tex., 202n, 203n

Prévost-Paradol, Lucien A. (French minister), 200, 200n–201n, 257n, 453
Price, Robert N. (U.S. Army), 334–35
Pride, George G., 234n
Priest, John G. (of St. Louis), 76, 77n
Prince, Charles H. (postmaster), 174n, 363
Prince Arthur (of Great Britain), 90 and n
Prince of Wales, Albert Edward: telegram to, June 23, 1870, 436
Princeton, N.J., 419
Princeton University, Princeton, N.J.: documents in, 248n, 366–67, 460; graduate of, 267n; commencement, 437
Prindle, Asa C. (commercial agent), 447
Pringle, Benjamin (of N.Y.), 402
Prisoners: Fenians, 115, 115n–18n, 222, 223n, 226n, 305, 306n–7n, 428; in Santo Domingo, 166 and n; in Cuba, 168, 169n–70n; in Edinburgh, 181n; during Civil War, 182n, 221; in N.C., 210n, 211n, 212n; Zacheus Allen, 246–47, 247n; in military custody, 410; murderer of blacks, 420–21; lynched, 423–24; black, 448, 456–57; seek pardon, 449–50
Protois, E. A., 385
Providence, R.I., 450, 459
Pueblos, 342–44, 409
Puerto Rico, 134n, 156, 397
Purviance, Samuel A. (of Pittsburgh), 64n

Quakers, 38–39, 119n, 395
Quapaws, 202n, 204n
Queenstown, Ireland, 117n
Quinby, Isaac F. (marshal), 151n–52n, 263n, 446
Quincy, Ill., 416
Quinn, William P. (African Methodist Episcopal bishop), 12n
Quinnebaug (U.S. Navy), 402, 444
Quito, Ecuador, 4n

Railroads: in Ecuador, 4n; Union Pacific, 5, 5n–6n, 150, 150n–51n, 230n–31n, 333–34, 388; in Europe, 36; influence Indian policy, 39, 100n–102n, 202n–8n; in Tex., 49; land grants to, 50n, 405; in Ga., 106n; in Mexico, 161n; bonds finance, 177; corruption involving, 231n; Kansas Pacific, 287n, 288n; Memphis, El Paso, and Pacific, 401; threatened in Kan., 415, 416, 417; Southern Pacific, 446; mentioned, 199n, 250n, 272n, 392
Raleigh, N.C., 176n, 210n, 211n, 212n, 338, 422
Ramsey, Alexander (U.S. Senator), 72n, 93n, 418, 441
Ranney, Nathan (of St. Louis), 360
Rawlins, Emily S. (daughter of John A. Rawlins), 97 and n, 98n
Rawlins, James B. (son of John A. Rawlins), 97, 98n
Rawlins, Jennie S. (daughter of John A. Rawlins), 97 and n, 98n
Rawlins, John A. (U.S. Secretary of War): fund supports family, 97, 97n–98n, 190; as secretary of war, 219n, 416, 417; discusses Union Pacific Railroad, 333; death of, 333, 348; active in politics, 365
Rawlins, Mary E. (wife of John A. Rawlins), 97, 98n
Ray, Charles H. (of Chicago), 229, 230n, 253 and n
Read, John Meredith, Jr. (U.S. consul-general), 268n
Reconstruction: in Ga., 19–20, 61, 61n–62n, 92n, 103, 103n–8n, 285, 289n–91n; in Miss., 20, 21, 40, 45n–46n, 96 and n; in Va., 20–21, 40, 45n, 373–74, 393, 412, 462–63; in Tex., 20, 21, 40, 132n, 162n, 449, 450; and Supreme Court, 53n, 54n; in Ala., 67n, 68n, 339–40; in Fla., 83n, 466–67; in Ark., 86n–87n, 435–36; Fifteenth Amendment completes, 91, 130–31, 132n–33n, 137, 138n; in N.C., 175–76, 176n, 210, 210n–13n, 422; in Tenn., 182n; readmission of states, 190; in S.C., 248, 248n–51n; Republicans support, 276n, 277n; military commission trial, 375; in Ky., 380–81
Reconstruction Acts: enforced, 21, 104n, 105n, 107n, 132n, 162n, 210n, 211n, 212n, 277n, 373–74, 375, 393; opposed, 211n, 391, 420; advocated, 422; interpreted, 448, 449, 450
Red Cloud (Sioux), 433

Red River, 397
Red River of the North, 92*n*, 381–82, 427
Reed, David (U.S. District Attorney), 333
Reed, Harrison (Gov. of Fla.), 352, 441, 466–67
Reemelin, Charles G. (of Cincinnati), 199*n*
Reims, France, 216*n*, 321*n*
Religion: Quakers, 38–39, 119*n*, 395; Catholics, 60*n*, 111*n*, 141*n*, 180*n*, 201*n*, 323*n*, 353; Methodists, 73, 73*n*–74*n*, 111*n*, 262*n*, 271 and *n*, 272*n*, 295*n*, 361; Mormons, 92*n*, 120*n*; Universalists, 98*n*; Russian Orthodox, 99*n*; Baptists, 141*n*, 221, 262*n*, 395; Congregationalists, 143*n*; atheist, 180*n*; missionaries, 205*n*, 295*n*, 395; Indian churches, 206*n*; churches burned, 211*n*; preacher, 280*n*; Moslems, 282*n*; Jews, 397–98; Young Men's Christian Association, 435; donations, 449, 459; Presbyterians, 461, 462
Rempel, Ferdinand F. (postmaster), 465
Republican Party: in Ky., 3*n*, 4*n*, 379, 380; in Tenn., 3*n*, 95*n*, 284 and *n*, 309*n*, 461; in Ind., 5*n*–6*n*, 93*n*, 200*n*, 457; supports blacks, 11*n*, 50*n*; in Washington, D.C., 51*n*, 138*n*; in Ark., 53*n*, 86*n*–87*n*, 95*n*; in Conn., 63*n*; in Pa., 64*n*, 333, 398, 462; in Md., 66*n*; in La., 66*n*, 400; in Mich., 68*n*; in Mo., 71*n*, 77*n*, 150*n*, 260, 269, 270*n*, 271*n*, 313–14, 314*n*, 315*n*, 468; 1860 convention, 84*n*; in Va., 87*n*, 345–47, 404–5; defections from, 90*n*, 284 and *n*, 293*n*–94*n*; in Miss., 95*n*; in Ga., 104*n*–5*n*, 106*n*, 174*n*–75*n*, 289*n*, 290*n*, 291*n*, 362–63, 437, 467; in Calif., 139*n*, 182*n*, 375; in New York City, 141*n*, 184*n*, 231*n*, 252*n*; Germans support, 141*n*, 413; supports Santo Domingo treaty, 164*n*, 183*n*; opinions on Cuba, 169*n*; in Mass., 187*n*–88*n*, 227*n*; USG complains about, 190; views USG as reelection candidate, 200*n*, 312–13; in N.C., 210*n*; in Ill., 221*n*, 253*n*–54*n*, 358; evaluated, 231*n*, 247, 323*n*; in S.C., 248, 249*n*–51*n*; in N.Y., 251–52, 261, 262*n*–63*n*, 426–27, 429;

supported, 271, 272*n*, 274, 275*n*, 276*n*, 277*n*; in Colorado Territory, 285, 286*n*; in Ala., 339–40, 341, 425; in Washington Territory, 351, 407; in Fla., 352, 466; in Ohio, 364–67, 403–4, 470; in New Mexico Territory, 375–78; in Alaska, 391; in Maine, 425; solicits funds, 451; in Wyoming Territory, 453; in Montana Territory, 453, 454; mentioned, 94*n*, 143*n*, 144*n*, 180*n*, 248*n*, 320*n*
Republican River, 334
Reynolds, John A. (of Albany, N.Y.), 63*n*–64*n*
Reynolds, Joseph J. (U.S. Army), 49, 132*n*, 133*n*
Rhode Island, 114, 162*n*, 450
Rhodes, Augustus L. (Calif. Supreme Court), 72*n*–73*n*
Ribet, E. (of Natchez), 445
Rice, Alexander H. (of Mass.), 86*n*
Rice, Benjamin F. (U.S. Senator), 83*n*, 84*n*
Richard, 259, 326, 327
Richard, John, Jr. (fugitive), 361
Richards, J. M. (of Chicago), 110*n*
Richardson, James, 368
Richardson, William A. (Asst. Secretary of the Treasury): administers dept., 215*n*, 253, 347, 429; letter to, Aug. 22, 1870, 253; prospective commissioner of Internal Revenue, 294*n*
Richmond, Lewis, 218*n*
Richmond, Ky., 380
Richmond, Va., 65*n*, 164*n*, 340, 345–47, 367, 393, 404, 412, 428–29
Richmond State Journal (newspaper), 345–46
Rickards, William (of Franklin, Pa.), 349
Rio de Janeiro, Brazil, 347, 402, 439
Ripley, Mr., 250*n*–51*n*
Ripley, Ohio, 273*n*
Rives, Alexander (of Va.), 317*n*
Roanoke Island, N.C., 457
Robb, Thomas P. (collector), 291*n*
Roberts, Mauricio Lopez (Spanish minister), 46*n*–47*n*, 348
Robertson, Thomas J. (U.S. Senator), 250*n*, 442
Robertson, William H. (of N.Y.), 141*n*
Robeson, George M. (U.S. Secretary of the Navy): administers dept., 41,

Robeson, George M. (*cont.*)
46*n*, 108*n*–9*n*, 122*n*, 198*n*, 337, 348,
357, 391, 394, 408, 423, 426, 430,
433, 436, 442, 444–45, 460, 464,
467, 474; policy toward Spain, 47*n*,
48*n*, 169*n*, 179, 400, 418, 419; advises USG, 55*n*; discusses amnesty,
133*n*; supports interoceanic canal,
135*n*, 136*n*; on Santo Domingo annexation, 158*n*; prepares Arctic expedition, 209 and *n*; dines with USG,
283 and *n*; influences appointments,
293*n*, 298*n*; discusses slave trade,
402; letter to, Sept. 20, 1870, 460;
telegram to, Sept. 19, 1870, 460; endorsement to, Oct. 27, 1870, 474
Robeson, John T. (U.S. consul), 181
and *n*, 182*n*
Robinson, José A. A. (U.S. Army),
434
Rochelle, Va., 462
Rochester, N.Y., 151*n*, 263*n*, 446
Rodgers, Alexander (U.S. Army), 395
Rodgers, Alexander P. (U.S. Army),
395
Rodgers, Andrew J. (attorney), 439–
40
Rodgers, C. R. Perry (U.S. Navy),
321*n*, 395
Roesing, Johannes (German consul),
223*n*
Rogers, H. W., Jr. (of Chicago), 353
Ronsaville, D. C. (engineer), 449
Rosecrans, William S.: during Civil
War, 86*n*, 320*n*; letter to, June 5,
1870, 160; urges investment in Mex-
ico, 160, 160*n*–61*n*
Rosenblatt, M. A. (of Mo.), 284*n*–85*n*
Ross, Edmund G. (U.S. Senator), 72*n*,
101*n*–2*n*
Ross, William P. (Cherokee), 205*n*–
7*n*
Rossa, Jeremiah O'Donovan (Fenian),
117*n*–18*n*
Rousselot, Peter (of Colfax, Colorado
Territory), 286*n*
Routt, John L. (marshal), 345
Rowland, W. S., 199*n*
Roxbury, Mass., 86*n*
Ruddy, James F., Rancho Mirage,
Calif.: document owned by, 88–89
Ruggles, Samuel B. (of New York
City), 419
Ruhm, John (of Nashville), 309*n*–10*n*

Runkle, Benjamin P. (U.S. Army),
460
Runnells, John S. (U.S. consul), 411
Ruple, James B. (assessor), 459
Russel, George (of Washington, Pa.),
459–60
Russell, Mr., 415
Russia, 35, 99 and *n*, 258*n*, 475
Rust, Mr., 272*n*
Rutledge, Ga., 290*n*

Sac and Fox, 100 and *n*, 102*n*
Sacket, Delos B. (U.S. Army), 162*n*
Sacramento, Calif., 214*n*
Saffold, Thomas P. (of Morgan Coun-
ty, Ga.), 174*n*
Saget, Nissage (president, Haiti), 12*n*,
14*n*
Saginaw River (Mich.), 271*n*, 272*n*
St. Anthony's Falls, Minn., 83*n*
St. Cloud, Minn., 120*n*
St. George Island, Alaska, 40, 99 and *n*
St. John, Henry (of Ark.), 85*n*
St. John's, Canada, 410–11
St. Louis, Mo.: USG investment in,
6–7, 76–77, 77*n*, 145–46, 149;
patronage in, 7*n*, 314*n*–15*n*; travel-
ers from, 110*n*, 111*n*; Winfield S.
Hancock seeks command at, 129*n*;
attorneys in, 140*n*; USG plans to
visit, 145, 178, 220 and *n*; court in,
147*n*; appointment in, 214*n*; William
T. Sherman wants hd. qrs. at, 219*n*;
USG visits, 222, 224–25, 227, 228*n*,
260, 269; mayor, 222*n*; cemetery,
224, 225; newspapers, 234*n*, 284*n*;
customhouse, 260, 269, 270*n*; Germans in, 270*n*; college in, 392;
Knights of St. Patrick, 392; mentioned, 72*n*, 120*n*, 128*n*, 137*n*, 138,
139*n*, 146*n*, 149*n*, 178*n*, 323, 326,
327, 344, 360, 377, 399, 417, 455
St. Louis County, Mo., 165, 224, 225,
315*n*, 326, 327 and *n*, 328, 344
St. Paul, Minn., 129*n*, 418
St. Paul Island, Alaska, 40, 99 and *n*
St. Petersburg, Russia, 437
St. Thomas, Danish West Indies, 75,
182*n*, 435
Salem, Ill., 221*n*
Salnave, Sylvain (president, Haiti),
9*n*, 10*n*, 12*n*, 13*n*–14*n*
Salomon, Edward S. (Gov. of Wash-
ington Territory), 350–52, 398
Salvador, 443

Samana Bay (Santo Domingo), 122*n*–23*n*, 155, 159*n*, 188, 189*n*

Sanborn, John B. (of St. Paul), 72*n*

Sandel, J. P. (of Albany, N.Y.), 140*n*

Sander, C. J. (of Philadelphia): letter to, March 7, 1870, 393

Sanderson, Silas W. (Calif. Supreme Court), 72*n*–73*n*

San Francisco, Calif.: fort in, 40; George W. Dent in, 139*n*, 140*n*, 145*n*, 146*n*, 147*n*, 177; alleged expeditions from, 223*n*; William T. Sherman visits, 228*n*; collector at, 373; mentioned, 128, 129*n*, 246, 338, 355, 369, 385

Sang, Mr. and Mrs. Philip D., River Forest, Ill.: document owned by, 135*n*

San Jose, Calif., 386

San Luis Valley (Colorado Territory), 288*n*

San Saba County, Tex., 463

Santa Cruz, Danish West Indies, 419, 420

Santa Fé, New Mexico Territory, 376, 378

Santiago, Chile, 336

Santiago de Cuba, 47*n*, 273 and *n*, 275*n*

Santo Domingo: annexation supported, 13*n*, 323*n*; USG urges annexation, 74–76, 121, 122*n*–23*n*, 153–57, 157*n*–59*n*, 163, 163*n*–64*n*, 171*n*, 176 and *n*, 311–12, 312*n*; Senate considers annexation treaty, 123–24, 124*n*, 133–34, 134*n*–35*n*, 163, 163*n*–64*n*, 179, 179*n*–80*n*, 183*n*, 187*n*, 188, 189*n*, 296*n*; Raymond H. Perry involved in, 162 and *n*; Davis Hatch imprisoned in, 166, 166*n*–67*n*; lease of Samana Bay, 189*n*

Santos, Brazil, 275*n*, 276*n*

Saranac River (N.Y.), 360

Sargent, Aaron A. (U.S. Representative), 88*n*, 182*n*

Sargent, Nathan (commissioner of customs), 393

Satterlee, Richard S. (U.S. Army), 382

Sault Ste. Marie, Mich., 427

Savage, John (Fenian), 115*n*–16*n*

Savannah, Ga., 175*n*, 291*n*, 384, 437, 467

Sawyer, Frederick A. (U.S. Senator), 55*n*, 442

Sawyer, Lorenzo (U.S. Circuit Judge), 73*n*, 92*n*

Sayles Brothers (of Conn.), 387

Sayre, Alfred (of Denver), 408

Schenck, Robert C. (U.S. Representative), 62*n*, 275*n*, 320*n*, 321*n*, 451, 468–69

Schneider, Edward F., 387

Schofield, John M. (U.S. Army): testifies concerning cadet warrants, 120*n*; as secretary of war, 219*n*; assists emigrants, 287*n*, 288*n*; recommends appointments, 383, 399; protects Kan., 415, 417

Schriver, Edmund (U.S. Army): note to, Sept. 8, 1870, 261; forwards cadet appointments, 261 and *n*; as inspector gen., 369, 448

Schurz, Carl (U.S. Senator): opposes Santo Domingo annexation, 157*n*–58*n*, 163*n*, 189*n*; USG despises, 180*n*, 296*n*, 314; letter to, July 18, 1870, 189*n*; opposes administration, 284 and *n*; active in politics, 376; during Civil War, 406

Scotia (steamship), 217*n*, 374

Scott, Hugh L. (U.S. Army), 426

Scott, John (U.S. Senator), 378

Scott, John N. (of Indianapolis), 457

Scott, Robert K. (Gov. of S.C.), 248, 249*n*–51*n*, 369

Scott, Thomas A. (Pennsylvania Railroad): letter to, July 13, 1870, 442

Scott, William M. (minister), 426

Scott, Winfield (U.S. Army), 229*n*

Scott County, Iowa, 360

Scovel, James M. (of Camden, N.J.), 132*n*

Sears, Edward H. (postmaster), 87*n*

Second Story Books, Washington, D.C.: document owned by, 216*n*–17*n*

Sedalia, Mo., 270*n*

Sedan, France, 216*n*, 217*n*

Selfridge, Alexander W. (Pa. Vols.), 354

Selfridge, Thomas O., Jr. (U.S. Navy), 122*n*

Sell, John M. (Pa. Vols.), 385

Seminole (U.S. Navy), 179

Seminoles, 202*n*

Senecas, 383

Settle, Thomas (of Raleigh, N.C.), 422

Seward, William H. (U.S. Secretary of State), 117*n*, 275*n*, 317*n*, 338, 371

Sewell's Point, Va., 430
Seymour, Horatio (presidential candidate), 87n, 314n, 426
Shanghai, China, 382, 425
Shannon, Scipio (murder victim), 448
Shannon, Thomas B. (of Calif.), 446
Sharp, Alexander (brother-in-law of USG), 220, 224
Shaw, Charles P. (attorney), 241n, 243n
Shaw, Oscar F. (of Ripley, Ohio), 273n
Shawnees, 395
Shelburne Falls, Mass., 8 and n
Sheldon, Benjamin R. (Ill. judge), 92n
Shellabarger, Samuel (of Ohio), 64n, 275n
Shepard, Isaac F. (appraiser), 260, 269, 270n–71n, 327
Shepherd, Alexander R. (of Washington, D.C.): letter to, Dec. 11, 1869, 51; identified, 51n
Shepley, George F. (U.S. Circuit Judge), 63n
Shepley, John R. (St. Louis attorney), 139n, 140n, 145, 146n, 147n, 149n, 178n, 224
Sheppard, Eli T. (U.S. consul), 275n, 276n
Sheridan, Philip H. (U.S. Army): letter to, Dec. 16, 1869, 59; presides over veterans, 59 and n; conducts Indian campaigns, 119n, 120n, 415; recommends appointment, 162n; letter to, July 25, 1870, 216; observes Franco-Prussian War, 216, 216n–17n, 318, 321n; USG supports, 230n; during Civil War, 462
Sherman, John (U.S. Senator): recommends appointments, 68n, 275n, 349–50, 397, 403–4, 465; letter to, March 30, 1870, 133–34; on Santo Domingo annexation, 133–34, 134n; visits USG, 298n
Sherman, William (of Calif.), 446
Sherman, William T. (U.S. Army): recommends appropriations, 40; administers army, 67n; recommends appointments, 77n, 412; protects chain of command, 96n; administers Reconstruction, 103n–4n, 105n, 106n–7n, 175–76, 176n, 338, 340, 380–81, 466; promotes aid to veterans, 109n; administers Indian policy, 119n–20n; letter to, March 10, 1870, 121; acquires house from USG, 121, 219n, 228n; arranges burial of George H. Thomas, 129n; rebukes Winfield S. Hancock, 129n–30n; letter to, June 17, 1870, 175–76; attends funeral of Lucien A. Prévost-Paradol, 201n; letter to, July 31, 1870, 218; protests status, 218, 219n, 227–28, 228n, 229n; letter to, Aug. 18, 1870, 227–28; assists emigrants, 287n–88n; during Civil War, 320n; discusses Union Pacific Railroad, 333–34; protects railroad, 417; letter to, June 6, 1870, 433; invited to Indian reception, 433; mentioned, 218n
Sherman, Tex., 207n
Ship Island, Miss., 420–21
Shorter, James A. (African Methodist Episcopal bishop), 12n
Shoshones, 474
Shriver, E. (of Frederick, Md.): letter to, Oct. 28, 1870, 328
Shumaker, Lindsay M. (Va. judge), 404–5
Sickles, Daniel E. (minister to Spain), 45n, 348, 418, 419
Sigel, Franz (U.S. Army), 320n
Sigerson (of St. Louis County), 145n
Simons, Nathan C., 263n, 264n
Simpson, Anna (daughter of Matthew Simpson), 79n
Simpson, James H. (U.S. Army), 449
Simpson, Matthew (Methodist bishop), 78n–79n, 272n, 317n
Sims, Clifford S. (U.S. consul), 85n
Singapore, 410, 411
Singer, John V., 447
Sioux, 361, 433
Sir Johns Run, West Va., 58n
Sitka, Alaska, 391
Slavery, 33, 60n, 75–76, 143n, 154, 156, 402–3, 405, 412, 426, 442, 445
Slevin, Patrick S. (collector), 473
Slocum, Henry W. (U.S. Army), 354
Smith (of Albany), 357
Smith, A. E. (of Glenwood, Iowa), 447–48
Smith, A. J. (of Harrisonville, Ill.), 464
Smith, Barnabas (assessor), 284, 285n
Smith, Caleb B. (U.S. Secretary of the Interior), 244n
Smith, Charles (slaveholder), 426
Smith, Charles J. (of Rochelle, Va.), 462–63

Smith, David R. (of D.C.), 412–13
Smith, E. Delafield, 17n–18n
Smith, E. Peshine (State Dept. law officer), 397
Smith, Edwin H. (assessor), 346
Smith, Emma (wife of William W. Smith), 57
Smith, J. Ambler (of Va.), 346
Smith, James W. (USMA cadet), 229n
Smith, John Somers (commercial agent), 163n
Smith, Richard M. (Indian agent), 272n
Smith, Robert M. (U.S. District Attorney), 309, 310n
Smith, William H. (Gov. of Ala.), 340
Smith, William R. (of Washington, D.C.), 337
Smith, William W. (cousin of Julia Dent Grant): letter to, Dec. 15, 1869, 57; receives invitations from USG, 57, 57n–58n, 452; telegram to, Sept. 5, 1870, 452
Smithsonian Institution, Washington, D.C.: possesses USG's property, 8n; document in, 350
Smith's Plantation, La., 257n
Smyth, John F. (postmaster), 140n
Smyth, William (U.S. Representative), 67n
Smythe, William H. (marshal), 475
Snell, William B. (D.C. police court), 440
Southard, Mr. (of Maine), 246
South Bend, Ind., 230n, 317n
South Carolina, 65n, 248, 248n–51n, 369, 448, 466
Southern Illinois University, Carbondale, Ill.: documents in, 159, 229–30, 230n, 318n–19n, 357, 430, 452
Southern Pacific Railroad, 446
Southern Union Land Co., 384
Spain: suppresses Cuban revolt, 25–28, 46n–47n, 48n, 167–68, 169n–70n, 348, 353, 394, 400, 446; captures U.S. vessels, 27, 167–68, 169n, 418–19, 440–41; at war in South America, 29, 47n–48n; U.S. consul in, 370–71; owes money to U.S., 389–90; wine from, 391; rules Puerto Rico, 397; U.S. minister to, 425; mentioned, 148n, 265n, 355
Spalding, Zephaniah S. (U.S. consul), 82n–83n

Spartanburg, S.C., 249n
Spartanburg County, S.C., 250n
Spaulding, Elbridge G. (of Buffalo), 263n
Speakman, Charles, 27–28, 46n
Speed, James (of Louisville), 54n, 389
Speed, John J. (of Ky.), 54n
Spence, William (marshal), 311n
Spence, William T. (of Ga.), 467
Spence and Thomson (tailors): letter to, Oct. 19, 1866, 220n–21n
Spencer, George E. (U.S. Senator), 55n, 425
Spencer, William M. (assessor): suspended, 378–79; letter to, Jan. 31, 1870, 379
Spiegel, Hamlin (USMA applicant), 397–98
Spiegel, Marcus M. (Ohio Vols.), 397–98
Spinner, Francis E. (U.S. Treasurer), 52n, 300n
Spofford, Paul N. (of New York City): letter to, Feb. 2, 1870, 97; administers Rawlins fund, 97, 97n–98n
Spofford, Tileston, and Co. (of New York City), 97n, 122n
Spooner, Benjamin J. (of Ind.), 59n
Spooner, W. B. (of Boston): letter to, May 10, 1870, 425
Spotted Tail (Sioux), 361, 433
Sprague, Royal T. (Calif. Supreme Court), 72n–73n
Springfield, Ill., 70n, 263n, 288n, 344
Springfield, Mo., 336
Springtown, N.J., 426
Stamford, Conn., 186n
Stanley, E. S. (of Newport, R.I.): letter to, Jan. 18, 1870, 369–70
Stanley, Edward H. (British foreign secretary), 152, 153n
Stanton, Benjamin (of West Va.), 64n
Stanton, Edwin M. (U.S. Secretary of War): nominated to U.S. Supreme Court, 54n, 56n, 77–78, 78n–80n, 92n; death of, 78, 80n, 92n; fund for family, 190; as secretary of war, 228n, 320n, 387, 435
Stanton, Ellen H. (wife of Edwin M. Stanton): letter to, Jan. 3, 1870, 77–78; receives condolences, 77–78, 78n, 79n; note to, Dec. 19, 1869, 79n
Starkweather, Henry H. (U.S. Representative), 185n

Starr, Solomon (land office receiver), 454

Starring, Frederick A. (State Dept. agent), 451

Staten Island, N.Y., 292n, 295n–96n

Staunton, Va., 87n

Stearns, Onslow (Gov. of N.H.), 401

Stephenson, James L., 375

Stevens, John L. (minister to Paraguay and Uruguay), 144 and n

Stevenson, John H. (U.S. Navy), 414

Stewart, Alexander T. (of New York City), 78n, 161n, 180n, 183n

Stewart, William M. (U.S. Senator), 88n, 158n, 245n

Stidham, G. W. (Creek), 433

Stillman, Mary, 234n

Stillman, Mr., 234n

Stockholm, Sweden, 339

Stokes, John G. (newspaper editor), 340

Stokes, William B. (U.S. Representative), 96n, 355–56, 396

Stone, Amasa, Jr. (of Cleveland), 280n, 370

Storer, George W. (U.S. Navy), 391

Storer, Samuel (of Sitka), 391

Stover, E. S. (Indian agent), 103n

Stow, Mr. (of Montgomery), 341

Strasbourg, France, 217n

Street, Hugh M. (Miss. representative), 420–21

Stribling, Cornelius K. (U.S. Navy), 354

Stringham, Silas H. (U.S. Navy), 460

Strong, James H. (U.S. Navy), 402

Strong, Julius L. (U.S. Representative), 185n, 399

Strong, William (U.S. Supreme Court), 55n, 56n, 57n, 64n, 323n

Struve, Henry G. (of Washington Territory), 407

Stuart, Alexander H. H. (of Va.), 65n

Stuart, George H. (of Philadelphia), 11n, 455

Suez Canal, 60n, 436

Sugar, 134n, 156

Sullivan, John M. (collector): letter to, March 1, 1870, 398

Sully, Alfred (U.S. Army), 119n–20n

Sumner, Charles (U.S. Senator): involved in appointments, 87n, 143n; on foreign relations committee, 93n, 180n; opposes Santo Domingo treaty, 122n, 123–24, 124n, 159n, 163,

163n–64n, 180n; sponsor of John L. Motley, 183n, 185n, 187n; proposed as minister to Great Britain, 185n; Reconstruction radicalism, 374

Sun Cliff, Pa., 464

Surratt, Mary E. (conspirator), 64n

Sutlers, 367

Swan Creek (Mich.), 271n, 272n

Swatara (U.S. Navy), 402

Swayne, Noah H. (U.S. Supreme Court), 95n

Swayne, Wager (U.S. Army), 362

Sweden, 35, 148n, 339, 418, 443

Swetland, J. G. (deputy marshal), 365

Swing, Philip B. (U.S. District Judge), 469, 470

Switzerland, 94n, 281n, 339

Sydney, Australia, 446–47

Tahiti, 85n, 223n

Tallahassee, Fla., 466, 467

Tampico, Mexico, 161n

Taney, John (of Richmond), 345

Tangier, Morocco, 181, 182n

Tate, Alexander (Haitian minister), 8–9, 9n–10n, 12n

Taxation, 22, 23, 44n, 160, 177 and n, 190, 343, 444

Taylor, 359

Taylor, Caleb N. (of Pa.), 87n–88n

Taylor, E. O., 245n

Taylor, James B. (of New York City), 231n–32n, 413

Taylor, James W. (U.S. consul), 381–82, 441

Taylor, Nathaniel G. (Commissioner of Indian Affairs), 103n

Telegrafo, 179 and n

Telegraph, 33, 44n, 436–37, 446

Telford, John G. (U.S. Army), 106n

Teller, Henry M. (of Denver), 408

Tenalleytown, D.C., 51n

Tennessee: diplomatic appointments from, 3 and n, 396; Unionists, 5n, 182n; appointments in, 94, 95n, 309, 309n–10n, 355; vols., 193; Nathan B. Forrest in, 211n; party strife in, 269, 284, 314; during Civil War, 353–54; Reconstruction politics in, 391–92; garrisoned, 466; mentioned, 381

Tennessee River, 391

Terrell, William G. (postmaster), 89n

Terrell County, Ga., 475

Terry, Alfred H. (U.S. Army), 103*n*–5*n*, 106*n*–7*n*, 339, 340
Texas, 20, 21, 40, 49, 132*n*–33*n*, 162*n*, 202*n*, 208*n*, 254*n*, 360, 449, 450, 463
Thackeray, Anne (daughter of William M. Thackeray), 321*n*
Thayer, John M. (U.S. Senator), 71*n*, 300*n*
Thiers, Louis Adolphe (of France), 255*n*, 258*n*
Thirteenth Amendment, 313
Thomas, Arad (of Albion, N.Y.), 372
Thomas, Charles G. (postmaster), 386
Thomas, Colonel, 342
Thomas, Frances K. (wife of George H. Thomas): letter to, March 29, 1870, 128; receives condolences, 128, 129*n*
Thomas, George H. (U.S. Army), 40, 59*n*, 128, 129*n*, 392
Thompson, Ambrose W. (International Steamship Co.), 197*n*–200*n*
Thomson, C. B. (postmaster), 147
Thomson, Joseph (tailor): letter to, Aug. 2, 1870, 220; clothes USG, 220, 220*n*–21*n*
Thornton, Edward (British minister), 158*n*, 268*n*, 338, 394, 428
Thrall, William R. (marshal), 364, 366–67
Tiedemann, Frederick (of Philadelphia), 406
Tientsin, China, 383
Tift, Nelson (of Ga.), 104*n*
Tinker, Dr., 48*n*
Tioga County, N.Y., 413
Tipton, Thomas W. (U.S. Senator), 72*n*
Tisdale, Horace C. (of Miss.), 421
Tisdale, Louis (of Miss.), 421
Tobacco, 74, 75, 156, 388, 389
Toledo, Ohio, 392, 473
Tomlinson, Reuben (S.C. auditor), 250*n*–51*n*
Townsend, Edward D. (U.S. Army), 218*n*, 219*n*, 406, 466
Townsend, Washington (U.S. Representative), 209*n*
Train, George Francis, 48*n*, 428
Treasure City, Nev., 245*n*
Treat, Samuel (U.S. District Judge), 7*n*, 149*n*, 314*n*
Trescot, William H. (of S.C.), 382
Tripoli, 182*n*

Trist, Nicholas P., 349
Trochu, Louis Jules (French army), 258*n*
Trowbridge, Charles A. (of New York City), 357
Trowbridge, Luther S. (of Detroit), 357
Troy, N.Y., 129*n*, 334, 392
Truman Library, Harry S., Independence, Mo.: document in, 342
Trumbull, Lyman (U.S. Senator), 94*n*, 222, 296*n*, 298*n*, 376, 458–59
Truth, Sojourner, 405
Truxtun, William T. (U.S. Navy), 88*n*, 108
Tucker, Charles L. (of Mo.), 270*n*
Tullock, Thomas L. (of Washington, D.C.), 451
Tunstall, England, 411, 412
Turkey, 4*n*, 35, 49*n*, 281*n*, 282*n*–83*n*, 436
Turks Island, 273*n*, 441
Tuscarora (U.S. Navy), 179 and *n*
Tuscola, Ill., 453
Tuttle, B. B. (of Washington Territory), 352
Tweed, John P. (of New York City), 80–81
Tweed, William M. (of New York City), 282*n*
Tybee (steamship), 122*n*
Tyler, John, Jr., 373–74

Uinta, 474
Union College, Schenectady, N.Y., 392
Union League Club (New York City), 97*n*, 283, 386
Union Pacific Railroad, 5, 5*n*–6*n*, 150, 150*n*–51*n*, 202*n*–8*n*, 230*n*–31*n*, 333–34, 344, 388
United States Army: supervises Indians, 39, 271*n*; appropriations, 39–40; reduced, 40–41; pensions, 42–43; enforces Reconstruction, 96*n*, 103*n*–5*n*, 107*n*, 132*n*, 133*n*, 210, 210*n*–12*n*, 249*n*, 250*n*, 251*n*, 290*n*, 339–40, 375, 380, 381, 393, 410, 420, 421, 428, 445, 448, 449, 466–67, 468; during Civil War, 115*n*, 192–95, 413, 415, 435, 438, 441, 449, 457, 462, 464, 465; in Utah, 120*n*; retirement, 191*n*, 235–36, 338, 413–14, 460; in Indian Territory, 214*n*; command structure, 218, 219*n*, 227–28,

United States Army (*cont.*)
228*n*, 229*n*; enforces neutrality, 223*n*, 309; Topographical Engineers, 261 and *n*; chaplains, 272*n*; assists emigrants, 287*n*–88*n*, 289*n*; quells Indian troubles, 414, 415, 416, 417; embezzlement in, 417–18; weaponry, 422, 449; reinstatements, 434, 442–43; deserters, 456–57; mentioned, 112*n*, 113*n*, 406, 446, 450, 461, 473
—1st Art., 434, 461
—2nd Art., 406
—4th Art., 261*n*
—6th Cav., 417
—7th Cav., 456
—10th Cav., 456
—1st Inf., 384
—2nd Inf., 339, 340
—4th Inf., 395
—8th Inf., 461
—10th Inf., 384
—12th Inf., 384
—17th Inf., 349, 367–68
—19th Inf., 380
—23rd Inf., 384
—24th Inf., 336
—25th Inf., 361
—43rd Inf., 336
—Veteran Reserve Corps, 414
United States Bureau of Refugees, Freedmen, and Abandoned Lands, 43, 404, 459, 462
United States Congress: controls Reconstruction, 16*n*, 19, 20, 21, 61, 61*n*–62*n*, 68*n*, 92*n*, 96, 103 and *n*, 104*n*, 106*n*, 107*n*, 130–31, 132*n*–33*n*, 174*n*, 175*n*, 211*n*, 212*n*, 373–74, 375, 393, 399, 420, 449, 450; receives USG's annual message, 18–44, 60, 292; considers treaties, 29, 30, 31, 32, 35, 82*n*, 135, 136*n*, 152–53, 153*n*, 341, 403, 442, 443; considers nominations, 37, 62 and *n*, 66*n*, 85*n*, 91, 92*n*, 93*n*, 94 and *n*, 108, 108*n*–9*n*, 143*n*, 174 and *n*, 183, 185*n*, 221*n*, 222, 282*n*, 291*n*, 323*n*, 342, 345, 349, 351, 376, 398, 400–401, 405, 407, 409, 411, 412, 413, 414, 419, 426, 442, 458, 470; provides pensions, 42; conducts census, 43; establishes land policy, 50*n*; reforms judiciary, 53*n*, 54*n*, 56*n*, 62*n*–67*n*, 70*n*–73*n*, 92*n*, 242*n*, 322*n*, 435, 439, 467, 468, 469; considers U.S. Supreme Court nominations, 54*n*–

55*n*, 57*n*, 92*n*, 172*n*; controls appropriations, 61*n*, 89–90, 90*n*, 372, 393; adjourns, 91, 159, 184*n*, 195–96, 247, 256*n*, 271*n*; USG's attitude toward, 91, 171*n*, 188*n*, 190, 274; elections to, 96*n*, 256*n*–57*n*, 286*n*, 289*n*, 405, 426–27, 453, 459; administers territories, 99, 391, 434; considers Indian matters, 100, 100*n*–101*n*, 102*n*, 103*n*, 118–19, 119*n*, 120*n*, 195–96, 202*n*, 205*n*–7*n*, 292*n*, 341, 383, 388–89, 403, 414, 417, 455–56; in foreign affairs, 115 and *n*, 118*n*, 135, 167–68, 169*n*–70*n*, 215*n*, 236, 255*n*, 257*n*, 281*n*, 341, 348, 350, 375, 398, 399–400, 410, 427, 430, 432, 440–41, 442, 443, 444; investigates sale of cadetships, 120*n*; considers Santo Domingo annexation, 121, 122*n*, 123–24, 123*n*, 124*n*, 133–34, 135*n*, 153–57, 157*n*–59*n*, 163, 163*n*–64*n*, 166, 166*n*–67*n*, 176, 179 and *n*, 180*n*, 185*n*, 188 and *n*, 189*n*, 311, 312*n*; asked to revive merchant marine, 124–26, 196 and *n*, 197*n*–200*n*, 255*n*, 257*n*, 446–47; considers interoceanic canal, 135, 136*n*; investigates Whiskey Ring, 150*n*; bill vetoed, 192–95, 362; controls railroads, 202*n*–8*n*, 388, 401, 405, 446; authorizes Arctic expedition, 209 and *n*; administers army, 218, 219*n*, 227, 228 and *n*, 229*n*, 382, 410, 414, 415, 434, 461; dislikes reform, 231*n*; considers McGarrahan claim, 240, 241*n*–42*n*, 243*n*–44*n*, 293*n*, 295*n*, 296*n*, 300*n*, 301*n*; criticized, 321*n*; sponsors art, 352, 353; considers private bills, 372, 387, 414, 423, 428, 429, 464; administers navy, 397, 408, 414, 433, 442; investigates slave trade, 402–3; revises laws, 422; creates dept. of justice, 450; enacts homestead law, 451, 452; mentioned, 3*n*, 4*n*, 15*n*, 111*n*, 112, 113*n*, 181*n*, 186*n*, 210*n*, 213*n*, 234*n*, 262*n*, 275*n*, 319*n*, 360, 380, 390, 394, 406, 462
United States Court of Claims, 390
United States Department of Justice, 242*n*, 310*n*, 450
United States Department of State: foreign service, 113*n*, 117*n*, 455, 457; role in Santo Domingo annexation, 122*n*, 124*n*; registers ratifica-

tions of Fifteenth Amendment, 132n, 133n; negotiates with Great Britain, 152–53; secretary may resign, 183n; employs consular agent, 214, 215n; processes paperwork, 214n, 447; conducts foreign policy, 223n, 225, 226n–27n, 240n, 268n, 398–99, 400, 428; sends mail, 252, 253, 255n, 256n, 257n, 258n; authorizes leaves, 282n; records, 307n, 312n, 386, 391; stocks books, 385; suppresses slave trade, 402–3; personnel, 406, 453; provides translations, 418; mentioned, 10n, 60 and n, 85n, 86n, 87n, 95n, 379, 411

United States Department of the Interior: Indian policy, 39, 119n, 202n–8n, 315, 388–89, 414, 434; asst. secretary, 69n; oversees railroads, 202n–8n; corrupt, 231n; maintains land office, 241n–46n, 276n–77n, 452; secretary resigns, 292, 292n–302n

United States Marine Corps, 88n, 355, 394, 430, 467

United States Military Academy, West Point, N.Y.: graduates, 83n, 261 and n, 325, 354–55, 426, 444; applicants, 112, 112n–14n, 182n, 221n, 363, 384, 388, 394, 395, 397–98, 404, 409, 412, 419, 425–26, 431, 441; sale of cadet warrants, 120n; USG visits, 159, 232, 233, 235, 251, 259, 283, 365; Frederick Dent Grant attends, 173 and n, 190, 232, 282, 319n, 325, 328–29, 329n; administration, 228n; black cadet, 229n; faculty, 328, 329n; cadets, 334–35

United States Naval Academy, Annapolis, Md., 350, 383, 388, 395–96, 409

United States Navy: appropriations, 41; pensions, 42, 43; patrols Cuba, 46n, 47n; in Hawaii, 82n, 88n; yards, 90 and n, 198n, 199n; promotions, 108, 108n–9n, 414, 426, 436; in Caribbean, 122n, 123n; at beginning of Civil War, 125; surveys interoceanic canal, 135n–36n; Arctic expedition, 209n; maintains neutrality, 306n, 309; surgeons disciplined, 348, 391; midshipman appointment, 395–96; rank, 397; suppresses slave trade, 402; ironclads, 408; patrols fisheries, 410; retirements, 426, 433, 442, 460, 464, 474; pay, 446; solicitor,

450; mentioned, 112n, 113n, 133n, 137n, 422, 423

United States Post Office Department: annual report, 41–42; postmasters, 83n, 87n, 89n, 214n, 221n, 232n, 277n, 290n, 291n, 438; in politics, 89n; contracts, 196n, 197n; international agreements, 196n, 339; in New York City, 221n, 248n, 321n; letter carriers, 372

United States Supreme Court: admits blacks to practice, 11n; salaries, 43; resignations, 52, 54n; nominations, 53n–57n, 70n–71n, 77–78, 78n–80n, 92n, 171n, 192n, 322n–23n; expanded, 62n; political activities, 95n, 339; decisions, 146n–47n, 177n, 241n, 242n, 244n, 300n, 389; considers claims cases, 439

United States Treasury Department: pursues fraud, 7n, 439–40; annual report, 23–24; statue for, 51, 52n; administers Alaska, 99n; bureau of immigration proposed, 199n; audits officials, 215n, 263n, 387; appointments, 253, 253n–54n, 298n, 407, 413, 414, 429, 431, 461; clerks, 294n; enforces neutrality, 306n; Whiskey Ring defrauds, 357–59; taxes Indians, 388–89; researches cotton claims, 390; bonds officials, 393; sells bonds abroad, 445

United States War Department: annual report, 39–41; appropriations, 40, 90n; funds interoceanic canal expedition, 135n, 136n; discharges cav., 193; issues orders, 219n, 228n; oversees emigrants, 288n; enforces neutrality, 306n; records, 319n–20n, 414, 421; administered, 404, 429, 457; clerks, 444

Universalists, 98n

Upson, William H. (U.S. Representative), 403

Uruguay, 144n, 396

Usher, John P. (U.S. Secretary of the Interior), 244n

Utah Territory, 92n, 120n, 474

Utes, 288n, 409

Utica, N.Y., 17n, 252, 261, 432

Valmaseda, Count, 28

Van Buren, Martin (U.S. President), 281n

Van Buren, Thomas B. (of New York City), 390
Van Cleve, Horatio P. (postmaster), 83n
Vanderbilt, Cornelius (of New York City), 334
Van Lew, Elizabeth L. (postmaster), 347
Van Nostrand, David (publisher): letter to, Dec. 15, 1869, 58; identified, 58n; letter to, July 7, 1870, 58n
Vansant, Joseph S. (of Olympia, Washington Territory), 351
Vashon, George B. (attorney), 11n
Vassar College, Poughkeepsie, N.Y.: document in, 328
Vaughan, George T. (of Linden, Tex.), 449–50
Vaughan, William R. (of Va.), 412
Veazie, Lewis, 253n
Venezuela, 398–99, 428, 435
Vera Cruz, Mexico, 161n
Vermont, 63n, 226n, 230n, 280n, 306n, 411, 458
Vermont, University of, Burlington, Vt.: document in, 280n
Versailles, France, 395
Versailles, Ind., 354
Veterans, 59 and n, 138n, 228n, 334, 369, 409
Viall, Jasper A. (Indian superintendent), 458–59
Vicksburg, Miss., 164n, 257n, 368, 397, 445, 458
Victor, James M., Broadview, Ill.: document owned by, 59
Victor Emanuel II (King of Italy), 148
Victoria, Queen: sons of, 90n, 436; as head of state, 151, 152, 186n, 319n, 337–38, 362; letter to, Jan. 11, 1870, 362
Vienna, Austria, 93n, 183n, 280n, 390, 447
Vinton, Henry C. (of St. Louis), 270n
Vinton County, Ohio, 365
Virginia: blacks in, 13n, 423–24; Reconstruction in, 20–21, 40, 45n, 360, 373–74, 393, 412, 462–63; courts in, 64n, 65n, 429; Republicans in, 87n, 269, 284, 314; during Civil War, 261n, 462; appointments in, 340–41, 345–47, 384, 399, 404–5, 436
Virginia, University of, Charlottesville,

Va.: documents in, 65n, 111n, 175n, 243n–44n
Visalia, Calif., 375
Von Steuben, Friedrich Wilhelm, 430

W. R. Carter (steamboat), 397
Wade, 403–4
Wade, Benjamin F. (of Ohio), 317n, 404
Wadsworth, William H. (of Maysville, Ky.), 3n–4n
Walcott, Iowa, 360
Walker, Francis A. (U.S. Census Bureau), 295n
Walker, Joe (prisoner), 448
Wallace, Lewis (U.S. Army), 354
Walter, G. Forrest (of San Francisco), 385
Walter Clayton (schooner), 447
Ward, J. Langdon (Union League Club): letter to, Feb. 9, 1870, 386
Ward, John E. (minister to China), 382
Warden, Robert B. (of Ohio), 471–72
Warmoth, Henry C. (Gov. of La.), 400
Warner, Willard (U.S. Senator), 67n, 341, 396, 425
War of 1812, 360, 384, 432
Warren, John (Fenian), 117n
Warren, William, 253n
Warren County, Va., 424
Washburn, Andrew (pension agent), 345, 346
Washburn, Cadwallader C. (U.S. Representative), 92n, 439, 440
Washburne, Adèle G. (wife of Elihu B. Washburne), 91, 92n, 190, 191n, 254, 255n, 258n, 406
Washburne, Elihu B. (minister to France): letter to, Dec. 17, 1869, 59–60; as diplomat, 59–60, 60n–61n, 91, 91n–92n, 93n, 110, 110n–11n, 268n, 280 and n, 401–2, 434–35, 452; advises USG, 61n, 93n, 405–6; recommends appointments, 70n–71n, 92n, 93n; letter to, Jan. 28, 1870, 91; health of, 92n, 255n, 258n, 406; letter to, Feb. 17, 1870, 110; letter to, [*April, 1869*], 110n; letter to, May 18, 1870, 110n; letter to, May 19, 1870, 110n–11n; letter to, June 22, 1870, 111n; letter to, Dec. 12, 1871, 111n; letter to, April 12, 1873, 111n; letter to, May 5, 1873, 111n; letter to,

July 7, 1876, 111*n*; discusses Robert Anderson, 190, 191*n*; receives political news, 190, 230*n*–31*n*; letter to, July 10, 1870, 190–91; letter to, Aug. 22, 1870, 254–55; during Franco-Prussian War, 254–55, 255*n*–59*n*; mentioned, 253

Washington, George (U.S. President), 131, 201*n*, 231*n*, 281*n*, 437

Washington, D.C.: blacks in, 11*n*, 138*n*; statue in, 51, 52*n*; local officials, 51*n*, 63*n*, 277*n*, 401, 412–13, 424–25, 436, 438, 440; newspapers, 51*n*, 119*n*, 164*n*, 208*n*, 301*n*; charities, 73 and *n*; U.S. Navy Yard, 90, 336–37; territorial government, 138*n*; USG house in, 219*n*; St. Andrew's Society, 337; Willard's Hotel, 369, 374; Wall's Opera House, 375; mentioned passim

Washington, Pa., 56*n*, 57*n*, 459, 474

Washington County Historical Society, Washington, Pa.: documents in, 57, 57*n*, 452, 459–60

Washington Territory, 281*n*, 350–52, 385, 407, 469

Wass, J. B., 473

Waters, Benjamin J. (New Mexico Territory Supreme Court), 378, 408

Watts, Henry M. (minister to Austria), 93*n*

Wausau, Wis., 449

Wayne, James M. (U.S. Supreme Court), 322*n*

Waynesboro, Va., 87*n*

Weaver, James R. (U.S. consul), 79*n*

Webb, 182*n*

Webb, Charles M. (U.S. District Attorney), 439

Webb, James Watson, 182*n*

Webb, Lewis W. (collector), 384

Webster, Daniel, 180*n*

Webster, Thomas (of Philadelphia), 10*n*

Webster, N.H., 419

Weed, Thurlow (of N.Y.), 140*n*

Weitzel, Godfrey (U.S. Army), 392

Welch, Adonijah S. (U.S. Senator), 83*n*

Welland Canal, 158*n*

Welles, George E. (assessor), 473

Wellington, Arthur Wellesley, Duke of, 337

Wells, Almer H. (USMA applicant), 394

Wells, Henry H. (U.S. District Attorney), 65*n*

Wells, Thomas H. (of Nev.), 245*n*

Wentworth, George E. (marshal), 352

Western and Atlantic Railroad, 106*n*

Weston, Mo., 110*n*

West Point, N.Y. *See* United States Military Academy

West Virginia, 64*n*, 65*n*, 381

Wet Mountain Valley (Colorado Territory), 286*n*, 287*n*, 288*n*

Wetter, Henry (secretary, New Mexico Territory), 376, 378

Wharton, Gabriel C. (U.S. District Attorney), 94, 95*n*

Wheeler, William F. (marshal), 98*n*

Wheeling, West Va., 58*n*

Whetstone Agency, Dakota Territory, 361

Whig Party, 53*n*, 93*n*–94*n*, 143*n*, 210*n*, 227*n*

Whiskey Ring, 150*n*, 357–59

Whitaker, John S. (of New Orleans), 66*n*

White, Alexander H. (of Ala.), 341

White, Andrew D. (Cornell University), 317*n*

White, Charles (secretary), 240, 241*n*, 244*n*–45*n*, 300*n*–301*n*

White, Horace (*Chicago Tribune*), 70*n*

White, Joseph W. (purchaser of USG farm), 260, 313

White, Rollin, 362

Whitefield, Maine, 425

Whitehead, J. R. (of Wyoming Territory), 433–34

Whiting, Billington C. (Indian superintendent), 431–32

Wilderness (Va.), battle of the, 164*n*, 458

Wilkins, Ross (U.S. District Judge), 68*n*, 356, 357

Willard, Charles W. (U.S. Representative), 432

Willey, Waitman T. (U.S. Senator), 64*n*, 65*n*

William I (Emperor of Germany), 217*n*, 238, 254

William II (King of the Netherlands), 281*n*

William and Mary, College of, Williamsburg, Va.: document in, 373–74
Williams, George H. (U.S. Senator), 274, 277n, 316n, 407
Williams, Jesse L. (Union Pacific Railroad), 5n, 6n
Williams, Thomas (of Allegheny County, Pa.), 398
Williams and Guion Steamship Co., 196n
Williams College, Williamstown, Mass.: document in, 80–81
Williamson, David J. (U.S. consul), 247n
Willmann, Andreas (assessor), 413
Wilson, Henry (U.S. Senator), 172n, 187n–88n, 451
Wilson, James F. (of Iowa), 67n–68n, 71n, 243n
Wilson, James H. (U.S. Army), 279n, 299n
Wilson, Joseph S. (General Land Office), 240–41, 243n, 244n–46n, 276n, 277n, 297n, 405
Winans, Benjamin L. (postmaster), 89n
Winans, James J. (U.S. Representative), 423
Winchell, Joseph R. (*Hannibal Courier*), 468
Windham County, Conn., 187n
Wing, E. Rumsey (minister to Ecuador), 3, 3n–4n
Winnipeg, Canada, 120n, 441
Winter, George (of Fiji), 430
Wirt, William (U.S. Attorney General), 174n
Wirtz, Horace R. (U.S. Army), 368–69
Wisconsin, 69n, 70n, 116n, 128, 392, 395–96, 438, 439, 440, 467
Wiswell, Edward R. (of New York City), 317n
Withey, Solomon L. (U.S. District Judge), 68n–69n
Wolf, Simon, 397
Women: in Ga., 61 and n; as hostesses, 90; political status, 107n; travel abroad, 110 and n, 111n; educated, 279n; manage orphanage, 335; seek husbands' employment, 336–37, 364, 437–38; appeal for pension, 337, 372, 406, 432, 451, 460, 475; pursue claims, 353–54, 355, 463–64; persecute illegitimate daughter, 368–69;

seek husband's body, 371–72; solicit son's USMA appointment, 397; seek clemency, 406, 445
Wood, Emma A., 372
Wood, George W. (collector), 253n–54n
Wood, George W. F. (U.S. Army), 372
Wood, Robert C. (U.S. Army), 383
Woodruff, Lewis B. (U.S. Circuit Judge), 16–17, 17n, 64n
Woods, William B. (U.S. Circuit Judge), 67n–68n, 171n
Woodstock, Conn., 186n, 187n
Woodward, Caroline Cates (of Huntsville, Tex.), 445
Woodwell, Joseph (of Pittsburgh), 333
Wool, John E., 334, 360
Woolsey, Melancthon B. (U.S. Navy), 414
Woonsocket, R.I., 473
Worcester, Mass., 227n
Worthington, Wilmer (appraiser), 349
Wright, William T. (U.S. consul), 275n, 276n
Wulsten, Carl (German Colonization Co.), 285n–89n
Württemberg, Germany, 341
Wyeth, Albert, 27–28, 46n
Wyllie, Robert C. (Hawaiian minister of foreign affairs), 86n
Wyoming Territory, 120n, 150n–51n, 234n, 354, 361, 433–34, 453, 457, 474

Yale University, New Haven, Conn.: students at, 11n, 261n; documents in, 63n, 64n–65n; graduates of, 67n, 248n, 355, 357
Yanceyville, N.C., 210n
Yates, Richard (U.S. Senator), 290n, 460
Yeaman, George H. (of Ky.), 69n, 92n
Yellow Fever, 372
Yorktown, Va., 201n
Young, Alfred N. (U.S. consul), 273 and n, 275n
Young, Brigham (Mormon president), 120n
Young, Francis G., 188n
Young, George W. (U.S. Navy), 108
Young, John (Gov. of N.Y.), 97n

Young, John Russell (*New York Tribune*), 230n–31n

Young, Jonathan (U.S. Navy), 108, 109n

Young, Mr. (U.S. Treasury Dept.), 199n

Younglove, Truman G. (of Albany, N.Y.), 140n

Young Men's Christian Association, 435

Ysleta Pueblo, New Mexico Territory, 342

Zagarizo, Gennaro (of Lecce, Italy), 449

Zimmer, Louis (of N.C.), 384

DATE DUE	131934	